TWENTY-FIRST CE
POPULATION, ECONOMY, HU
AND THE ENVIRONMENT

TWENTY-FIRST CENTURY INDIA
POPULATION, ECONOMY, HUMAN DEVELOPMENT, AND THE ENVIRONMENT

Edited by

TIM DYSON • ROBERT CASSEN • LEELA VISARIA

OXFORD
UNIVERSITY PRESS

OXFORD
UNIVERSITY PRESS

Great Clarendon Street, Oxford OX2 6DP

Oxford University Press is a department of the University of Oxford.
It furthers the University's objective of excellence in research, scholarship,
and education by publishing worldwide in

Oxford   New York
Auckland   Cape Town   Dar es Salaam   Hong Kong   Karachi
Kuala Lumpur   Madrid   Melbourne   Mexico City   Nairobi
New Delhi   Shanghai   Taipei   Toronto

With offices in
Argentina   Austria   Brazil   Chile   Czech Republic   France   Greece
Guatemala   Hungary   Italy   Japan   Poland   Portugal   Singapore
South Korea   Switzerland   Thailand   Turkey   Ukraine   Vietnam

Oxford is a registered trade mark of Oxford University Press
in the UK and in certain other countries.

Published in the United States
by Oxford University Press Inc., New York

British Library Cataloguing in Publication Data
Data available

Library of Congress Cataloging in Publication Data
Data available

ISBN 019 924335 2
ISBN 019 928382 6 (Pbk.) 978 0 19 928382 8 (Pbk.)

Printed in Great Britain
on acid-free paper by
Biddles Ltd
King's Lynn. Norfolk
Published in India by OUP India
This edition is not for sale in
India, Bangladesh, Nepal, Bhutan, Sri Lanka and Burma

This book is dedicated to the memory of Pravin Visaria. At the start of the project which led to this book, Pravin was a leading member of the research team, and would have been a co-author and editor. We have incorporated here some of the work he left behind, and have tried to maintain in this volume a standard of which he would have approved. But we are all too aware of the cost of his tragically early death. His knowledge of the subject matter had few parallels. An appreciation by Tim Dyson of Pravin's life and work appeared in the *Economic and Political Weekly*, Vol. 36, No. 33, August 2001. His going is a severe loss not only to his family and colleagues, but also to scholarship and to India.

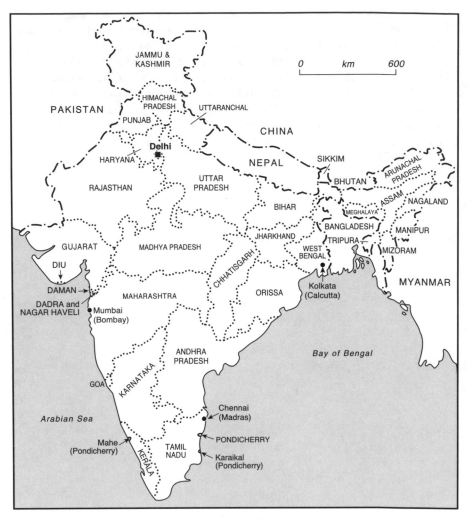

Map of India
States and Selected Cities

Note: The map shows the three new states Uttaranchal, Jharkhand, and Chhatisgarh, created
        in November 2000.

Source: Registrar General, India (2001a).

Preface

This book is the outcome of a research project, generously funded by The Wellcome Trust (grant number 053660), which was designed to examine the nature and consequences of the future growth of India's population.

This may not be the first book on India's population and development. But it is the first to present them in an integrated manner. Inevitably, despite four years of work by a team of authors and researchers, the coverage is incomplete. But many of the questions that might occur to anyone pondering India's future find a response here.

When the project began the principal researchers were Pravin and Leela Visaria, Tim Dyson, and Robert Cassen, with Cassen in the role of project coordinator. We appointed the rest of the team. Their names appear in the list of contributors. After the demise, due to sudden illness, of Pravin Visaria, we engaged three consultants to share some of the work he would have contributed to: Shankar Acharya, Ramaswamy Iyer, and Jeemol Unni, each of whom has made major inputs to specific chapters. We are particularly grateful to them for stepping in at short notice and giving generously of their time. In addition, a fourth consultant, Mari Bhat, has provided valuable advice, documents, and studies which have significantly assisted our demographic work.

There are many others whose help we acknowledge with warmth and gratitude. None of them should be held responsible for any anomalies that we may have made in the writing of this book. They include:

Bina Agarwal, G. Ananthapadmanabhan, P. Arokiasamy, M.D. Asthana, Roli Asthana, Montek Singh Ahluwalia, Isher Ahluwalia, Jayanta

Bandyopadhyay, Shilpi Banerjee, Jayant Banthia, Suman Beri, Joy de Beyer, A.D. Bhide, Ashish Bose, Marty Chen, Kanchan Chopra, Biplab Dasgupta, Monica Das Gupta, Angus Deaton, Mahendra Dev, Jean Drèze, Malathy Duraisamy, S.K. Gadkari, P.S. George, Anne Goujon, Ashima Goyal, Simon Gregson, Ashok Gulati, Shreekant Gupta, S. Janakarajan, D. Jayaraj, Dayanatha Jha, P.L. Joshi, S.N. Joshi, Ramesh Kanbargi, Ashok Khosla, Ramesh Kohli, Dilip Kumar, Praduman Kumar, Amitabh Kundu, Murari Lal, François Leclercq, Michael Lipton, Arup Maharatna, P. Malhotra, Ajay Mathur, Tony McMichael, Rakesh Mohan, Madan Mohan Jha, Mina Moshkeri, Chandan Mukherjee, Aswini K. Nanda, Amulya R. Nanda, Sunita Narain, Ajay Narayanan, K.S. Natarajan, B.N. Navalawala, K. Navaneetham, R.K. Pachauri, Theodore Panayotou, Jyoti Parikh, Kirit Parikh, Lubina Qureshi, U. Raghupati, K.N. Raj, S. Irudaya Rajan, K.V. Raju, Radhika Ramasubban, Charlotte Ramsey, Uma Rani, C.H. Hanumantha Rao, M. Govinda Rao, P. Parthasarathy Rao, Martin Ravallion, Gopinath Ravindran, S.K. Ray, Bhanwar Rishyasringa, T.K. Roy, Sumeet Saksena, Zeba Sathar, David Seckler, B. Seshadri, Tushaar Shah, Abusaleh Shariff, Amani Siyam, K. Srinivasan, P.V. Srinivasan, S. Subramanian, M.H. Suryanarayana, Madhura Swaminathan, Suresh Tendulkar, Robin Vanner, Prem Vashishtha, S.M. Virmani, and Hania Zlotnick.

We would also like to thank all the contributors to the Delhi Workshop held in January 2002 to review the project's principal findings, and the participants of the London School of Economics (LSE) Workshop on Poverty in India, held in October 1998 under the auspices of the UK Development Studies Association.

We are indebted to a number of institutions in India which received us as visitors and/or contributed in other ways to our work: in Ahmedabad, the Indian Institute of Management and the Gujarat Institute of Development Research; in Chennai, the Madras Institute of Development Studies; in Delhi, the Delhi School of Economics, the India International Centre, the Institute of Economic Growth, and the Tata Energy Research Institute; in Hyderabad, the International Crops Research Institute for the Semi-Arid Tropics and the Centre for Economic and Social Studies; in Mumbai, the Indira Gandhi Institute of Development Research and the International Institute for Population Sciences; in Pune, the Gokhale Institute of Politics and Economics; and in Thiruvananthapuram, the Centre for Development Studies.

We owe special thanks to our three project administrators: Lucy Wright who set up our basic systems, Nikki East who carried them forward, and Lisa Rabanal who maintained them to the end and did further sterling work organizing the production of this book. We are also indebted to the late Jean Ingram, Departmental Manager of the Social Policy Department at LSE, which has housed our project, and Michael Oliver and Gavin Smart of the Research and Projects Division. At the Wellcome Trust, we would like to thank

Wendy Ewart, Sam Balakrishnan, Gunvanti Goding, Ian Scott, and Martin Sexton for all their help.

Lastly, a word on the organization and presentation of this book. The first chapter provides a brief summary of the book's main results. Chapters 2–6 address population matters. Chapters 7–10 deal with key aspects of human and economic development. Chapters 11–15 tackle issues relating to food and the environment. Chapter 16 discusses implications for policy. Given the importance of the subject, we have tried to keep the text as informal and accessible as possible.

Tim Dyson
Robert Cassen
Leela Visaria

Contents

Contributors

Project Team:

Dennis Anderson, Imperial College of Science, Technology, and Medicine, London

Robert Cassen, London School of Economics, UK

Tim Dyson, London School of Economics, UK

Amresh Hanchate, Harvard School of Public Health, Boston, USA

Geeta Gandhi Kingdon, University of Oxford, UK

Pramila Krishnan, Jesus College, University of Cambridge, UK

Kirsty McNay, Pauling Centre for Human Sciences, University of Oxford

Bhaskar Vira, Fitzwilliam College, University of Cambridge, UK

Shiraz Vira, University of Cambridge, UK

Leela Visaria, Gujarat Institute of Development Research, Ahmedabad

Consultants:

Shankar Acharya, Indian Council for Research on International Economic Relations, Delhi

P.N. Mari Bhat, Institute of Economic Growth, Delhi

Ramaswamy R. Iyer, Centre for Policy Research, Delhi

Jeemol Unni, Gujarat Institute of Development Research, Ahmedabad

Figures

Tables

Abbreviations

AIDS	Acquired Immuno-deficiency Syndrome
ASI	Agricultural Statistics of India
BAU	Business as usual
BCM	Billion cubic metres
BOD	biological oxygen demand
CDS	current daily status
CF	correction factor
CNG	compressed natural gas
CPCB	Central Pollution Control Board
CPHEEO	Central Public Health and Environmental Engineering Organization
CPR	common pool resources
CSE	Centre for Science and Environment
DALYS	disability adjusted life-years
DFID	Department for International Development (UK)
DOTS	Directly Observed Treatment—Short course (TB)
DPAP	Drought Prone Areas Programme
DPEP	District Primary Education Programme
DPT	diphtheria, pertussis, and tetanus (triple antigen vaccine)
EAS	Employment Assurance Scheme
EFA	Education for All
EKC	Environmental Kuznets curve
EPTRI	Environment Protection, Training, and Research Institute
FAO	Food and Agriculture Organization (of the United Nations)
FBS	Food Balance Sheet (produced by the FAO)

FDI	Foreign Direct Investment
FRBM	fiscal responsibility and budget management
GM	genetically modified
GW	Gigawatts
ha	hectares
HC	hydro carbons
HIV	human immuno-deficiency virus
HUDCO	Housing and Urban Development Corporation
HYV	high yielding variety
ICDS	Integrated Child Development Scheme
ICMR	Indian Council for Medical Research
IDFC	Infrastructure Development Finance Company
IEC	Information, Education, Communication
IIPS	International Institute for Population Sciences
IMR	infant mortality rate
IPCC	Intergovernment Panel on Climate Change
IRDP	Integrated Rural Development Programme
ISAR	in school attendance rates
IUD	intra uterine device
IWV	India Water Vision (2025)
JRY	Jawahar Rozgar Yojana
LFPR	labour force participation rate
LPCD	litres per capita per day
LPD	litres per day
LPG	liquefied petroleum gas
LSE	London School of Economics
Mg/cum	microgrammes per cubic metre
MLD	million litres per day
MMR	maternal mortality ratio
mmt	million metric tonnes
MOEF	Ministry of Environment and Forests
MSW	municipal solid waste
MWR	Ministry of Water Resources
NAAQM	national ambient air quality monitoring
NAS	National Accounts Statistics
NCAER	National Council for Applied Economic Research
NCERT	National Council of Educational Research and Training
NCIWRD	National Commission on Integrated Water Resources Development
NCRPB	National Capital Region Planning Board
NEERI	National Environmental Engineering Research Institute
NFHS	National Family Health Survey
NIUA	National Institute of Urban Affairs

NNMB	National Nutrition Monitoring Board
NSS	National Sample Survey
NSSO	National Sample Survey Organization
OBC	other backward classes
OECD	Organization for Economic Cooperation and Development
O&M	Operation and Maintenance
ORT	Oral Rehydration Therapy
PDS	Public Distribution System
PFI	Population Foundation of India
PHC	primary health centre
PM	particulate matter
PROBE	Public Report on Basic Education
PV	photovoltaic
QR	quantitative restrictions
RBI	Reserve Bank of India
R&D	research and development
RPDS	Research Programme in Development Studies, Woodrow Wilson School, Princeton University
SC	Scheduled Caste
SDP	State Domestic Product
SEB	State Electricity Board
SHG	self help groups
SIDA	Swedish International Development Authority
SPM	suspended particulate matter
SRS	Sample Registration System
SS	suspended solids
STICERD	Suntory and Toyota International Centres for Economics and Related Disciplines
SWM	solid waste management
TERI	Tata Energy Research Institute
TFR	total fertility rate (live births per woman)
TN	total nitrogen
TOE	tonnes of oil-equivalent energy
TP	total phosphorous
TPDS	targeted public distribution system
TWh	terawatt hours
UA	urban agglomeration
UEE	universal elementary education
UNCHS	United Nations Centre for Human Settlements
UPSS	usual principal and subsidiary status
VEC	Village Educational Committee
VOC	Volatile organic compound
WCD	World Commission on Dams
WG	working group

1
Overview

India's population has trebled since its independence in August 1947, and seems headed inexorably towards a total of at least 1.5 billion by the middle of the twenty-first century. Our study examines how population growth will affect India's future development in the light of recent experience, and how India can manage this last phase of its demographic transition. It covers three broad sets of questions. What is happening to India's population in terms of fertility, mortality, and urbanization, and what can we say about future trends? How does population growth affect economic growth; does it have any bearing on poverty and human development? What will be the impact of population growth on the environment?

INDIA'S POPULATION: THE PAST

India's population grew slowly in the past. It reached about 211 million by the first decennial census in 1871. The next five decades saw an alternating pattern of growth—relatively fast during one decade, slow or negative during the next—largely due to huge famines in the 1870s and 1890s and the influenza epidemic of 1918. But despite these disasters the population reached approximately 251 million by 1921. In each subsequent intercensal decade the scale of the population addition rose, from about 28 million during 1921–31 to 180 million during 1991–2001, a figure roughly equal to the total population of Indonesia in 1991.

In the past, the rate of India's population growth was controlled by high mortality from infectious and parasitic diseases, epidemics, and famines.

However, improvement in the mortality rate from around 1921—which accelerated sharply after 1947—led to an increasing concern with the high birth rate. As a result, in 1952, India became the first nation to adopt an official family planning programme. For much of the twentieth century the country pioneered new approaches to the mass provision of birth control. Nevertheless, although the birth rate has been falling since the 1960s, it was only during 1991–2001 that it fell significantly faster than the death rate—bringing about a clear reduction in the rate of demographic growth. Overall the period 1947–2001 saw a trebling of the population.

Several of the basic features that characterize India's population growth have deep roots. The Gangetic plain has been the demographic centre of gravity of the Indian subcontinent for over two thousand years, and it will remain so for the foreseeable future. Similarly, the origins of the familiar north–south demographic divide probably date back equally far. Historical perspective also sheds light on the phenomenon of son preference, and helps to explain why the demographic transition is significantly more advanced in the country's south. Finally, India's middling rate of fertility decline since the 1960s accounts for its present still fairly young age structure—a feature which will ensure considerable future population growth.

HEALTH AND MORTALITY

During the period 1947–70, the mortality rate fell considerably due to reductions in several major communicable diseases and the absence of major famines. However, many infant and childhood diseases remained prevalent, tuberculosis (TB) contributed to high levels of adult morbidity (and significant mortality), and malaria began to re-emerge after a period when it had seemed to have been brought under control.

The mortality rate continued to decline fairly steadily during the last three decades of the twentieth century. Both the crude death rate and the infant mortality rate (IMR) almost halved, the former falling from 16 to less than nine per 1000, and the latter from 134 to about 70 infant deaths per 1000 live births. Life expectation rose from 50 to 62 years.

This period saw considerable progress against communicable diseases such as gastro-enteritis, dysentery, tetanus, polio, and leprosy. But regional differentials in mortality remained, mortality and health conditions generally being more favourable in the south than in the north. Contamination of water supplies, inadequate management of liquid and solid wastes, and the high levels of crowding typical of urban slums contributed to the continuation of infections in the general population, though urban mortality remained lower than rural.

The resurgence of malaria, the spread of drug-resistant forms of TB, and the menacing rise of HIV/AIDS from the mid-1980s (a development which has probably contributed to the resurgence of TB) all serve to illustrate how important infectious diseases remain in the country's mortality and health profile. Indeed, although there has been a marked shift towards greater prominence of non-communicable diseases (for example, cancers and circulatory ailments) in the country's overall pattern of cause of death, at the start of the twenty-first century India suffers from a double burden of communicable and non-communicable diseases. Widespread nutritional and reproductive health problems, reflecting conditions of great poverty, coexist with illnesses linked to the adoption of new patterns of behaviour. These include reduced levels of physical activity and more obesity among the better off in urban areas, and greater consumption of tobacco. Respiratory ailments remain prominent and stubbornly high, in part because of increased levels of atmospheric pollution.

FERTILITY

Given the scale and diversity of India's population, a decline from around six births per woman in 1970 to almost half that level within a span of 30 years is a significant achievement. Fertility has declined throughout the country, though at a varying pace in rural and urban areas and in different states, with Kerala and Tamil Nadu already reaching about the replacement level. Changes in fertility behaviour have diffused through space and time, conditioned by socio-cultural and historical patterns rather than neat administrative boundaries. Fertility has fallen at all ages; at younger ages due to a rise in the age at marriage and at older ages due to control of fertility within marriage through family planning (mainly sterilization). This has resulted in a very short time-span of childbearing in some states.

Fertility in India has fallen under a wide range of socio-economic and cultural conditions. Rising levels of education, the influence of the media, economic changes, continuing urbanization, and declines in infant and child mortality have all contributed to fertility decline. The diffusion of new ideas and greater aspirations for their children have led even uneducated parents to limit their family size. However, fertility variation between regions is likely to persist for some time, although 'a trend towards broad convergence in levels of fertility between the states is under way.

INDIA'S POPULATION: THE FUTURE

India's population reached 1027 million in 2001. The prospects for its further growth are explored using state-level projections. It is likely to be in the vicinity of 1.4 billion by 2026, and could well approach 1.6 billion by 2051, as depicted in Figure 1.1. These projections employ what some would regard as fairly optimistic assumptions about the pace of future demographic progress—namely, that for the country as a whole the total fertility rate (TFR) will fall

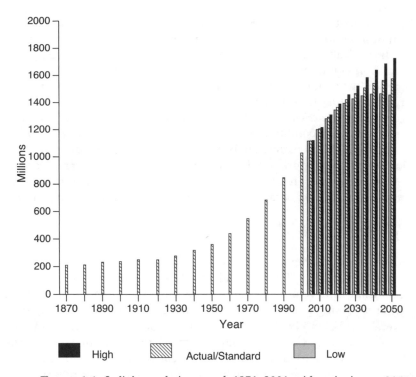

FIGURE 1.1: *India's population growth 1871–2001, with projections to 2051*
Source: Registrar General, India (2000a) and Table 5.10, this volume.

to around 2.1 births per woman by 2016–21, when life expectation will be approximately 67 years for males and 70 for females.

Alternative population projections, however, which also incorporate fairly plausible assumptions about future fertility, suggest that the population could reach 1.7 billion by 2051 and still be increasing. Yet other projections, which incorporate extremely optimistic assumptions about future fertility, indicate a population of at least 1.4 billion before it starts to decline. It appears that the only way a population of 1.4 billion will not be reached is through an event such as an unexpectedly severe HIV/AIDS epidemic or perhaps, a full-scale nuclear war.

A population of about 1.4 billion in 2026 represents an addition of some 400 million over 25 years. Around half of this is likely to occur in the northern states of Bihar, Madhya Pradesh, Rajasthan, and Uttar Pradesh. The populations of these states will increase by 45–55 per cent during 2001–26. Uttar Pradesh alone—including Uttaranchal—will reach some 270 million by 2026. The future fertility declines of these four states with relatively high levels of fertility will be particularly crucial in determining by how much India's population will grow in the decades beyond 2026. Most other states in the country already have moderate or low fertility, and their populations thus seem set to increase by only around 20–30 per cent in the period to 2026, and to grow only modestly thereafter.

Fertility decline will ensure that the proportion of the population below 15 years of age will fall considerably during 2001–26. Indeed, most population growth during this period will take place at ages above 15 years. Consequently the median age of the population will rise appreciably, from perhaps 22 years in 2001 to around 31 by 2026. The proportion of India's population aged 60 years and over is projected to rise from about 7 to 11 per cent during 2001–26. But because of the substantial fall in the proportion of the population at younger ages the overall dependency ratio of the population will decline significantly, that is, the ratio of those aged under 15 and over 59, to those aged 15–59.

MIGRATION AND URBANIZATION

India's level of urbanization is projected to rise from about 28 per cent in 2001 to 36 per cent by 2026—when the total urban population could number roughly half a billion. Indeed, because there is considerable scope for reclassifying rural areas as 'urban', these figures could turn out to be underestimates. Whereas in 2001 there were 35 'million-plus' cities, it seems likely that there will be nearly 70 such cities by 2026, and because the urban population is becoming increasingly concentrated, these 70 cities could contain around half of all the country's urban inhabitants. The largest urban agglomerations— Delhi and Greater Mumbai—will probably each contain 30 million people. Everywhere urban populations will grow much faster than their rural counterparts; more than half of all India's population growth in the period to 2026 is likely to end up living in the urban sector. More demographically and socio-economically advanced states like Maharashtra and Tamil Nadu will have relatively modest rises in the sizes of their rural populations, while less advanced states like Uttar Pradesh and Bihar will have considerable increases in the sizes of both their urban and their rural populations.

The volumes of people involved in different types of migration may increase in the coming decades, but many migration rates seem set to decline. Thus short-term 'circulatory' migration rates will probably fall as such movements are increasingly replaced by the rise of commuting. Interstate migration rates may also fall partly because the growing number of million-plus cities will mean that people can move to such places without having to leave their home state. Continued urbanization will ensure that migration flows become more and more urban-oriented. Uttar Pradesh and Bihar will remain the most important exporters of people, but it seems unlikely that major north-to-south migration flows within the country will develop soon. That said, short distance migration—which is dominated by women, and primarily for reasons of marriage—will continue to be the most frequent type of human movement.

Finally, international migration will continue to be negligible compared to the size of India's population. But the number of people leaving for North America, Europe, and Australia seems certain to continue to rise in the period to 2026, as does the number of migrants entering India from Nepal and Bangladesh. International migration will probably have increasing social, economic, and political implications for India in the next few decades.

EDUCATION AND LITERACY

The recent progress in Indian education makes a welcome contrast with the past. The legacy of illiteracy and educational neglect inherited at the time of independence led the new Indian state to resolve that it would provide free and compulsory education to all children up to age 14 by 1960. Since that time, the target date for achieving the goal has repeatedly been extended, yet at the start of the new millennium the country is far from attaining its elusive goal. However, some encouraging signs from the 1990s could bode well for the future. Between the censuses of 1991 and 2001, the overall literacy rate of the population over 7 years of age rose by 13 percentage points, to 65 per cent—the highest decadal rise ever. Age-specific literacy rates measured in 1993 and 1999 also show a 10 percentage point increase in literacy among 6–19 year olds, quite substantial for a six-year period. Even in the four large and educationally backward northern states of Bihar, Madhya Pradesh, Rajasthan, and Uttar Pradesh, there was marked acceleration in the literacy rate, among the 10–14 year olds, which increased by 18 percentage points. Current school attendance also grew rapidly. For example, among rural 6–10 year old girls, it increased by a full 20 percentage points during the same six years.

The factors that are likely to have contributed to this progress are grouped into two broad categories: increases in the demand for schooling and improvements in the quantity and quality of the supply of schooling. The increase in demand over the 1990s is linked to the combined effects of falling poverty, fertility decline, and brighter economic prospects due to greater openness to international trade and investment. These trends promise stronger demand in the economy for educated employees and thus higher economic returns to education. Improvement in the supply of education is linked to better management through decentralization, the initiation of centrally and externally financed education projects, the use of para-teachers to expand access, and the rapid spread of private schooling. Different parts of the country, however, have experienced different patterns of educational provision, with varying degrees of reliance on the public and private sectors.

Population growth has made the task of educating India's children more difficult. Some states have, in fact, already experienced declines in their school-age numbers, while others will have growing school-age populations up to 2026. Projections are shown for the educational distribution of the population in 2026 in two cases—Bihar and Tamil Nadu. Our study of education ends with a discussion of the problems of the near future, such as low and static or falling per capita real public expenditures on education across many states; low quality in terms of poor school facilities; high pupil–teacher ratios and dull curricula; the spread of private primary schooling; and a tendency for poorer children, lower castes, and girls to have access only to lower quality schooling.

EMPLOYMENT

Despite rapid economic growth, the 1990s have in many ways been a disappointing decade for employment: there was a slowdown in the rate of employment generation and a corresponding increase in unemployment. The declining capacity of agriculture to absorb labour, together with absolute job losses in the public sector, have been the main culprits. Employment growth in other sectors like trade, financial services, and some manufacturing activities have been unable to compensate. Persistently high unemployment among those with high job aspirations remains, although with some improvement. State-level dispersion in unemployment rates appears to have increased. There is also evidence that employment quality has deteriorated with an informalization and casualization of the workforce. However, research shows increasing labour productivity in the unorganized sector during the 1990s, together with an increasing growth rate of incomes. There is also evidence of an increase in the real wage earnings of casual workers.

This book's population projections indicate that the working age population will be approximately 1.5 times as large in 2026 as it was in 2001. This future growth is incorporated in employment projections. To estimate future labour force size, the growing population is combined with estimates of changes in the labour force participation rate, with particular attention to women's participation. If women's participation increases, there will be an average annual addition of approximately 8 million people to the labour force between 2001 and 2026. And if recent trends in economic growth and the employment intensity of output continue until 2026, there will be a significant increase in unemployment. Even an annual economic growth rate of 8 per cent up to 2026 will not avoid future increases in unemployment.

These are, of course, only mechanical projections, not a forecast of worsening employment prospects. But they do suggest that if such prospects are to be avoided, policy must ensure that the economic climate becomes much more employment-friendly.

THE CONDITION OF THE PEOPLE

Poverty in India has been diminishing, though at an uncertain rate. The numbers in income poverty are in the region of 300 million. In today's understanding, poverty is not just a lack of income but includes deprivation in health, education, and other aspects of well-being. Only two indicators have shown accelerated improvement in the last decade—fertility decline and education—although nearly a third of the population is still illiterate. Nutrition has also improved modestly in recent years, but malnutrition is still widespread, despite slowly improving diets. It seems to be only partially a problem of income. Other aspects of health also show only modest improvements, and there is even some worsening due to environmental factors and HIV/AIDS.

There are numerous inequalities: most poverty is rural, and there are large discrepancies in well-being between different regions and social groups. The numbers in poverty are still projected to be 190 million in 2026, if the trends of the recent past continue. Again, these are mechanical projections—much can be done to improve this prospect. The country shows divergent progress, with the better-off states making significant improvements, and the worse off (and most populous) experiencing only slow changes. Recent research suggests there is a link between high fertility and poverty at the family level, and even at the macroeconomic level. Unfortunately, the states where poverty is worst and economic growth slowest are also mostly those where population growth is fastest. Continuing fertility decline should contribute to the amelioration of poverty.

THE ECONOMY

India's economy grew at about 6 per cent a year during the decade up to 2001—an increase in performance over previous decades. But there are some worrying signs that raise questions about whether the speed of growth can be maintained. The economic reforms of the 1990s played a considerable part in the acceleration of economic growth, but the large agenda of reforms still to be completed is stalled, mainly for political reasons. Difficulties in the export sector, partly related to the backlog of reforms, and lack of human capital and infrastructural investment, are also likely to impede future growth.

Progress has been mixed at the state level, with some southern and western states growing much faster than others, particularly those in the Gangetic plain. Many of the same factors explain this differential performance, with the additional problem of poor economic management in several states. A key issue is the heavy subsidies for electricity and water, which together account for a large portion of the fiscal deficits of several states. They deplete the resources which might be available for expenditure on health and education, which are the province of state governments, and they hinder environmental conservation. Resource constraints also hamper much-needed social and economic investment.

One positive factor for the future is the so-called 'demographic bonus' that results when the labour force grows faster than the dependent population of younger people, permitting increased savings and investment. This presents an opportunity that has to be grasped over the next 30 years, before a larger ageing population begins to reverse the early benefits of fertility decline.

FOOD AND AGRICULTURE

What of the country's food prospects? Population growth and increases in food production are intimately entwined. During 1951–2001, India's population grew by 285 per cent and cereal production by 441 per cent—figures which suggest that over half of cereal production growth was attributable to rising demand from population growth. The data are often patchy and inconsistent. By 2026, the level of total cereal demand is projected to be roughly 250 million tonnes, of which perhaps 30 million will be needed to cover feed, seed, and wastage. There should be no insurmountable obstacles to producing this quantity of cereal, which will require an average yield in 2026 of just over 3 metric tonnes per hectare (ha).

People are diversifying their patterns of food consumption. Taste, lifestyle, income, and other changes are contributing to particularly fast demand growth for non-cereal foods such as vegetables, fruit, and milk, while consumption of coarse cereals and pulses is either constant or declining. This trend towards diversification will continue, especially in vegetable and fruit production. This will mean that farmers working close to major towns and in agriculturally more productive states like Punjab and Haryana, may shift land out of cereal cultivation. Growers everywhere will have to be much more careful in their use of water. The application of chemical fertilizers per hectare will probably double by 2026. There could be a small but significant loss of agricultural land due to urban growth, but this loss will be more than outweighed by the expansion of the harvested area that will come from increased multiple cropping. Indeed, by 2026 India's gross harvested area will probably significantly exceed 200 million ha.

It is clear that current policy stances towards agriculture are unsustainable. Despite the political difficulties, they will have to change. For many farmers electricity and water are going to become increasingly expensive in the years ahead. Government food support prices for wheat and rice, which have produced mountains of wasted grain, will be reduced. With a general reduction in agricultural subsidies, policies will also have to target the poor—whether farmers needing water pumps in Bihar, or cultivators of coarse grains and oilseeds in the country's semi-arid regions, or the poorest sections of society who rely upon fair price shops. Farmers will face increased international competition as trade barriers come down; the country's production of sugar, for example, is profligate with water. But export possibilities will also arise, such as in fruits, vegetables, and pulses.

The outlook for India's food situation will be one of slow, modest improvement. There will probably be fewer hungry people in 2026 than in 2001, despite considerable population growth. But there may still be several hundred million people suffering from mild or moderate nutritional problems. Meat consumption will probably rise, but average levels of per capita meat consumption will remain extremely low by international standards.

These expectations are for average results over the whole country and over a long time horizon. There can be considerable fluctuations from year to year, and India's many different regions will inevitably face varying fortunes. A particular source of variation will arise from climate change, the main feature of which may be to make the future less predictable, and possibly more volatile. In late 2002, 13 of India's states were gripped by one of the worst droughts of recent years. Failure to address the difficult policy problems confronting agriculture, especially water, would compromise potential gains.

MODELLING THE ENVIRONMENT

Energy use is likely to grow very considerably as both the economy and the population expand. In the recent past the use of commercial energy has been increasing considerably faster than population, indicating that it is economic growth, and the pattern of growth, that has been the driving force. But population is a strong background factor adding to demand. Hitherto growing energy use has been accompanied by significant pollution, but the analysis here suggests that this trend need not continue. Cleaner technologies already exist and are becoming steadily less expensive. Future expansion is modelled with clean technologies introduced at different stages; the earlier they are introduced, the lower the levels of pollution reached. This effect is dominant, considerably outweighing demographic growth. The economics of introducing the beneficial technology is the key factor: it is assessed here as eminently affordable. The conclusion is that India can aspire to a greatly improved environment and a higher rate of economic growth. In fact, on account of the economic benefits of environmental improvement, which are likely to exceed the costs by an appreciable margin, India's economic prospects would be improved.

Similar accounts are suggested for other sources of pollution, including industry and transport. The message is a positive one. There is no need for India to become a polluting giant. But there are caveats. The results apply mainly to large-scale production; the small-scale sector is polluting, and has not benefitted to nearly the same extent from improved technologies. The analysis only describes what is possible. Whether India undertakes the appropriate investments and policies is another question. In some cases the cleaner technologies pay for themselves, so the producers should take them up. In others there are costs to the investor, while the benefits are to the wider society: then it is up to the government to regulate or give appropriate incentives by taxation and subsidy.

THE URBAN ENVIRONMENT

Urban environmental quality in India is set to become an increasingly important issue. Towns and cities draw heavily on natural resources such as water, forests, and soils. Where not properly managed, urban areas generate waste in a manner that pollutes air and water sources, and degrades renewable resources. Many of these problems of waste, air and water pollution have increased beyond both the absorptive capacity of nature and the handling capacity of institutions.

Solid waste is a major problem. The expanding volume of waste comes both from rising numbers of people and increasing per capita generation of waste; but most of the country's towns and cities are not coping successfully with its growth: uncollected refuse, unmanaged disposal sites, and the presence of hazardous waste are all too common, while land for disposal becomes ever scarcer. Options do exist; successful examples of good management can be found, commonly with the involvement of non-governmental organizations (NGOs), and some remarkable recycling is carried out, not least by poorer households. It is possible to manage waste and in many cases to generate wealth at the same time.

Urban water and sewage, linked to population growth, present further challenges. A large proportion of India's towns and cities lack sewage disposal, and water supplies are inadequate, especially for the poor, and often unsafe. All urban areas experience rising volumes of human and municipal liquid waste, commonly growing faster than treatment capacity. This presents considerable dangers to health. The threat to water-courses is very considerable.

Air pollution is a scourge of most urban areas. The main culprits are vehicle traffic, industry, and thermal power production, which have all grown much faster than population. Domestic burning of low-grade fuels and vegetable matter makes a further contribution. There is a considerable variety of experience across India, with some notable improvements, not least in Delhi during the recent past. Cleaner fuels and improved vehicle and manufacturing technologies can make major differences.

The combination of a lack of institutional capability, demographic pressures, and economic growth explains the current state of the environment in India's cities. Future trends will depend on the way in which demographic factors change, but also very largely on the ways in which urban governance is transformed over the coming decades. India has positive experiences to show in all fields of urban environmental management; the challenge is to have these best practices more widely spread.

WATER

Perhaps the strongest of all population impacts is on the demand for water. There will be growing needs for residential and industrial supplies, but it is agriculture which takes most of India's water, and as long as the country tries to remain broadly self-sufficient in food, demand for water may grow with the population requiring to be fed. Yet India will not have more water available in future than it has now and, as a result of pollution, it could well have less. Climate change could produce more rainfall, although with greater seasonal fluctuations and uncertain impacts on the Himalayan snowmelt and glacier flow. Very large increases will be needed in the efficiency with which water demand is met.

A number of studies have examined the future balance between water supply and demand, and found that growing national demand can be met. Apart from uncertainties linked to climate change, the account here takes the same view. But much depends on the manner in which demand is met. At present there is little incentive for farmers or residential consumers to conserve water. On the contrary, the mix of prices and subsidies in agriculture favours excessive water use without provision for maintenance of supplies, while better-off urban consumers have mostly free or subsidized water, and only the poor pay. At the same time, pollution is affecting the quality and quantity of useable water, and the situation is worsening rather than improving. Water is not just a problem for the future: it is already apparent in water scarcity, and frequent conflicts over water use in cities and countryside alike. The challenge is considerable: to find ways of overcoming pollution, and to give the right incentives to consumers that will induce them to conserve water, while not hurting the poor.

Much policy has been directed at supply management. There has been an engineering tradition of building large-scale dams and water works, now giving way to increasing emphasis on smaller-scale schemes, watershed development, and water harvesting. The view taken here is that large dams will almost certainly still be required, but they should be regarded as instruments of last resort, and only adopted with far more sensitivity to environmental concerns and the care and resettlement of affected populations than has been shown in the past. More attention to demand management is also needed; indeed, as water problems become more acute, lifestyle changes may well be required as part of any solution. Water policy is complex, and not to be seen in simple demand and supply terms. It involves laws, institutions, society, and politics. But, however difficult, there will have to be change. 'Business as usual' is not an option for India where water is concerned.

COMMON POOL RESOURCES

Fuel-wood, fodder, crop wastes, cow-dung, forest products, water—these and other common pool resources (CPRs) make valuable contributions to people's livelihoods, especially of rural populations, and, most importantly, in arid and semi-arid areas and the Himalayan region. They may be the principal assets of landless people, but they are subject to conflicting claims, including those from industry and commerce. One study suggests that these resources contribute on average 3 per cent of household expenditures, but there has been a quinquennial rate of decline in the land area of CPRs of close to 2 per cent in recent times; more detailed local studies show higher rates of decline, and higher contributions to household expenditures, especially for the poor.

Population growth contributes to increasing demand on these resources; at the same time, income growth can lead to changing preferences and demand switching to other products. There are possibilities of substitution also, and supplies can regenerate as well as be depleted. An index is developed here for access and use of these resources; Bihar and Uttar Pradesh turn out to be the worst placed states in terms of the combination of population growth and poverty relative to the availability of CPRs.

While there has been much emphasis in the past on the safety-net and livelihood functions of CPRs, the analysis here suggests a need for a wider focus, including market-based opportunities for their use, and their role in the provision of ecological services. At the same time, the main philosophy of management, stressing decentralized local governance and collective institutions and values, sits uneasily with national and global forces pointing to an expanding and individualized market economy. Need for a major effort of reconceptualizing the issues and reformulating policy is foreseen if the problems of conflicting claims are to be resolved.

POLICIES

India is presented with a number of challenges by its future population growth. This book closes with a chapter outlining the policies the authors consider most important to prepare for these challenges. Many of them will be familiar to observers of India. There are few issues the book covers for which the government does not already have well articulated policies and policy legislation, usually with strong support from commissions and studies by officials, academics, and NGOs. It is not for the absence of good analysis and policies that India still lags behind many other low-income countries in health and education, and in the extent of poverty. The difficulties have mostly been in implementation.

There are some policy issues of overarching importance. First, it is clear that the country will benefit from slower population growth, and, therefore, there is an urgent need for higher quality services in reproductive health and family planning, together with a host of supporting measures. Lower fertility will benefit the poor, especially poor women. It will make it easier to bring education of better quality to the whole population. It will reduce urban growth, and the growth of the labour force, making it easier to provide a better quality of urban life and satisfactory levels of employment. It will enhance economic growth. It will reduce pressure on environmental resources. Since the large, poor states of north India are where fertility is highest, women are most disadvantaged, and services are still weak, it is in these states that improved services are most needed.

Second, the excessive subsidies to electricity and water must be reduced. These are a fiscal problem and diminish economic growth. They also reduce the resources of the states which may be used to invest in health and education; and they contribute to environmental damage.

Third, water emerges as the greatest challenge posed by population growth. Here, while there are impressive government documents on water policy, many detailed policies are not, in fact, agreed to at a technical level. And where there is agreement that something needs to be done to control pollution, to regulate the use of groundwater, to regulate or price water for irrigation and domestic use, there is nothing resembling an implementable strategy for the whole country backed by political commitment.

Lastly, when it comes to atmospheric and chemical pollution arising from production and transport, this study finds that for the most part any negative effects of economic growth and growing population can be neutralized by the introduction of clean technologies. While there are public bodies with powers to control many forms of pollution, these powers are only used to a very limited extent. And as for the kinds of taxation and subsidy needed to support the introduction of clean technologies—where these do not pay for themselves (as they often do)—appropriate policies have still to be formulated.

This is not a pessimistic book, in the sense of finding insuperable difficulties lying ahead. Even with 1.5 billion people India can become a more prosperous country, with less poverty and better health and education, and a better conserved environment. Whether it does or not, only the people and the government of India can decide.

2
India's Population—The Past

Tim Dyson

This chapter reviews India's population history. It begins with the time before the year 1800, when it is only really appropriate to consider the subcontinent as a whole. It then considers the nineteenth and twentieth centuries, when the key points of divide are around 1871 (with the initiation of decennial censuses) and independence in 1947. These more recent periods are considered in greater depth, and the focus shifts to the territory of contemporary India. Finally, the chapter comments on some implications of the country's population history for the present and the future.

ANCIENT AND MEDIEVAL TIMES

Virtually nothing is recorded about the population history of the subcontinent during ancient and medieval times. Some societies collected relevant information, usually for purposes of taxation or military assessment. The *Arthashastra*, written by Kautilya around 325 BC, mentions population counts (Bhattacharya 1989: 348). However, no data from these or similar sources survive. Much later in history, even the Mughal emperors showed little interest in counting the people under their control. The famous *Ain-i-Akbari*, compiled by Akbar's minister Abul Fazl in 1595–6, provides information about the cultivated area, and it has been used to estimate the subcontinent's population. But such estimation involves large assumptions, not least because the *Ain-i-Akbari* did not cover the south (Habib 1982). As the data is either non-existent or, at best, highly fragmentary, we will probably never have more than a crude impression of the subcontinent's population in ancient and medieval times.

Nevertheless, it is possible to make some generalizations about the region's early demographic history. Before the advent of agriculture, say around 12,000 years ago, the subcontinent was inhabited solely by hunter–gatherers, and the population density was extremely low. One estimate puts the total population at roughly 100,000 (McEvedy and Jones 1978: 182). By around 5000 years ago, when the first major civilization in the semi-arid north-west region of the subcontinent had thrown up cities like Harappa and Mohenjodaro, the region's population may have been about 4–6 million (Bhattacharya 1989: 348; McEvedy and Jones 1978: 185). The great majority formed part of the Indus Valley Civilization.

The coming of the so-called 'Aryan' tribes is thought to have occurred around 3500 years ago. And the subcontinent's population is believed to have remained at only a few million until the period of late Aryan settlement (Bhattacharya 1989: 350). However, the Aryan migrations were to have two long-lasting consequences for the region's demography. First, there occurred a fundamental shift in the demographic centre of gravity from the Indus valley into the Gangetic plain. Indeed, from the sixth century BC onwards the Gangetic plain has been the subcontinent's most densely settled part. Second, the Aryan expansion eventually had a huge impact on the subcontinent's social geography. Indo-European languages became predominant throughout the north and west, leaving Dravidian languages to be spoken mainly in the south. In addition, whereas Aryan kinship laid great stress upon the male line and the tight control of women, southern kinship systems allowed women greater social freedom (Sopher 1980: 199). This fundamental north–south divide has resonances which are still detectable. Using data from the 2001 Census of India, Figure 2.1 shows that in the north and west the child population tends to be abnormally masculine. This reflects excess female mortality and the abortion of female foetuses. In the south and east, however, the balance between boys and girls is generally closer to normal.

By the time of the *Ain-i-Akbari* the subcontinent's population is thought to have reached about 130–50 million (Bhattacharya 1989: 352; McEvedy and Jones 1978: 185). Little is known about the region's demographic trajectory during the preceding centuries. Historians who have estimated the population size at particular moments have generalized from scraps of information. Perhaps swayed by the grandeur invoked by ancient texts, some have concluded that there were at least 100 million people as early as 230 BC. However, another estimate puts the figure at around 22–37 million as late as the seventh century AD, which may be more plausible because it suggests a population-growth trajectory broadly comparable to that indicated by the better data available for China (Durand 1977: 290). Indeed, the Chinese data, and those for western Europe, reveal a remarkable synchronicity of trend, with populations generally growing during times of planetary warming, and stagnating or

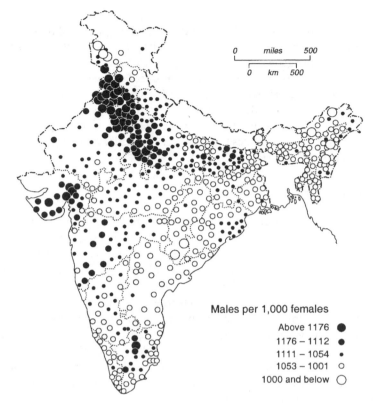

FIGURE 2.1: *Sex ratios by district, for children aged 0–6, 2001*

Source: Registrar General, India (2001b).

declining during times of cooling (Galloway 1986: 16). The subcontinent's demographic trajectory was probably also influenced by changes in climate, although not necessarily in the same way as in Europe and China. Furthermore, the occasional appearance of new diseases presumably brought about periods of population decline.

Most scholars believe that the seventeenth century—the age of the great Mughal rulers—saw some demographic growth (Durand 1977: 267). The population may have risen by 30 million or more. Mughal India appears to have contained a relatively developed urban hierarchy. Perhaps 10–15 per cent of people lived in towns. Partly from the observations of European travellers, it is thought that places like Agra and Delhi may have had several hundred thousand inhabitants (Habib 1982: 168–71). Besides remarking on the crowded cities, early travellers often commented on the extreme poverty experienced by most people. The observation that the subcontinent is populous and poor is long-standing (Cassen 1978: 1–5).

The rate of population growth during the eighteenth century was probably lower than it was during the seventeenth. Indeed, there may have been periods in the eighteenth century when—with the disintegration of Mughal rule and wars against intruders (notably the British)—the subcontinent experienced no demographic growth at all. During the 1770–2 famine in Bengal—if one contemporary account is believable—one-third of the entire population, some 10 million people, perished (Visaria and Visaria 1982: 528). Looking at the eighteenth century as a whole, it seems likely that the population was marginally larger at its end than at its start. However, the size of the population in 1800 remains uncertain; estimates fall between 160 and 214 million (Durand 1977: 267; Visaria and Visaria 1982: 466).

1800 TO 1871

During the early nineteenth century, East India Company administrators became increasingly interested in the populations under their control. Therefore the quantity and quality of the available data improve. For example, in rural areas Company officials conducted population counts and land surveys—again, often for purposes of raising taxation.

Some of the administrators who wanted such data collected were former students of Thomas Robert Malthus at the East India Company's college at Haileybury between 1805 and 1834. Although he wrote little on the subject, Malthus was certainly interested in the subcontinent's population, and he had a profound influence upon how the region's population came to be viewed. Thus in 1826, and after he had compiled evidence that marriage was both early and universal, Malthus wrote:

The population would thus be pressed hard against the limits of the means of subsistence, and the food of the country would be meted out to the major part of the people in the smallest shares that could support life. In such a state of things every failure in the crops from unfavourable seasons would be felt most severely; and India, as might be expected, has in all ages been subject to the most dreadful of famines (quoted in Caldwell 1998: 680).

Several population counts were conducted in the early 1850s. These contributed to the estimate (probably too low) of 181 million for the combined populations of the areas under Company control and the so-called 'native' states which was presented to the British Parliament in the mid-1850s (Raghavachari et al. 1974: 2). Such early census data provide rough figures. However, taken together, they suggest that the period 1800–71 may have seen unprecedented demographic growth. Comparison of 10 sets of estimates of population increase between 1800 and 1871 reveals considerable disagreement about the precise scale of the change. But the mean increase indicated is about 40 per cent, which would imply an average annual growth rate of about 0.5 per cent. Certainly the subcontinent's population was approaching, or had reached, about 255 million by 1871 (Visaria and Visaria 1982: 466).

The most likely reason for this faster demographic growth is that the death rate fell slightly. Average vital rates prevailing in the subcontinent during 1800–71 were certainly very high. Only a small fall in the death rate was required to raise the population growth rate towards 0.5 per cent. Perhaps the most plausible general explanation for a decline in the death rate is an increase in social stability which came, eventually, with British rule.

As in previous times, periodic famines occurred. Some—such as that of 1837–8 in the north—caused great loss of life. However, even a modest reduction in famine mortality could have made a significant contribution towards the minor rise in the population growth rate. And in certain locations, such as the Doab region of what is now Uttar Pradesh, limited famine relief operations, together with improvements in grain transport and irrigation, combined to reduce mortality from famines and raise population growth, particularly after about 1840 (Commander 1989: 65–7).

Another significant development was the introduction of smallpox vaccination in 1802. Smallpox probably accounted for at least 10 per cent of all deaths in the subcontinent at the start of the nineteenth century. The task of getting vaccination available to, and then accepted by, the general population was immense. There was, however, limited success in the decades before 1871, although it was the 1870s and 1880s which saw major improvement (Banthia and Dyson 1999).

Other developments of this period had more mixed implications for mortality. The expansion of irrigation was considerable. This provided employment and raised agricultural production. But from the 1830s, engineers remarked on a link between irrigation and the spread of malaria. Road and rail works were also implicated, in as much as they left stagnant pools of water stretching across the landscape which both heightened mosquito breeding and spread different strains of malaria around (Klein 1972). Cholera is a similar case. In earlier times outbreaks tended to occur mostly on the eastern side of the subcontinent. However, from the early nineteenth century onwards, British-imposed patterns of military movement and trade augmented the spread of cholera within the subcontinent (McNeill 1977: 241–2).

1871 TO 1947

The half-century which followed 1871 was punctuated by several major disasters which probably reduced the rate of population growth compared to the preceding seven decades. Also, the amount of available data, both from vital registration and census-taking, increases from around this time. Therefore it becomes possible to examine developments in greater detail.

Tables 2.1 and 2.2 provide census statistics and demographic estimates for India from 1871. As census-based estimates tend to obscure short-term fluctuations, Figure 2.2 plots annual registered vital rates for the Berar region

TABLE 2.1: *Census statistics for India, 1871–2001*

Year	Population (millions)	Increment (millions)	Average annual growth rate (per cent)	Population sex ratio (males per 1000 females)	Per cent aged 0–14	Per cent aged 15–44	Per cent aged 45+	Per cent urban
1871	211.7	–	–	1059	–	–	–	8.7
1881	213.5	1.8	0.08	1039	38.4	47.0	14.6	9.3
1891	234.0	20.5	0.92	1039	38.8	46.5	14.7	9.4
1901	238.3	4.3	0.18	1029	38.0	46.9	15.1	10.8
1911	252.0	13.7	0.56	1038	37.8	47.0	15.2	10.3
1921	251.2	–0.8	–0.03	1047	38.7	45.9	15.4	11.2
1931	278.9	27.7	1.05	1053	38.5	46.0	15.5	12.0
1941	318.5	39.6	1.33	1058	39.1	44.3	16.5	13.9
1951	361.0	42.5	1.25	1057	38.4	45.1	16.5	17.3
1961	439.1	78.1	1.96	1063	41.0	43.1	15.9	18.0
1971	548.2	109.1	2.22	1075	41.9	41.9	16.2	19.9
1981	683.3	135.1	2.20	1071	39.5	43.2	17.2	23.3
1991	846.3	163.0	2.14	1076	37.2	44.9	17.9	25.7
2001	1027.1	180.6	1.93	1072	34.4	47.1	18.5	27.8

Notes: Data from the 1867–72 censuses have been taken as representing 1871. The populations for 1871, 1881, and 1891 constitute 0.8995 of those derived by Davis (1951); this adjustment derives from a comparison for the censuses of 1891–1901 of his figures which relate to India and Pakistan with those derived by Mukherjee (1976) which relate to India's current area. The sex ratio and per cent urban statistics for 1871 relate to India, Pakistan, and Bangladesh combined. Statistics for 2001 are provisional. The age data for 2001 are estimates derived from the 1991 age distribution.

Sources: Davis (1951); Mukherjee (1976); Visaria and Visaria (1982, forthcoming); Census of India, *Other Social and Cultural Tables*, New Delhi: Registrar General and Census Commissioner (various years); Registrar General, India (2001a; 2001d).

TABLE 2.2: *Mortality and fertility estimates for India by intercensal decade*

Decade	Life expectancy at birth Male	Life expectancy at birth Female	Crude death rate (per 1000)	Crude birth rate (per 1000)	Total fertility per woman
1881–91	26.3	27.2	37.2	46.4	5.81
1891–01	22.2	23.4	43.9	45.7	5.78
1901–11	25.3	25.5	40.3	45.9	5.77
1911–21	21.8	22.0	45.4	45.1	5.75
1921–31	29.6	30.1	34.9	45.4	5.86
1931–41	29.5	29.6	33.2	46.5	5.98
1941–51	31.0	31.8	32.4	44.9	5.96

(contd...)

(Table 2.2 continued)

Decade	Life expectancy at birth		Crude death rate (per 1000)	Crude birth rate (per 1000)	Total fertility per woman
	Male	Female			
1951–61	36.8	36.6	25.9	45.5	6.11
1961–71	44.0	43.0	21.3	43.5	6.50
1971–81	50.0	49.0	16.0	38.0	5.40
1981–91	55.5	56.0	13.6	35.0	4.60
1991–2001	60.8	62.3	9.3	28.2	3.50

Notes: The life expectancies, crude birth rates, and total fertility rates for 1881–1961 are the 'Indian standard' estimates of Bhat (1989). For 1881–1961 the crude death rates were derived by subtracting from the birth rates the rates of natural increase implied by the population growth rates in Table 2.1. For 1961–91 the figures shown are averages of Bhat's (1998) 'integrated' estimates. The figures for 1991–2001 are based on SRS data. The 1991–2001 life expectancies are the averages of those for 1992–6 and 1996–2001 presented in Chapter 5; the death and birth rates and the total fertility rate are based on SRS estimates for 1991–8. The SRS figures may slightly overestimate life expectation and slightly understate the death, birth, and total fertility rates.

Sources: Bhat (1989, 1998); Registrar General, India (1999a, 2000).

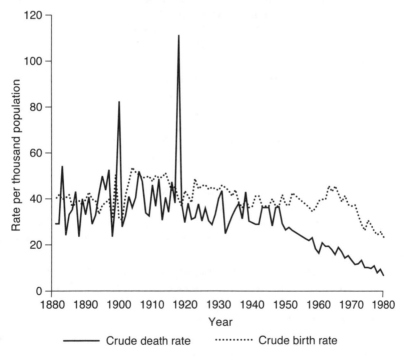

FIGURE 2.2: *Registered crude birth and death rates in Berar, 1881–1980*

Source: Dyson (1989b).

of central India by way of illustration. This region had unusually good registration, and it experienced a demographic trajectory which broadly resembled that of the country as a whole (Dyson 1989a). Notice, for example, the reduction in fluctuations of the death rate which happened after about 1921.

Five disasters during 1871–1921 require special mention. The massive famine of 1876–8, which was particularly severe in the south, probably caused between 5 and 8 million deaths. Then in the 1890s, the western and central areas were hit by two more major famines. Estimates of mortality from the famine of 1896–7 vary between 2.5 and 5 million; and that of 1899–1900 probably caused between 2 and 4.5 million deaths (Maharatna 1996: 15). Another major disaster was the bubonic plague which was introduced into Mumbai (then Bombay) by ship in 1896. Plague became a great problem in western India and Punjab, causing over 12 million deaths in the years to 1921, after which it subsided (Davis 1951: 46). The final disaster was the influenza pandemic. Also entering through Mumbai, it caused 17–18 million deaths in the subcontinent during the last four months of 1918. The probability of dying from an episode of flu was much greater in the north and west; consequently it was in these areas where most deaths occurred (Mills 1986).

India's population grew by 18.7 per cent between 1871 and 1921. The corresponding rate of annual increase was just 0.3 per cent. There was virtually no population increase during the 1870s and 1890s due to famine, and there was a slight decline in population during 1911–21 due to influenza (Table 2.1). However, the intervening decades 1881–91 and 1901–11 witnessed positive growth. The populations in the east of the subcontinent and, at least after 1876–8, in the south, were unaffected by major crises during 1871–1921 and these regions experienced growth rates close to 0.5 per cent. In contrast, the west was hit by everything: famine, plague, and influenza; therefore its population barely increased (Visaria and Visaria 1982: 490).

Table 2.2 shows that average life expectation during the worst decades of 1891–1901 and 1911–21 fell to roughly 22 years. However, in the Bombay Presidency, in 1918, influenza reduced life expectancy to only about 6 years (Mills 1986). And in Berar, in 1900, famine raised the IMR to 415 infant deaths per 1000 births, with a corresponding life expectancy of just 9 years (Dyson 1989b). The death rate fluctuations in Figure 2.2 underscore how extremely insecure life was.

As in earlier periods, famines and epidemics interacted synergistically to augment each other. Thus the conditions which accompanied famines (such as mass wandering) helped generate epidemics (for example, of cholera) to which many famine victims succumbed. Similarly, in western India the occurrence of influenza in 1918 disrupted agricultural operations and contributed to the declaration of famine in 1919 (Mills 1986).

Whether the famines of 1876–8, 1896–7, and 1899–1901 were the greatest ever to afflict India is moot (McAlpin 1983: 195–8). Over the long sweep of history some earlier famines probably raised death rates by more in percentage terms. However, by the late nineteenth century India's population had grown considerably; and if there were 5–8 million deaths during the famine of 1876–8 there can have been few previous famines which caused more. Throughout the nineteenth century, British interventions during times of famine were generally ad hoc, miserly, and hampered by a false confidence in the efficacy of free markets to deal with the problem. Also the opinions of colonial administrators were sometimes influenced by a Malthusian view that spending money on famine relief might only exacerbate India's population problem in the longer run. Thus the Governor General, Lord Edward Lytton, told the Legislative Council in 1877 that the population 'has a tendency to increase more rapidly than the food it raises from the soil' (Ambirajan 1976: 6). However, the Famine Commission Report of 1880, and the later Famine Reports of 1898 and 1901, established administrative procedures and systems of relief which played a role in reducing the effects of famine, especially after 1901 (Drèze 1990: 13–55).

During 1921–41, India's population growth accelerated at an unprecedented rate (Table 2.1). The growth was due to a modest improvement in mortality. Average life expectancy rose to nearly 30 years, while the birth rate remained about 45. Enhanced understanding of disease transmission, plus limited government efforts to improve public health (for example, in relation to cholera and plague) probably had a beneficial effect (Davis 1951: 45–52). But the scale of, and reasons for, the mortality improvement varied from place to place. In many areas of the country most of the gain probably came from a reduction in famines and epidemics. However, in Bengal, for example, the 1920s and 1930s saw a sustained fall in the death rate because of which, and boosted by some in-migration, the population was growing at the fairly fast annual rate of 1.9 per cent by 1931–41. Finally, it is important to remember that mortality decline is a complex *process*. Just as before 1921 one crisis might generate or augment another, so after 1921 the reduction in famines and epidemics provided a platform upon which various public health advances could have certain beneficial effects—effects which could begin to reinforce each other.

In the early 1940s, the attention of the colonial administration was distracted by the events of World War II. Consequently, rather than continuing to experience the slightly improving trend of the 1920s and 1930s, many areas of India experienced a rise in death rates (Figure 2.2). The Bengal Famine of 1943–4, which caused about 2.1 million deaths (Dyson and Maharatna 1991), was the most extreme expression of this. Also, the 1940s witnessed the massive disruptions and migrations consequent upon the Partition of 1947. Nevertheless, the rate of population growth was only slightly less than in the 1930s, and the total volume of growth, some 42 million, may have been slightly greater (Table 2.1).

The period 1871–1947 saw almost a doubling of the level of urbanization.

Specific crises, like major famines and the Partition, produced minor spurts (Table 2.1). During the nineteenth century and the first decades of the twentieth, urban death rates were much higher than those in rural areas. Indeed, the very existence of the towns depended upon an inflow of migrants coming from rural areas. Kolkata (then Calcutta), and especially Mumbai, both of which had populations of about 1 million in 1911, were virtual death traps. The IMR in Mumbai was roughly 50 per cent, possibly the highest in the world. Recognition of the extreme seriousness of the situation led to efforts to improve urban health conditions, and by the 1940s urban–rural mortality differentials had narrowed considerably (Dyson 1997: 123–31).

Four additional comments about the period 1871–1947 should be made. First, although average levels of mortality and fertility were high, they were probably not quite as high, or as exceptional, as has sometimes been believed. Previous work has suggested a very 'high pressure' demographic regime in which a very high death rate was counterbalanced by a very high birth rate (Mukherjee 1976). Recent research, however, has moderated this conclusion somewhat (Bhat 1989; Dyson 1989c). Thus, although the estimates of life expectation in Table 2.2 for 1871–1947 are low, they are not quite as low as some earlier estimates. At times, during the nineteenth century, several European populations experienced similar mortality levels (Dopico 1987; Preston et al. 1972). A corollary is that levels of fertility were probably not quite as high as was previously thought. Table 2.2 indicates that average levels of total fertility were under six births per woman. Many factors restricted the birth rate: breastfeeding was universal and prolonged; traditional beliefs promoted sexual abstinence; widow remarriage could be very difficult; and, given widespread child marriage, many women became widows while still extremely young, so curtailing their reproductive lives. Poor health conditions and infectious diseases also acted to depress fertility.

Second, demographic variation existed at several different geographical levels. At the broadest level, studies reveal that birth and death rates were somewhat lower in the south than in the north (Mukherjee 1976; Visaria and Visaria 1982). There is probably some correspondence between this finding and the general north–south variation shown in Figure 2.1. There were also considerable differences in the demographic experiences of different provinces, such as that of Bengal during 1921–41, as we saw earlier; Punjab was another area which experienced mortality decline at this time, leading to a relatively early fall in fertility (Das Gupta 1995); and Kerala appears to have experienced relatively favourable mortality from early in the twentieth century (Bhat and Rajan 1990). At the district level, work by Geddes (1947) shows that variation in patterns of population growth during 1871–1947 was so great that the country resembled a veritable patchwork of different demographic regimes. For example, large areas of West Bengal, Bihar, and eastern Uttar Pradesh experienced 'population stagnation' due to the presence of endemic malaria.

Most of Rajasthan and Gujarat, plus the drought-prone areas of Maharashtra and Karnataka experienced 'recurrent crisis'. Populations would grow for several years, only to be cut back by periodic famines or epidemics. Yet another growth pattern was that of 'high natural increase' which prevailed in much of Kerala, Tamil Nadu, and Andhra Pradesh. Populations in these areas grew fairly steadily because they were relatively free of malaria and their birth rates were significantly higher than their death rates. Then again, in parts of Punjab and Assam there was quite rapid population growth due to 'colonizing immigration', prompted, for example, by the extension of irrigation canals or the development of plantations (Geddes 1947).

A third comment relates to excess female mortality, a phenomenon which still exists, especially in the north and west, and which, understandably, continues to attract attention. As noted earlier, this feature has deep historical roots. At its most acute, female death rates can be sharply heavier than those of males from mid-infancy through to the end of the childbearing years and beyond. In the nineteenth century the phenomenon was sometimes compounded by the practice of female infanticide. However, looking at the country as a whole, it appears that India was only briefly a land where male life expectation exceeded that of females. Mari Bhat's estimates used in Table 2.2 suggest that this was true in the 1950s, 1960s, and 1970s, but not in earlier or later periods. During the first half of the twentieth century, male life expectation rose marginally more than that of females. Possible explanations include: (i) the increasing control of famines (which had tended to kill men slightly more than women), (ii) an increase in TB, which took a heavier toll of women (Bhat 1989), and (iii) that in a generally male-dominated society it was men who took first claim of what few health and other improvements occurred.

A final development of the period 1871–1947, with immense import for the future, was a gradual change in attitudes towards population growth. If the famines of the late nineteenth century were viewed by many as proof that the country was overpopulated, the increasing realization that modern contraceptive methods were being used in western countries, combined with knowledge that India's population was expanding, spurred a growing neo-Malthusian conviction that birth control, plus economic and social development, constituted the best way forward (Ambirajan 1976: 13). The early stirrings of the birth-control movement can be dated to around 1916 with the formation of a students' Eugenics Association in Chennai (then Madras). The first private family planning clinic was opened in Pune (then Poona) in 1925. The Maharajah of Mysore established the world's first government-sponsored family planning clinics at state hospitals in Mysore in 1930. The National Planning Committee, formed in 1935 and chaired by Jawaharlal Nehru, supported family planning through sexual abstinence and also through contraception. And in the same year the All-India Women's Conference called for the establishment of a national birth-control programme. Yet another significant development was the support for birth control provided by the Bhore Committee (so called after its chair, Sir Joseph Bhore) which published its report in 1946 (Visaria and Jain 1976).

From the 1920s onwards India was in the vanguard of the family planning movement in the developing world (Caldwell 1998: 688–90; Thapar 1963: 4–7). Of course, early efforts to promote contraception were questioned by those who, like Mahatma Gandhi, favoured sexual abstinence. The early birth-control clinics were few in number and overwhelmingly urban in location. However, by the 1940s, the practice of contraception was certainly spreading among better-off people living in the major towns (Davis 1951: 71).

AFTER 1947

At the time of its independence in 1947, India's population was about 345 million. Life expectancy was around 33 years, and the TFR was close to six births (Tables 2.1 and 2.2). The decades following the 1940s have seen great changes.

The most important change relates to mortality. With control of its own affairs, the Government of India now placed greater stress upon improving the health of its people. Figure 2.2 illustrates what has subsequently occurred almost everywhere—death rates have fallen, more or less continuously. At the start of the twenty-first century, at perhaps 62 years, life expectancy is almost double that of 1947.

Many factors contributed to this mortality reduction. Even the poorest people experienced some improvements in their living conditions. For example, average levels of calorie availability and income have risen (Table 2.3). Water supplies, sanitary facilities, and rural electrification have all progressed. People have been able to purchase an increasing number of modern medicines. Since these and other developments have tended to be greater in the towns, urban death rates have fallen appreciably more than in rural areas.

In addition, the control of certain communicable diseases has been important. Programmes aimed at cholera, filariasis, leprosy, smallpox, and TB were incorporated into the government's early five-year development plans, albeit with varying degrees of success. Smallpox was eradicated in 1975, but TB remains a huge problem, and malaria deserves special mention. In the 1940s, there were tens of millions of malaria cases and perhaps hundreds of thousands of malaria deaths each year. However, the National Malaria Control Programme began in 1953 and, largely through house-wall spraying with DDT, by 1965 there were estimated to be only 100,000 active malaria cases and perhaps no deaths (Learmonth 1988). Malaria has subsequently revived, but the situation is not nearly as serious as in the late 1940s. In broadly similar vein, the national child immunization programme against common diseases (such as diphtheria and tetanus) was started in the mid-1970s and made a

TABLE 2.3: *Selected indices for India, around 1951 and recent years*

	1951	1986–2001	
Female literacy (%)	7.9	54.2	(2001)
Male literacy (%)	25.0	75.8	(2001)
Number of hospitals	2,694	15,097	(1995)
Hospital beds per 1000 population	0.32	0.94	(1995)
Registered ancillary health personnel (000s)	76.5	506.9	(1996)
Per capita income (in 1980–1 Rs)	1127	2804	(1997)
Per capita daily calorie availability	2073	2417	(1999)
Female age at marriage (years)	15.4	18.8	(1986–91)

Notes: The literacy rates for 1951 and 2001 relate to the populations aged five and seven years and over respectively. Hospital bed figures include beds in dispensaries, health centres, etc. Ancillary health personnel are nurses, health visitors, and auxiliary nurse midwives. The initial health personnel figure and daily calorie estimate shown relate to 1961. The initial marriage figure relates to 1951–6.

Sources: Agrawal et al. (1993); Bhat (1998); Food and Agriculture Organization, *Food Balance Sheets,* Rome: Food and Agriculture Organization (various years); Jain (2000); Registrar General, India (2001a).

major contribution to the fall in infant and child mortality during the 1980s and 1990s. There has also been a considerable expansion of health and medical facilities (Table 2.3). Government expenditure on public health service provision has increased greatly. There are many more doctors and hospitals (private as well as public), and the establishment of a nationwide network of primary health centres and sub-centres has markedly raised people's access to advice and treatment. Another development which, augmented by rising levels of education, has helped to underpin the overall mortality improvement has been the gradual secularization of people's attitudes towards disease. In former times illness was sometimes either accepted, or treated by religious propitiation, but now, increasingly, there is understanding that practical steps can often lead to its control (Caldwell et al. 1983).

The reduction in the death rate after 1947 resulted in a significant rise in the rate of population growth, which reached almost 2 per cent during 1951–61. In the following three decades it remained fairly constant at around 2.2 per cent. Plainly, the birth rate was more resistant to change than the death rate. Indeed, it was only really during the 1991–2001 intercensal decade that the birth rate fell faster than the death rate—so bringing about a significant decline in the rate of population growth (Tables 2.1 and 2.2).

The mortality decline of the 1950s and 1960s reduced the proportion of the population aged 15–44 (Table 2.1). However, research suggests that around this time the level of total fertility per woman was rising, and the birth rate may have risen too (Bhat 1998; Dyson 1989c; Figure 2.2). Perhaps for the first time since decennial censuses began the country's TFR may have exceeded six births (Table 2.2). The concurrent improvements in mortality may have contributed to this fertility rise. Thus, the reduction in malaria could have reduced the incidence of foetal loss and raised the level of coital frequency. The mortality decline also contributed to a reduction in widowhood. Finally, it is possible that traditional practices of sexual abstinence and breastfeeding were beginning to erode.

The debate about population growth and family planning received impetus in the late 1940s not only due to the publication of the Bhore Committee Report, but also because of the occurrence of several poor harvests which necessitated the importation of food. Moreover, the 1951 Census revealed significant demographic growth. It was against this background that Nehru announced that India would initiate a national family planning programme. The final document of the First Five-Year Plan, presented to Parliament in 1952, referred specifically to a programme for 'family limitation and population control'. So, effectively, India became the first country in the world to adopt an official national population policy in support of family planning (Caldwell 1998; Visaria and Jain 1976).

During the 1950s, the government allocated modest sums of money to the population programme, much of which went to research into the rhythm method. Looking back, it is easy to dismiss such early efforts as cautious and ineffectual. But it should be recalled that many people had reservations about the promotion of modern contraception. And India was a *pioneer*; there was little previous experience on which to draw. However, there were other significant developments in the 1950s. Thus there was increasing achievement in promoting contraception in the larger towns. The government of Madras state began endorsing vasectomy with success, and it was soon followed in this by Kerala, Mysore, and Maharashtra. Madras also began making compensation payments to poor people who were sterilized (Thapar 1963; Visaria and Jain 1976). By the time of the Third Five-Year Plan (1961–6) the 'objective of stabilising the growth of population [within] a reasonable period' was put 'at the very centre of [India's] planned development'. The Third Plan document also noted the important role that voluntary sterilization might make towards achieving this. The budgetary outlay was significantly increased. Sterilization camps began to be used to promote vasectomy. There was also a shift in the emphasis of family planning delivery, from a clinic-based approach to a wider community extension strategy. The late 1960s also saw the increasing adoption of timebound—and often unrealistic—demographic 'targets'. In 1968 a goal was set to reduce the birth rate from 41 to 23 per 1000 within ten years (Visaria and Jain 1976). But at the start of the twenty-first century the birth rate was still about 25.

The period of the Fourth Five-Year Plan (1969–74) saw increased concern over the rate of demographic growth. Anxiety was heightened by the 1971 Census which showed a decadal increment of 109 million (Table 2.1).

Consequently, there was an increased emphasis upon targets, compensation payments, and male sterilization. This continued into the Fifth Plan, and culminated in the atmosphere of urgency which characterized Indira Gandhi's declaration of Emergency in 1975–7. The language of the 1976 National Population Policy as quoted in Cassen (1978: 182) is revealing of the time:

To wait for education and economic development to bring about a drop in fertility is not a practical solution. The very increase in population makes economic development slow and more difficult of achievement. The time factor is so pressing, and the population growth so formidable, that we have to get out of this vicious circle through a direct assault upon this problem as a national commitment.

The Emergency saw a massive increase in vasectomies. But there was later a backlash against the programme, particularly in the northern states, which lasted into the 1980s. Subsequently, although the government family-welfare programme has continued to emphasize sterilization, it has been mainly tubectomy which has been provided.

The rhetoric of population control largely disappeared with the Sixth Plan (1980–5). Since the Seventh Plan in particular (1986–90) there has been increasing recognition of the requirements: to tailor the family-welfare programme to the conditions prevailing in individual states; to adopt a multi-sectoral approach which recognizes the linkages between birth control and programmes in other areas (such as education); and to involve the private sector more in contraceptive delivery. Incentive payments and targets have largely been eliminated. Furthermore, following the 1994 Cairo Population Conference, somewhat greater account has been taken of the reproductive health needs of women.

India's various population policies and programmes have certainly facilitated the fall in fertility. The idea of birth control has been legitimated, and modern contraceptive methods have been made more accessible. Furthermore, other factors—perhaps most notably the rising levels of female education (Table 2.3) and the spread of new models of sexual and reproductive behaviour through channels like films and television—have been extremely important in promoting contraception (still predominantly female sterilization). Such processes have generally had stronger sway in the towns, and so fertility levels are significantly lower in urban areas.

If India's TFR was about six in 1947, by the start of the twenty-first century it had fallen to almost half that level. The rise in the age of women at marriage has made only a small contribution to this fall, which has occurred mostly due to increased use of contraception. Because of fertility decline, from the 1981 Census onwards there has been a significant reduction in the proportion of the population aged 0–14 years. The start of a trend towards population ageing, appreciably more advanced in the country's south, is discernible (Table 2.1).

Nevertheless, this record of progress in reducing mortality and fertility cannot hide the size of the many challenges which remain. And by many indicators of mortality, health, and fertility, India compares rather poorly in international terms. The population has trebled since 1947, and around the year 2001 it was probably increasing by about 17 million each year. These facts certainly complicate the task of reducing the number of people living in poverty and ill-health.

Finally, although the level of urbanization has risen since 1947, it remains fairly low (Table 2.1). Even so, the 2001 Census indicates that 285 million people live in urban areas. In 1951 only five towns had populations in the vicinity of, or larger than, one million (Kolkata, Mumbai, Chennai, Delhi, and Hyderabad). The 2001 Census, however, identified 35 urban areas with populations of one million or more.

SOME IMPLICATIONS

This chapter has provided only a sketch: its prime purpose has been to give some background and perspective. In conclusion, four points are underscored.

First, several key features of India's contemporary population have very deep historical roots. The Gangetic plain has constituted the subcontinent's demographic heartland for over two millennia, and will remain so during the foreseeable future. The north–south demographic divide is also of long-standing. Many measures of fertility and mortality are significantly higher in the north. To generalize, at the start of the twenty-first century the south is two or three decades ahead in terms of its fertility decline and its completion of the demographic transition. It has been in the most densely settled, inland northern states, notably Uttar Pradesh and Bihar, that health care and reproductive behaviour have been slowest to change. India is heading down a path of eventual demographic convergence where levels of fertility and mortality in both the north and south will be relatively low. However, this convergence will take considerable time to happen.

Second, history provides valuable perspective on the dynamics of the various processes that are currently under way. This is especially true of the demographic transition. During the nineteenth century, the high and highly variable death rate was the predominant demographic feature; and governmental concern, such as it was, was directed mainly at countering famines and epidemics. It was the reduction in these which laid the basis for the limited mortality improvements of the 1920s and 1930s, with much greater gains coming after 1947. But because it resulted in a growing population, the reduction in mortality was paralleled by an increasing concern with the birth rate. The fertility decline which, for the country as a whole has been happening since the 1960s, is essentially a response to the decline in the death rate: India's concern with family planning policies basically arose from this. That said, there is tremendous variation in demographic experience within the country. The fact that some populations (such as in Kerala and Punjab) experienced a greater measure of mortality decline and population growth at a relatively early time probably helps to account for their relatively early fertility declines. So different parts of India are experiencing different versions of the same overarching demographic transition.

Third, there are the key related issues of population growth and population scale—the latter, of course, resulting from past growth. Here, history certainly provides perspective. The 2001 Census indicated the addition of 180 million people since 1991. Despite the fall in the growth rate, the absolute addition to the population in just ten years is the greatest since censuses began. At well over a billion, the population was almost five-fold that of 1871 (Table 2.1).

Finally, history bequeaths yet another legacy, because the age structure of the population is largely the outcome of the country's past record of reducing its birth rate. And at the start of the twenty-first century the age structure is still fairly young (Table 2.1). This virtually guarantees the addition of another 500 million people, at least, during the decades which lie ahead.

3

Mortality Trends and the Health Transition

Leela Visaria

$\sim$

I ndia is experiencing interrelated demographic and epidemiological transitions. These processes are transforming the country's mortality and health profile; they will have major implications for prevailing disease patterns and the composition of the population in the years ahead. It is worth noting that while the materials available to study mortality are reasonably robust, the data pertaining to causes of death are both more limited and less precise. Nevertheless, if considered in conjunction with other data sources, the cause of death material can still be helpful in gauging likely future developments.

MORTALITY AND HEALTH TRENDS

Changes in India's record in mortality and health are best understood in historical perspective. This section begins by briefly considering the period from India's independence in 1947 until around 1971. It then examines the period since 1971 in greater depth, because future trends will be more heavily influenced by the more recent developments.

Chapter 2 has shown that the country's mortality improved quite significantly during the first 25 years following independence. Indeed, between the mid-1940s and the mid-1960s average life expectation at birth probably increased by about 12 years, which was considered a significant achievement. It was also during these 25 years, however, that the mortality and health disadvantages suffered by females became much more evident because, for the first time since estimates became available, Indian females began to experience lower average levels of life expectancy than males.

Parts of the country experienced intermittent failures of the monsoon rains, but these did not result in the widespread famine mortality that had occurred in earlier times. Improvements in transport and relief meant that food was distributed to regions experiencing shortages, basic employment opportunities were provided, and food prices were generally kept under control (Drèze 1988). In addition, both plague and smallpox diminished. Advances in sanitation and housing helped to check plague; increased vaccination reduced the incidence of smallpox, and eventually led to the eradication of the disease: the last recorded case was in 1975 (Banthia and Dyson 1999, 2000).

However, many preventable childhood diseases like tetanus, pertussis (whooping cough), poliomyelitis, measles, plus a host of respiratory and diarrhoeal ailments continued to cause heavy mortality. The generally dismal levels of maternal health and nutrition meant that conditions such as low birth weight and prematurity remained important contributors to high levels of early age mortality, as were birth injury and asphyxia. It is probable that most improvements in infant mortality in the period between 1947 and 1971 were seen at post-neonatal ages (after the first month of life, but before the first birthday) and, therefore, the contribution of neonatal deaths (those in the first month of life) to overall infant mortality increased.

In the 1950s many of India's policy-makers and planners believed that malaria could be eradicated through the wider availability of quinine-based drugs and, still more, through the spraying of mosquito breeding-places with insecticides like DDT. When the National Malaria Control Programme was introduced in 1953, the annual incidence of malaria cases was estimated at around 75 million, with about 800,000 deaths. The programme proved to be highly successful, and within five years the annual incidence of cases had dropped to roughly 2 million (Sharma 1996). There is little doubt, therefore, that the reduction in malaria was a major factor behind the decline in the national crude death rate from around 32 deaths per 1000 population during the 1940s to about 21 by the mid-1960s. That said, neither the growing resistance of mosquitoes to the new insecticides nor the other harmful effects on human health of indiscriminate DDT spraying were anticipated. The euphoria of the 1960s regarding the possible eradication of malaria proved to be short-lived, and in the 1970s the disease re-emerged.

Two other diseases which were addressed by government health initiatives during this period merit mention. The number of registered deaths from cholera fell from over 2 million in the 1940s to under 150,000 during 1959–68 (Ragavachari et al. 1974: 44). The provision of safer water supplies and the closer monitoring of congregations of pilgrims were important to this significant advance. Even so, cholera continues to prove difficult to control completely, especially in the eastern areas of the country. Whenever there is a calamity, like a flood or an earthquake, the threat of an outbreak persists. The national programme to control TB was initiated in 1962. It aimed at detecting cases of TB at an early stage by means of sputum microscopy and X-rays; this was to be followed by provision of effective domiciliary treatment using standard chemotherapy regimes. However, the programme did not succeed in arresting the prevalence of TB. Sufferers did not comply with treatment both because of the stigma attached to having TB and because of the lengthy process of cure which could last up to 18 months. High dropout rates from treatment both increased the chances of re-infection and contributed to the growth of drug-resistant forms of TB (Pathania et al. 1997).

During the period 1971–2001, the quantity and quality of the data available to study India's mortality and health circumstances improved greatly. In particular, the Sample Registration System (SRS) came into existence in the late 1960s. Since that time, the SRS has provided annual estimates of all the main demographic measures. These estimates are generally thought to be fairly reliable and are, therefore, used in the text that follows.[1] From about the same time sample data on causes of death also began to be collected for rural areas of the country.[2] Two major National Family Health Surveys (NFHS) were conducted in 1992–3 and 1998–9. In addition there were quite a few smaller studies and surveys related to health conditions.

The decades 1971–2001 saw unparalleled population growth. Most attention during this period was, therefore, directed to the analysis of fertility data. Mortality and morbidity remained of secondary interest. It was thought, perhaps, that the various public health programmes aimed at controlling diseases like malaria and smallpox were generally achieving their objectives. It is only recently—with the resurgence of certain diseases, the increasing prominence of various non-communicable ailments, and the new threat posed by HIV/AIDS—that studies of mortality and health conditions have at last received greater attention.

Perhaps the most important fact to record is that the steady decline in mortality that was clearly evident in the 1950s and 1960s continued during the last three decades of the twentieth century. The SRS estimates for all-India summarized in Table 3.1 indicate that the crude death rate declined from almost 16 deaths per 1000 population during 1971–5 to under 9 per

[1]The SRS employs a 'dual record' mechanism to collect information on vital events (births and deaths) in a large, representative sample of villages and urban blocs. There is thus a continuous enumeration of vital events by a local enumerator, the results of which are then checked and updated through retrospective half-yearly surveys conducted by investigator-supervisors who visit the sample units from outside. Data from these two sets of records are matched and the unmatched events are verified in the field. For more information on the SRS see Registrar General, India (1999a, 2000). For evaluations of SRS event coverage see Bhat (1998, 2000b).

[2]This is the so-called Model Registration Scheme, Survey of Causes of Death (Rural). Under this scheme paramedical staff attached to primary health centres (PHCs) collect information regarding the probable cause of death from the families of the deceased. This survey was initiated on a limited basis in 1965 in 10 states and by 1977 all the major states were covered.

1000 by 1999. During the same period, the estimated IMR fell from about 134 infant deaths per 1000 live births to a figure of around 70; this represents quite an impressive fall of almost 50 per cent. Furthermore, life expectation at birth for both sexes combined rose from about 50 years in 1971–5 to around 61 years by 1993–7 (Registrar General, India 1999a: 16). During 1971–5, male life expectation exceeded that of females by more than one year, but by the mid-1990s the situation had reversed. Between the early 1970s and the end of the twentieth century the gains in female and male life expectancy were about 12 and 10 years respectively.

Neonatal and post-neonatal mortality rates also continued to fall significantly at this time, although the pace of the declines varied (Figure 3.1). Between 1971 and 1997 the post-neonatal rate fell from about 54 to 25 deaths per 1000 (that is, by 54 per cent), whereas the neonatal mortality rate fell from 75 to 46 deaths per 1000 (that is, by 39 per cent) (Registrar General, India 1999a: 16). This meant that neonatal mortality continued to contribute an increasing share of overall infant mortality, and was partly to be expected because neonatal mortality is inherently more difficult to reduce. However,

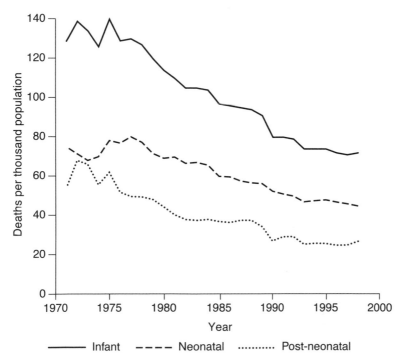

FIGURE 3.1: *Infant, neonatal, and post-neonatal mortality rates from the SRS, all-India, 1971–98*

Source: Registrar General, India (1999a).

Table 3.1: Mortality estimates for all-India and by rural–urban residence, 1971–2000

Period	Crude death rate (per 1000)			Infant mortality rate (per 1000 live births)			Life expectancy at birth (years)					
							Male			Female		
	Total	Rural	Urban	Total	Rural	Urban	Total	Rural	Urban	Total	Rural	Urban
1971–5	15.5	17.1	9.8	134	144	83	50.5	48.9	58.8	49.0	47.1	59.2
1976–80	13.8	15.0	8.9	124	134	74	52.5	51.0	59.6	52.1	50.3	60.8
1981–5	12.1	13.3	7.9	104	113	64	55.4	54.0	61.6	55.7	53.6	64.1
1986–90	10.6	11.6	7.3	91	99	59	57.7	56.1	62.0	58.1	56.2	64.9
1991–5	9.5	10.4	6.6	76	83	50	59.7	58.5	64.5	60.9	59.3	67.3
1996	9.0	9.7	6.5	72	77	46	60.1	58.9	64.9	61.4	59.8	67.7
1997	8.9	9.6	6.5	71	77	45	60.4	–	–	61.8	–	–
1998	9.0	9.7	6.6	72	77	45	–	–	–	–	–	–
1999	8.6	9.4	6.3	70	75	44	–	–	–	–	–	–
2000	8.5	9.3	6.3	–	–	–	–	–	–	–	–	–

Notes: For each period the rates shown are averages of respective annual estimates. The life expectations shown against the year 1996 actually relate to the period 1992–6 and those shown against the year 1997 relate to 1993–7.

Sources: Registrar General, India, *Sample Registration Bulletin*, Ministry of Home Affairs, New Delhi (various years); Registrar General, India (1999a).

it also reflected the fact of only limited improvements in the utilization of antenatal and obstetric services and the continuing young ages of females at marriage.[3]

These figures for all-India conceal differential rates of progress for different sections of society. For example, Table 3.1 shows that mortality rates have generally been appreciably higher in rural areas. In the mid-1990s, the life expectation of males in urban areas was some six years greater than that of their rural counterparts; and with an average life expectation of almost 68 years, urban females in the mid-1990s had a life expectation that was almost eight years higher than the figure prevailing in rural areas. Considering the period of almost 30 years starting from 1971–5, the proportional decline in the IMR was actually fairly similar between rural and urban areas, but gauged in terms of the estimated absolute rise in life expectation, there was, in fact, greater progress in reducing mortality in rural areas. During 1971–5, the urban population of India outlived the rural population by about 10.9 years; by 1992–6 this differential had fallen to just 6.9 years (Registrar General, India 1999a: 16; Table 3.1).

Interstate mortality differentials are quite wide too. In general, states in the south of the country tend to experience more favourable levels of mortality than states in the north. Kerala, in particular, does outstandingly well, and among the northern states both Punjab and Haryana are also rather exceptional. Three–year averages of the SRS infant mortality rates for the period 1997–9 suggest that in Madhya Pradesh and Orissa, for example, over 90 out of every 1000 live births died before reaching their first birthday (Table 3.2). Both Rajasthan and Uttar Pradesh also had IMRs exceeding 80 per 1000. However, Kerala's IMR during 1997–9 was just 14. The IMR was less than 60 in Karnataka, Maharashtra, Tamil Nadu, West Bengal, and Punjab. Estimates of life expectation give a broadly similar picture. In 1993–7, estimated life expectancy was over 70 years in Kerala; in Haryana, Punjab, Karnataka, Maharashtra, West Bengal, and Tamil Nadu it was around 63–5 years; but in the populous northern states of Madhya Pradesh, Bihar, and Uttar Pradesh it was only about 55–8 years (Table 3.2).

All states experienced significant declines in mortality during the last three decades of the twentieth century. The basic regional pattern of inter-state differentials persisted, although there was also some reduction in mortality differentials. Over the period 1971–5 to 1993–7, gains in life expectation, expressed in terms of years, tended to be somewhat greater in states with initially low relative levels of life expectancy. For example, the SRS suggests that Uttar Pradesh and Orissa experienced rises in life expectation of around 14 and 13 years respectively, whereas in Kerala, Punjab, and Haryana the

[3] According to data from the 1991 Census the mean age at marriage of women who married during the period 1986–91 was 18.3 years (Registrar General, India 1998a: 52). In poorer parts of the country many women are married at much younger ages.

TABLE 3.2: *Mortality estimates for the major states and all-India, 1971–99*

	Crude death rate (per 1000)		Infant mortality rate (per 1000)		Life expectancy at birth (years)			
	1971–3	1997–9	1971–3	1997–9	1970–5		1993–7	
					Male	*Female*	*Male*	*Female*
Andhra Pradesh	15.8	8.4	109	65	48.4	49.3	61.2	63.5
Assam	17.3	9.9	137	76	46.2	44.8	56.6	57.1
Bihar	13.7	9.5	110	68	54.2	51.5	60.4	58.4
Gujarat	15.7	7.8	144	63	48.8	48.8	60.9	62.9
Haryana	11.3	8.0	90	69	59.0	55.6	63.7	64.6
Karnataka	12.4	7.7	93	56	55.1	55.3	61.6	64.9
Kerala	8.9	6.3	58	14	60.8	63.0	70.4	75.9
Madhya Pradesh	17.1	10.9	145	94	46.3	47.6	55.6	55.2
Maharashtra	12.9	7.5	107	48	54.5	53.3	64.1	66.6
Orissa	17.9	11.0	134	97	46.0	45.3	57.1	57.0
Punjab	11.7	7.5	112	53	59.0	56.8	66.7	68.8
Rajasthan	16.2	8.7	131	83	49.2	49.2	59.1	60.1
Tamil Nadu	14.5	8.2	114	53	49.6	49.5	63.2	65.1
Uttar Pradesh	21.7	10.4	182	85	45.4	40.5	58.1	56.9
West Bengal	10.6	7.4	87	53	56.4	58.0	62.2	63.6
All-India	15.9	8.9	134	71	50.5	49.0	60.4	61.8

Notes: For each period the rates shown are averages of respective annual estimates. Because SRS event coverage in Bihar and West Bengal was particularly poor during the 1970s for these two states the rates shown for 1971–3 actually relate to 1981–3 and the life expectations shown for 1970–5 relate to 1981–5.

Sources: Registrar General, India, *Sample Registration Bulletin*, Ministry of Home Affairs, New Delhi (various years); Registrar General, India (1999a).

increases were only about 11, 10, and 7 years respectively (Table 3.2). So, as with the urban–rural contrast, here too there is some suggestion that absolute mortality differentials may have narrowed a little.

There is particular concern about trends in infant mortality. The pace of decline in the all-India IMR during the 1990s appeared to be slow compared to the 1980s (Figure 3.1). In particular, the SRS infant mortality rate fell from 114 infant deaths per 1000 live births in 1980, to 80 in 1990, but it had only declined to 70 by 1999. Many analysts attributed this apparent slowdown in the 1990s to a decline in the provision of immunizations and other basic health interventions (Claeson et al. 1999;

Measham et al. 1999).[4] Data on immunizations and the utilization of infant and maternal health services provided by the two NFHS survey rounds in the 1990s gave some support for this viewpoint. For example, there was only a marginal improvement—from about 52 per cent in 1992–3 to 55 per cent in 1998–9—in the proportion of children aged 12–23 months who were protected by three doses of triple antigen vaccine (DPT) covering diphtheria, pertussis, and tetanus (Table 3.3). The DPT vaccine coverage in each of the

TABLE 3.3: *Percentages of children aged 12–23 months who had received specific vaccinations at any time before the interview, major states and all-India, 1992–3 and 1998–9*

| | Type of vaccination | | | | | | | |
| | BCG | | DPT(3) | | Polio(3) | | Measles | |
	1992–3	1998–9	1992–3	1998–9	1992–3	1998–9	1992–3	1998–9
Andhra Pradesh	73.9	90.2	66.1	79.5	68.0	81.6	53.8	64.7
Assam	48.2	53.5	31.0	37.5	32.7	37.9	25.8	24.6
Bihar	33.9	37.7	29.1	24.2	31.6	41.0	14.6	16.6
Gujarat	77.1	84.7	63.8	64.1	62.9	68.6	55.9	63.6
Haryana	77.4	86.8	66.8	71.1	67.7	74.3	60.9	72.2
Karnataka	81.7	84.8	70.7	75.2	71.4	78.3	54.9	67.3
Kerala	86.1	96.2	73.7	88.0	75.2	88.4	60.5	84.6
Madhya Pradesh	56.8	64.9	43.7	37.0	46.6	56.7	40.7	35.5
Maharashtra	86.9	93.7	83.1	89.4	81.6	90.8	70.2	84.3
Orissa	63.3	84.7	56.3	61.9	56.7	68.4	40.2	54.0
Punjab	77.4	88.7	73.6	82.0	73.4	83.6	64.8	76.5
Rajasthan	45.7	53.9	29.7	26.1	32.8	44.6	31.2	27.1
Tamil Nadu	91.7	98.6	86.5	96.7	85.3	98.0	71.6	90.2
Uttar Pradesh	48.9	57.5	34.1	33.9	37.1	42.3	26.3	34.6
West Bengal	63.1	76.5	51.9	58.3	56.0	61.7	42.5	52.4
All-India	62.2	71.6	51.7	55.1	53.4	62.8	42.2	50.7

Notes: The figures relate only to surviving children from among the two most recent births in the three years preceding the survey. The BCG vaccine provides immunization against tuberculosis; DPT provides immunization for diphtheria, pertussis (whooping cough), and tetanus. For DPT and polio the figures refer to those who had received a third vaccine dose.

Sources: International Institute for Population Sciences (IIPS) and ORC Macro (1995, 2000).

[4]It is worth recording that during the 1970s too there was a widespread impression that the pace of mortality decline in India had slowed down (Ruzicka 1984). However, this suggestion was rejected by the authors of the US National Academy of Sciences report on India's demography (Bhat et al. 1984).

four populous northern states of Bihar, Madhya Pradesh, Rajasthan, and Uttar Pradesh, which contain about 41 per cent of the country's total population and where, in 1998–9 about 51 per cent of all births took place, actually fell between the first and second NFHS survey rounds. Furthermore, the trends with respect to measles were not much better (Table 3.3).

However, most states did experience increases in immunization coverage for most vaccines during the 1990s. While contrasting IMR trends in the 1990s with those in the 1980s, it should not be forgotten that the 1980s was a decade of major activity in immunization. The country's Expanded Programme of Immunization was initiated in 1978, and in 1985–6 the so-called Universal Immunization Programme was introduced. These programmes were also stimulated by the global immunization efforts of UNICEF (Cassen 2002). In absolute terms the fall in mortality inevitably becomes shower as mortality rates decline. In Kerala, for example, there is only restricted scope for more reductions in the IMR. Finally, changes in the SRS sampling frame and variations in the system's coverage of births and deaths may also have obscured real trends in early-age mortality during the 1990s.[5]

In concluding this section it is worth making several points of relevance for the future. First, it is clear that at the start of the twenty-first century levels of infant and child mortality in India were still fairly high, and there is huge scope for further reductions. For example, the achievement of universal immunization, and the control of basic diarrhoeal diseases, can both bring about significant falls in early-age death rates in the years ahead. It seems probable that in the country's poorest states the full impact of basic health measures in the past has often been limited by low levels of nutrition, high infection loads in the general environment, and various socio-economic and infrastructural limitations (for example, low levels of maternal education, poor water quality, and inferior transport facilities). Here, too, some progress can be expected as socio-economic and infrastructural conditions improve. There are distinct possibilities for health 'virtuous circles' (for example, reductions in infectious diseases contributing to improvements in child nutrition and vice versa).

Second, as we see in the following chapter, levels of fertility are declining in every state in the country. This should benefit mortality and health conditions in the future, for example, by lowering exposure to the risks of pregnancy and thereby contributing to falls in maternal mortality. Fertility decline should also help to improve the average survival chances of infants and young

[5]A change in the SRS sampling frame tends to affect the resulting demographic estimates because the new sample tends to be younger in its age composition than the old sample. In this context it is worth noting that earlier periods (for example, 1971–8) were also times of slower IMR decline at the all-India level (Figure 3.1).

children, for example, because there will be fewer births at high parities and at high maternal ages in the coming decades.

A final point for discussion relates to gender differentials in mortality. For all-India, Figure 3.2 plots the ratios of male to female death rates for five-year age groups. The ratios are below 1 for age groups in childhood and young adulthood, meaning that female death rates at these ages are higher than those of males.[6] Measured in this way, and compared to experience elsewhere in the world, excess female mortality in the 0–4 and 5–9 age groups is exceptional, and it tends to be especially so in the country's northern states. Notice from the plots for 1971, 1986, and 1996 that there has been no improvement in the relative death rates of females at childhood ages; indeed, if anything, the situation has worsened.

Preference for sons is widespread in India, particularly in the north. Many studies have shown that behavioural factors, including care-seeking practices, operate against young female children. Girls are less likely to receive medical attention than boys, and if they do get treatment then it tends to be at a later stage of illness and to be provided by less qualified personnel. Many of the discriminatory practices involved are subtle and lie deep within intimate family behaviour (Chatterjee 1990; Filmer et al. 1998; Visaria 1988).

In addition, there is mounting evidence that high levels of son preference are increasingly manifesting themselves in female-specific abortions in some parts of the country (Booth et al. 1994; Ganatra et al. 2001; George and Dahiya 1998). The sharp rise in the masculinity of the child population aged 0–6 years in the states of Haryana, Punjab, Gujarat, and Maharashtra indicated by the results of the 2001 Census is strongly suggestive of sex-selective abortions (Dyson 2001). According to the reports of women interviewed in the 1998–9 NFHS survey, the ratio of male to female last births in the country as a whole was 1.43, compared to a more normal figure of 1.07 reported for all previous births. The NFHS data for 1998–9 suggest that women are much more likely to have experienced ultrasound and/or amniocentesis during an ante-natal check-up if they have no living sons than if they have one or more sons, and this is especially so in the states with high son preference mentioned earlier (Arnold and Roy 2002).

That said, adult female mortality has been improving appreciably faster than male. Figure 3.2 shows that the age group at which the male death rate exceeds that for females dropped from 40–4 in 1971 to 30–4 by 1996. This trend has been fairly steady and seems likely to persist in the future. In part, it probably reflects the morbidity and mortality benefits to women which stem

[6]It should be noted, however, that during the first six months of life, and probably largely for innate biological reasons, the death rate of males tends to be higher than that of females in most areas of India.

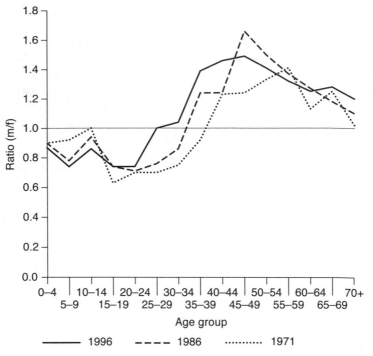

Figure 3.2: *Ratios of male to female age-specific death rates from the SRS, 1971, 1986, and 1996*

Source: Registrar General, India (1999a).

from continuing fertility decline. However, Figure 3.2 suggests that adult male mortality may be a subject of greater concern in the years ahead.

We now consider trends in patterns of cause of death in India since around 1971.

CAUSES OF DEATH

Epidemiological theory postulates that as mortality declines so there is a marked shift in the distribution of causes of death, from those due to infectious diseases to those caused by non-communicable ailments. To examine the extent of this transition we consider data at five–year intervals from 1966 to 1995 from the survey of causes of death in rural areas referred to earlier.[7] It should be stressed

---

[7]Data for 1995 were the most recent available. This annual survey collects information through the 'lay diagnosis reporting' method for deaths in villages where a sample of PHCs are located. Around 1994, the sample involved 1731 PHC villages and about 37,000 deaths. See also footnote 2 of this chapter.

that comparisons over time are often complicated, among other things, by variations in the specific causes of death used in the survey, and because of changes in diagnostic practices.[8] However, the information provides some broad indications regarding changes in disease patterns.

Table 3.4 summarizes how the proportional mix of causes of deaths has altered. Several points arise. Deaths attributed to 'senility' (including 'old age') increased fairly steadily from 1966–7. The abrupt drop in 1994–5 was probably related to the simultaneous rise in the proportion of deaths attributed to 'other clear symptoms'. This latter category includes several major disease groups such as cancer, diabetes, cirrhosis, and other chronic liver diseases, which tend to affect older people more. Table 3.4 shows that the share of deaths due to 'accidents and injuries' also rose progressively from about 3.9 to around 9.5 per cent between 1966–7 and 1994–5. This rise may partly mirror an increasing degree of mechanization in the economy. Some of it also reflects increasing mortality due to vehicular accidents, especially from the 1980s onwards. Notice too that the share of deaths due to 'disorders of the central nervous system' and 'diseases of the circulatory system' (a category which includes deaths from heart disease) both increased steadily. Again, this can be seen as reflecting a progressive shift towards greater prominence of non-communicable ailments in the country's overall cause of death profile. The share of deaths due to 'digestive disorders' fell from about 10.4 per cent around 1966–7 to 6.2 per cent by 1994–5. In part this may reflect some decline in mortality from diarrhoeal diseases. Deaths related to 'child birth and pregnancy' constitute a tiny fraction of the total, although, as might be expected, their share too declined slightly with time.

The proportional contribution of 'coughs' (diseases of the respiratory system) and 'causes peculiar to infancy' hardly changed. Prominent in the first category are deaths involving TB, bronchitis, and asthma. Table 3.4 shows that respiratory ailments continued to account for about a fifth of all deaths during the entire period 1966–95 and that this was probably the single most important general cause of death category. Causes of death peculiar to infancy accounted for roughly 10 per cent of deaths, again with signs of a marginal decline from the 1980s.

The extent and nature of the transition from communicable to non-communicable diseases can be seen in Table 3.5 which shows percentages relating to 15 specific cause of death categories. Collectively these 15 causes of death accounted for about 34 per cent of rural deaths in 1969–71 and 55 per cent in 1994–5. The cause of death categories shown relate to six

[8]For example, in the 1960s, diseases of the circulatory and central nervous systems were not identified separately. Accordingly, deaths from these causes were often included under the general category of 'fever' although fever is a symptom which accompanies deaths from many causes. See also the notes to Table 3.4.

TABLE 3.4: *The percentage distribution of deaths by major cause of death groups, rural India, 1966–95*

Cause of death group	1966–7	1969–71	1974–6	1979–81	1984–6	1989–91	1994–5
Accidents and injuries	3.9	3.9	4.7	4.9	6.3	8.0	9.5
Child birth and pregnancy	1.4	1.2	1.2	1.1	1.1	1.0	1.0
Fever	21.7	18.4	12.6	8.6	10.0	7.3	7.3
Digestive disorders	10.4	8.6	9.6	9.0	7.7	6.4	6.2
Coughs (disorders of respiratory system)	21.1	23.8	20.7	20.3	20.4	19.5	20.1
Swellings	7.3	8.5	–	–	–	–	–
Disorders of the central nervous system	–	–	3.3	3.6	3.9	4.5	4.8
Diseases of the circulatory system	–	–	7.5	8.9	9.5	11.0	11.9
Other clear symptoms	4.9	5.6	7.9	8.0	8.4	8.3	11.4
Causes peculiar to infancy	10.3	11.1	12.5	13.1	10.6	9.9	9.7
Senility	14.8	18.9	16.6	20.5	22.1	24.1	18.1
Rest	4.2	–	3.4	2.0	–	–	–
Average annual number of deaths	18,936	19,432	15,026	16,947	17,793	22,742	37,315

Notes: The major cause of death groups shown are those employed by the Registrar General. Here and in Table 3.5 notice that some groups were either dropped, or introduced, at different times. It should also be borne in mind that all such data on cause of death are only broadly indicative. Moreover, the figures reflect, among other things, population ageing; and because they are percentages a decline in one cause of death will produce rises in the figures for others.

Sources: Registrar General, India, *Survey of Causes of Death (Rural)*, New Delhi, Office of the Registrar General (various years).

communicable and six non-communicable disease groups. Also included are two specific causes associated with maternal and perinatal health conditions, plus vehicular accidents.

Table 3.5 shows that overall the share of communicable diseases in rural India's cause of death profile fell from about 47.7 per cent in 1969–71 to 22.1 per cent by the mid-1990s. This very significant change was partly because of the decline in the importance of diseases such as gastro-enteritis, dysentery, and tetanus, but it also reflected declines in other communicable diseases like leprosy and kala-azar (leishmaniasis). Leprosy was the object of intensive prevention measures which resulted in a sharp decline in its prevalence and associated mortality, especially in Andhra Pradesh, Tamil Nadu, and

TABLE 3.5: *The percentage contributions to total deaths of deaths from selected specific major causes of death, rural India, 1969–95*

Disease/disease group	1969–71	1974–6	1979–81	1984–6	1989–91	1994–5
Communicable diseases						
1. Tuberculosis of the lungs	6.1	5.3	5.6	5.5	5.5	5.3
2. Gastro-enteritis/dysentery	6.3	5.3	4.2	4.1	2.9	3.0
3. Typhoid	2.1	3.3	2.7	2.0	1.8	1.8
4. Malaria	0.4	0.8	1.0	1.8	0.9	1.7
5. Pneumonia	9.1	6.0	5.4	5.4	5.0	4.7
6. Tetanus	2.3	1.9	1.8	0.6	0.4	0.4
Total of 1 to 6	26.3	22.6	20.7	19.4	16.5	16.9
Other communicable diseases	21.4	13.6	9.1	9.9	6.6	5.2
A. All communicable diseases	47.7	36.2	29.8	29.3	23.1	22.1
Non-communicable diseases						
7. Bronchitis and asthma	4.5	8.7	9.0	8.8	8.2	9.3
8. Heart attack	3.1	2.9	4.6	5.0	5.7	6.6
9. Cancer	3.3	1.9	2.5	2.8	3.3	4.0
10. Paralysis	–	2.2	2.5	2.6	3.0	3.4
11. Acute abdominal problems	–	–	–	1.5	1.8	1.8
12. Congestive and other problems	–	–	–	–	–	2.2
Total of 7 to 12	10.9	15.7	18.6	20.7	22.0	27.3
Other non-communicable diseases	25.0	27.1	29.6	28.1	33.9	27.6
B. All non-communicable diseases	35.9	42.8	48.2	48.8	55.9	54.9
Maternal and perinatal causes						
13. Prematurity	3.0	4.0	4.4	4.5	4.9	5.0
14. Anaemia	–	3.3	3.8	3.5	3.2	3.1
C. All maternal and perinatal	12.5	16.3	17.1	15.6	13.0	13.7
Accidents and injuries						
15. Vehicular accidents	0.5	0.7	0.9	1.4	1.8	2.3
D. All accidents and injuries	3.9	4.7	4.9	6.3	8.0	9.3
% of all deaths due to causes 1 to 15	33.9	46.2	48.4	49.5	48.6	54.9
Total of A, B, C, and D	100.0	100.0	100.0	100.0	100.0	100.0

Notes: For 1969–71 the figure listed for cause 7 relates only to bronchitis, that for cause 8 relates to 'congestive heart disease', and that for cause 9 is inclusive of cirrhosis of the liver. See also the notes to Table 3.4.

Sources: Registrar General, India, *Survey of Causes of Death (Rural)*, Ministry of Home Affairs, New Delhi (various years). Data for 1994–5 were kindly made available in electronic form by P. N. Mari Bhat.

Maharashtra. However, the disease continues to be fairly prominent in Orissa, Bihar, and Uttar Pradesh (Planning Commission 2000a: 255). Kala-azar exhibited a particularly serious revival in Bihar during the early 1970s. Periodic outbreaks continue in some districts of Bihar and West Bengal, predominantly in districts adjoining the Ganga, but at the start of the twenty-first century deaths from kala-azar were rare (Ministry of Health and Family Welfare 2000a).

Pulmonary tuberculosis, typhoid, and malaria have remained important causes of mortality throughout the period 1970–95 (Table 3.5). The country has the dubious distinction of having the largest number of TB cases in the world. It is estimated that 2–4 million Indians develop the disease every year—most of them young adults in the most economically productive years—and that about half a million people die from it (Ministry of Health and Family Welfare 2000a: 174–7). The long duration over which treatment needs to be administered leads to premature discontinuation and results in many deaths. In fact, recent estimates suggest that TB is probably the most important single infectious cause of death in the country (Krishnaswamy 2000).

With the spread of HIV/AIDS, the number of TB cases is almost certainly on the rise. A strategy for its effective treatment and control is required urgently. At the start of the twenty-first century, the government is hoping that the so-called DOTS strategy (directly observed treatment—short course) will help to overcome the limitations of traditional self-administered chemotherapeutic approaches (Dholakia 1997). Under DOTS a trained monitor is supposed to ensure that the patient's drug treatment regime is adhered to. However, to make this strategy effective the diagnosis should be accurate, the supply of drugs regular, and there should be systematic evaluation and monitoring of the programme. Experience from other countries, including China, suggests that DOTS can have a high success rate in both case-holding and eventual cure, and holds out some prospect that India too may be able to bring TB under manageable control. However, this will require considerable political and administrative commitment.

The resurgence of malaria since the mid-1960s epitomizes the problems of the re-emergence of infectious diseases. The total number of reported malaria cases briefly surpassed 6 million during the mid-1970s, and it has remained at around 2–3 million in the 1980s and 1990s (Ministry of Health and Family Welfare 2000a: 164). The number of deaths from malaria is not great, although Table 3.5 suggests that the disease has been causing a rising share of deaths.[9] There is concern too over the loss of economic productivity due to malaria

[9]According to the 1998–9 NFHS survey, the reported prevalence of malaria in the population was 3.7 per cent, with rural areas reporting levels twice those of urban areas (IIPS and ORC Macro 2000: 199).

sickness. Under the National Malaria Control Strategy in 1994 the central government appointed a committee to identify high-risk areas and suggest remedial schemes. However, the resurgence of malaria, even in parts of the country where it was not previously endemic, points to flaws in the control strategies.

A study in Kerala found that the presence of ill-ventilated housing, open dug wells, and non-compliance with drug treatment regimes were important factors which increased the risk of malaria (Devi and Das 1999). While in the short run the spraying of larvicides interrupts the transmission of the disease, other prevention strategies, such as steps to eliminate potential mosquito breeding sites, are also required to control it. There has been evidence for some time that anti-malarial drugs and insecticides are showing reduced efficacy (Akhtar and Learmonth 1985). Development projects and urban expansion have sometimes created new vector breeding grounds and malaria control has become a complex business.[10] Many analysts consider that in the future the management and control of the disease will require locally based community participation approaches to help restrict its transmission.

Although the contribution of gastro-enteritis and dysentery to overall mortality appears to have declined over time, diarrhoeal diseases continue to be an important cause of morbidity and mortality, especially in childhood (Table 3.5). The NFHS survey of 1998–9 found that almost one-fifth of children aged under three years had suffered a bout of diarrhoea during the two–week period prior to the survey (IIPS and ORC Macro 2000: 220). All the main infectious agents causing diarrhoea are transmitted via the faecal–oral route, and through contaminated water. Efforts to promote the use of oral rehydration therapy (ORT) to control diarrhoea can have limited beneficial effects; the NFHS data demonstrate clearly that most women are aware of the importance of providing sick children with extra fluids and about ORT. However, only about half of those children who had suffered from diarrhoea had actually been treated with a solution made from oral rehydration salt packets. It is clear that significant future progress can be made with ORT, but what is essential is safe water provision and more hygienic means of disposal for human excreta. And these measures are still not available to much of India's population.

Measles remains a substantial cause of morbidity and mortality. Although measles immunization is a proven and cost-effective primary health care intervention, and a single dose of the vaccine is enough to afford protection, only about half the children aged between 12 and 23 months were reported to have been immunized according to the 1998–9 NFHS survey. The use of

[10]For example, the spread of irrigation canals in the desert areas of Rajasthan, where malaria was not previously endemic, was widely held to be responsible for the serious epidemic of plasmodium falciparum malaria there in 1994.

vaccine by the states varies, and coverage is especially unsatisfactory in the main northern states of Bihar, Madhya Pradesh, Rajasthan, and Uttar Pradesh (Table 3.3). The scope for future progress is very apparent.

Finally, polio deserves mention here because its eradication seems a distinct possibility. This is mainly due to the 'pulse' polio immunization campaign which began in 1995 and is based on the repeated administration of oral polio vaccine to children aged under five years. This campaign required the establishment of a cold chain stretching throughout the country; instructions were given to health workers to discard supplies of vaccine if they were left unused for more than a few hours. In spite of the well coordinated efforts of voluntary agencies, the national and state governments, and international donor agencies, performance in states like Bihar and Uttar Pradesh lagged behind. Nevertheless in 1999 there were only 2214 cases of confirmed polio in the whole country (Ministry of Health and Family Welfare 2000a: 63).

Mortality from many communicable diseases has declined, although morbidity from them often remains quite high. Contaminated water supplies and minimal liquid and solid waste management, coupled with high levels of overcrowding in urban slums, contribute to maintaining infections. The continuing high level of communicable diseases has led some to suggest that India is currently experiencing a double burden of disease. On the one hand there is the unfinished agenda of health problems related to under-development and poverty: in this category come infectious diseases, nutritional deficiencies, and reproductive health problems. On the other hand there is an emerging agenda involving lifestyle-induced illnesses linked to new patterns of behaviour. Here the rise of cigarette smoking, and greater alcohol consumption and drug abuse, are very important (Gwatkin 1993; Murray and Lopez 1996). Health problems related to environmental factors and HIV/AIDS are also taking their place on the emerging agenda. We now turn to some of these topics.

Table 3.5 indicates that the share of non-communicable diseases in rural mortality rose from about 35.9 per cent in 1969–71 to 54.9 per cent in 1994–5. Bronchitis and asthma, heart attack, cancer, and paralysis (including stroke) all became more important in the overall mortality profile. In urban areas especially, coronary heart disease and hypertension have emerged as prime cardiovascular disorders, and they seem to be related to changing lifestyles.[11]

Non-communicable diseases often require long-term and costly interventions, which most people cannot afford. They also exert new pressures on already overburdened health systems. Almost certainly the share of non-communicable diseases in India's total disease burden will continue to increase.

---

[11]The greater susceptibility to coronary heart disease of people of Indian descent living in Western countries, compared to the general populations of those countries (Shaukat et al. 1997) may foreshadow what may happen in India as lifestyle changes spread and urbanization and Westernization increase.

This will reflect continued progress in controlling infectious diseases, and population ageing. Disease patterns are also altering because of urbanization and industrialization.

A shift from rural to urban living implies changes in exposure to indoor cooking pollutants, toxic industrial chemicals, and various contaminants, such as airborne lead associated with motor vehicles. Recent decades have seen the number of cars in Delhi increase at an average annual rate of 12 per cent, while the population increased at just 4 per cent (McMichael 2001). Levels of air pollution in the city have been so bad that many incoming airline flights have been cancelled due to poor visibility. At the same time several behavioural risk factors are increasing, particularly in urban areas, and are contributing to premature mortality. Lifestyles have become more sedentary and diets increasingly involve a high intake of saturated fats; by the late 1990s almost one-tenth of women in Delhi were estimated to be obese, and another 25 per cent were overweight. The problem of obesity is increasingly afflicting rural populations too, especially in northern India (Agrawal 2002). Increasing levels of diabetes, for example, will certainly follow these trends.

The health implications of urbanization are complex. Benefits from improved sanitation and better access to health care facilities have to be set against the negative effects stemming from increased pollution and crowding. Although urban death rates are significantly lower than rural rates (Table 3.1), socio-economic disparities in death rates within urban areas are certainly considerable.

To illustrate how lifestyle changes will affect future disease patterns, it is worth considering tobacco—the source of one of the major health burdens that India will face. There is huge potential for increased cigarette sales in the country. Smoking has major delayed effects on mortality and health (for example, through lung cancer and ischaemic heart disease). Estimated tobacco-related deaths increased from 129,000 to 383,000 during 1990–8; and estimated tobacco deaths as a proportion of all deaths increased from 1.4 to 4.1 per cent during this same period (Murray and Lopez 1996; World Health Organization 1999).

The number of people sick and disabled due to tobacco-related illnesses could be three to four times the number that die. It has been estimated that 154,300 new cases of lung, larynx, oral cavity, pharynx, and oesophagus cancer developed in 1996 due to the use of tobacco (Rath and Chaudhry 1999); and that in 1996 tobacco caused 4.2 million of India's 15.7 million cases of coronary artery disease, and 3.7 million cases of chronic obstructive lung disease (Gupta and Gupta 1996). It also contributes to tuberculosis mortality. Tobacco is likely to be one of the country's largest killers early in the twenty-first century. Indeed, perhaps 13 per cent of all deaths in 2020 may be attributable to it (Murray and Lopez 1996), tripling the current level.

Of course, tobacco is consumed in several ways besides smoking. For example, it is chewed and eaten in the form of *gutka*—a new product introduced to the market around the 1990s. Overall, an estimated 184 million Indians used tobacco products in 1996. According to the National Sample Survey (NSS) of 1998, nearly 45 per cent of men above age 10, and 7 per cent of women, were regular users (Sudarshan and Mishra 1999). Men generally smoke, whereas women chew or inhale. The 1998–9 NFHS found that 28 per cent of males over the age of 15 years chewed tobacco and 29 per cent smoked, with corresponding rates for women being 12 and 2.5 per cent (IIPS and ORC Macro 2000: 41–5).[12] Interestingly, the overall incidence of use is greater among disadvantaged socio-economic groups and in rural areas.

Tobacco consumption is almost certainly on the rise. Yet a comprehensive strategy to curb its use is still to be developed and implemented, particularly given strong opposition from the tobacco industry and many farmers. Because a significant proportion of tobacco consumed is in the form of *bidis*, which are produced in the unorganized sector, heavy taxation on cigarettes has yielded only limited results.[13] A careful study of the outlays on treatment for major tobacco-related diseases, and the losses of income due to illness and premature deaths, put the total cost of tobacco to the country in the late 1990s at Rs 277,611 billion (over US$ 5 billion) (Rath and Chaudhry 1999).

More generally, levels of outdoor and indoor air pollution are alarmingly high in much of India. The major source of indoor air pollution is the cooking stove. According to the 1991 Census, nearly 75 per cent of rural households cooked with unprocessed solid fuels such as dried animal dung, crop residues, wood, charcoal, and coal. When these substances are burnt in traditional and inefficient stoves large amounts of hazardous pollutants are created (Parikh et al. 1999; Smith 1996). Women invariably do the cooking in poorly ventilated areas, and harmful smoke is released into the general living space. A second, somewhat less prevalent source of indoor air pollution, comes from space heating with biomass fuels, which are used especially in high altitude areas during winter.

There is a strong relationship between levels of household air pollution and acute respiratory infections in children and chronic obstructive pulmonary disease among adults (Chen et al. 1990; Smith et al. 1999).[14] An analysis of

---

[12]It is likely that some respondents both chew tobacco and smoke, so these percentages cannot be added to give total use prevalence.

[13]A *bidi* consists of 0.2–0.3 grams of tobacco flakes rolled in a tendu leaf, the ends of which are then folded and tied. Some environmentalists and activists have objected to taxes on the sale of *bidis* because their production gives employment both to farmers who cultivate the special tobacco required and women who roll *bidis* at home.

[14]Accumulating evidence from epidemiological studies shows that indoor household smoke is a substantial health hazard. The concentration of smoke particles (total suspended particulates) can be more than ten times higher than accepted air quality guidelines and the concentrations of specific chemicals, such as benzo-alpha-pyrene (in wood smoke) or sulphur dioxide (in coal smoke) can be higher still.

data from the 1992–3 NFHS found that children aged under three in households that used traditional cooking fuels (such as dung or wood) experienced risks of acute respiratory infection that were 30 per cent greater than those of children living in households that used cleaner fuels (Mishra and Retherford 1997). In the city of Ahmedabad in western India the incidence of cough, cough with expectoration, and lung abnormalities was found to be appreciably higher among women who cooked with smoky fuels. Also, many women complain about the irritating effects of smoke, particularly on the eyes (National Institute of Occupational Health 1979).

In the future, increasing use of cleaner fuels and stoves may reduce the health hazards to which women and children, especially, are exposed within the home. However, the cost of these alternative sources of energy is often beyond the reach of poor households in both rural and urban areas. Nevertheless, it is almost certainly the case that the aggregate cost of treating respiratory ailments arising from the use of unprocessed solid fuels far exceeds the cost of making cleaner fuels available at affordable rates.

The quality of urban air, especially, is also affected by vehicular emissions and by atmospheric pollutants released by industrial units which are frequently dispersed throughout residential locations. Efforts to improve public transport, and so reduce vehicular emissions, and to relocate industries to specific sites away from inhabited areas, have generally been ineffectual in the past, and they are likely to remain so for the foreseeable future, although there have been significant improvements in Delhi recently (Chapter 13 of this book). Since the adverse consequences for human health are rarely evident in the short run, both individuals and the government tend to underestimate the gravity of the situation.

Among the other major cause of death groups represented in Table 3.5, the share of deaths attributed to maternal and perinatal causes remained little changed at roughly 14 per cent. India certainly has one of the highest levels of maternal mortality in Asia. The 1998–9 NFHS estimated the country's maternal mortality ratio (MMR) to be approximately 540 maternal deaths to women aged 15–49 years per 100,000 live births. This figure represented a rise compared to the estimate of 424 obtained from the 1992–3 NFHS, although because the associated sampling errors are large the difference is not statistically significant (IIPS and ORC Macro 2000: 196). Other work using SRS data suggests that the national MMR declined slightly, by about 5 per cent, between 1972–6 and 1982–6. Fertility decline accounted for about one quarter of the associated decline in the maternal death rate (Bhat et al. 1995). Rates of maternal mortality are exceptionally high in Bihar, Madhya Pradesh, Rajasthan, and Uttar Pradesh (Ministry of Health and Family Welfare 2001a: 52). It is probably safe to conclude that the risk of maternal mortality fell only modestly in India during the final decade of the twentieth century, a conclusion which is supported by estimates from various micro-level studies.

Table 3.5 shows that the proportion of deaths attributed to prematurity increased steadily between 1969–71 and 1994–5. In this context it is significant that estimates suggest that 33 per cent of all live births in India have birth weights under 2500 grams; this proportion is very much greater than that estimated for any other country in the world, with the exception of Bangladesh (UNICEF 2000: 88–91). Data from the 1998–9 NFHS survey suggest that only about two-thirds of Indian women (two in five in rural areas) had received even one ante-natal check-up from a doctor or other health professional; only 54 per cent of pregnant women were fully immunized against tetanus, and only about half had received iron supplements. Furthermore, untrained birth attendants attended two out of three deliveries, and three out of four births were delivered at home, usually in unhygienic conditions (IIPS and ORC Macro 2000: 280–99). Clearly the scope for improvements in all these areas is great.

Finally, Table 3.5 shows that deaths from motor accidents have assumed increased importance in the past several decades: the share rising from about 0.5 per cent around 1970 to 2.3 per cent in 1994–5. This increase probably largely reflects the rise in the number of vehicles.

The subject of HIV/AIDS is treated more formally in Chapter 5. This disease, however, could well become the country's leading cause of death at some point during the first or second decade of the twenty-first century. There is little hope of either a cure or an effective vaccine for the near future. So the spread of HIV/AIDS will certainly act to slow the overall rate of decline of mortality in India. At the start of the twenty-first century there may have been 4 to 5 million persons infected. And one estimate suggests that there could be about 500 thousand deaths each year from HIV/AIDS by around the year 2010 (Murray and Lopez 1996). The experience of other countries indicates strongly that the increasing presence of HIV/AIDS in the general population will stimulate and interact with other infections such as hepatitis, diarrhoea, malaria, and, especially, TB.

Although Mumbai appears to have been the main focus of HIV/AIDS, the disease is no longer restricted to the major metropolitan areas. It is spreading to rural parts, carried, for example, by migrant labourers and workers, such as lorry drivers, in the transport sector. It has been estimated that in 81 per cent of AIDS cases in India the probable source of infection was through unprotected heterosexual sex, in about 5.5 per cent of cases the source was infected blood or blood products, and in about 5.2 per cent of cases it was through the sharing of needles/syringes associated with intravenous drug use (National AIDS Control Organization 2000a: 7). HIV has spread rapidly among high risk groups; levels of infection among commercial sex workers in Maharashtra reportedly increased from around 3 per cent in 1987 to over 70 per cent in 1997 (National AIDS Control Organization 2000a: 4). Levels of HIV prevalence appear to be somewhat higher in the country's southern states. But the most severely affected location is the small north-eastern state of Manipur, bordering the so-called Golden Triangle region of South East Asia. In Manipur, HIV has spread very rapidly by way of intravenous drug use: a practice which, fortunately, is not widespread elsewhere in India.

It is likely that the HIV/AIDS epidemic will eventually have a significant impact on the economy. Clearly, there may well be losses of productivity, both because the disease involves long periods of sickness, and because people in the prime working ages tend to be most severely affected. Since tubectomy (female sterilization) is the primary method of birth control, and levels of female autonomy are often extremely low, it is very difficult for women to insist on the use of condoms by their husbands in order to gain some measure of protection from infection. Therefore it can be predicted that the future will see increasing levels of HIV infection among Indian women who, largely monogamous themselves, have virtually no control over their husbands' sexual behaviour. The number of children infected through vertical transmission will certainly increase too, as larger numbers of women become infected (breastfeeding is virtually universal). Drugs which might restrict vertical transmission (for example, AZT and Nevirapine) are rarely available, even in urban areas (Bloom and Godwin 1997; Gupta 1998).

That said, there are signs of success, although limited, in certain specific locations. For example, between 1992 and 1998 condom use among commercial sex workers operating in the Sonagachi area of Kolkata rose from virtually zero to over 70 per cent. Serious efforts have also been made to improve blood safety (National AIDS Control Organization 2000a). Fairly simple and inexpensive measures can significantly reduce the risks of mother-to-child transmission (Gray 1998). However, according to the 1998–9 round of the NFHS only about 40 per cent of ever-married women aged 15–49 had heard about AIDS. Not surprisingly, levels of awareness were appreciably greater among women living in urban areas, those with higher levels of education, and those living in the country's southern states. But in states like Bihar, Madhya Pradesh, Rajasthan, and Uttar Pradesh only about one-fifth of women, or less, had heard of the disease (IIPS and ORC Macro 2000: 230–9). There is considerable room for levels of knowledge about HIV/AIDS and its modes of transmission to improve, but greater knowledge by itself will be of only limited benefit.

IMPLICATIONS OF MORTALITY DECLINE FOR THE FUTURE

Despite the many concerns expressed here, there is no doubt that there is huge scope for further mortality decline in India during the decades which lie immediately ahead. The scale of the potential is underscored by the size of the mortality differentials which exist, for example, between states and between urban and rural areas. The more favourable levels of mortality already experienced by other large Asian countries, like Indonesia and China, demonstrate that further improvements are possible.[15]

These statements probably hold true even when allowance is made for the future impact of HIV/AIDS, although the longer one looks into the future the greater must be the measure of uncertainty regarding this disease. Nevertheless, in Chapter 5 it will be argued with some confidence that life expectation at birth in India will continue to rise, reaching perhaps 69 years by 2021–6, when the female advantage in longevity may be about three years. Also, partly because of differences in the prevalence of HIV in the late 1990s, there will probably be reductions in the mortality advantage which the southern states have had hitherto. From the trends which have been examined here, it seems probable that differences in the levels of life expectation experienced in rural and urban areas are set to decline still further in the years ahead.

The consequences of continuing mortality decline need to be considered. Average life expectation at age 60 in India increased from less than 14 years in 1970–5 to over 16 years by the mid-1990s (Registrar General, India 1999a) and it will rise further during the coming decades. There were 72 million people over age 60 in 2001; according to our projections, that figure will rise to 165 million by 2026. Gains in survivorship at older ages will have implications for the kinds of illnesses (many of them chronic) which will prevail, the nature of the health services that will be required, and the costs and burdens of care. For example, 6 per cent of people over age 65 and 20 per cent of those over 80 can be expected to suffer from dementia, including Alzheimer's disease (Cayton et al. 2002).

Women are going to live appreciably longer than men (Figure 3.2). The psycho-social dimensions of this will need policy consideration because most older woman in India are not economically self-sufficient, and typically they have few savings or assets of their own. The traditional practice of elderly women living with, and depending upon, other family members to meet their physical, financial, and emotional needs is likely to face increasing stress with continuing urbanization and the growth of individualism. Moreover, fertility decline means that there will be fewer children around to look after elderly parents in the future. The state, in conjunction with voluntary organizations, will have to address the matter of providing basic requirements for those elderly people with no family or other support.

India will face many health challenges in the first quarter of the twenty-first century. The control of major communicable diseases like malaria and TB will require considerable financial and administrative resources, concerted efforts, and political will. The country must also increase rapidly its levels of

---

[15]Life expectancy in the year 2000 was close to 70 years in both Indonesia and China. The estimated IMRs were 31 and 46 infant deaths per 1000 live births respectively (Population Reference Bureau 2001).

basic immunization coverage for the major preventable diseases of childhood. Health sector reforms will need to address the significant disparities which exist in relation to the availability of basic health care facilities; this must involve increased investment in rural areas and in those states which are presently under-served. Analysis of NSS data reveals that the level of untreated illness among the country's poor has increased because of increasing financial constraints. The divide between rich and poor households in terms of untreated illness and expenditures on health has grown. Better-off households have become the major users not only of private, but also of public hospitals (Sen et al. 2002).[16] Increased drug costs and rising medical fees in both the private and public sectors seem to have played a major role in these developments. The rising costs of health care services can have especially adverse consequences for the poor, for example, leading to reductions in their food consumption, increased levels of indebtedness, and heightened gender selectivity when seeking medical care. Women in India find it particularly difficult to access formal health care services and tend to leave untreated conditions which are chronic, but perhaps not completely incapacitating. Examples include reproductive tract infections, mental health problems, and anaemia. According to the 1998–9 NFHS about half of all women have iron-deficiency anaemia to some degree (IIPS and ORC Macro 2000: 249). Indeed, the many widespread and persistent gender biases in health care provision must be addressed.

There are even greater concerns for India and, indeed, many other countries. The re-emergence of old diseases and the appearance of new ones raise questions about the path of development that the country is pursuing, and what other paths may be preferable if improving the health and well-being of the population is seen as the ultimate aim of the state. True, advances in biotechnology raise hopes of fresh means of conquering certain ailments. But there is also increasing evidence of the extraordinary capacity of many viruses and bacteria to adapt to new circumstances through mutation, and so hinder the task of controlling other diseases. Future efforts to improve the health of India's people are going to have to go beyond matters of narrow specialization. They must address wider considerations of lifestyles and the environment.

CONCLUSIONS

In conclusion, levels of mortality in India will probably continue to improve in the period 2001–26. However, the objectives specified in the National

[16]Until the mid-1980s public hospitals were still the dominant providers of in-patient care, especially for the poor, although patients were increasingly resorting to the private sector for outpatient services. Although the situation varied considerably between states, public hospitals provided an important alternative to the private sector and at significantly lower cost. By the mid-1990s, however, there is clear evidence that the private sector had become dominant in terms of both out-patient and in-patient services.

Population Policy of 2000—such as reducing the IMR to 30 and the MMR to 100 by the year 2010 (Ministry of Health and Family Welfare 2000b: 2)—seem rather unrealistic. And although mortality may continue to decline it is quite conceivable, perhaps even likely, that levels of morbidity will not show a commensurate improvement.

Differentials in life expectation between urban and rural populations, and between states, will in all likelihood continue to reduce; although one probable exception to this is that females are likely to experience an increasing advantage in life expectation relative to males. The shift in the balance between communicable and non-communicable diseases in causing deaths will in all probability be sustained. Indeed, some infectious diseases, polio, guinea worm, yaws, and perhaps even leprosy, could be eradicated. Levels of childhood immunization should certainly improve, leading to further falls in the incidence of diseases like tetanus and measles. Socio-economic progress—in particular, rises in levels of education and average incomes, and improvements in infrastructure—should also contribute to a continuing reduction in mortality from certain types of infectious disease, such as some forms of diarrhoea and respiratory infection. Fertility decline too should bring benefits to the conditions influencing maternal and child death rates.

India's efforts aimed at controlling infectious diseases are likely to show only partial success. Malaria, for example, will continue to be a serious, perhaps increasing, threat, particularly given the probable absence of an effective vaccine. Tuberculosis however, will constitute an even more formidable challenge as drug-resistant forms proliferate and the spread of the disease is fuelled by HIV/AIDS. Moreover, to reiterate, HIV/AIDS could well become the leading cause of death perhaps as early as in the first decade of the twenty-first century. The greater prevalence of HIV in urban areas, and in the country's south, at the beginning of the century, will be one factor underlying the narrowing of mortality differentials envisaged over the medium term. What will happen in the longer run, say beyond 2016, is even harder to gauge. But it is certain that HIV/AIDS will become increasingly prevalent in rural areas, and in the country's north.

Finally, it is virtually certain that various degenerative and other non-communicable ailments will continue to become increasingly prominent in India's overall cause of death and health profiles. Important here will be most types of cancer, heart, and circulatory problems, diabetes, hypertension, mental health disorders, and dementia. The rise of these health problems will largely be related to urbanization, changes in lifestyles, and, especially over the longer run, population ageing.

4
The Continuing Fertility Transition

Leela Visaria

This chapter considers India's fertility transition. It reviews present fertility trends and differentials, the socio-economic and cultural explanations for the transition, and discusses future fertility trends and some of the implications.

FERTILITY TRENDS AND DIFFERENTIALS

Before the mid-twentieth century, average levels of human fertility were high. Indeed, given high death rates, birth rates had to be appreciable simply to maintain the population (Davis 1951). Although for women marriage was both early and universal, and there was little or no practice of deliberate birth control, fertility levels were restricted in several ways. High death rates meant that many females were widowed while still young, and restrictions on remarriage meant that their childbearing lives were curtailed. There were also various traditional curbs on the frequency of sexual intercourse (for example, relating to the postpartum period, and during times of ritual importance). The practice of female infanticide, common among certain castes in areas of the north-west, also restricted the birth rate.[1]

Research suggests that during 1901–51 the crude birth rate averaged about 45–7 births per 1000 population, with rates probably slightly lower in the

---

[1]Female infanticide tended to reduce the birth rate by reducing the number of women in the population. The practice was declared illegal in British India as early as 1795, but it proved difficult to eradicate.

south (Visaria and Visaria 1982). The birth rate probably fell somewhat during 1941–51, reflecting the 1943–4 Bengal famine and the effects of Partition. There may have been a modest rise in fertility during the 1950s and 1960s (Bhat 1998), possibly linked to the advances which were being made against malaria.

Comparatively robust, direct estimates of fertility are only available from around 1970. Figures produced by the SRS suggest that the birth rate for all-India fell from about 37 in 1971–2 to around 25.8 in the year 2000 (Registrar General, India 1999a, 2002a). Corresponding estimates of the TFR suggest that it dropped from about 5.0 births per woman in the early 1970s to 3.5 births in 1994–6 (Table 4.1), and further to 3.2 in 1998 (Registrar General, India 2002a). The SRS may have been especially deficient in its coverage of births in the early 1970s (when it was still in its formative years), and the true level of fertility then may have been closer to 6.0 births (Bhat 1998). It seems reasonable to conclude that, in less than three decades, fertility per woman probably declined by nearly 50 per cent. Given the scale and diversity of India's population, this is not poor progress.[2]

The SRS suggests that for all-India, the urban TFR was about 30 per cent lower than the rural TFR throughout most of the period 1971–99.[3] The

TABLE 4.1: *Fertility measures by place of residence, all-India, 1971–99*

Period	Crude birth rate			Total fertility rate		
	All Areas	Rural	Urban	All Areas	Rural	Urban
1971–5	35.6	37.2	29.3	5.0	5.2	3.9
1976–80	33.4	34.7	28.1	4.5	4.8	3.4
1981–5	33.6	35.2	28.1	4.5	4.8	3.4
1986–90	31.4	33.0	26.1	4.0	4.3	3.0
1991–3	29.1	30.7	23.7	3.6	3.9	2.7
1994–6	28.2	29.9	22.5	3.5	3.8	2.6
1997–9	26.6	28.2	21.1	3.3	3.6	2.4

Notes: Total fertility rates for 1999 were not available at the time of writing, so the figures shown for 1997–9 actually pertain to 1997–8. The SRS measures shown here and in Table 4.2 may be slight underestimates, but the implied extent of such underestimation is uncertain, and varies between the many fertility estimates made by different authors. Also the degree of birth under-registration in the SRS has probably varied over time.

Sources: Registrar General, India (1999a, 2002a).

[2]Some observers have been concerned because the censuses indicate that the all-India population growth rate remained fairly constant, at about 2.2 per cent per year, during 1961–91. This was because the decline in the birth rate was offset by the decline in the death rate. It is worth noting, however, that the population growth rate during this period was relatively low compared to that in many countries.

[3]Before the mid-twentieth century, urban–rural fertility differentials may have been small. But it is clear from Table 4.1 that by the early 1970s the urban TFR was appreciably lower than the rural TFR.

rural–urban differential persisted because both the rural and urban TFRs declined by similar proportions. Almost certainly, fertility fell first in urban areas at some time during the 1960s. But for all-India, the rural population was not far behind in both the timing and pace of fertility decline. Between the early 1970s and the late 1990s the urban TFR fell from about 3.9 to 2.4; and the rural fall was from 5.2 to 3.6 (Table 4.1).

Total fertility has declined in all states since the early 1970s. By the late 1990s TFRs were close to the approximate replacement level of 2.1 births in Kerala and Tamil Nadu (Table 4.2). Moreover, the estimated urban TFRs were close to the replacement level not only in Kerala and Tamil Nadu, but also in Andhra Pradesh, Karnataka, Maharashtra, Punjab, Orissa, and West Bengal. For the remaining major states, urban TFRs in 1996–8 were generally between 2.5 and 4.0 births. SRS data indicate that rural TFRs have declined in every state. In Kerala and Tamil Nadu, by the late 1990s rural fertility was close to if not below replacement, and any rural–urban fertility differential had largely disappeared (if gauged in absolute terms). Thus, for 1996–8 the SRS put the TFR in both rural and urban areas of Kerala at 1.8; rural TFRs of around 3 births were reported for Andhra Pradesh, Gujarat, Karnataka, Maharashtra, Punjab, and West Bengal (Registrar General, India 1999a).

TABLE 4.2: *Estimated total fertility rates, major states and all-India, 1970–98*

State	Total fertility rate				Decline
	1970–2	*1980–2*	*1990–2*	*1996–8*	*(per cent)*
Andhra Pradesh	4.7	3.9	3.0	2.5	46.8
Assam	5.5	4.1	3.4	3.2	41.8
Bihar	–	5.7	4.6	4.4	22.8
Gujarat	5.7	4.4	3.2	3.0	47.4
Haryana	6.4	5.0	3.9	3.4	46.9
Karnataka	4.4	3.6	3.1	2.5	43.2
Kerala	4.1	2.9	1.8	1.8	56.1
Madhya Pradesh	5.7	5.2	4.6	4.0	29.8
Maharashtra	4.5	3.7	3.0	2.7	40.0
Orissa	4.8	4.2	3.3	3.0	37.5
Punjab	5.3	4.0	3.1	2.7	49.1
Rajasthan	6.3	5.4	4.5	4.2	33.3
Tamil Nadu	3.9	3.4	2.2	2.0	48.7
Uttar Pradesh	6.7	5.8	5.2	4.8	28.4
West Bengal	–	4.2	3.2	2.6	38.1
All-India	5.2	4.5	3.7	3.3	36.5

Notes: Rates shown are three–year averages. The SRS estimates for Bihar and West Bengal for years before 1980 are particularly questionable; accordingly, figures for 1970–2 are not shown for these states and the corresponding declines refer to the period since 1980–2.

Sources: Registrar General, India (1999a, 2002a).

In 1996–8, fertility levels were appreciably lower in the country's southern states, particularly compared to the main northern states (Table 4.2). Indeed, if anything, during 1970–98 regional fertility differentials widened, because TFRs tended to decline by more in states with initially relatively low levels of fertility. Although Kerala was the first major state to approach replacement fertility, Tamil Nadu may have had a lower TFR in 1970–2. In Andhra Pradesh, Gujarat, Karnataka, Maharashtra, Orissa, Punjab, and West Bengal it is likely that total fertility declined from around six (or more) births during the late 1950s to between 2.4 and 3.0 births by 1996–8. It is particularly significant that, despite their general socio-economic backwardness, fertility has fallen in the major northern states of Bihar, Madhya Pradesh, Rajasthan, and Uttar Pradesh. The TFRs in these populous states in 1996–8 were estimated by the SRS to range between 4.0 (Madhya Pradesh) and 4.8 births (Uttar Pradesh). However, during 1971–98, total fertility appears to have fallen by roughly 30 per cent in these states, appreciably below the national figure of about 36.5 per cent.

Several analyses have studied fertility at the district level (where data permit). They allow a more detailed assessment of the role of socio-cultural and historical factors in the fertility transition; and they also shed light on how changes in fertility behaviour have diffused through space and time. These studies show that the transition has not followed neat administrative boundaries; rather, its diffusion has been heavily conditioned by socio-cultural and historical considerations. Bhat (1996) has mapped district TFRs for the 1970s and 1980s and observed that fertility levels were often similar in contiguous districts, despite being located in different states. He showed that fertility fell first in coastal areas of southern India, and that the decline then moved inland. Guilmoto (2000) reached similar conclusions. Changes in fertility behaviour came late to the country's heartland, that is, in and around the Gangetic valley. In the late 1960s, north Punjab, Haryana, and Himachal Pradesh emerged as a second area of fertility decline, from which diffusion also occurred. Guilmoto and Rajan (2001) suggest that the spatial dimension of the fertility transition became more intense as the transition progressed. A detailed analysis of NFHS data by Bhat and Zavier (1999) also indicates that in the 1970s and 1980s fertility decline was faster in a contiguous belt comprising the country's southern areas, and vast areas of the west and east. In India's Gangetic core, however, fertility decline has been late and, hitherto, slow.

FERTILITY VARIATION BY AGE

Figure 4.1 illustrates how age-specific fertility rates for all-India have changed since the early 1970s.[4] The broad trends shown were experienced in both rural and urban India.

---

[4]The NFHS surveys provide data on age-specific fertility. They confirm the broad changes discussed here. See also Chapter 5.

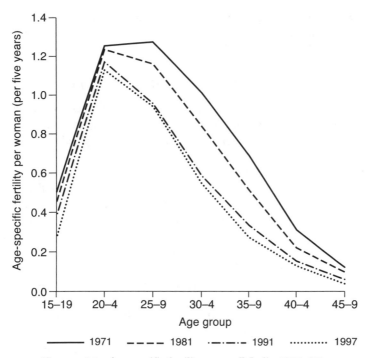

FIGURE 4.1: *Age-specific fertility rates, all-India 1971–97*

Source: Registrar General, India (1999a).

Fertility fell for women of all ages. The greatest falls, however, occurred for the 25–9, 30–4, and 35–9 age groups. These changes are strongly indicative of increasing control of fertility within marriage through the adoption of family planning. At 15–9, the decline in age-specific fertility mainly reflects a rise in the age of female marriage, which increased from around 17 years in 1971 to probably about 20 years for women marrying around 2001. The 1961 Census indicated that 71 per cent of women aged 15–19 were married, and the 1991 Census gave a figure of 35.3 per cent (Registrar General, India 1998a). Figure 4.1 also reveals a shift in the age pattern of childbearing. Around 1971, levels of fertility in the 20–4 and 25–9 age groups were similar. But by the late 1990s the significantly greater fall for the 25–9 age group meant that the age-specific fertility distribution peaked at 20–4.

These changes mean that the average span of childbearing (measured in years) has declined considerably. In the southern states especially, with relatively low and, generally, still falling levels of fertility, childbearing has become concentrated into a very short period. Women marry, have their children, and then get sterilized, in just a few years. According to the 1998–9 NFHS survey, in Tamil Nadu the median ages at first marriage and sterilization were 18.7 and 25.3 years respectively (a difference of 6.6 years). In the major northern states, with relatively high levels of fertility, the gap between marriage and sterilization was much longer; the corresponding figures for Uttar Pradesh were 15.0 and 28.3 years (a difference of 13.3 years).[5]

PROXIMATE DETERMINANTS OF FERTILITY

Changes in socio-economic and related factors often account for changes in fertility. But such factors can only affect fertility through intermediate, that is proximate, variables, the most important of which relate to marriage, breastfeeding, and contraception (Bongaarts 1978). Various policy interventions have attempted to influence factors such as the age at marriage (the minimum legal age for women has been raised to 18 years), the availability of family planning methods, and access to legal abortions. Using NFHS data it is possible to examine how fertility changes have been influenced by changes in the proximate determinants. As background for discussion, Table 4.3 presents relevant measures obtained by the 1998–9 NFHS survey.

Virtually all childbearing in India occurs within marriage and, other things equal, an increase in the age of marriage for women, or in the proportions remaining single, will tend to reduce fertility. Although the age at marriage has risen, marriage is still virtually universal. By age 25 about 94 per cent of Indian women are married. There are, however, significant interstate variations. The 1998–9 NFHS survey found that the median age of marriage for women aged 20–49 years was roughly 16 years in Bihar, Madhya Pradesh, Rajasthan, and Uttar Pradesh, but it was over 18 in Assam, Gujarat, Kerala, Punjab, and Tamil Nadu, and in most of these states 10 per cent or more of women were not married by age 25 (Table 4.3). Data from the 1991 Census confirm the broad regional picture; women marry relatively late in the south, especially in Kerala, and in the north they marry relatively late in Gujarat, Punjab, and Haryana (Registrar General, India 1998a). With continuing socio-economic development (for example, increases in female education, and the spread of more modern, urban-based values through the mass media) there is considerable scope for the age of marriage to rise further in those states where it is still relatively low; clearly, this will have an inhibiting influence on fertility in the 15–19 age group.

The length of breastfeeding is the principal determinant of the period of postpartum amenorrhoea. In general, lengthy durations of breastfeeding tend to have a powerful negative effect on levels of fertility. Breastfeeding in India is prolonged and virtually universal (Jain and Adlakha 1982; Visaria et al. 1995).

---

[5]These differences, based on the data in Table 4.3, may be inflated because the marriage figures used in the calculation refer to the experience of all women aged 25–49. Also, in the main northern states the onset of cohabitation often occurs a year or two after the formal marriage ceremony. Traditional practices (for example, *gauna*) which involve a lag between marriage and cohabitation are waning. (IIPS and ORC Macro 2000: 56).

TABLE 4.3: *Measures relating to the proximate determinants of fertility, ideal family size, and son preference, major states and all-India, NFHS, 1998–9*

	Median age at marriage, females (years)	Per cent of women ever-married by age 25	Duration of breastfeeding (months)	Per cent currently using contraception (any modern method)	Per cent of currently married women sterilized	Median age at sterilization (years)	Mean ideal number of children, by age group of ever-married women aged:		Per cent who want more sons than daughters
							20–4	30–4	
Andhra Pradesh	15.1	96.8	25.0	58.9	52.7	23.6	2.1	2.4	19.8
Assam	18.1	85.9	≥ 36.0	26.6	15.7	26.7	2.6	2.9	38.2
Bihar	14.9	97.9	≥ 36.0	22.4	19.2	27.7	3.0	3.4	47.9
Gujarat	17.6	94.2	22.0	53.3	43.0	26.5	2.4	2.4	33.2
Haryana	16.9	96.2	24.3	53.2	38.7	26.5	2.3	2.5	37.5
Karnataka	16.8	91.7	20.0	56.5	51.5	24.2	2.2	2.2	13.0
Kerala	20.2	82.0	24.5	56.1	48.5	26.4	2.4	2.4	14.6
Madhya Pradesh	14.7	95.5	≥ 36.0	42.6	35.7	26.4	2.7	3.0	42.5
Maharashtra	16.4	93.9	23.8	59.9	48.5	25.0	2.2	2.3	27.1
Orissa	17.5	93.8	≥ 36.0	40.3	33.9	26.3	2.5	2.7	37.6
Punjab	20.0	90.5	21.2	53.8	29.3	27.1	2.1	2.2	29.1
Rajasthan	15.1	98.5	25.5	38.1	30.8	27.0	2.6	2.8	47.5
Tamil Nadu	18.7	90.3	16.1	50.3	45.2	25.3	2.0	2.0	9.6
Uttar Pradesh	15.0	97.3	25.8	22.0	14.9	28.3	2.9	3.2	53.3
West Bengal	16.8	92.2	≥ 36.0	47.3	32.0	25.1	2.1	2.4	20.7
All-India	16.4	93.7	25.4	42.8	34.2	25.7	2.5	2.7	33.2

Notes: The figures on age at marriage refer to the age at first marriage of married women aged 25–49 at the time of the survey. The breastfeeding statistics refer to the median duration of any breastfeeding, based on children aged under three years at the time of the survey; figures shown as ≥ 36.0 months are for states for which the exact median could not be computed because the percentage of children breastfeeding did not fall below 50 in any age group of children aged less than three. The data on contraception (which are exclusive of induced abortions) and sterilization refer to currently married women aged 15–49. In the case of sterilization the median ages shown have been calculated inclusive of the ages of wives of sterilized men at the time of their sterilization. The mean ideal numbers of children were reported by ever-married women. The percentages who wanted more sons than daughters relate to ever-married women aged 15–49 years.

Source: International Institute for Population Sciences (IIPS) and ORC Macro (2000).

Table 4.3 shows that in the late 1990s the median duration was about 25.4 months. Urban women, however, breastfed for a somewhat shorter median duration (21.8 months) than rural women (26.3 months). Breastfeeding durations are fairly long everywhere, but they are especially so in the eastern states (Table 4.3). Breastfeeding for such lengthy periods does not protect women completely from the risk of becoming pregnant, in part because its intensity wanes as children are introduced to other foodstuffs (the length of exclusive breastfeeding, inclusive of the provision of water, was only 5.3 months (IIPS and ORC Macro 2000: 262)). The average birth interval according to SRS data is still quite long, with about 70 per cent of second or higher order births occurring at intervals of 24 months or more (Registrar General, India 1999a: 10). There is little doubt that breastfeeding plays a significant role in accounting for this; NFHS data suggest that the median duration of postpartum amenorrhoea was almost nine months (IIPS and ORC Macro 2000: 108). Durations of breastfeeding are declining in much of the country, and they will probably continue to fall (Visaria 2002). A district-level study in Gujarat showed that urban women from higher socio-economic groups breastfed their children for significantly shorter durations than did poor rural women (Visaria et al. 1995).

Induced abortion has been legal in India since 1972. But no reliable estimates of the number of abortions exist, in part because many women attend private clinics for this service. The incidence of induced abortions reported in demographic surveys is unrealistically low. According to NFHS and other survey data, only 1 or 2 per cent of all pregnancies end in an induced abortion. But some micro-studies suggest that the figure in some parts of the country may be as high as 9 to 14 per cent (Ganatra et al. 2001). It is likely that the current incidence of abortion is high and on the increase, especially in areas of the south, but data deficiencies mean that it is difficult to assess the influence of induced abortion on fertility trends.

This brings us to contraception, which has undoubtedly been the major cause of India's fertility decline. At the national level the use of modern contraceptives only really began to spread after the late 1960s. Between 1970 and 2000 the estimated 'couple protection rate' (a measure broadly analogous to the contraceptive prevalence rate), derived from official family planning programme statistics, rose from about 10 to over 45 per cent. Method-specific estimates derived from the official programme statistics also imply that the use of reversible contraceptives has been increasing since the mid-1980s (Figure 4.2). However, as Table 4.4 shows, survey data do not fully support this; there may have been little change in condom use and only a slight rise in use of the pill.

During the Emergency period of 1976–7, male sterilization (vasectomy) was promoted with zeal. This accounts for the sharp rise in the couple protection rate at that time (Figure 4.2). But in the 1980s, female sterilization (tubectomy) became the main contraceptive method, and it has remained so since. Indeed, in the late 1990s survey data suggest that female sterilization accounted for almost 80 per cent of all current use of modern methods of contraception (Table 4.3). Research has shown that reported use levels of reversible contraceptives were exaggerated when local health workers were given method-specific contraceptive targets to achieve, in the era before such targets were officially discontinued in 1996 (Visaria et al. 1995). On balance it seems probable that the official family planning programme estimates overstate the use of reversible methods.

The data in Table 4.3 show that female sterilization is the dominant method of contraception in all states. Note that in Andhra Pradesh and Karnataka in the late 1990s the estimated median age of currently married women at sterilization was about 24 years. The regional pattern of contraceptive use corresponds to, and largely explains, the regional pattern of fertility variation. The proportion of women using contraception was around 55 per cent or

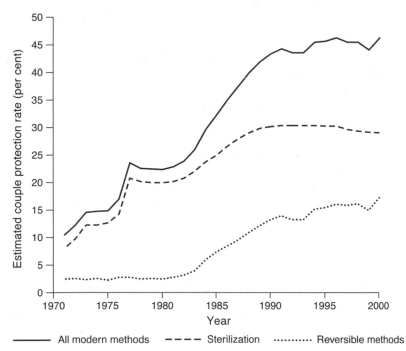

FIGURE 4.2: *Trends in contraceptive use according to family planning service statistics, all-India, 1971–2000*

Note: The main modern reversible methods are the IUD, condoms, and the pill.
Source: See Table 4.4.

TABLE 4.4: *Percentages of couples estimated to be using contraception, by method, according to service statistics, and survey data, all-India, 1980–99*

Contraceptive method	1980		1988		1992–3		1998–9	
	Service statistics	*Survey data*	*Services statistics*	*Survey data*	*Service statistics*	*Survey data*	*Service statistics*	*Survey data*
Sterilization	19.9	22.1	28.9	29.6	30.3	29.9	29.3	36.1
IUDs	1.4	0.3	5.5	1.9	6.3	2.0	7.3	1.6
Condoms	1.0	4.4	4.2	5.2	4.9	2.6	5.0	3.1
Oral pills	n/a	0.8	1.5	1.3	2.0	1.3	3.8	2.1
All modern methods	22.3	27.1	40.1	38.0	43.5	35.8	45.4	42.8

Notes: The service statistics figure shown for 1998–9 actually pertains to 1997–8. The sterilization figures relate to both sexes. However, according to the 1998–9 NFHS survey the contributions of female and male sterilizations to the figure of 36.1 per cent were 34.2 and 1.9 per cent respectively.

Sources: The service statistics are based on data taken from Ministry of Health and Family Welfare, *Family Welfare Year Book*, New Delhi (various years). The survey-based estimates are from Operations Research Group (1983, 1990) and International Institute for Population Sciences (IIPS) and ORC Macro (1995, 2000).

more in Andhra Pradesh, Gujarat, Haryana, Karnataka, Kerala, Maharashtra, Punjab, and West Bengal, mostly southern and eastern states. Tamil Nadu, with its exceptionally low fertility, is absent from this list (its use level was 50 per cent) and that is almost certainly accounted for by an unusually high level of induced abortion.[6] Table 4.3 shows that elsewhere in the country contraceptive use levels were generally appreciably lower, especially in Bihar and Uttar Pradesh where the figure was around 22 per cent.

An application of the Bongaarts (1978) fertility framework to state-level data from the 1992–3 and 1998–9 NFHS surveys confirms that India's fertility transition has been achieved overwhelmingly through increased use of modern contraceptive methods, primarily female sterilization. Even in states with relatively high levels of fertility, increased sterilization was responsible for most of the fertility decline. The influence of changes in female marriage patterns has been very limited (Visaria 2002). Data of the NFHS suggest that the postpartum period of infecundability changed little in the 1990s. It is to be expected that in the future educated women, especially, will reduce the length of time when they breastfeed their children, but that for spacing purposes these reductions will be offset by greater use of reversible forms of contraception.

[6]The 1998–9 NFHS survey estimated that 5.2 per cent of all pregnancies among ever-married women in Tamil Nadu ended in an induced abortion, compared to a national figure of 1.7 per cent. (IIPS and ORC Macro 2000: 95).

ACCOUNTING FOR THE FERTILITY TRANSITION

Several approaches have been adopted to try to account for India's fertility transition. Some analysts have examined socio-economic changes in particular states in order to understand how they have affected fertility behaviour. Others have taken advantage of district- and regional-level data to study associations between various measures of fertility on the one hand, and a range of socio-economic, demographic, and family planning measures on the other. Finally, researchers have studied the motivations behind childbearing and contraceptive use in local settings. We examine these three strands of research.

The role of development and culture: For obvious reasons the case of Kerala has attracted much attention. Scholars saw a close link between its early fertility decline and the pattern of social development which began in the nineteenth century. Efforts to provide universal education were initiated at the start of that century. Religious reforms were introduced to break the rigidities of the caste system; they also helped the spread of education among lower castes. Later, land reforms, the setting of minimum wages, and the provision of public health care, all contributed to the growth of a fairly egalitarian social structure. Changing perceptions of the costs of children's care and education were significant in the control of fertility. So a 'human development' path of fertility transition occurred (Krishnan 1998; Srinivasan 1995). In the 1950s and 1960s, the spread of female education and the related rise in the marriage age were major factors behind the gathering fertility decline. Family planning became important only after about 1965. Fertility decline continued apace in the 1970s and 1980s (Zachariah 1994). Virtually all social and occupational groups had low fertility by the late 1990s.

Tamil Nadu, however, pursued a more mixed path, involving elements of both social and economic development (Kishor 1994; Ramasundaram 1995). Levels of education and health in the state were comparatively favourable, but because the state's population did not have particularly high levels of income, some analysts argued that Tamil Nadu's fertility decline was 'poverty driven' (Basu 1986; Mencher 1980). For example, Kishor (1994) maintained that poor parents were left with little choice but to invest in their children's education to enable them to get urban employment. Rising material aspirations probably gave impetus to the desire to reduce fertility. Strong backing from the state's political leaders, a relatively efficient public service, effective communication, and a good transportation network, all assisted the health and family planning programmes. Studies found that the media also had a strong negative influence on fertility in Tamil Nadu (Ramasundaram 1995; Srinvasan 1995; Visaria 2000).

Punjab too experienced fertility decline from relatively early on; economic development seems to have been important. From the late 1960s, Punjab prospered from the Green Revolution in agriculture. This supported the rise of a flourishing industrial sector, and average incomes in the state rose significantly. Fertility was reduced even though levels of female literacy were low, levels of child mortality were relatively high, and there was a very strong degree of son preference (Das Gupta 1995). It was only in the 1980s and 1990s that more broad-based social development (for example, increases in levels of female education) really began.

It has been argued that India's large northern states, perhaps especially Bihar and Uttar Pradesh, have lagged behind in the fertility transition due to their lower levels of female literacy, slower declines in mortality, and poorer performance in family planning. These weaknesses have probably reinforced each other. The slow pace of both social and economic development in these states has meant that policies and programmes which proved relatively effective elsewhere did not work well throughout much of the north (Satia and Jejeebhoy 1991). In the populous northern states fertility decline began some two decades after the official family planning programme was initiated.

Also relevant is Dyson and Moore's (1983) study which attributed the lower fertility levels and earlier fertility declines of the south to the region's less patriarchal kinship structures and the higher status accorded to women. Basu's (1992) work among migrants from both the north and south living in the same neighbourhood of Delhi, supported these ideas. She observed that southern migrant women enjoyed greater autonomy in their decision-making, had more interaction with the non-domestic world, and lower fertility than their counterparts from northern India. The idea of personal autonomy is complex; it is, moreover, hard to practise in a patriarchal society, particularly at the individual level. One survey-based study found little difference between women from Gujarat and Kerala in their levels of autonomy. It also found a weak relationship between autonomy and levels of contraceptive use and fertility (Visaria 1996). An analysis by Krishnan (2001), however, found that indices of female autonomy and the extent of patrilineal kinship were significant in accounting for regional differences in fertility between the major northern and southern states.

Statistical analyses of fertility trends and differentials: Statistical data have been analysed to identify the correlates of fertility variation. Jain's (1985) state-level analysis highlighted the strong associations between levels of female education, infant mortality, and fertility. The effects of higher levels of female education, and lower levels of infant mortality, in reducing fertility remained strong, even when the influence of other factors was controlled for. The theoretical arguments on these associations are convincing.[7] A quantitative

[7]For example, increased education keeps girls longer in school, so helping to raise their age at marriage; it may also give young women greater awareness of services, and confidence in requesting them both for themselves (for example, advice regarding contraception) and their children (for example, relating to health care). Levels of maternal education and child survival

study by Bhat and Rajan (1990) concluded that increased levels of female education were very important in accounting for Kerala's fertility transition. Greater education heightened women's perceptions of the costs and benefits of having children. A district-level study by Bhat (1996) found that less than 10 per cent of fertility variation within the country was attributable to structural economic factors. However, differences in exposure to the mass media and levels of female education accounted for 40 per cent of the variation. Murthi et al. (1995) and Drèze and Murthi (2001) also found that the level of female literacy was an important factor in accounting for fertility variation both between regions and over time. In contrast, general development and modernization variables were found to have small effects.

Most studies have emphasized the role of female education as a factor contributing to lower fertility. But the widespread adoption of contraception by illiterate women in the 1990s has raised questions about the role of education as the prime mover in the fertility transition. Bhat (2002b) found that 65 per cent of all fertility decline in India between 1981 and 1991 occurred among women with no education. He attributed the decline of fertility among these women to ideational change, brought about through the influence of the mass media. A multi-level analysis by McNay et al. (2003) also found that fertility in some parts of India had declined among uneducated women due to increased use of contraception. The diffusion of new ideas and aspirations for their children is leading even uneducated parents to limit the size of their families.

Finally, the family planning programme has played an important independent role in lowering the level of fertility. Several decomposition analyses have attributed a significant share of the overall decline in fertility to the effective implementation of state-sponsored family planning efforts, leading to greater use of contraception (Rao et al. 1986; Das and Dey 2000). Andhra Pradesh seems a particularly convincing instance where, despite low levels of female literacy and a relatively young age of female marriage, rapid fertility decline in the 1980s and 1990s was to a considerable extent the result of effective family planning programme efforts (James 1999). Politicians in Andhra Pradesh have initiated fairly aggressive targets and incentive-driven strategies to promote the greater uptake of sterilization. These approaches run against current mainstream opinion in India as to how family planning services should be provided. It is hard to gauge how these developments will turn out, but they may play an accelerating role for fertility transition. It is possible that other states may adopt similar approaches in the future, in a context in which state-level population policies are likely to play an increasingly prominent role in family planning provision.

---

tend to be positively associated, and, in turn, improvements in child survival may reduce the demand for large numbers of children. For research on these issues in south India see Caldwell et al. (1982 and 1985).

Qualitative accounts: Finally, brief mention should be made of relevant qualitative investigations. In a detailed study of a community in Uttar Pradesh, Jeffery and Jeffery (1996) found that women's autonomy and fertility were poorly correlated. Significantly, decisions regarding fertility and sterilization were made at the household level, following negotiations between different family members. An ethnographic study by Säävälä in rural Andhra Pradesh argues that young women have turned increasingly to sterilization not because of the availability of cash compensation payments, but rather to gain prestige, to defy and undermine the authority of household elders, and to improve their position relative to their mothers-in-law. In addition, socio-economic changes and political movements in the state have raised general levels of confidence, even among downtrodden sections of the population (Säävälä 2001). A series of qualitative studies in Tamil Nadu suggests that the aspirations of young couples to provide better levels of education and health care for their offspring, compared to what they themselves received as children, have increased. At the same time, however, decisions related to childbearing were taken largely by men. Women had very little say, and if they expressed a view that they wanted to postpone or terminate a pregnancy then they risked facing anger from the family (Ravindran 1999).

FUTURE DEVELOPMENTS

It is clear that India's fertility transition is well established and that it will continue. The many developments in the country, for example, rising levels of education, the considerable and growing influence of the media, economic changes, and continuing urbanization, all point in this direction. There is little reason to believe that the country's TFR will 'stall' or 'plateau' for long at a level that is far above replacement.

These conclusions are supported by the measures of ideal family size presented in Table 4.3. Around 1998–9 there was no state where ever-married women aged 20–4 gave a figure above three as their ideal number of children. Significantly, in most states women aged 20–4 reported a lower number as ideal than those aged 30–4. Moreover, the women's responses were probably influenced upward by the existence of children already born (that is, in a process of rationalization). So while one should not put great confidence in the precise figures, it seems reasonable to suppose that views regarding the ideal number of children are fast approaching a two-child norm, although it will take somewhat longer for this to apply to the major northern states.

There is a positive relationship between levels of fertility and levels of son preference (Arnold and Roy 2002). Notice from Table 4.3 that in the populous northern states of Bihar, Rajasthan, and Uttar Pradesh, roughly half of all ever-married women reported that they wanted more sons than daughters. In contrast, in the southern states the extent of son preference is very much less. In Tamil Nadu, for example, less than 10 per cent of women revealed any partiality for having sons. An analysis of NFHS data collected during the 1990s concluded that levels of son preference were declining. This was true even for northern and western states like Punjab and Gujarat (Lahiri and Dutta 2002). Furthermore, the experience of these states demonstrates that fertility can fall despite relatively high levels of son preference. Thus the undoubted existence of a positive cross-sectional relationship between levels of son preference and levels of fertility should not be used to make dynamic inferences regarding the prospects for future fertility decline. Moreover, it seems probable that, even in the major northern states, fertility decline will eventually help to generate a more balanced view of the desirability of having daughters, a development which itself should facilitate continuing fertility decline.[8]

During the medium term, basic regional differences in levels of total fertility per woman are likely to persist to some degree. But over the longer run, say by the year 2026, the main northern states will have largely caught up with the others in terms of their levels of fertility. So the size of any absolute differences in TFRs between states (that is, expressed in terms of births per woman) will be relatively small. In other words, a trend towards broad convergence in levels of fertility between the states is under way. Similarly, in much of the country, perhaps especially the south, the extent of any difference between urban and rural areas in their fertility levels will probably be negligible by the year 2026. Processes of convergence will happen somewhat faster if appropriate policy and programme measures are introduced. In the future such measures may be increasingly tailored to take account of how circumstances vary at the district level.

Remnants of the basic north–south fertility contrast may still persist in 2026, if only because fertility in major northern states like Bihar and Uttar Pradesh has a long way to fall. But it would be wrong to rule out the possibility of fairly rapid fertility declines even in these populous and relatively backward states. Indeed, the world's demographers have something of a history of over-caution with respect to predicting future fertility declines (Eberstadt 1981). Whether the north–south fertility contrast will remain in the middle of the twenty-first century is debatable. It may not persist with respect to the level of fertility then. But given the huge socio-economic, cultural, and kinship differences which are still likely to exist in the country, it would not be surprising if certain more subtle residual differences relating to reproductive and marital behaviour remained.

A key issue, which is addressed in more detail in Chapter 5, is just how low fertility may fall in the coming decades. From the evidence assessed here, it

---

[8]However, it should be noted that some researchers have argued that with fertility decline the level of son preference may increase (Das Gupta and Bhat 1997).

seems clear that average levels may fall below the approximate replacement figure of 2.1 births. Experience from Europe, and from a significant and rising fraction of Asia's population, supports this position. And we have seen that throughout the 1990s SRS estimates for two states, Kerala and Tamil Nadu, put the TFR at about two births per woman.

A question can be asked about the future of the family planning programme. Since its inception in the early 1950s one of its main objectives has been to help reduce levels of fertility to around the replacement level. Indeed, probably over-ambitiously, the National Population Policy 2000 lists the achievement of replacement level fertility as a national demographic goal for the year 2010 (Ministry of Health and Family Welfare 2000b: 2). In many states there is still some way to go before this objective is achieved. Nevertheless, in the coming one or two decades a growing number of states will experience levels of fertility that are around, or below, replacement. It seems unlikely that this will lead to a reduction in the commitment to family planning provision. Population growth will continue; and there will probably be a continued commitment to the provision of family planning services (perhaps with greater involvement from the private sector) despite circumstances of replacement, or below replacement fertility.

At the start of the twenty-first century, the family planning programme was dominated by female sterilization in all states. The procedure is quick and is usually effective in providing long-term protection from pregnancy. But women who have a tubectomy often have minimal understanding of precisely what is involved, including the importance of follow-up care and the possible adverse effects on their health. India's family planning programme will have to address these issues in the future. It will have to widen its remit so that women and men both have greater access to safe, effective, and affordable methods of contraception in addition to sterilization. The mix of methods provided by the programme must receive greater priority. It seems likely that the next couple of decades will see greater provision and use of reversible forms of contraception, such as the pill, IUD, and—perhaps increasingly influenced by the spread of HIV/AIDS—condoms. Induced abortion too may become more prevalent. Even so, the dominance of female sterilization is so great that it may still be the most important single method of contraception employed in 2026.

The uneven pace of fertility decline between different regions, and the consequent implications for future population growth and age structure, deserve greater attention from the country's politicians and planners. There should be more recognition of the long-term implications of such disparities. Estimates for the late 1990s suggest that in states like Uttar Pradesh and Bihar only about half of total demand for family planning was being satisfied (IIPS and ORC Macro 2000: 174). These states will require greater investments and more innovative family planning programmes. While political will is important, so also are good governance, committed and dedicated administrators, and responsive NGOs.

It has been argued in this chapter that fertility is falling because of a wide range of socio-economic and cultural conditions. The fact that during the 1990s the fertility of many illiterate women declined too, especially in much of the country's south, points to some inadequacies with the conventional list of socio-economic variables (for example, levels of income, female education, etc.) which have usually been employed to account for fertility decline. These variables are often significant facilitators of the fertility transition, but they are not necessarily its ultimate cause. It is undeniable that couples are reducing their fertility in a whole range of different economic, cultural, and kinship contexts—contexts which themselves will change over time. We have noted that family planning efforts have played a facilitating role in fertility decline. In addition, couples absorb new fertility norms and forms of behaviour in response to new ideas and the behaviour of others around them. However, in the last resort it appears reasonable to presume that India's continuing fertility transition, in all parts of the country, is basically a response to the massive improvements in mortality, the origins of which lie in the first half of the twentieth century.

It is difficult to forecast likely future developments regarding marriage. In general the institution will still be both early and universal in the year 2026. But the age of female marriage will probably rise further during the coming decades. Measured in years, rises can be expected to be relatively large in those states where in the late 1990s the age of female marriage was still relatively low (Table 4.3). Also, with rising levels of female education and other socio-economic developments, some women may find the alternatives to a domestic life of marriage and childbearing increasingly attractive. The proportions of women who are not married by age 25 can be expected to increase. It seems probable that a life which does not revolve around marriage and childbearing may gradually become more socially acceptable, especially in urban areas and parts of the country's south.

Moreover, even for the vast majority of women who will still marry and have children, the childbearing phase of life is going to be very much shorter than it has been in the past. We have seen that the trend in India appears to be towards women marrying, having a small number of children, and then getting sterilized. The age span of fertility is becoming increasingly concentrated. This too should have beneficial effects for women's levels of autonomy and status over the longer run.

5

India's Population—The Future

Tim Dyson

This chapter presents population projections for India's major states to the years 2026 and 2051. These state-level projections underpin virtually all the work presented elsewhere in this book. When summed and adjusted for the existence of smaller states and union territories, they also provide population projections for all-India.

The present projections constitute a best assessment of how India's population will grow. But it should be made clear that they are only projections, not predictions. That is, they involve making assumptions about how trends in fertility and mortality might unfold. Actuality will certainly depart from what is assumed and projected here: the more so because 15 state populations are involved. Nevertheless, we can gain some broad indications regarding the country's demographic future.

PREVIOUS POPULATION PROJECTIONS

Several institutions make population projections for India. Table 5.1 summarizes the assumptions and results from those of the Population Foundation of India (PFI), the United Nations (UN), the United States Census Bureau, and the World Bank. Data from the projections made by the Registrar General of India's Technical Group on Population Projections (Registrar General, India 1996) are not shown chiefly because they extend only to the year 2016. However, by extension, the Registrar General's projections imply a population total for the year 2026 similar to the figures shown for the US Census Bureau

TABLE 5.1: *Summary results and assumptions from selected population projections for India*

Projection	Population (millions)			TFR (births per woman)			Life expectation (years)		
	2001	2026	2051	2001–6	2021–6	2046–51	2001–6	2021–6	2046–51
Population Foundation (PFI)	1012	1414	1646	2.85	2.15	1.85	65.0	71.8	76.5
United Nations: Low	1009	1262	1298	2.8	1.6	1.6	64.2	70.5	75.4
Medium	1009	1351	1572	3.0	2.1	2.1	64.2	70.5	75.4
High	1009	1460	1888	3.1	2.6	2.6	64.2	70.5	75.4
US Census Bureau	1016	1408	–	2.95	2.3	–	63.0	74.0	–
World Bank	1016	1343	1572	2.9	2.2	2.1	63.2	67.0	71.1

Notes: The United Nations and World Bank figures relate to years and periods ending in zero and five (for example, 1995, 2000–5). The World Bank figures shown for 2046–51 actually relate to 2040–5. The population totals shown for the US Census Bureau relate to years 2000 and 2025; the TFRs are averages for the years bounding the corresponding periods ending in zero and five (for example, that shown for 2001–6 is the average of the figures assumed for 2000 and 2005); and the life expectation shown for 2001–6 is the Census Bureau estimate for 1998. The assumed TFRs of the PFI are weighted averages for the 15 major states. Other minor adjustments have been made to some figures to assist comparability.

Sources: Natarajan and Jayachandran (2001); Population Foundation of India (2000); United Nations (2001); US Bureau of the Census (1999); World Bank (2000b).

and the PFI. It should be noted that none of these projections incorporate data from the 2001 Census.

The UN, the US Census Bureau, and World Bank projections were made for all-India, as part of larger exercises which involved projecting the populations of many different countries. But the PFI projections (and those of the Registrar General) entailed making separate population projections for all the major states, and the results were then summed up to produce all-India totals. Whether they were conducted at the national or state levels, all these projections involved developing relatively simple rules which, when combined with a measure of judgement, were used to generate fertility and mortality assumptions across different (national or state) populations. This applies to the present projections too.

The UN medium variant and World Bank projections suggest that around the year 2026 India's population will be about 1.35 billion, and that by 2051 it will be about 1.57 billion. However, the US Census Bureau and PFI projections, and by implication those of the Registrar General, imply that the population will exceed 1.4 billion by 2026. And the PFI projections indicate that it may be significantly higher than 1.6 billion by 2051 (Table 5.1).

Small differences in the assumed levels of the TFR produce sizeable differences in the projected populations. The UN's three variant projections illustrate this. According to them, if the TFR were to decline to 1.6 births per woman by 2021–6 then India's population might never exceed 1.3 billion. However, if total fertility falls to only 2.6, and remains there, then the population will be well over 1.4 billion by 2026 and approaching 1.9 billion by 2051 (Table 5.1). So the pace of fertility decline, and its eventual level, will be hugely important in determining the scale of future demographic growth.

This basic point can be made retrospectively too. For example, if India had experienced China's TFR trajectory since 1950 then its population at the 2001 Census would have been smaller by roughly 200 million.[1] This difference is the more striking because until about 1970 both countries had similar levels of fertility.

Until recently most population projections for India have assumed that the TFR will fall to, and then remain at, the approximate replacement level of 2.1 births per woman. The World Bank and UN medium-variant projections illustrate this convention. And the US Census Bureau projection does not envisage total fertility dropping below 2.3 before 2021–6. However, with an increasing number of countries in Europe and Asia approaching or experiencing below-replacement fertility, the UN low-variant projection assumes a lower 'floor' of just 1.6 births (Table 5.1). The state-level projections of the Registrar General and the PFI also use a floor of 1.6, although not all states reach this TFR within the periods of the projections. Clearly, the implications of assuming a particular lower boundary become more important the longer the period of projection.

An important point, illustrated by the projections of the PFI, is that a state-level approach to projection tends to imply that the level of national total fertility will decline more slowly than does an all-India approach. The main explanation is that assumed lower TFR floors come into play earlier when making state-level projections. The resulting difference can be appreciable. Thus, when the state-level TFR assumptions of the PFI are weighted to produce a national TFR for the quinquennium 2021–6, the resulting figure is 2.15 births (Table 5.1); but a figure of just 1.65 would have been obtained if the fertility assumptions had been generated using all-India data (Registrar General, India 1996: 35; Natarajan and Jayachandran 2001: 40). Although it is more complex, a state-level approach to projection is preferable.

Finally, all the projections in Table 5.1 assume that the mortality level will continue to improve. The US Census Bureau assumption seems particularly buoyant, with life expectation reaching 74 years by around 2025. The Registrar General's assumption that life expectation will reach 69 years by 2011–6 is

---

[1]This figure results from comparing two population projections for all-India. The first used the life expectations and TFRs estimated for India by the UN for the period 1950–2000 (United Nations 2001) and gave a population of 989 million in the year 2000. The second projection was identical, except that the UN's estimated TFRs for China were used and the resulting population was 779 million.

similarly optimistic (Registrar General, India 1996: 43). And the PFI assumption is fairly optimistic too. Thus, whereas the PFI foresees an average life expectancy of nearly 72 years being attained by 2021–6, the UN assumes a figure of 70.4, and the World Bank only 67. Some of the explanation for these differences may derive from differing assessments regarding the future impact of HIV/AIDS. Only the UN projections appear specifically to incorporate a modest—inevitably rather speculative—allowance for this disease.

In summary, previous projections suggest that India's population will be around or between 1.34 and 1.41 billion by 2026, and around or between 1.57 and 1.65 billion by 2051. Only one projection results in an eventual population under 1.5 billion, and its fertility assumptions are extreme. State-level projections suggest that fertility will decline more slowly than if assumptions are formulated at the national level. Other matters for consideration are how low total fertility will fall, and the impact of HIV/AIDS.

STATE-LEVEL PROJECTIONS TO 2026

The present projections pertain to the 15 most populous states as they were constituted before the creation of Jharkhand, Chhatisgarh, and Uttaranchal. Therefore these projections relate to the *former* territories of Bihar, Madhya Pradesh, and Uttar Pradesh. No estimates for fertility and mortality levels exist for the new states. So it makes sense to project them as part of the populations to which they previously belonged. It is worth noting, however, that according to the 2001 Census, Jharkhand, Chhatisgarh, and Uttaranchal comprised respectively 24.5, 25.6, and 4.9 per cent of the former populations of Bihar, Madhya Pradesh, and Uttar Pradesh. Compared to the states to which they formerly belonged the new states each experienced appreciably lower population growth rates during 1991–2001, had less masculine populations, and lower population densities (Dyson 2001).

The cohort component method of projection is used here, in particular, the computer package *People* (Overseas Development Administration 1993a, 1993b). Five-year age cohorts of the population are projected forwards five years at a time, subjecting them to assumptions regarding levels of fertility, mortality, and migration. This section develops simple, yet plausible, rules which, with a few minor amendments, are used to generate these assumptions.

The main demographic data sources used are the census and the SRS. The census provides information on the size and structure of India's population. And the SRS remains the only source which, for each of the country's major states, supplies a regular time series of fairly reliable estimates of all the main demographic measures. While the SRS may suffer from a modest degree of birth under-registration, for present purposes this is partly offset by some degree of death under-registration. Certainly, when allowances are made for likely migration flows and changes in census coverage, then the rates of population growth indicated by the SRS are usually close to those indicated by the censuses (Dyson 2001).

Population size and distribution: The present projections use provisional population totals from the 2001 Census. The final totals are unlikely to be much different.[2] In 2001, 10 states had populations exceeding 50 million. Former Bihar and Uttar Pradesh each had populations exceeding 100 million, and together comprised 27.7 per cent of India's total population (Table 5.2).

It will be some time before the age distributions from the 2001 Census are available. So those summarized in Table 5.2 were derived from the 1991 Census. Specifically, the 1991 age distributions were smoothed and brought forward to 1996 by the Registrar General's Technical Group, and they were then brought forward again to 2001 using SRS data (Dyson and Hanchate 2000). These age distributions are probably acceptable, although hardly exact, representations of the true distributions.[3] Some states, notably those which are most advanced in the fertility transition, especially Kerala and Tamil Nadu, have relatively small proportions of their populations aged under 15 years, and comparatively large proportions aged 50 and over. But states which are behind in the transition, like Bihar, Madhya Pradesh, Rajasthan, and Uttar Pradesh, have relatively high proportions aged under 15 years (due to their higher fertility). India's population in 2001 was still fairly young, with over 34 per cent aged less than 15. It may be noted that Bihar, Gujarat, Maharashtra, Rajasthan, and Uttar Pradesh all have fairly masculine populations. The sex ratios are extraordinarily high, around 1.15 males per female, in Haryana and Punjab (Table 5.2). These high ratios reflect high levels of excess female mortality and the abortion of female foetuses. They may also reflect a slightly greater degree of under-enumeration of females in the census (Bhat 2001b; Dyson 2001). Indeed, the true population of India in 2001 was probably somewhat larger than 1027 million.

Fertility: There are two sources of data on state-level fertility. The first and second rounds of the cross-sectional NFHSs, held respectively during the early and late 1990s, are one. The second is the dual record SRS which has been operational since about 1970.

Using the 'own children' approach (a form of reverse survival), Retherford and Mishra (2001) have generated 15-year aggregated ratios of estimated TFRs from the NFHS to those obtained from the SRS. For all-India the ratio for the first NFHS survey round is 1.067 and for the second it is 1.020.

[2]In 1991 the provisional and final population totals were 843.9 and 846.4 million respectively.

[3]Slight adjustments were made to some age distributions for reasons of consistency. The distributions in Table 5.2 are similar to those projected by the Registrar General for 2001 (Registrar General, India 1996) although they may understate slightly the youthfulness of India's population (Bhat 2001a).

TABLE 5.2: *Summary of baseline population data and assumptions, major states and all-India*

State	Population 2001 (000s)	% of all-India	Density (per sq. km) 2001	Population age distribution (per cent)			Population sex ratio 2001	Net migration rate (per 1000)
				0–14	15–49	50+	m/f	
Andhra Pradesh	75,728	7.4	275	31.7	53.4	14.9	1.023	-0.04
Assam	26,638	2.6	340	36.3	52.6	11.1	1.073	0.07
Bihar (fmr)	109,788	10.7	632	38.6	48.5	12.9	1.080	-1.10
Gujarat	50,597	4.9	258	31.8	54.6	13.6	1.086	1.09
Haryana	21,083	2.1	477	35.9	51.6	12.5	1.161	1.04
Karnataka	52,734	5.1	275	31.7	54.0	14.3	1.038	0.29
Kerala	31,839	3.1	819	25.8	57.0	17.2	0.945	-0.64
Madhya Pradesh (fmr)	81,181	7.9	183	37.1	49.8	13.1	1.067	0.64
Maharashtra	96,752	9.4	314	32.0	53.1	14.9	1.084	1.24
Orissa	36,707	3.6	236	32.7	52.6	14.7	1.029	-0.19
Punjab	24,289	2.4	482	31.6	53.5	14.9	1.145	0.35
Rajasthan	56,473	5.5	165	38.3	49.2	12.5	1.085	-0.38
Tamil Nadu	62,111	6.0	478	26.5	56.2	17.3	1.014	-0.45
Uttar Pradesh (fmr)	174,532	17.0	593	38.7	48.1	13.2	1.109	-1.32
West Bengal	80,221	7.8	904	32.9	53.8	13.3	1.071	1.05
All-India	1,027,015	100.0	324	34.4	51.7	13.9	1.072	–

Notes: The all-India figures above include smaller states and union territories. As mentioned in the text, the projections for Bihar, Madhya Pradesh, and Uttar Pradesh relate to their former (fmr) jurisdictions. Only summary age/sex distributions are given above; those actually used in the projections for 2001 were in five-year age groups. The net migration rates are expressed per 1000 population per year and were calculated from 1991 census data.

Sources: Registrar General, India (1996, 1998a, 2001a).

These figures, which are essentially NFHS-based correction factors (CFs) for the SRS TFRs for the same years, may be underestimates. Nevertheless they can be taken to suggest that during the late 1990s there was probably only a modest degree of underestimation of the national TFR by the SRS. The decline in the implied CF between 1990–2 and 1996–8 could reflect deterioration of birth coverage between the NFHS survey rounds and/or some improvement in SRS birth coverage. For most states, however, the CFs obtained from the second NFHS survey round—the closest in time to the baseline period employed here—are near to unity, that is, they imply that the SRS TFRs are generally reasonably accurate. The main exceptions are Tamil Nadu (1.095) and Kerala (1.157). However, the absolute size of the implied TFR adjustment is fairly modest because both these states have comparatively low fertility. In fact, the implication is that in the late 1990s both Tamil Nadu and Kerala had TFRs close to the replacement level (Retherford and Mishra 2001: 36–9).

Employing various procedures and combinations, Retherford and Mishra (2001) applied the 15-year aggregated CFs from the two NFHS survey rounds to the SRS TFRs for 1990–2 and 1996–8. This provides an impression of the extent of TFR decline. For all-India most of these applications suggested a similar quantum of fertility decline as the SRS. Most of the state-level comparisons were also fairly similar. Therefore, analysis of the NFHS data can be taken to provide broad support for the use of SRS fertility estimates here. Moreover, where the NFHS raises questions regarding the SRS figures it does not provide clear alternatives. So, partly because the SRS TFRs are generally close to the levels indicated by the second round of the NFHS, and partly because they are available annually, it is they which form the basis of the TFR assumptions used here. Table 5.3 gives SRS-based TFRs for the baseline period 1996–2001.

The age patterns of fertility produced by the SRS may, however, be less reliable than those of the NFHS. The SRS age-specific fertility rate distributions tend to be located at older ages than is appropriate (Narasimhan et al. 2001). A likely explanation is systematic age exaggeration of women in the SRS—a phenomenon which, incidentally, tends to raise the resulting TFRs and so partially offsets the effects of any birth under-registration in the SRS (Retherford and Mishra 2001). However, because the NFHS placed considerable emphasis on ascertaining the ages of women who were to be interviewed, its results probably give a better indication of the true age patterns of fertility.

Accordingly, data from the 1996–8 NFHS surveys were used here to derive baseline age patterns of state-level fertility. Gompertz relational models—in which α reflects the age location of the fertility schedule, and β its degree of concentration across the female reproductive years (United Nations 1983: 25–6)—were fitted to the 1996–8 data. The resulting parameters, shown in Table 5.3, are generally very high, reflecting an unusually young and extremely concentrated age pattern of fertility. Moreover, between the first and second

TABLE 5.3: *Summary of baseline fertility indices and assumptions, major states and all-India*

State	TFR 1996–2001	α	β	Period when TFR = 1.8 is reached (or TFR during 2021–6)	Sex ratio at birth (m/f)			
					SRS 1981–90	NFHS1 1978–92	NFHS2 1984–98	Assumed
Andhra Pradesh	2.34	1.00	1.66	2001–06	1.047	1.02	1.07	1.06
Assam	3.16	0.41	1.36	2016–21	1.064	1.07	1.08	1.06
Bihar (fmr)	4.28	0.30	1.31	2.11	1.117	1.04	1.05	1.06
Gujarat	2.93	0.59	1.67	2016–21	1.113	1.06	1.07	1.08
Haryana	3.31	0.54	1.61	2016–21	1.150	1.09	1.14	1.13
Karnataka	2.41	0.90	1.73	2006–11	1.073	1.06	1.05	1.06
Kerala	1.80	0.42	1.79	1996–2001	1.055	1.03	1.05	1.06
Madhya Pradesh (fmr)	3.93	0.52	1.36	1.88	1.082	1.08	1.06	1.06
Maharashtra	2.63	0.99	1.87	2011–6	1.085	1.04	1.10	1.08
Orissa	2.89	0.42	1.55	2011–6	1.062	1.06	1.06	1.06
Punjab	2.64	0.42	1.98	2011–6	1.132	1.15	1.20	1.16
Rajasthan	4.13	0.34	1.28	2021–26	1.141	1.13	1.10	1.08
Tamil Nadu	1.96	0.79	1.87	2001–06	1.049	1.02	1.04	1.06
Uttar Pradesh (fmr)	4.73	0.25	1.29	2.32	1.116	1.08	1.09	1.08
West Bengal	2.44	0.70	1.57	2006–11	1.056	1.01	1.06	1.06
All-India	3.21	0.50	1.46	2016–21	1.095	1.06	1.08	–

Notes: The TFRs for 1996–2001 are averages of (i) the published SRS rates for 1996–8 and (ii) linear extrapolations for years 1999–2000 based on the SRS TFRs for 1986–98. In the standard run the TFR for Kerala was fixed at 1.8 throughout, and that for Tamil Nadu reaches 1.8 in the first projection period (that is 2001–6). The α and β values derived from the 1996–8 NFHS data are taken here as pertaining to the baseline period 1996–2001. The figures shown for all-India are those obtained using all-India data, that is, they are not weighted averages of state-level results.

Sources: Registrar General, India (1996, 1999a, 2000); IIPS and ORC Macro (2000).

NFHS survey rounds the values of α and β increased in most states, implying that the age location of fertility declined and became even more highly concentrated during the 1990s. Related to this, both features, that is the very young age location and high degree of concentration, tend to be greater in states with lower TFRs.[4] Data from the second NFHS round indicate that except for Punjab, Bihar, and Uttar Pradesh (the last two states still with fairly high fertility) around half of all the TFR schedule is located at ages below 25. In Andhra Pradesh and Maharashtra this fraction approaches 70 per cent.

The strong implication is that as fertility declines in the future so its age location will tend to fall and become more highly concentrated. As noted in Chapter 4, in much of India, women appear to be moving towards a pattern of behaviour where they get married, still at a fairly young age, have two children in quick succession, and then get sterilized.

According to the SRS, the level of total fertility has been falling in most states since the early 1970s or earlier (Figure 5.1). The TFRs sometimes fluctuate, reflecting real events and/or changes in data collection procedures. The estimated TFRs for Bihar and West Bengal were especially doubtful before 1981, and the trend in the SRS TFR for Assam has also been particularly questionable. It is to be noted that the pace of fertility decline seems to have slackened in those states with the lowest levels of fertility. In Kerala, with the lowest fertility of all, the SRS indicates that the TFR briefly touched 1.7 births during 1992–4, but that it subsequently rose to 1.8. However, it may be recalled that analysis of NFHS data suggests that total fertility in Kerala and Tamil Nadu in the late 1990s may have been around, or slightly above, replacement. So there seems to be no strong reason for setting a lower floor for total fertility that is less than 1.8 births, the figure which is assumed in the standard run projections here. This view is supported by the strong son preference which characterizes Indian society. Moreover, it is only recently that any country has experienced below-replacement fertility for more than a relatively short period; and in many countries which have TFRs below replacement there are grounds to believe that the cohort rates may be around replacement or slightly higher (Teitelbaum 1997). Also, even a figure of 1.8 is below the floor employed by most projections. So use of this figure here may itself prove to be too low as a long-term lower average.

To assign an appropriate age pattern of fertility to this TFR floor in the standard-run projections, linear regressions were employed across the parameter estimates in Table 5.3 to give values appropriate for a TFR of 1.8 births.[5]

[4]Kerala is the only exception. Its age pattern of fertility is not highly concentrated at young ages. Therefore in the standard-run projection, the α and β parameters for Kerala were held constant at the values shown in Table 5.3.

[5]The same procedure was used to produce parameters for the alternative TFR floors used in the variant projections considered below. The results were: TFR=2.1 (α=0.73, β=1.79), TFR=1.5 (α=0.84, β=1.92).

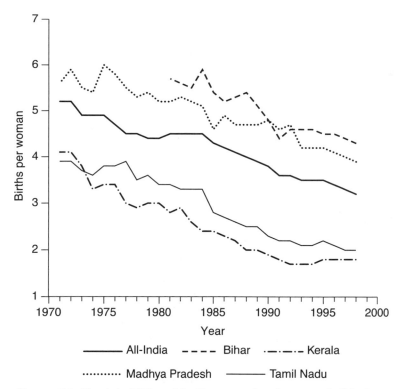

FIGURE 5.1: *Trends in SRS total fertility rates, selected states and all-India*

Source: Registrar General, India (1999a, 2000).

Figure 5.2 shows the resulting target age-specific fertility distribution towards which states are assumed to move over time. Interestingly, the parameters of the target schedule ($\alpha=0.79$, $\beta=1.85$) are very similar to those of Tamil Nadu, which has the second lowest TFR (Table 5.3). Figure 5.2 also illustrates how closely the Gompertz models fit the observed baseline age-specific fertility rates.

There remains the crucial issue of the *pace* of future fertility decline. The projections of the PFI and the Registrar General assumed that in several major states, notably Bihar, Madhya Pradesh, Rajasthan, and Uttar Pradesh, TFR declines will be very slow. Thus in the PFI projections the TFR for Uttar Pradesh was assumed to be as high as 3.5 births in 2026 (Natarajan and Jayachandran 2001: 37). Even more extreme, the assumptions of the Registrar General's projections imply that Uttar Pradesh will not reach replacement fertility for over 100 years (Registrar General, India 1996: 12). Indeed, the use by both these sets of projections of a TFR floor as low as 1.6 seems to have been required in order to counterbalance the very slow rates of fertility

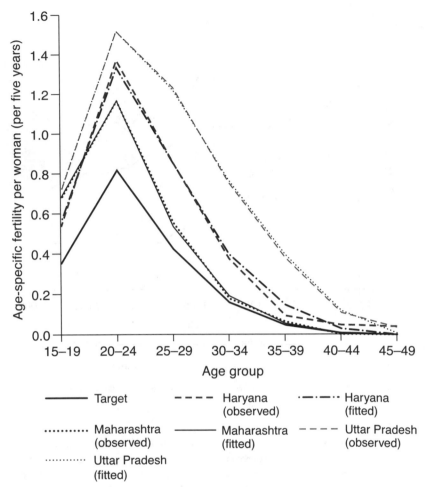

FIGURE 5.2: *Target, and observed and fitted age-specific fertility rates, selected states*

Note: The observed fertility distributions are those from the NFHS surveys for 1996–8.
Source: IIPS and ORC Macro (2000).

decline which were assumed for certain states. Clearly, what is needed is an approach which avoids the use of an extremely low floor, but which permits a reasonable pace of fertility decline in all states.

Several approaches to this issue were considered. The most satisfactory turned out to be to fit linear regressions to the state-level SRS TFRs for 1986–98 and to use these to extrapolate the future trend in total fertility until it reached the floor level of 1.8. With a few minor amendments this approach produced reasonably brisk TFR declines for most states.[6] However, for Uttar Pradesh, it produced an unusually slow pace of decline, implying that total fertility would be around 3.2 births during 2021–6, while in all other states it would be about or below replacement. Yet if linear extrapolation produces a TFR for Bihar in 2021–6 of 2.1 it seems improbable that the TFR in Uttar Pradesh will be over one birth higher. Therefore it was assumed here that the TFR in Uttar Pradesh during 2021–6 will be 10 per cent higher than that in Bihar (as applied during 1996–2001). This admittedly arbitrary adjustment implies that the TFR of Uttar Pradesh will fall linearly to about 2.3 births in 2021–6 and means that this key state is not left as the sole significant outlier. Figure 5.3 illustrates several state-level TFR trajectories, including some of the more difficult cases. For all states the assumptions,

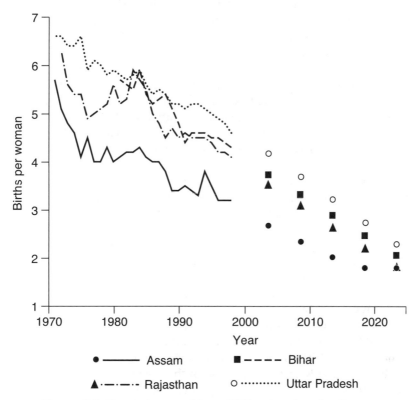

FIGURE 5.3: *Past and assumed future TFR trajectories, selected states*

Source: Registrar General, India (1999a, 2000).

[6]Due to discontinuities in the SRS TFRs, the years 1994 and 1995 were omitted from the procedure in the case of Assam; for Rajasthan the period used was 1984–98.

expressed mainly in terms of the quinquennium when a TFR of 1.8 is attained, are summarized in Table 5.3.[7]

A final fertility assumption relates to the sex ratio at birth. In most human populations this ratio is biologically determined, usually varying between 1.05 and 1.07 male births for every female. The projections in Table 5.1 generally assumed a ratio of 1.06. Those of the Registrar General, however, took the average sex ratios at birth registered by the SRS during 1981–90. Table 5.3 shows that for eight—mainly northern—states these ratios are exceptionally masculine.

Because the numbers of births reported in the NFHS surveys are relatively small, one must be cautious in drawing conclusions about state-level sex ratios at birth from NFHS data. Nevertheless, analysis of these data suggests that the abnormally masculine ratios indicated by the SRS for states like Bihar, Rajasthan, and Uttar Pradesh probably reflect the under-registration of female births to a considerable extent (Griffiths et al. 2000). That said, Table 5.3 shows that the NFHS data themselves indicate that the ratios for Punjab, Haryana, Maharashtra, Rajasthan, and Uttar Pradesh are unusually masculine. And although the time periods to which the NFHS data relate are very broad, comparison of data from the first and second survey rounds suggests that there have been sharp rises in the masculinity of births in the first three of these states. In addition, for these three states, and Gujarat, the 2001 Census results imply that there has been a substantial rise in the masculinity of the child population (Dyson 2001).

There is strong evidence of sex-selective abortion in much of northern India. The practice of aborting female foetuses probably increased during the 1990s due to the spread of scanning and amniocentesis techniques (Das Gupta and Bhat 1998). Its extent is hard to gauge, and very difficult to foresee. In the short run, at least, the sex ratio at birth may continue to become more masculine in some states. Over the longer run, however, one might anticipate that a reaction may set in: for example, if, with changes in the labour market or shortages of women in the marriageable ages, daughters become more highly valued (Dyson 2002a).

Despite these uncertainties some allowance for the phenomenon has been attempted here. Looking across the three sets of available sex ratios in Table 5.3, for nine states there is no real basis for using a figure other than 1.06. For Uttar Pradesh and Rajasthan, because of the suspicion that to some degree the high ratios reflect under-reporting of female births in both the SRS and the NFHS, a figure of 1.08 has been assumed. Finally, for the remaining

[7]For each projection period the state-level TFRs were converted into age-specific fertility rates on the assumption that the respective baseline values of α and β will change regularly towards those of the target distribution. The changes were made with respect to the time periods when the TFR floor was reached or would be reached.

states the average of the three sets of sex ratios has been used, although for Punjab and Haryana these ratios may actually understate the level of birth masculinity.

Mortality: Population projections for India usually incorporate a single path for mortality, framed in terms of life expectancy at birth (Table 5.1). Both these practices are followed here.

However, if the task of making population projections has become more complicated by the rise of sex-selective abortions, the same is true because of the appearance of HIV/AIDS. The UN has estimated that in 1997 there were 4.1 million sero-positive adults (people aged 15 years and over) in India. This was the largest estimate for any country at that time, although it represented only 0.65 per cent of the adult population (United Nations 1999a: 28). There are many uncertainties involved in gauging the current level of HIV prevalence and the future spread and demographic impact of this slow, new disease. It is especially hard to anticipate developments in technology, such as vaccines and medicines, and human behaviour, such as sexual conduct.

Nevertheless, for a growing number of countries the UN makes tentative short-term population projections which permit comparison of what it is estimated will happen 'with' the effects of AIDS with what might have happened 'without' it (that is, if the disease had not occurred). These projections give a rough idea of the potential demographic effects of the disease and hold out some prospect of allowing for its impact at the state level. The UN projections for India assume that by 2010–15 life expectation will be 67.9 years, compared to 68.9 years 'without AIDS'. The associated projection results suggest that by 2015 the population will be 1230 million, compared to 1239 million 'without AIDS'. The projected reduction of 9 million is large in absolute terms, but small as a proportion of the country's population. If the reduction is decomposed then about 70 per cent of it is attributable to an increase in deaths and the remainder is due to the occurrence of fewer births because of the early deaths of females (United Nations 1999a, 2001).

Turning to the issue of developing state-level mortality assumptions, the SRS provides estimates of life expectation. To minimize sampling errors these relate to periods of several years. Those for 1992–6 are given in Table 5.4. Although the figures are probably more accurate for some states than for others, the SRS is thought to provide fairly good estimates of life expectation for all-India (Bhat 1998: 47–52). Accordingly, SRS data have been used here. The first step involved producing sex-specific estimates of life expectancy for the baseline quinquennium 1996–2001. Linear extrapolation of estimates over the period 1986–96 produced implausibly high figures for a few states with relatively high life expectations. This was because such an approach fails to reflect the fact that in absolute terms improvements tend to occur more slowly as life expectancy rises to comparatively high levels. Therefore the figures for

1996–2001 shown in Table 5.4 are averages of the linearly extrapolated estimates and figures generated for the same period from an earlier projection exercise (Dyson and Hanchate 2000). For most states the differences produced by these two approaches are minimal. But the averages shown have the advantage of moderating the rise in life expectation between 1992–6 and 1996–2001 for a few states.

Several procedures exist to generate future trajectories for life expectation in populations unaffected by HIV/AIDS. The UN approach is used here. To develop its mortality assumptions the UN employs three models which reflect plausible future paths for mortality. For India, in the absence of AIDS, and taking account of the pace of mortality decline in the past, the UN adopts the so-called 'medium' model of improvement (United Nations 1999b: 197). Table 5.4 presents sex-specific life expectations for 2011–6 which result when this model is employed for India's major states. Note that, quite plausibly, the procedure implies some degree of convergence in life expectation over time, because states with lower life expectations are assumed to experience greater improvements per quinquennium. For all-India the (unweighted) values of life expectation in 2011–6 derived by this approach increase by 5.5 years to 67 years for males, and by 6.8 years to 69.9 years for females. These results for 2011–6 are similar to those derived by the Registrar General and the PFI (Natarajan and Jayachandran 2001: 40; Registrar General, India 1996: 13–5).

However, some allowance is required for the impact of HIV/AIDS. In this context Table 5.4 gives state-level estimates of the number of adult HIV infections as estimated by the National AIDS Control Organization (2000b). The figures relate to the central year of the present baseline projection period (that is, 1998) and they have been converted to levels of adult prevalence. It may be noted that the estimated total number of infected adults (2.9 million) is below the UN figure mentioned previously, a fact which underscores the tentative nature of the available information. Nevertheless, the data suggest that around 1996–2001 levels of adult sero-prevalence were probably approaching or were above 1 per cent in the five southern states, with Maharashtra and Andhra Pradesh being the worst affected. The disease appears to be less advanced in states outside the south, but there is little doubt that prevalence levels are rising in most states (National AIDS Control Organization 2000a, 2000b). Although men are infected more than women (for all-India in a ratio of 1.75), in the more badly affected states the sex ratio of infection is approaching unity (that is, equality), presumably because the infection has spread more into the general population (Table 5.4).

To help gauge what impact these levels of infection may have on future levels of state-level mortality, UN data for all countries for which 'with' and 'without AIDS' estimates of life expectation have been made, and with estimated levels of adult HIV prevalence in 1997 below 2 per cent, were

TABLE 5.4: *Summary of baseline mortality indices and assumptions, major states and all-India*

State	SRS life expectations (years) 1992–6		Baseline life expectations (years) 1996–2001		Life expectations from UN model (years) 2011–6		Estimated adults with HIV		Sex ratio of infection 1998	Reduction in life expectation (years) 2011–6		Assumed life expectations in future periods (years) 2011–6		2021–6	
	m	f	m	f	m	f	1998 (000s)	1998 (%)	(m/f)	m	f	m	f	m	f
Andhra Pradesh	60.8	63.0	61.7	64.2	67.2	71.0	567	1.16	1.38	2.9	2.1	64.3	68.9	65.2	71.5
Assam	56.1	56.6	57.5	58.2	64.5	65.7	29	0.19	3.49	0.6	0.2	63.9	65.5	66.0	68.0
Bihar (fmr)	60.2	58.2	62.7	60.9	68.2	68.2	114	0.20	3.46	0.7	0.2	67.6	68.0	69.2	70.4
Gujarat	60.5	62.5	62.3	64.3	67.8	71.1	82	0.26	2.23	0.8	0.4	67.0	70.7	68.6	72.9
Haryana	63.4	64.3	64.0	65.6	69.0	71.9	34	0.29	3.60	1.0	0.3	68.0	71.6	69.4	73.6
Karnataka	61.1	64.5	61.4	65.3	66.9	71.8	310	0.93	1.37	2.3	1.7	64.6	70.1	65.7	71.7
Kerala	70.2	75.8	71.2	76.1	74.0	78.9	169	0.74	2.96	2.4	0.8	71.6	78.1	71.8	78.8
Madhya Pradesh (fmr)	55.1	54.7	56.1	56.1	63.1	63.6	138	0.29	3.45	1.0	0.3	62.1	63.3	64.1	65.7
Maharashtra	63.8	66.2	64.8	67.4	69.5	73.2	747	1.27	1.36	3.2	2.3	66.3	70.9	66.9	72.0
Orissa	56.9	56.6	58.3	58.2	64.8	65.7	45	0.19	3.35	0.6	0.2	64.2	65.5	66.1	67.9
Punjab	66.4	68.6	67.3	69.6	71.0	74.3	44	0.29	3.47	1.0	0.3	70.0	74.0	71.0	75.5
Rajasthan	58.6	59.6	60.5	61.7	66.5	69.0	50	0.16	3.83	0.6	0.1	65.9	68.9	67.8	71.2
Tamil Nadu	62.8	64.8	64.1	66.8	68.8	72.6	308	0.72	1.37	1.8	1.3	67.0	71.3	68.0	72.8
Uttar Pradesh (fmr)	57.7	56.4	59.8	58.9	66.3	66.4	109	0.11	3.68	0.4	0.1	65.9	66.3	68.0	68.8
West Bengal	61.8	63.1	62.9	64.7	68.4	71.5	117	0.24	2.22	0.7	0.3	67.7	71.2	79.3	73.4
All-India	60.1	61.4	61.5	63.1	67.0	69.9	2934	0.50	1.75	1.4	0.8	65.6	69.1	67.0	71.1

Notes: The life expectations shown above for all-India for 2011–6 and 2021–6 are unweighted; they are included for reasons of completeness and did not result from the state-level projections. The HIV prevalence figures have been computed on the basis of estimates of state populations aged 15 years and over as of mid-1998. In the projections linear interpolation was used to derive intermediate life expectations for quinquennia between the baseline period and the above figures for 2011–6 and 2021–6.

Sources: Registrar General, India (1999a); National AIDS Control Organization (2000b).

examined. Specifically, the estimated levels of HIV prevalence in 1997 were compared with the estimated future reductions in national life expectations for the period 2010–5 (Dyson and Hanchate 2000). This exercise suggested that, on average, for every 1 per cent increase in adult HIV prevalence in 1997 the level of life expectation during 2010–5 would be reduced by 2.15 years. Table 5.4 gives the implied reductions in future state-level life expectation which arise when this indication is applied to the estimates of HIV prevalence in the major states in 1998. In most cases the implied decreases are small, but in the southern states they are quite significant. Thus in Maharashtra, the suggestion is that, compared to the situation 'without AIDS', male and female life expectations may be reduced by 3.2 and 2.3 years respectively. When these state-level reductions are applied to the previously generated 'without AIDS' life expectancies for 2011–6, the result is to produce a further degree of convergence in future mortality, particularly for males. This is because over the period to 2011–6, HIV/AIDS will have a greater impact in the southern states; and these are states which otherwise would have tended to experience relatively favourable levels of mortality. It has been shown in Table 5.4 that in Kerala male life expectation only rises from 71.2 to 71.6 years between 1996–2001 and 2011–6 because the assumed impact of HIV/AIDS offsets most of the relatively modest rise in life expectation that would otherwise have occurred. The average of the unweighted male and female life expectations generated for all-India 'with AIDS' in 2011–6 (67.3 years) is close to the figure used by the UN for 2010–15 (67.9). Finally, an extension must be made to 2021–6. Here the UN considers that the prevalence of HIV among adults may rise from 0.65 per cent to about 1.2 per cent between 1998 and 2007 and that sero-prevalence levels will then start to decline (United Nations 1999a: 96–8). This and other evidence that sero-prevalence is rising would lead one to expect that AIDS will further restrict the rise in life expectation during the period to 2021–6. It has been assumed here that between 2011–6 and 2021–6 state-level life expectations will rise at half the rates assumed for the period between 1996–2001 and 2011–6.[8] Table 5.4 summarizes the resulting state-level mortality assumptions.

Lastly, a particular model age pattern of mortality for the projections is needed. Following the Registrar General and PFI, the so-called 'South Asian' model has been employed (United Nations 1982), except for Kerala and Tamil Nadu where following the Registrar General (1996: 15) a 'West' model is used. The South Asian model has the advantage that it was partly derived

---

[8]For the period 2011–6 to 2021–6 this assumption restricts the rise in life expectation by more (measured in terms of years) for females than for males, and for those states which in 1998 were still relatively unaffected by HIV/AIDS. However, both these features seem reasonable as the disease may spread more into the female population in particular in the years ahead, and into those states which in 1996–2001 had relatively low levels of infection.

using SRS data. The age pattern of mortality in much of India may well move towards the West model if mortality in infancy and early childhood declines relatively fast in the future. But the issue is uncertain and of relatively minor significance.

Migration: The projections of the Registrar General and the PFI made no allowance for interstate migration. The stated justification was that the 1991 Census data on duration of residence 0–9 years and place of last residence indicate that net interstate migration flows are negligible (Natarajan and Jayachandran 2001: 40; Registrar General, India 1996: 15). For most states the migration rates resulting from these data, summarized in Table 5.2, support this position. The overall pattern of flows revealed, however, is almost certainly genuine (see Chapter 6). Therefore, although migration is notoriously hard to measure and project, and although the data are inevitably somewhat dated, it was thought best to make some allowance for it here. Accordingly these net interstate migration rates were assumed to remain constant throughout the projection periods, the numbers of migrants being adjusted the whole time so that they summed to zero for the country as a whole.[9] The rationale for making such an allowance about net interstate migration is that long-standing flows, generally out of poorer states to those where employment is more readily available, are likely to persist. The next section will show that for the main 'sending' and 'receiving' states the implications of continued migration stretching over a period of 25 years are significant. However, no allowance was made for international migration, which for a population exceeding one billion can probably be safely regarded as negligible for projection purposes.

Summary: In concluding this section the inevitable elements of uncertainty, compromise, and arbitrariness involved in formulating projection assumptions should be clear. Thus, perhaps, fertility in Uttar Pradesh will not decline as fast as is being assumed here. Perhaps a total fertility floor of 1.8 is too low. There is also considerable uncertainty regarding the future course of HIV/AIDS; about all one can say is that the assumptions used here are similar to those of the UN. Clearly, it is impossible to make separate projections for every possible variation and combination of assumptions which might conceivably be entertained. However, for all-India, the penultimate section will consider the issue of variation around the standard run.

RESULTS OF THE STANDARD RUN PROJECTIONS TO 2026

All-India: The standard run results for all-India arise from summing the results for the 15 major states. However, with the exception of the statistics relating

[9]The migration rates used were sex-specific and they were distributed on the *People* projection package's standard age pattern.

to the projected population age distributions (and the TFRs and life expectancies which are population-weighted figures arising from the state-level input assumptions) the all-India figures in Table 5.5 have been adjusted to take account of the existence of smaller states and union territories. Together these states and territories comprised 4.51 per cent of the population in 2001. And it has been assumed here that this proportion will rise at the average rate experienced during 1961–2001 until it reaches 5.29 per cent in 2026.[10]

TABLE 5.5: *Projected population characteristics for all-India, 2001–26, standard run*

	2001	2006	2011	2016	2021	2026
Population (000s)	1,027,015	1,114,745	1,204,451	1,290,327	1,362,021	1,419,203
Males	531,227	575,816	621,132	664,172	699,706	727,552
Females	495,738	538,929	583,319	626,155	662,315	691,651
Sex ratio (m/f)	1.072	1.068	1.065	1.061	1.056	1.052
Age distribution:						
% aged 0–14	34.4	31.0	28.8	27.7	25.7	23.2
% aged 15–49	51.7	54.3	55.0	54.4	54.4	54.9
% aged 50–9	6.9	7.5	8.1	8.9	9.7	10.3
% aged 60+	7.0	7.2	8.1	9.0	10.2	11.6
Median age (years)	22.7	24.0	25.6	27.5	29.6	31.6
Density (per sq. km)	324	352	380	407	430	448

	2001–6	2006–11	2011–6	2016–21	2021–6	–
Births per interval (millions)	132.68	136.26	133.37	122.46	111.91	–
Deaths per interval (millions)	44.90	46.51	47.46	50.75	54.72	–
Population growth rate (%)	1.64	1.55	1.38	1.08	0.82	–
Crude birth rate (per 1000)	24.8	23.5	21.4	18.5	16.1	–
Crude death rate (per 1000)	8.4	8.0	7.6	7.7	7.9	–
TFR (births per woman)	2.84	2.55	2.33	2.13	1.94	–
Life expectation (males)	63.2	64.6	66.1	66.9	67.6	–
Life expectation (females)	64.8	66.8	68.7	69.7	70.7	–

Notes: Except for the statistics relating to age composition and the TFRs and life expectations (which are appropriately weighted averages of the state-level assumptions) the figures above have been adjusted to take account of the existence of smaller states and union territories. The TFRs have been weighted on the projected state female populations aged 15–49.
Source: Projection output.

[10]The proportion was 3.2 per cent in 1961. Most such states and union territories have grown faster than the national population (partly due to in-migration), and assuming a figure of 5.29 for 2026 could be an underestimate. According to the 2001 Census, Delhi, Jammu and Kashmir, and Himachal Pradesh together comprised 64.6 per cent of the total population in this category (Registrar General, India 2001a).

According to the standard projection, India's population will increase from 1027 to 1419 million during 2001–26, a total rise of 38 per cent or 1.3 per cent per year (Table 5.5). The crude birth rate will decline appreciably because of falling total fertility. But population ageing will mean that there will be little change in the crude death rate, despite improving mortality. Indeed, the total number of deaths will increase steadily, and by 2021–6 the death rate may have started to rise slightly. The population growth rate is set to decline significantly because of the falling birth rate. However, the projection implies that it will not be until 2021–6 that the quinquennial growth rate falls below 1 per cent. During 2001–6 the average annual increment to the population (the excess of births over deaths) will probably be around 17 million; by 2021–6 there will still be an annual addition of about 11 million.

Despite the assumption of quite masculine sex ratios at birth for some states, the sex ratio of the total population is projected to decline slightly (Table 5.5). This is partly because of the more favourable levels of overall mortality that are envisaged for females (compared to males) and partly because of population ageing (the projected population is progressively more feminine at older ages).

The proportion of the total population aged 0–14 years is set to decline considerably. During 2001–26 it falls from 34.4 to 23.2 per cent. However, the absolute size of the population aged 0–14 will also fall from about 353 to 329 million. So *all* of the country's future demographic growth will occur at middle and older ages. A modest reduction in the annual number of births is projected from around 26 million during 2001–6 to 22 million during 2021–6. The median age of the population rises appreciably from 22.7 to 31.6 years. The proportion of the population aged 60 years and over rises from about 7 to over 11 per cent (Table 5.5).

The population-weighted TFRs and life expectations which emerge from the assumptions and projection results for all-India suggest that total fertility will be close to replacement by the quinquennium 2016–21, and below replacement by 2021–6. However, the all-India TFR does not reach 1.8 births during the period under review. Life expectation for both sexes combined is about 69 years by 2021–6. The female advantage then will be approximately three years (Table 5.5).

Major states: There will be considerable variation in the scale of demographic growth between states (Table 5.6). For those states which in the baseline period already had relatively low TFRs—Andhra Pradesh, Karnataka, Kerala, Maharashtra, Orissa, Punjab, and West Bengal—projected growth during 2001–26 is in the range 20–30 per cent. The smallest increase is for Tamil Nadu where out-migration, very low fertility, and not particularly high life expectancy contribute to a rise of only 15.5 per cent.

In contrast, the populations of the former states of Bihar and Madhya Pradesh, and of Rajasthan are projected to rise by about 45–50 per cent. The

TABLE 5.6: *Projected population totals (thousands), major states and all-India, 2001–26, standard run*

State	2001	2006	2011	2016	2021	2026	2001–26 Change (per cent)
Andhra Pradesh	75,728	79,278	83,274	87,070	89,883	91,693	21.1
Assam	26,638	28,912	31,229	33,266	34,745	36,022	35.2
Bihar (fmr)	109,788	121,762	134,716	147,433	157,975	166,221	51.4
Gujarat	50,597	55,068	59,255	62,801	65,561	68,123	34.6
Haryana	21,083	23,070	24,998	26,642	28,066	29,396	39.4
Karnataka	52,734	55,727	58,663	61,519	63,820	65,508	24.2
Kerala	31,839	33,668	35,302	36,652	37,674	38,451	20.8
Madhya Pradesh (fmr)	81,181	89,423	98,001	106,190	112,928	117,953	45.3
Maharashtra	96,752	103,558	109,308	115,088	120,034	123,871	28.0
Orissa	36,707	39,060	41,112	42,871	44,314	45,453	23.8
Punjab	24,289	26,025	27,510	28,842	30,026	31,001	27.6
Rajasthan	56,473	62,652	69,062	75,048	79,841	83,324	47.5
Tamil Nadu	62,111	64,827	67,393	69,512	70,889	71,717	15.5
Uttar Pradesh (fmr)	174,532	194,768	216,245	237,314	255,723	271,046	55.3
West Bengal	80,221	85,183	90,497	95,975	100,662	104,311	30.0
All-India	1,027,015	1,114,745	1,204,451	1,290,327	1,362,021	1,419,203	38.2

Source: Projection output.

increase for the former state of Uttar Pradesh is 55 per cent; this state's population may be in the vicinity of 271 million by 2026. With Haryana, these four states are projected to experience proportional growth above the all-India average. The remaining states, however, are likely to experience proportional growth below the national average (Table 5.6).

Nearly a quarter of the total population increase of 392 million during 2001–26 is projected to occur in Uttar Pradesh (Table 5.7). The projections suggest that Bihar will add perhaps another 56 million to its population, and that Madhya Pradesh and Rajasthan may together contribute some 63 million. Therefore, around 55 per cent of total demographic growth during this period is projected to happen in these four states. Maharashtra and West Bengal are each likely to experience additions of roughly 25 million. The projections also imply that the combined population of the country's smaller states and union territories will rise by some 28 million at an annual rate of 1.9 per cent— which seems plausible because there will probably be continued net in-migration to them.

So the key factor determining the volume of state-level demographic growth will be the future course of the birth rate. And the projected birth rates are essentially the outcomes of the assumed TFR trajectories and the projected numbers of women of reproductive age that there will be in the years ahead. In turn, these numbers are determined largely by the baseline age/sex distributions (Table 5.2). The younger these distributions are the greater will be the contribution of age-structural population momentum to future demographic growth.

One way of gaining an idea of the degree to which future growth will be due to such momentum is to compare the present state-level projected populations for 2026 with those arising from projections in which the TFR is assumed to drop immediately (that is, by 2001–6) to the replacement level of 2.1 and then remain there.[11] In the latter projections practically all growth is due to momentum. For Andhra Pradesh, Karnataka, Kerala, Tamil Nadu, and West Bengal, however, such immediate replacement level fertility projections are unnecessary because the standard run projections already incorporate levels of fertility that are below replacement from 2001–6. So, provided total fertility falls as has been assumed here, the implication is that virtually all future growth in these states will be due to momentum. Also, as column (iv) of Table 5.7 shows, for Maharashtra, Orissa, and Punjab the assumption of immediate replacement fertility results in a larger population in 2026 than does the standard run. The explanation is that for these states the standard projections soon embody TFRs that are significantly below replacement. So given the present fertility assumptions for these states, it can also be concluded that most growth in them will be due to momentum as well. In addition, for Assam, Gujarat, and Haryana the results of the immediate replacement fertility projections imply that at least 95 per cent of future population growth will be due to momentum (column (v) of Table 5.7).

However, for Bihar, Madhya Pradesh, Rajasthan, and Uttar Pradesh the indications are rather different. In these states population momentum is projected to be responsible for only 50–70 per cent of growth in the period to 2026. It is in these four states, especially, that efforts to speed fertility decline could have a major impact on limiting future growth. Overall Table 5.7 suggests that roughly 75 per cent of India's population growth over this period may be due to momentum. However, this figure depends upon the fertility assumptions of the standard run. Of course, should the level of fertility fall more slowly, then momentum will account for a smaller proportion of the country's total future demographic growth.

Table 5.7 also allows comparison of the state-level results from the standard run with alternative projections which incorporate no assumptions regarding interstate migration. Comparison of columns (i) and (vi) reveals that the allowance made for migration in the standard run causes a significant difference to the projected populations of some states. Thus in the standard run the populations of Gujarat, Haryana, Madhya Pradesh, Maharashtra, and West

---

[11]All other assumptions were assumed to remain constant. See the notes to Table 5.7.

TABLE 5.7: *Analysis of projected population growth during 2001–26, major states and all-India, standard run*

State	Projected population 2026 (millions)	Increase during 2001–26 (millions)	Contribution to all-India increase (per cent)	Projected population 2026 (TFR=2.1) (millions)	Increase due to momentum (per cent)	Projected population 2026 (no migration) (millions)	Influence of migration on population size in 2026 (per cent)
	(i)	(ii)	(iii)	(iv)	(v)	(vi)	(vii)
Andhra Pradesh	91.7	15.9	4.1	91.7	100	91.8	-0.1
Assam	36.0	9.4	2.4	35.7	96	36.0	0.1
Bihar (fmr)	166.2	56.4	14.4	143.6	60	170.1	-2.3
Gujarat	68.1	17.5	4.5	67.8	98	66.1	3.0
Haryana	29.4	8.3	2.1	29.0	95	28.5	3.0
Karnataka	65.5	12.8	3.3	65.5	100	65.0	0.8
Kerala	38.4	6.6	1.7	38.4	100	39.0	-1.4
Madhya Pradesh (fmr)	117.9	36.8	9.4	105.9	67	115.7	2.0
Maharashtra	123.9	27.1	6.9	128.4	100	119.8	3.4
Orissa	45.5	8.7	2.2	46.5	100	45.6	-0.4
Punjab	31.0	6.7	1.7	31.9	100	30.7	0.8
Rajasthan	83.3	26.9	6.8	75.3	70	84.0	-0.8
Tamil Nadu	71.7	9.6	2.4	71.7	100	72.4	-0.9
Uttar Pradesh (fmr)	271.0	96.5	24.6	223.3	50	279.1	-2.9
West Bengal	104.3	24.1	6.1	104.2	100	101.3	3.0
All-India	1,419.2	392.2	100.0	–	75	–	-0.1

Notes: For Andhra Pradesh, Karnataka, Kerala, Tamil Nadu, and West Bengal the figures in column (iv) result from using the same assumptions as in the standard run. But for these states the figures in column (iv) differ slightly from those in column (i) because of the integrated nature (for example through migration) of the projection. For Maharashtra, Orissa, and Punjab it has also been assumed that *all* future growth will be due to momentum (see text) which, given the standard run fertility assumptions for these states, is only a slight exaggeration. The all-India figures in columns (v) and (vii) result from calculations relating only to the 15 major states. All the figures, especially in column (iv), should be regarded as only broadly illustrative. The negative figure for all-India in column (vii) reflects the fact that in the standard run projection interstate migration redistributes people from states with relatively high to states with relatively low fertility. It may actually understate the extent to which interstate migration will reduce the volume of national population growth.

Source: Projection output.

Bengal in 2026 are larger by about 2–3 per cent compared to the projections with no migration; and Bihar and Uttar Pradesh are smaller by similar proportions as shown in column (vii). While these figures may seem modest, they are more significant if expressed in absolute numbers or as a proportion of total projected population growth. For example, in the standard run Maharashtra's population in 2026 is larger by 4.1 million because of the assumption of continuing net in-migration. The implication is that such migration will be responsible for about 15 per cent of the state's total demographic growth during 2001–26. The difference of 4.1 million stems from total net in-migration of about 3.3 million; the remainder comes from the natural increase of the in-migrants themselves. Conversely, net out-migration from Uttar Pradesh results in a population that is smaller by some 8 million (compared to the projection with no migration). Yet during 2001–26 net loss for Uttar Pradesh due to migration is only about 5.6 million. However, the out-migrants do not contribute to the state's natural increase after they leave. Of course, one should not read too much into these figures. But it is clear that migration will have an appreciable effect upon future population growth for certain states.

Finally, Table 5.8 presents some of the more detailed state-level results.[12] The crude birth rate is set to decline considerably in all states. It should be noted, however, that in absolute terms the greatest declines will occur in those states with relatively high levels of fertility. By 2021–6 no state is projected to have a birth rate above 20 per 1000, and in most it will be in the range 10–15. In every state the total number of deaths occurring per quinquennium is set to rise. But while some states, including those which are demographically least advanced (such as Bihar and Uttar Pradesh), seem set to experience a reduction in their crude death rates, others, including those more advanced (such as Andhra Pradesh and Punjab), are going to experience significant rises in their death rates, despite generally improving levels of life expectation. Clearly, this reflects a greater degree of population ageing.

With falling birth rates and roughly constant (sometimes increasing) death rates, state population growth rates will decline. And, again, the largest declines in absolute terms will generally occur in the least advanced states. Nevertheless, the projections suggest strongly that in 2021–6 the fastest growing state will be the former Uttar Pradesh where, despite net out-migration, the annual rate of growth will still amount to 1.16 per cent. Bihar's growth rate too may exceed 1 per cent (Table 5.8). Interestingly, by 2026 the average population densities for the former territories of both Bihar and Uttar Pradesh are projected to be well over 900 persons per square kilometre, greater than the population density of both Kerala and West Bengal in 2001 (Tables 5.2 and 5.8). As seen earlier, Tamil Nadu will be the slowest growing state in 2021–6, with a projected

[12]For further state-level results see Dyson (2002b).

TABLE 5.8: Selected population characteristics, major states, 2001–26, standard run

State	Density (per sq. km) 2026	Population age distribution (per cent) 2026			Median age (years)		Population sex ratio 2026	Birth rate (per 1000)		Death rate (per 1000)		Population growth rate (per cent)	
	2026	0–14	15–49	50+	2001	2026	m/f	2001–6	2021–6	2001–6	2021–6	2001–6	2021–6
Andhra Pradesh	333	19.7	54.5	25.8	24.1	35.9	0.997	16.8	12.9	7.6	8.9	0.92	0.40
Assam	459	21.3	57.4	21.3	21.3	32.5	1.048	25.0	14.5	8.7	7.4	1.64	0.72
Bihar (fmr)	956	27.0	54.7	18.3	20.2	27.7	1.055	29.8	17.5	8.2	6.6	2.07	1.02
Gujarat	348	20.1	55.6	24.3	23.8	33.7	1.071	23.3	13.9	7.5	7.2	1.69	0.77
Haryana	665	20.8	57.9	21.3	21.5	32.4	1.138	24.3	14.4	7.4	6.2	1.80	0.93
Karnataka	342	19.7	55.0	25.3	23.8	35.3	1.008	18.3	13.3	7.6	8.3	1.10	0.52
Kerala	989	18.8	50.6	30.6	27.1	37.6	0.945	17.6	12.2	5.9	7.8	1.12	0.41
Madhya Pradesh (fmr)	266	24.8	56.2	19.0	21.4	29.0	1.057	29.4	16.1	10.7	8.1	1.93	0.87
Maharashtra	403	19.9	54.8	25.3	24.3	34.7	1.065	19.3	13.4	6.9	8.2	1.36	0.63
Orissa	292	20.0	55.8	24.2	23.7	34.4	1.020	22.1	13.9	9.5	8.7	1.24	0.51
Punjab	616	19.2	54.9	25.9	24.0	35.0	1.126	19.9	13.1	6.4	7.0	1.38	0.64
Rajasthan	243	24.6	56.7	18.7	20.3	29.0	1.061	29.4	15.3	8.4	6.5	2.08	0.85
Tamil Nadu	551	18.9	52.1	29.0	27.0	37.1	0.985	16.9	12.3	8.0	9.7	0.86	0.23
Uttar Pradesh (fmr)	921	28.5	54.4	17.1	20.2	26.2	1.083	32.7	19.4	9.7	6.9	2.19	1.16
West Bengal	1175	20.3	54.6	25.1	23.4	34.9	1.039	17.7	13.4	6.7	7.1	1.20	0.71
All-India	448	23.2	54.9	21.9	22.7	31.6	1.052	24.8	16.1	8.4	7.9	1.64	0.82

Source: Projection output.

annual growth rate of 0.2 per cent. Andhra Pradesh and Kerala are the only two other states which are projected to be growing at less than 0.5 per cent per year at that time.

The results imply that the population of virtually every state will be slightly less masculine in 2026 than was the case in 2001 (Tables 5.2 and 5.8). This applies even to Punjab and Haryana where highly masculine sex ratios at birth have been assumed. That said, population sex ratios change relatively slowly. So the broad regional pattern of noticeably greater population masculinity in the northern states will not diminish much.

Clearly, future population ageing will be greatest in those states which experience the lowest levels of fertility. But all states will undergo some ageing in the period under review. In Uttar Pradesh, for example, the median age of the population is projected to rise from about 20 to 26 years; and Kerala and Tamil Nadu are projected to experience rises from around 27 to 37 years (Table 5.8). There will be big reductions in the proportion of the population aged 0–14 in all states, sizeable increases in most in the proportion aged 50 years and over, and relatively modest changes in the proportion aged 15–49. Even so, population ageing in the current European or Japanese sense will be some way off in most of India in 2026. In that year only Kerala and Tamil Nadu will have around 30 per cent of their populations aged 50 and over. Indeed both these states will experience sizeable reductions in the proportion of their populations aged 15–49 (Tables 5.2 and 5.8). The results suggest that, because of the assumed reductions in total fertility, most states will experience declines in the absolute size of the 0–14 age group by 2026. For example, in states like Andhra Pradesh, Haryana, Karnataka, Maharashtra, and Tamil Nadu this will amount to a reduction of roughly 20 per cent. However, in Bihar the size of the 0–14 age group in 2026 is projected to be about 6 per cent larger than it was in 2001. In Uttar Pradesh it will be greater by about 14 per cent.

To illustrate the range of population ageing implied by the standard run, Figure 5.4 shows the projected proportional age/sex distributions for Andhra and Uttar Pradesh in 2026. In Andhra Pradesh, where total fertility has fallen fast and is assumed to reach the floor from the first projection period, the age distribution falls away below the age group 35–9, and about 52 per cent of the population is aged 35 years or more. The quantum of demographic ageing that Andhra Pradesh may experience in the quarter century following 2026 is clear. In contrast, in Uttar Pradesh the population pyramid remains fairly broad-based in 2026, and it falls away just below the age group 10–14; only about 36 per cent of the projected population is aged over 35. In 2026, each of the populous northern states of Rajasthan, Madhya Pradesh, and Bihar will have projected age distributions tending towards that shown for Uttar Pradesh.

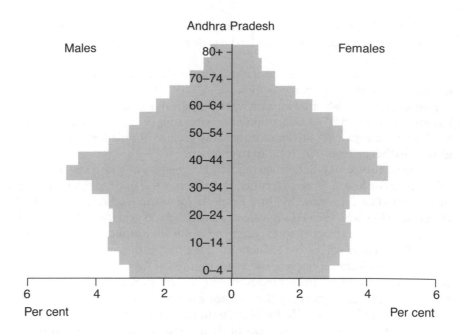

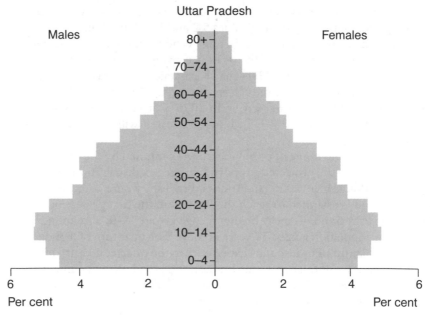

FIGURE 5.4: *Projected proportional age and sex distributions for Andhra Pradesh and Uttar Pradesh, standard run, 2026*

Source: Projection output.

VARIANT PROJECTIONS TO 2051

The standard projection can readily be extended to 2051. In the standard run only three states have TFRs above 1.8 in 2021–6 (Table 5.3). It is straightforward to extrapolate their TFRs until they too reach this lower floor— which they do soon thereafter. Also, state-level mortality trajectories after 2026 can be generated by applying the UN medium model of improvement. Essentially this means that in all states during 2026–51 life expectation resumes its upward march at the pace which would have applied in the absence of HIV/AIDS, although, of course, from a lower base.

The assumptions of the standard run can also be varied to produce high and low fertility variant trajectories. This has been done by varying the level of the TFR floor. In the high variant, the lower boundary for total fertility has been set at 2.1 births. In this variant, Andhra Pradesh, Karnataka, Kerala, Tamil Nadu, and West Bengal all experience a TFR of 2.1 from the first projection period (2001–6). For Kerala and Tamil Nadu this represents an increase in fertility compared to the levels generated from SRS data for the baseline period (1996–2001). However, as previously noted, it may be that the true TFRs for these two states were actually around replacement at that time. Partly with considerations of symmetry in mind, in the low fertility variant the floor for state-level fertility was set at 1.5. It should be emphasized, however, that this is an exceptionally low TFR—below that employed by other projections. Nevertheless, in the low variant, the linear extrapolation of the SRS estimates means that Kerala attains a TFR of 1.5 during 2001–6, and it is joined by Andhra Pradesh, Karnataka, Tamil Nadu, and West Bengal during 2006–11. In summary, the high fertility variant uses a floor for state-level total fertility that is the norm in most other projections; and the low variant incorporates a floor which is extraordinarily low. In both variants the age pattern of fertility for the respective TFR floors was derived as in the standard run; the variant projections also incorporated the same age patterns of mortality and migration rates.[13]

Table 5.9 summarizes the implications of these fertility and mortality assumptions for demographic trends at the all-India level.[14] The figures shown arise when the state-level assumptions are weighted by the respective state populations projected for each future time period. In the high variant India's TFR almost reaches 2.1 by 2021–6; in the standard run this happens during 2016–21; in the low variant it occurs during 2011–6. Since only a single mortality trajectory has been assumed for each state, the resulting national life expectations shown in Table 5.9 are those of the standard run. Life

[13]See footnote 5, this chapter. The proportion of the population in smaller states and union territories was held constant at 5.29 per cent after 2026.

[14]For further variant projection results see Dyson (2002b).

TABLE 5.9: *Total fertility rates and life expectations (by sex), long-run variant projections, all-India, 2001–51*

Period	TFR (per woman)			Life expectation (years)	
	High	Standard	Low	Males	Females
2001–6	2.92	2.84	2.81	63.2	64.8
2006–11	2.68	2.55	2.46	64.6	66.8
2011–6	2.48	2.33	2.20	66.1	68.7
2016–21	2.30	2.13	1.98	66.9	69.7
2021–6	2.14	1.94	1.78	67.6	70.7
2026–31	2.10	1.81	1.59	69.0	72.3
2031–6	2.10	1.80	1.50	70.2	73.7
2036–41	2.10	1.80	1.50	71.2	74.9
2041–6	2.10	1.80	1.50	72.2	76.0
2046–51	2.10	1.80	1.50	73.2	77.0

Notes: The TFRs are the assumed state-level TFRs in each variant projection weighted by the corresponding projected female populations aged 15–49. The life expectations are derived from the assumed state-level life expectations weighted by the projected state-level populations in the standard run. The differences in all-India life expectancy between the three variants are extremely small.

Source: Projection output.

expectation for both sexes combined reaches about 75 years by 2046–51. This figure is similar to that assumed in other projections (Table 5.1).

The results of the long run variant projections suggest that by 2026 the population will lie somewhere between 1392 and 1456 million (Table 5.10). The standard run implies that the population will surpass 1.5 billion around the year 2036, and that if state-level TFRs remain at around 1.8 then the population will be approaching 1.6 billion by 2051, although it may not surpass this figure. In contrast, the high fertility run produces a population in 2051 that is larger by 152 million. Within this scenario India's population will exceed 1.7 billion by the middle of the twenty-first century, when it will still be growing at about 0.5 per cent per year. The low fertility variant projection is the only one in which the population does not reach 1.5 billion; and it is the only projection which involves an eventual slight decline in the country's population size before the year 2051.

All three projections suggest that the population will still be growing at around 1 per cent per year during 2016–21. It is in later periods when differences in the assumed fertility trajectories really translate into more significant differences in the rates of growth (Table 5.10). In all scenarios the population is set to age, but differences between the variants in the proportions at later ages only become appreciable in the period after about 2026 (Dyson 2002b). If 'dependents' are defined as persons who are aged under 15, and those who are aged 60 years and over, then in all variants dependents will form a slightly smaller proportion of the population in 2051 than was the case in 2001. That said, by the middle of the present century at least 20 per cent of

TABLE 5.10: *Comparison of long-run variant projection results for all-India, 2001–51*

Year	Population (millions)			Population growth rate (per cent)		
	High	Standard	Low	High	Standard	Low
2001	1027	1027	1027	–	–	–
2006	1118	1115	1114	1.70	1.64	1.63
2011	1214	1204	1199	1.65	1.55	1.47
2016	1307	1290	1278	1.48	1.38	1.28
2021	1387	1362	1343	1.19	1.08	0.99
2026	1456	1419	1392	0.97	0.82	0.72
2031	1521	1465	1425	0.87	0.64	0.47
2036	1585	1508	1449	0.82	0.58	0.33
2041	1642	1543	1463	0.71	0.46	0.19
2046	1690	1566	1467	0.58	0.30	0.05
2051	1731	1579	1458	0.48	0.17	-0.12

Source: Projection output.

India's population will be aged 60 years and over, and this figure, in all likelihood, will be increasing fairly fast. Figure 5.5 shows the projected trend in the dependency ratio in the standard run. The ratio falls until about 2031, due to the quite sharp decline in the number of younger dependents. However,

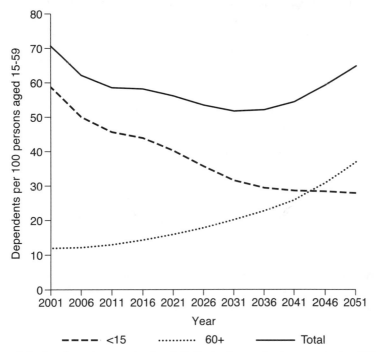

FIGURE 5.5: *Age dependency ratios for all-India in the standard run projection, 2001–51*
Source: Projection output.

thereafter, it rises fairly sharply because of increasing dependency at later ages (60+) combined with a flattening out of the dependency ratio at young ages.

It seems almost certain that India's population will be in the vicinity of 1.4 billion by 2026 and that it will subsequently exceed 1.5 billion. The main way in which 1.5 billion might not be attained is if total fertility falls to—and then remains at—levels which until recently have been virtually unknown anywhere in the world. The only other scenario in which the population might not reach 1.5 billion is if there should be an unexpectedly calamitous path for future mortality, for example, an HIV/AIDS scenario resembling that of Africa where life expectation has been roughly constant since about 1980. While some African countries have experienced major reductions in life expectancy others, less affected by the disease, have continued to experience some improvement. Like India, Africa as a whole is an heterogeneous place. So a rough analogy for India might be if there were to be no future mortality improvement at all, that is if life expectation were to remain constant as in 1996–2001. Yet even on such a depressing scenario India's population in 2026 would only be smaller by about 4 per cent (1366 million) and by 2041 it would still exceed 1.4 billion.[15]

TABLE 5.11: *Projected population totals (millions), major states and all-India, long-run variant projections, 2000–51*

State	2001	2026			2051		
		High	Standard	Low	High	Standard	Low
Andhra Pradesh	75.7	97.2	91.7	87.5	108.8	93.9	82.6
Assam	26.6	36.9	36.0	35.5	43.1	39.4	36.6
Bihar (fmr)	109.8	166.1	166.1	166.1	204.6	194.2	185.0
Gujarat	50.6	69.8	68.1	67.1	82.4	75.4	70.0
Haryana	21.1	30.2	29.4	28.8	36.5	33.3	30.7
Karnataka	52.7	68.9	65.5	62.6	78.5	68.6	60.4
Kerala	31.8	40.7	38.5	36.2	45.0	39.0	33.6
Madhya Pradesh (fmr)	81.2	118.9	118.0	118.0	146.4	137.2	129.9
Maharashtra	96.8	129.3	123.9	119.8	150.2	133.0	119.7
Orissa	36.7	47.2	45.5	44.1	53.0	47.4	42.9
Punjab	24.3	32.2	31.0	30.1	36.5	32.7	29.8
Rajasthan	56.5	84.2	83.3	83.2	103.4	96.6	91.3
Tamil Nadu	62.1	76.1	71.7	68.0	83.1	71.3	61.7
Uttar Pradesh (fmr)	174.5	271.1	271.0	271.0	336.7	319.3	306.6
West Bengal	80.2	110.0	104.3	99.5	130.5	113.7	100.0
All-India	1027.0	1455.8	1419.2	1391.6	1730.6	1578.6	1458.0

Source: Projection output.

[15]These statements arise from a comparison of two projections for all-India. The first incorporated and held constant the baseline life expectations shown in Table 5.4. The second

Finally Table 5.11 gives the projected state populations according to the three variants. For states like Bihar, Madhya Pradesh, and Uttar Pradesh there are virtually no differences in the projected populations by 2026. This is because levels of total fertility in these states are still above those at which the respective floors come into operation. The standard run suggests that the population of former Bihar will be approaching 200 million by 2051 and that the population of former Uttar Pradesh will probably surpass 300 million. In the standard projection only Tamil Nadu will have a smaller population in 2051 than in 2026. Indeed, of the 45 state-level projections summarized in Table 5.11, only one—the low fertility variant for Tamil Nadu—will result in a smaller population in 2051 than was enumerated in 2001. Even in the low variant about half of the states have larger populations in 2051 than in 2026. According to the standard run only Andhra Pradesh, Karnataka, Kerala, Orissa, Punjab, and Tamil Nadu will have negative demographic growth by 2046–51: the populations of the remaining nine states will still be growing. However, by 2051 population ageing in the aforementioned states will become extreme—with between 25 and 30 per cent of the populations being aged 60 years and over (Dyson 2002b).

CONCLUSIONS

The present projections are just one attempt to explore the future. They involve an inevitable element of arbitrariness. Indeed, it is hard to assemble a consistent representation of the country's demographic situation during the baseline period, let alone accurately forecast its future. Even the precise size of the population in 2001 is uncertain. Therefore, projections such as these are intended to elucidate likely broad developments; the more detailed their examination, the more sure they are to be wrong. However, these caveats made, several remarks and conclusions arise.

The present projections are based on the provisional totals from the 2001 Census. These totals may be amended. However, such amendments are likely to be small. It will take some time for the detailed census age data to be published, but even they are unlikely to change much the main indications and conclusions drawn here. So these projections have the potential to remain relevant for some length of time.

The projections have been made at the state level. The importance of this cannot be underplayed. The demography of India involves such scale and variation that it really must be approached state by state. Just one aspect of

incorporated the standard run life expectations shown in Table 5.9. In both projections the standard run TFR trajectory was assumed (Table 5.9). The first projection produced populations in 2026 and 2041 that were respectively 96.3 and 91.9 per cent of those projected by the second. For further discussion of use of an analogy between India and Africa, see Dyson and Hanchate (2000).

this is that a state-level approach to framing fertility assumptions results in a slower rate of fertility decline than when assumptions are developed for all-India.

State-level population projections cannot afford to ignore migration. For several states it will have an important influence on the quantum of future demographic growth. There is sufficient stability to patterns of interstate migration to make some allowance for it; and it is probably better to do so than not.

These projections have also attempted to make some allowance for the impact of HIV/AIDS. Because UN estimates have been used to achieve this, it is perhaps not surprising that the present results chime fairly closely with those of the UN. In proportional terms the impact of the disease may be modest during the next few quinquennia, although in absolute terms the number of people afflicted will be great. In most states HIV/AIDS is unlikely to have much impact on life expectation by 2011–6. But in Andhra Pradesh, Karnataka, Kerala, Tamil Nadu, and Maharashtra it may well do so. However, even in these states the disease is envisaged to moderate—not reverse—the overall improvement in mortality. Because HIV/AIDS is generally more prevalent in the south of the country there will probably be a reduction in the mortality advantage hitherto seen in the southern states.

The population will be about 1.4 billion by 2026. The likely range of variation around this figure is not great. The population will probably reach about 1.5 billion by 2036. It is worth emphasizing that these results arise from assuming rather rapid fertility declines. Furthermore, there is a good chance that the population will be approaching 1.6 billion by the middle of the century, although it may not surpass this level. That said, for India to avoid having a population of 1.6 billion will require the occurrence of widespread below-replacement fertility. An eventual population approaching 1.7 billion is not inconceivable.

The levels and trends of future fertility are crucial to India's population prospects. In the most demographically advanced states most future growth will be due to population momentum; it is worth noting that there are significant amounts of this momentum remaining to be played out. However, in the standard run projection, 55 per cent of all population growth during 2001–26 occurs in Bihar, Madhya Pradesh, Rajasthan, and Uttar Pradesh. Indeed, the population of former Uttar Pradesh is projected to rise by about 55 per cent by 2026 (that is, by 96.5 million). It will be in the fertility trajectories of these four states that India's demographic future will largely be determined.

These projections illustrate how the full consequences of current demographic trends take many years to unfold. Comparison of the variant projections shows that differences in population size and age structure are initially quite modest. But they become much more significant over the medium run (Table 5.10). Interestingly, if India had experienced China's fertility trajectory since about 1970 then in 2001 its population would have been smaller by around 200 million. This difference, when carried forward and compared with some of the figures projected here for 2051, could easily translate into an eventual difference in population size of roughly 600 million.

It is important to note that the present projections suggest strongly that India's future population growth will mostly happen at adult ages. In the standard run projection, the size of the 0–14 age group is set to fall significantly by 2026. The great majority of all future growth will occur in the age group 15–64 years. However, even in the high variant projection, the size of the population aged 0–14 is only slightly larger in 2026 than it was in 2001, and virtually all of the increase of 430 million in that projection occurs at ages of 15 and above.

As regards levels of fertility and mortality, it is very probable that India's states are heading towards an increasing degree of demographic convergence in the period to 2026. However, primarily because of differential past levels and trends in fertility, this is much less true regarding matters of population growth and age structure. Indeed, population growth differentials between the major states may widen a little over the medium run. And the populations of the most demographically advanced states are going to age to an appreciably greater degree than those of the less advanced states.

Finally, under all future projection scenarios the country's age dependency ratio is set to decline fairly significantly during 2001–26. Clearly, this must be considered a good thing. But for India's eventual population to remain well below 1.6 billion, as opposed to, say, growing beyond 1.7, will involve appreciably sharper population ageing during the period 2026–51. Particularly in the longer run, there is an inevitable element of trade-off between less growth and greater ageing.

6

Migration and Urbanization
Retrospect and Prospects

TIM DYSON AND PRAVIN VISARIA[1]

T his chapter reviews what is known about migration and urbanization
and assesses how these processes will unfold. It argues that the future
of both phenomena will be one of increasing dynamism and complexity.

MIGRATION

The Indian census includes questions on people's place of last residence and
their duration of residence at the place of enumeration.[2] In the resulting
tabulations, a migrant is someone with a place of previous residence which
differs from their place of enumeration. In fact, the data miss many movements—
for example, within the same town (Skeldon 1986). But they do capture the
broad features of migration.

Table 6.1 shows that about 60 per cent of migrants have made intra-district
moves, that is, over relatively short distances. The next most common type of
migrant are those who move between districts, again, often over short distances
(for example, between adjacent districts). About 11 per cent of migrants move
between states. Much smaller proportions report their place of last residence
as in another country. Females form the great majority of migrants, especially
over shorter distances. This is because, particularly in north India, women
usually move to their husband's village at marriage. Thus, according to the

---

[1]This chapter draws from material left by Pravin Visaria, although it contains much else
besides. He may not have concurred with everything here.

[2]At the time of writing, migration data from the 2001 Census were unavailable.

TABLE 6.1: *Summary migration figures for India based on census data on place of last residence, 1971–91 (thousands)*

Census	Total population	All migrants	Intra-district migrants	Inter-district migrants	Interstate migrants	International migrants
1971						
Number	528585	161812	101225	35009	18293	6653
(per cent)	–	(100.0)	(62.6)	(21.6)	(11.3)	(4.1)
Males per 100						
females	107	46	33	60	104	116
1981						
Number	659300	206486	126469	50521	23448	6045
(per cent)	–	(100.0)	(61.3)	(24.5)	(11.4)	(2.9)
Males per 100						
females	107	43	31	53	91	114
1991						
Number	816154	226705	137065	57469	26202	5673
(per cent)	–	(100.0)	(60.5)	(25.4)	(11.6)	(2.5)
Males per 100						
females	108	38	28	45	80	107

Notes: Census data on place of last residence and duration of residence were first collected in 1971. The numbers 'unclassifiable' (that is those which could not be categorized by the particular type of movement) are omitted above, but were 633, 3, and 297 thousand respectively in 1971, 1981, and 1991. Due to disturbed conditions Assam and Jammu and Kashmir were not enumerated in the censuses of 1981 and 1991 respectively. Therefore, these states are omitted here and in Table 6.2.

Sources: All figures are based on data from Table D-2 of the Census of India. See Registrar General, India (1979, 1988, 1998a, 1998b).

1991 Census, for every 100 female migrants there were only 38 males. And for intra-district, inter-district, and interstate migrants the corresponding figures were 28, 45, and 80. It should be noted that females have become increasingly prominent in all forms of migration.

In 1971 migrants accounted for almost one third, that is, 30.6 per cent, of the total population. But this figure fell to 27.8 per cent in 1991. The total number of internal migrants rose by 29.7 per cent between 1971 and 1981, but the corresponding rise was only 10.1 per cent between 1981 and 1991. So there are signs that, at least as it is defined by the census, the propensity to fit the criteria of a migrant is declining (Kundu and Gupta 2000). Table 6.1 shows that there has been a long-run decline in the proportion of migrants in the international category. This reflects the dwindling number of survivors from those who moved from the newly-created Pakistan (including what is now Bangladesh) at partition. By 1991 this group constituted only 2.5 per cent of migrants. However, the overall decline in the proportion of the population classed as migrants between 1981 and 1991 chiefly reflects changes relating to internal movements.

When the data are classified by the length of time migrants report they have been living at their places of enumeration, it becomes clear that there has been a significant decline in both the number and the proportion of migrants classed at the shortest durations. Thus in 1971, about 11.4 million internal migrants (7.4 per cent of the total) gave their durations of residence as less than one year (Skeldon 1986). By 1991, however, the number had fallen to 6.7 million (3.1 per cent). The census data show that females predominate at all durations of residence. Only at durations of less than one year do males even begin to approach the representation of females in migration.

Overall the census data suggest that short-term, short-distance migration, which can be described as 'circulatory' or 'turnover' in character (Bose 1980) and which is usually undertaken by men has declined greatly in importance. During the 1960s and 1970s travel was generally so difficult, and expensive, that people often preferred to engage in such circulatory movement. More recently, however, improvement in transport systems means that they can make a trip to a town for just a few days, or hours, duration and then return home. And, conditioned by subsidized transport and difficult urban housing conditions, the practice of *commuting* has increased significantly.

Table 6.2 gives the numbers of migrants who have resided at their places of enumeration for less than 10 years by the types of intersectoral movement. Women moving at marriage are prominent in all the flows shown, especially in rural-to-rural transfers. Other rural-to-rural migrants include those moving in response to development initiatives (such as irrigation projects) and, over shorter durations, those travelling for reasons of seasonal employment. Among people migrating from rural to urban areas are those seeking permanent employment, plus some who are moving to improve their education; in this category too are short-term circular migrants. Urban-to-urban movers include people moving up the urban hierarchy—again, often for employment reasons. This stream also contains some older adults, around the end of their working lives, moving from bigger to smaller towns closer to their places of birth (Skeldon 1986). Finally, the urban-to-rural flow includes those returning to their home villages at the end of their working lives, and turnover migrants returning after a period working in a town.

TABLE 6.2: *Net intercensal intersectoral migration flows according to data from the 1971 and 1991 censuses (thousands)*

	1971			1991		
	Number	(per cent)	(m/f)	Number	(per cent)	(m/f)
All internal						
Rural-to-rural	40355	62.0	47	44756	57.2	31
Urban-to-rural	5086	7.8	91	6013	7.7	66

(contd...)

(Table 6.2 continued)

	1971			1991		
	Number	*(per cent)*	*(m/f)*	*Number*	*(per cent)*	*(m/f)*
Rural-to-urban	10775	16.6	121	16504	21.1	93
Urban-to-urban	8867	13.6	109	10978	14.0	88
Total	65083	100.0	65	78251	100.0	50
Interstate						
Rural-to-rural	2671	30.1	88	2828	26.1	58
Urban-to-rural	911	10.3	133	925	8.5	91
Rural-to-urban	2430	27.4	172	3541	32.6	125
Urban-to-urban	2870	32.3	122	3558	32.8	91
Total	8882	100.0	122	10852	100.0	90

Notes: The figures are 'intercensal' because they relate to migrants of durations of residence in their places of enumeration of less than 10 years. Thus the 1991 figures pertain to the 1981–91 decade. Migrants who could not be assigned to a particular intersectoral flow are omitted. Data from the 1981 Census are not shown for reasons of space, but this does not affect the conclusions drawn in the text.

Sources: See Table 6.1.

Table 6.2 shows that during 1981–91 about 57.2 per cent of internal migrants were rural-to-rural movers. Next were rural-to-urban migrants (21.1 per cent) followed by urban-to-urban migrants (14.0 per cent). The smallest stream was composed of urban-to-rural movers. Comparing the periods from 1961–71 to 1981–91 there has been a general decline in the importance of rural-bound movement, and a rise in the importance of urban-bound movement, especially from rural to urban areas. Indeed, between 1961–71 and 1981–91 the data indicate that the net intercensal addition to urban areas from migration rose from 5.7 to 10.5 million. Nevertheless, the net rural out-migration rate may have declined slightly (Papola 1997), again, possibly conditioned by improvements in transport and rises in commuting.

However, for interstate intersectoral migration, which often involves travel over considerable distances, the situation is rather different (Table 6.2). Here rural-to-urban and urban-to-urban flows are of similar weight, together accounting for around two-thirds of all moves during 1981–91. Rural-to-rural migrants accounted for roughly a quarter (26.1 per cent) of movements, with the least frequent move again being that from urban to rural areas.

The pattern of interstate intersectoral migration flows is changing systematically. Rural-to-rural and urban-to-rural flows are becoming relatively less important, while urban-to-urban and especially rural-to-urban flows are becoming more prominent. Females have become more represented in all types of movement, even those that are urban-bound. Indeed, the sex ratios for the 1981–91 decade indicate that nearly every type of intersectoral migration stream contained more women than men (Table 6.2).

It is probable that with transport improvements, and an increase in dowry marriages, women are now more likely to move to a different place when they marry than they were in the past. The geographical spread of Indian marriage fields is reported to have increased (Skeldon 1983). And, comparing census data for 1981 and 1991, the proportion of females for whom 'marriage' was given as the reason for migrating rose significantly for intra-district, inter-district, and interstate migrants (Singh 1998). In addition, whereas during the 1950s and 1960s men might have migrated alone to find employment, it seems that increasingly they are being accompanied, or joined, by their wives. Also, at least in the more economically advanced and urbanized parts of the country recent employment growth, for example in light industry, has sometimes favoured females. In this context National Sample Survey (NSS) data suggest that more than half of all women employed in so-called 'million-plus' cities (that is urban areas with populations of one million or more) work in the service sector (Visaria 1998b). It has also been suggested that education is an increasingly important reason for young women to migrate to urban areas (Skeldon 1986). On the other hand, the modest rise in the relative representation of female migrants at short durations of residence probably partly reflects a reduction in male short-term circulatory moves. That said, the census data confirm that 'employment' and 'business' are the major reasons for male migration, especially over longer distances. And this is increasingly so over time (Singh 1998). These trends are consonant with the expansion and growing complexity of the Indian economy.

Using data from the 1991 Census, Figure 6.1 details the main interstate migration flows. Four features are particularly prominent. First, notice the large net outflows from Uttar Pradesh, which experienced a net loss of 911,000 migrants during the quinquennium 1986–91. Uttar Pradesh exports people to almost every state. The main destinations are Delhi/Haryana, Maharashtra, and, to a lesser extent, Madhya Pradesh. A second feature is the role of Bihar as the next most important exporter. Like Uttar Pradesh, Bihar loses migrants to almost every state, and its net loss during 1986–91 amounted to 519,000. West Bengal (with Kolkata) is the most important destination, followed by Delhi/Haryana and Uttar Pradesh, for out-migrants from Bihar. A third feature is the powerful attracting role of Delhi/Haryana. During 1986–91 Delhi alone experienced a net addition of about 657,000 people, and it gained them from virtually every other state. Finally, there is the attraction exerted by Maharashtra (including Mumbai). This state experienced a net gain of about 475,000 during the same five years. The pull exerted is so strong that Maharashtra attracts people from almost every state—especially Uttar Pradesh and, to a lesser extent, Karnataka. Gujarat is the only state to which Maharashtra lost people during 1986–91. But this loss should be seen in the context of the increasingly dynamic and integrated urban system which is developing in western India. Indeed, after Delhi and Maharashtra, Gujarat received the largest net addition to its population from in-migration during 1986–91 (247,000).

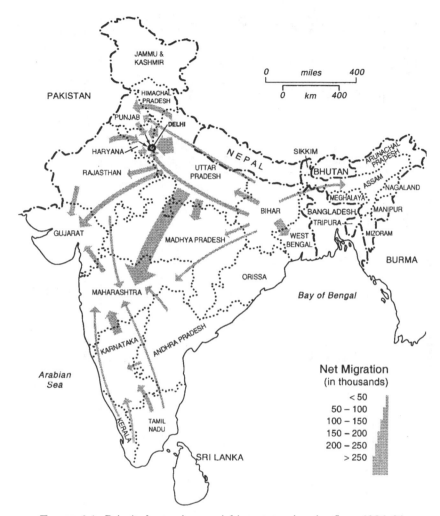

FIGURE 6.1: *Principal net quinquennial interstate migration flows, 1986–91*

Source: Registrar General, India (1998a, 1998b).

Of course, the migration streams out of Uttar Pradesh and Bihar are of long standing. However, whereas Delhi and Mumbai have become the centres of intensively urbanized regional migration systems, this has been much less true of Kolkata. Consequently, West Bengal has lost much of its previously strong attractive force (Chapman and Pathak 2000). However, although recent decades have seen increasing economic disparities between states, this does not seem to have generated a rise in out-migration rates from poor states, or in-migration rates to better-off states (Kundu and Gupta 2000). The increasing assertion of cultural and political identities may have

TABLE 6.3: *Summary measures of internal migration and urbanization, major states and all-India, 1991–2001*

State	Migrants in 1991 (per cent)	Per cent of internal migrants in 1991 that were:				Per cent urban	
		Female	Rural–rural	Rural–urban	Urban–urban	1991	2001
Andhra Pradesh	29.4	68.0	62.6	20.2	11.2	26.9	27.1
Assam	23.0	62.4	78.6	10.7	6.5	11.1	12.7
Bihar (fmr)	24.7	89.0	80.8	12.8	3.9	13.1	13.4
Gujarat	32.9	69.5	54.8	24.4	14.9	34.5	37.4
Haryana	29.8	77.6	61.5	17.7	14.7	24.6	29.0
Karnataka	29.7	65.6	57.2	17.7	15.9	30.9	34.0
Kerala	27.9	64.2	58.8	15.5	8.4	26.4	26.0
Madhya Pradesh (fmr)	32.5	73.0	67.3	16.4	10.9	23.2	25.0
Maharashtra	32.0	62.6	52.3	25.2	15.0	38.7	42.4
Orissa	26.4	77.4	77.6	13.2	5.3	13.4	15.0
Punjab	31.9	73.4	59.8	16.8	16.5	29.6	34.0
Rajasthan	28.5	79.9	70.3	13.6	9.8	22.9	23.4
Tamil Nadu	23.4	65.9	49.8	19.7	20.2	34.2	43.9
Uttar Pradesh (fmr)	21.1	85.4	74.9	11.5	8.7	19.8	21.0
West Bengal	22.3	73.4	67.9	18.0	8.8	27.5	28.0
All India	26.9	72.9	64.2	17.7	11.7	25.7	27.8

Notes: Figures on migration for 1991 pertain to all types of internal migrant at all durations of residence. The state-level percentages relate to the resident state populations (for example 29.4 per cent of the population enumerated in Andhra Pradesh in 1991 were migrants). All-India figures for 1991 include estimates for Jammu and Kashmir. The proportions given for intersectoral moves have been calculated on totals which include small numbers for whom the place of last residence was 'unclassifiable'. For 2001 the data for Bihar, Madhya Pradesh, and Uttar Pradesh are inclusive of Jharkhand, Chhatisgarh, and Uttaranchal respectively, that is, they relate to the former (fmr) jurisdictions.

Sources: On migration see Table 6.1. The 1991 urbanization figures are from Visaria (2000b). The 2001 urbanization figures are provisional and come from Registrar General, India (2001d).

constrained the growth of interstate migration. Also, sharpened intra-state socio-economic inequalities may sometimes have encouraged intra-state (rather than interstate) movement.

Table 6.3 illustrates how migration patterns vary between states. The populations of economically advanced states (such as Punjab and Gujarat) are slightly more likely to be migrants. In contrast, people enumerated in Uttar Pradesh and Bihar are less likely to be migrants. In both these states a particularly high proportion of migrants are female, reflecting the especially strong influence of village marriage exogamy. Females form a noticeably smaller fraction of migrants in the southern states. The particularly developed urban system of western India is reflected in the measures for Maharashtra and Gujarat, where rural-to-rural movers comprise a relatively low, and rural-to-urban and urban-to-urban movers a relatively high, proportion of migrants. It may be noted that, with the exception of Kerala, urban-bound movements tend to be somewhat more important in the southern states, reflecting their generally higher levels of urbanization. The proximity of Delhi helps to account for the relatively high proportions of urban-to-urban migrants shown for Punjab and Haryana. Finally, it is noticeable that in Bihar and Uttar Pradesh (and Assam and Orissa) the frequency of rural-to-rural movers is relatively high, and the frequency of rural-to-urban and urban-to-urban migrants is relatively low, reflecting their comparatively low levels of urbanization.

URBANIZATION AND URBAN GROWTH

Urban areas in India are of two main types. Most important are 'statutory towns' which are deemed to be urban because of their form of local self-government (for example, they have municipal status). In 1991, statutory towns contained 87.4 per cent of the urban population. In addition there are so-called 'census towns' which should meet several basic demographic and employment criteria. There is little doubt, however, that the populations of many areas which match these criteria prefer to retain their rural status (partly because of concerns about paying higher taxes). Moreover, the criteria themselves are fairly stringent by international standards.

These considerations suggest that India's 'true' level of urbanization may be somewhat higher than the official figures indicate. In 1991, for example, there were 13,376 'villages' with populations of 5000 or more. Were the 113 million inhabitants of these villages to have been treated as urban then the level of urbanization would have risen from 25.7 to 39.1 per cent (Visaria 2000a). Furthermore, there is considerable scope to raise the level of urbanization even within the existing criteria: for example, through the more rigorous application of the census town criteria, or through the wider granting of municipal status. The census also uses the concept of an 'urban agglomeration' (UA). As its name implies a UA tries to cover the population of a single large and complete urban area (such as two or more contiguous towns). In 1991, there were 3768 'urban areas and towns'. This figure comprised 381 UAs (taking in a total of 1301 towns) and 3387 towns. According to the 2001 Census the number of 'urban areas and towns' rose quite substantially to 4378. However, the number of UAs increased only slightly to 384 (Registrar General, India 2001c).

Table 6.4 summarizes trends in urbanization. The chief impression is of a relatively low level and slow pace of urbanization. Whereas 17.3 per cent of the population lived in urban areas in 1951, by 2001 this figure had risen to only 27.8 per cent. The average annual growth rate of the rural population has been relatively constant, although it fell slightly during the 1990s. In contrast, the urban growth rate has been far from constant, and always significantly higher than the rural rate. Thus the urban growth rate peaked at 3.79 per cent during 1971–81, but declined to 2.71 per cent during 1991–2001. Consequently, India's *tempo* of urbanization has fallen quite appreciably since 1971–81. The gain in the percentage urban has declined as the growth rate of the urban population has fallen. Even so, the urban population still increased by 68 million during the 1990s, giving a total of about 285 million in 2001.

TABLE 6.4: *Summary measures of India's urbanization, 1951–2001*

Census	Population (millions)	Urban population (millions)	Urban increment (millions)	Per cent urban	Gain in per cent	Average annual population growth rate (per cent)		
						Total	Urban	Rural
1951	361.0	62.4	–	17.3	–	–	–	–
1961	439.1	78.9	16.5	18.0	0.68	1.96	2.34	1.88
1971	548.2	109.1	30.2	19.9	1.94	2.22	3.24	1.98
1981	683.3	159.5	50.3	23.3	3.43	2.20	3.79	1.77
1991	846.3	217.6	58.1	25.7	2.37	2.14	3.11	1.83
2001	1027.0	285.3	67.7	27.8	2.07	1.94	2.71	1.65

Notes: Figures include estimates for Assam and Jammu and Kashmir. Here and subsequently all data for 2001 are provisional.

Sources: The census data for the period 1951–91 are as summarized in Visaria (2000b). The data for 2001 are from Registrar General, India (2001d).

The population of urban areas can grow by three basic mechanisms: (i) the natural increase of the urban population (the excess of births over deaths); (ii) migration from rural areas; and (iii) the reclassification of rural areas as urban. Several analyses provide similar conclusions on the sources of urban growth in India (Pathak and Mehta 1995; Visaria and Kothari 1985). Table 6.5 summarizes estimates for 1961–91, by Jain, Ghosh, and Kim (1993) together with our preliminary estimates for 1991–2001. It shows that during recent decades the natural increase of the urban population has accounted for most of the urban growth. Thus during 1991–2001 about 55.8 per cent of urban growth was due to urban natural increase, a figure which is similar to the estimate shown for 1981–91. However, there are signs that growth in the decadal volume of urban natural increase is beginning to slow. Thus, whereas between 1971–81 and 1981–1991 the estimated contribution of urban natural increase to urban population growth rose from around 24 to about 33 million, between 1981–91 and 1991–2001 it rose to only 38 million. The main explanation for this development is the fairly sharp fall in the urban birth rate. According to the SRS, between 1981–91 and 1991–2001 the birth rate in urban areas fell from about 27.1 to around 22.6 and consequently the urban rate of natural increase fell from around 19.5 to 16.0 per 1000 (from 1.95 to 1.60 per cent per year). The reduced tempo of urbanization during 1991–2001 was partly due to this fall in the urban rate of natural increase. Table 6.5 also suggests that the contribution of rural-to-urban migration to urban population growth rose from about 6 to 12 million between the 1960s and the 1980s. These numbers would probably have been greater if commuting had not increased. Data of the NSS for 1987–8 indicate that around 4 per cent of the urban workforce were rural-based commuters, and this proportion has probably risen since (Visaria 1997). Finally, the net reclassification of localities from rural to urban has played a fairly significant role in urban population growth. Its role, and possibly that of net rural-to-urban migration, may become relatively more important in the future.

Table 6.3 shows that Tamil Nadu and Maharashtra were the most urbanized major states in 2001, with Gujarat not far behind. Karnataka and Punjab were the only other states with levels of urbanization significantly above the national average. That said, the comparatively low level indicated for Kerala is rather artificial because in this densely populated place the distinction between rural and urban is especially difficult. Thus in 1991, around 90 per cent of Kerala's people inhabited 'villages' with populations exceeding 10,000 (Visaria 1997). It is clear that states in the country's south and west are generally more urban than are those in the north and east. Levels of urbanization are particularly low in Assam, Bihar, Orissa, and, to a lesser extent, Uttar Pradesh. In 2001, despite the presence of Kolkata, even West Bengal was only slightly more urban than the national average.

Between 1991 and 2001 most states experienced only modest gains in the percentage urban (Table 6.3). The level for Kerala actually fell, presumably reflecting some urban declassification. Gujarat, Haryana, Karnataka, Punjab, and Maharashtra all experienced fairly strong rises—increases which appear consonant with what is known about the comparative socio-economic advancement of these states. However, the rise indicated for Tamil Nadu— from 34 to 44 per cent—reflects a significant degree of reclassification of rural areas as urban. Tamil Nadu is undoubtedly relatively urban, but the indicated change is too large and abrupt to be due to the operation of demographic and socio-economic processes alone.

TABLE 6.5: *Estimated contributions of the components of urban growth in India, 1961–71 to 1991–2001*

Component	1961–71		1971–81		1981–91		1991–2001	
	Number (millions)	Per cent	Number (millions)	Per cent	Number (millions)	Per cent	Number (millions)	Per cent
Absolute increase	30.2	100.0	49.9	100.0	57.7	100.0	67.7	100.0
Net reclassification from rural to urban	4.6	15.6	9.8	19.0	9.8	17.0	–	–
Net rural–urban migration	6.3	20.9	9.8	19.6	12.5	21.7	–	–
Natural increase								
(i) of initial urban population	18.8	62.2	24.5	46.1	33.5	58.0	37.8	55.8
(ii) of intercensal migrants	0.7	2.3	1.1	2.2	1.9	3.3	–	–
Residual	–0.3	–1.0	5.0	10.0	–	–	–	–

Notes: For 1971–81 and 1981–91 there are slight differences in the absolute increases shown compared to those in Table 6.4 due to the exclusion here of Assam and Jammu and Kashmir. However, estimates for 1991–2001 include Assam and Jammu and Kashmir. The estimate of 55.8 per cent is based on the assumption that the urban vital rates from the SRS for 1991–9 can be taken to apply to the period 1991–2001.

Sources: Jain et al. (1993). The estimates shown for 1991–2001 use census data from Registrar General, India (2001d) and SRS data from Registrar General, India (1999a and 1999b).

Data on the distribution of India's UAs and towns according to the size-class categories employed by the census show that there has been a long-run rise in the number of urban units in the larger size-class categories, but comparatively modest changes in the number of units in the smaller size-class categories. The explanation is that population growth has shifted many units into the larger size-class categories. But, partly because of a reluctance to be classed as urban, there have been relatively few new entrants at the lower end of the distribution. Consequently the urban population has become increasingly top heavy with time. Between 1951 and 2001, the proportion of the urban population living in cities (units with populations of 100,000 or more) increased from 46 to 68 per cent. Analysis reveals little variation in the average population growth rates of urban units in most size-class categories. For example, during 1981–91, urban units in most categories grew by about 30 per cent. However, the cities grew at the somewhat faster rate of about 35 per cent (Visaria 1997, 1998b).

The largest type of urban unit, the so-called 'million-plus' city, deserves special mention. In 1951 there were only five: Kolkata (4.7m.), Mumbai (3.2m.), Chennai (1.5m.), Delhi (1.4m.), and Hyderabad (1.1m.) (Visaria 2000b). However, the 2001 Census listed no less than 35 (Registrar General, India 2001c). Three had more than 10 million inhabitants: Greater Mumbai (16.4m.), Kolkata (13.2m.)—having fallen into second place—and, coming up fast, Delhi (12.8m). In addition, Chennai, Bangalore, and Hyderabad had populations of 6.4, 5.7, and 5.5 million respectively. Together these six UAs contained some 60 million people in 2001, about 21 per cent of the entire urban population. The remaining 29 million-plus cities ranged in size from Ahmedabad with 4.5 million, to places like Amritsar and Rajkot, each with just over one million.

FUTURE TRENDS

The following consideration of future prospects builds on the foregoing analysis. Projected levels of urbanization are combined with the results of the population projections from Chapter 5.

Urbanization: Table 6.6 summarizes 2001 Census data on the urban–rural population distributions of the major states. The projected urbanization levels for 2026 and 2051 have been generated using the 'urban–rural growth differential' method, which essentially involves making a logistic extrapolation of the average urban–rural population growth rate difference observed during the period 1971–2001 (Registrar General, India 1996; United Nations 2000). Of course, these projections provide only broad indications.

Assuming that there are no major changes in the ways in which areas are categorized as urban then India's level of urbanization will rise to roughly 36 per cent by 2026 (Table 6.6). Indeed, given the country's hitherto low level

TABLE 6.6: *Projected levels of urbanization and the size of the urban and rural populations, major states and all-India, 2001–51*

State	Per cent urban			Population, 2001 (millions)		Population, 2026 (millions)		Per cent change, 2001–26	
	2001	*2026*	*2051*	*Urban*	*Rural*	*Urban*	*Rural*	*Urban*	*Rural*
Andhra Pradesh	27.1	34.9	43.6	20.5	55.2	32.0	59.7	55.9	8.1
Assam	12.7	17.0	22.4	3.4	23.2	6.1	29.9	81.0	28.6
Bihar (fmr)	13.4	16.9	21.0	14.7	95.1	28.0	138.2	90.9	45.3
Gujarat	37.4	45.9	54.7	18.9	31.7	31.3	36.9	65.5	16.3
Haryana	29.0	41.1	54.4	6.1	15.0	12.1	17.3	97.7	15.6
Karnataka	34.0	43.3	53.0	17.9	34.8	28.3	37.2	58.2	6.8
Kerala	26.0	36.5	48.5	8.3	23.6	14.0	24.4	69.8	3.6
Madhya Pradesh (fmr)	25.0	34.3	44.9	20.3	60.9	40.4	77.6	99.2	27.3
Maharashtra	42.4	52.5	62.3	41.0	55.7	65.0	58.9	58.4	5.7
Orissa	15.0	23.3	34.3	5.5	31.2	10.6	34.9	92.3	11.8
Punjab	34.0	43.9	54.3	8.2	16.0	13.6	17.4	64.9	8.5
Rajasthan	23.4	29.1	35.5	13.2	43.3	24.2	59.1	83.5	36.6
Tamil Nadu	43.9	56.1	67.6	27.2	34.9	40.2	31.5	47.6	–9.6
Uttar Pradesh (fmr)	21.0	28.6	37.6	36.7	137.8	77.5	193.6	111.2	40.4
West Bengal	28.0	31.0	34.0	22.5	57.7	32.3	72.0	43.6	24.7
All India	27.8	35.6	44.3	285.4	741.7	505.8	913.5	77.2	23.2

Notes: The all-India figures for 2026 and 2051 have been derived using national data for 1971–2001. However, a population-weighted estimate for 2026 based on the state-level estimates gives a figure of 33.9 per cent, which is increased to around 36.5 per cent if the figure for Delhi in Table 6.7 is factored in.

Sources: Registrar General, India (2001d) and the standard run population projection results from Chapter 5.

and slow pace of urbanization it is difficult to arrive at a substantially different conclusion (Bhat 2001a; Visaria 1999b).[3] Even by 2051 less than half the country's population will live in urban areas—a conclusion which accords with other projections (Becker et al. 1992). By 2026 only Maharashtra and Tamil Nadu are projected to be more than 50 per cent urban, and even by 2051 this proportion will apply in only six states. On the other hand, the levels of urbanization in Assam, Bihar, and Orissa (all eastern states) in 2051 are projected at under 25 per cent.

Table 6.6 gives the projected sizes of the urban and rural populations in 2026, based upon the standard run population projections from Chapter 5. All states will experience very appreciable proportional additions to their urban populations. At the low end of the spectrum, West Bengal's urban population is projected to rise from around 22 to 32 million during 2001–26, that is, by 44 per cent. Tamil Nadu and Andhra Pradesh will experience slightly larger proportional rises. At the high end of the spectrum, however, the urban populations of Bihar, Haryana, Madhya Pradesh, Orissa, and, above all, Uttar Pradesh may roughly double in size. In the case of Uttar Pradesh, the projected addition amounts to some 41 million, an increase of 111 per cent. The relatively large proportional rises indicated for the urban populations of these states reflect their current comparatively low levels of urbanization and, in most cases, their considerable projected future demographic growth. For India as a whole the urban population is estimated to be around 506 million by 2026, which corresponds to an average annual rate of growth of 2.2 per cent (compared to a rate of 2.7 per cent during 1991–2001). Furthermore, if the standard run projection holds, then by 2051 India's urban population will be about 700 million.

The size of the urban population in the future will largely reflect the amount of overall population growth which occurs. Thus, if instead of using the standard run projection results, the all-India levels of urbanization in Table 6.6 are combined with the results of the low variant projection, then the urban population in the years 2026 and 2051 becomes 496 and 646 million respectively. However, if the high variant projection results are used then the corresponding numbers are 520 and 767 million. To express the point in a different way: the slower India's birth rate comes down in the future the more the urban population will grow through its own natural increase, and the larger will be the urban-bound migration flows coming from rural areas (Preston 1979). Moreover, the figures in Table 6.6 imply that about 56 per cent of all population growth in India in the period to 2026 will end up living in the urban sector.

---

[3] The United Nations (2000) projects a figure of 42 per cent for 2025, but this estimate is influenced by the assumption that a 'world norm' of what constitutes an urban area will increasingly come into play.

Several states, for example, Andhra Pradesh, Karnataka, Kerala, Maharashtra, and Punjab, will probably experience only modest increases in the size of their rural populations during the period to 2026, and Tamil Nadu may even see a decrease (although this result is influenced by the major rural reclassification evident in 2001). In these states, especially, the implication is that most of the relatively limited demographic growth which will occur will finally inhabit the urban areas; to a considerable extent it will either take place in these areas, or it will migrate there. A related inference is that in these states problems of rural labour absorption should be relatively manageable. In contrast, as well as facing an approximate doubling of their urban populations, both Bihar and Uttar Pradesh are likely to experience rural population growth of roughly 40 per cent. However, for India as a whole, the rural population is projected to increase by 23 per cent, at an annual rate of about 0.8 per cent (Table 6.6).

Of course, if the criteria used to classify a place as urban are modified, or interpreted differently, then the levels of urbanization and the sizes of the urban population could be appreciably greater than is suggested here. We can probably safely conclude that the broad relative levels of urbanization between different regions will persist during the medium term: for example, the country's east will remain relatively rural. Furthermore, reclassification aside, urban natural increase will continue as the main factor behind urban population growth. The mass media will surely make rural people more aware of the superior average living conditions which sometimes exist in urban areas. But town dwellers, with generally higher levels of education, are in a better position to compete for urban jobs. And for many of the rural poor the likely living conditions, were they to move to an urban area, will often be worse than those available in rural areas. So, while its proportionate contribution to urban population growth could well increase, it is unlikely that rural-to-urban migration will overtake urban natural increase as the chief cause of urban growth in the period to 2026 (Visaria 1998b, 1999b).

Urban growth: The expected expansion of India's urban population, a projected increase of 77 per cent in 25 years, will be spread over virtually all urban units in all size-class categories. There are likely to be many more towns by 2026. The number of cities will continue to increase as smaller towns expand and shift across size-class boundaries. Moreover, the trend towards increasing urban concentration should continue (Bhat 2001a: 15). All these considerations point to a considerable increase in the scale and complexity of the urban hierarchy.

One way of exploring these issues is to consider the future of the country's million-plus cities. To get an approximate idea of how many there may be, the 115 cities and UAs with populations of 300,000 or more in 2001 were selected for analysis. For each unit the three intercensal population growth rates experienced during 1971–2001 were examined in order to provide an appropriate rate with which to project the population to 2026. Growth rates which were high or out of line with the other two were usually ignored. For 82 units the urban growth rate experienced during 1991–2001 was selected, and for most of the remaining 33 cases the average of the urban growth rates experienced during 1971–81 and 1981–91 was used. For only six of these 33 units did this averaging procedure involve assuming a higher rate of UA/city growth than applied during 1991–2001; for 25 units it involved assuming a lower rate. Nevertheless, because in a majority of the 115 cases the assumed rate of urban population growth was that which applied during 1991–2001 the current assumptions may tend to slightly overestimate future UA/city growth. On the other hand, by ignoring growth rates which were high or out of line we have effectively discounted the influence of some past rural-to-urban reclassifications, a consideration which would work in the opposite direction.[4]

Table 6.7 summarizes the results. Clearly, for any individual UA/city the projected population sizes are only very broadly indicative. And some of the smaller units shown may not actually attain populations of one million during the period under review. However, several general conclusions can be drawn. Thus by 2026 there are likely to be approximately 70 million-plus cities. This broad supposition is strengthened by the fact that 12 new million-plus cities emerged during 1991–2001, implying that perhaps 30 more could emerge during 2001–26. Roughly half of all million-plus cities in 2026 will have less than two million people. Perhaps 20 will lie in the range between two and five million. And there may be another eight or so very large units with populations of between five and 15 million. That, very tentatively, Pune and Surat could both emerge with roughly similar populations to places like Bangalore, Hyderabad, and Chennai in 2026 is somewhat unexpected. But in 2001 they had populations of 3.8 and 2.8 million respectively, and both have experienced consistently high growth rates since 1971.[5] In contrast, Bangalore, Hyderabad, and Chennai all had somewhat lower population growth rates during 1991–2001 compared to 1981–91.

The projections suggest that India's three largest UAs will remain the same, but that their rankings will change. Thus, with about 20 million people, it seems likely that Kolkata will fall into third place. However, the population of Delhi could increase to challenge, or surpass, that of Greater Mumbai. In this context it should be borne in mind that Mumbai's rate of population growth has been falling since 1971, whereas that of Delhi has been fairly constant and significantly higher than that of Mumbai. People can migrate to Delhi from several directions and the city too can expand in several directions, but this cannot happen to Mumbai because of its coastal location.

[4]Here such reclassification has largely been ignored. See Dyson and Visaria (2002) for further details.

[5]Moreover, the assumed annual growth rates for Surat and Pune were both below those actually experienced during 1991–2001.

TABLE 6.7: *Projected 'million-plus' urban agglomerations and cities in 2026, ranked by approximate population size*

	Size range (millions)			
1.0 to 1.9	2.0 to 4.9	5.0 to 14.9	>15.0
35–38 Chandigarh, Durg-Bhilainagar, Guwahati, Raipur (1.9)	12 Kanpur (4.8)	4 Bangalore (13.0)	1 Delhi (36.2)
39–42 Amritsar, Bhiwandi, Srinagar, Varanasi (1.8)	13 Ghaziabad (4.6)	5 Surat (11.3)	2 Greater Mumbai (31.7)
43–45 Allahabad, Jodhpur, Ranchi (1.7)	14 Faridabad (4.1)	6 Hyderabad (10.5)	3 Kolkata (21.3)
46 Vijayawada (1.6)	15 Patna (4.0)	7 Chennai (10.1)	
47–48 Madurai, Solapur (1.5)	16 Nagpur (3.9)	8 Pune (10.0)	
49–54 Gwalior, Jalandhar, Kota, Kozhikode, Salem, Siliguri (1.4)	17 Indore (3.8)	9 Ahmedabad (9.9)	
55–57 Mysore, Tiruchirappalli, Tiruppur (1.3)	18 Nashik (3.7)	10 Jaipur (6.8)	
58–61 Bareilly, Cuttack, Hubli-Dharwad, Jammu (1.2)	19 Bhopal (3.2)	11 Lucknow (5.1)	
62–63 Gorakhpur, Jalgaon (1.1)	20–21 Ludhiana, Vadodara (3.1)		
64–74 Amravati, Bhavnagar, Bikaner, Dehradun, Firozabad, Gulbarga, Jamnagar, Mangalore, Nanded-Waghala, Tirupati, Warangal (1.0)	22 Agra (3.0)		
	24–25 Meerut, Rajkot (2.6)		
	26–27 Aurangabad, Coimbatore (2.5)		
	28–29 Jamshedpur, Visakhapatnam (2.4)		
	30–33 Bhubaneswar, Dhanbad, Kochi, Trivandrum (2.1)		
	34 Jabalpur (2.0)		

Notes: The projected 2026 urban populations are given in brackets. The illustrative nature of the projections should require no emphasis. Units sharing the same approximate size (for example 1.0 million) are listed in alphabetical order.

Sources: UAs/cities with populations in 2001 of 300,000 or more were taken from Registrar General, India (2001e and 2001f).

It may well be that the growth rates of these vast UAs will fall somewhat as they expand. Nevertheless, it seems reasonable to conclude that both will have populations in the vicinity of 30 million by 2026. Rather than relying upon a single central urban core, such immense agglomerations will contain an increasing number of major urban sub-centres, a process which is already well under way. Even for the year 2000, the UN has ranked Mumbai and Delhi as respectively the third and eighth most populous UAs in the world (United Nations 2000). And whatever may be the problems of definition and international comparison, they should both be within the top five by 2026.[6]

In 1951 the five million-plus cities contained about 16 per cent of the urban population. By 2001 this figure had increased to 38 per cent. The present projections imply that by 2026 over half of the total urban population will be residing in about 70 million-plus cities. Indeed, the combined populations of Delhi, Mumbai, and Kolkata could contain over 15 per cent of the urban total. The only way this trend towards increasing concentration is likely to be moderated is if there is much greater rural reclassification elsewhere in the country than has occurred in the past.

Internal migration: India is experiencing several related, structured changes in its patterns of migration, which are likely to continue.

Because the country's population is set to increase considerably, the absolute numbers of people involved in most types of migration flow may also tend to increase. This will certainly be the case, other things being equal. Thus the volume of net rural-to-urban migration will probably continue to rise during most of the period to 2026. And most of the major net interstate migration flows, particularly those emanating from Uttar Pradesh and Bihar, should continue to grow in absolute terms.

The projected trends in urban growth and urbanization have clear implications for migration. Thus, underpinned by increasing urbanization, rural-bound movements will continue to decline in relative importance, while urban-bound movements—both rural-to-urban and urban-to-urban—will tend to increase. In addition, and initially in some of the southern and western states, the absolute size of the rural population will start to fall, especially in the years beyond 2026, and this will be reflected in increasing rates of rural out-migration.

With perhaps 70 million-plus cities dotted around the country, for many

---

[6]The UN (2000) has projected the size of India's UAs to 2015. For that year the projected population of Mumbai (26.1 million) is the second largest in the world. Kolkata (17.3m) ranks tenth, and Delhi (16.8 m) eleventh. The UN lists 44 million-plus UAs in India in 2015. However, these UN projections do not take the 2001 Census results into account. Thus the population of Mumbai in 2000 is put at 18.1 million, whereas the census revealed 16.4 million. Another limitation of the UN projections is that with the exception of Faridabad, Jaipur, and Ludhiana, they relate only to urban units which were classed as UAs in 1991. Thus they omit places like Chandigarh and Solapur which even by 2001 were fast approaching one million.

potential rural out-migrants such a city will be significantly closer and more accessible in 2026 than it was in 2001. This will be a major countervailing factor working against a general increase in interstate movements. Also, commercial firms may increasingly perceive cities of intermediate size as benefitting from basic transport and communications facilities, whilst also offering economies of scale, and cheaper office space. In contrast, the biggest UAs usually suffer badly from problems of congestion and pollution. This is not to say that the absolute numbers of migrants to the largest UAs will decline, but there may well be changes in the propensity of rural out-migrants to move to particular types of destination. The very largest urban areas may become a little less appealing to potential migrants.

In 2026 the vast majority of migrants will still be those who have made intra-district moves. However, aided by better transport (especially buses) inter-district migrants may form a significantly larger fraction of all migrants than was the case in 2001. The prominence of women in internal migration— especially over short distances, and for marriage and family reasons—is unlikely to diminish. But increasing levels of education and economic growth will probably augment the frequency of migration for employment, business, and educational reasons, not only for men, but also for women. In addition, the data suggest strongly that circulatory migration (which is often picked up by the census) is being increasingly replaced by commuting (which in the past has not been picked up). These trends too are likely to persist. The continuing rise of commuting may also contribute to a continued slight decline in the fraction of all migrants who have made intra-district moves. Almost certainly the actual frequency of daily movements, including commuting, will increase greatly. However, future census statistics may well imply that there has been a fall in the proportion of the total population who are classed as migrants.

It has been suggested that with much greater population growth in the north, and greater economic growth and urbanization in the south, the future may see migration of labourers from the poorer northern states towards farmlands in the south (Bhat 2001a). While this possibility cannot be discounted entirely, there are reasons to consider that, at least in the period to 2026, such north to south migration will not develop on a very large scale. Thus, with an increasing number of million-plus cities in northern India, rural-to-urban migration within the north (often within the same state) is likely to prove an increasingly attractive option. Also, the continued growth of regional cultural and political identities in the south, and their expression in educational and language restrictions, may tend to discourage such migration. Finally, the southern states tend to be net exporters of people, and there are currently no major migration streams from north to south. We anticipate that the dominant interstate movements portrayed in Figure 6.1 will continue into the medium-term future.

International migration: International migration has always been numerically small compared to the size of India's population. Therefore it has had, and will have, only marginal influence upon the country's future population growth.

Of course, there are populations of Indian origin scattered around parts of Asia, Africa, and the Caribbean which were established during the colonial era. Starting from the 1960s there was increased out-migration from India to the UK, the US, Canada, and Australia, mainly in search of better employment and, more recently, educational opportunities. Many of these migrants have professional or technical qualifications and the citizenship of the countries in which they reside. There are thought to be over a million persons of Indian origin living in both the UK and the US (Visaria and Visaria 1994). The 1996 Canadian census revealed that of the 235,000 people born in India, 70,000 had entered during the period 1991–6 (Statistics Canada 2001). From the late 1970s there has also been considerable out-migration to the oil-producing countries of the Persian Gulf and, to a lesser extent, other countries in West Asia and North Africa. This migration tends to be contractual and relatively short term. It rarely results in permanent residence (Weiner 1982). However, annual remittances from the two million or so Indian workers thought to be residing in the Middle East amount to several billion dollars.

International migration flows can be very difficult to foresee. The 1990 conflict involving Iraq, for example, led to the sudden return of perhaps 125,000 Indian workers from various Gulf states (Visaria and Visaria 1994). Similar migration could happen again. However, it seems reasonable to expect that an increasing awareness of overseas employment opportunities, and easier air travel, will tend to raise the number of better-educated young people who leave India for North America, Europe, and Australia. Yet for every flow there is a counter-flow. The liberalization of the Indian economy has created new investment opportunities in India for Indians resident overseas. There are high-tech jobs in places like Bangalore and Mumbai, and high-capacity telephone lines to all the major cities. Such developments may attract back (and help to retain) a relatively small, but growing number of specialized skilled workers in India.

However, perhaps the most profound effect on India's population arising from out-migration since the 1960s has occurred through the introduction of radically new ways of thinking and behaving, not least, with respect to aspects of family and personal life (including birth control). International migration has, through mechanisms like the return visits of Indians resident overseas (and their children), had an inordinate influence by helping to spread elements of a so-called 'Western' lifestyle. The results are particularly evident among better-off young people living in the major cities. And, increasingly, similar influences have also been broadcast by the media (something which will happen even more in the years ahead).

Finally, there is the matter of immigration. The main inflows are from Bangladesh and Nepal. The UN (2001) projects that during the period 2000–25 the populations of these countries will grow from 137 to 211 million, and from 23 to 49 million respectively. These increases, which in proportional terms are significantly greater than those projected for India, will tend to raise substantially the volumes of future immigration both from Bangladesh and Nepal.

CONCLUSIONS

Much of India, particularly in the south, has the feel of being rather more urban than the census statistics convey. The 2001 Census results for Tamil Nadu underscore the scope for rural reclassification to become a more important cause of urban growth. Should other states follow this lead then this will alter the basic premise upon which projections of urbanization, such as those here, are made.

Nevertheless, we can be confident about many of the general prospects for India's urbanization and population migration. In 2026 the country will be significantly more urban, and the size of the urban population will be much greater. Urban natural increase will probably continue as the main engine of urban population growth, and the country's urban population will grow faster than the rural population.

However, the rate of urban growth will probably continue to fall because of the declining urban birth rate. The urban population will grow fastest in states like Bihar and Uttar Pradesh, which have comparatively low levels of urbanization. The explanation is simply that future demographic growth, urban and rural, will be greatest in these states. Conversely, more urbanized states, like Maharashtra and Tamil Nadu, will tend to experience lower rates of urban growth because their populations will not grow as fast. Moreover, the rural populations of such states will not increase by much (relatively speaking). The projections suggest that around half of all India's population growth in the period to 2026 will end up living in urban areas. And the coming decades will see an increasing concentration of the urban population too. There may be about 70 million-plus UAs/cities by 2026. Consequently, the country's urban hierarchy will become much more developed, particularly around Delhi/Haryana and in western and southern India. One aspect of this is that much future de facto urban growth will occur in urban corridors formed along the transport routes linking major cities. Indeed, there is clear evidence of such corridors already (Centre for Policy Research 2001). By 2026 Delhi and Mumbai could each have populations of 30 million.

Migration will become more urban-oriented, but increasingly this will happen within expanding regional urban systems. Movements to reside in a million-plus city, for example, will be over shorter distances than applied in the past. However, most urban growth in the period to 2026 will not be due to rural-to-urban migration. There will be more commuting, but less turnover movement (the one partially offsetting the other). But when households migrate, in the sense of moving home, their moves may well be more enduring. Other things being equal, the numbers of people engaged in most types of migration stream will tend to increase in proportion to the rise in the size of the 'sending' population. This will apply, for example, to out-migration from Uttar Pradesh and from Bangladesh. In the future, as in the past, there will be social and political repercussions from such trends.

As was implied at the outset, the picture is one of increasing complexity and dynamism. The broad developments sketched here are largely inevitable. The slower India's urban population growth is in the coming decades the better things are likely to be because rapid growth places great strains on urban infrastructures. However, the fact that the country will experience an increasingly urban future is probably in itself a good thing because urbanization is a sign of development. Scale economies and benefits of concentration mean that in most respects urban living is comparatively efficient. And an urban lifestyle is one which younger people, in particular, tend to prefer. It is important to recognize this. Nevertheless, India may well be alone among the world's major countries in still being predominantly rural in 2026.

7
Education and Literacy

Geeta Kingdon, Robert Cassen,
Kirsty McNay, and Leela Visaria

The case for education requires little elaboration. Apart from its obvious intrinsic worth, education has powerful instrumental value, both in terms of increased individual productivity and in terms of the considerable social benefits of education such as lower fertility and child mortality. Moreover, literacy is an essential tool of self-defence, participation, and empowerment in a modern society (Drèze and Sen 2002). Thus, the centrality of education—at least of basic education—in bringing about economic and social change, is clear.[1]

In this light, it is one of the tragedies of India's development that the country still lags behind educationally, both absolutely and in comparison with some developing countries at similar income levels. It has 17 per cent of the world's population but some 40 per cent of the world's illiterates. While it has emerged as an important player in the worldwide information technology (IT) revolution, it is home to millions of out-of-school children. However, there is a silver lining in this cloud: the 1990s saw a perceptible acceleration in the pace of educational progress, which bodes well for the future.

---

[1]Some recent empirical literature questions the economic benefits of education (Pritchett 2001). This is something of a minority view. It is based on cross-country growth regressions which do not show a consistent effect of basic education on economic growth. One reason for the lack of a consistent relationship between education and the growth rate is that data on education are poor and not comparable across countries. For example, 'percentage of children enrolled' in primary or secondary education in various countries does not tell us anything about the quality of schooling or levels of learning across the countries.

This chapter provides an assessment of the current educational situation and the progress made in this field in recent years, and examines potential future trends. We consider whether the conditions and public and private interventions that led to particularly rapid educational improvement in the 1990s are likely to be sustained in the future.

THE HISTORICAL BACKGROUND

At the time of its independence in 1947, India inherited an appalling legacy of illiteracy and educational neglect. The first post-independence census in 1951 indicated that only 9 per cent of the female population and 27 per cent of males were literate.[2] British rule made some contributions to Indian education, but mainly for the purpose of providing for an élite which would help administer the country—perhaps policies were also influenced by the relatively low regard for education that Britain had shown at home.[3]

The past neglect led to a resolve at the time of independence that the new Indian state would endeavour to provide free and compulsory education to all children up to age 14 by 1960, as reflected in Article 45 of the Indian Constitution. Although the Sargeant Commission just before independence had suggested a 40–year period for achieving the goal of universal elementary education, the framers of the Indian Constitution felt that the country could not wait that long. However, as several analysts have noted, education policy in India has been characterized by a chronic inconsistency between stated intentions and actual action, between rhetoric and platitudes on the one hand and practical steps to achieve the goals on the other (Drèze and Sen 2002; Weiner 1990).

The ambitious goal of education for all up to age 14 has been reiterated time and again and absurd target dates for its achievement have been set repeatedly. For example, the Education Commission 1964–6 set a period of 20 years for the achievement of universal elementary education (UEE).[4] The 1986 New Policy on Education set 1990 as the target year for the achievement of universal primary education and the year 1995 as the target year for the achievement of UEE. In 1991, at the Jomtien World Education Conference,

[2]At the time of the 1901 Census, less than 1 per cent of women were literate in every single province of British India (Drèze and Sen 2002: 189).

[3]OECD (2001) shows the UK still performing worse than most other OECD countries in some aspects of education.

[4]Primary education in India typically refers to the first five years of schooling (corresponding to ages 6–10); junior education refers to the next three years of schooling (corresponding to ages 11–14); elementary education refers to primary and junior schooling combined (ages 6–14); and secondary education refers to the last four years of schooling before university entrance (corresponding to ages 15–18). This last is often divided into two years of lower secondary and two years of upper secondary schooling.

India signed up to the declaration on Education for All (EFA) by 2000. However, at none of these junctures did public policy spell out in earnest the practical steps that would be put in place—apart from a few specific measures such as schools for villages—and the resources that would be made available to make the stated aims a reality. By the turn of the century, some 50 years after its adoption, the goal of education for all up to age 14 remained far from being fulfilled.

RECENT PROGRESS

Literacy rates in the population aged seven or older for 1991 and 2001 are presented in Table 7.1. They show that the literacy rate rose quite substantially in the last decade of the twentieth century from 52 per cent to 65 per cent, an increase of 13 percentage points. This is the highest absolute increase in any decade since records began in 1881.[5] Figure 7.1 shows that there was a visible acceleration in the growth of literacy over the 1990s, especially for

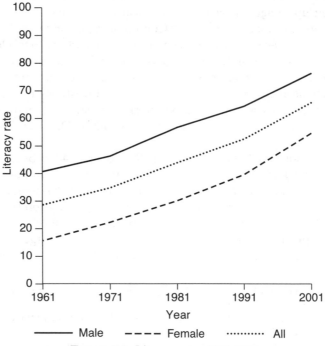

FIGURE 7.1: *Literacy rates, 1961–2001*

Source: Census data.

[5]Literacy rates increased by 6.2 percentage points in the 1960s, 9.2 points in the 1970s, and 8.5 points in the 1980s.

women. For the first time the gender gap began to close perceptibly in the 1990s. Table 7.1 shows that in some states the literacy increase was particularly impressive. For example, in Rajasthan and Madhya Pradesh, literacy rates rose by 22 and 20 percentage points respectively.[6] The increase in female literacy was especially large in these states as well as in Andhra Pradesh and Uttar Pradesh, but Bihar, starting from the lowest base among all states in 1991, made disappointing progress, as did Gujarat.

Literacy rates for the population above seven years of age as a whole are more a reflection of past educational achievements, and those for the younger age groups more an indication of current achievements. The most recently available age-specific literacy data from the NFHS in 1998–9 show encouraging trends (IIPS and ORC Macro 2000).[7] Table 7.2 shows that between 1992–3 to 1998–9, literacy rates in the young age groups rose quite rapidly for girls. For example, for rural girls aged 6–19, literacy rates rose by about 14–16 percentage points over just a six–year period. Taking rural and urban areas together, female literacy in the youngest age group 6–10 rose by nearly 14 percentage points. Overall, the national literacy rate for males and females aged 6–19 years increased by about 10 percentage points, quite substantial for a six–year period. It is particularly encouraging that literacy gains were the greatest in the youngest age groups. Any major improvement in national literacy in the future will depend crucially on its progress among young persons in the four large north Indian states of Bihar, Madhya Pradesh, Rajasthan, and Uttar Pradesh which have lagged behind seriously in the past. Table 7.3 shows a marked acceleration in 10–14 year old literacy

TABLE 7.1: *Increase in literacy rates by state and gender*

	Male			Female			Persons		
	1991	*2001*	*Increase*	*1991*	*2001*	*Increase*	*1991*	*2001*	*Increase*
Andhra Pradesh	55.1	70.9	15.8	32.7	51.2	18.5	44.1	61.1	17.0
Bihar	52.5	62.2	9.7	22.9	35.2	12.3	38.5	49.2	10.7
Gujarat	73.1	76.5	3.4	48.6	55.6	7.0	61.3	66.4	5.1
Haryana	69.1	79.3	10.2	40.5	56.3	15.8	55.9	68.6	12.7
Himachal Pradesh	75.4	84.6	9.2	52.1	67.1	15.0	63.9	75.9	12.0

(contd...)

[6] Indeed, the growth in literacy rate was so remarkable over the short 6–year period between the NFHS-1 and NFHS-2 of 1992–3 and 1998–9, that some have even questioned the validity of the statistics showing the improvements. However, comparisons between Census 2001 (Registrar General, India 2001a), NFHS-2 (1998–9) and NSS (1997) literacy data show a good deal of consistency across data-sets and generate confidence that the growth in literacy rates is genuine.

[7] As of June 2003, the 2001 Census age-specific literacy figures were not available.

(Table 7.1 continued)

	Male			Female			Persons		
	1991	2001	Increase	1991	2001	Increase	1991	2001	Increase
Karnataka	67.3	76.3	9.0	44.3	57.5	13.2	56.0	67.0	11.0
Kerala	93.6	94.2	0.6	86.1	87.9	1.8	89.8	90.9	1.1
Madhya Pradesh	58.4	77.0	18.6	28.9	51.0	22.1	44.2	64.4	20.2
Maharashtra	76.6	86.3	9.7	52.3	67.5	15.2	64.9	77.3	12.4
Orissa	63.1	76.0	12.9	34.7	51.0	16.3	49.1	63.6	14.5
Punjab	65.7	75.6	9.9	50.4	63.6	13.2	58.5	70.0	11.5
Rajasthan	55.0	76.5	21.5	20.4	44.3	23.9	38.6	61.0	22.4
Tamil Nadu	73.8	82.3	8.5	51.3	64.6	13.3	62.7	73.5	10.8
Uttar Pradesh	55.7	70.9	15.2	25.3	43.9	18.6	41.6	58.1	16.5
West Bengal	67.8	77.6	9.8	46.6	60.2	13.6	57.7	69.2	11.5
India	64.1	75.6	11.5	39.3	54.0	14.7	52.2	65.2	13.0

Note: The old boundaries of Bihar, Madhya Pradesh, and Uttar Pradesh have been used for 2001, that is, including Jharkhand, Chhatisgarh, and Uttaranchal, respectively.
Source: Census 1991; Census 2001, preliminary estimates, both taken from Table 4.1 (Planning Commission 2002a: 186).

TABLE 7.2: *Increase in age-specific literacy rates, by area and gender*

	Rural			Urban			Total		
	1993	1999	Increase	1993	1999	Increase	1993	1999	Increase
MALES									
Age Group									
6–9	59.8	70.0	10.2	77.5	83.8	6.3	64.0	73.1	9.1
10–14	79.1	85.0	5.9	90.5	93.0	2.5	82.1	87.0	4.9
15–19	77.0	83.0	6.0	89.7	91.2	1.5	80.5	85.3	4.8
FEMALES									
Age Group									
6–9	47.1	63.6	16.5	74.9	80.3	5.4	53.6	67.4	13.8
10–14	57.1	71.4	14.3	84.3	90.7	6.4	64.1	76.1	12.0
15–19	47.2	61.3	14.1	80.8	86.6	5.8	56.2	68.2	12.0
TOTAL									
Age Group									
6–9	53.7	66.9	13.2	76.2	82.1	5.9	59.0	70.4	11.4
10–14	68.5	78.5	10.0	87.5	91.8	4.3	73.4	81.8	8.4
15–19	61.8	72.2	10.4	85.2	89.0	3.8	68.1	76.9	8.8

Source: Compiled from NFHS-1 (Table 3.8) and NFHS-2 (Table 2.7), National Final Reports (IIPS and ORC Macro 1995, 2000).

TABLE 7.3: *Literacy rates in the 10–14 age group, 1961–99*
(Bihar, Madhya Pradesh, Rajasthan, and Uttar Pradesh)

Year	Average 10–14 literacy rate	Percentage point increase over previous decade	Annual percentage increase over previous decade (per cent)
1961	31	–	–
1971	37	6	1.8
1981	43	6	1.5
1991	57	14	2.9
1999	75	18	3.5

Note: For any given year, the literacy rate figure in the first column is the simple average of the literacy rates for the four states in that year. It is not weighted by the respective populations of the states.

Source: 1961–91 figures: calculations from census data reported in Table 21.2 (Govinda 2002); 1998–9 figures: State reports of the National Family Health Survey-2, (IIPS and ORC Macro, 2000).

rates in these states over time. Whereas the literacy rate among the young increased by only 6 percentage points in each of the two decades of the 1960s and 1970s, it increased by 14 points in the 1980s and by 18 points in the 1990s. This is perhaps the most informative statistic when attempting to foresee the future of literacy among the Indian population in the next quarter century.

Enrolment and school attendance rates are more sensitive than literacy rates to the current spread of education. Of the two, current school attendance rates are the more reliable indicator, since large enrolment rates, if taken at the start of the school year, can mask any drop-out later in that school year. Table 7.4 shows current school attendance rates from the two rounds of the NFHS in 1992–3 and 1998–9 (IIPS and ORC Macro 1995, 2000). Between the short six–year period 1993 and 1999, current school attendance among rural 6–10 year old females and males increased by 20 and 12 percentage points respectively; these are substantial increases. In the rural 11–14 year age group, increases were more modest but still substantial, especially for rural girls, at 13.7 per cent. Urban increases were smaller. Andhra Pradesh, Madhya Pradesh, Rajasthan, and Uttar Pradesh achieved quite spectacular improvements in their current school attendance rates, particularly in rural areas where, in each of these four states, attendance rates increased by over 25 percentage points in a 6–year period. Overall, nearly 80 per cent of all 6–14 year olds were attending school in 1999. While attendance rates themselves are not a guarantee of grade completion or of achieving minimum levels of learning, these are nevertheless encouraging trends, suggesting that perhaps a corner has been turned.

TABLE 7.4: *Increase in current school attendance, by state, gender, and residence*

| | Rural | | | | | | Urban | | | | | |
| | Age 6–10 | | | Age 11–14 | | | Age 6–10 | | | Age 11–14 | | |
	1993	*1999*	*Increase*	*1993*	*1999*	*Increase*	*1993*	*1999*	*Increase*	*1993*	*1999*	*Increase*
MALE												
Andhra Pradesh	68.9	86.3	17.4	63.5	68.8	5.3	86.0	94.4	8.4	83.4	77.0	–6.4
Bihar	57.0	68.0	11.0	64.9	71.6	6.7	83.0	81.0	–2.0	86.2	78.6	–7.6
Gujarat	78.9	83.9	5.0	78.7	73.9	–4.8	89.8	91.4	1.6	88.4	87.2	–1.2
Haryana	85.9	92.5	6.6	85.8	88.3	2.5	91.9	92.7	0.8	89.3	90.9	1.6
Himachal Pradesh	94.0	98.9	4.9	93.1	98.2	5.1	97.9	99.5	1.6	94.0	98.2	4.2
Karnataka	76.4	84.8	8.4	67.2	72.2	5.0	87.6	94.3	6.7	80.1	81.3	1.2
Kerala	94.9	96.7	1.8	94.8	96.2	1.4	95.8	98.3	2.5	93.0	99.4	6.4
Madhya Pradesh	61.0	80.1	19.1	69.7	75.4	5.7	83.9	92.8	8.9	85.9	86.6	0.7
Maharashtra	84.9	90.7	5.8	80.8	86.0	5.2	91.9	96.2	4.3	89.2	88.5	–0.7
Orissa	75.8	85.4	9.6	72.9	79.9	7.0	89.7	85.2	–4.5	86.2	78.3	–7.9
Punjab	83.8	92.7	8.9	77.4	87.0	9.6	90.2	97.5	7.3	87.1	93.7	6.6
Rajasthan	69.9	87.4	17.5	75.2	82.8	7.6	82.5	88.5	6.0	87.0	88.9	1.9
Tamil Nadu	90.8	95.5	4.7	77.7	83.3	5.6	94.4	96.4	2.0	78.5	87.6	9.1
Uttar Pradesh	69.5	83.0	13.5	75.1	80.4	5.3	77.3	87.1	9.8	76.8	81.3	4.5
West Bengal	68.9	82.8	11.4	68.1	74.6	6.5	83.3	88.2	4.9	83.4	78.5	–4.9
All India	71.4	83.2	11.8	73.4	78.5	5.1	86.2	91.7	5.5	84.2	85.1	0.9
FEMALE												
Andhra Pradesh	51.9	79.3	27.4	37.1	47.0	9.9	82.0	93.8	11.8	67.7	79.1	11.4
Bihar	34.0	53.0	19.0	33.0	48.7	15.7	69.3	72.1	2.8	65.6	78.2	12.6
Gujarat	64.0	74.9	10.9	57.9	54.8	–3.1	84.4	90.0	5.6	78.4	76.5	–1.9

(contd...)

(Table 7.4 continued)

| | Rural | | | | | | Urban | | | | | |
| | Age 6–10 | | | Age 11–14 | | | Age 6–10 | | | Age 11–14 | | |
	1993	1999	Increase	1993	1999	Increase	1993	1999	Increase	1993	1999	Increase
Haryana	71.9	89.3	17.4	65.8	77.3	11.5	89.9	92.0	2.1	87.3	86.8	-0.5
Himachal Pradesh	88.5	98.9	10.4	85.1	95.3	10.2	95.2	98.1	2.9	92.0	97.7	5.7
Karnataka	64.8	81.9	17.1	46.4	60.7	14.3	85.4	93.0	7.6	72.5	82.9	10.4
Kerala	95.0	97.7	2.7	93.6	96.3	2.7	97.1	98.8	1.7	95.4	98.8	3.4
Madhya Pradesh	47.3	73.9	26.6	44.5	54.9	10.4	81.7	87.8	6.1	81.4	80.0	-1.4
Maharashtra	77.5	88.5	11.0	56.2	78.3	22.1	89.8	93.3	3.5	85.1	89.9	4.8
Orissa	63.0	81.0	18.0	52.5	64.8	12.3	78.8	82.7	3.9	78.2	77.0	-1.2
Punjab	77.5	92.7	15.2	67.5	79.6	12.1	91.4	97.7	6.3	85.9	95.5	9.6
Rajasthan	36.4	66.0	29.6	28.6	44.9	16.3	72.4	82.7	10.3	71.2	75.5	4.3
Tamil Nadu	83.6	94.5	10.9	62.8	76.3	13.5	94.7	98.0	3.3	75.7	87.1	11.4
Uttar Pradesh	45.4	71.4	26.0	38.2	57.1	18.9	70.3	83.3	13.0	68.4	80.0	11.6
West Bengal	63.5	80.8	17.3	55.0	66.9	11.9	77.5	87.9	10.4	65.0	74.9	9.9
All-India	55.0	75.1	20.1	47.9	61.6	13.7	81.8	89.1	7.3	75.7	82.8	7.1

Source: NFHS-1 and NFHS-2 state and all-India reports (IIPS and ORC Macro 1995, 2000).

LIKELY CAUSES OF ACCELERATED PROGRESS

The faster progress in the rate of literacy and school attendance in the 1990s can be traced to a number of factors, though it is not possible to estimate their relative importance without further statistical analysis. These factors can be grouped into two broad categories: acceleration in the demand for education and improvements in the quantity and quality of supply of education.

Demand for education: The faster progress in basic education and literacy is consistent with an increase in demand for education. The Public Report on Basic Education (PROBE) report (PROBE Team 1999: 19) reported a broad-based surge in educational aspirations in the 1990s. Demand for education can increase with a fall in poverty, which makes it possible for the poor to realize their educational aspirations for their children; it can also increase if fertility levels fall and there is a trade-off between the number of children and the education of each child within the family; demand for education can also increase if the perceived benefits of education—its private economic rates of return—increase.

There is controversy about the extent of the decline in poverty in the 1990s. Nevertheless, as discussed in Chapter 9, income poverty did fall, and there was progress, although uneven, in other indicators of well-being. It is likely that poverty reduction helped to boost the effective demand for education. Expenditure data from the NSS are consistent with the story that the proportion of households incurring positive expenditure on education has been rising as poverty levels have been falling. For example, according to national accounts statistics for India, the share of private expenditure on education in total private consumption expenditure increased from around 2.5 per cent in the early 1980s to over 3.5 per cent in the late 1990s (Planning Commission 2002a: 60). In three different Indian micro-studies examining the budget share of education, figures for Maharashtra are available for the years 1983, 1988, and 1994. These show that the proportion of households incurring any positive expenditure on education rose from 11 per cent in 1983 to 30 per cent in 1988 and further to 55 per cent in 1994 (Kingdon 2002a; Subramanian 1995; Subramanian and Deaton 1991). It is likely that the national picture is broadly similar, though there will inevitably be inter-state differences.[8]

Second, as discussed in Chapter 4, the rate of fertility decline has accelerated over the 1990s. As the factors associated with this decline intensify in the next two decades—factors such as increases in women's education, falling IMRs, greater exposure to media, and improved access to and acceptance of

---

[8]Studies of various parts of the country suggest poverty itself may induce parents to send children to school, as a means to improve the family's situation. (Irudaya Rajan and Mishra (1996); Kishor (1994); Säävälä (2001).)

contraception—so the fall in TFRs can be expected to continue further. A number of studies worldwide suggest that there is a quantity–quality trade-off between numbers of children and the education (or quality) of children (Hanushek 1992; Knodel et al. 1990; Montgomery et al. 1995). There is evidence of this trade-off in India too: Bhat (2002b) calculates that almost two-thirds of all recent fertility decline in India is attributable to illiterate women, and finds evidence that they are using contraception to reduce family size so that they can send their children to school. Given this trade-off, falling TFRs—projected to reach replacement level of 2.1 within 2016–21 (Chapter 5 and Bhat 2002a)—suggest that demand for the education of children will continue to strengthen in India in the future.

Third, demand for education may increase if the perceived or actual returns to education rise. There are no estimates of such returns for India using recent data and it is not possible to say whether returns have increased in the post-1991 reform period. Earlier estimates suggest that, contrary to conventional wisdom, returns to education generally rise with education level in India, at least up to the secondary level (Duraisamy 2000; Kingdon 1998; Kingdon and Unni 2001; Wood and Calandrino 2000).[9] Moreover, Duraisamy (2000) finds that between the ten-year period 1983 to 1993, returns to education for men and women remained fairly stable, except for women at the upper primary level of education where they fell from 14 per cent to 10 per cent and at the secondary level of education where they rose from 24 per cent to 26 per cent. It may be thought that low returns to elementary education would imply a low demand for it. However, any increase in the demand for secondary education (which has high and somewhat increasing returns) must lead to an increase in demand for elementary education which is a necessary input into secondary education (Appleton et al. 1996).

A bright picture of India's potential economic future is painted in a recent paper by Adrian Wood with Michele Calandrino (2000: 4691) who foresee India as potentially one of the world's two economic giants, the other being China. They estimate that reduction in trade barriers could multiply India's exports five-fold and double its per capita income over two decades. The paper argues that greater openness would substantially raise employment demand for educated workers in India, partly by shifting employment towards more skill-intensive sectors (especially away from agriculture), but mainly by increasing the need for more educated workers within each sector, because of the wider diffusion of modern products and methods of production. Wood and Calandrino project that over the next decade or two, the employment demand for illiterate workers would fall by about a fifth and, among literate

---

[9]Kingdon (1998) uses 1995 data from Uttar Pradesh; Duraisamy (2000) uses 1983 and 1993 NSS data for India as a whole; Wood and Calandrino (2000) also use the 1993 NSS data for India; and Kingdon and Unni (2001) use 1987 NSS data from Tamil Nadu and Madhya Pradesh.

workers, the increases in demand would be proportionally larger, the higher their level of education. This expansion in demand for educated labour should increase the economic return to education, strengthening financial incentives for children to acquire education.

Supply of education: The acceleration in educational progress over the 1990s, in terms of faster paced growth in literacy and school attendance, is also consistent with an improvement in the supply of education over the period, both in terms of the quantity and the quality of education. There are a number of aspects to this improvement, including centrally- and externally-funded education projects, improved management via decentralization measures, the use of para-teachers to expand schooling, and the spread of private schooling. We briefly examine each one in turn.

Centrally- and externally-funded projects: While state per capita spending on elementary education has stagnated or even fallen in some states in the 1990s (Table 7.7) owing to the large fiscal deficits of state governments, central government funding has risen. This has been supplemented with relatively small amounts of foreign funds for primary education from the World Bank, the UK Department for International Development (DFID), and other European bilateral aid under the District Primary Education Project (DPEP) which targets low literacy districts for educational investments. The centrally-sponsored schemes included a mid-day meal programme started in 1995; the introduction of Minimum Levels of Learning; and Total Literacy Campaigns. The DPEP has included upgrading of school facilities, provision of books, training of teachers, and the development of locally relevant curricula. Although there are a number of critiques of the DPEP (Kumar et al. 2001a; Govinda 2002), the accelerated progress in current school attendance in states covered by Phase I of the DPEP suggests that the project has, together with other interventions, made a contribution to improved educational outcomes in India. The fact that the Government of India has recently brought the various schemes of external funding and centrally-sponsored programmes under the banner of the new *Sarva Shiksha Abhiyan* (Education-for-All Campaign) and reiterated its commitment to Education-for-All in its Tenth Five-Year Plan suggests that it wants to build on the momentum of educational progress generated in the past decade.

Decentralized management of education: An important change in the 1990s was in the institutional environment in which education functions in India. The powers of local government or Panchayati Raj institutions were extended by the states, devolving a number of educational responsibilities to them from 1993 onwards. While in principle this form of community participation is expected to contribute to educational improvements—since teachers are likely to be more accountable to local managers than to remote central authorities—the jury is still out on whether, in practical terms, panchayat decentralization has improved the management of primary schooling.[10] While some analysts are sceptical about any beneficial effects, Drèze and Kingdon (2001) believe there may be some positive effects. Using PROBE data from five north Indian states, they find that villages with Village Education Committees—these have panchayat representation (Sinha 1998)—were significantly more likely to have mid-day meal schemes and that mid-day meals had a very significant positive effect on child schooling participation. By adopting a district-specific approach to planning primary education, the DPEP also strengthened decentralized management of education.

Use of para-teachers: In the 1990s, several states also initiated individualized programmes to promote primary schooling, involving the use of low-cost professionally unqualified teachers known as *shiksha karmis, shiksha mitras,* etc.[11] Kumar et al. (2001b) report that between 1994 and 1999, about 220,000 such 'para-teachers' were appointed across 10 states but that this number had 'more than doubled' by 2001. Under these schemes, persons with relatively low levels of schooling are employed on low pay to make schooling available in small hamlets and to increase the number of instructors in single-teacher schools. Although the model varies from state to state, the instructors are typically paid between Rs 1000 and Rs 2500 per month by the village panchayat—one-fifth to half the salary of a regular teacher—and the jobs are tenable for 10 months per year, with possibility of renewal each school year.

The schemes have raised a number of concerns mainly to do with the

[10]For instance, Acharya (2002) and Mathew (2002) represent conflicting views. In his study of panchayat decentralization and its effects on education in West Bengal, Acharya (2002) notes that through the panchayat, 'a class of new mandarins have emerged in the village society who are unscrupulous in the extreme and heinously power-hungry. Unfortunately, primary teachers being a major group of panchayat members, are also involved in this unholy power game. This has also vitiated the primary [education] system' (p. 796). Mathew (2002) takes issue with this view, arguing that panchayats have 'played an effective role in monitoring the functioning of schools', played 'a crucial role in organizing and monitoring the functioning of *Shishu Shiksha Kendras* in villages where there are no schools or [which] have locational disadvantages'. She argues that 'Kerala, with a history similar to that of West Bengal in terms of ideological persuasion, provides examples where certain panchayats have taken initiatives like teacher training, developing a revised curriculum, training modules, setting up of library and other activities'. Leclercq (2002) finds that in rural Madhya Pradesh, political decentralization (the empowering of panchayats) had had less effect on the progress of education than 'administrative decentralization', that is, than the effect of local educational institutions such as Block and Cluster Resource Centres that provide support to local teachers.

[11]Rajasthan had already initiated the Shiksha Karmi (education worker) project in 1987. Several states devised their own versions of Shiksha Karmis in the 1990s. For example, under its Education Guarantee Scheme, Madhya Pradesh utilized such 'para-teachers' called *guruji,* building on the Alternative School Programme initiated in 1994–5, the Rajiv Gandhi Prathmic Shiksha Mission (Govinda 2002: 52). Uttar Pradesh had a Shiksha Mitra project. Other states that utilized para-teachers on a large scale in the 1990s were Andhra Pradesh, Gujarat, Himachal Pradesh, and West Bengal.

ethical, legal, and political difficulty of sustaining two different standards of employment between regular teachers and informal instructors. Some authors have also raised concerns about the quality of teaching provided by these less-qualified instructors (Kumar et al. 2001b). Others have pointed to a compensating feature, namely that para-teachers generally have much greater accountability due to the (welcome) closer community involvement and because of the (less welcome) insecurity of their job-contracts. A recent report based on a survey of schools and communities in West Bengal[12] found that compared with schools that have regular teachers, schools with para-teachers (*shishu shiksha kendras*) had higher child attendance rates, lower teacher absenteeism rates and higher rates of parental satisfaction with teachers. Leclercq (2002) found that in Madhya Pradesh, average achievement levels of children taught by para-teachers were no lower than those of children taught by regular teachers. Drèze and Sen (2002) believe that the contribution of these low-cost schemes so far is uncertain and that it is premature either to applaud or dismiss them since some schemes have failed (such as the Non-Formal Education schemes) but some have made significant contributions (such as the Education Guarantee Scheme in Madhya Pradesh). The use of para-teachers and 'second-track arrangements' is very likely to be an increasing feature of India's educational future. It is envisaged that this type of teacher recruitment will continue in the future on an enlarged scale as state governments' fiscal capacities to increase the number of 'regular' teachers is undermined by continued budgetary difficulties and high/rising salaries demanded by state teacher unions (Kingdon and Muzammil 2002).

Growth and greater utilization of private schooling: Another significant development in Indian education over the recent past has been a growth of fee-charging private schooling.[13] Table 7.5 shows the enrolment share of private schools in rural and urban India, according to both official school returns data and household survey data. The last two columns show the corresponding figures for Uttar Pradesh, a state with quite high levels of private school participation.

According to official statistics, in 1993, only 2.8 per cent of all rural primary school students in India were studying in private schools but, according to

[12]Pratichi Trust (2002).

[13]There are three main school types in India: government, aided, and private. Schools run by the central, state or local governments are referred to as 'government' schools. Schools run by private managements but with heavy government influence and funded largely by government grant-in-aid are known as 'private aided' or just aided schools. Their teachers are paid at government-teacher salary rates directly from the state government treasury, and their teacher recruitment is usually determined by a state-appointed Education Service Commission. Schools under private management and run without state aid are known as 'private unaided' schools. These run entirely on fee-revenues and have little government interference in matters such as teacher recruitment. For the purposes of this chapter, we refer to these simply as 'private' schools rather than by their full name of 'private unaided'.

household survey data for the same year, 10.1 per cent of all rural 6–10 year old school attendees went to a private school, a figure that is more than three times as high as the official estimate.[14] Overall, 9.8 per cent of all 6–14 year old rural Indian school-goers went to private schools (Shariff 1999). Table 7.5 shows that in rural Uttar Pradesh, official estimates put the 1993 enrolment share of private primary schools at 8.8 per cent but that according to the 1993–4 National Council of Applied Economic Research (NCAER) household survey, the actual share was 30.7 per cent, again, more than three times as high as the official estimate. By the time of the PROBE survey in 1996, 36 per cent of all primary-age students (6–11 year olds) in rural Uttar Pradesh attended private schools (PROBE Team 1999). The reasons for the large discrepancy between household survey estimates and official estimates of the size of the private schooling sector in India are discussed in Kingdon (1996a) and Kingdon and Drèze (1998), where it is argued that the role of private schooling in India is seriously underestimated in official data, particularly at the primary education level.[15]

TABLE 7.5: *The enrolment share of private schools in India*

	India		Uttar Pradesh	
	1993 Official Data	1993 Household Survey Data	1993 Official Data	1993 Household Survey Data
RURAL				
Primary	2.8	10.1	8.8	30.7
Junior	6.5	7.9	28.3	23.3
Secondary	6.8	10.1	10.9	14.4
URBAN				
Primary	25.7	26.2*	53.3	49.7*
Junior	18.8	15.4*	29.6	25.1*
Secondary	11.5	11.2*	5.3	11.3*

Source: Official data are based on a census of all schools in the Sixth All-India Education Survey (NCERT 1998). Rural household survey figures are based on calculations from the NCAER survey of 1993–4 in rural areas of 16 major states in India (Kingdon 2002b). The urban household survey figures marked *are taken from NSS 1995–6, published data from NSSO (1998: A69–A82).

[14]The two sources are not exactly comparable since it is possible that some school-going 6–10 year olds may attend pre-primary or junior classes.

[15]First, government and government-aided school teachers have an incentive to over-report their enrolments, which reduces the apparent enrolment share of private schools; second, the school survey is carried out only in the registered and government-'recognized' private schools and there is no requirement on private schools to be registered or recognized: it seems that many private primary schools do not register or get recognized.

It is worth noting that according to the (more reliable) household survey data in Table 7.5, the size of the private school sector is proportionately largest at the primary level, smaller at the junior level, and smallest at the secondary level.[16] Since the children of the poor are best represented at the primary education level, this pattern is clearly perverse from the point of view of equity.

The most telling statistic for looking at recent trends, however, is not the share of private schooling in the stock of total school enrolment but, rather, the share of private schooling in the total recent *increase* in school enrolment at different levels. Table 7.6 presents the proportion of the total enrolment increase (over time) that is absorbed by private schools. It shows the percentage of all new enrollees who choose private schooling. It shows that in urban India 61 per cent of all the increase in total primary school enrolment in the period 1986–93 was 'absorbed' by private schools. Government and aided schools together absorbed only 39 per cent of the new primary enrolment over the period. This suggests a massive growth of private primary schooling in urban India. In rural India, the rate of expansion of private primary schooling is slower: only about one-fifth (18.5 per cent) of the rural total increase in primary students was taken up by private schools. However, there was a marked acceleration in the growth of rural private primary schooling in this period compared to the previous 8–year period of 1978–86, when only 2.8 per cent of the total increase in enrolment was absorbed by rural private schools. It is important to emphasize that these figures are all underestimates since they do not include new enrolments in the unrecognized private primary schools (Kingdon 1996a).

In some states, the acceleration in the growth of private schooling has

TABLE 7.6: *Proportion of total enrolment increase (over time) absorbed by private schools*

	Urban		Rural	
	1978–86	*1986–93*	*1978–86*	*1986–93*
INDIA				
Primary	56.8	60.5	2.8	18.5
Junior	35.7	31.8	7.2	12.8
UTTAR PRADESH				
Primary	75.3	93.9	9.3	41.9
Junior	63.7	15.8	34.0	54.3

Source: Calculations from the Fourth, Fifth and Sixth All-India Education Surveys (NCERT 1982, 1992, 1998).

[16]This pattern arises because government controls over private schools—in terms of requirements on schools to be government recognized and to pay their teachers state-prescribed salaries, etc.—are progressively greater as one goes to higher levels of education. The political economy reasons for this are discussed in Kingdon and Muzammil (2002).

been spectacular. Figures for Uttar Pradesh are included in Table 7.6 to illustrate this. In urban Uttar Pradesh, 94 per cent of all new primary school enrolment over the 7-year period between 1986 and 1993 occurred in private schools. Even this dramatic statistic is likely to be an underestimate since, as stated before, it takes no account of new enrolments in the numerous unrecognized private schools that are unregistered and thus excluded from the official statistics cited in Table 7.6. The table also shows that in rural Uttar Pradesh, the percentage of total enrolment increase accounted for by private schools rose from 9 per cent in the period 1978–86 to 42 per cent in the period 1986–93 at the primary level and from 34 per cent to 54 per cent at the junior level. If this trend has continued, it is likely that the role of private schooling increased further from the middle to late 1990s, and particularly so in some states.

The growth of private schooling offers a plausible explanation for the fact that despite falling or static per capita public education expenditure in some states (Table 7.7) these states have improved their educational outcome indicators in the 1990s. It seems that accelerated educational progress in the 1990s was partly due to the contribution made by the rapidly growing private school sector, which represents increased private expenditure on education by households. Various reasons have been suggested by different analysts as to why households—even many below the poverty line—are increasingly bypassing the free public school option to send their children to private fee-charging schools (Pradhan and Subramanian 2000). Reasons given rarely include the lack of a government-funded school in the vicinity; they more frequently refer to the perceived better quality of schooling available in private schools. As the PROBE Report found, the major attraction of private schools was that, unlike government primary schools, private schools provided active teaching: when investigators visited these schools, teachers were almost always in class and teaching (PROBE Team 1999). If the fiscal squeeze in state budgets continues in the future, parents who can afford it will turn increasingly to private schools to educate their children, and the private sector is likely to continue to grow relative to the public education sector. The optimism engendered by the enrolment increases of the 1990s must be tempered by the worrying rapid growth of the supply of private schooling at the basic education level.

Supply models—Kerala, Uttar Pradesh, and Himachal Pradesh: A more detailed look at the cases of Kerala, Uttar Pradesh, and Himachal Pradesh is revealing. They have been described as three 'models':[17] Kerala shows a successful mix of public and private education, Uttar Pradesh has a poor record in public education and a growing reliance on the private sector, and Himachal Pradesh uses the public sector almost entirely. A number of features of Kerala's experience

[17]By Jean Drèze, in a comment at the Wellcome Workshop, New Delhi, January 2002.

stand out. There is a record of concern for public action in health and education in Kerala going back to the nineteenth century.[18] Of more practical, but still limited, effect was the work of various missionary societies, which set up numerous schools including several for members of lower castes. The matrilineal character of some of Kerala's castes also contributed to the greater regard for females in various aspects of Kerala's social life.

It was not until the 1960s that the majority of females became literate, or that literacy for males and females 'spread to the backward districts and to the rural poor' (Ramachandran 1997). In addition to the historical factors seen earlier, several others played a part. There was significant pressure to establish the economic and social rights of backward castes; the rural movements for improved rights and agrarian reforms gave many people the experience of successful social action, and did achieve a degree of security for many of Kerala's poorer sections. In the post-independence period a Communist government was in power for several years, elected because it stood for a platform of equality and social development. Although it was in office for a relatively short time, it succeeded in setting the agenda for subsequent governments in Kerala. Since the 1960s Kerala has spent a considerably higher proportion of both development and non-development expenditure on education than the average for Indian states (Ramachandran 1997). Credit must be given to the activity of local NGOs, not least in launching the Total Literacy Campaign in the late 1980s, a campaign that shows how difficult it is to reach the most excluded.[19] Kerala, in 2001, showed only a 1.1 per cent improvement in literacy over 1991, moving from just under to just over 90 per cent—though that is still an achievement unmatched elsewhere in India.

Uttar Pradesh, in contrast, shared none of the attributes that contributed to Kerala's achievements. When it comes to female subordination, Uttar Pradesh, it is said, is not just backward by international and Indian standards, but is 'virtually in a league of its own' (Drèze and Gazdar 1997). In every dimension of female development—health, fertility, education, or employment—Uttar Pradesh ranks lowest or among the lowest in India. Its women are, obviously with exceptions, essentially confined to domestic life and subject to male domination. Agrarian reform has been very limited, and backward castes are subject even today to worse oppression than in most other states. Uttar Pradesh's expenditures on education are among the lowest in India, and the state has never had governments with any kind of broad welfare agenda.

The principal culprit in what might be called the proximate causes of the

[18]Richard Franke, cited in Ramachandran (1997).
[19]Even Sweden today has 7 per cent adult illiteracy, according to data from the International Adult Literacy Survey.

poor educational record of Uttar Pradesh is the dismal quality and performance of its government schools. Although more than half of the small villages are without schools, 89 per cent of the rural population were within one kilometre of a primary school in 1986, and 98 per cent within two kilometres. But many of the schools are little more than designated spaces; where there are buildings they are often in poor condition and without facilities. A very common failing is the non-appearance of teachers; researchers visiting schools unannounced found no teaching in progress in a large proportion of cases (Drèze and Gazdar 1997; PROBE Team 1999).

Teachers and teachers' associations and unions have become politically powerful in Uttar Pradesh. They are well represented in both Houses of the State Legislature, and have also conducted frequent agitations and strikes, especially in the 1970s and 1980s. At one time they were motivated by the need to redress the poor pay and conditions of teaching in British India, but they became an interest group mainly bent on securing higher pay for themselves. The result has been a major growth in teachers' salaries at the expense of the rest of educational provision. Teachers' unions in Uttar Pradesh have resisted attempts to subject teachers to accountability to the local panchayats. While such accountability would reduce teacher absenteeism and negligence, the Uttar Pradesh state government has lacked the political courage to push through measures to achieve this because of the resistance of teachers' unions (Kingdon and Muzammil 2002). Poverty is a further factor, but not a dominant one. The head-count ratio of poverty in Uttar Pradesh is no higher than in several other states where educational performance is much better. Caste is undoubtedly still important: Drèze and Gazdar (1997) note that keeping lower caste or *dalit* children out of school altogether is largely a thing of the past; but there are other ways in which these children are disadvantaged, by the inaccessibility of the school, or the treatment they receive at the school. The rates of schooling for these children are well below even the Uttar Pradesh average.

Himachal Pradesh has made the most remarkable strides in education in the last two decades. Some 90 per cent of rural males and 82 per cent of rural females aged 5–14 attended school in 1993–4. Prior to the 1980s, Himachal Pradesh's record was not remarkable (NSSO 1997).[20] Many of the factors which have helped education in Kerala have been present in Himachal Pradesh and some of those which have hindered it in Uttar Pradesh are absent. Unlike Kerala, Himachal Pradesh did not have a background of relatively good educational performance before the recent period. The ingredients of success appear to have been a number of mutually reinforcing factors. Perhaps

[20]Figures of 47.5 per cent (males) and 37.3 per cent (females) are derived in Swaminathan and Rawal (1999) from NSS data for 1987–8, but as the authors note, the figures are not strictly comparable.

the first is a relatively homogeneous society. There is much less class and caste division than in many parts of India, and less exploitative relations between different classes and castes. Very significantly, gender relations have long been more equal than in much of India. Himachal Pradesh has a high female–male ratio, and female child mortality is lower than male. Women also have a high presence in the labour force, that is, in employment outside the home.

Himachal Pradesh's per capita expenditure on education is double the average for Indian states, and so are its teacher–child ratios, including a good proportion of female teachers. There is strong commitment by the state government and parents and village communities support their schools, often making up for deficiencies in public provision. There is very little private schooling at the primary level, because the government schools work well. Teachers teach, and schools are on the whole well managed. There has been an effort to reduce disparities between districts, and to raise standards even in remote tribal areas. Himachal Pradesh is one of the states where Operation Blackboard has been followed through: one of its goals was to get away from single-teacher schools, which accounted for 28 per cent of all schools in the state in 1986; they were only 2 per cent by 1995.[21] It is tempting to say that what Himachal Pradesh has achieved, others can too. But some of the 'enabling factors' are not in place elsewhere, in particular when it comes to caste and gender relations. When these are divisive, it will take time to generate the political will for change which lies behind educational success.

POPULATION GROWTH AND SCHOOLING

Population growth has made the task of educating India's children more difficult. But different states have tackled the problem in different ways. The primary-school age population (6–10) for India as a whole kept growing until it levelled out at the 1991 Census. The birth rate has been declining for decades, but on an ever larger total population, so the absolute number of births kept rising. The projections in Chapter 5 imply that the 6–10 age group will remain more or less stable up to 2026, although there are signs that it may start to decline from 2021. Similarly, the 11–17 age group continued to grow till 2001, and will also be stable up to 2026.

The pattern differs considerably by state: in Kerala both primary and secondary age groups have already started to decline. Andhra Pradesh, Gujarat, Haryana, Himachal Pradesh, Karnataka, Maharashtra, Orissa, Punjab, Tamil Nadu, and West Bengal will see stability or decline in both their 6–10 and 11–14 age groups between now and 2026; in Bihar, Madhya Pradesh, Rajasthan, and Uttar Pradesh both primary and secondary age groups will rise till 2026. While the better-off states and one of the poorer ones (Orissa) will enjoy a 'demographic bonus' in the shape of falling school-age populations

[21]These paragraphs depend heavily on The PROBE Report (PROBE Team 1999).

in the near term, this improvement is postponed in four of the five poorest states. The implications of this contrast are considerable. The backlog of unmet need makes the task of ensuring education for all a huge one, even in better-off states. Some of the states that are both poor and most educationally deprived confront the additional task of a school-age population that will go on growing at least for the next 25 years.

THE PROBLEMS OF EDUCATION IN THE NEAR FUTURE

One of the main problems of education in the short to medium term is expenditure on education. Another, related, problem is the low quality of education.

Data for state elementary educational expenditure are given in Table 7.7. As can be seen, the figures are low as a percentage of state domestic product (SDP) in the latest year available, that is, 1997–8: 1.8 per cent on average for the 15 major states. The trends are not encouraging either: this share declined marginally in the 1990s, though experience varied in the various states, some rising, some falling. The rate of growth of state real expenditure per capita on elementary education in the 1990s is more troubling: it was slow in Madhya

TABLE 7.7: *Trends in public educational expenditure in the 1990s*

	Growth rate of real per capita expenditure on elementary education	Share of elementary education expenditure in state domestic product	
	1990–1 to 1997–8* *(per cent per year)*	*1990–1*	*1997–8*
Maharashtra	5.9	1.2	1.3
Orissa	4.9	2.5	2.8
Assam	4.6	2.6	3.7
Karnataka	4.3	2.0	1.9
Himachal Pradesh	3.3	4.1	-
Rajasthan	3.3	2.4	2.5
Haryana	2.8	1.2	1.1
Gujarat	2.7	1.9	1.6
Tamil Nadu	1.5	2.3	1.8
Madhya Pradesh	0.9	2.0	1.9
Andhra Pradesh	0.7	1.5	1.2
Kerala	0.7	3.3	2.1
Bihar	0.4	3.3	3.6
Uttar Pradesh	-1.8	2.5	2.0
West Bengal	-2.5	1.5	1.0
15 states combined	1.4	2.0	1.8

Note: *Using wholesale price index deflator.
Source: Table 5.3 in Drèze and Sen 2002: 169.

Pradesh, Andhra Pradesh, Kerala, and Bihar and actually fell in Uttar Pradesh and West Bengal. This is partly the result of a fiscal squeeze in the states—though that squeeze has not affected other, less essential, items. The states have also partly relied on centrally-funded initiatives such as the DPEP.

These expenditure levels and trends imply that there could have been little progress made in the quality of education. The overwhelming bulk and increasing share of education expenditure is on teachers' pay, with very little going to other facilities such as instructional materials, school resources, etc. Table 7.8 shows that between 1960 and 1981 (the latest year for which evidence is available), the share of salary expenditure in total recurrent education expenditure rose secularly. The implied share of non-salary expenditure fell from 28 per cent to 10 per cent in secondary education; from 15 per cent to 6 per cent in junior education; and from 12 per cent to a mere 3 per cent in primary education. Yet research internationally, as well as for India, shows that these non-salary school investments are much better associated with enhanced educational outcomes than are teacher salaries (Fuller 1986; Hanushek 1986, 1995; Kingdon 1996b).

Another aspect of quality of schooling is the number of students per

TABLE 7.8: *Salary expenditure as a proportion of total education expenditure*

Year	Recurrent as a per cent of total educational expenditure	Salary as a percentage of total recurrent educational expenditure (per cent)		
		Primary	Junior	Secondary
1960–1	74.7	87.9	85.1	72.3
1965–6	79.4	90.7	89.2	75.3
1969–70	85.0	92.3	90.4	85.6
1974–5	87.1	96.6	94.3	87.1
1981–2	94.8	96.7	93.8	89.9
1987–8	97.3	NA	NA	90.7

Note: The figures published for the year 1987–88 for primary and junior education levels are not comparable with figures published in previous years because for 1987–88, non-teaching staff salaries have been lumped together with the item 'other' giving the implausibly low figures of 94.0 per cent and 91.6 per cent for primary and junior education respectively. After the late 1980s, the publication of the breakdown of total educational spending into salary, consumables, and other expenditure has been discontinued, that is, it does not appear to be published any more, perhaps because it became too embarrassing to publish such a breakdown. For instance, the 1994–5 copy of 'Education in India', published in the year 2000, had no such table. Note that prior to 1960–1, expenditure information in published documents was not presented by item of expenditure (salaries, consumables, others, etc.) but rather by expenditure on boys' schools and expenditure on girls' schools, etc., or expenditure by source.

Source: Table 13.13 from Kingdon and Muzammil (2002).

available teacher.[22] Class sizes remain excessive in many areas as the big increase in enrolments has outstripped teacher appointments. For example, according to 1999–2000 data from the District Information System for Education initiated under the DPEP, 26 per cent of all India's primary schools had a pupil–teacher ratio above 60 (Drèze and Sen 2002).[23] An offset to this has been the rise of para-professional teachers, valuable perhaps as a means of getting children into school in ill-served locations, as in the Madhya Pradesh Educational Guarantee Scheme. However, these schemes have their own attendant problems, such as the proliferation within each village of schools of different types that are typically too small to be efficient, and problems of equity raised by the coexistence of different school-types (Leclerq 2002). Despite recent progress, the country is still a depressingly long way from providing public primary education of reasonable quality for the great mass of children whose numbers in some states are set to grow substantially for two more decades.

THE OUTLOOK

We have seen that India made encouraging progress in some educational outcomes during the 1990s. However, it would be a serious mistake to think that it is close to achieving universal elementary education or that that will be attained easily.

At the turn of the century in rural India, 25 per cent of female children aged 6–10 and 38 per cent of female children aged 11–14 were not attending school (IIPS and ORC Macro 2000); the corresponding figures for male children were 17 per cent and 21 per cent, respectively. Thirty per cent of rural and 16 per cent of urban children aged 11–14 were still not currently attending school (IIPS and ORC Macro 2000). Even current attendance among a high proportion of students does not necessarily mean completion of primary or junior schooling levels given premature drop-out. There were large drop-out rates in 1998–9: only 60 per cent of ever-enrolled children

---

[22]There has been a lively debate about whether class-size matters to student achievement. Fuller (1986) and Hanushek (1986, 1995) find that smaller class-sizes are not consistently associated with higher student achievement scores. For India, Kingdon (1996b) also finds this to be the case—though class-size did matter to numeracy skills in her study. However, using better statistical techniques that take into account the potential endogeneity of class-size, Case and Deaton (1999), Angrist and Lavy (1999), and Krueger (1999) each find that larger class-sizes do significantly reduce student achievement in South Africa, Israel, and the US respectively. It seems reasonable to suppose that very large class-sizes are not conducive to learning.

[23]Average class-size in government primary schools in the 188 villages in the PROBE survey of 1996 was 50 students per teacher. Among 16 per cent of the sample schools, the pupil–teacher ratio was above 75. This was partly because teacher posts in less attractive areas were not easily filled (PROBE Team 1999).

reached the end of primary schooling; only 43 per cent the end of elementary schooling; and only 33 per cent the end of lower secondary.[24] While the overall increase in literacy rates is very welcome, the fact remains that by the turn of this century, the overall literacy rate was a mere 65 per cent of the population aged seven and over. Forty-six per cent of women and 24 per cent of men were still illiterate, showing that much remains to be done.

Moreover, there were stark inequalities in educational access and attainment along gender, caste, and rural–urban lines, as well as across states and districts. For instance, district female literacy rates ranged from 18.5 per cent in Kishanganj (Bihar) to 94.5 per cent in Kottayam (Kerala). There was a 22 percentage-point gender disparity in the overall national literacy rates in 2001, which were 76 per cent for males and 54 per cent for females (Table 7.1). This disparity was particularly large in Rajasthan (32 percentage points). The rural–urban disparity of 15 percentage points nationally was smaller than the gender disparity but still substantial.

To estimate some possible future patterns of progress in education we project the educational composition of the populations of India's main states to 2026.[25] The 2001 state-level age- and sex-specific populations from Chapter 5 are the starting populations on which our projections are based. The population of each state in 2001 is sub-divided by four levels of educational attainment, according to census categories; 'illiterate', 'primary and lower', 'junior', and 'secondary and higher'. Unfortunately, the 2001 Census data on state-level educational attainment are as yet unavailable. We therefore used equivalent data from the NFHS-2 conducted during 1998–9 for age groups between 5 and 49.[26] For age groups beyond 50, for which there are no NFHS-2 data, data from the 1991 Census are applied, taking account of population ageing between 1991 and 2001. We then estimated three sets of age- and sex-specific educational transition rates. These are the age-specific probabilities for young males and females to move from the category of illiterate to primary, from primary to junior, and from junior to secondary and higher education. The transition rates were translated into adult educational distributions, again accounting for population ageing. For each transition, it was assumed that the rate of increase observed between NFHS-1 (1992–3) and NFHS-2 (1998–9) in school attendance rates (ISAR) would continue in the future. So, for example, the ISAR for males and females aged 6–10 were applied to the

[24]Annual Report 1999–2000, Department of Education, The Union Ministry of Human Resource Development (pp. 142, 178, and 179), cited in Planning Commission (2002a: Tables 4.21, 4.22, 4.23 on pp. 206, 207, and 208).

[25]Our thanks go to Anne Goujon at The Institute for Demography of The Austrian Academy of Science for running these projections. See Goujon (2002) for details of our methodology and Lutz and Goujon (2001) for similar research in a global context.

[26]Some adjustments had to be made because for the age groups 20–49, the NFHS-2 data are only available for 10–year rather than 5–year age groups.

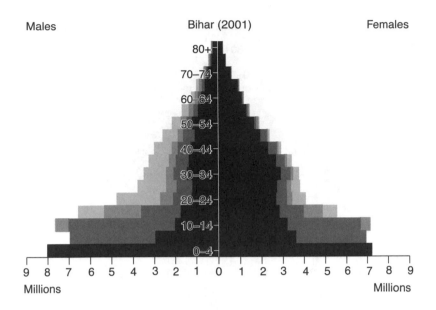

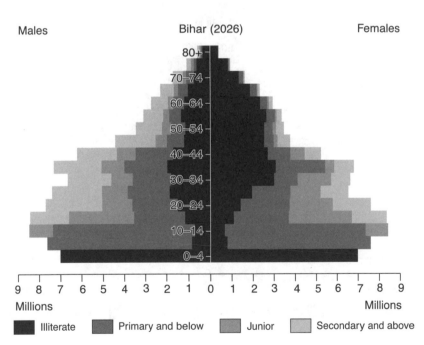

FIGURE 7.2a: *Educational composition of the population, 2001 (Bihar) and projected educational composition of the population, 2026 (Bihar)*

Source: Goujon and McNay (2003).

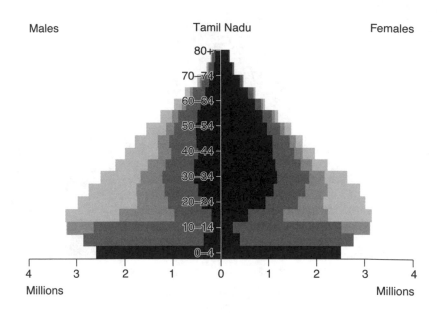

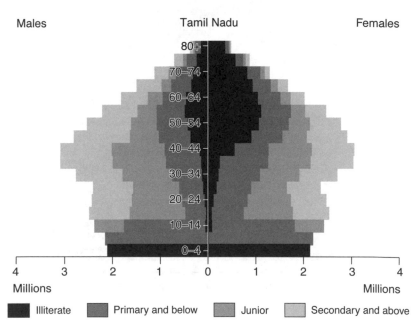

FIGURE 7.2b: *Educational composition of the population, 2001 (Tamil Nadu) and projected educational composition of the population, 2026 (Tamil Nadu)*

Source: Goujon and McNay (2003).

transitions from illiterate to 'primary and lower'.[27] All projections follow the fertility, mortality, and migration paths as defined by the population projections of Chapter 5.

We illustrate our results for two quite different north and south Indian states (Bihar and Tamil Nadu) as population pyramids for 2001 and 2026 shown in Figures 7.2 a and b. For Bihar (7.2a), the pyramids show that significant growth in the school-age population, and the accompanying challenge of getting increasing numbers of children into school, still lie ahead. For Tamil Nadu (7.2b), the task of schooling everybody is made easier because the size of the school-age population will shrink. Nevertheless, we can expect to see educational progress in Bihar, although in 2026 there is still a sizeable proportion of children and working-age people who will be illiterate or without completed elementary education (usually completed by age 14). For boys, our projections show that the proportion of 15–19 year olds without completed elementary education will fall from 55 per cent in 2001 to 42 per cent in 2026; for girls the fall is from 72 per cent to 44 per cent. Based on our assumptions therefore, gender differences in educational attainment narrow. Tamil Nadu's superior educational record is clearly visible, although even here our projections show that completed elementary education may not be universal among 15–19 year olds by 2026. For boys, the proportion without it falls from 30 per cent in 2001 to 19 per cent in 2026, and for girls the fall is from 41 per cent to 29 per cent.[28] These projections are sobering: they suggest that even in the relatively educationally-advanced states such as Tamil Nadu, universal elementary education will not be achieved even by 2026. They should not, however, be taken as predictions. They represent the likely scenario of educational attainments in 2026 if efforts to improve schooling access, retention, and quality are not stepped up.

A number of factors continue to pose threats to the universalization of elementary education. Physical accessibility remains a serious problem since the proportion of villages with an upper primary school is very low. It was only 29 per cent in the PROBE survey of north Indian villages (PROBE Team

---

[27]For most states during the 1990s, the ISAR for females has been higher than for males, leading to large gaps in levels of educational attainment in favour of females by 2026. We, therefore, decided to apply the ISAR for males and females separately until the proportions of males and females moving to the next educational levels equalized, and then apply the ISAR of males for both sexes. In addition, to obtain the most realistic results, we varied the length of time during the projection period over which the ISAR for the transition from junior to secondary and higher education were applied (Goujon 2002).

[28]In our most optimistic scenario, in which we maximized the length of time during the projections period in which the ISAR was applied to the most advanced educational transition, the proportion of 15–19 year olds without complete elementary education in 2026 is smaller; it ranges from 10 per cent for males in Tamil Nadu to 16 per cent for males in Bihar and 16 per cent for females in both states.

1999). The high pupil–teacher ratios and the inappropriateness of a dull and over-stretching curriculum pose quality concerns as well. Education spending seems to be falling or is growing too slowly. The proportion of gross domestic product (GDP) spent on schooling fell during the 1990s—from 4.4 per cent in 1989 to 3.6 per cent towards the end of the 1990s. The proportion of total education spending going to non-salary expenses of schools is less than 3 per cent in primary education, with serious implications for schooling quality.

We attempted to estimate the recurrent costs of achieving universal primary education in 2026 for our two contrasting states, Bihar and Tamil Nadu. Predicting costs is hazardous to undertake because many assumptions are required.[29] For each state, we estimated the number of 6–10 year olds in 2026 using the population projection results in Chapter 5. To estimate the unit recurrent costs of primary education for the mid-1990s, we combined information on monthly salary costs as agreed by the Fifth Pay Commission on 1 January 2001 with data on class size obtained from the Ministry of Education's annual publication *Selected Educational Statistics*.[30] We assumed an additional 3 percentage points to represent other recurrent costs and then a further 25 percentage points to represent the expenditure required to reach out-of-school children. We then used state-level price indices for Bihar and Tamil Nadu extrapolated to 2026 to estimate the unit recurrent costs in 2026. We multiplied the 2026 unit costs by the number of 6–10 year olds in 2026. We extrapolated SDP trends to 2026 to estimate total 2026 educational costs as a proportion of 2026 SDP for the two states. Our estimates indicate that achieving universal primary education in 2026 will be more costly in both absolute terms and as a proportion of SDP for Bihar compared to Tamil Nadu because Bihar's educational attainment has been more lacking to date, its school-age population is still to increase, and its 2026 SDP is extrapolated to be smaller than that of Tamil Nadu's. In addition, our estimates indicate that Bihar will have to spend a higher proportion of its 2026 SDP on primary education than the proportion it spent in the early 1990s if it is to achieve universal primary schooling.

We can conclude that despite encouraging leaps in literacy and current school attendance over the 1990s, the situation at the start of the twenty-first century leaves much to be desired. It is clear that a lot remains to be done to achieve universal elementary education. The central government's new emphasis on elementary education under its Sarva Shiksha Abhiyan initiative (albeit still to be tested) and the promise of continuation of the enabling conditions of the 1990s give grounds for optimism in the medium

[29]Ramachandran et al. (1997).

[30]We have used the monthly salary rates for teachers agreed by the Uttar Pradesh government, the only rates to which we had access. Those in Bihar and Tamil Nadu may well differ.

term. However, even if progress towards universal elementary education is rapidly achieved, education of a decent quality for all will remain a challenging goal. In particular, developments such as the increasing employment of para-teachers in small or marginal communities and the rapid growth of private education give rise to concerns about 'hierarchies of access', with those who are poorer and subject to discrimination being frequently left with the lower-quality options in primary schooling.[31] The achievement of better education for all will require still greater social action and public commitment than has been given to education so far.

[31]The phrase 'hierarchies of access' is used by Ramachandran (2001).

8

Employment

KIRSTY McNAY, JEEMOL UNNI, AND ROBERT CASSEN

T
he task of ensuring employment for the labour force has been a
persistent concern throughout India's post-independence
development. Demographic trends contribute to the difficulty of the
task. Between 1971 and 2001 the 15–59 working-age population grew faster
than the population as a whole, and comprised 602 million people in 2001,
more than double its size in 1971. Whereas the growth rate of the total
population has already started to slow, the working–age population will reach
its peak growth rate only during 2001–6. It will continue to grow faster than
total population to 2026, when it will be about 1.5 times as large as in 2001,
comprising 925 million people. At the same time, despite economic growth
and optimism from pro-reform analysts about the employment implications
of liberalization, the economy's ability to provide employment during the
1990s has in many ways proved disappointing. According to the NSS, the
number of people counted as unemployed on the 'current daily status' (CDS)
basis increased from 20 million in 1993–4 to nearly 27 million in 1999–2000.
In addition, there is evidence that the quality of available work has deteriorated.
Although there have also been several positive trends, given that economic
reform and liberalization are set to continue, concern should be given to the
future. To capitalize on the benefits of a growing labour force and avoid a
significant worsening of the employment situation in the future, policies are
required that boost both the generation and quality of jobs as well as equip
workers with the skills to undertake new opportunities.

In this chapter, we focus our discussion around the NSS data as these
provide the most detailed information on employment and unemployment.

We then project the labour force to 2026 and show the implications for unemployment if the economic and employment conditions of the 1990s are extrapolated into the future. We use both the recent trends and the projections to suggest some future employment policy priorities.

RECENT TRENDS IN THE EMPLOYMENT SITUATION

Aggregate employment growth: Table 8.1 shows the rate of growth of aggregate employment (the workforce) between the NSS quinquennial employment–unemployment surveys since 1972–3.[1]

TABLE 8.1: *Workforce and labour force annual growth rates*

	Annual growth rate of workforce[a]	Annual growth rate of labour force[a]
1972–3—1977–8	2.92	3.11
1977–8—1983	1.85	1.75
1983—1987–8	1.62	1.81
1987–8—1993–4	2.42	2.30
1983—1993–4[b]	2.14	2.13
1993–4—1999–2000	0.95	1.02

Notes: [a] Growth rates calculated by log method.
[b] We include this longer period because NSS data for the shorter periods 1983—1987–8 and 1987-8—1993–4 may have been affected by the drought conditions of 1987.
Sources: NSSO, *Employment and Unemployment Survey*, various rounds, and Census of India, various years.

A sharp drop in the rate of employment generation from 2.14 per cent per annum to 0.95 per cent per annum between 1983 to 1993–4 and 1993–4 to 1999–2000 is evident. The slowdown in employment generation has led to much concern that the economic growth of the 1990s has been of a 'jobless' variety (Planning Commission 2001b). The slowdown in the rate of employment generation is corroborated by other definitions of employment. The Planning Commission's Special Group calculates that on CDS terms employment growth fell from 2.70 per cent to 1.07 per cent during the same period, implying a yearly decline in the labour intensity of output of 5.5 per cent during 1993–4 to 1999–2000 compared with 2.2 per cent during 1983

[1]The data are for the 'usual status' definition of employment including both principal and subsidiary workers, that is, Usual Principal and Subsidiary Status (UPSS). See Planning Commission (2001b) or (2002b) for detailed explanations of the different definitions of employment and unemployment.

to 1993–4 (Planning Commission 2002b). The faster rate of employment growth on CDS terms compared with Usual Principal and Subsidiary Status (UPSS) terms suggests that new job opportunities tend to be of short duration (Chadha and Sahu 2002).[2] The slowdown in employment generation has been more severe in rural than in urban areas and has been worse for females than for males (Chadha and Sahu 2002; Sundaram 2001a, 2001b, 2001c).[3]

Sector-specific employment growth: Disaggregating NSS data by sector indicates that the slowdown in total (UPSS) employment growth during the 1990s has been associated primarily with negative growth in agriculture, still by far the largest single employment provider in India.[4] Even in CDS terms, agriculture has almost stopped absorbing labour (Planning Commission 2002b). The slowdown in the rate of agricultural growth may partly explain this trend; in Chapter 10 we note that annual agricultural growth was 3.6 per cent during 1981–2 to 2000–1, falling to 3.2 per cent for 1992–3 to 2000–1 (and only 2.7 per cent during 1991–2 to 2000–1.) Chadha and Sahu (2002) relate the declining capacity of agriculture to absorb labour to increasing marginalization of land holdings, faster mechanization and changing cropping patterns. At the same time, there has also been a slowdown in the growth rate of non-farm employment in rural areas, particularly among females (Kundu 2002). This trend signals a deceleration of the process of rural diversification, widely seen as being directly and indirectly beneficial (via a tightening of the rural labour market and a consequent boosting of agricultural wages) for rural development and poverty reduction (Lanjouw and Shariff 2002; Ravallion and Datt 1999). The deceleration in employment growth in the rural non-farm sector may well have been largely associated with reform-induced declines in government rural expenditure, which had been important to its expansion during the 1980s

---

[2]The provisional results of the 2001 Census confirm a slowdown in the generation of employment which qualifies for 'main work' that is, work which employs a person for the major part of the preceding year. However, according to the census, the rate of growth of marginal workers, those employed for less than the major part of the preceding year, has speeded up in the 1990s. While the total size of the 2001 Census workforce is comparable to that of the 1999–2000 NSS round, the census has a significantly higher proportion of marginal workers than the analogous category (subsidiary workers) in the NSS (Kumar and Sharma 2002a).

[3]It is worth noting that the NSS's story of deterioriating employment generation has been questioned by Hirway (2002). She argues that some of the slowdown in employment growth may be associated with an increase in 'difficult to measure' work over the 1990s. Hirway asserts that such work, like women's home-based or informal work, is unlikely to be wholly captured by the NSS. Her view is consistent with evidence on trends in informalization and casualization of work (which are discussed later in this chapter), and the growth in short duration employment. Although it suggests a lessening of the extent of any slowdown in employment generation, her view has important implications for employment quality.

[4]Previous censuses provide a sectoral breakdown for main workers only. However, the 2001 Census provides it for main and marginal workers combined, making inter-censal comparisons of the sectoral distribution of workers difficult.

(Chadha and Sahu 2002; Sen 1998). In this context, the fall in agricultural employment during the 1990s is not necessarily a positive structural trend because the ability of the rural secondary and tertiary sectors to absorb labour has also been limited.

More positively, employment growth rates in trade, construction, financial services, and transport, storage, and communication have increased, along with their share of employment. Employment growth in manufacturing declined, but its employment share increased marginally. Within this sector, significant gains in employment were experienced in export-oriented areas such as garments and in industrial organic and inorganic chemicals and plastic products (Chaudhuri 2002; Tendulkar 2002). The post-1993 slowdown in the rate of employment growth in community–social–personal services probably reflects declining public expenditure (Chadha and Sahu 2002). But some service areas did well; the expansion of software development and IT-enabled services is a well-known Indian success story.

Unemployment: Table 8.1 shows that during 1993–4 to 1999–2000, the slower rate of employment growth did not keep pace with the rate of growth of the labour force. This differential is reflected in a higher rate of (UPSS) unemployment in 1999–2000 compared with 1993–4. According to the Planning Commission's Task Force, the unemployment rate increased from 1.9 per cent in 1993–4 to 2.2 per cent in 1999–2000.[5] Unlike in earlier periods, the increase in unemployment is apparent for all different definitions of unemployment; according to CDS it increased from 6.0 per cent in 1993–4 to 7.3 per cent in 1999–2000.[6] For all measures of unemployment, the increase is evident in both rural and urban areas, although the rise has been sharper in rural areas. In CDS terms, rural unemployment increased from 5.6 per cent in 1993–4 to 7.2 per cent in 1999–2000, whereas the corresponding change in urban areas was from 7.4 per cent to 7.7 per cent. The rise in rural unemployment relates to the trends which explain why agriculture has become less able to absorb labour, and to the shift in the composition of employment from self-employment to casual labour that these trends entail (Sundaram

[5]The increase in unemployment is not as large as would be expected from the decline in the work participation rate (the percentage of workers to the corresponding population). The discrepancy implies declining labour force participation rates (Table 8.5), resulting in a slowdown in the rate of growth of the labour force which has been faster than the deceleration in population growth. It is worth noting that unlike the NSS, the 2001 Census shows increasing work participation rates for both males and females during the 1990s (Registrar General, India 2002b). The increase is explained largely by the increase in the proportion of marginal workers in the census.

[6]UPSS is generally regarded as a measure of chronic open unemployment during the reference year. In an economy like India's where casual wage employment and self-employment predominate, it is likely to hide considerable underemployment. CDS is a more comprehensive unemployment measure which includes both chronic unemployment and underemployment in terms of time allocated to work within the reference week.

2001a). Rural–urban unemployment differentials have consequently narrowed considerably during the 1990s. Both males and females experienced the increase in rural unemployment over the 1990s, as did urban males. But urban females enjoyed a decline in unemployment, although their rate of unemployment remains higher than among urban males. Chadha and Sahu (2002) suggest that the decline may be associated with a rise in demand for short duration work, for which females may be preferred to males.

Youth and educated unemployment: Certain groups tend to have significantly higher unemployment rates than that of the labour force as a whole. Two such groups are the young (ages 15–29) and the educated. It is important for policy purposes to try to understand why these groups are particularly prone to unemployment.

The problem of youth unemployment is not a recent one (Visaria 1998a). However, for all groups except urban females, it has increased significantly over the 1990s (Planning Commission 2002b). The 1999–2000 NSS data indicate that the (CDS) youth unemployment rate was 12.1 per cent compared with 7.3 per cent for the total labour force (Planning Commission 2001b). The higher youth unemployment rate is generally attributed to a mismatch between available jobs and the expectations and aspirations of young job-seekers.

A similar phenomenon is probably reflected in the relatively high rate of educated unemployment, although this coexists with the finding that the rate of return to education in terms of access to both better quality jobs and earnings rises with educational level (Kingdon and Unni 2001). There is also an interaction effect between age and education, with young educated job-seekers having some of the highest unemployment rates. The rates of both educated unemployment and educated youth unemployment have fallen during the 1990s, probably reflecting an expansion of skilled employment in some areas, for example manufacturing, during the period (Dev 2000). At the same time, there are still shortages in certain skilled sectors (Planning Commission 2002b). This is not surprising given that in the 1990s almost 44 per cent of the labour force was illiterate, only 10 per cent of male rural workers and 6 per cent of female rural workers possessed a specific marketable skill and only 5 per cent of the labour force aged 20–4 had received formal vocational training (Planning Commission 2001b, 2002b).

The mismatch between the type of work sought by young and educated job-seekers and the type of work which is available suggests that much of the latter is of insufficient quality. Simultaneous skill shortages in other areas raise questions about the extent to which such job-seekers are trained to do available work.

Regional aspects of employment: The all-India slowdown in employment genera-tion during the 1990s has been evident in most states, by varying magnitude

(Chadha and Sahu 2002). The sectoral patterns discussed earlier have also been generally widespread, although with some variation. For example, although the slowdown in the rate of growth of rural non-farm employment has been common, employment growth increased in several states, including Bihar, Haryana, Kerala, and Uttar Pradesh, testifying to this sector's employment potential (Chadha and Sahu 2002).

Of particular note at the state-level has been the persistence of huge differentials in unemployment between the states (Bhalotra 2002). The ranking of Kerala, West Bengal, and Tamil Nadu as the highest unemployment states and Himachal Pradesh, Rajasthan, and Uttar Pradesh as the lowest has been stable over time. In 1999–2000, Kerala's (CDS) unemployment rate was 21 per cent, whereas that of Himachal Pradesh was 3 per cent. However, despite rank order stability, dispersion across the states has increased during the 1990s. One explanation for Kerala's high unemployment rate is that there are few new jobs arising because of the adverse climate of labour relations (Bhalotra 2002). But as Bhalotra (2002) notes, this explanation does not account for why labour does not leave Kerala, prompting a convergence of state-level unemployment rates. Bhalotra (2002) argues that in the absence of significant barriers to migration this may be because Kerala has characteristics which compensate for its high unemployment, including educational, health, and social security provision which is superior to that in other states. She also argues that interstate urban unemployment differentials are maintained because intrastate rural–urban migration offsets interstate urban–urban migration. Finally, Bhalotra (2002) argues that wage differentials between states are upheld by substantial interstate inequality in infrastructure and human capital as well as labour bargaining power.

Most states have experienced an increase in unemployment during the 1990s. Only three states—Gujarat, Karnataka, and Haryana—achieved a decline. Among these states, Gujarat and Karnataka combined high rates of economic growth with relatively high employment elasticity of output (Planning Commission 2002b). Despite also having high economic growth, Tamil Nadu and West Bengal have been unable to prevent a rise in unemployment, something which is perhaps associated with their relatively low employment elasticities of output. Kerala's already high unemployment rate also rose during the 1990s in the context of a relatively high employment elasticity but comparatively low rate of economic growth (Planning Commission 2002b).

Organized and unorganized employment: The picture of employment trends presented so far does not capture important changes in the quality of employment. Employment quality is associated with two distinct, though related, structural features of the employment situation in India. The first is the distinction between employment in the organized and unorganized sectors and the second is the distinction between wage and self-employment.[7] Among wage workers, there is also a distinction between regular and casual workers.

According to the Planning Commission's Special Group, nearly 92 per cent of employment (and 59 per cent of GDP) is in the unorganized sector (Planning Commission 2002b). The self-employed, consisting of employers, own account workers, and contributing family members, can more or less be identified as such workers. Unorganized sector workers pursue economic activities with lower productivity than organized sector workers, resulting in lower incomes. In addition, the activities of unorganized sector workers, the self-employed, and casual workers have less stable employment contracts and fewer social security benefits than those of other workers. Casual workers, who may be employed in either organized or unorganized enterprises, tend to have lower levels of education and skill than regular wage earners. Changes in the structural pattern of employment may, therefore, have significant implications for employment quality, labour productivity, and workers' earnings and security. In this section, we examine recent changes in the structure of employment according to the distinction between the organized and unorganized sectors.

In Table 8.2, we use NSS and National Accounts Statistics (NAS) data to examine the structural pattern of non-agricultural employment in the periods 1983 to 1993–4 and 1993–4 to 1999–2000, disaggregating it by organized and unorganized sectors.[8]

TABLE 8.2: *Trends in non-agricultural organized and unorganized sectors*

	Annual growth rate of NDP	*Annual growth rate of employment*	*Annual growth rate of labour productivity*
	Non-agricultural organized sector		
1983–1994	7.17	1.21	5.97
1994–2000	8.35	0.40	7.93
	Non-agricultural unorganized sector		
1983–1994	5.66	3.92	1.74
1994–2000	7.21	3.20	3.97

Sources: National Accounts Statistics, various years, and NSSO, *Employment and Unemployment Survey*, various rounds.

[7]According to the National Accounts Statistics (NAS), the organized sector comprises of enterprises in the public sector, private corporate sector and cooperatives, manufacturing units registered under the Indian Factories Act, 1948 or the Bidi and Cigar Workers Act, 1966 and recognized educational institutions. Enterprises which do not belong to any of these categories are unorganized sector units.

[8]We concentrate on changes in the non-agricultural sector because agriculture provides almost no organized sector employment. Unorganized sector employment is calculated by the residual method. See Unni (2002) for details.

In the organized sector, there has been low and declining employment growth between the two periods. Coupled with rapid income growth (net domestic product (NDP)), this has resulted in growth in labour productivity, particularly in the second period. The pattern of employment growth in the organized sector is explained by absolute job losses in the public sector since 1993–4. These losses have occurred as the public sector has begun to shed excess labour in response to financial constraints and the need to become more competitive, and has physically withdrawn from several areas. On the other hand, the rate of employment growth in the organized private sector has increased beyond the rate of total employment generation, resulting in the creation of high quality jobs. However, scope for the organized private sector to contribute significantly to aggregate employment generation is limited because it provides less than 3 per cent of total employment and its labour intensity of output is comparatively low.

In the unorganized sector, there has also been income growth, although at a slower pace than in the organized sector. However, employment grew at more than 3 per cent in both periods, indicating that it is this sector which has been the prime labour absorber during the 1990s and which has the higher labour intensity of output. So while the share of the unorganized sector in non-agricultural GDP declined across the two periods, its share of non-agricultural employment rose. A process of informalization of employment has occurred and the unorganized sector is absorbing labour more quickly than it is generating output compared to the organized sector.

Given the characteristics of organized and unorganized sector work, these trends imply an overall deterioration in employment quality during the 1990s. However, as Table 8.2 shows, labour productivity in the unorganized sector increased between the two periods, although more slowly than in the organized sector. This, together with an increasing income growth rate points to some positive features of India's economic growth since the implementation of reforms. There are perhaps some favourable linkages between the organized and unorganized sectors involving a shift of activities from the former to the latter. It is likely that only high productivity managerial and technologically superior activities are retained in the organized sector, while others are shifted to the unorganized sector, raising its productivity.

However, the extent and nature of these linkages differ between various industry groups. In organized manufacturing, employment growth picked up in the 1990s following the 'jobless growth' of the 1980s (Bhalotra 1998; Nagaraj 1994). This growth has involved a significant shift in employment from the public sector to small and medium-sized enterprises in the private sector (Bhalotra 2002; Goldar 2000). However, during the 1990s the rate of employment growth as well as income and productivity has been faster in unorganized manufacturing, suggesting that favourable linkages are leading to convergence between the two sectors. Linkages can occur through changes in the activity mix within manufacturing industry between the organized and unorganized sectors. One example is via subcontracting out parts of the production activities of formal units to smaller units in the unorganized sector. Restructuring of manufacturing industry within the unorganized sector itself may also have contributed to convergence. It seems that as competitive forces have been unleashed with reforms and liberalization, smaller inefficient units have been weeded out and larger, more productive enterprises have expanded (Unni 2001). This restructuring process has been associated with the decline in traditional, more labour-intensive activities and the switch towards more modern manufactured products (Bhalla, S. 2001). Such a shift could account for the small decline in the rate of employment growth (as well as the increase in labour productivity) which has occurred in the unorganized manufacturing sector during 1993–4 to 1999–2000.

Conversely, while there was a quantum jump from 6.2 per cent to 16.0 per cent in the rate of growth of NDP in the organized trade and hotel industry during the reforms period, the NDP growth in the unorganized sector rose from 5.3 per cent to 7.6 per cent. In the organized sector, the rate of employment growth was minimal. However, there has been rapid absorption of employment in the unorganized sector. The result is a sharp increase in labour productivity in the organized sector and a much smaller increase in the unorganized sector. Unlike manufacturing, there seems to be a process of divergence in income and productivity occurring in this industry. Similarly, there is little evidence of positive linkages operating in the community-social-personal services industry. Again, divergence in income and productivity between organized and unorganized sectors is happening here.[9]

Status distribution of workers: Besides the distinction between organized and unorganized sectors, the second important structural feature of India's employment situation is the distinction between wage and self-employment. In this section, we examine recent changes in the structure of employment according to this distinction, and among wage workers, between regular and casual employment.

It is generally agreed that the proportion of casual workers in the Indian workforce has been increasing since the early 1970s and that this has been largely at the expense of self-employment (Planning Commission 2001b). In Table 8.3 we show a variety of patterns behind these broad trends. The table illustrates changes in the status of total male and female workers, both agricultural and non-agricultural, as well as only non-agricultural male and female workers for rural and urban areas since 1983.

[9]Part of the increase in incomes in the services sector is spurious and results from the higher pay scales due to the Fifth Pay Commission decision. The Pay Commission effects are spread mainly over the three years 1997–8, 1998–9, and 1999–2000 (Acharya 2002a). This impact is felt in the organized sector and widens the gap between organized and unorganized sectors.

TABLE 8.3: *Percentage distribution of employment status of workers*

	Male			Female		
	Self Employed	*Regular Employee*	*Casual Employee*	*Self Employed*	*Regular Employee*	*Casual Employee*
	All workers, rural					
1983	60.5	10.3	29.2	61.9	2.8	35.3
1987–8	58.6	10.0	31.4	60.8	3.7	35.5
1993–4	57.9	8.3	33.8	58.5	2.8	38.8
1999–2000	54.9	8.9	36.2	57.4	3.1	39.6
	All workers, urban					
1983	40.9	43.7	15.4	45.8	25.8	28.4
1987–8	41.7	43.7	14.6	47.1	27.2	25.4
1993–4	41.7	42.1	16.2	45.4	28.6	26.0
1999–2000	41.5	41.7	16.8	45.4	33.3	21.4
	Non-agricultural workers, rural					
1983	49.3	29.6	21.1	58.3	14.6	27.1
1987–8	46.5	27.6	25.9	50.1	14.1	35.8
1993–4	47.6	27.7	24.7	58.7	15.8	25.5
1999–2000	45.6	26.5	27.9	62.0	17.0	21.0
	Non-agricultural workers, urban					
1983	40.7	44.3	15.0	45.4	26.3	28.1
1987–8	41.6	43.7	14.7	47.1	27.5	25.4
1993–4	41.6	42.1	16.2	44.8	29.1	26.1
1999–2000	41.4	41.6	16.8	45.3	33.2	21.3

Source: NSSO, *Employment and Unemployment Survey*, various rounds.

Overall, self-employed workers continue to form the largest category of the workforce in both rural and urban areas. But their proportion has been declining especially among males and in rural areas. There has been a corresponding casualization of the rural workforce which many researchers associate with the displacement of marginal cultivators and their conversion to agricultural labour (Sundaram 2001a; Visaria 1999a). However, Table 8.3 shows that for rural males casualization involves non-agricultural as well as agricultural work. For rural females, casualization among the non-agricultural workforce has declined. The male urban and non-agricultural workforces have also witnessed casualization, but the opposite is true for female urban and non-agricultural workers.[10] There is a current trend of

[10]Bhalotra (2002) argues that the rate of casualization has been no quicker since the onset of reforms. Our data support her view. However, other researchers assert that casualization has been accentuated in the post-reform period (Chadha and Sahu 2002; Dev 2000).

females being increasingly absorbed into regular employment everywhere, unlike males. This may reflect their incorporation into the formal health sector, formal and informal education, and public administration (Unni 2001). The decline in regular wage employment since 1983 has essentially been a male phenomenon. Unni (2002) argues that it is associated with the decline in the share of the organized sector in total employment and implies a deterioration in employment quality. Despite these different trends among males and females, the female workforce continues to have a higher proportion of casual workers and a lower proportion of regular wage workers than the male workforce.

Wage earnings: There is evidence that the casualization of the workforce has been accompanied by an increase in the average daily real wage earnings of casual workers in both the agricultural and non-agricultural sectors since the mid-1980s (Sundaram 2001a, 2001b). As Chapter 9 shows, this increase has coexisted with a decline in poverty. However, these favourable developments are tempered by evidence of widening inequalities in the real wage earnings of casual workers compared to regular salaried workers. Table 8.4 shows that in both agricultural and non-agricultural sectors in rural and urban areas, the earnings of the former have increased more slowly than those of the latter.

TABLE 8.4: *Real wage and salary earnings of regular and casual workers (rupees per day at 1993–4 prices)*

		Rural earnings				Urban earnings		
	1983	1987–8	1993–4	1999–2000	1983	1987–8	1993–4	1999–2000
				Regular workers				
Agriculture	17.96	24.86	26.68	41.50	29.99	46.15	50.71	83.15
Non-agriculture	43.00	60.28	62.85	90.94	56.27	70.67	76.63	105.31
All	35.37	51.66	55.12	78.95	55.69	70.49	75.78	99.53
				Casual workers				
Agriculture	14.68	17.71	19.25	22.69	17.13	18.85	21.78	25.85
Non-agriculture	21.03	25.54	27.66	35.40	24.18	27.84	30.67	36.80
All	15.82	19.64	20.54	25.34	22.67	25.88	28.77	34.96

Source: NSSO, *Employment and Unemployment Survey*, various rounds.

It seems to be lower status workers who have benefitted least from the process of reforms and economic growth. These widening wage differentials are reflected in growing divergence in labour productivity between the organized and unorganized sectors; while organized sector productivity was about six times that in the unorganized sector in 1983, it grew to nearly nine times in 1999–2000 (Unni 2002).

However, disaggregating by industry groups shows different patterns in earnings differentials for different industries, although we have been able to obtain disaggregated earnings data for urban workers only. In manufacturing, the differential in earnings between casual workers and regular salaried workers declined between 1983 and 1999–2000. This convergence probably reflects the effects of the positive linkages between the organized and unorganized sectors in this industry and the restructuring of the latter which we discussed earlier. Conversely, in both the trade and hotels industry and in services, earnings differentials have increased during the reforms period. Unlike manufacturing, the lower wages of the least advantaged workers lag increasingly behind those of regular salaried workers, reflecting the rapid growth of value added and labour productivity in the organized sectors of these industries.

Deaton and Drèze (2002) also find evidence of widening wage inequality between different occupational groups during the 1990s by comparing the annual growth rate of real wages of agricultural labourers with that of the salaries of public sector workers. Real agricultural wages have increased by 2.5 per cent per year whereas public sector salaries have increased by almost 5 per cent per year. Deaton and Drèze's findings support our view that less advantaged workers have prospered least in the reforms environment.

Summing up recent trends in the employment situation: In the aggregate, the economic growth of the 1990s has not been employment friendly. In terms of generation of jobs, the situation appears to have deteriorated and this is reflected in increased unemployment, however measured. The slow growth of employment mainly reflects the decline in agricultural employment coupled with sluggish growth in organized sector employment. The latter has been a result of absolute job losses in the public sector. The quality of available employment also seems to have declined as the share of unorganized and casual work in total employment has increased. Unni's (2002) employment quality index, based on assigning different weights to different types of work, shows that the decline in employment quality has been particularly sharp in the 1990s. This trend is likely to have been associated with an increase in the problem of underemployment. The fact that about 28 per cent of the population in 1999–2000 were poor whereas the (CDS) unemployment rate was only 7 per cent suggests that this is the case; the earnings of many of the employed are insufficient to lift them (or their dependants) out of poverty. The inadequate quality of much employment is also reflected in the particularly high unemployment rates among those with higher aspirations. There have also been some positive trends, including the rising rate of employment growth in the organized private sector and the increase in real wages, including those of casual workers. Individual sectors, including a range of manufacturing activities and several services, have also shown their potential as future sources of employment expansion.

FUTURE EMPLOYMENT SCENARIOS TO 2026: THE PROSPECT OF INCREASING UNEMPLOYMENT

In this section we present some future employment scenarios to 2026. Our projections provide an idea of the unemployment implications of extrapolating the economic and employment conditions of the recent past to 2026.

India's labour force to 2026: The size of India's future labour force will depend on the size and age structure of the population and the labour force participation rate (LFPR). Between the 1971 and 1991 censuses the population in the most active working ages 15–59 years increased from 285 million (52 per cent of total population) to 602 million (59 per cent of total population). The population projections in Chapter 5 show that this absolute increase will continue to 2026. The working age population will be approximately 1.5 times as large in 2026 as in 2001, increasing to 925 million (65 per cent of total population). In addition, India's 60 plus population, many of whom are also in the labour force, will also increase absolutely and as a proportion of the total population. These changes in the age structure of the population reflect India's demographic past and will be associated with future increases in labour force size.

Table 8.5 shows past and projected future trends in the male and female LFPR together with the absolute size of the labour force. Looking at past trends, between 1972–3 and 1999–2000 the LFPR shows reasonable stability, although there is an overall declining trend for females. The decline for both males and females during the 1990s is reflected in the slowdown in the growth

TABLE 8.5: *Labour force participation rates (LFPR) and labour force sizes, projected to 2026*

	LFPR (all ages, per 1000)			Labour force (000s)		
	Males	Females	Persons	Males	Females	Persons
1972–3	545	286	420	161,660	78,899	240,560
1977–8	560	310	440	184,849	95,483	280,332
1983	545	291	423	206,610	104,364	310,974
1987–8	545	290	422	223,640	110,427	334,067
1993–4	556	287	427	258,777	124,066	382,843
1999–2000	541	258	404	581,373	125,404	406,777
2006	546	317	435	313,679	170,840	484,520
2011	544	329	440	337,804	191,912	529,716
2016	543	341	445	360,611	213,519	574,130
2021	542	353	450	379,272	233,797	613,070
2026	541	361	453	393,709	249,686	643,395

Sources: NSSO, *Employment and Unemployment Survey*, various rounds, and the results of the population projections described in Chapter 5.

rate of the labour force shown in Table 8.1. The LFPR trends in Table 8.5 are for all ages combined and they mask different patterns in age-specific LFPRs. There has been a clear decline among the younger age group 10–29 (Planning Commission 2001b). Some experts on the subject are optimistic, stating that this reflects increasing school attendance rates (Chadha and Sahu 2002; Visaria 1999a). Chadha and Sahu point out that the most evident decline in the LFPR has been in Himachal Pradesh, where, as noted in Chapter 7, there has been substantial educational progress during the 1990s. Other experts tell a pessimistic story involving the withdrawal of people from the labour force in the face of unfulfilled employment aspirations (Ghose 1999; Kundu 2002). In this context, the long-term decline in the female LFPR and the 'masculinization' of the labour force that it implies has been a matter of concern. Given the LFPR trends, the absolute growth of the labour force to 1999–2000 has resulted solely from demographic change, specifically the increase in the population of working age.

We project the male LFPR to 2026 by extrapolating the trend since 1972–3 forwards. As Table 8.5 shows, this results in a marginally declining rate. There are many scholars who argue that the future size of the labour force will depend primarily on what happens to the female LFPR. Many believe its decline will be reversed in the future as fertility continues to fall and more women become freer to seek and engage in economic activities (Bhat 2001c; Dyson 2002b). There are other reasons why participation of females in the labour force may rise in the future. These include better access to employment via increased schooling opportunities for females, rising opportunities for employment in sectors such as manufacturing, services, health, and education and increasing social acceptance of women's work, fostered by globalization and mass media exposure. It is difficult to project accurately the extent of a reversal in the direction of the female LFPR trend. But to proceed with our calculations, we need to get an idea of future rates. To do this, we use the inverse relationship between the female LFPR and fertility which already exists across India's main states.[11] We assume that this relationship remains constant to 2026 and combine it with the state-level total fertility rate projections from Chapter 5 to produce estimates of state-level female LFPRs. We multiply these rates by the female population projections from Chapter 5 to estimate the absolute size of the female labour forces in the states. We then sum the state-level labour forces and populations and divide the former by the latter to obtain estimates of the female LFPR for India.[12]

[11]We observe this inverse relationship between the NSS's state-level female LFPR data for 1999–2000 and the state-level total fertility rate data for 2001.

[12]The all-India labour forces are estimated by applying the LFPR described earlier to Dyson's population projections for all-India presented in Chapter 5. We acknowledge that this method has limitations. For example, the inverse relationship between state-level fertility and female LFPR may not necessarily reflect a causal relationship from the former to the latter. Instead,

Table 8.5 shows that the method produces an increasing female LFPR trend which reaches 361 per 1000 in 2026, closing the gap with the male rates. The resulting growth in the total labour force implies that between 2001 and 2026 there will be an average annual addition of approximately 8 million people to it.[13] To avoid increasing unemployment, this growth necessitates the generation of the same number of jobs, to say nothing of what is required to take care of the existing backlog of unemployment and underemployment. For comparison, we also project the labour force by holding the female LFPR at 287 per 1000—the average level across the six NSS surveys from 1972–3 to 1999–2000—and by extrapolating the declining trend in participation rates across the surveys to 2026. These comparative scenarios are shown in Table 8.6. Both the future size and the growth rate of the labour force vary significantly depending on our assumptions about female participation.

Economic growth and employment to 2026: To project employment, we focus on its macroeconomic relationship with economic growth. We then undertake a straightforward comparison of the number of jobs relative to the size of the labour force. In other words, we project the demand for labour independently of its supply, and do not take account of the likely labour market adjustment mechanisms that operate in response to their interplay. In our approach, a growing shortfall of jobs relative to the labour force is depicted by an increase in the (UPSS) unemployment rate, whereas in the real world it may well be underemployment which increases as surplus labour is absorbed into residual sectors. Conversely, we illustrate a tightening of the labour market by a fall in unemployment, whereas what may actually happen would be an increase in real wages and shifts to labour-saving technologies. As a result of our method, we are interested less in the actual rates of future unemployment and more in how they compare with the 1999–2000 rate.[14]

We combine our labour force projections with an assumed 'business as usual' annual economic growth rate of 6.5 per cent to 2026, that is, we extrapolate the economic growth experience of the 1990s into the future.[15] To

---

some third external factor, such as women's status, could be influencing both variables. However, despite such limitations, the resulting female LFPR projections seem reasonable.

[13] The average annual additions to the labour force will decline over time. Between 2001 and 2006, an average of approximately 9 million people will join the labour force each year but between 2021 and 2026, annual additions fall to approximately 6 million. These labour force projections are higher than those made by the Planning Commission's Task Force for 2007 and 2012 (Planning Commission 2001b). Using an assumed annual rate of labour force growth of 1.8 per cent, its estimate for 2007 is 462 million and for 2012 it is 505 million. Our estimates for these years are 494 million and 539 million. The differences arise because our rate of labour force growth is slightly higher than that of the Task Force due to our treatment of female participation.

[14] In the same sense, it does not really matter that our projections are based on the UPSS measure of unemployment rather than the more comprehensive CDS measure.

[15] Within this aggregate rate of 6.5 per cent, we use the Planning Commission's (2001b) sectoral growth rates.

TABLE 8.6: *Alternative labour force participation rates (LFPR) and labour force sizes, projected to 2026*

	LFPR (all ages, per 1000)				Labour force (000s)			
	Females		Persons		Females		Persons	
	constant from 1999–2000 to 2026	extrapolating past trend to 2026	with female LFPR constant from 1999–2000 to 2026	with female LFPR extrapolating past trend to 2026	with female LFPR constant from 1999–2000 to 2026	with female LFPR extrapolating past trend to 2026	with female LFPR constant from 1999–2000 to 2026	with female LFPR extrapolating past trend to 2026
1972–3	286	286	420	420	78,899	78,899	240,560	240,560
1977–8	310	310	440	440	95,483	95,483	280,332	280,332
1983	291	291	423	423	104,364	104,364	310,974	310,974
1987–8	290	290	422	422	110,427	110,427	334,067	334,067
1993–4	287	287	427	427	124,066	124,066	382,843	382,843
1999–2000	258	258	404	404	125,404	125,404	406,777	406,777
2006	287	263	420	409	154,673	141,931	468,352	455,610
2011	287	258	419	406	167,413	150,295	505,217	488,099
2016	287	252	419	403	179,706	157,761	540,318	518,372
2021	287	246	418	399	190,084	163,095	569,357	542,367
2026	287	241	417	396	198,504	166,375	592,213	560,083

Sources: NSSO, *Employment and Unemployment Survey*, various rounds, and the results of the population projections described in Chapter 5.

estimate the employment generated from this rate of economic growth, we use the sectoral (UPSS) employment elasticities calculated for 1977–8 to 1983, 1983 to 1993–4, 1993–4 to 1999–2000, and 2002 to 2012 by the Planning Commission's Task Force (Planning Commission 2001b). The elasticity of employment indicates the percentage growth in employment (or sectoral employment) associated with a 1 per cent growth in GDP (or sectoral GDP). An employment elasticity of zero indicates that output can be expanded with no employment generation.

In India, most sectoral elasticities have declined over time. These declines may reflect productivity improvements, but very low elasticities may also imply underemployment. The elasticity declines have been especially sharp in the 1990s and reflect the coexistence of the deceleration in employment growth shown in Table 8.1 with accelerating GDP growth. As noted earlier, there has been a lack of recent employment growth in agriculture and the Task Force estimates that the elasticity for this sector during 1993–4 to 1999–2000 was zero. The Task Force's projected employment elasticities for 2002–12 incorporate its assumptions about future productivity changes and the

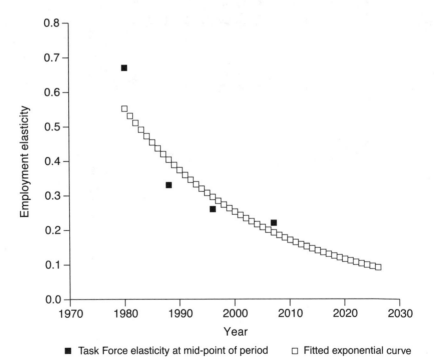

FIGURE 8.1: *Estimated employment elasticities for the manufacturing sector*

Source: Task Force elasticities are from Planning Commission (2001b).

relationship between technological change and labour use.[16] For several sectors we continue the declining trends in employment elasticities to 2026. In other words, we assume that their secular downward trends continue in the future, and do not account for potential sectoral policies which may increase them. For manufacturing, construction, trade, transport and storage, and services we fit exponential trends to the Task Force's data and use the fitted values as our annual elasticity estimates from 2001 onwards. To illustrate, our method is shown for manufacturing in Figure 8.1.

For mining and quarrying, and electricity, gas, and water we continue the Task Force's projected elasticities of zero to 2026. For agriculture, the Task Force projects a small positive elasticity of 0.1 to reflect a future structural shift towards more labour-intensive non-cereal agriculture. We continue this value to 2026.[17] For each sector we obtain the number of workers and calculate the overall (UPSS) unemployment rate relative to our projected labour forces. Figure 8.2 shows the unemployment profiles under the different labour force sizes. Table 8.7 summarizes the future employment scenarios.

Figure 8.2 indicates that the range and pattern of unemployment is considerable under the different labour force size assumptions, indicating that what happens to women's participation in the labour force will have a crucial bearing on the level of unemployment in the future. However, the main story which emerges from our projections is that with a continuation of the economic growth rate of the 1990s and an extrapolation of long-term trends in employment elasticities, a significant worsening of India's employment situation seems inevitable.[18] Although the unemployment rates peak before 2026 for all three projected labour forces, it is only with the unlikely assumption of declining female LFPR that unemployment is lower in 2026 than in 1999–2000.[19] Even with the assumption of an annual economic growth rate of 8

[16]These assumptions are not repeated here. They can be found in Planning Commission (2001b).

[17]There is some debate about the future capacity of agriculture to absorb labour. Some experts suggest that the employment elasticity may be higher than that assumed here. See Asthana (2002) and Planning Commission (2002b). However, like the Task Force, others believe that agriculture's future employment elasticity will remain relatively low because of considerable underemployment in the sector (Chadha and Sahu 2002).

[18]This conclusion is consistent with those of the Planning Commission's Task Force and Special Group, who both project employment and unemployment to 2012, the latter on CDS basis (Planning Commission 2001b, 2002b).

[19]The unemployment rate projections estimated by the Planning Commission's Task Force assume an annual economic growth rate of 6.5 per cent and constant employment elasticities for the period 2002–12. For 2012, the unemployment rates range from 4.0 per cent to 7.4 per cent, the range being due to different labour force growth rate assumptions (Planning Commission 2001b). Our unemployment rate estimates for 2012 range from 5.2 per cent (declining female LFPR), 8.5 per cent (constant female LFPR), and 13.0 per cent (increasing female LFPR).

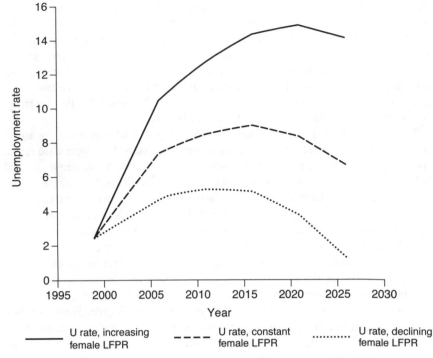

FIGURE 8.2: *Future unemployment rate scenarios for different female LFPR assumptions*

Note: The NSS female LFPR for 1999–2000 is unusually low (see Table 8.5). This means that our estimate for 2001 seems too high (although it is in line with the NSS rates for survey years prior to 1999–2000). The LFPR discontinuity between 1999–2000 and 2001 means that there is a corresponding jump in the unemployment rate between 1999–2000 and 2001. For ease of presentation, we therefore show the unemployment trend between 1999–2000 and 2006 as a linear increase.

Source: Own calculations (see text).

TABLE 8.7: *Summary of future employment scenarios*

	Unemployment rate in 2026	Peak year of unemployment	Unemployment rate in peak year
Increasing female LFPR after 1999–2000	14.05	2021	14.82
Constant female LFPR after 1999–2000	6.63	2016	8.93
Declining female LFPR after 1999–2000	1.27	2011	5.21

per cent to 2026, our calculations show that unemployment in 2026 is still higher than in 1999–2000 under the assumption of increasing female LFPR. With a constant female LFPR, it is higher than the 1999–2000 rate until 2022 and with declining female LFPR, it is higher until 2012. These results indicate that although it makes a key difference, economic growth by itself is not the answer to India's future employment situation. With a more realistic annual economic growth rate of 5 per cent (see our medium-term economic growth forecasts in Chapter 10), the 2026 unemployment rate is higher than that in 1999–2000 for all three labour force sizes, and is still rising in 2026 with the assumption of increasing female LFPR. These scenarios imply that future levels of underemployment are also likely to increase, with adverse implications for employment quality. They also suggest that under the assumptions we have made, the backlog of existing unemployment will not be touched. Our projections, therefore, have an important policy implication: to minimize any worsening of the employment situation in the future, policy must ensure that the economic climate becomes more employment friendly. Both our projections and the recent trends in India's employment situation suggest directions in which such a strategy should focus. As well as fostering rapid economic growth, these include identifying and encouraging strategic labour-intensive areas, improving employment quality in the unorganized sector, amending labour laws to stimulate employment expansion in the organized private sector, and developing labour force skills. These policies are discussed in Chapter 16.

CONCLUSIONS

Providing quality employment for India's growing labour force will continue to be testing. The future will present some new challenges: the working-age population will reach its peak growth rate during 2001–6 and the participation of women in the labour force will probably rise, both trends increasing the number of job-seekers. At the same time, the ability of agriculture, India's largest single employer, to increase its labour absorptive capacity significantly and productively is a matter of debate and the government's direct role as an employment provider will diminish further as public sector downsizing continues. So, in a context of growing international and domestic competition, an increasingly disproportionate share of future employment will be found in labour-intensive activities in the unorganized sector. Policy must address these issues to ensure that rather than wasting its human potential, India capitalizes on the enormous comparative advantage that its labour force potentially represents.

9

The Condition of the People

ROBERT CASSEN AND KIRSTY MCNAY

This chapter assesses the effects India's development has had and will have on the quality of life of its people. Naturally there is some concentration on the way population growth has influenced these aspects of development; but it can be said at the outset that while population has been a factor in the unsatisfactory progress India has experienced in human welfare, it is only one among many, and not by any means a dominant one.

One of the most pervasive findings of all our research is the large and in some cases growing inequalities in India, in several dimensions, and the threat that these will worsen. If one looks across India's main states, one sees significant and sometimes widening discrepancies in income poverty and other social indicators, in demographic characteristics, and in economic growth. These discrepancies are reinforced by the situation of population groups: there is clear discrimination by gender, by caste and tribe, and by other groupings. Discrimination is often worse in the economically worst performing geographical areas. There is a clear danger of India's continuing to show a pattern of divergent development, with parts of the country making progress on many fronts, and other parts stagnating. There are five large states—Bihar, Madhya Pradesh, Orissa, Rajasthan and Uttar Pradesh—with more than their fair share of poverty, together with poor health and nutrition and a low level of education, and where the disadvantaged suffer severe discrimination. These states also mostly have slower economic growth, and faster population growth, than the Indian average. It is true, though, that there are large pockets in other states where conditions are equally bad just as there are parts of these poor states where there is positive progress. And there are many dimensions of inequality: big gaps between standards are common, between rural and urban, between rich and poor, between males and females, between Scheduled Castes (SCs) and Scheduled Tribes (STs), and others.

Significant differentials are also found between Hindus and Muslims. Typically Muslims have lower educational levels than Hindus (excluding Scheduled Castes), though the gaps have mostly been narrowing in recent years. They are small in southern and western states, wider in the north and east. Muslims also have lower income and asset levels: the mean for their incomes was about three-quarters of that for non-SC Hindus, and their land ownership was not much more than half that of non-SC Hindus (Kulkarni 2000; the data are for 1994). The economic differences, though, are described as only 'moderate' in Bihar, Himachal Pradesh and Uttar Pradesh and 'moderately high' in other states. Gujarat and Punjab, however, show 'very high disparity, with means for Muslims generally below half the means for [non-SC] Hindus' (Kulkarni 2000: 26).

THE PERSISTENCE OF POVERTY

There is much evidence that historical inequalities persist geographically and within social groups, in part because of people's passing on advantages, not least the ability to acquire human capital (Benabou 1994; Eswaran and Kotwal 1994). Many of the characteristics which render people liable to discrimination in India are theirs at birth. Much of the analysis of earlier chapters indicates the nature of these inequalities. Fertility decline has been found to be related to improvements in infant and child mortality, in education, especially female education, and to the spread of family planning and reproductive health services. All these factors have been relatively weak in the poorer states. While some progress has been made, it has been much slower in these states than elsewhere in India. Similarly with education and health, whose spread has been found to be related to a number of factors that are in short supply in the poorer states. The same is true of poverty. All these features of the backward states are inter-related, contributing to each other.

Poverty in contemporary discussion has acquired broader dimensions than just shortage of income. It refers to people's capacities to function as full members of society: they may not have adequate incomes, but the quality of their lives also depends on whether they enjoy access to important public goods, whether they are educated, healthy, free of insecurities to life and property, and possess various basic rights and freedoms (Sen 1985). While people's incomes are strongly connected to many of these other capabilities, the level of income cannot be taken as a proxy for them. The great bulk of discussions and measurements of poverty in India, though, are about income poverty, and that is where we begin.

TABLE 9.1: *Selected state indicators*

| | Literacy 2001 | SDP per capita 1997–8 | SDP 1992–3 to 1999–2000 | | Poverty 1999–2000 | Pop. growth 1991–2001 | Share of total pop. 2001 |
| | | | Growth rate | Per capita growth | | | |
	% of pop.	Rs per year	% per year	% per year	(per cent)	% per year	(per cent)
Bihar*	**47.5**	**4,654**	**4.22**	**1.79**	**46.9**	**2.43**	**10.7**
Madhya Pradesh*	**64.1**	**8,114**	**5.15**	**3.08**	**36.8**	**2.07**	**7.9**
Orissa	**63.6**	**6,767**	**3.5**	**1.51**	**46.3**	**1.49**	**3.6**
Rajasthan	**61.0**	**9,356**	**6.7**	**4.17**	**20.4**	**2.53**	**5.5**
Uttar Pradesh*	**57.4**	**7,263**	**5.2**	**2.91**	**33.0**	**2.29**	**17.0**
Andhra Pradesh	61.1	10,590	5.56	4.35	18.8	1.21	–
Gujarat	70.0	16,251	6.29	4.24	15.4	2.05	–
Haryana	68.6	17,626	5.46	2.06	11.8	2.50	–
Himachal Pradesh	77.1	10,777	6.28	4.65	17.5	1.63	–
Karnataka	67.0	11,693	7.25	5.65	25.6	1.60	–
Kerala	90.9	11,936	5.38	4.37	14.5	1.01	–
Maharashtra	77.3	18,365	5.78	3.72	33.67	2.06	–
Punjab	69.9	19,500	4.26	2.44	11.80	1.82	–
Tamil Nadu	73.5	12,989	6.83	5.76	20.10	1.07	–
West Bengal	69.2	10,636	7.36	5.7	32.10	1.66	–
India	65.38	**10,508	**5.73	**3.8	28.64	1.93	100

Notes: *Adjusted to correspond to pre-2001 boundaries. States listed alphabetically with five poorest shown separately.
** Population weighted.

Sources: Literacy figures from Census 2001. Population figures from Census 2001. State Domestic Product (SDP) figures from Planning Commission data. Poverty figures from Deaton (2001).

HISTORICAL TRENDS IN INCOME POVERTY, AND DATA PROBLEMS

Measured by income alone, India has the largest number of poor people of any country in the world. It also has a longer history of concern for the poor in public action, and more voluminous studies of poverty, than can be found in most developing countries.

The most common index of poverty is the headcount ratio, the proportion of people with incomes too low to afford the minimum necessities of life. The 1950s are the first period for which we have data on poverty consistent with the recent period.[1] During 1950–5, the headcount ratio averaged over 50 per cent, a situation which continued (with fluctuations below 45 per cent and above 60 per cent) till the early 1970s. It is from this time that a systematic decline in the headcount index began, lasting until the mid-1980s, after which further fluctuations can be observed, around a modestly declining trend. While the percentage of the poor has fallen, the numbers in poverty have risen with the increase in population: around 300 million today, compared with some 200 million in the early 1950s.

There have been increasing debates about the recent findings of the NSS. One of the problems is that they give a level of aggregate consumption below what is shown in national accounts. However, the national accounts cover some different categories of consumption, and there are doubts about their estimates too.[2] There is another data set that is collected by the NCAER. It covers a larger sample of people than the NSS, and also goes back several decades. It does not, however, cover the same items as the NSS, being designed for different purposes. Calculations based on its data have been made, attempting to derive from it a poverty measure similar to that of the NSS, and showing declines in poverty (Lal et al. 2001). The main deficiency of this source, however, is that it asks respondents to remember their income, a notoriously unreliable method.

There is a further source in the NSS itself: its employment rounds give data on period of employment and real wages. These too show declines in poverty, but again questions of comparability arise. One cannot make sense of the detailed results without further enquiry, and we return to them next. Table 9.2 gives the historical trend in the headcount ratio, but the uncertainties in the figures should be borne in mind.

---

[1]India's headcount index is based on a nutritional norm; the data are derived from the NSS of household expenditure. Someone is 'poor' if their expenditure is insufficient to cover this dietary 'minimum', which is set at a low level, plus some allowance for non-nutritional needs. Adjustments are made for price variations between India's states.

[2]While other scholars have claimed that these discrepancies cast serious doubt on the NSS data, Deaton and Drèze (2002) state firmly that too much should not be made of them.

TABLE 9.2: *Decline in poverty rates over time, by state*

	Poverty rates				Annual rate of decline in poverty		
	1973–4	1983–4	1993–4	1999–2000	1973–83	1983–93	1993–9
Andhra Pradesh	48.9	28.9	22.2	18.8	5.1	2.6	2.7
Assam	51.2	40.5	40.9	39.6	2.3	−0.1	0.5
Bihar	61.9	62.2	55.0	46.9	0.0	1.2	2.6
Gujarat	48.2	32.8	24.2	15.4	3.8	3.0	7.3
Haryana	35.4	21.4	25.1	11.8	4.9	−1.6	11.8
Himachal Pradesh	26.4	16.4	28.4	17.5	4.6	−5.6	7.8
Karnataka	54.5	38.2	33.2	25.6	3.5	1.4	4.2
Kerala	59.8	40.2	25.4	14.5	3.9	4.5	8.9
Madhya Pradesh	61.8	49.8	42.5	36.8	2.1	1.6	2.4
Maharashtra	53.2	43.4	36.6	28.7	2.0	1.7	4.0
Orissa	66.2	65.3	48.6	46.3	0.1	2.9	0.8
Punjab	28.2	16.2	11.8	11.8	5.4	3.1	10.7
Rajasthan	46.1	34.5	27.4	20.4	2.9	2.3	4.8
Tamil Nadu	54.9	51.7	35.0	20.1	0.6	3.8	8.8
Uttar Pradesh	57.1	47.1	40.9	33.0	1.9	1.4	3.5
West Bengal	63.4	54.9	35.7	32.1	1.4	4.2	1.8
All-India	54.9	44.5	36.0	28.6	2.1	2.1	3.8

Sources: Figures for 1973–4 to 1993–4 from Annexure Table 1.2., 9th Five–Year Plan (Vol. 1),
(Planning Commission, 1997); Tables 2.19 and 2.21, Planning Commission (2002a).
Figures for 1999–2000 are from Deaton (2001), and growth-rate calculation in the last
column use both sources.

ACCOUNTING FOR PAST TRENDS IN INCOME POVERTY

The most widely accepted account of year-to-year changes in income poverty
incidence up to the 1970s was their relationship with the annual harvest
(Ahluwalia 1978). This is hardly surprising. Even today the great majority of
the poor arc rural. The size of the harvest is a major factor in employment and
earnings for small landholders and agricultural labourers, and also for off-
farm rural employment. The harvest also affects the price of food grains, which
is a major factor in poverty-related price indices: most of the poor are net
buyers of grain.

There is also a reasonable consensus about the declines in poverty incidence
from the 1970s to the mid-1980s: they relate quite clearly to economic growth.
Sectoral evidence confirms this, but also makes it clear that it was the primary
and tertiary sectors that were responsible. India's manufacturing development
under its pre-reform strategy of import-substituting industrialization not only

did little for economic growth; it also did little for poverty. The linkages within the economy have remained basically rural to urban. Good harvests do not now generate much additional employment directly. The employment elasticity of agricultural output is quite low in agriculture itself. But they are still a considerable factor in off-farm employment and in urban sector growth: 'from the point of view of India's poor—it is the dog (the rural economy) that wags the tail (the urban sector), not the other way around' (Ravallion and Datt 1996: 19). Real rural wages rose during this period in virtually all states, despite the continuing increases in the labour force (Repetto 1994). This reflects in particular a rise in rural non-farm employment.

A variety of other evidence bears out this general story. There was a considerable variety of performance in poverty reduction across the states of India, but it was fastest where the rural sector grew most. Progress in human development in some cases—Kerala is the most notable—was able to substitute for economic growth in other forms, though poverty would have diminished faster if agricultural productivity had risen faster as well. As the World Bank (1997a) observes, none of the states strongly pursued both of these key factors together.[3] The states where poverty reduction has been slowest, such as Bihar, are those where neither has advanced sufficiently. Agro-climatic features also play a significant part. Areas suffering from drought or other adverse agricultural conditions had the worst poverty and the least reduction in poverty.

Government action for agriculture and rural development has also made considerable inroads on poverty, though not mainly by its anti-poverty programmes, as we will discuss next. The government launched the Green Revolution, which was the key to much of the rural growth when poverty began to fall. Studies have shown strong links between poverty reduction in the period 1970–93 and expenditure on rural infrastructure, agricultural research and extension, education, and irrigation. This expenditure both raised agricultural productivity and benefited the poor; and when it lessened, poverty reduction slowed (Fan et al. 1999). Arguably, further reform to the agricultural sector could bring more benefits to the poor (World Bank 2000a).

Other explanations for poverty include ill health and lack of education (Desai 1995; Gaiha 1988). These are, of course, in many cases, consequences as well as causes of poverty, but neither are purely functions of income; they are also related to a number of other factors, not least the quality of public services, as Chapters 3 and 10 make clear.

Recent years have seen some narrowing of the gap between the urban and rural proportions in poverty; but the main structural factors in poverty are still in the conditions of rural life. The poor are the landless or those who

[3]See also Datt and Ravallion (1998), who further point out the significance of initial conditions in infrastructure and human development.

survive on marginal landholdings. Other structural factors are also important, however, though here too the associated conditions are usually more severe in rural areas. Being female, and belonging to other groups subject to discrimination, in particular, the SCs and STs, very commonly translates into acute poverty. Fifty-two per cent of the landless are poor, and 68 per cent of the landless are wage earners; half the 206 million population of SCs and STs are poor (NCAER 1996).[4] It is these structural reasons which make poverty so resistant to change; growth alone is not the answer.

Many of these features come together in Uttar Pradesh, which has the largest number of poor people amongst all Indian states. It is the most populous state, with a very high proportion of SCs and STs—24 per cent of the population, and one-third of the poor according to the NSS 55th Round (1999–2000). It has a weak record, as we note, on most indicators of female welfare, and the highest human fertility of all Indian states. It is growing slowly economically and fast demographically. It has very deficient public services in general, and publicly-provided education and health facilities are of particularly poor quality, so that measures of education and health status are among the worst in India. Above all it suffers from weak and deteriorating governance, which makes the rectification of policy defects difficult. The prospects for Uttar Pradesh are uncomfortable to contemplate. With a population possibly approaching 270 million by 2026 on our projections (including Uttaranchal), it faces a difficult future unless social conditions improve.[5]

POPULATION AND POVERTY

An interesting question is whether population itself is a factor in income or other aspects of poverty. Chapter 10 discusses the negative effect of population growth until recently on the growth of per capita income. Given that slower income growth is likely to mean slower reduction of poverty, there is a clear implication that population is a factor in poverty. Eastwood and Lipton (2001) were the first to find an association of population growth with poverty internationally, and ruled out the possibility that poverty was inducing high fertility rather than the other way round. The magnitude of the effect of high fertility on growth, and thence on poverty, was considerable; and there was an effect of similar magnitude operating via the effect of high fertility on distribution. 'The average (developing) country in 1980 had a poverty incidence

---

[4]There is some (modest) evidence that SCs have fared somewhat better than STs under the various programmes of positive discrimination initiated in recent years. This has been attributed to the fact that the former are socially and geographically less removed than the latter from mainstream society (Xaxa 2001). For other estimates of discrepancies among different population groups, see Kulkarni (2000).

[5]On all this see World Bank (2002).

of 18.9 per cent; had it reduced its fertility by 5 per 1000 throughout the 1980s (as did many Asian countries), this figure would have been reduced to 12.6 per cent' (Eastwood and Lipton 2001: 218). The authors point to additional effects which suggest that this finding may underestimate the true reduction of poverty.

There is an association between population growth and poverty across states in India too, found in three studies: it is not clear from the first of them which is cause and which is effect (Van de Walle 1985), but the second ruled out reverse causation, that is, running from poverty to population growth (Evenson 1993). The third found a negative correlation between population growth and the rate of poverty reduction, but the explanatory power of the population factor was not large (Chelliah and Sudarshan 1999). One would expect, given the importance of land as a productive asset, that demographic pressure on land, as well as its distribution, would be a significant factor in rural poverty; and one study has indeed shown that poverty incidence was lower where land per head was higher, after allowing for the productivity and distribution of the land; but it was made some time ago, and there seems to be little more recent research (Sundaram and Tendulkar 1988). Our own study of state-level economic growth found population to be a negative factor (see Chapter 10).

At a broader level, it seems clear that the growth of the labour force has been a factor exerting downward pressure on wages and living standards. As Chapter 8 has shown, although employment has kept up with population growth and real rural wages have risen, there has not been anything resembling adequate creation of secure and well-paid jobs. In general it seems clear that population growth has made poverty reduction more difficult in India's states, but only as one among several factors, and it is far from being the most important of them.

At the micro-level, the distribution effects of high fertility arise from two sources: a dependency effect, by which if extra births are concentrated in poorer households, the distribution of consumption is adversely affected through the 'dilution' of household income which occurs when there are more dependents per working family member. There is also what Eastwood and Lipton (2001) call an 'acquisition' effect, that is, where fertility affects the income of non-dependents, through their savings or earnings capacity. The acquisition effect could come from child costs, increased labour supply reducing wages, or other effects via savings or factor rewards—for all of which the authors find evidence.

There is a positive association between family size and poverty; this could be a result of mutual causation, since poor people in India commonly have higher fertility than the better off. But is high fertility also a cause of poverty at the household level? If there are scale economies of consumption in large households, they could outweigh the poverty effect, as some have claimed;

there are, though, doubts about the magnitude of any scale effect (Drèze and Srinivasan 1995).[6] There are quite a number of household studies, however, which show clearer findings—in particular, negative relations between the number of surviving siblings and children's health, nutrition, and education prospects, especially for female children: high fertility seems to have some adverse welfare effects at the household level (Lloyd 1993).[7] It does appear that fertility reduction can benefit the poor at the micro- as well as the macro-level.

ANTI-POVERTY PROGRAMMES

India has for a long time had several anti-poverty programmes. They account for sizeable expenditures nationally: they averaged a little under 6 per cent of Central Plan Budgetary Expenditures during 1990–1 to 1992–3, and close to 8 per cent from 1993–4 to 1995–6. State-level spending adds a further 20–25 per cent to the outlays (World Bank 1997a: 26). But their potential impact on poverty is limited in each case by a variety of defects. A large number of the poor are missed, and a large proportion of benefits under the programmes leak to the less poor.

A case in point is the Public Distribution System (PDS), intended to provide subsidized grain rations to the poor through ration cards. The cards, though, were not restricted to the poor; and the evidence suggests both that poor states and poor individuals made less use of the PDS than better-off states and individuals: 50–60 per cent of PDS beneficiaries were non-poor. Benefits were stronger in urban than rural areas; and the cost of transmitting a rupee's worth of subsidy income is more than four rupees. A large proportion of the foods allocated to the programme, 36 per cent of wheat, 31 per cent of rice, and 23 per cent of sugar, did not reach the beneficiaries. A large proportion of the allocation was not even taken up: the quota for the poor was doubled to 20 kg per household per month in April 2000, but 46 per cent of the allocated food grains, 2.2 million tonnes, were not taken up (Saxena 2000). The other main food subsidy is the school meals programme. This does reach quite a large number of poor and less poor children where the programme is properly implemented.

Another main type of programme is for employment generation through rural public works, social forestry projects, and similar measures. These include

---

[6]Anand and Morduch (1998) suggest that only small economies of scale could negate the size effect; but Eastwood and Lipton (2001) doubt that there are any for poor families, most of whose consumption expenditure is on food. It would be different if they spent major amounts on, say, consumer durables. They cite evidence from a variety of (non-Indian) sources strongly suggesting a lack of scale economies for poor families.

[7]Anand and Morduch (1998) also find, based on Bangladesh data, that females are the main sufferers from high fertility.

the Integrated Rural Development Programme (IRDP), the Drought Prone Areas Programme (DPAP), the Jawahar Rozgar Yojana (JRY), and the Employment Assurance Scheme (EAS). While both IRDP and DPAP have helped poor people in poor areas (the IRDP benefits 2.5 million households annually), they were both captured to a degree by locally powerful interests: vote-getting is all too often the determining factor in allocation of resources and identification of eligible areas and beneficiaries. The DPAP was by no means confined to the districts with the lowest rainfall; on the contrary, politics rather than actual thirst seems to have determined allocations (Sainath 1996). The IRDP was also found to suffer from a variety of defects, including defective targeting, allocation to the non-poor, 'indifferent' delivery of credit by banks, and even rising indebtedness among intended recipients (Saxena 2000). The JRY, the largest programme, is estimated to provide one billion paid employment days annually; but the beneficiaries are predominantly male, and 18 per cent of them are non-poor, in part because the contractors do not keep to the self-selecting low wage prescribed. The latter fault also afflicts the EAS. In general there is a large leakage from such programmes: 'Today Rs 60 out of Rs 100 in wage schemes is reserved for wages, but in reality only Rs 10 to 15 actually goes to the poor worker, the rest is illegal income for bureaucracy, contractors and politicians' (Saxena 2000: 3629).

In recent years there have been some reforms to anti-poverty programmes. The IRDP together with some small self-employment programmes was absorbed into the Swarnjayanti Gram Swarozgar Yojana (SGSY). The latter concentrates on lending to self-help groups, as opposed to individuals: given that group lending has a better record than individual lending, this may be a positive move. The PDS has also been reformed into the Targeted Public Distribution System (TPDS), and it appears to be having good results in ensuring a higher proportion of subsidized food reaching the poor (World Bank 2000a: 19).

Altogether anti-poverty programmes make some dent on acute poverty, but not at all efficiently in proportion to the resources expended (Harriss et al. 1992; World Bank 1997a).

OTHER DIMENSIONS OF POVERTY

Health, nutrition, and food security: Inequality of incomes is combined with inequality of access to public services, and severe inequalities of outcomes in health and nutrition. The poorest fifth of the population had 2.5 times the infant mortality of the richest fifth in 1992–3, and experienced nearly 75 per cent higher malnutrition (World Bank n.d.: 23). There are several other inequalities between the poorest and the richest fifth: under-five mortality is 2.8 times worse among the poorest than among the richest fifth; underweight children are 2.7 times more common; and children without immunization are six times more common. The total fertility of the poorest fifth was almost twice that of the richest fifth, and fertility of mothers aged between 15–19 years was three times higher, with implications for maternal mortality (World Bank n.d.). We cite these figures not simply to display the disparities, but to indicate the relatively good levels achievable in India by those with better incomes and better access to public services. Most of those in the top quintile, some 200 million people, are not wealthy by the standards of developed countries. The average woman born in Bihar can expect to live 15 fewer years than one born in Kerala (Table 5.4).

As noted in Chapter 3, maternal mortality is a particular scourge in India. At about 540 maternal deaths per 100,000 live births in the late 1990s, it is one of the highest rates in the world, on a par with some of the poorer African countries such as Tanzania or the Gambia, though better than the very poorest within South Asia, such as Bangladesh (IIPS and ORC Macro 1995; World Bank 1997b: Table 2.14). It is partly related to poor nutrition, and partly to unsatisfactory birth practices and lack of medical attendance at and before birth. The proportion of women having two or more antenatal care visits in the poorest fifth of the population (about one third) is far lower than among the richest fifth (over 90 per cent). Only 12 per cent of the poorest fifth have deliveries attended by a medically trained person, compared with nearly 80 per cent of the richest fifth (Harriss et al. 1992; World Bank 1997a).

Malnutrition is an exceptional problem in India. It has made less progress than most other features of well-being, and is far from fully explained by low incomes or even low intake of calories. In 1989 a survey by the Indian Council of Medical Research (ICMR) found that 87 per cent of all pregnant women tested were anaemic (ICMR 1989). NFHS data for 1992–3 found 53 per cent of children under four to be moderately or severely undernourished. These figures are much higher than the proportions of poor people in the population; it is clearly a problem not confined to the poor, even if it is far worse among the poor. Malnutrition in a child may start with a malnourished mother who is of small stature and has a low birth-weight baby (Haddad 2002). People may eat enough, but suffer from gastric disease, which depletes their nutritional levels; or they may follow deleterious eating habits. For example, it is commonly observed that many pregnant women 'eat down' out of concern about the size of their baby and possible complications in pregnancy. The concern may be well-founded up to a point, given the dangers of maternal mortality, but the cure is the wrong one. Properly supervised births can take care of babies of any normal size; malnutrition of the mother is in fact one of the causes of birth problems. And low birth-weight babies themselves have diminished life-chances. Another common problem is the feeding of babies with flour- or sugar-water as well as or instead of mother's milk, and late weaning onto other, more nutritious, foods. Thus while malnutrition is often a result of low caloric intake, it is also significantly affected by hygiene, water-quality, sanitation, and eating and child-feeding practices, and this will be true even among those whose incomes or food-intakes are otherwise adequate.

Of course, some progress has been made with nutrition. But the combined figure for severe and moderate malnutrition in children aged 1–5 was still 49 per cent in 1996, according to National Nutrition Monitoring Board data, even if it was down from 63 per cent in 1975 (Measham and Chatterjee 1999: 10). Again, there are discrepancies by income: children aged 0–4 with low height for age were 55.6 per cent of the poorest fifth, as against 30.9 per cent among the richest fifth; those severely underweight were 29 per cent among the poorest fifth, 10.8 per cent among the richest fifth (Harriss et al. 1992; World Bank 1997a). The fact that these figures are still quite high among better-off people shows once more that this is not just an income issue.

Education: Despite considerable progress in the 1990s, the dismal record of basic education in India remains, especially in the poorest states and among disadvantaged groups. The gains in Bihar still left 66 per cent of women illiterate in 2001. Chapter 7 has pointed out the many dimensions of educational deprivation and its consequences. Education is among the most important of capabilities, for its own sake and for all the advantages it brings, everywhere from health to social and political participation. This is not just what social scientists think; it is what the deprived in India feel themselves: education is 'widely perceived by members of socially or economically disadvantaged groups as the most promising means of upward mobility for their children' (Drèze and Sen 2002: 143; and see other references they cite). Lack of education makes considerable contributions to monetary poverty. It deprives people of the ability to acquire skills and better jobs; it contributes to ill-health and, therefore, to diminished productivity.

The environment as a factor in poverty: Poverty is sometimes responsible for environmental degradation; less commonly noted is the impact that environmental degradation has on the poor. Some of the worst effects of environmental degradation are in India's cities, where just in the last two decades, air and water pollution has reached dangerous levels. Delhi, until recently, had the third worst air-pollution measures among the world's cities, with very high levels of suspended particulate matter (SPM), contributing to high levels of respiratory disease, now one of India's largest sources of morbidity and mortality. Domestic cooking technology and fuel also plays a major part in respiratory disease, both urban and rural. This has a gender dimension: respiratory diseases (other than tuberculosis) are among the biggest sources of mortality and morbidity in India, and the figures show they are more prevalent among women than men. While a considerable fraction of it is due to tobacco, women smoke relatively less, and so a major share of their respiratory illnesses must come from domestic air pollution (see Chapters 3 and 13).

Water supplies in India's cities are also heavily polluted. Apart from high levels of industrial waste, the river Jamuna has a count of 7500 coliform bacteria per decilitre as it enters Delhi and 350,000 per decilitre as it leaves. Skin diseases and gastric disorders are the common result of biological pollution. Better-off people are relatively protected from these conditions; they may have air-conditioned homes or at least cook with less noxious fuel, and they enjoy better sanitation and cleaner water. Evidence suggests some 21 per cent of communicable diseases, or 11.5 per cent of all disease, come from unsafe water (World Bank 1993a). And excess deaths from air pollution (indoor and outdoor) have been assessed at 800,000 a year, or about one-eighth of all deaths (Smith 2000).

Another major impact on the poor comes from the diminution of forest and other natural resources. The poor derive as much as 25 per cent of their livelihoods from environmental sources and these resources have declined by as much as a third on a per capita basis in the last twenty years. (This is only partly due to the increase in population numbers, but, importantly, also due to development and, not infrequently, to unscrupulous selling-off of protected or public lands (Repetto 1994; also Chapter 15.))

WELL-BEING IN THE 1990s

Income poverty: It is unfortunate that the most recent full data-round of the NSS for the years 1999–2000 gave an unclear result. The survey had been eagerly awaited, as there was so much controversy about the social impact of the economic reforms. But its results were compromised by a methodological flaw, to do with the period of recall for food-expenditure data. Poverty was now officially estimated at 26.1 per cent, the figure cited in the 2001 Government of India *Economic Survey*. The figure could possibly be correct. But we do not know that it is.[8]

In 2001, Angus Deaton re-worked the NSS 55th Round data to produce a revised poverty estimate comparable to the 1993–4 estimate. His adjusted figures for the headcount ratios came to 30.2 (rural) and 24.7 (urban); for India as a whole this comes to 28.8 per cent compared with the 'official' figure of 26.1 per cent. In his words: 'Instead of there being a drop in rural poverty since 1993–4 of 10.2 percentage points, the adjusted figures show a reduction of only 7.0 percentage points, so that a little more than two-thirds of the official reduction appears to be real'. Similarly Deaton (2001) estimates for urban poverty that '7.9 percentage points of the official reduction of 9.1 percentage points is real'. As he notes, the revised estimates raise some questions, since in individual states the changes from the official estimates are not all in the

---

[8]For discussions on the data issues, see Sen (2000), Deaton (2001), Deaton and Drèze (2002), and Cassen (2002).

same direction, though they are all fairly small; and there are assumptions in his method which are open to discussion. Still, the results may be taken to lend credibility to the belief that there has probably been a reduction in income poverty in the latter half of the1990s even on the basis of the NSS data. We have adopted these figures in this chapter.[9]

An entirely different approach was taken by Datt and Ravallion (2002). They modelled the economy at the state level, examining factors most strongly related to poverty reduction. 'Higher farm yields and higher development spending reduce the incidence of poverty .... Higher non-farm output per person lowers poverty in all states. Inflation is poverty-increasing' (Datt and Ravallion 2002). But the most interesting finding was how much the elasticity of poverty reduction to non-farm output varied among states, that is, the extent of the impact of non-farm output on poverty. The impact was greatest in Kerala, lowest in Bihar. Neither farm nor non-farm output grew fastest where it would have had the greatest impact on poverty, that is in the high poverty states. Thus one can explain the seemingly modest impact on poverty of India's high national growth in the 1990s: it to some extent bypassed the poorest states; and the growth those states did achieve produced less poverty reduction than it did elsewhere. Nevertheless their model implies a reduction of poverty from the 39.1 per cent in 1993–4 to 34.3 per cent in 1999–2000. This is still a rate of poverty reduction similar to that of the 1980s; and it is in the middle of the range of rates found by other estimates. We can only conclude that it is highly likely that income poverty did continue to fall in the 1990s, and at rates similar to those in the past: indeed, in Datt and Ravallion's 2002 study, the rate of descent seems relatively unchanged since the 1970s. But exactly where it now is we do not know. Somewhere in the region of 30 per cent seems plausible.

Whatever the pace of income poverty decline in the 1990s, the decade seems to have witnessed increases in inequality of incomes. As well as divergent growth between states—on which we have more to say in Chapter 10—with the poorer states growing more slowly than the better-off, Deaton and Drèze (2002) note increasing inequality within states. They observe that this is one of the reasons for the fact that growth has produced less poverty reduction than expected. There have also been widening rural–urban disparities, and an increase in inequality of consumer expenditure among the urban population. As they note, these increasing inequalities are significant in magnitude, all the more so as they follow a period of relative stability in measures of inequality.

[9]Deaton and Drèze (2002) recast the whole NSS data series for the quinquennial rounds from 1987–8, going back to the original quantities of goods purchased as recorded by the NSS, and adjusted price indices. These adjustments give a national headcount ratio for all-India in 1999–2000 of 22.1 per cent, but the previous years' figures are also adjusted downwards. We do not use these figures as they are not comparable with the longer series of the NSS going back to the 1970s.

As we discuss next, the relations between the NSS data and the true state of poverty seem more and more uncertain. There was virtually no growth in real consumption in the 1990s as measured by the NSS, during a period of rapid national growth. It could be that growth was so unequal that all of it accrued to the upper income brackets; but at least one study has shown this is improbable: it imputes only 25 per cent of consumption growth apparent from other evidence to the growth of income in upper income-brackets (Banerji 2002). Nevertheless, the top income percentiles have enjoyed income increases vastly in excess of those of the lower income groups, and have captured a very sizeable share of the growth in personal incomes. And the reductions in poverty do not reflect major improvements in consumption, since in many cases they are the result of movements from just below to just above the poverty line.

Employment and wages: Recent employment rounds of the NSS give data on period of employment and real wages. While employment may have fallen in the 1990s, the 55th Round (1999–2000) notes that wages have risen more, indicating a rise in incomes. These data permit an estimate of poverty: the net result from this source is that the proportion of the population below the poverty line declined by 2.5 percentage points between 1993–4 and 1999–2000. Rural poverty declined in eight major states: Andhra Pradesh, Bihar, Gujarat, Haryana, Kerala, Punjab, Rajasthan, and Uttar Pradesh. In others it rose or was unchanged. For all-India the decline was three percentage points; the list for urban poverty is different. Half the states that had declines in rural poverty also showed declines in urban poverty; Bihar, Haryana, Kerala, and Uttar Pradesh did not. And some states where rural poverty did not decline showed falls in urban poverty: Karnataka, Madhya Pradesh, Maharashtra, Orissa, and Tamil Nadu. For all-India urban poverty only declined by 1.6 percentage points (Sundaram 2001a, 2001b).[10]

An additional data source, *Agricultural Wages in India*, published by the Ministry of Agriculture, lends credence to these figures. They show agricultural wages growing at 2.5 per cent in the 1990s, slower than the 5.5 per cent recorded for the 1980s, but consistent with poverty decline in the 1990s of the magnitude suggested by Deaton (2001).[11]

Infant and child mortality: Other indicators shed light on the trends of the 1990s. That of infant mortality might be the first to be considered. It has declined in the 1990s, but according to SRS data, slower than in the 1980s. Does this bear on the debate about trends in monetary poverty in the 1990s? The answer seems to be: probably not. According to SRS data, the IMR was at 110 in 1981 and had come down to 80 by 1990 and 1991, but only declined a further

[10]Others have disputed these results, but they seem consistent with related evidence.
[11]More detail is given in Deaton and Drèze (2002).

10 points, to 70, by 1999 (Registrar General, India 1999a, b). However, this does not really support any particular view of the trend in income poverty.

As noted in Chapter 3, some doubts attach to the SRS data. NFHS data give a somewhat different view: slightly larger declines in a shorter period, and starting from a higher level: male infant mortality fell from 88.6 in NFHS-1 (1992–3) to 74.8 in NFHS-2 (1998–9), and female from 83.9 to 71.1. This is a decline of approximately 13 points in six years, equal to a decline of more than 20 points in 10 years. That would suggest little falling off in performance. In any case it is accepted by demographers that the IMR can be resistant to major improvements in socio-economic conditions. A relevant study is Woods (2000),[12] who showed that the IMR in nineteenth century England and Wales remained high for a considerable period despite prolonged improvements in living conditions and mortality declines among other age groups. So the behaviour of India's IMR is not evidence one way or another about income poverty: the slowdown, if such it is, does not mean poverty has failed to fall, and the decline of the IMR in the 1990s—albeit apparently relatively modest—does not imply that poverty has fallen.

Something similar is true of child mortality. The SRS figures show a much greater decline in the 1980s than in the 1990s (Table 9.3). But perhaps some of the same factors are at work. Again NFHS data show a somewhat different picture: male child mortality fell from 29.4 in NFHS-1 to 24.9 in NFHS-2, and female from 42.0 to 36.7, that is, as with infant mortality, a higher initial level than the SRS data show, and a slightly greater rate of decline over six years. This is not a full decade of data for the 1990s; and the lower the level of mortality, the slower, eventually, must be its further decline. Still, there is perhaps something to be explained. Part of the explanation may lie in HIV/ AIDS, the first case of which was only discovered in India in 1986. (It is not clear, however, whether this could be a major factor: the standard calculation is that HIV-positive mothers pass the infection to their children in one-third of cases, and half of these children will die before age five, that is one-sixth of children born to HIV-positive mothers will add to child mortality. If the official estimate of about 3 million adults with HIV in 1998 is correct (Table 5.4), AIDS has not yet added greatly to infant and child mortality.) Another

TABLE 9.3: *Mortality age 0–4*

	Rural	Urban	All-India
1981	45.5	20.4	41.2
1991	29.1	16.0	26.5
1997	25.6	13.1	23.1

Note: The figures refer to annual deaths per 1000 children aged 0–4.
Source: Registrar General, India (1999a).

[12]See also Woods (1988).

part of the explanation may lie in environmentally-caused illness; environmental degradation has been seriously worsening in recent times.

Health: More broadly there has been little change in the rate of rise of overall life expectancy during the past decade, on an all-India basis. The data, such as they are, show shifts in the pattern of cause of death, but, again, nothing—when all factors are taken into account—implying a slowdown in poverty reduction in the 1990s. And there have been some major improvements, such as the large drop in leprosy cases.

Fertility: Fertility has continued to decline in the 1990s, at a rate somewhat faster than in the past: according to SRS data, the TFR fell from 4.5 in the early 1980s to 3.3 in 1996–7. From 1970 to 1980 the fall had been only from 5.0 to 4.5. (If the NFHS is to be believed, the TFR fell from 3.39 in 1992–3 to 2.85 in 1998–9, but there is suspicion that the latter figure is an underestimate.) This decline is in itself an indicator of improving well-being: there is gathering evidence that high fertility is a factor in poverty, with adverse effects on mothers and surviving children (Eastwood and Lipton 2001; Lloyd 1993). Perhaps most remarkable, given the long association of fertility decline with improvements in female education, is that the majority of fertility decline in the 1990s (65 per cent of it, in fact) has been among uneducated women, reflecting considerable social change and aspirations for a better life, not least a desire on the part of parents to educate their children (Bhat 2002b).

Literacy: One of the welcome features of the 2001 Census was the considerable increase in literacy it showed relative to 1991. It rose by 13 percentage points, from 52.2 per cent to 65.2 per cent—a much larger increase than in the 1980s, which recorded a rise of only 8.6 points (Registrar General, India 1999a). There is independent confirmation of the census figures from the NFHS.

The 2001 Census literacy figures break into 75.6 for males, 54.0 for females. NFHS-2 (1998–9) gives 75 per cent for males, 51 per cent for females aged six and above. The comparable figures in NFHS-1 (1992–3) were 69 per cent (males) and 43 per cent (females), confirming the increase in the mid- to late-1990s. Various Employment–Unemployment Rounds of the NSS, which give marginally higher literacy estimates than the Census, also support a very similar level and trend of literacy improvement in the 1990s.[13] Despite doubts about precise adult numbers, it is hard not to believe in a major increase in literacy for the general population in the 1990s, and indeed, as Chapter 7 has pointed out, an acceleration in progress.

Education: Chapter 7 has extensively documented the state of education, and the improvement in attendance in the 1990s. One should not be carried away by these figures, however. Attendance is not everything. Significant proportions

---

[13]See, for example, the 43rd Round for 1987–8 and the 50th Round for 1993–4.

of young people dropped out of school in the period covered: between ages 6 and 17, over 10 per cent of rural boys and 12 per cent of rural girls. And 9 per cent of rural boys aged 6–17 had never attended school; the figure for rural girls was 25.7 per cent. It is well known that the quality of schooling remains dismal in many places. And the chapter reported other worrying trends: the extent of improvement in schooling in Uttar Pradesh and elsewhere which is in the private sector, and the growing spread of 'para-teachers' where there should be fully trained staff, not to mention inadequately growing or even falling public expenditure on schooling at the state level. Nevertheless, the improvement in schooling across India, much of which is schooling for the poor, cannot be doubted. This is a field where the influence of population growth is obvious; it has clearly made it harder for every state to bring education to all, and will continue to do so in the states where major growth of the school-age population still lies ahead.

Food and nutrition: If one seeks to round out the picture of trends in well-being in the 1990s by examining the data on food consumption and nutrition, one enters once again on a shifting sand of data problems. Our own study (Hanchate 2001) has assessed food consumption by going to the actual quantities of the main food items reported as consumed, derived from NSS data.[14] It found a significant decline in per capita cereal consumption on an all-India basis between 1972–3 and 1993–4, with a gradually reducing income elasticity of demand for cereals. There was also a significant decline in the proportion of household income spent on food: for the richest fifth of the population the decline over that period was from 61 to 50 per cent; for the poorest fifth, from 81 to 76 per cent. However, for the poorest fifth the quantity of cereals consumed rose, though only slowly: at 0.25 per cent per year; the rise occurred in six of the largest 15 states, though the quantity consumed fell in the other nine states.

A key factor has been the decline in the consumption of coarse cereals (sorghum, millet, etc.) by all expenditure groups. Among the poor, though, increases in rice and wheat consumption more than compensated for it. As for pulses, six out of the 15 states recorded an increase in consumption, nine a decrease: but in all but four states, the poorest fifth increased their consumption. When we look at the poor it is clear that their consumption of cereals and pulses mostly rose during the two decades, but their consumption of other foods grew faster: fruit, vegetables, and milk. At the same time the price of cereals was falling relative to the price of all other foods, except pulses. The NSS quinquennial surveys also give information about 'subjective hunger': it is worth noting that the proportion reporting that they had two square meals a day rose from 81.1 per cent in 1983–4, to 94.5 per cent ten years later, and

[14]Actual quantities were used for cereal consumption, and other quantities were generally estimated using price data.

96.2 per cent in 1999–2000; the percentage reporting never having two square meals a day fell from 2.4 in 1983–4 to 0.7 in 1999–2000.

When one translates these trends in food consumption into nutrient intakes, the picture is positive for the poor: an increase in the protein and calorie intakes of the two lowest quintiles, growing at 1 per cent and 0.3 per cent per year respectively. Calories and proteins were flat for the middle quintile, and declined for the upper two quintiles (though still leaving the highest quintile with intakes 80 per cent above those of the lowest). Fat intakes have also grown for all expenditure groups. The gains in nutritional intakes for the two poorest quintiles occurred in all states except Haryana, Punjab, and Tamil Nadu.

A considerable headache in the data is that one can calculate nutritional intakes directly from the estimated quantities of food consumed: if one does this, one gets a picture of nutritional intakes completely different from that provided by the standard NSS procedure. That is, the quantitative food intake measure gives an account wholly different from one based on expenditures. The rural headcount ratio in column 1 of Table 9.4 bears little relation to the caloric intake ratios for the rural population in column 8, though the headcount ratio is supposed to indicate people not achieving a nutritional norm: and both are calculated by the NSS from NSS data. The numbers not meeting the 2400–2100 standard measured by expenditure are wholly different from those measured by food intake. Rajasthan has one of the highest poverty ratios, 47.5 per cent not achieving caloric sufficiency by the expenditure measure; but when measured by actual food intake, only 19.6 per cent fail to achieve it. The problem is not just with Rajasthan; there is little correlation between the two measures (Hanchate 2001).

Food consumption estimates are further complicated by the issue of meals taken in kind. Suryanaryana (2002) has argued that the NSS overestimated poverty in the 1970s because of missing this factor, and underestimated it later. Meals in kind have been diminishing as a factor in the payment of rural labour as a result of changing social relations and increasing monetization of the labour market. The NSS attributes meals in kind to the providing, not the consuming household. Hanchate (2001) makes an adjustment for this and finds the amount in caloric equivalent to be significant: 'For India as a whole this adjustment leads to daily calorie intake rising by 59 calories for the poorest quintile and falling by 206 calories for the richest quintile' (Hanchate 2001: 4).

The upshot of all this is that although alternative data are generally lacking one must be concerned about food consumption as measured by the NSS. Further, experiments with recall periods for food consumption have shown that a seven–day period gives a consistently higher estimate than the 30-day period on which the NSS normally relies.[15] Most commentators have not taken this

[15]There is also evidence of considerable gaps between NSS and national accounts estimates of food consumption; for further discussion, see Cassen (2002) and Chapter 11.

on board. The seven–day data do not give us a series for NSS consumption which is comparable over time; but no one has refuted the claim that the 30-day recall figures underestimate consumption. The original caloric baseline is still a useful monetary definition of poverty, as a parsimonious benchmark with more than a 20-year history; but it seems increasingly divorced from a measure of current food or caloric deprivation.

It is evident from this account that there have been major shifts in food consumption patterns across India, mainly in the shape of shifting into foods regarded as being of higher quality. We have not been able to complete this study for the latter half of the 1990s, but we have no reason to think the trends have worsened. The trends up to 1994 are consistent with what we know about income poverty—that it declined, and that the poverty gap also fell, that is, with some improvements in the living standards even of many of those below the poverty line. NFHS measurements of anthropometric nutritional status show distinct improvements between 1992–3 and 1998–9, as noted in Chapter 11.

Of course, the food and nutritional status of the country as a whole is far from satisfactory. We know that there are large proportions of people with inadequate food consumption, with protein and calorie deficits and micronutrient deficiencies. But for many of the poor the picture is, on average, one of slow improvement.

TABLE 9.4: *Poverty and nutritional availability*

State	Head count ratio		Poverty gap		Calorie availability (30th percentile)		NSS calorie availability	Per cent population below norm
	Level (1)	Growth (2)	Level (3)	Growth (4)	Quantity (5)	Growth (6)	(7)	(8)
South								
Kerala	31.1	−3.82	7	−6.18	1990	0.71	1965	45.7
Tamil Nadu	36.7	−2.25	8.6	−3.45	1762	−0.44	1885	51.3
Andhra Pradesh	28.9	−3.81	5.8	−5.99	1932	0.18	2052	40.9
Karnataka	41.0	−1.72	9.8	−3.11	1929	0.24	2073	42.7
West								
Maharashtra	47.8	−2.89	13.2	−4.15	2053	0.84	1939	49.7
Gujarat	35.4	−2.69	7.4	−4.89	1981	0.08	1994	46.4
Rajasthan	47.5	−1.27	11.8	−2.43	2649	0.58	2470	19.6
North								
Punjab	20.9	−0.98	3.2	−2.94	2134	−0.61	2418	24.4
Haryana	30.2	−0.12	7.4	0.04	2377	−0.85	2491	25.9
Uttar Pradesh	41.6	−1.32	10.2	−1.99	2165	0.07	2307	26.5
Madhya Pradesh	45.4	−2.02	11.4	−3.59	2130	0.13	2164	35.6

(contd...)

(Table 9.4 continued)

State	Head count ratio		Poverty gap		Calorie availability (30th percentile)		NSS calorie availability	Per cent population below norm
	Level (1)	Growth (2)	Level (3)	Growth (4)	Quantity (5)	Growth (6)	(7)	(8)
East								
Bihar	63.5	−0.59	17.2	−2.02	1995	0.2	2115	37.3
West Bengal	27.3	−4.06	4.7	−7.25	2090	1.73	2211	32.2
Orissa	40.3	−2.54	8.7	−4.98	1988	1.05	2199	30.9
Assam	49.0	−1.48	9.6	−2.09	1847	0.07	1983	49.4
India	43.5	−1.45	10.9	−2.7	2063	0.29	2153	36.9

Notes: Columns (1)–(4): Rural poverty estimates for 1993/4; from Özler et al. (1996) and Datt and Ravallion (1998).

Columns (5)–(6): Calorie availability for 30th percentile for 1993/4; note that this refers to the mean of the second quintile.

Column (7): Per capita daily calorie availability for 1993/4 (mean for state; rural); from *NSSO Sarvekshana* (1996).

Column (8) per cent of rural population with less than 2430 kcal (90 per cent of normal requirement level of 2700); from NSSO *Sarvekshana* (1996).

Environmental factors: If we can point to many aspects of welfare that have been getting better in the 1990s, there are some that did not. Air and water pollution have negative effects on most people, but they hurt the poor more than most. The better-off can protect themselves more easily. Environmental damage to health and productivity has begun to be measured relatively recently, and comparative data over time are scarce. But there are data on environmental deterioration, which has undoubtedly worsened in almost every respect throughout the 1990s: recent improvements in Delhi's air quality, if sustained, would be a rare exception.

Another feature is the impact of population growth, developmental change, and environmental damage on common property resources. The poor, especially in rural areas, have traditionally derived significant shares of their livelihoods from these resources. Population growth is far from being the most important factor in what is happening. But greater numbers have to share resources whose availability or productivity are shrinking rather than rising; this is once again a factor that has probably led to worsening in the living conditions of many of the poor. These topics are covered in greater detail in Chapter 15.

CONCLUSIONS ABOUT THE 1990s

It is not possible to add up all the positive and negative indications about socio-economic progress in India in the 1990s. Broadly there are positive signs to be found in improving literacy and school attendance, declining fertility, rising real rural wages, and in economic growth. Many of these trends have benefitted poor people. It would be mistaken to infer from our lack of certainty about the precise path of income poverty that no real progress has been made in that too. At the same time, the faltering of employment growth, and the lack of improvement in job quality are major concerns, as are the continuing inequalities in the school system, the low quality of much education, and the continuing, if slowly diminishing deficits of female education.

Environmental degradation has to be set against any general picture of improvement, since it has been worsening in the 1990s and mostly in ways detrimental to the poor, that is, to their health and their livelihoods. Health in general has not made adequate progress in the 1990s, but some of the apparent slowdown in improvement, if not a statistical artefact, may be due to HIV/AIDS and environmental factors rather than other social conditions.[16] The food and nutrition data are in a state from which it is hard to derive solid conclusions; but the trends up to 1993–4 are of improvements for the poorer sections over a 20-year period, and there is little in the data for the remainder of the 1990s to suggest that things have deteriorated, and some signs of continuing improvement.

Set in this broad context, it is hard to see the poverty debate as it has recently been posed, a debate between proponents and opponents of India's liberalization policies in the 1990s. We discuss in Chapter 10 the trends in social expenditures, which were adverse in many states. But these trends existed in the 1980s (Shariff et al. 2002); and the fiscal squeeze that exacerbated them in the 1990s resulted in part from retrenchment after the crisis of 1990–1, but much more to mismanagement of state level finances, and the large shares of states' indebtedness due to misguided electricity, water, and transport subsidies. Liberalization may be to blame for some of the adverse trends in employment; but not for the poor economic performance of the poorer states; and as is noted elsewhere, the disparities in income between the poorest and the best-off states have been widening since 1950, not just since 1991. The continuance of poverty in India is due to age-old problems.

One further point deserves emphasis: all the improvements discussed here, though welcome, are nothing to be complacent about. The huge numbers of people deprived of so many of the requisites of a decent life are a sad reflection on India's half-century of independent development.

FUTURE PROSPECTS FOR INCOME POVERTY

Looking to the future, the following simulation suggests that India's inequalities and slow progress in redressing the conditions of the poor must be a subject

---

[16]Suryanarayana (2001) cites various other indicators from the NFHS, including the proportion of houses with electricity, a toilet, or drinking water from a pump or pipe, all of which show modest improvements, as does the proportion of *pucca* houses.

of major concern. We have projected poverty on an all-India basis up to 2026, using the levels from Deaton (2001) for 1993–4 to 1999–2000. Taking India's economic growth rate and the growth–poverty elasticity during this period and assuming both hold for the next two-and-a-half decades, we obtain a poverty rate of 10.6 per cent in 2026, or some 150 million people given the 2026 level of population we project in Chapter 5.

However, as with population projections, a more trustworthy method is to do it state by state. Using the same method but state-level data for the initial headcount ratios, growth rates, and growth–poverty elasticities, we obtain a poverty rate for India in 2026 of 13.3 per cent, or nearly 190 million people. Today 56 per cent of the poor are in the five states of Bihar, Madhya Pradesh, Orissa, Rajasthan, and Uttar Pradesh. Their combined headcount ratio was 35.9 per cent in 1999–2000, and declines to just below 18 per cent in 2026; but the ratio for the remaining states declines from 23.5 per cent to 9.6 per cent, because the poorer states have lower economic growth (except for Rajasthan), lower growth–poverty elasticities, and faster population growth. Thus in 2026 the poorer states' headcount ratio will be almost double that of the remainder; they will have 144 out of the total of 190 million poor people.

We emphasise that these are simply mechanical projections, assuming all the parameters—which are uncertain to begin with—remain unchanged. And it is looking only at overall growth, while we know poverty responds both to the sectoral pattern of growth, and to many other things besides growth. Still, the projections give a very rough guide to what could be the future of poverty if current trends remain unchanged. Clearly in the decades ahead India faces major tasks just in combatting income poverty. As Chapters 7 and 8 show, the same is true for other dimensions of well-being, such as education and employment. These other dimensions deserve much greater prominence in debates about the character of India's development, including the impact of reforms. Apart from other considerations, the data on income poverty are now contested: the discrepancies between various data sources seem to be widening, and in the NSS data themselves, always regarded as the most authoritative, there are distinct problems. It is essential to take a rounded view of deprivation by considering all its dimensions. When this is done it rapidly becomes clear that unless something happens to change the fate of the poor in the most deprived areas, India's economic growth may continue to pass them by.

CONCLUSIONS

The conditions described here shed light on some of the debate of the 1990s and since, and whether economic reforms were worsening or improving social conditions. The reforms may have raised the rate of national economic growth though even that is questioned (Nagaraj 2000). But if 6 per cent annual economic growth in the 1990s has not made much of an impact on widespread deprivation, at least some of that fact is due to the entrenched nature of poverty in all its forms. If so much of poverty can be traced to its geographical persistence, then the economic reforms are not the main thing to be blamed, though obviously if they make private investment more important, those parts of the country which are unattractive to private investors will have their disadvantages reinforced.

So much has been written about poverty in India. There have been so many measurements, analyses, exhortations, and policy prescriptions. One can find so much valuable work that it is hard to believe one can improve on it. If anything has been added here, it is on the analytical side, and giving a greater presence to demographic considerations than is often the case. As far as policies are concerned, past writings have said most of what needs to be said.

An excellent summary was provided by S. Guhan, one of India's most acute social commentators. Writing in 1986, he said:

Most simply, development policy as a whole and in each of its aspects, that is, in a systemic manner, will have to be directed towards increasing entitlements to the rural poor from ownership and exchange. This will entail redistribution and transfer of assets in their favour, improving returns from assets and enterprise, increasing real earnings for wage labour, and the provision of social consumption and the safety net of social security (Guhan 1986: 39).

Guhan's (1986) assessment of past efforts was 'mainly negative'. The direct programmes for poverty alleviation were found wanting; they missed many if not most of their intended beneficiaries and wasted money on a grand scale. Social consumption measures, by which he referred to health, education, and other basic welfare provision, or social consumption, had also commonly failed the poor. Nor had the character of growth brought much benefit to poor people.

Seventeen years later there is not a great deal to add. Assessment of direct programmes remains negative, as does assessment of health and education measures, even if there is some progress to report. Perhaps growth has at last trickled down somewhat to the poor, and considerable strides have been made in education. But there was one aspect of current poverty missing from Guhan's analysis: growth has also brought with it environmental damage which has harmed the poor. There is much to redress.

10

The Economy—Past and Future

Shankar Acharya, Robert Cassen, and Kirsty McNay

I ndia's economy grew at about 6 per cent a year over the decade up to 2001—an increase in performance over previous decades. This chapter examines the prospects for continued rapid growth in the Indian economy in the medium term. It also considers growth at the state level, and the record in social expenditure.

THE CAUSES OF GROWTH

The economic literature is replete with analyses of the causes of growth—most of which have been shown to be false or at best only partially true. For a long time the prime candidate was physical capital: countries had mainly to achieve an adequate level of investment and then they would 'take off' into sustained growth (Lewis 1954; Rostow 1960). Clearly investment is an important ingredient of growth. Countries need infrastructure, and labour has to work with equipment to become more productive. But research has shown that countries can invest without growing very much, and grow without investing very much, at least for considerable periods. As early as the 1950s, Robert Solow had shown that long-run growth could not be determined by investment: if labour were in fixed supply, there must eventually be diminishing returns to increasing the amount of capital. Then only technological change could maintain or increase the rate of growth (Solow 1957).

Another prime candidate for the cause of growth is 'human capital', people's acquisition of education and skills. Certainly many studies of growth have shown impressive contributions of education to growth—in East Asia for example (World Bank 1993b). But, as with investment, there are plenty of cases of countries improving their human capital without improving growth. Once again, part of the problem may be diminishing returns. Additions to human capital may only reduce the rewards to those who possess it if the further things that make it productive are missing. Developing countries are only too familiar with the problem of 'educated unemployment'. (This of course is not to question the importance of education, which has many valued purposes; only to clarify that it does not offer an automatic route to growth.)

The question of diminishing or increasing returns has acquired a key importance in the modern understanding of growth. When conditions are favourable, investments in both physical and human capital can complement each other and yield increasing returns; that is why, for example, production often takes place in 'clusters'—England's nineteenth-century textile and pottery towns, or today's Silicon Valleys. The question is what makes conditions favourable or unfavourable?

A valuable recent study has termed this question 'the elusive quest for growth' (Easterly 2001). The most general answer it gives is that the incentives for growth have to be present. This is not a simple 'market' philosophy. If increasing returns are present, individuals and firms will not necessarily make the best possible choices, since the combined effects of all the choices are greater than what each investor can know. Coordinated investments may have returns higher than each individual investor would calculate; and it is impossible for parents and young people to tell in advance what the value of education and training will be. There is thus a role for governments. But they must have the right incentives too.

Markets have much to do with it; few countries have achieved sustained growth for any length of time with command or socialistic economies; and openness to trade and foreign investment have survived research fairly well as key features of growth, not least because they help to transfer technology and provide markets which again allow economies of scale. Commonly there are gains and losses from openness to trade, but over the long run the gains greatly outweigh the losses.

Apart from setting the production and trade environment, another critical role for the government is management of the macro-economy. Large fiscal deficits, high rates of inflation, misaligned exchange rates are all inimical to growth. This much is fairly uncontroversial. Less easy to determine is the appropriate role for the government in correcting market failures. The East Asian example of successful collaboration between business and government to achieve the investment coordination just mentioned has proved hard to copy—and it contained the very faults which led to the 'crashes' in East Asia in the 1990s. Skilfully directed credit became crony capitalism. 'Miracle' economies were overtaken by failed financial regulation and corruption.

Beyond these factors in growth lie more intangible dimensions. Rule of law and well-enforced property rights are important to growth. Income and asset equality has been found to be good for growth; ethnic division is bad for it, though less so when fairly resolved in a democratic framework. Democracy itself has on the whole been found to be positively associated with growth, though there can be combinations of circumstances when democratic politics may interfere with good policies. These are some of the issues that determine whether governments themselves are led by appropriate incentives which foster growth.

Given the complexity of the causes of growth, it is hardly surprising that countries have often found growth hard to achieve. In addition to the factors already listed, adverse shocks have to be reckoned with too, such as sudden changes in major export or import prices, natural disasters, and, as many countries have learned in the last two decades, vulnerability to financial instability. Perhaps the surprising thing has been the confidence of economists that they know how to promote growth.

THE ROLE OF POPULATION

One of the major debates in development economics has been over the issue of the macroeconomic role of population growth. In the twentieth century the seminal work was Coale and Hoover's 1958 study using the example of India (Coale and Hoover 1958). It compared two paths for the economy, one with higher fertility than the other, and reached a powerful conclusion: not only was the growth of per capita income lower under the high fertility variant, but also even the growth of aggregate gross national product (GNP) was lower. The result derived from two assumptions in their model: one was that the burden of dependency, the ratio of non-workers to workers in the population, was greater under high fertility and led to reduced savings; and the other was that investment had to be spread over larger numbers instead of raising the amount of physical or social capital per worker. This was called 'capital widening versus capital deepening', that is, if population were growing more slowly, the same amount of capital would be used to improve the quality of schooling or health services received by each individual, instead of being diluted by having to extend coverage to more people; or there would be more or better capital for each worker in the work-place.

These findings were hotly disputed; attempts to measure the burden-of-dependency effect on savings suggested it might be quite small, and similar questions were raised about the capital-dilution argument. There could be benefits from high fertility too, such as a younger and more adaptable labour force, economies of scale, and other positive effects.[1] Above all, until the 1980s,

---

[1]For an early survey disputing the Coale–Hoover view, see Cassen (1976).

most attempts to measure the effect of population on growth (either in the aggregate or per capita) suggested the impact was small or non-existent; any negative influence could easily be outweighed by other factors (Kuznets 1974).

Research in the last few years, as noted in Chapter 9, has brought a swing of the pendulum in the macroeconomic discussion. The first article in the field was by Blanchet (1991). A major inter-country study by Kelley and Schmidt (1994) followed, showing a negative relationship between population growth and the growth of per capita income, though only for the 1980s; for the 1960s and 1970s they found little effect (Kelley and Schmidt 1994). This '1980s reversal' attracted attention. There was a series of studies looking in more detail at the East Asian and other economies, which found that reductions in the burden of dependency had a significant effect on savings. Reductions in the school-age population also permitted increases in the quality of schooling, with valuable effects on 'human capital', to which a large share of East Asia's rapid growth up to the 1990s was attributed. These positive influences of fertility decline acquired the label of a 'demographic bonus', even if it was one which would eventually be put into reverse by population ageing. Rising life expectancy could also have positive effects, through increasing savings and also the productivity impacts of a healthier population.

It should be noted that these recent studies do not show a relationship between the rate of population growth per se and economic growth; it is rather certain demographic features which may matter—fertility, the age distribution, and life expectancy. Some of the models incorporate simultaneous relationships, with economic growth affecting the demographic variables and vice-versa, giving rise to virtuous or vicious circles of rapid or slow growth (Bloom et al. 2000).

For data and other reasons we have not been able to carry out a study of population effects on the Indian economy as a whole over time. We report here on the results of our research and those of others on growth at the state level. It is not clear that India will enjoy much of a demographic bonus from its fertility decline; the effect on savings is quite likely to be a modest one,[2] and while the reduction in school-age population provides the potential for increases in the quality of education, India's poor record in that field does not suggest the opportunity will necessarily be grasped. Nonetheless, the role of educational aspirations in reducing fertility and the recent gains in literacy may show that important forces are at work here: the desire of parents to educate their children may be one of the keys to India's fertility decline, and the decline in fertility may in turn be assisting parents to achieve their desire.

---

[2]Bloom and Williamson (1997) did not expect that India would enjoy a large demographic bonus because of the low productivity of the economy, and slow demographic progress. See also papers by Kelley and Schmidt (1994); Williamson (2001); Lee et al. (2001); and Bloom and Canning (2001).

INDIA'S MEDIUM-TERM GROWTH PROSPECTS

Historical perspective: To form a view of growth possibilities and prospects in future some appreciation of past performance is clearly necessary.[3] Table 10.1 presents the basic facts of India's growth performance over the last 50 years. The three decades from 1950–1 to 1980–1 saw economic growth average close to 3.5 per cent per year, the infamous 'Hindu rate of growth': per capita GDP growth averaged hardly 1.5 per cent a year.

There was a welcome acceleration of economic growth in the 1980s to 5.6 per cent a year, based on a clear acceleration of growth performance in all the three constituent sectors of agriculture, industry, and services. Per capita growth averaged a healthy 3.4 per cent per annum, bringing about a significant improvement in average living standards. Unfortunately, the growth acceleration of the 1980s was accompanied by the emergence of unsustainable fiscal deficits, continuation of a costly anti-export bias in trade policy and growing reliance on external borrowing to fund a widening current account deficit in the balance of payments (BOP). The 1990 Gulf War and the resulting surge in oil prices triggered a full-fledged BOP crisis, which brought growth to a grinding halt in 1991–2 and plunged the economy into considerable disarray.

TABLE 10.1: *Average growth of real GDP over 50 years (per cent)*

	1951/2– 1960/1	1961/2– 1970/1	1971/2– 1980/1	1981/2– 1990/1	1991/2– 2000/1	1992/3– 2000/1
Agriculture and Allied	3.1	2.5	1.8	3.6	2.7	3.2
Industry	6.3	5.5	4.1	7.1	5.7	6.4
Services	4.3	4.8	4.4	6.7	7.5	7.8
GDP (factor cost)	3.9	3.7	3.2	5.6	5.6	6.1
Per capita GDP	2.0	1.5	0.8	3.4	3.6	4.0

Note: Industry includes Construction.
Sources: Central Statistical Organization, *National Accounts Statistics*, Back Series 1950/1, 1992/3, April 2001 and *Economic Survey 2001/2*.

The new Congress government of June 1991 undertook emergency measures to restore external and domestic confidence in the economy and its management. The rupee was devalued, the fiscal deficit was cut and special BOP financing mobilized from the International Monetary Fund (IMF) and the World Bank. Even more importantly, the government seized the opportunity offered by the crisis to launch an array of long overdue and wide-ranging economic reforms. They encompassed external sector liberalization, deregulation of industry, reforms of taxation and the financial sector and a more commercial approach to the public sector.

[3]For a comprehensive assessment of India's macroeconomic performance in the 1990s, see Acharya (2002a).

The economy responded exceptionally well to these initiatives, with growth quickly recovering to nearly 6 per cent by 1993–4. For the 1990s as a whole, GDP growth averaged 5.6 per cent. And if the crisis year of 1991–2 is omitted (as it reasonably should be) growth in the nine years between 1991–2 and 2000–1 averaged 6.1 per cent—the fastest decadal growth in India's recorded history (Table 10.1). Furthermore, per capita growth accelerated to 4 per cent per annum, taking India into the ranks of the 10 fastest growing countries in the world. The lumbering Indian elephant seemed to be breaking into quite an impressive canter, with the promise of sustained rapid growth in the decades ahead.

Growth in the 1990s: Closer examination of growth trends during the 1990s provides interesting insights and tempers optimism about the future. Table 10.2 subdivides the record for the 1990s into an initial high growth period of five years (corresponding to the Eighth Plan period) and the subsequent four years. First, comparing the performance of the post-crisis nine years of the 1990s to the pre-crisis 1980s, it is interesting to note that the acceleration of GDP growth from 5.6 per cent to 6.1 per cent is entirely attributable to the services sector where growth surged to 7.8 per cent from an already high 6.7 per cent in the 1980s. Indeed, the growth of both agriculture and industry averaged a little lower in the post-crisis nine years compared to the pre-crisis decade. Second, the acceleration of GDP growth to 6.7 per cent in the quinquennium 1992–7 from the pre-crisis decadal average of 5.6 per cent is quite remarkable. Third, it is noteworthy that in this high growth Eighth Plan period all major sectors (agriculture, industry, services) grew noticeably faster than in the pre-crisis decade. The acceleration in the growth of agricultural value added is particularly interesting in the light of the oft-repeated criticism that the economic reforms of the early 1990s neglected the agricultural sector.

What are the factors which explain this remarkable and broad-based

TABLE 10.2: *Growth of GDP and major sectors*

	Share in Real GDP 1993–4 prices (per cent)	Average Annual Growth Rates			
	Average of 1994/5–1996/7	1981/2– 1990/1	1992/3– 2000/1	1992/3– 1996/7	1997/8– 2000/1
	(1)	(2)	(3)	(4)	(5)
Agriculture	28.9	3.6	3.2	4.7	1.2
Industry	27.6	7.1	6.4	7.6	4.8
Services	43.5	6.7	7.8	7.6	8.1
GDP (factor cost)	100.0	5.6	6.1	6.7	5.4

Sources: Central Statistical Organization, *National Accounts Statistics*, Back Series 1950/1–1992/9, 1992–3, April 2001, and *Economic Survey*, 2001/2.

growth surge in the period 1992–7? In the absence of authoritative research, we can suggest the following factors:

- Productivity gains resulting from the deregulation of trade, industry, and finance, especially in the sectors of industry and some services;
- The surge in export growth at about 20 per cent per year (in dollar terms) for three successive years beginning 1993–4, attributable to the substantial devaluation in real effective terms in the early 1990s and a freer policy regime for industry, foreign trade, and payments;
- The investment boom of 1993–6 which exerted expansionary effects on both supply and demand, especially in industry. The investment boom itself was probably driven by a combination of factors including the unleashing of 'animal spirits' by economic reforms, the swift loosening of the foreign exchange bottleneck, confidence in broadly consistent governmental policy signals, and easier availability of investible funds (both through borrowing and new equity issues);
- The partial success in fiscal consolidation, which kept a check on government borrowings and facilitated expansion of aggregate savings and investments;
- Improvement in the terms of trade for agriculture resulting from a combination of higher procurement prices for important crops and reduction in trade protection for manufactures;
- Availability of capacity in key infrastructure sectors, notably power; and
- A buoyant world economy which supported expansion of foreign trade and private capital inflows.

But economic growth fell to 4.8 per cent in 1997–8, 4.3 per cent if the 'Pay Commission effect' is netted out (see next). Agriculture recorded negative growth in value added, while the growth of manufacturing slumped to 1.5 per cent from 9.7 per cent in the previous year. Only services boomed at 9.8 per cent. Although industrial expansion remained subdued, GDP growth recovered smartly in 1998–9 thanks to a strong rebound in agriculture and continued buoyancy in services. Growth was sustained in 1999–2000 by a temporary recovery in industry. In 2000–1, renewed industrial deceleration and virtual stagnation in agriculture pulled GDP growth down to 4.0 per cent.

As a result, average GDP growth dropped to 5.4 per cent in the four years 1997–8 to 2000–1 (Table 10.2). Much more disquieting is the collapse of agricultural growth to 1.2 per cent (from over three times the rate in the Eighth Plan period) and the significant fall in industrial growth down to 4.8 per cent. Indeed, the drop in GDP growth in these four years would have been much steeper but for the extraordinary buoyancy of services which averaged growth of 8.1 per cent. This growth in services was much faster than industry, a pattern which is quite different and novel compared to past experience and, at the very least, raises questions of sustainability.

A part of the services sector growth in the last four years was 'spurious' in the sense that it simply reflected the revaluation of the value added in the sub-sector 'Public Administration and Defence' because of higher pay scales resulting from decisions of the Fifth Pay Commission. It is a peculiarity of national income accounting conventions that value added in non-marketed services is estimated on the basis of cost. These Pay Commission effects (including knock-on effects in the states) were spread mainly over three years, 1997–8, 1998–9, and 1999–2000, when 'real' growth of 'Public Administration and Defence' soared to 14.5 per cent, 10.3 per cent, and 13.2 per cent, respectively, compared to an average growth in the previous five years of less than 4 per cent. Subtracting the trend growth from the exceptionally high reported growth rates gives a measure of the 'spurious' (or Pay Commission affected) growth in these years, which we also subtract from overall GDP growth in the relevant years. This adjustment reduces GDP growth by 0.5 per cent in 1997–8 and 1999–2000 and by 0.4 per cent in 1998–9. The adjusted (net of Pay Commission effect) GDP growth becomes 4.3 per cent in 1997–8, 6.0 per cent in 1998–9 and 5.7 per cent in 1999–2000. As a result of these adjustments, the average GDP growth in the four years 1997–8 to 2000–1 drops to 5.0 per cent, which is below the 5.6 per cent average for the pre-crisis decade and substantially lower than the 6.7 per cent achieved in the post-crisis quinquennium.[4]

From a macroeconomic perspective, 1997 witnessed negative developments in three key areas of exports, investment, and fiscal balance. Export growth in dollar terms dropped to 5 per cent from 20 per cent in the previous three years, partly because of the real appreciation of the rupee between 1993 and 1995 and partly because of the surge in Chinese exports to the world, which took away market share from all other Asian competitors. Industrial investment stalled for several reasons. First, the investment boom of the previous three years had built up large capacities which discouraged further expansion. Second, real interest rates had risen in 1995–6 because of a sharp decline in inflation and a temporary rise in nominal interest rates driven by Reserve Bank of India (RBI) interventions in the foreign exchange market to stabilize a suddenly wobbly rupee. Third, the advent of coalition governance had probably heightened uncertainty and damped business confidence. Fourth, and related, the reform programme lost momentum and consistency after the mid-1990s.

On the fiscal front, after 1996–7, the consolidated fiscal and revenue deficits deteriorated steadily, with about half the worsening due to the phasing in of increases in government pay scales following the Fifth Pay Commission. Both the fiscal deficit and the revenue deficit increased by about 3 per cent of GDP between 1995–6 and 1999–2000. This sharp widening in deficits

---

[4]It could be argued that, for strict comparability, similar adjustments should be made to the growth in previous periods following previous Pay Commission decisions. However, the scale of the pay increases of the Fifth Pay Commission is of a different order.

was fully reflected in the decline of public savings from 2 per cent of GDP in 1995–6 to minus 0.9 per cent in 1999–2000. This, in turn, explained the drop in gross domestic savings from its peak of 25.1 per cent of GDP in 1995–6 to 23.2 per cent in 1999–2000. Over this period, there was a decline of similar magnitude in gross domestic investment, partly for reasons noted earlier and partly because of continued high real interest rates shored up by growing fiscal deficits.

From India's perspective the international economic environment also weakened after 1997. The Asian crisis of 1997–8 hurt exports and private capital inflows. The problems were compounded by the economic sanctions which followed the nuclear tests in May 1998. In the next two years the surge in international oil prices (much of it passed on, with lags, to Indian energy users) exerted negative effects. Finally, from the last quarter of 2000, the global economic slowdown took its toll of India's economic performance.

Other, more structural factors influenced the deceleration of growth. This probably included the petering out of productivity gains from economic reforms, which clearly slowed after 1994. Although reforms continued throughout the decade, they never regained the breadth and depth of the early 1990s. First, key reforms in the financial sector, infrastructure, labour laws, trade and industrial policy, and privatization remained unfinished or undone. Second, despite good intentions, the bottlenecks in infrastructure became worse over time. Third, the low quality and quantity of investment in rural infrastructure combined with distorted pricing of some key agricultural inputs and outputs to damp the growth of agriculture. Fourth, the continuing decline in governance and financial discipline (especially, but by no means exclusively) in the populous states of the Gangetic plain constrained growth prospects for over 30 per cent of India's population.

Growth prospects—Some relevant dimensions: What can one say about India's growth prospects in the next five, ten, or twenty years? Crystal-ball gazing is intrinsically uncertain. It becomes especially difficult against the background of the last 10 years when growth accelerated to nearly 7 per cent in the first five years and then decelerated markedly to around 5 per cent in the next five. The qualitative approach adopted here will be to assess briefly the likely evolution of some of the key dimensions which normally influence growth and then form some judgments on that basis.

Savings, investment, and fiscal imbalance: Growth is dependent on many factors but no one would deny the role of investment in augmenting productive capacity, embodying new technology, and as a key component of aggregate demand. Gross domestic investment peaked in the mid-1990s at around 26–7 per cent of GDP and has since retreated to around 24 per cent of GDP, which is not very different from the average recorded in the late 1980s. The prospects for an early revival are not promising, especially in view of the record on aggregate savings.

Gross domestic savings also peaked in the mid-1990s, at around 25 per cent of GDP, and has since subsided to about 23 per cent of GDP. This is noticeably better than the late 1980s record. More interestingly, private savings held up remarkably well, even during the growth slowdown since 1997. Having climbed from 18 per cent of GDP in the late 1980s to about 23 per cent by the mid-1990s, private savings remained strong and even increased further to 25 per cent of GDP by 2000–1. This strong record of private savings was propelled by the buoyancy of household savings (including unincorporated enterprises), which rose by almost five percentage points of GDP in the past decade. Indeed, if public savings (that is, of government and enterprises) had maintained its late 1980s level, we could well have seen aggregate savings and investment at record levels of 27 and 28 per cent respectively by 2000–1.

Unfortunately, over the past decade and especially since the mid-1990s, public savings collapsed from a modest 2 per cent or higher of GDP to minus 1.7 per cent in 2000–1. The financial performance of public enterprises did not improve, while dissaving by government deteriorated badly. The consolidated revenue deficit of central and state governments worsened from 3.2 per cent of GDP in 1995–6 to over 6 per cent in each of the three years 1998–9 to 2000–1. This was certainly a serious breach of the oft-cited golden rule of public finance which admonishes governments to borrow only to finance investment (that is, have zero revenue deficits).

In 2002, despite widespread recognition of the high costs of large fiscal and revenue deficits, the prospects for an early turnaround were not good for several reasons. First, in December 2000 the central government had introduced the Fiscal Responsibility and Budget Management (FRBM) bill in Parliament, but it eventually dropped the mandatory benchmarks for deficit reduction and some other tough elements. Second, the large pay increases following the Fifth Pay Commission continued to bloat government revenue expenditures, especially in the states. Third, there was no obvious reason to expect early improvement of the recent record of low tax buoyancy. Fourth, the pressure of competitive populism in democratic politics did not augur well for the implementation of long overdue cost recovery efforts for reducing subsidies in the public provision of various goods and services, including power, water, state transport, higher education, and fertilizers.

Private savings (especially household savings), on the other hand, could see a further modest secular increase as a ratio of GDP. The main reason for this expectation is that, with continued increase in per capita GDP and labour supply, the proportion of income recipients in the population with rising discretionary incomes is likely to continue to increase for the next couple of decades or so.

Depending on what happens to foreign savings, the considerations here suggest a moderate improvement in the rate of gross domestic investment in the medium term, perhaps to the levels attained in the mid-1990s. However, this is only a mildly positive expectation and abstracts from the eventuality (not impossible) of a serious crisis in either government finances or the financial system.

The financial system itself is in fact part of the problem, increasingly impacting on the real sectors of the economy. Bhattacharya and Patel (2002) argue that the dominant government role in the sector, coupled with high regulatory forbearance and the absence of efficient bankruptcy procedures, contributed significantly and negatively to the slowdown in industrial investment and growth in recent years. The need for serious reforms in the financial sector is clear and growing. Unfortunately, this is another area of stalled reform. In late 2002 there had been little progress in the legislature with the government's proposed amendments to banking laws, and these in any case did not go far enough. Until privatization of government-owned financial institutions becomes a major plank of economic policy, the prospects for serious financial sector reform and better financial sector performance are likely to remain cloudy.

External sector—resources and competitiveness: As noted earlier, India's export growth decelerated sharply after 1996. The prospects for an early resumption of rapid export growth are not bright given the sluggish pace of world trade growth, the growing domination of China in labour-intensive manufactured exports, the anti-export bias in India's trade policies, high infrastructure costs, unusually rigid labour laws, 'reservation' of hundreds of labour-intensive manufactured items for small-scale producers and relatively high regulatory hassles. Many of these impediments are amenable to policy reforms but the near-term outlook has to be cautious.

Foreign trade and payments policies merit some elaboration. Between 1991 and 1996 there was substantial policy reform in the form of the transition to a broadly market-determined exchange rate system, major reductions in India's extraordinarily high customs tariff rates, phased removal of quantitative restrictions (QRs) on imports and liberalization of foreign investment. These reforms underpinned the exceptional external sector performance of those years. After 1996, although the phased elimination of QRs was continued to its logical conclusion (under World Trade Organization auspices), average import weighted tariffs actually increased. Furthermore, the management of the floating exchange rate was such as to allow appreciation of the rupee in real effective terms, especially when currency depreciations of Asian competitor countries are factored in. Future reduction in the anti-export bias of trade policies will depend crucially on implementation of announced plans for reducing customs tariffs and a more competitive exchange rate policy.

Measured by the ratio of the current account deficit to GDP, the level of foreign savings inflow into India was low in the five years up to 2002, around 1 per cent. Inflows in the form of net external assistance have declined secularly as a proportion of GDP, reflecting increasing levels of aid-weariness in the world. Foreign direct investment (FDI) inflows grew rapidly (from negligible levels) between 1991 and 1997 and then sputtered. In the five years 1996–2000, FDI into India amounted to only US $13 billion, compared to US $209 billion to China, US $123 billion to Brazil and US $26 billion to Malaysia. The factors impeding export growth also constrained FDI. In addition there were all the reasons which discouraged domestic investment. Any upsurge in FDI will remain heavily dependent on policy reforms which successfully boost domestic investment and stimulate resurgence of export growth.

Nor does recent experience in international and Indian capital markets hold out much promise for a sustained boom in foreign portfolio investment. All in all, the medium term prospects for inflows of foreign savings are fairly subdued, with little chance of such flows exceeding 1 to 2 per cent of GDP for a sustained period. So, on present trends and policies, neither exports nor foreign savings are likely to be important sources of growth dynamism in the medium term.

Economic reforms and productivity: Is there scope for growth acceleration through rapid increases in productivity? After all, key sectors of the Indian economy have enjoyed bursts of productivity increase in the past. This is a very large topic and we can only touch upon it here. Quite clearly, economic reforms have a lot to do with productivity increases. By now there are several inventories of 'second generation reforms' that India needs to undertake.[5] Typically, they include reforms of labour laws, bankruptcy provisions, small scale industry (SSI) reservations policy, external sector reforms of the kind noted earlier, financial sector reforms, revamping of infrastructure, overhaul of education and health sector policies, and much more.

The problem is not with compiling lists of plausible reforms for improving economic performance but with navigating them through the perilous shoals of political expediency, vested interests and administrative capacity. If the last five years are any guide, we are more likely to see reforms going forward in fits and starts than in a rapid, sustained manner across a broad front. Correspondingly, the favourable influence on productivity is also likely to be sporadic and attenuated.

Infrastructure constraints: India's infrastructure problems are legendary. There is little doubt that past economic performance has been constrained by weaknesses in availability and quality of infrastructure services, even if rigorous

[5]One such is contained in the Planning Commission's Employment Task Force report, (Planning Commission 2001b).

studies of the timing and severity of such constraints are hard to come by. There is some qualitative evidence to suggest that in key sectors such as electric power, roads, and railways the situation may have worsened in recent years because of mounting fiscal pressure on budgets of public sector entities, continuing problems of chronic under-pricing and economically unsound cross-subsidization policies and insufficient progress with regulatory reforms. The real issue is what are the prospects for the medium-term?

The answer probably varies substantially across infrastructure sectors. The outlook is most promising for the telecom sector, which has made the most progress in the transition from a public monopoly paradigm to a model where public and private service providers compete in the same market subject to an independent regulator. After a somewhat tortuous process of reform of the regulatory and investment framework, the telecom sector is now benefiting from substantial new investments and productivity gains from new technology and competition. This process should continue in the medium term, bringing widespread benefits from better tele-connectivity, including the allied IT sector.

Connectivity will also improve from growing investments in the national highway network, although the old problems of maintenance and upkeep remain challenging. The outlook for state highways and rural roads is more problematic (see the following paragraph). There has been much less progress in railways, which remain a public monopoly, burdened by unrealistically low tariffs, massively uneconomical cross-subsidization of passengers by freight, insufficient investment in track and rolling stock, and declining safety performance. Despite several high-level reviews and reports, the prospects for early corrective action are not bright.

Progress has been slowest in the sector of electric power, even though it is the sector in which it is most urgently needed. The problems are well known and include grossly inefficient State Electricity Boards (SEBs), a long history of massive under-pricing to agricultural users, very high levels of power theft, cross-subsidies which hit large- and medium-scale industry, declining levels of investment in generation and transmission and widespread incidence of brownouts and blackouts. One recent survey of over 1000 industrial firms in India found the average cost of power to users (after allowing for blending from the public grid and private generators) to be over Rs 4 per unit, compared to less than Rs 2 in North America and around Rs 2.50 in Korea and Taiwan (World Bank 2002: CII). 70 per cent of survey respondents had to resort to running their own generator sets. Although there has been some reform of the regulatory environment, the basic problems of inefficient, loss-making SEBs and unsustainable pricing and distribution policies remain far from being solved.

Taken together, the summary medium-term outlook for infrastructure performance is not promising. It is even possible that the constraints might get worse before they get better.

Problems in agriculture: Much is being made of the strong growth of agriculture in 2001–2. According to the recently published Advance Estimates of National Income the agriculture sector (broadly defined) was projected to grow by a very healthy 5.7 per cent. Indeed, without this buoyancy in agriculture overall GDP growth would have been well below 5 per cent. However, the current revival masks some worrying longer-term trends. For a start, it comes after two successive years of poor performance, including negative growth in 2000–1. In a somewhat longer perspective, in the nine years after the crisis of 1991–2 the growth of agricultural value added averaged 3.2 per cent, slightly slower than the 3.6 per cent achieved in the 1980s. What is more, while the first five post-crisis years, 1992–7, saw agriculture boom at an average growth of 4.7 per cent per year, the next four years, 1997–2001, recorded a dismal average of only 1.2 per cent. Even if we add the very preliminary estimate for 2001–2, the Ninth Plan average annual growth is only 2.1 per cent, less than half the Eighth Plan average of 4.7 per cent. No wonder GDP growth in the Ninth Plan averaged barely 5 per cent per year, once we adjust for the spurious growth attributable to government pay increases. Experience from all over the world (and India's own Eighth Plan experience) suggests that for a country to sustain economic growth at around 7 per cent or higher, agriculture has to grow at 4 per cent or more.

Similar concerns emerge if we look at the growth of production and yield in principal crops which account for about 70 per cent of value added in the agriculture and allied sector (the rest is attributable to livestock, dairying, fishing, and forestry). Table 10.3 presents comparative data for the 1980s and 1990s. The average growth rate of crop production almost halved from 3.2 per cent a year in the 1980s to 1.7 per cent in the 1990s. And the decline was entirely due to the sharp fall in yield growth from 2.6 per cent per year in the 1980s to 1.0 per cent in the 1990s. Furthermore, the deceleration in production and yield affected both food grains and non-food crops (each accounting for about half of crop production). Food grain growth has dropped below the rate of population growth, while the non-food growth rate has halved from 3.8 per cent in the 1980s to 1.9 per cent in the 1990s. Growth of food grain yields has halved and that of non-food crops has plummeted to only a quarter of the 1980s rate. Assuming a reasonably good correlation between the value added

TABLE 10.3: *Principal crops: Growth of production and yield (per cent per annum)*

	Production		Yield	
	1980/1–1989/90	*1990/1–2000/1*	*1980/1–1989/90*	*1990/1–2000/1*
Foodgrains	2.85	1.66	2.74	1.34
Non-Food Crops	3.77	1.86	2.31	0.59
All Crops	3.19	1.73	2.56	1.02

Source: Economic Survey 2001/2.

data and the crop production data, it would be reasonable to infer that most of the observed deceleration in the growth of production and yield has occurred in the period 1997–2001; indeed the Eighth Plan period may have seen some acceleration.

So what was amiss? Since agriculture accounts for 60 per cent of India's labour force and a quarter of GDP, one might have expected intense scholarly research to yield an authoritative answer to this question. Although there has been a fair amount of research, the answers are still tentative.[6] In the absence of definitive answers to the puzzle of the agricultural slowdown, the following likely reasons can be put forward.

First, real public investment in agriculture (mostly in major and medium irrigation projects) actually fell by a fifth between 1994–5 and 2000–1. Over the same period there was a 25 per cent increase in real private investment (mainly in farm equipment and minor irrigation), taking the share of private investment in total to over three-quarters. The rise in total real investment has been modest, reflected in the fall in the ratio of agricultural investment to agricultural value added to a meagre 5 per cent or so.

Second, the operation and maintenance (O&M) of irrigation systems in most states has deteriorated, partly because of very weak cost recovery as well as widespread entropy in the effectiveness of irrigation departments. The post-Pay Commission pay increases have starved departments of funds for non-salary inputs for O&M. As a result, the management and distribution of the critical resource of water probably worsened.

Third, in most states the rural roads and state highways programmes have not gone anywhere fast for much the same reasons that bedevil irrigation departments. Yet the creation and sustenance of road linkages is crucial for the development of well-functioning agricultural markets.

Fourth, the systems of agricultural research, development, and extension services (which played such a crucial role in the Green Revolution of the 1970s and 1980s) are generally perceived to have become bureaucratic, unaccountable (to farming needs) and unmotivated. The Pay Commission effect of starving non-salary inputs also took its toll.

Fifth, although the terms of trade remained favourable to agriculture as a whole, the natural and necessary diversification away from wheat and rice was retarded by the pattern of inappropriately high procurement-price increases for these crops. They have also created the costly food mountains in public godowns.

Sixth, there is growing evidence that high levels of urea subsidy for many years distorted the use patterns of nitrogen-phosphates-potassium in a way which was cumulatively detrimental to soil fertility.

Seventh, especially in the more populous states, agricultural productivity

---

[6]Bhalla (2001a), Gulati and Bathla (2001), Radhakrishna (2002) and Vaidyanathan (2000).

was hurt by continuing fragmentation of land holdings arising partly from India's peculiarly slow shift of labour force from agriculture to non-agriculture. This peculiarity, in turn, is largely attributable to rigid labour laws (in the organized sector) and SSI reservations, which seriously damaged the expansion of employment in manufacturing (we have only to compare this with the much better experience of East Asian countries).

If these are the right reasons, the solutions to the problems are implicit and clear. But they will not be easy to implement.

Labour supply and demand: As noted in Chapter 8, the economically active population in the age group 15–59 will increase rapidly in the next 25 years. At one level, this addition to the potential labour supply and an associated decline in the dependency ratio offers an opportunity for faster growth of output. However, whether the potential is transformed into reality will depend crucially on the effectiveness of policies to stimulate labour demand and policies to foster good health and skill acquisition, and also on what happens to savings and investment.

The beginning of the potential demographic bonus was in the 1970s, when the labour force first began to grow faster than the total population. The difference between the two growth rates reaches a peak of 0.6 per cent from 2001–11, and declines to 0.07 per cent by 2021–31, according to Bhat (2001c), after which it peters out as the population begins to age. But these are all-India figures. Individual states experience their 'bonus' at different times: the growth difference for Kerala and Tamil Nadu peaked in 1991–2001, and becomes negative after 2011. In gcneral in states with lower fertility the growth difference peaks earlier and declines sooner. Uttar Pradesh and Bihar will still be enjoying a positive growth difference in 2021–31, when it will have become negative elsewhere.

The economic magnitude of the bonus is hard to determine. Bhat (2001c) calculates that it could be as much as 3 per cent per year additional growth in per capita incomes over the period 2001–51. But as he clearly states, this depends on a number of assumptions. One per cent of the 3 is attributed to the growth of labour supply, and four-fifths of that to an increasing female labour-force participation rate, which as he says, and as we have seen in Chapter 8, is highly uncertain in its timing as well as in its magnitude. Further, one has to assume that all the additional labour force will be employed, and with at least the same productivity as in the past. A number of factors militate against this.

First, India's rigid labour laws in the organized sector protect the jobs of the 8–9 per cent of the labour force in this sector and actively discourage fresh employment. The problem is compounded by the pattern of relatively high formal sector wages in government employment. Second, the peculiar policy of reservation of a large range of labour-intensive products for SSI has seriously damaged the rapid development of labour-intensive manufactured exports, in sharp contrast to the favourable experience of a number of East Asian countries, including China. It has also frustrated the development of mutually beneficial and commercially sustainable linkages between small units and large to medium scale ones. Third, the policies in the education sector have been quite weak in fostering the development of skills and productivity, as we have discussed in Chapter 7.

This is the pure labour contribution to the bonus; there is also the potential for increased savings, which could in Bhat's calculation contribute a further 2 per cent to per capita growth. Declining dependency burdens point to a substantial possible increase in savings, but for the demographic bonus to be realized, as Bhat (2001c) again makes clear, there must be no decline in per capita savings rates, and the savings have to be translated into productive capital. As this chapter suggests, one cannot assume this will happen automatically.

Achieving a growth dividend from the anticipated work force increase and associated expansion of savings requires an end to policies which restrict labour demand and dilute skill formation, and improvements in all the factors governing the growth and productivity of savings and investment. As already remarked, some experts have for these reasons questioned the potential significance of India's demographic bonus. It is there, but it has to be grasped.

Governmental performance: Government has an important role in providing a range of public and quasi-public goods and services, in conducting national economic policy and in assuring an institutional framework for expert and independent regulation of economic activity in many areas. But are the governmental departments and agencies up to the job? And what is the outlook for the medium term?

There is plenty of anecdotal evidence to suggest that the quality of public administration in India has been declining steadily, if slowly, over the last several decades. In the relatively simple matter of implementing development projects, there is growing evidence of falling standards. In part, this is linked to growing politicization of civil services and the rising tide of corruption in the politico-bureaucratic nexus. Even the effectiveness of the basic administration of law and order has deteriorated. Ahluwalia (2002) writes

Tensions associated with economic and caste stratification in parts of the country, especially in rural areas, have created disturbed conditions in some of the slow growing states. ... There are reports of urban mafias engaged in extortion, various types of protection rackets, and even kidnapping in parts of some states ....

What is more, the impressionistic evidence suggests that such problems are worst in the poorest and slowest growing states. This, in turn, means that effective implementation of development programmes is weakest where they are most needed.

Aside from general quality, there is also the important issue of expertise in public administration. There is widespread agreement that for too long India has relied on a generalist civil service tradition (especially in executive–management levels) inherited from the British colonial legacy. Despite numerous official reports, there has been little reform of civil services, not counting the legally mandated policies of reservations for backward castes. Although modern governance clearly requires more and more technical knowledge in various fields, India's governance machinery has yet to adapt to this fact. Consequently, the capacity for conceiving, designing, and implementing necessary reforms in various dimensions of economic governance is woefully inadequate in most relevant public agencies. This lacuna is likely to exact a growing toll of development performance in the years ahead.

Finally, and perhaps most importantly for growth performance, coalition governance seems to have become a continuing feature of India's central government since 1996 and of growing importance in the states as well. The experience so far certainly suggests that coalition governments find it harder to take tough, but necessary, economic and financial decisions, especially when they require legislative action. Furthermore, they may be more vulnerable to the pressures of competitive populism. None of this augurs well for either strong fiscal consolidation or bold economic reforms in the medium term.

GROWTH PROSPECTS—AN OVERVIEW

What can we say about the medium-term future? Based on the earlier analysis, there is a reasonable possibility of a mild increase in aggregate savings and investment, if the recent steady decline in government savings can be arrested. On present trends, there is little prospect of a rise in foreign savings or of significant productivity gains from more openness. While there is potential for sizeable productivity gains from major economic reforms, the realistic prospects for quickly translating this potential into reality are not high. Infrastructure, especially power, is likely to be a tightening constraint and agriculture is unlikely to recover the buoyancy of 1992–7. Realization of the potential growth gains from the demographic bonus will depend crucially on the speed and depth of reforms in labour laws, industrial reservation policy, and trade policy. Overall governmental performance could become more of a drag on economic performance. On the other hand, the 1990s have wrought important favourable changes, including reduction of dysfunctional government controls over investment, production, and prices in large chunks of the modern economy. Policy reforms have made the external sector more resilient. Technological advances reach India faster and modern financial practices are more prevalent. However, the possibility of fiscal or financial crisis is greater in 2002 than it was 10 years ago.

On balance it might be reasonable to expect growth to fluctuate in the range of 4–6 per cent, perhaps averaging close to 5 per cent, in the next five years. This is significantly lower than the growth recorded in the 1980s and the 1990s and well below the Eighth Plan period (1992–7) achievement of 6.7 per cent per year. And even this 5 per cent projection might turn out to be optimistic if there is a serious economic crisis, whether triggered in the financial sector, government finances, or as a result of war or international turbulence.[7]

STATE-LEVEL GROWTH

India's reasonable recent progress at the macro level masks a diversity of experience at the state level. There are concerns about progress in the slowest growing, typically the poorest, states; about divergence between the states' rates of growth; and about whether the economic reforms that began in the 1990s may have increased that divergence. Research carried out for the present study provides insights into all these questions (Baddeley et al. 2003).

TABLE 10.4: *India's regional economic growth, 1970–97*

State	SDP	SDP	SDP	% Annual growth	% Annual growth	% Annual growth
	1969–71	1990–2	1995–7	1970–97	1970–90	1991–7
North						
Bihar	555	754	741	1.62	2.13	0.79
Haryana	1190	2120	2579	3.12	2.69	4.58
Madhya Pradesh	730	1169	1324	2.80	2.53	3.32
Punjab	1431	2464	2930	2.85	2.41	3.41
Rajasthan	760	1057	1313	2.18	1.18	5.79
Uttar Pradesh	803	1116	1244	2.03	2.08	2.95
East						
Assam	687	1182	1114	2.57	3.14	−0.94
Orissa	746	1143	1233	2.65	2.76	0.93
West Bengal	1065	1509	1771	2.24	1.89	3.52
West						
Gujarat	1042	1619	2245	3.25	2.80	7.77
Maharashtra	1013	1920	2498	3.80	3.58	5.85
South						
Andhra Pradesh	848	1527	1867	3.50	3.02	4.09
Karnataka	937	1461	1767	3.07	2.69	3.88
Kerala	725	1210	1441	2.74	2.26	3.51
Tamil Nadu	878	1576	1923	3.78	3.15	4.20

Note: Sources and methods for the data in Table 10.4 are described in Baddeley et al. (2003).
Columns 1–3 are real per capita state domestic product (SDP) in Rupees.

[7]A more detailed discussion of the prospects for medium-term growth can be found in Acharya (2002b).

Table 10.4 summarizes the economic growth experience for India's 15 main states in 1970–97 in three periods: the pre-reform period 1970–90, the post-reform period 1991–7, and the entire period 1970–97. During 1970–90, Maharashtra, initially relatively wealthy, was the fastest growing state. Tamil Nadu, Andhra Pradesh, and Gujarat followed. Haryana and Punjab, the two wealthiest states, ranked next, along with Karnataka. Bihar, the poorest state, was also the slowest growing and grew at less than half the rate of Maharashtra. Uttar Pradesh and Rajasthan, also poor states, experienced slow growth.

From 1991 onwards, Gujarat and Maharashtra were the fastest growing states and enjoyed rates of growth comparable with the East Asian economies. Rajasthan also did relatively well. According to our data, Assam experienced negative growth during the post-reform period. Bihar also continued to grow slowly, at a rate nearly ten times lower than Gujarat; it remained the poorest state. Punjab and Haryana remained the two wealthiest states by 1995–7.

Table 10.4 indicates the considerable diversity in state-level growth rates, and that this diversity increased in the 1990s. Other writers have also noted the increasing dispersion in economic growth rates across the states since 1991 (Ahluwalia 2000). Widening gaps in state per capita incomes were also found over the period 1950–80 (Rao 1983). The situation seems to be more one of divergent growth than of convergence (Easterly 2001; Pritchett 1997).

Our data also indicate that some of the most reform-orientated states have enjoyed the fastest rates of growth in the post-reform period. This finding also accords with other writer's views (Bajpai and Sachs 1999). There were numerous elements of state-level reform: infrastructure, industrial policy, and provision of investment incentives. Power sector reform was a significant component of infrastructural reform and has involved tariff revision, unbundling and restructuring of SEBs, and introduction of regulation. Industrial policy reform included introducing simpler and speedier procedures for clearance, and investment incentives were aimed at encouraging private participation and included fiscal inducements such as capital subsidies and tax exemptions. However, the extent of reform varied greatly among the states.

Andhra Pradesh, Gujarat, Karnataka, Maharashtra, and Tamil Nadu can be classified as the most reform-oriented states, Haryana, Orissa, and West Bengal as intermediate reformers, while Assam, Bihar, Kerala, Madhya Pradesh, Punjab, Rajasthan, and Uttar Pradesh are the slowest reformers (Bajpai and Sachs 1999). So growth and reform appear to go hand-in-hand for states such as Gujarat and Maharashtra. Perhaps it is not really surprising that once inter-state competition and private investment assumed greater importance, already prosperous states governed by higher quality administrations were able to capitalize and build on their advantages, though Rajasthan's experience suggests that growth can occur in a less reform-oriented environment. But after 1991, the growth rate in Punjab, another slow reformer, was notably below what would have been expected given its 1990–1 income level, the highest of any state.

Accounting for these differences is complex. Although after controlling for factors explaining states' long-run equilibria our research found evidence of convergence of growth rates, it also showed that convergence has slowed down since the onset of reforms. This does not mean that the reforms were wrong from a growth point of view; only that the poorer states were ill-equipped to profit from them. The central government has found it difficult to intervene in ways that would enhance their growth prospects—so much is due to their politics and deep-seated problems of governance. Our research also confirmed the significance of demographic factors. The higher the dependency rate at the state level (as measured by the ratio of the non-working-age population to the total population of each state), the lower was the rate of economic growth (Baddeley et al. 2003).

GROWTH AND EXPENDITURES ON SOCIAL SECTORS AND POVERTY ALLEVIATION

One of the international concerns of recent years has been the impact of structural adjustment and liberalization on parts of the economy affecting the poor. Chapter 9 has examined the most recent trends in poverty and associated welfare indicators. Here we examine expenditures on the social sectors, which various authors have pointed to as commonly being compressed by reform and adjustment policies.[8] India's performance has not been wonderful. But on this score it is hard to attach much blame to these policies. Social sector expenditures have increased in real terms in the 1990s, but a closer look, especially at the state level, reveals some unhappy tendencies. The reasons for them lie mainly in the character of state politics.

Responsibility for the social sectors is divided between the central government and the states, with the states playing a major role in all of them, while the central government is responsible for schemes that require a national approach. Thus the states have the main role in health, but the centre is in charge of the malaria programme, for example. The centre also supplements resources at the state level for promoting priority concerns, and drives much of the emphasis of policy at all levels; even for central programmes, however, the state government is commonly the implementing agency. For all social sector expenditures the states bear 80 per cent, and for poverty alleviation schemes, 60 per cent. The changes under various heads of expenditure are given in Table 10.5. (It must be borne in mind that social expenditure trends at the state level in real terms are very misleading in recent years because of the post-Pay Commission wage–pension increases, which are spread over 1998–2001 at different times in different states. Thus expenditures may be going

[8]Stewart and Morissey (1995).

TABLE 10.5: *Social sector real expenditure (centre and states) 1991–2 to 1999–2000*

	Period change in expenditure (per cent)	Central share (per cent)		Actual expenditure* (per cent)	
		1991–2	1999–2000	1991–2	1999–2000
Education, sports and arts	199	19	11	37	50.5
Health and family welfare**	81	21	24	11.8	16.1
Medical and public health	71	12.4	19.4	9.7	13.2
Water supply and sanitation	86	21.5	18.8	5.4	7.4
Rural development	50	30	35	11.6	15.8
Urban development	228	28	19	2.8	3.8
Welfare of SCs, STs & OBCs	64	23	17	4.7	6.4

Notes: *Rs 1000 crore in 1993–94 prices
** Family welfare is entirely funded by the centre; medical and public health is a sub-total of health and family welfare.
Source: Shariff et al. (2002) from Budget & Reserve Bank data.

up but deliverables going down where less money is available for non-wage items. We have not been able to correct for these effects.)

It can be seen first, that all sectors enjoyed a real increase, and second, that the central share increased in all social sectors other than urban development and welfare of SCs, STs, and Other Backward Classes (OBCs). Education, health, and rural development are much the biggest items in expenditure terms. With the exception of education, however, growth rates in expenditure on the main items have been low for a period of rapid growth in GNP; education fell slightly as a share of GNP from 3.4 per cent in 1991–2, but climbed from 1997–8 to reach 3.7 per cent in 1999–2000. Health and family welfare, however, started at a dismal 1.2 per cent of GNP, fell below that to 1.1 per cent, only climbing back to 1.2 per cent in 1999–2000.

The increase in the central share reflects two trends: first, a variety of moves at the centre to change priorities and policies in a number of areas; and second, a need to supplement troubled state budgets. Some of the shifts in priorities have been reflected in other chapters. In education, for example, there has been a major effort by the centre to promote primary education, including substantial support for school-meal programmes (though this seemed to have reduced priority after 2000). The health sector has had a major increase in funding for the HIV/AIDS programme, and the 2001–2 budget allocated a further large increase to health, most of it to the family welfare programme. Considerable re-directions have been set in train under various heads of poverty alleviation: in rural development, from special programmes and rural employment to a rural roads programme, with the aim of creating more durable assets for development; and in the change from the PDS for food subsidies to the poor to the TPDS, which has itself acquired sub-programmes designed to reach the ultra-poor and the old.

The reorienting of all these expenditures is welcome in the main, reflecting a number of concerns about failure of many of the old programmes to achieve the intended results, including large leakages, failure of expenditures to reach the intended beneficiaries, the provision of benefits to the less needy, and the failure to pursue urgent priorities. There have also been considerable reductions in a number of government subsidies that have suffered from a variety of inefficiencies, with efforts to protect poor people from any adverse consequences. Some of the major initiatives, notably for example in HIV/AIDS prevention and the DPEP, have benefited from substantial support by foreign aid donors. At the same time, the picture is far from healthy. As pointed out in previous chapters, performance in various sectors is wholly insufficient, with huge deficiencies in the basic provision of education and health, and only modest impacts of public programmes on poverty. Seventy-five per cent of all expenditure on health is private, as is 40 per cent of expenditure on primary education, with very considerable inequalities of access as a result. Several individual states have experienced adverse trends in expenditures on health and education, and many have seen increasing shares of expenditure taken up by wages, with little left over for infrastructure and supplies.

At the same time, some 10 per cent of budgeted allocations to the states for these sectors are never taken up. Some of this reflects the plethora of programmes and schemes which makes implementation difficult; but a large share of it is due to the poor fiscal performance of state governments. The centre has laid down two rules: one, that many of its allocations are on a part-grant, part-loan basis, and the states can often not afford to take on the loan share, given their indebtedness; and two, that states must have spent 75 per cent of the previous year's allocation before they are allowed new funding in the next. The states' debts are due in very large part to massive subsidies for electricity, water, and transport, which are in turn due to populist politics. Deficits of the SEBs are believed to amount to some 2 per cent of GDP; they arise because of large-scale thefts from the grid as well as subsidies. They are a considerable macroeconomic problem, and can plausibly be said to be a major factor by themselves in the lack of public provision for human welfare.

ENVIRONMENT AND GROWTH

What growth is doing or will do to the environment is treated in Chapter 12. This section is concerned with what the environment may do to growth, and whether environmental protection is affordable. Part of the problem of examining this issue is that growth as traditionally measured takes virtually no account of the environment. Gross national product or GDP measure only market transactions. Most environmental effects are not priced or marketed. Value added to natural resources by processing is counted; their depletion is not. The cost of vehicle repairs is included in the national income; the part of their deterioration due to acid rain is not. Various proposals have been made to calculate a 'green GNP' that would take account of environmental costs. There are as yet no settled methods for doing this, and no international data set of green national accounts.

Estimates have been made for the environmental costs of growth. One for India in Brandon, Homman and Kishor (1995) finds that annual losses due to the environment are of the order of 4.5 per cent of GDP—that is to say that if the economy grows at 6 per cent, it loses three-quarters of that growth in environmental damage. However, if one looks closely at this estimate, it turns out that the figure of 4.5 per cent is a mid-range point of judgment between the 'high' estimate of damage (over 9 per cent of GDP) and the 'low' estimate (some 2 per cent or more). Most of the difference between the two extremes of the estimate is due to alternative methods of evaluating the health costs of environmental damage. Every link in the chain of such calculations is weak: in air pollution, say, one measures the amount of emissions from various processes entering into the GDP, transport or manufacturing for example; then the health impact of those emissions, and then the value of the health impact. It is the last item that is the most insecure.

The lowest value one could put on a life is the earnings potential of the individual. But surely life is worth more than a person's wages? Indeed it is. Even if one took only wages, should they be Indian wages? But then an Indian life would be worth less than an American or European life, which is unthinkable. Surely all lives are equally valuable—but then, what are they worth in money terms? There is no real answer to this question. One might well wish to say that any person's life is infinitely valuable, beyond financial estimation. There are really only two ways to go. One is to take the earnings estimate, and accept that it is not the value of a life, but simply the lower bound to that value from a national income point of view: a life is worth at least that much. The other is to consider how society actually values a life, in the sense that society makes (or fails to make) expenditures to save lives, and that puts an implicit valuation on life—again, this is not the 'true' value of a life, just what value society implicitly puts on it from this (limited) point of view. This avoids the America/India comparison, since one can look at the value Indian society places on the lives of Indian citizens. What the Indian government is prepared to spend to save a life is some measure of this implicit valuation; it takes account not only of the value of lives but what the government can afford.

Unfortunately even if one adopts this as a procedure, a large range of values will be found. It will rapidly become clear that different government actions place widely varying implicit valuations on life. These are not just questions of *whose* life. Obviously much more is spent on keeping the president of India out of harm's way than protecting the man in the street; there are also many other questions of distribution and access when it comes to services which are designed to save lives. But if one were to look across the whole range of things society does to protect the lives and health of its citizens, one would find little economic rhyme or reason to it. No-one has gone through every item and ensured that the marginal rupee is allocated to provide the greatest amount of protection. More is spent on this, less on that. Take the horrible fires that occur every so often in public buildings and kill dozens of people: there are building and safety regulations, and inspections to try to ensure they are observed. But no-one has ever worked out the appropriate amount to spend so that life-saving by building inspection saves as many lives per rupee as life-saving by standards of road illumination—this is true not just in India but virtually anywhere.

This is an important topic, because it bears on the relations between growth and the environment. Chapter 12 shows that a great deal of India's past environmental damage has been due more to economic growth and its character than to population growth, even if the latter has been a significant background factor. This is quite likely to continue to be the case in the near future at least. But we also show that curbing further damage can be achieved in most areas at a fairly modest cost, at least as far as concerns energy and the majority of vehicle and industrial pollution.

But will India be willing to bear these costs? Many of the new technologies *will*, in fact, be introduced because they are actually cheaper options for the investor. But some have costs to the investor, while the benefits accrue to the population at large or economic actors other than the investor. Some investments will appeal to companies even if the benefits accrue to others because they find it in their interests to be seen as environmentally responsible— the presence of consumer movements in the West has much to do with this; so far in developing countries NGOs have made more of the running. But when these are not effective, green investments will only be adopted if the government acts on the grounds that the benefits outweigh the costs. In some cases the government will find that the costs fall on the productive sector itself, with measurable impact that they will find it worthwhile to prevent. But what if the costs are measured in ill health or early death? This is the case at present, but the government is not taking many of the actions that will reduce environmental health damage.

That is where the evaluation of health and lives comes in. The government could of course simply decide that it wanted to improve health by environmental policy action, provided that it was not too expensive. It is essentially a political question, and one that is not likely to receive a positive answer unless those who suffer from environmentally induced disease have political weight. Commonly they do not. The better-off classes can often protect themselves from air or water pollution; they have air-conditioners at home, air filters in their cars; they can easily buy pure water or purify it for themselves. The poor are the least able to protect themselves. But few Indian politicians have as yet adopted the interests of the poor as the source of their political base—for any cause, let alone environmental ones.

The government might act on more limited grounds than a full evaluation of the health benefits. They might take the value of health and lives as measured by forgone wages as a lower limit of what it is worth spending. If they are spending a given amount in their health budget on curative medicine, say for respiratory disease, they might take environmental action as a means of saving medical costs. Environmental prevention might be cheaper than medical cure. These are hard-hearted calculations. But they do suggest that even without estimating the wider benefits of health on a full ethical basis, the benefits would very frequently outweigh the costs of green policies.

This discussion abstracts from wider considerations. When it comes to issues of the global environment, it can be—and often is—argued that poor countries cannot be expected to act altruistically in the world's interest, especially when richer countries are responsible for the lion's share of such things as carbon emissions leading to global warming. It is the argument of Chapter 12, however, that India will be able to achieve and afford higher emission standards without detriment to its economic performance, indeed with enhancement of performance. It need not sacrifice economic growth and higher living standards to improve its own environment and its contribution to global environmental protection.

11

Prospects for Food Demand and Supply

Amresh Hanchate and Tim Dyson

T his chapter assesses whether India's food production can be raised to match the growth in demand which will arise from population growth. It also considers alterations in demand which will come from factors like urbanization and changes in people's lifestyles. The data are frequently rough and inconsistent. Often all that can be done is to address issues with a broad brush. Moreover, the canvas is huge, so the need to simplify should require no explanation.

PAST TRENDS

Food production: Cereals form the main component of the Indian diet accounting for approximately 60 per cent of calorie and protein supplies (Hopper 1999). Food and Agriculture Organization (FAO) statistics indicate a considerable rise in annual cereal production, from 43.5 million tonnes in 1949–51 to 191.8 million tonnes in 1999–2000 (FAO 2000a). A rough estimate is that more than half of this cereal production growth was attributable to demand arising from demographic growth (Dyson and Hanchate 2002).

Following the approach of Evans (1998: 91), Figure 11.1 plots the relationship between the size of India's population and the average cereal yield. For the population to have grown there must have been a broadly commensurate increase in cereal availability. Because there are limits to the country's cultivable area, and because the importation of cereals on a massive scale has been deemed unrealistic, population growth has necessarily stimulated a rise in the average yield. These basic facts help explain why the government assumed a central role in food production from 1947, and why it took such an early interest in family planning. Moreover, the relationship is sufficiently tight to suggest that if the population reaches 1.42 billion in 2026 then the average cereal yield (with rice as paddy) will be roughly 3.2 tonnes per hectare.

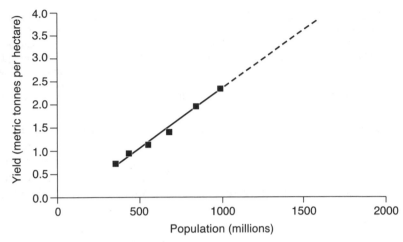

FIGURE 11.1: *Population size and the average cereal yield in India since 1951*
(with simple linear extrapolation)

Note: The cereal yields used above are 3-year averages of output data in production form, that is, with rice as paddy.

Sources: Food and Agricultural Organization, *FAO Production Yearbook*, Rome (various years); Registrar General, India (2001a).

Between 1950 and 2000 annual cereal production per capita rose from 121.5 to 191.0 kg (Table 11.1). There were increases for rice, and especially wheat, but FAO data suggest a 30 per cent decline for coarse cereals. Nevertheless, the overall increase in per capita cereal output has underpinned the considerable improvement in food security since 1947.

TABLE 11.1: *Estimated per capita production of the main foodstuffs in India, 1950–2000*
(kg per person per year)

	1950	1960	1970	1980	1990	2000
Rice	60.3	82.4	77.6	73.8	88.9	88.5
Wheat	18.2	25.4	38.7	51.4	63.8	72.2
Coarse cereals	43.0	53.1	50.7	43.2	37.4	30.3
Total	121.5	160.8	167.0	168.4	190.1	191.0
Pulses	23.7	29.8	21.1	15.6	16.1	14.0

(contd...)

(Table 11.1 continued)

	1950	1960	1970	1980	1990	2000
Vegetables	–	42.2	47.6	52.9	57.8	61.4
Fruits	17.0	31.4	30.4	31.0	33.6	49.0
Milk, etc.	54.7	47.1	40.0	47.4	65.0	76.9
Meat, etc.	3.6	6.5	7.4	8.3	10.5	12.4

Notes: Most estimates are based on three–year averages. However, for cereals and pulses those for 2000 are based on production figures for 1999 and 2000, and for vegetables, fruits, milk, and meat the figures are based on figures for 1999. Here and in all subsequent tables rice is expressed as milled equivalent, milk includes milk products, and meat is inclusive of eggs and fish.

Sources: Food and Agriculture Organization (1987, 2000a) and Registrar General, India (2001a).

Total cereal production has risen mainly because of increased yields. Figure 11.2 shows that from the late 1960s, first for wheat, and then for rice, yields began to rise faster. This reflected the influence of the so-called 'Green Revolution' when high-yielding varieties (HYVs) of cereals were introduced from international agricultural research stations. Subsequent research in India

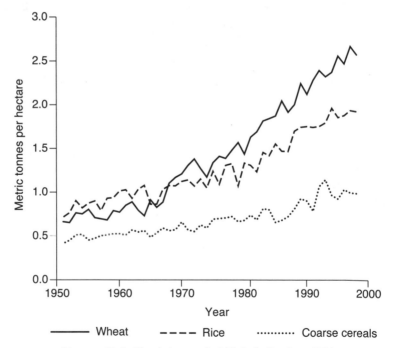

FIGURE 11.2: *Trends in cereal yields in India since 1951*

Note: For reasons of comparability the rice yield is expressed in milled equivalent form.
Source: Food and Agricultural Organization, *FAO Production Yearbook*, Rome (various years).

has built on these advances, and wheat yields, especially, have risen at a fair pace. There has, however, been no comparable rise for coarse cereals. Indeed, in absolute terms, this may never happen because coarse cereals are grown on rain-fed land, which restricts their capacity to benefit from chemical fertilizers.

The importance that successive governments have attached to raising national cereal output, and the substantial promise of wheat and rice to help achieve this, help explain why so much financial support has gone to farmers in Punjab, Haryana, and western Uttar Pradesh—areas with considerable potential for these crops.

Table 11.1 suggests that the per capita production of pulses has fallen considerably, but the record is better for other foodstuffs. During 1960–2000, estimated per capita vegetable production rose by 45 per cent. That for milk, and milk products, rose by 41 per cent during 1950–2000. The per capita production of fruits has almost tripled. In percentage terms the production of 'meat', here inclusive of eggs and fish, appears to have risen too, although from an extremely low base. There have also been rises in the supplies of sugar and vegetable oils (Hopper 1999). So, except for coarse cereals and pulses, trends in per capita production have generally been positive, although for most foodstuffs the levels remain low.

The FAO converts estimates of national food output into annual indices per capita of (i) food production, an index which reflects the monetary value of production, and (ii) calorie availability. Time series of these indices suggest little progress with respect to either measure in the 1960s and 1970s (Dyson and Hanchate 2002). Indeed Table 11.1 indicates that the period 1960–80 saw little change in the per capita production of fruits, milk, and meat and declines for rice, coarse cereals, and pulses. However, after 1980 there were modest rises in both indices. By the late 1990s average per capita calorie supplies were about 20 per cent higher than in the 1960s and 1970s, and the corresponding food production index was about 30 per cent higher. This suggests that during the 1990s farmers increasingly turned to the cultivation of higher value food crops. But the rise in the monetary value of the harvest was not matched by a commensurate rise in its nutritional content.

In this context Figure 11.3 extends the work of Mitchell et al. (1997) and shows that average incomes have more than doubled since 1980, while the estimated price of a representative 'food basket' has remained fairly constant. However, people are spending a significantly greater share of their higher incomes on non-food items (Joshi 1998: 12–3). And, in relation to food, they are buying fewer coarse cereals and pulses (which tend to be nutritionally valuable), but greater quantities of comparatively expensive 'quality' foods, especially milk, fruits, and vegetables. So in some respects the dietary situation seems to be improving, although in other respects it may be getting worse.

Food consumption: Two types of food consumption estimate exist for India. Both are really estimates of food *availability* because neither makes allowance

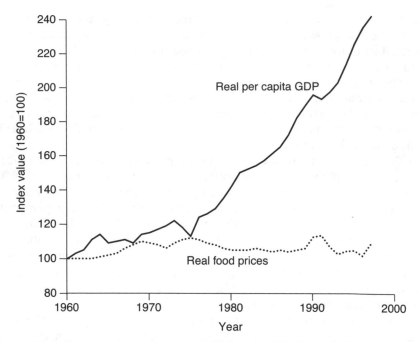

FIGURE 11.3: *Comparison of real per capita GDP and real food prices in India since 1960*

Sources: Mitchell, Ingco and Duncan (1997: 21); International Labour Office, *Yearbook of Labour Statistics*, Geneva (various years); International Monetary Fund, *International Financial Statistics*, Washington DC (various years).

for losses within the home (for example, in preparation). The first type comes from FAO food balance sheets (FBS). FBS estimates of the quantities of food available for 'domestic utilization' derive from FAO's food production estimates—with allowances for the quantities imported, exported, added to or taken from stocks, used for seed and feed, lost in storage prior to being sold, etc. The second type of estimate arises from NSS 'quinquennial' surveys of household food consumption which have occurred every five years since 1972–3. The cereal consumption data from these surveys generally relate to household consumption during the previous 30 days, and are available in quantity form for the surveys from 1972–3 to 1999–2000. For non-cereal foods we have used household-level information to get direct estimates of the amounts purchased for the quinquennial surveys of 1983, 1987–8, and 1993–4. For the surveys of 1972–3 and 1977–8, however, it was necessary to use expenditure and price data to get estimates.[1]

[1]For non-cereals these approaches were not possible for the 1999–2000 survey, which was also complicated by methodological problems. The NSS data on food consumption are collected by male interviewers mainly from male respondents, which underscores the caution with which they should be viewed.

Figure 11.4 compares estimates of the annual per capita quantities of cereals sold through retail outlets (FBS) and reported as purchased by household heads (NSS). For rice and wheat there were modest rises in consumption between 1972–3 and 1999–2000; fairly similar levels of per capita consumption are indicated for 1993–4 and 1999–2000 by both sets of estimates. Coarse cereal consumption has fallen, although by appreciably more according to the NSS. Consequently for coarse cereals the estimated levels of annual per capita consumption differ appreciably: for 1999–2000 the FBS estimate is almost twice that of the NSS.

The differences regarding coarse cereals are significant because of their influence on estimated trends in overall cereal consumption. According to the NSS annual consumption of all cereals combined fell from 175 kg per

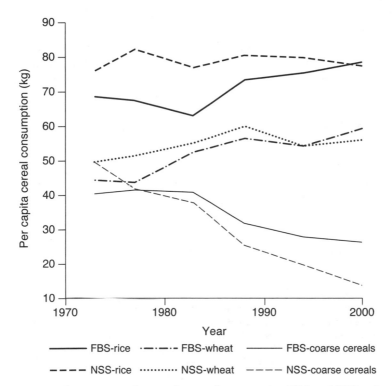

FIGURE 11.4: *Average annual per capita cereal consumption, FBS and NSS estimates, India, 1972–3 to 1999–2000*

Notes: Except for 1983 the NSS estimates plotted above relate to 12 month periods covering two calendar years. To obtain corresponding FBS figures the annual estimates for the same two years were averaged. The sole exception is for 1999–2000, where due to data unavailability the FBS estimates shown are the averages for 1998 and 1999. For reasons of comparability the FBS rice estimates pertain to rice in milled form.

Sources: Food and Agricultural Organization (2000a); Joshi (1998); NSSO (2001).

person during 1972–3 to about 147 kg during 1999–2000. The FBS figures, however, suggest that consumption rose slightly from around 153 kg in 1972–3 to about 157 kg in 1993–4, before increasing to 164 kg in 1999–2000. The discrepancies with respect to coarse cereals are difficult to resolve (Suryanarayana 2002). However, it is worth emphasizing that around 1993–4 both sources were in close agreement with respect to overall levels of consumption: the FBS and NSS estimates were 157 and 154 kg respectively.

Comparison of trends for non-cereals is more problematic, partly because categories like 'vegetables' and 'fruits' are artificial composites. Nevertheless Table 11.2 shows that for 1993–4 there is rough agreement with respect to estimated consumption levels for pulses, vegetables, and milk. Both types of estimate indicate that pulse consumption has fallen, and that levels of vegetable, fruit, milk, and meat consumption have increased. The largest discrepancies relate to fruit and meat consumption levels. There is little doubt that NSS data fail to reflect much fruit consumption in the form of snacks outside the home. Regarding meat, it has been suggested that people may under-report its consumption in supposedly vegetarian India (Sen 2000). However, the NSS does not include questions on certain types of meat consumption, and this is probably relevant too (Kulshreshtha and Kar 2002).

TABLE 11.2: *Comparison of estimates of food consumption, FBS, and NSS, 1972–3 to 1993–4 (kg per person per year)*

Survey year	Pulses		Vegetables		Fruits		Milk etc.		Meat etc.	
	FBS	NSS	FBS	NSS	FBS	NSS	FBS	NSS	FBS	NSS
1972–3	15.4	12.3	51.9	28.0	25.7	5.4	35.2	35.4	7.6	3.4
1977–8	15.3	11.0	57.0	35.5	25.9	6.7	38.5	46.6	8.2	4.1
1983	14.5	12.1	62.3	46.9	27.1	7.1	47.2	49.3	8.6	4.5
1987–8	13.4	12.1	67.0	54.2	28.3	11.8	53.0	49.6	9.4	4.8
1993–4	13.1	10.6	67.2	72.4	34.9	9.0	59.9	57.2	11.1	5.1
Ratio	0.90	0.98	1.15	1.57	1.15	1.46	1.32	1.19	1.19	1.20

Note: The ratio is an index of change. Specifically it is the ratio of the average levels of consumption indicated for 1983, 1987–8, and 1993–4 compared to the average level indicated for 1972–3, 1977–8, and 1983.

Sources: Food and Agriculture Organization (2000b); Jain and Minhas (1991); NSSO *Sarvekshana*, New Delhi (various years).

In summary, there has been increasing diversification of food consumption patterns in India. This reflects urbanization, lifestyle changes, the influence of the media, and the increasing range of foodstuffs available in local markets (Bansil 1999; Dyson and Hanchate 2000). For all-India the data suggest only modest improvement, or even some stagnation, in the nutritional content of the average diet during recent decades. Analysis of NSS data suggests little change in per capita calorie or protein availability between 1972–3 and 1993–4. The poorest sections of the population experienced modest rises in their supplies, mainly because as the relative price of cereals fell so they purchased greater amounts; but the better-off sections seem to have experienced modest declines in calorie and protein availability, partly because they are buying fewer coarse cereals (Hanchate 2001).

The nutritional status of the population is influenced by other factors too. For example, health conditions and water supplies have improved which should favour some nutritional advance. Direct estimates of the population's nutritional status indicate a lamentable situation, although with evidence of improvement. Thus body mass indices for adults show signs of progress (FAO 2000c: 1). According to NFHS data between 1992–3 and 1998–9 the percentage of children aged under four who were underweight fell from 52 to 47 (IIPS and ORC Macro 2000: 267). That said, focusing on average measures is insufficient, because if we are concerned with the total number of undernourished people then any improvement must be weighed against the country's population growth. The scale of stark hunger has certainly declined hugely. But the number of people affected by mild and moderate nutritional problems may not have declined by much.[2]

PROJECTIONS OF FOOD DEMAND

We now present some rough projections of food demand to 2026. The procedures are kept simple because neither the data nor the length of time being considered warrant sophistication. The cereal projections are made at the state-level. However, since smaller physical quantities are involved, the projections for other foodstuffs are made for four regional groupings of states. The NSS data on per capita food consumption underpin the projections because they provide the only state-level figures. Furthermore, except for coarse cereals, fruits, and meat, around 1993–4 the FBS consumption estimates were comparatively close to those of the NSS.

Direct cereal demand: Direct cereal demand refers to consumption in forms like cooked rice and bread. Table 11.3 shows that levels of consumption are invariably higher in rural areas, and that consumption is somewhat greater in the eastern states. Also, people from better-off states (such as Punjab and Maharashtra) tend to consume smaller quantities than people from poorer states (such as Bihar and Orissa). The statistics on changes in monthly consumption are based on data from the NSS surveys from 1972–3 to 1993–4.

---

[2]The FAO (2000c: 1, 2) estimates that the percentage of people whose energy requirements were unsatisfied fell from 36 to 21 between 1969–71 and 1990–2, implying a reduction in numbers undernourished only from 197 to 178 million.

TABLE 11.3: *Levels, trends, and projections to 2026 of direct cereal consumption/demand, rural and urban areas, major states and all-India*

Region/state	Per capita consumption, kg per month				Change in monthly consumption (kg) per year, 1972–3 to 1993–4		Total direct cereal consumption/demand (millions of metric tonnes)	
	1993–4		1999–2000					
	Rural	Urban	Rural	Urban	Rural	Urban	1993–4	2026
South								
Kerala	10.11	9.46	9.89	9.25	0.108	0.064	3.64	4.62
Tamil Nadu	11.72	10.05	10.66	9.65	−0.144	−0.064	7.82	9.41
Andhra Pradesh	13.27	11.30	12.65	10.94	−0.113	−0.082	10.74	14.04
Karnataka	13.15	10.87	11.53	10.21	−0.122	−0.067	7.14	9.69
West								
Maharashtra	11.39	9.37	11.32	9.35	−0.055	0.022	10.67	15.57
Gujarat	10.66	8.96	10.19	8.49	−0.133	−0.083	5.33	8.19
Rajasthan	14.85	11.52	14.19	11.56	−0.159	−0.049	8.04	14.07
North								
Punjab	10.78	9.01	10.58	9.21	−0.213	−0.090	2.66	3.77
Haryana	12.92	10.46	11.37	9.36	−0.158	−0.087	2.63	4.26
Uttar Pradesh	13.91	11.08	13.62	10.79	−0.136	−0.059	24.04	43.20
Madhya Pradesh	14.20	11.32	12.94	11.09	−0.123	−0.074	11.55	18.96
East								
Bihar	14.31	12.82	13.75	12.70	−0.066	−0.044	15.44	28.43
West Bengal	14.96	11.64	13.59	11.17	0.055	0.029	12.23	17.68
Orissa	15.93	13.36	15.09	14.51	0.015	−0.020	6.27	8.48
Assam	13.17	12.05	12.63	12.26	−0.058	−0.050	3.76	5.69
All-India	13.40	10.63	12.62	10.42	−0.086	−0.034	137.67	217.59

Notes: Here and in Table 11.4 the consumption estimates relate to a period of 30 days. The annual changes shown are based on the absolute differences between the average level of cereal consumption obtained from the first three NSS quinquennial rounds and the average level indicated by the last three rounds (data for the 1983 survey being represented in both averages). Here and in subsequent tables the all-India figures were obtained by summing from the state-level up and they include an allowance for smaller states and union territories. The illustrative nature of all the present projections should require no emphasis.

Sources: Cereal data are from Joshi (1998) and NSSO (2001). For the state-level projections of population and urbanization used in the above projections see Chapters 5 and 6.

They indicate that cereal consumption has fallen in both urban and rural areas of most states. Moreover, between 1993–4 and 1999–2000 consumption continued to fall in most states.

The complex nature of the seeming move away from consuming cereals, despite rising incomes, suggests that future levels of direct cereal demand cannot be projected using expenditure demand elasticities. Indeed, NSS data have been used to generate very different estimates of such elasticities (Bhalla et al. 1999). However, extrapolating to 2026 on the basis of the changes summarized in Table 11.3 is also problematic, because if the state-level changes were to continue then levels of per capita cereal consumption soon diverge in improbable ways (Dyson and Hanchate 2000). Accordingly, here we have simply assumed that for the rural and urban populations of each state levels of per capita consumption will remain constant as in 1993–4. For all-India this corresponds to annual consumption of 154 kg per person— a figure which is almost identical to the average of the NSS and FBS estimates for 1999–2000. Table 11.3 shows that using the projected state rural and urban populations for 2026 then total direct cereal demand will increase to about 217 million metric tonnes (mmt). The NSS data suggest that our assumption of constant per capita consumption may err on the high side. But this may be prudent when estimating the future amount of cereals that will be required.

Non-cereals: We have seen that patterns of food consumption have been diversifying. Table 11.4 presents monthly per capita consumption estimates for non-cereal foods for 1993–4 and summary statistics on changes in consumption since 1972–3. It also gives total consumption figures for 1993–4 and demand projections to 2026. Several procedures were explored to gain an idea of how levels of demand might develop, but simple linear extrapolation was found to be preferable (Dyson and Hanchate 2002).

Table 11.4 suggests strongly that urban populations consume more non-cereal foodstuffs than their rural counterparts; and urban populations have generally experienced greater rises in non-cereal food consumption.

Pulses are consumed in significant quantities everywhere, and are a key source of protein. Recent changes in pulse consumption have generally been modest; indeed, at the national level the NSS data suggest little change. The national projected demand figure in Table 11.4 arises from combining the projected monthly per capita consumption figures with the projected state-level rural and urban populations in 2026. From about 9.5 mmt, demand is projected to rise to 16 mmt.

Table 11.4 shows substantial regional variation in vegetable consumption. Average monthly vegetable consumption for all-India increased substantially between 1972–3 and 1993–4; the increases were particularly great in the north and east. Given the regional disparities in consumption which existed in 1993–4, the projected levels for 2026 evince even greater absolute disparities.

TABLE 11.4: *Levels, trends, and projections to 2026 of consumption/demand of major non-cereal foodstuffs, by region and for all-India*

Region	Per capita consumption, kg per month, 1993–4		Projected per capita consumption (demand), kg per month, 2026		Change in monthly per capita consumption, kg per year, 1972–3 to 1993–4		Total annual consumption (millions of metric tonnes)	
	Rural	Urban	Rural	Urban	Rural	Urban	1993/4	2026 (projected)
Pulses								
South	0.75	0.87	1.17	1.22	0.013	0.011	1.94	3.87
West	0.92	0.97	1.07	1.07	0.004	0.003	1.96	3.57
North	1.08	1.11	0.70	1.25	−0.011	0.004	3.39	4.80
East	0.63	0.76	0.74	0.54	0.003	−0.007	1.72	2.97
Vegetables								
South	4.05	4.64	7.98	8.40	0.119	0.114	10.48	26.54
West	4.48	6.18	8.88	11.22	0.133	0.153	10.58	33.18
North	6.18	7.51	11.96	14.56	0.175	0.213	20.19	69.94
East	7.23	8.88	14.03	16.14	0.206	0.220	19.90	62.08
Fruits								
South	0.82	1.19	1.60	2.39	0.024	0.036	2.30	6.32
West	0.44	1.13	0.49	1.40	0.002	0.008	1.41	2.98
North	0.56	1.13	1.48	3.10	0.028	0.060	2.13	10.91
East	0.39	0.96	0.64	1.87	0.008	0.028	1.30	3.90
Milk, etc.								
South	2.95	4.40	3.88	5.83	0.028	0.043	8.40	15.33
West	6.51	7.20	6.50	11.83	0.000	0.140	14.14	29.58
North	6.55	7.43	7.66	12.95	0.034	0.167	21.03	51.12
East	1.83	3.45	2.57	5.17	0.022	0.052	5.59	13.44

(contd...)

(Table 11.4 continued)

Region	Per capita consumption, kg per month, 1993–4		Projected per capita consumption (demand), kg per month, 2026		Change in monthly per capita consumption, kg per year, 1972–3 to 1993–4		Total annual consumption (millions of metric tonnes)	
	Rural	Urban	Rural	Urban	Rural	Urban	1993/4	2026 (projected)
Meat, etc.								
South	0.60	0.65	0.94	1.00	0.010	0.011	1.52	3.15
West	0.19	0.37	0.30	0.78	0.003	0.012	0.53	1.70
North	0.16	0.23	0.18	0.26	0.001	0.001	0.54	1.15
East	0.50	0.84	0.67	1.32	0.005	0.015	1.47	3.48
All-India								
Pulses	0.85	0.94	0.74	1.06	−0.003	0.004	9.52	16.04
Vegetables	5.66	6.75	11.08	12.42	0.164	0.172	64.51	201.32
Fruits	0.57	1.20	1.14	2.39	0.017	0.036	7.54	25.31
Milk, etc.	4.38	5.97	6.03	9.64	0.050	0.111	51.87	115.49
Meat, etc.	0.38	0.53	0.57	0.79	0.006	0.008	4.29	10.00

Notes: The figures relating to milk are in litres (in the last two columns, billions of litres). As elsewhere all figures are only broadly indicative. Thus while fruit consumption may increase by a factor of say three or four between 1993–4 and 2026, as noted in the text the total amount of fruit consumed is very uncertain.

Sources: Consumption estimates for the last three NSS rounds were calculated from household-level data; those for the first two rounds were derived from expenditure data in NSSO, *Sarvekshana*, New Delhi (various years) and Jain and Minhas (1991).

For all-India the respective projected levels of consumption are 11.1 and 12.4 kg in rural and urban areas. Total demand is projected to rise from about 64.5 to 201 mmt.

Table 11.4 suggests considerable regional variation in fruit consumption too, which, interestingly, occurs in broadly the opposite direction to that for vegetables. At the all-India level fruit consumption has grown substantially. There was considerable variation between regions, however; in absolute terms greater growth occurred in the north and south. Assuming these absolute changes in consumption continue, then by 2026 monthly per capita fruit consumption will be roughly 1.1 kg and 2.4 kg in rural and urban areas respectively. Total demand will be around 25 mmt—a more than three-fold rise compared to 1993–4.

Around 1993–4 per capita monthly consumption of milk is estimated at about 4.38 and 5.97 litres in rural and urban areas (Table 11.4). Notice that levels of consumption are especially great in the north and west (reflecting notably high consumption in Punjab, Haryana, and Gujarat). However, milk consumption has risen appreciably in most regions. For all-India, monthly consumption increased at an annual rate of 0.05 of a litre in rural areas and 0.11 of a litre in urban areas. National levels of consumption are projected to rise to about 6.0 and 9.6 litres in rural and urban areas by 2026. And total demand will more than double, increasing to about 115 billion litres.

Lastly, there is 'meat', including eggs and fish. NSS data suggest that egg consumption is trivial, being only 0.64 and 1.48 eggs per person per month in rural and urban areas respectively in 1993–4. However, roughly half of all meat consumed is actually fish, the consumption of which is quite high in Kerala and West Bengal. Even so, levels of meat consumption for all-India are extremely low. Consumption is somewhat greater in the south and east regions (largely due to Kerala and West Bengal respectively), but in the west and north meat is rarely eaten. It is noteworthy that Punjab, Haryana, and Gujarat—all states with comparatively high incomes—have the lowest levels of meat consumption, although they consume a lot of milk. In addition, growth in meat consumption across the country has been negligible in absolute terms. Levels of per capita meat consumption are projected to rise to 0.57 and 0.79 kg for rural and urban areas, and total demand is projected roughly to double to about 10 mmt (Table 11.4).

Indirect cereal demand: Cereals will also be required for feed, seed, and to offset wastage. Feed requirements have attracted particular attention because of the notion that India's population may acquire a significant liking for meat and other livestock products (Bhalla and Hazell 1997). In our view, however, the data just reviewed do not support this. Nor do we believe that the experience of other countries, such as China, provides much guidance about what will happen here. The borrowing of cereal/livestock product conversion factors derived for other countries is also inappropriate. As Bansil (1999) notes, there is little evidence on livestock feed for India although the use of cereals is certainly tiny. Instead, most milk and meat production relies upon dry and green fodder, kitchen and agricultural waste, scavenging and grazing. The only real exception is commercial chicken and egg production, where the use of maize will probably increase.

We employed two approaches to estimate future indirect cereal requirements. First, since the late 1950s the Ministry of Agriculture has assumed that 5 per cent of total cereal output is used for feed, 5 per cent for seed, and 2.5 per cent is wasted—giving a total figure of 12.5 per cent. If direct cereal consumption in 2026 is 217.6 mmt then these factors imply that 31 mmt will be needed. Second, for the organized food production sector Bansil (1999: 12–14) uses feed rates of 0.167 kg of cereals for 1 kg of milk, and 1.2 kg of cereals for 1.0 kg of eggs and meat, excluding fish. If, exceptionally, we assume that for the period 1993–4 to 2026 all of the projected growth for milk and meat in Table 11.4 arises from the organized sector, and use these feed rates, then cereal feed requirements in 2026 will be 10.6 mmt for milk and 4.1 mmt for meat. Adding an allowance of 7.5 per cent of production (18.8 mmt) for seed and wastage gives a figure of about 33 mmt.

So this analysis suggests that in 2026 direct cereal demand will be roughly 220 mmt, with another 30 mmt being needed for other uses, giving a 'ballpark' total of 250 mmt.

Most other cereal demand projections extend to 2020. The present exercise implies that total cereal demand then will be around 237 mmt, a figure which, particularly when allowance is made for the use of different population projections, is similar to some estimates (for example, Kumar 1998; Rosegrant et al. 1995) although lower than others (such as that of 296 mmt by Bhalla et al. 1999). A major reason for appreciably higher estimates of future demand is the inclusion of large feed requirements. However, in our view, even an estimate of 237 mmt may be too high, especially if levels of direct cereal consumption decline, and there are efficiency gains in the use of cereals for seed, and reductions in wastage.[3]

Virtually all of the rise in demand for cereals and pulses is likely to come from population growth. Demand for meat may double, but from a very low base. Demand for milk may double too. There may be roughly a threefold rise in the demand for fruits and vegetables fuelled, especially, by changes in tastes and incomes. The fact that fruit and vegetable consumption are already appreciably higher in urban areas points strongly in this direction.

PROJECTIONS OF FOOD SUPPLY

We now consider the prospects for production, again using a straightforward approach.

[3]For comparisons of cereal demand estimates for 2020 see Thamarajakshi (2001) and Dyson and Hanchate (2000).

Cereals: Table 11.5 shows that around 1996–8 the northern region produced 47.5 per cent of the total cereal harvest, although it contained only 29 per cent of India's population. Punjab is particularly striking: with 2.4 per cent of the population it produced 11.8 per cent of national cereal output. In fact, the east, south, and west regions are all net cereal importers from the north. Punjab is the largest exporter by far, followed by Haryana and Uttar Pradesh. As previously indicated, cereal production in these states has been boosted by significant subsidies to cultivate wheat and rice.

The north accounted for 77 per cent of wheat production in 1996–8. Rice cultivation, however, is fairly dispersed; every region (except the west) produces significant quantities. Coarse cereal cultivation is chiefly restricted to the rain-dependent, semi-arid areas of Rajasthan, Gujarat, Maharashtra, Karnataka, and Madhya Pradesh. Average annual wheat production growth rates during 1954–98 in the north have varied between 3.8 per cent in Madhya Pradesh to 6.3 per cent in Haryana. Production growth rates for rice have been quite diverse. In Punjab and Haryana rice output grew at rates of 9.7 and 7.8 per cent respectively, well above the all-India figure of 2.7 per cent. Rice production continues to grow in most states. Coarse cereal production growth rates, however, are generally low.

Around 1996–8 the total harvested cereal area (almost 40 per cent of it located in the north) was about 101 million hectares (Table 11.5). This figure had changed little since the late 1960s, although the share devoted to wheat increased appreciably (from 13 to 25 million hectares) while that of coarse cereals fell. However, for all types of cereals the average annual growth rate of the harvested area has tended to decline. Thus for rice the area growth rate was 0.8 per cent in the 1950s and 0.5 per cent in the 1990s; for wheat the figure was 3.0 per cent in the 1950s and 1.5 per cent in the 1990s; and for coarse cereals the figure was 1.5 per cent in the 1950s and –1.8 per cent in the 1990s.

Table 11.5 shows that in 1996–8 cereal yields (with rice in milled form) ranged from 1.05 tonnes in Maharashtra to 3.75 tonnes in Punjab. The mix of cereals grown influences the average yield: the greater the share of coarse cereals, the lower the yield. Thus in Maharashtra, Rajasthan, Karnataka, and Gujarat over 60 per cent of the cereal area is devoted to coarse cereals. But states with relatively high yields, like Punjab, Haryana, and Tamil Nadu, specialize in wheat and/or rice. Cereal yield growth rates during 1954–98 were above 2 per cent in most states. Not surprisingly, the highest rates occurred in Haryana, Punjab, and Uttar Pradesh. More generally, in many states yield growth has benefitted from a substantial decline in the area allocated to coarse cereals and pulses. Notice that Bihar, Orissa, Madhya Pradesh, and Assam all have comparatively low cereal yields although they do not specialize in coarse cereals. Interstate differences in yields for the same type of cereal are often considerable.

TABLE 11.5: *Projections of cereal area, yield, and production for the year 2026, major states and all-India*

Region/state	Harvested area			Yield			Production		
	1996–8 (millions of hectares)	Average annual growth rate 1985–98 (per cent)	Projected area in 2026 (millions of hectares)	1996–8 (metric tonnes per hectare)	Average annual growth rate 1985–98 (per cent)	Projected yield in 2026 (metric tonnes per hectare)	1996–8 (million metric tonnes)	Projected for 2026	Average annual growth rate (per cent)
South									
Kerala	0.40	–4.4	0.23	1.83	0.7	1.90	0.7	0.4	–1.70
Tamil Nadu	3.28	–0.8	3.19	2.49	2.4	3.37	8.2	10.8	0.96
Andhra Pradesh	5.40	–1.2	5.44	2.27	3.7	3.13	12.3	17.0	1.15
Karnataka	5.52	–0.6	5.28	1.56	4.2	2.30	8.6	12.2	1.22
West									
Maharashtra	9.99	–0.9	8.85	1.05	3.4	1.66	10.6	14.7	1.16
Gujarat	3.10	0.0	3.05	1.57	6.6	2.38	4.9	7.3	1.39
Rajasthan	9.03	0.5	8.90	1.21	4.9	1.82	10.9	16.2	1.41
North									
Punjab	5.81	1.0	7.00	3.75	1.4	4.48	21.8	31.2	1.26
Haryana	3.81	1.6	4.67	3.00	2.5	4.02	11.3	18.8	1.79
Uttar Pradesh	17.70	0.3	18.84	2.21	2.7	2.95	39.1	55.6	1.24
Madhya Pradesh	12.73	–0.1	13.69	1.21	2.7	1.61	15.4	22.1	1.27
East									
Bihar	8.03	–0.1	8.01	1.58	2.6	2.30	12.7	18.4	1.31
West Bengal	6.29	0.8	7.08	2.23	2.6	3.24	14.0	22.9	1.75
Orissa	4.67	–0.5	4.79	1.18	1.2	1.39	5.5	6.6	0.67
Assam	2.58	0.3	2.71	1.33	1.9	1.73	3.4	4.7	1.14
All-India	101.28	–0.1	104.73	1.82	2.9	2.54	184.2	265.8	1.30

Notes: The projected area, yield, and production figures for wheat, rice, and coarse cereals in 2026 were summed in order to obtain the figures given above. As mentioned in the text, for both area and yield the growth rates actually used in the projections were half the past rates summarized above. Also in a few cases extremely high growth rates (relative to those prevailing in neighbouring states) were substituted by the next highest growth rate found for a state within the same region. For example, the area harvested of wheat in Rajasthan grew at 7.0 per cent per year during 1985–98, but for the projection this was replaced by the corresponding growth rate for Maharashtra of 0.7 per cent. In all cases higher numbers were substituted by substantially smaller numbers.

Sources: Ministry of Agriculture (1997, 2002).

Two considerations were important for the present projections. First, past growth of cereal areas and yields have been far from uniform. In this context more recent trends are probably better indicators of future changes. Accordingly, we selected 1985 as a cut-off year and the cereal projections are based on yield and area growth rates for the period since. Second, if area and yield growth rates have tended to decline, then, given a rather distant projection date (2026), it seems appropriate to allow for further declines. Therefore, for each cereal crop in each state, we assumed that in the period to 2026 the average annual growth rate of harvested area and yield will be half that experienced during 1985–98—a reduction which seems suitably cautious, although it will not apply to all states.

Although the projections dealt with rice, wheat, and coarse cereals separately (since their area and yield trends can vary in magnitude and sign) the results in Table 11.5 are given for all cereals combined. Notice that one result of working from the state-level up is that the area of cereals harvested for the country is projected to rise slightly, although it fell slightly during 1985–98. The average cereal yield for all-India (with rice in milled form) is projected to rise to 2.54 tonnes in 2026. This corresponds to 3.1 tonnes if rice is counted as paddy, and 3.2 tonnes if there is no increase in the harvested cereal area. Cereal production is projected to rise to around 265 mmt by 2026, a figure which compares favourably with the demand estimate of 250 mmt.

The largest rises in cereal production seem set to occur in Uttar Pradesh, Punjab, West Bengal, Haryana, Madhya Pradesh, and Bihar. Indeed, the four northern states are envisaged to account for 49 per cent of the total production increase, with West Bengal and Bihar together contributing another 18 per cent. However, in Uttar Pradesh, Madhya Pradesh, and Bihar future demographic growth may well mean that these cereal production increases do not translate into clear surpluses. Also, comparison of these results with those for demand (and making some allowance for indirect cereal demand and requirements for other uses) suggests that Maharashtra and Gujarat, in particular, may become significantly more dependent upon cereals grown elsewhere. That said, the projected output figures for Punjab, Haryana, and, to a lesser extent, West Bengal are all significantly bigger than the corresponding demand figures. So these states may become even more important for the national cereal supply. Lastly, comparing 1996–8 and 2026, the share of wheat in total cereal output rises from 37.0 to 40.8 per cent, rice rises from 44.0 to 45.6 per cent, but coarse cereals fall from 19.0 to 13.6 per cent.

Non-cereals: The total area harvested of pulses was constant during 1985–98 (Table 11.6). However, adopting the same projection approach as for cereals implies that this area will increase modestly to about 26 million hectares, and that the average yield will rise from 0.65 to 0.81 tonnes. Total pulse production increases from 15.0 to about 23.7 mmt in 2026. If, as for cereals, we allocate 12.5 per cent of output for feed, seed, and wastage then 20.7 mmt remains

TABLE 11.6: *Projections of non-cereal food production for the year 2026, regions and all-India*

Region/food	Harvested area			Yield			Production	
	1996–8 (millions of hectares)	Average annual growth rate 1985–98 (per cent)	Projected area in 2026 (millions of hectares)	1996–8 (metric tonnes per hectare)	Average annual growth rate 1985–98 (per cent)	Projected yield in 2026 (metric tonnes per hectare)	1996–8 (million metric tonnes)	Projected for 2026
Pulses								
South	3.88	−0.2	3.81	0.44	1.0	0.56	1.7	2.1
West	8.52	2.5	12.28	0.55	3.4	0.86	4.7	10.6
North	8.34	−0.4	8.01	0.77	1.5	0.98	6.4	7.9
East	2.36	−4.0	2.13	0.59	0.0	0.84	1.4	1.8
All-India	23.04	0.0	26.15	0.65	1.5	0.81	15.0	23.7
Vegetables								
South	0.91	0.7	1.16	16.37	1.8	23.50	14.9	27.4
West	0.58	7.3	1.62	11.91	−2.4	8.78	6.9	14.2
North	1.17	2.7	1.80	15.65	1.1	17.75	18.3	32.0
East	2.71	3.0	3.50	13.13	2.1	15.77	35.5	55.2
All-India	5.66	1.8	8.53	13.83	2.5	19.82	78.4	133.5
Fruits								
South	1.14	3.2	2.21	14.79	3.3	22.63	16.8	50.0
West	0.57	7.0	1.63	16.11	0.4	17.38	9.2	28.4
North	0.68	1.7	0.91	9.62	2.5	14.22	6.6	12.9
East	0.75	3.3	1.43	10.00	0.4	6.20	7.5	8.9
All-India	3.67	3.5	7.22	11.60	1.7	14.84	42.6	106.4

Notes: Due to data limitations the growth rates for vegetables and pulses shown are for 1991–8. The high all-India yield growth rate for vegetables (relative to the regional rates) arises from the published data. As for cereals the area and yield growth rates used in the projections were half the past rates summarized above and in a few cases very high growth rates (relative to those prevailing in neighbouring states) were substituted by the next highest growth rate for a state in the same region.

Sources: Ministry of Agriculture (1997, 2002); National Horticulture Board (2000).

for human consumption: a figure which compares favourably with the demand estimate of 16 mmt. Notice that because of strong area and yield growth the share of total production in the western region is projected to rise sharply.

Table 11.6 shows that in all regions the area harvested of vegetables increased considerably during 1991–8 (detailed production data exist only from 1991). The rate of increase was especially high in the west, although the corresponding yield there appears to have fallen quite significantly (trends which probably reflect data problems and are partly offsetting). The present projections suggest that vegetable output will rise to about 133.5 mmt by 2026, at an annual rate of 1.82 per cent. On this basis it appears that production may fall well short of demand because the figures in Table 11.4 imply that demand will increase at an average rate of 3.5 per cent. That said, the shallow time depth of the data available on vegetable production may be part of the problem, particularly when the growth rates of harvested areas and yields are halved for projection purposes.

Turning to fruits, the harvested area has grown even faster than for vegetables. All regions experienced area increases. However, yield growth rates have been more modest. The projections suggest that total fruit production may rise from 42.6 mmt in 1996–8 to about 106.4 mmt by 2026, a figure which is four times the demand estimate. We have also seen that NSS consumption data probably understate fruit consumption a lot. Therefore, again, it is better to compare projected growth rates of demand and supply. In this context the projections suggest that fruit demand will rise at 3.7 per cent per year, which is somewhat above the projected supply growth rate of 3.2 per cent. Notice that the contribution of the southern region to fruit production increases substantially (Table 11.6).

During the 1990s, milk production grew at an annual rate of 4.1 per cent (Table 11.7). In 1997–8 output reached 72.3 billion litres with the northern states producing almost 42 per cent. In the mid-1990s, the average daily yield per milch animal was 5.9 litres, but Punjab and Gujarat had yields of

TABLE 11.7: *Production and projections for milk, regions and all-India*

Region	Production (billions of litres)			
	1992–3	*1997–8*	*Average annual growth rate (per cent)*	*Projection for 2026*
South	11.28	15.13	6.1	35.42
West	12.74	15.88	4.5	30.01
North	25.33	30.35	3.7	51.04
East	7.56	8.51	2.4	11.88
All-India	59.14	72.29	4.1	132.79

Notes: State-level data on milk production are available from 1992. Again, both the area and yield growth rates used in the projections were half the past rates summarized above.
Source: Ministry of Agriculture (1999).

8.9 and 8.2 litres respectively (Ministry of Agriculture 1999). However, recent growth in milk production has been greatest in the south. Assuming that state-level production growth rates in the period to 2026 are half those of the 1990s then total output will increase to 132.8 billion litres which compares favourably with the demand projection of 115.5 billion.

Turning finally to meat, inclusive of eggs and fish, state-level production data are unavailable, so here we employ national estimates from FAO (1987, 2000a). They indicate that production increased from 1.3 to 12.5 mmt between 1950 and 1999, at an annual rate of 4.5 per cent. In the 1990s the growth rate was about 3.9 per cent. The NSS-based meat demand estimate for 2026 in Table 11.4 is actually below FAO's production estimate for 1999 (reflecting the extremely low levels of consumption recorded by the NSS). So, perhaps, all we can safely conclude is that if past meat production growth rates are sustained then that should meet future demand growth which is projected to rise at 2.6 per cent per year.

DISCUSSION

Patterns of food consumption will continue to diversify in India. Growth in cereal and pulse demand will be comparatively moderate and mainly due to demographic growth. For both these foodstuffs, supply seems well capable of matching demand. Milk and meat demand will probably grow faster but, again, there appear to be no insurmountable problems for supply to keep pace. If supply side difficulties are raised by these illustrative projections then they relate to fruits and, still more, vegetables—crops which can be fairly water intensive. Here, particularly, strong projected demand growth largely reflects changes in people's lifestyles, incomes, tastes, and so on. The foregoing analysis also points to comparative advantages in agricultural production. Punjab and Haryana, in particular, have good soils and relatively sophisticated farming infrastructures and are potentially strong producers of many food crops. More generally, the western region appears to have an advantage in pulses, and the southern in fruits. A related conclusion emerges for milk where, in the 1990s, production methods pioneered in the northern and western states were fast being adopted in southern states such as Karnataka.

Of course, in reality demand and supply interact through prices. And, over the long run, demand and supply are essentially one. Moreover, projections based on past trends have their limitations because new influences may come into play to affect future developments. Accordingly, here we qualify the foregoing results, taking particular account of the main factors of production and likely changes in the policy environment.

Human labour for agriculture is plentiful and will remain so. Problems of labour oversupply and land fragmentation are especially severe in parts of eastern India (for example, Bihar) and in rain-fed areas where coarse cereals are cultivated. Although the share of the total working population employed in agriculture will continue to fall, rural population growth will ensure that in most states labour will be abundant: the more so because agricultural mechanization will increase significantly in the period to 2026. To the extent that labour shortages develop in specific locations, rural migration will fill the gap.

The land area used for cultivation (that is, the net area) has changed little since the late 1960s. In 1997–8 it was 142.0 million hectares, about 11.6 per cent of which was used for non-food crops (Ministry of Agriculture 1997, 2002). Some states have been able to expand their net areas (for instance, through forest clearance), but land degradation (for example, salinization, waterlogging) has worked—and will work—in the opposite direction. Urbanization is relevant too. Assuming the 1991 urban population density (3370 persons per sq km) then India's projected urban expansion of 220 million by 2026 could, allowing for the fact that about 55 per cent of the country's total land area is not used for agriculture, reduce the net cultivated area by 2.9 million hectares (2 per cent). That said, there is enormous scope for regenerating degraded land, which can also produce much needed rural employment (Kothari 2002). So it seems reasonable to conclude that the net cultivated area will not reduce by much.

However, the situation is different with respect to the gross (that is, harvested) area which will certainly expand considerably. In 1950–1 only 13 per cent of the net cultivated area was harvested more than once each year. Therefore, the country's gross cultivated area then—about 17 per cent of it irrigated—was 131.9 million hectares. By 1997–8, however, the gross area had risen by 45 per cent to 190.8 million hectares, with about 38 per cent irrigated (Ministry of Agriculture 1997, 2002). Moreover, the gross area has continued to expand and will certainly surpass 200 million hectares well before 2026. Our projections suggest that there may be a slight rise in the harvested area for cereals, but there will be significant rises in the areas devoted to fruits and vegetables. This seems probable, given the envisaged strong demand growth for these foodstuffs and likely improvements in associated transport and storage facilities. Therefore, we anticipate that in areas of the greatest agricultural potential, especially Punjab, but also Haryana, western Uttar Pradesh and, for vegetables, Himachal Pradesh, the long-anticipated diversification of food production will increasingly happen. And in such locations, and areas close to major towns, land will be switched out of cereals into other food crops.

Water resources and management issues will be crucial to India's future agricultural development (see also Chapter 14). Irrigation promises higher yields, but there is mounting concern about the rapid growth of groundwater extraction and falling water tables. Data on these matters are scarce. However, Figure 11.5 illustrates trends in the net and gross irrigated areas and underscores the particular expansion of the latter. The area irrigated from canals has more than doubled since 1950, but groundwater irrigation saw remarkable growth largely due to the spread of tube-wells from the 1960s. Thus while the area irrigated by canals increased at an annual rate of 0.9 per cent between 1980 and 1992, that for tube-wells grew at 4.3 per cent. By the start of the twenty-first century the tube-well area probably surpassed the canal area.

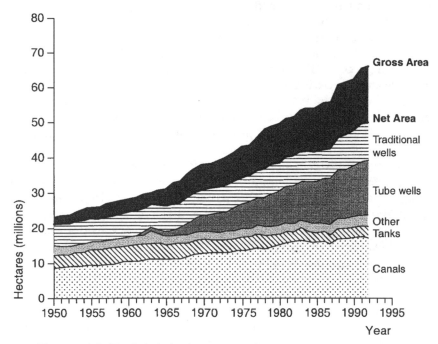

FIGURE 11.5: *Trends in irrigation source and coverage, 1950–1 to 1992–3*

Source: Centre for Science and Environment (1999c).

The northern region alone accounts for nearly half the country's gross irrigated area. Of the total area under groundwater irrigation, predominantly through tube-wells, 63 per cent was located in the north. Punjab, Haryana, and Uttar Pradesh all have high proportions of their net cultivated areas under irrigation; in 1992–3 the figures were 93.0, 75.8, and 67.1 per cent respectively (CSE 1999c: 7).

Most canals are constructed and maintained by governments. In theory farmers should be charged levies to help meet the costs of provision. But this rarely happens, and often they get their water free (Vaidyanathan 1999). Canals also restrict the control growers have of their water. In contrast, tube-wells are installed privately, often with subsidized loans, and give farmers much greater control. These advantages are often reinforced by the provision of free electricity for pumping. In the future tube-wells will be more important to the growth of multiple cropping than will canals, even though in some places excessive extraction rates are leading to declines in groundwater levels. The spread of tube-wells explains why between the 1980s and the 1990s the growth rate of the net irrigated area rose from 0.9 to 1.9 per cent. Because tube-wells are privately owned, superior economic returns should result from the continuation of this trend, although this will probably occur with a reduction in associated subsidies.

There is still some potential for the expansion of surface irrigation in certain river basins. But the installation of major canal systems in most regions would involve high costs. Estimates suggest that the irrigation potential from groundwater sources is about 64 million hectares, of which about 55 per cent was being utilized by 1993 (World Bank 1998a: 9). Eastern India, especially, has significant promise. Tube-well growth in this region has the potential to address serious environmental problems (such as water logging) and help reduce rural poverty. There are promising signs in eastern Uttar Pradesh (where the pump subsidy scheme has been reformed) and West Bengal. Other developments may involve the introduction of new ways of collecting electricity charges and better pumps, plus the possibility of growing a large summer crop (Shah 2000). Moreover, should Punjab and Haryana not raise their cereal production at the rates envisaged in the present projections (for example, if farmers switch to growing vegetables, perhaps because wheat and rice support prices are reduced) then West Bengal, and also Bihar and eastern Uttar Pradesh have considerable potential to raise cereal output and help bridge any gap.

The period to 2026 will certainly see a shift towards improving the performance of existing irrigation facilities. This will involve restructuring canal administrations to make them more responsive to growers, much greater use of canal water charges, and major reductions in electricity subsidies. Using such approaches, schemes in Orissa and Karnataka have already resulted in substantial expansion of the irrigated area and significant increases in agricultural production. Efficiency improvements by themselves could add the equivalent of several million hectares of irrigated land without drawing on any additional water resources (World Bank 1998b).

It is notable, concerning water, that the 1990s saw a quite unexpected reduction in the annual volatility of India's cereal harvest. This reflected the spread of tube-wells, the continued decline in growing coarse cereals, plus a series of relatively good monsoons (Dyson and Hanchate 2002). Most climate models indicate increased temperatures and greater monsoon rainfall for India during the twenty-first century, although possibly with reductions in winter rainfall and more flash-floods. With other effects (for example, sea-level rise, and increased concentrations of atmospheric carbon dioxide (CO_2)) such developments will eventually have significant implications, both negative and positive, for Indian agriculture (Lal 2000). However, the changes are expected to be small within the time horizon under review.

Turning to agricultural technologies, the HYV cereals introduced in the late 1960s spread rapidly, helped by various forms of subsidy. By 1997 the proportion of the total foodgrain area harvested of HYVs reached 85 per cent (90 and 73 per cent for wheat and rice respectively). This development provided powerful stimulus for the rapid expansion of the country's agricultural research establishment, which in turn facilitated both the adaptation of HYVs to Indian conditions and the development of new cross-bred seeds. Today, India's research establishment is one of the largest in the world. And the role of the private sector in seed research has grown, especially in relation to fruits, vegetables, oilseeds, and cotton (Singhal 1999).

There is actually considerable scope for future yield growth using seeds and agricultural techniques which already exist. And conventional plant breeding programmes are likely to remain the chief source of improved crops for the next decade or so. However, greater gains are achievable through genetically modified (GM) crops. These are already widely grown, for example, in the United States (US) and China, although because of possible health and environmental risks they have not been widely adopted in India yet. That said, the country has substantial capacity in agricultural biotechnology. There has been considerable laboratory work, and field trials, for instance, for cotton and sorghum. As GM crops are increasingly cultivated elsewhere in the world so it is probably inevitable that some will be introduced in India step by step. This development will be fuelled by competition, as international trade barriers are reduced under World Trade Organization (WTO) rules.

Much greater use of chemical fertilizers will be another key part of the country's agricultural future. India's use of fertilizers is comparatively low. In the mid-1990s use per hectare was only about 25 per cent that of China (World Resources Institute 1998: 267). However, fertilizer applications are increasing inexorably, rising from 67 to 86 kg per hectare between 1991–2 and 1997–8. Moreover, interstate variation is considerable. In 1997–8 use per hectare ranged from 18 kg in Assam to 171 kg in Punjab (Fertilizer Association of India 1998). With probable growth in access to irrigation, especially in eastern India, there will certainly be increasing returns for farmers from greater fertilizer use. The average use rate of chemical fertilizers per hectare could well double by 2026, and in areas of high application this will probably provoke increasing health and environmental problems ranging from nitrate contamination of ground and surface water supplies to eutrophication. Such problems are not inevitable, but avoiding them will require much greater attention to these environmental issues than has been apparent hitherto. Analysis by Evenson et al. (1999) reveals that yield growth in India has also benefited from agricultural extension work, and that higher literacy levels have probably enabled faster dissemination of new technologies and better farming practices. Yield growth tends to be greater in areas with superior food marketing networks and, related to that, better road infrastructure. These findings suggest that improvements in all these spheres will contribute to raising food crop yields in the years ahead.

Finally, a few words are required regarding future policies. As we intimated at the outset, several key government policies pertaining at the start of the twenty-first century are unsustainable. This applies, for example, to the high support prices which farmers receive for wheat and rice, and to the extensive fertilizer and electricity subsidies. The former have led to massive food grain stocks—exceeding 60 million tonnes in 2001—which are wasteful and expensive to maintain. The latter have had adverse environmental consequences, on soil fertility and groundwater levels, for example. In the future subsidies will be reduced and used more selectively to help the poor. Thus a transference of support price subsidies towards coarse cereals would benefit farmers in rain-fed areas (Asthana 2001). Similarly, in Bihar, money which is frequently wasted on minor irrigation schemes could be better used to give poor farmers pumps (Shah 2000). The country's system of fair price shops often fails the poor most in the country's poorest states; the future will surely see increased targeting of subsidized food-grain provision. Indeed, the germs of such policy shifts are already detectable, although they will sometimes involve tough decisions and take years to unfold.

Lastly, there is the issue of international trade. The new century is seeing small, but increasing, volumes of some fruits and vegetables being imported into India under WTO rules. This trend will continue, and the country's long-standing policy of food self-sufficiency is going to crumble away inexorably at the edges. Indian farmers cannot compete internationally, for example, in growing sugar cane (which is costly in terms of water consumption). But they have comparative advantages in growing pulses (Hopper 1999) and certain fruits and vegetables. In future trade negotiations one key priority will be to protect the interests of India's poor farmers, for example, those growing coarse cereals and oilseeds on rain-fed land.

CONCLUSIONS

India's food prospects are extremely complex. We have only scratched the surface here. It is clear that the country will be able to feed its rising population, although population growth will remain a major influence on Indian agriculture in the period to 2026. Nevertheless, we expect that average levels of food consumption will improve somewhat; the average diet will be a little richer especially in vegetables, fruits, and milk. But increasing agricultural mechanization and urbanization mean that patterns of human activity are changing fast: obesity is already a significant and growing problem in the major towns. The present conclusions regarding food prospects are broadly consistent with the anticipated reductions in poverty discussed in Chapter 9. India will certainly contain many undernourished people in 2026, but probably fewer than existed at the start of the century. Cereal output of 250 million tonnes is an eminently attainable figure. Indeed, it could well be surpassed. The average cereal yield (with rice as paddy) will be just over three metric tonnes.

However, one reason for confidence that the projected food demand volumes will largely be met is that they are so pitifully low. Moreover, the evidence suggests that rising levels of income have often not been used in ways that improve the diet; but then people do not always do what is good for them. So, while there will be modest gains, there will be no radical transformation of India's food situation in the period to 2026.

12

Modelling the Environment: The Production and Use of Energy[1]

DENNIS ANDERSON

B y reference to the technologies and practices for the prevention and control of environmental damage, this chapter seeks to show why India may aspire to a greatly improved environment and a higher rate of economic growth. In fact, on account of the economic benefits of environmental improvement, which are likely to exceed the costs by an appreciable margin, India's economic prospects would be improved. This conclusion is supported through an in-depth analysis of the economic and environmental problems arising from energy production and use, and evidence which shows that energy is not a special case.

FIVE PROPOSITIONS ON THE ENVIRONMENT, POPULATION, AND ECONOMIC GROWTH

The five propositions considered below are:

On pollution and economic prosperity: Addressing environmental problems will lead to an improvement, not a diminution, of India's economic prospects, and

[1]Aside from friends and colleagues working on the study, the author is especially grateful to R.K. Pachauri, Ajay Mathur (now with the World Bank), and Lubina Qureshy of the Tata Energy Research Institute (TERI) for their hospitality and generosity in sharing ideas during a visit to Delhi in 2000; to Robin Vanner and Charlotte Ramsey who did their MSc projects under my supervision as part of this project and were able to gather and analyse much valuable material; and to Richard Perkins and Robert Cassen for their thoughtful and detailed comments on the drafts.

the goal of achieving economic prosperity in India can be fully reconciled with that of reducing pollution to low levels.

On population and the environment: If environmental policies were in place, the 'population effect' on harmful emissions and effluents would be relatively small.

On income distribution and the environment: The worst environmental problems facing India afflict the lowest income groups the most, and it is evident that environmental policies would be beneficial for distribution and growth.

On the role of technical progress in pollution abatement: Technical progress, together with the policies which induce it, is by far the most important factor in enabling countries to reconcile economic growth with environmental improvement. It is the capacity of technologies and practices to prevent and control pollution that explains the preceding propositions.

On the benefits of addressing environmental problems sooner rather than later: Introducing policies sooner rather than later would reduce the peak intensity of pollution by a factor of five or more in most cases, and lead to environmental problems being solved a generation or more earlier.

The propositions are first supported through case studies of energy production and use covering local and regional air pollution from electricity generation, urban transport and household fuels, water pollution, and 'global' pollution from CO_2 emissions. Evidence on some other sectors is then discussed. The findings given here echo those of several other studies, most recently those of the Tata Energy Research Institute (TERI) (1997, 2001), the World Energy Assessment of the United Nations Development Programme, and World Energy Council (2000), and, in relation to carbon emissions abatement, Grubb (1997), Grubler (1998), Goldemberg (1998), and the scenarios of low emissions of the Intergovernmental Panel on Climate Change (IPCC) in all three of its Assessment Reports.

TECHNOLOGIES FOR POLLUTION ABATEMENT: EVIDENCE FROM ENGINEERING AND ENVIRONMENTAL STUDIES

If high levels of economic output are to be reconciled with low levels of pollution, it is evident that technologies and resource management practices having low levels of emissions per unit of output need to be developed and deployed. Table 12.1 lists examples of such technologies now commonly in use or under development in relation to the following sources of pollution and environmental damage:

Electricity generation: PM and sulphur dioxide (SO_2) emissions from the combustion of coal, and the emission of nitrous oxides (NO_x) from the combustion of gas and coal in power generation.

Motor vehicle emissions from petrol engines: a range of tailpipe emissions from vehicles.

Traditional fuels: wood, crop residues, and dung-cakes used for household cooking to be replaced by the use of liquefied petroleum gas (LPG), kerosene, or biogas. As the traditional fuels are a source of soil erosion and nutrient loss, two indicators of the abatement efficiencies and costs are included in the table, one relating to the abatement of smoke, the other to the reduction of soil erosion.

Carbon dioxide: the table lists some renewable energy technologies now under development.

Industrial and municipal wastewaters: the reduction of biological oxygen demands, suspended solids, faecal coliforms, phosphorous and nitrogen from municipal wastewaters.

TABLE 12.1: *Pollution intensities and costs of technologies for the prevention and control of air and water pollution, relative to those of the polluting technologies they displace*

Source and type of emissions or effluents	Index of pollution per unit output (polluting practice = 100)		Indicator of added costs, per cent	Comments on nature of low-polluting practice (see also the table's footnotes)
	Polluting	Low-polluting		
Electricity Generation:				
PM only	100	< 0.1	< 0 to 2.0	Natural gas; 'clean coal'
PM and SO_2	100	0 to 10 [a/]	< 0 to 8 [a/]	technologies; low-sulphur fuels;
PM, SO_2, and NO_x	100	10 to 30 [a/]	<0 to 10[a/]	low-NOx boilers and emission control catalysts.
Motor Vehicle Emissions:				
Lead	100	0		Unleaded and reformulated fuels,
Volatiles (VOCs)	100	4		and catalytic converters (petrol
CO	100	4		engines). Low-sulphur fuels
NO_x	100	20	≈3.5%	and particulate traps (diesel).
SO_2 (diesels)	100	5		The 3.5 per cent figure is relative
PM (diesels)	100	<10		to total discounted lifetime vehicle and fuel costs and is roughly the same for diesel and petrol engines.
Renewable energy technologies for reducing CO_2 emissions:				
Wind (electric power)	100	0	0 to 30	Costs declined 5-fold since 1985.
Biomass (electric power)	100	<0	0 to 100	Costs vary with source of fuel.
Biomass (ethanol)	100	0	≈50	Brazilian data. Costs declined by factor of 3 since 1980s.
Photovoltaics (off-grid)	100	0	≤ 0	High insolation areas. Relative

(contd...)

(*Table 12.1 continued*)

Source and type of emissions or effluents	Index of pollution per unit output (polluting practice = 100)		Indicator of added costs, per cent	Comments on nature of low-polluting practice (see also the table's footnotes)
	Polluting	*Low-polluting*		
Photovoltaics (grid)	100	0	0 to >400	costs vary greatly with application. Costs of PVs have declined 50-fold in the past 25 years.
Solar-thermal (electricity)	100	0	≈50–100	High insolation areas only. Costs also declining with technical progress.
Geothermal (electricity)	100	0	≤ 0	Costs location specific.
Fuel Cells (electricity and vehicles)	100	0	Not available	Emissions assume renewable energy source for hydrogen.

Industrial and municipal wastewater treatment (primary, secondary and tertiary treatment):

Primary and Secondary:

BOD	100	5	1–2 per cent	Based on costs of US $1.9 per m^3
Suspended solids (SS)	100	5	of value	and typical volumes of waste-
Total phosphorous (TP)	100	5	added	water per unit value added in
Total nitrogen (TN)	100	65	in cities	municipal areas.

As above plus tertiary:

BOD	100	3	1.5–3 per cent	Ditto, at costs of US $2.5 per m^3.
Suspended solids (SS)	100	5	of value	
Total phosphorous (TP)	100	5	added	
Total nitrogen (TN)	100	13	in cities	

Household fuels in developing countries:

Smoke from firewood and dung	100	0 <1 to 5	< 0	Gas, LPG, and kerosene. Stoves with flues.
Soil erosion (sediment yield)	100	<0 to 1	< 0	Agro-forestry and erosion-prevention practices.

Notes: [a]The index of pollution here refers to SO_2 only, since the figure for PM is provided in the preceding row. Similar remarks apply to NO_x in the following row. The estimates of added costs are for PM in the first row, PM and SO_2 in the second row, and for all three pollutants in the third row.

Source: See Anderson (2001) for details.

The data on abatement efficiency show the emissions per unit output of the low polluting practice listed as a percentage of the emissions of the technology or practice displaced (the latter is indexed at 100). With the partial exception of emissions from vehicles in times of congestion, such data are fairly reliable. They are not based on laboratory experiments in ideal conditions, but on verification tests when new plant and equipment are being commissioned, the monitoring activities of environmental agencies, and field studies of the technologies in use.

Data on the costs of abatement are more uncertain, and the indicators in

Table 12.1 are put forward with the customary qualifications. With the possible exception of CO_2, the extra costs of achieving high levels of abatement amount to small percentages of the costs of supply or value added in the industry. In some cases costs have turned out to be negative because unanticipated sources of cost-efficiency were discovered. The substitution of gas as a domestic and industrial fuel and, more recently, for power generation is one example. Industrial wastewater treatment is another area where reductions in wastes are often accompanied by reductions in costs.[2] In other cases the cost savings from general improvements in efficiency, for example, in the thermal efficiencies of power stations and energy conversion processes in industry, have swamped any added costs of pollution prevention and control.

The technologies and practices mentioned here were developed in response to environmental problems encountered in the industrial countries in the nineteenth and twentieth centuries. It is their widespread use, more than any other factor, which explains why local air and water pollution levels are orders of magnitude lower than in the developing countries, even though their economic outputs per capita are an order of magnitude higher.

MODELS FOR THE ANALYSIS OF OPTIONS

Recent studies suggest that pollution and environmental damage will grow exponentially for several decades in developing countries—in India, for most of this century—before they are eventually brought under control and reduced to tolerable levels. Correlating per capita incomes with pollution levels across countries economists have estimated so-called inverted 'U-shaped' curves for several pollutants, which indicate that for long periods pollution rises with per capita incomes, peaks at a high income level, and then begins to decline.[3] Estimates of the per capita incomes at which the peaks occur vary appreciably between studies. In 1985 purchasing power parity prices they are in the ranges:
- US $3000 to US $13,400 for SO_2,
- US $3300 to US $16,000 for SPM,
- US $5000 to US $6200 for smoke,
- US $5500 to US $21,800 for nitrogen oxide,
- US $6200 to US $35,000 for carbon monoxide,
- US $2700 to US $8500 for dissolved oxygen in rivers,
- US $1400 to US $8000 for faecal coliform in rivers, and
- an out of sample value of US $35,000 per capita for CO_2.[4]

These are roughly the income ranges obtaining in the industrial countries when the pollutants noted peaked or (in the case of CO_2) are expected to peak.

[2]See for example the report by Nilsen (1998) on a paper mill in Finland.
[3]Sometimes referred to as Environmental Kuznets Curves (EKCs).
[4]See the reviews of Ekins (1997) and Chua (1999), which cover all pollutants noted except CO_2; for CO_2, see Holtz-Eakin and Selden (1995).

India's per capita income in purchasing power parity prices was approximately US $1000 in 1990, so if this analysis were correct, taking the midpoints of these ranges as a basis, her per capita income would have to rise 5- to 10-fold before local pollution began to peak, and 40-fold before CO_2 emissions began to peak. CO_2 emissions would still be rising exponentially in a century's time.

Such estimates are, however, open to question.[5] They are based on curve-fitting exercises in which emissions are fitted to quadratic or cubic functions of per capita incomes across countries. There are no variables to represent the influence of prices, technical progress, or even of environmental policy on emissions. It is tacitly assumed that policies will not be put in place until per capita incomes approach the levels comparable to those of the industrial countries when the latter began to address their pollution problems. On this assumption, the introduction of environmental policies in India would be delayed for another half century or so, by which time pollution would rise to extraordinary levels. Yet, as shown in Table 12.1, the technologies are available to reduce and sometimes eliminate pollution at costs that are small in relation to output. Furthermore, the extent of current research on environmental policies in India—and indeed, of some policy measures already in place—give grounds for encouragement that India will not wait for another 50 years before policies are established.[6]

To make progress, we need a model with equations to represent the following:

(i)   The demand for the product or service in question, as a function of per capita incomes, prices, population, and other variables;
(ii) The outputs of the technologies and practices making up the total supply;
(iii) Costs;
(iv) Prices, based on costs plus or minus taxes or subsidies, and plus or minus the imputed taxes or subsidies arising from regulation or public policy, to feed into the demand and technical choice relationships (i) and (ii);
(v)   Emissions, which can be derived from the outputs from the technologies and practices making up total supply times their emissions co-efficients;
(vi) The accumulation of pollutants in the ecosystems, estimated from emissions, the natural rates of recovery of the ecosystems, and the effects of remediation policies;
(vii) The costs of environmental damage, as a function of (vi);
(viii) The net effects of (vii) minus (iii) on growth.

[5]Dasgupta, Laplante, Wang, and Wheeler (2002), Ekins (1997), Pearson (1994), Chua (1999), Moomaw and Unruh (1997), and Anderson and Cavendish (2001).
[6]See also Panayotou (1998), who has attempted to estimate the impact of policies on the turning point of the EKC.

This is the approach on which the results discussed next are based, with the following differences.[7] Instead of making the technical choice variables in (ii) an endogenous function of prices, the possible patterns of technology choice over time are specified exogenously as 'scenarios'. The marginal costs are estimated from the technical choice equations, from which we can estimate the prices required to bring any given scenario about, and the total costs of moving from one scenario to another.

The mathematical features and structure of the model are outlined in the appendix to this chapter. It has several simplifications. For example, the population effect is represented by a single variable, population size. In practice the effects of population on growth and the environment are of course more complicated than this, and vary with the age distribution, average family size and composition, education, and other factors. However, we lack evidence on the precise relationships between these quantities and the demands for energy to model the effects at the present time, and have had to concentrate on the aggregate effects of population growth instead.

Changes in income distribution are another area where quantitative research is difficult. What is known is that the overriding effects of environmental damage bear overwhelmingly on the poor. The emissions of pollutants from household fuels, the absence of safe water supplies and sanitation facilities, the incidence of emissions from traffic and industry, the effects of depletion of groundwater in agricultural areas on the landless are all examples of where the poor would benefit the most from enlightened environmental policies. Changes in income distribution could also affect demand, for example, for different types of energy. We have not been able to incorporate these features in our model.

CASE STUDIES OF ENERGY PRODUCTION AND USE

It is necessary to distinguish between different sources and kinds of pollution. The following considers sulphurous and PM emissions and other residues from coal, gas, nuclear power, the alternatives of renewable energy, household fuels, emissions from urban transport, and climate change.

SO_2 and particulate matter emissions from electricity generation: Output from electric power stations in India in 1996–7 was approximately 435 Terawatt hours (TWh), of which two-thirds (290 TWh) were from coal-fired stations and the rest from gas and hydro-electric stations. This is only 15 per cent more electricity than was generated in the United Kingdom (UK), although India's population is nearly twenty times greater. With economic growth and the extension of service to unserved urban and rural populations, electricity demand and production is doubling every decade or so, and is expected to continue

---

[7]A full exposition of the model used for the following studies is provided in Anderson and Cavendish (2001).

to rise exponentially for several decades ahead, with coal continuing to be the predominant fuel.

India has been introducing measures to control PM emissions from power stations for nearly 20 years, though emissions of most pollutants continue to rise. Aggregating the emissions of PM, SO_2, and NO_x, TERI (1997) report that the total estimated pollution load from thermal power stations increased almost 50-fold from 0.3 million tonnes in 1947 to 15 million tonnes in 1997. Emissions per unit output from coal and gas stations in the industrial countries are less than one-tenth of those in India, and are declining rapidly. Can India aspire to comparable reductions in the face of rising demands for electricity?

Using the co-efficients provided in Table 12.1, the simulations summarized in Figure 12.1 show how the time paths of PM emissions might vary under alternative policy assumptions.[8] Similar results apply to SO_2. Two options are considered. The first is with no policy introduced for the next 25 years. In this case emissions rise exponentially in step with output growth, peaking at 2.5

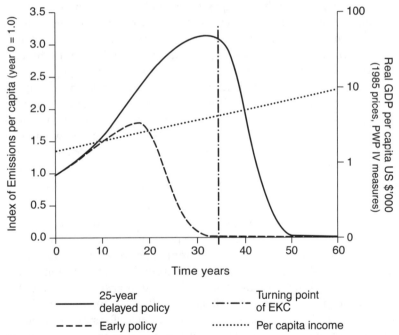

FIGURE 12.1: *Effects of environmental policy on emissions: Simulation results for PM emissions with early and delayed policies. Case: Initial real GDP per capita US $1500, growth rate: 3 per cent per annum*

Note: Here and in Figures 12.2 to 12.5 PWP IV measures relate to the world purchasing power parity prices in the Penn Mark IV World Tables found in Summers and Heston (1991).
Source: Anderson (2002).

[8] The results are presented in a Working Paper (Anderson 2002) accompanying this chapter.

times today's levels in the case of PM, and 6–7 times today's levels in the case of SO_2. The turning points of peak intensities are about the same as those that would emerge from estimates of the EKC, as shown.

With early policies, in contrast, pollution would peak much earlier and at appreciably lower levels. There is still a two-decade long lag before the policies begin to have their full effect, on account of the time it takes to retire and replace the older, more polluting, stations, whose economic lifetimes are typically 30 years.

Further analysis shows the costs of reducing PM would be relatively small, those to reduce SO_2 would be somewhat higher.[9] The increase in the long-run marginal costs of electricity generation would be about 3 per cent for PM and 8 per cent for SO_2.

Such costs could be more than offset by gains in economic efficiency from the elimination of subsidies.[10] India has long followed a policy of subsidizing coal and electricity production and distribution, which has both reduced the capacity of the industry to meet electricity demands, and led to appreciable economic losses. There is also scope for cost savings arising from the reduction of electrical losses in electricity transmission and distribution, which currently are around 20–30 per cent of generation, more than double the losses one would expect in good practice situations.

There are thus good economic and environmental reasons for supporting an early policy, and good technical reasons for expecting that the effects would be just as dramatic as those now being experienced in the Organization for Economic Cooperation and Development (OECD) countries, where PM and acid deposition have declined appreciably in recent decades, partly, it must be admitted, on account of the use of gas for power generation, but in no small measure on account of the development of clean coal technologies.

Coal: In an important respect, the simulations given here oversimplify the situation. Indian coal has a relatively low sulphur content (0.5 per cent by weight) but a very high ash content (30–45 per cent depending on type). Current coal consumption is around 250 million tonnes per year. The 'fly ash' emerging from the boiler exhausts is estimated to be around 45 million tonnes per year; the 'bottom ash' is likewise discharged in huge quantities in water slurries.

Given the growth of demand, these quantities are small in relation to the problem ahead. Coal reserves appear to be sufficient for several decades, even allowing for expansion; commercially proven reserves are sufficient for nearly 250 years at current rates of extraction. The ash content of coal is also rising and the average calorific value declining. It is estimated that if coal continues as the primary fuel for power generation, the total annual consumption would

[9]Anderson (2002).
[10]Anderson and Cavendish (1994).

reach 1400 million tonnes by the middle of the century, producing over 350 million tonnes of fly ash and nearly 100 million tonnes of bottom ash.[11]

Yet from the perspectives of engineering and economics, studies of the subject are not pessimistic, and the common concern is less whether the problem can be addressed, than whether the policies will be put in place. There are several possibilities:[12]

Coal washing: To remove inert mineral matter at the mine, and raise the average calorific value of the coal delivered to the power stations. Coal washing is widely practised in the industrial countries; India introduced coal washing plants at coal fields in Talcher and North Karanpura in the late 1990s.

Coal cleaning: Tavoulareas and Charpentier (1995) describe this as a well-proven practice, highly suited for developing countries. It consists of crushing the coal and the separation of the inerts (ash) and sulphur compounds before the coal is finally pulverized and blown into the boilers for combustion.

Ash utilization: Dry ash has economic applications in agriculture as an absorbent, artificial aggregate, fertilizer, and soil conditioner; in building materials, for aggregates, bricks, building blocks, tiles, paving materials, and panelling; for cement and concrete; in civil engineering as an aggregate, and for foundations, road construction; and in industry, for abrasives, ceramics and filler materials.[13] It is widely used for such purposes in the industrial countries. India uses only 11 per cent for such purposes as land development, dyke raising, industry and construction, as compared with 25 per cent in China, 20 per cent in the US and 85 per cent in Germany.[14] The studies by TERI (1997) show that there are good economic returns to ash utilization; in the UK its use has been encouraged by a landfill tax.

India is also looking to other energy sources for electricity generation, and improved technologies for exploiting coal. The latter include the production of methane from coal beds, in situ gasification of coal (in the coal seams), and integrated coal-gasification combined-cycle technologies for power generation. Gas is another possibility, but reserves are small and are thought to amount to no more than the quantity of coal India consumes every four years; it is imported in liquefied form, and there are also possibilities for pipelines from gas-rich regions.

Nuclear power: In India nuclear power accounts for 1.6 gigawatts (GW) of generation capacity and 3 per cent of electricity supply. The average load

[11]TERI (1997)

[12]See UNDP/World Bank Energy Sector Management Assistance Programme (1998); TERI (1997).

[13]UNDP/World Bank Energy Sector Management Assistance Programme (1998).

[14]Ibid. Tables 2.78 and 2.79.

factor in 1996 was 40 per cent,[15] less than half of what should be expected of a base load plant; historically availability has been as low as 25 per cent. On this basis the costs of nuclear power in India are over five times those of coal plant, after several decades of effort. At no time in the past 50 years, and in no country, has nuclear power not required immense subsidies for investment and waste disposal.

It will be difficult for nuclear power to compete economically. A study by the OECD in 1992 indicated that costs ranged from 4.5 US cents per kWh in France and Canada, to 6–7 US cents per kWh in the US and UK, to 8–9 US cents per kWh in Germany and Japan.[16] A more recent study puts costs in the same range.[17] The lower end of this range of figures suggests that costs are 50 per cent higher than those of gas and coal, the higher end more than twice the costs.

With the possible exceptions of programmes in France and Finland, construction and operating experience have fallen short of expectations, and costs ex post have frequently proved to be several times ex ante estimates.[18] Construction times in the 1970s used to be 5–6 years, but in the 1980s rose to over 10 years in the US and the UK (though remained at 6 years in France). There is, in fact, no commercial interest in the technology outside state-run electricity sectors.

It is thus hard to defend a scenario in which nuclear capacity expands 200-fold over the next 50 years, which is what it would have to do if it were to meet even half of India's electricity requirements. The subsidies required would be enormous. Nuclear power is not a viable solution to India's energy and environmental problems, quite the opposite; nor, after 50 years of development, has it proved itself to be an economic alternative to fossil fuels.

Renewable energy: India's renewable energy resources are immense. With the technical developments discussed next, they are capable of meeting India's energy needs in perpetuity. So far, the main efforts to exploit the resource for commercial use have concentrated on hydro electricity.[19] Hydroelectric generation was 90 TWh in 1996–7, about 20 per cent of electricity supplies. The technical potential is thought to be three to four times this amount. A further constraint arises from inundation and the displacement of people from habitable and often fertile lands, which has been controversial in India. This can be mitigated somewhat by redesigning the hydro schemes to give high

[15]World Energy Council (1998).

[16]*Projected Costs of Generating Electricity: Update, 1992*, Paris: OECD. These figures use a 10 per cent discount rate and are in 1991 prices.

[17]Nuclear Energy Agency (2000).

[18]United States National Research Council (1992). See also Pearson and Pena-Torres (2000) on costs in the UK.

[19]Policies toward biomass as a cooking fuel are discussed in the section 'Emissions from Urban Transport'.

power–energy ratios, such that the rate of water throughput is greater, less storage and land area are needed, and the schemes can make a greater contribution to meeting peak demands while producing the same amount of electricity. In relation to the growth of electricity demand, however, hydro's contribution is unlikely to exceed 10 per cent of supplies given the availability of sites.

The solar energy resource is virtually unlimited, by comparison, and there is an appreciable potential in other renewable energy forms.[20] The incident solar energy in India is approximately 2500 kWh per square metre per year. Modern photovoltaic (PV) modules (which are manufactured in India) can convert 7–15 per cent of this energy—and prospectively 20 per cent—into electricity. Solar-thermal power stations, in which the radiation is focused onto heat-receiving elements to generate high temperature steam, can convert 15 per cent of the incident energy into kWh using today's technologies (parabolic solar trough, parabolic dish, and central receiver systems). In theory, the current electricity demand of 450 TWh per year could be met on an area of land equal to 35 square kilometres (1225 km^2), or 0.036 per cent of India's land area, or 0.06 per cent of the land currently under crops and pasture.

An additional advantage is that solar schemes are modular, and need not occupy valuable land at all. Thermal solar and PV schemes in the desert areas of Rajasthan have been under review for some time; PV modules are also suitable as 'rooftop' devices, and there are also demonstration projects showing their use as cladding materials.

The main issues concern cost and, in the longer-term, storage. The costs of renewable energy have declined by 20–30 per cent with each doubling of the cumulative volume of production. Engineering studies and studies of the learning curve have pointed to scope for significant cost reductions,[21] on three grounds:

- Assessments of the scope for further improvements in conversion efficiency, which has increased by 50 per cent over the past decade.
- The modularity of the technology, coupled with scope for batch production.
- Further innovations in designs and materials.[22]

In the long term, it will also be necessary to solve the problem of storing renewable energy so that it can be used as and when it is needed. There are several possiblities: mechanical storage, pumped storage, and electrochemical, thermal, and thermo-chemical devices. But the most promising option is the production of hydrogen.[23] Hydrogen is also the ideal fuel for the fuel cell,[24] which is among the most promising of the emerging technologies for electricity

[20]For a technological exposition of new renewable energy technologies see Johansson et al. (1993), Turkenburg (2000), and IPCC (2001).

[21]See Turkenburg's review, in UNDP/WEC (2000).

[22]Ahmed (1994), Archer and Hill (2001).

[23]A recent review is provided by Ogden (1999).

[24]See the review of fuel cell technologies by Srinivasan et al. (1999).

generation and transport; it offers the prospect of a very low emission energy system in the long-term. The Indian scientific and engineering communities are well aware of such options, and are undertaking experimental and demonstration projects.[25]

Household fuels: The dependence of low-income households on what are alternatively called 'non-commercial' or 'traditional' fuels—logs, twigs, dung-cakes, and crop residues—is stubbornly persistent in India, and will continue as long as poverty persists. It is one of the leading sources of pollution-related mortality in India, particularly amongst children, women, and the elderly. The problem is not wholly related to income, since ease of access also explains the much higher share of use by low income groups in rural as compared with urban areas (Table 12.2).

TABLE 12.2: *Percentage share of total household energy consumption in rural and urban areas in 1985*

Area and Fuel	Income Group (Rs per annum per household)				
	Up to 3000	3001– 6000	6001– 12,000	12,001– 18,000	>18,000
Rural:					
traditional	86	85	83	84	82
modern	14	15	17	16	18
Urban:					
traditional	63	44	30	23	16
modern	37	56	70	77	84

Source: Ramsey (2000), from whose report this table is taken, comments that recent data by the NSSO show a slight increase in modern fuel use at the highest income levels (Government of India (1997) Fifth Quintennial Survey on Consumer Expenditure—Energy Used by Indian Households 1993–4. NSSO, Department of Statistics: Calcutta), but generally reflects the same association with income distribution as seen in the NCAER study.

The percentage share of traditional fuels in total energy consumption fell from just over 70 per cent in 1951 to around 35 per cent in the 1990s, on account of the rapid growth of modern fuels in the country's energy supplies. But in absolute terms the energy they provided rose from 60 million tonnes of oil-equivalent energy in 1951 to nearly 100 million tonnes by 1996.[26] (Compare this with the consumption of coal, which was around 150 million tonnes of oil-equivalent energy in 1996.) In rural areas, household energy use continues to be reliant on traditional fuels, mostly for cooking, and there

[25]TERI is responsible for several such experimental and demonstration projects. The Ministry of Non-Conventional Energy Resources also supports projects in these areas.
[26]Planning Commission (1997).

is little penetration of modern energy sources in low and even middle and higher income households. In urban areas the opportunities for substitution are far greater, and consequently substitution is proceeding more quickly.

The use of traditional fuels has not peaked, and there is a dispute about the sustainability of the continued dependence on them by many people. It is well summed up by Ramsey (2000) as follows:

The woodfuel crisis of the early '70s was prompted by a government report that described the growing problem of rising rural populations, all dependent on woodfuels that would deplete resources leading to a ... biofuel deficit .... Despite this prophesy of doom, thirty years on the shortage has yet truly to manifest itself as being a serious problem (Agarwal 1998). This is primarily due to the initiation of coping mechanisms such as moving to fuels down the energy ladder (e.g. twigs and leaves) or simply through careful management of privately owned woodfuel resources (Natarajan 1995 and 1990). This shows that it is unlikely that dependence on biofuels would ultimately lead to a dire fuel shortage across the nation. As a fuel becomes scarce it is likely to lead to an increase in costs (for non-marketed fuels this will be the cost of collection, i.e. having to spend more time looking farther afield for fuel), it then becomes viable for people to invest in energy sources elsewhere. Households either make an energy transition or change their biofuel using habits to suit the available resources.

Nevertheless forest resources are becoming more depleted, and there is an increasing use of fuelwood gathered from farmlands and wastelands. In addition, there is a rising contribution of animal dung and crop wastes for fuel, which together account for about one-third of rural energy supplies.

India's policy is to secure a sustainable supply of traditional fuels by improving land management practices, and to reduce the damage they inflict on people's health. Practices encouraged are:

- the establishment of public and private plantations;
- the establishment of vegetative barriers, hedgerows, and shelterbelts on farmlands, complemented by bank and ditch structures and terracing on sloping lands, as part of an integrated land management programme.

Such practices currently account for over half of fuelwood supplies. Their primary benefits are to increase organic matter in the soils and improve soil structure and water retention. This in turn raises yields in agriculture. Fuelwood is in many respects a by-product. The consensus is that improved land management practices can, in principle, secure an adequate supply of traditional fuels for as long as they might be needed. In doing so, they will also improve the yield of land and help to improve water resources. The extent to which they will be adopted remains in question, but the government is surely right in the general direction of its policies.

To reduce the damage to people's health from the burning of fuelwood,[27] the government has introduced a number of programmes:

[27]Saksena et al. (1992), TERI (1997), Smith (1993), and Holdren and Smith (2000).

- An improved *chula* (a traditional Indian cookstove) programme, initiated in 1983, to burn fuel more completely and efficiently. It is estimated that 30 million improved *chulas* have been constructed, and that a further 12 million would be installed by the end of the Ninth Five-Year Plan (Natarajan 1998).
- A rural biogas programme. The plants make use of animal and some plant waste to produce a clean gas for cooking and, as a by-product, a rich fertilizer that can be ploughed back into the soil.
- Subsidies for kerosene and LPG.

The emissions of PM from the improved *chula* are one-quarter to one-half of that of its predecessors, and one-tenth if fitted with a flue. In the case of biogas, emissions are reduced 50 to 100-fold, comparable to those of LPG and kerosene.[28] Furthermore, these are emissions per unit of 'energy delivered to the pot'; per unit of fuel used they are much lower, on account of improvements in efficiency.

Although there has long been much disquiet about the ways the programmes are implemented, most post-evaluations propose ways of improving their cost-effectiveness, not the abandonment of the programmes. The two main proposals are (i) avoidance of subsidies, which have undermined private initiatives to develop and sell stoves, and (ii) involvement of women and the rural extension and educational services in the programmes, to heighten people's awareness of the benefits.

The subsidies for modern fuels such as kerosene and LPG have been widely criticized on two grounds: they mainly benefit the higher income households, and they have led to supplies being restricted (effectively rationed) by the subsidies available. Among other things they led to kerosene fuel being used to adulterate (and make more polluting) diesel fuels for transport (Srivastava 1997). When Hyderabad reduced subsidies in the early 1990s, there was a rapid uptake of the LPG alternative (World Bank 1996). As Leach (1992) concluded from his survey, 'quite minor and low cost interventions, or changes in market conditions, can greatly accelerate the ... pace of the energy transition which occurs during the normal development process as a result of improving infrastructure for distributing modern fuels ... and rising incomes to overcome the high costs of buying modern fuel appliances.'

Emissions from urban transport: Emissions from transport in India grew 70-fold between 1947 and 1997, from 0.15 million tonnes to 10.3 million tonnes per year; they are presently not far short of aggregate emissions from coal-fired power stations,[29] and are currently trebling every decade, in step with the growth of transport. The main local pollutants are carbon monoxide, hydro

[28]Pandey et al. (1990).
[29]A summary of the statistics quoted in this paragraph is provided in TERI (1997).

carbons, lead compounds, PM, and SO_2, altogether a more potent mix than those from coal-fired power stations and, being mainly in urban areas, affecting the health of large and rapidly growing populations. The emissions stem from scooters, motorcycles, auto-rickshaws, cars, jeeps, taxis, and buses. The number of vehicles in the late 1990s was approaching 40 million, having increased from 5 million in 1981.

There are two ways by which pollution from urban transport can be reduced. First, use of cleaner fuels and emission control technologies. Such programmes have been introduced widely in the industrial countries, and are now beginning to appear in developing countries. Second, policies can be made to encourage greater use of public transport, bicycles, and pedestrian traffic; these would include congestion management and charging policies, such as permits for use of vehicles in cities, parking restrictions, parking charges, and congestion tolls.

The options for policy have been analysed by Bose (1998), who developed a simulation model for the purpose. He develops four scenarios:

• A business as usual (bau) scenario in which the present trends in vehicle use continue, and fuel efficiencies and emissions co-efficients remain unchanged.

• A public buses scenario, in which their share of passengers per km of transport rises to 80 per cent in all the cities.

• Promotion of cleaner fuels and improved engine technologies, in which there are significant shifts towards the cleaner fuels and technologies by all categories of vehicles shown in Table 12.1.

• A combination of the last two.

His results show that striking reductions in the trends and levels of pollution from vehicles could be achieved by encouraging the use of public transport on the one hand, and changes in engine technologies and fuels on the other. The main barrier is neither technological nor economic. As Richard Perkins has commented,[30] India already has stringent standards for new vehicles, and the main problems arise with the poor monitoring and enforcement of policies, which include poor enforcement of fuel standards. Nevertheless, the point remains that pollution from vehicles is not an unaddressable problem in India (see also Chapter 13).

The results of similar studies for the paths of volatile organic compounds (VOCs) and carbon monoxide are shown in Figure 12.2.[31] The effect of the 'early policies' would be to reduce the peak intensity of the emissions by a factor of four; the rate of growth of emissions would also be substantially reduced, and the peak intensity reached in 15–20 years time, as compared with 50–60 years if nothing were done.

[30]Personal communication.
[31]See also Anderson (2001).

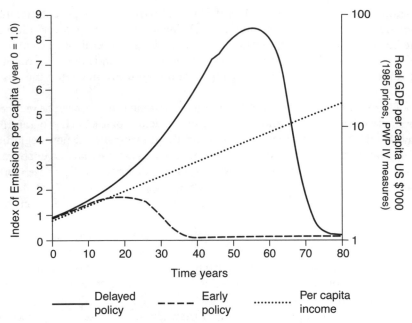

FIGURE 12.2: *Effects of environmental policy on emissions: Simulation results for vehicle emissions. Case of VOCs and CO. Initial real GDP per capita US $1500. Per capita income growth rate: 3 per cent per annum*

Notes: Rate of improvement in the abatement efficiency in the emissions control technology is taken to be 2 per cent per year relative to an initial bass level of emissions per unit fuel use of 0.04 times the level without controls. An annual rate of improvement can be justified both in terms of improvements in catalytic converters and engine design, and the emergence of hybrid and fuel cell engines over the long-term. If anything, the assumed rate of improvement is conservative since zero VOC and CO emission are feasible with fuel cell vehicles, and very low emissions with hybrids.

Source: Anderson (2002).

The costs of introducing the cleaner engines and fuels in new vehicles would not be small in absolute terms. But in relative terms they would be quite small (Table 12.1), amounting to 3–4 per cent of the lifetime capital, fuel, and maintenance costs of vehicles. In addition, there would be the non-trivial costs of setting up a testing and certification system, and all the difficulties and dangers of ensuring that vehicle owners comply with it.

There are also two other economic benefits of over-riding importance. There would be reductions in the damage to people's health and to buildings. Second, if congestion management and pricing were to be introduced, there would be the benefits of reduced congestion—the reduction of accidents, noise, and the savings in the time people spend travelling (Anderson and Cavendish 1992; Maddison et al. 1996). The policy, first of changing the engine technology and fuel mix through environmental taxes and regulations, and second of introducing congestion pricing and management to encourage a more rational and efficient urban transport system, would leave India considerably better off economically, and with a much improved urban environment.

Climate change and CO_2 abatement: Should India begin to address the climate change problem? Emissions are bound to rise for some time given the growth of demand for energy and the dependence of electricity on coal and of transport on oil. A review of the scientific evidence on climate change and its possible impacts on India is provided by Lal (2000), who suggests there is a 'strong possibility' of more intense monsoon rainfall events over the plains of central India and a significant decline in the winter time rainfall. He concludes: 'Perhaps the best course of action at this stage would be for the developed countries to implement strict measures to control emissions of greenhouse gases into the atmosphere and for the developing countries to formulate their future development activities in a sustainable manner conserving their natural resources and adopt advanced technologies on efficient energy uses.'

But should India and other developing countries do more than this and embark on long-term programmes to reduce greenhouse gas emissions? Over the long term such emissions could eventually be stabilized and then reduced to zero using renewable energy and a range of other technologies and practices discussed above. Would the costs be too high? There would be economic and environmental advantages to India if she were to embark on such a programme.

To begin with, the technologies and practices required to mitigate climate change are becoming attractive prospects for investment. For example:[32]

- PVs for off-grid applications such as solar home systems, street lighting, rural health clinics, water pumping, telemetry, and so forth.
- Solar water heaters for domestic and industrial processes.
- PVs for peak load supplementation on grids or for backup supplies. The frequency of brown outs and black outs from central supplies is high. As Chapter 10 noted 'One recent survey of over a thousand industrial firms in India found the average cost of power ... to be over four rupees per unit, compared to less than two rupees in North America. Seventy per cent of the survey respondents had to resort to running their own generator sets.'
- Electricity generation from wind and solar-thermal power stations, which could also be used as a complement to the hydro-plant already in place. The renewable energy could be used for pumped storage in these schemes and/or to reduce the rate of drawdown of the water in the dry season.
- Agro-forestry and biomass production projects, having the multiple purposes of arresting land degradation and restoring the fertility of soils,

[32]Further options for reducing CO_2 emissions include the reforming of natural gas or coal-bed methane to produce hydrogen and CO_2 with the hydrogen being used for combustion or fuel cells and the CO_2 sequestered on a non-net carbon emitting cycle (Socolow 1997).

protecting watersheds, and reducing surface run-off, thus offering a measure of adaptation to climate change, and providing wood for fuels and building materials, with carbon sequestration as a by-product.

• Emerging technologies such as fuel cells for electricity generation and transport, and solar desalination.

Figure 12.3 shows two simulations, using the model developed for this study. In the first, it is assumed that no policies are introduced until India's per capita income reaches that of the rich countries today; in the second, policies are introduced to encourage the emergence and use of the technologies and practices just described (the early policies scenario shown). As shown, it would put India on course for a zero-carbon energy system.

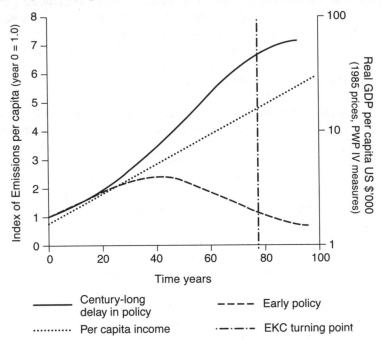

FIGURE 12.3: *Effects of environmental policy on emissions: Simulation results for CO_2 emissions contrasted with the EKC. Initial real GDP per capita US $1500, growth rate: 3 per cent per annum.*

Source: Anderson (2002).

It does not seem that the costs would be prohibitive. The effects on average prices would be initially small, since the share of renewable energy in overall supplies is small.[33] By the time the share is large, the unit costs relative to those of fossil fuels would be much reduced.

The positive externalities arising from such a policy would be appreciable,

---

[33]The simulation studies are fully discussed in Anderson (2002).

and would well justify India introducing tax and regulatory incentives to support the development and use of the technologies. Elimination of the subsidies for coal, hydro schemes, nuclear power, and rural electrification would also facilitate the emergence of renewable energy technologies.

A closer look at the 'population effect' on emissions from energy use: The effects of population growth on emissions are complex, since they depend not only on the size of the population itself, but on family size, composition, age distribution, location and other factors (Lutz and Sanderson 2002). However, a rough estimate can be made by considering alternative values of the population variable in the simulation model outlined earlier. All the runs for the pollutants discussed here so far took an average population growth rate of 1 per cent per year, which, over a 50-year period, would correspond to India's population rising to around 1.6 billion people—as is suggested by the population projections in Chapter 5. We can ask the hypothetical question, which is, what would be the difference if the population did not grow at all over this period?

Some results are shown for the case of emissions of VOCs and CO from transport in Figure 12.4.[34] For the case of vehicle emissions, the model was

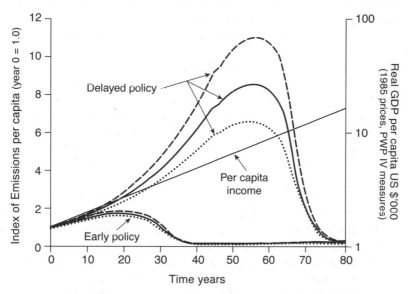

FIGURE 12.4: *Profiles of emissions of VOCs and CO from vehicles with 'early' and 'delayed' policies for average population growth rates of 2 per cent, 1 per cent and a hypothetical 0 per cent per year (the dashed, solid, and dotted lines respectively)*

Notes: Initial real GDP per capita US $1500. Per capita income growth rate: 3 per cent per annum. The case of 1 per cent population growth rate is the same as for Figure 12.2.
Source: Anderson (2002).

[34]Anderson (2002).

re-run assuming a 2 per cent population growth rate on the grounds that the bulk of the damage from vehicle emissions is in urban areas, and is more closely correlated with the urban population growth rate than the national average.

The over-riding conclusion is that the population effect on emissions from energy production and use is significant only if no environmental policies are put in place. Without environmental policies, the effects of population growth would be, as one might expect, to intensify greatly the effects of pollution. On the other hand, if policies were put in place, the induced changes in the technologies and practices of pollution abatement would be enough virtually to eliminate the effects of population growth.

A closer look at the 'scale effect' of economic growth on emissions: Suppose India were able to raise its long-run per capita growth rate from the current level of 3 per cent per year to 5 per cent, through a combination of infrastructure pricing and investment policies, and the financial and macroeconomic reforms discussed in Chapter 10. There were signs in the 1980s and 1990s that India's growth rate was headed in this direction, though Acharya and Srinivasan conclude the long-term per capita growth rate is still likely to be less than 4 per cent so long as contradictions in policies persist. However, let us consider the case of a 5 per cent per capita income growth rate and compare this with the case of 3 per cent.

The curves in Figure 12.5 show the results for the case of PM emissions from electricity generation.[35] They are compared with the results shown in Figure 12.1 (3 per cent growth) to show the net effects. Again, both early and delayed policies are considered as before. Three points stand out:

- With delayed policies, there is a near-doubling of the rate of growth of emissions at the higher economic growth rate, and a more than doubling of the peak intensity of local emissions, from the already high levels discussed earlier. This is not surprising since a 2 percentage point improvement in the rate of per capita income growth translates into 2.7–fold increase in per capita incomes and consumption over a 50-year period. All else constant, pollution would be bound to intensify; indeed the effect of emissions from transport, industry, and households in urban areas would be much greater on account of the higher population growth discussed earlier.
- With early policies, there would also be a period in which emissions would grow more rapidly—and the peaks would be somewhat higher with higher per capita income growth. However:
- Even with the higher population levels, pollution from energy production

[35]The results for the cases of transport emissions and CO_2 are reported in Anderson (2002).

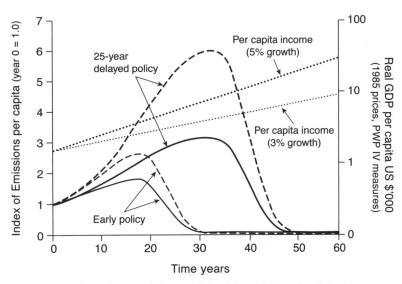

FIGURE 12.5: *Profiles of PM emissions with 'early' and 'delayed' policies for an average per capita growth rate of 3 per cent per year (the solid lines) and a higher per capita growth rate of 5 per cent per year (the dashed lines)*

Notes: All results assume an initial real GDP per capita of US $1500. The population growth rate is averaged at 1 per cent year over the 50 year period. The solid lines repeat the results of Figure 12.1.

Source: Anderson (2002).

and use can still be reduced to low levels using the technologies and policies discussed so far.

• High growth policies would thus merit stronger and earlier—not weaker and later—environmental policies, and would indeed be helped by them.

Assessment: To return to the five propositions set out in the introduction, the preceding analysis suggests that India should be able to enjoy much higher levels of per capita income and energy use, and on a broader basis, than it does today, with an improved environment (Propositions 1–3). For all the cases discussed the technologies and practices are available for reducing pollution per unit of energy use by orders of magnitude, at costs not far removed—and in some cases below—the polluting alternatives they would displace (Proposition 4). Furthermore, India's economic prospects would be improved by early policies to encourage the development and use of the low-polluting technologies and practices discussed here (Proposition 5). There are grounds for encouragement that several policy initiatives are in place or in train, for example, with respect to household fuels, renewable energy, and the reduction of PM from power stations.

IS ENERGY A SPECIAL CASE?

If we look at other sectors—for example, water for agriculture, industry and domestic use, wastewater treatment, and wastes—where some of India's most pressing problems arise, similar conclusions emerge to those just reached for energy production and use. The technologies and practices for pollution prevention and control have long been developed; the costs are not prohibitive; there is ample scope for efficiency improvements and further technological development; and widespread use of the technologies and practices would be beneficial to people's health, the environment and the economy. The main concern in the literature is whether policies will be pursued vigorously enough, and whether contradictions in structure (such as often arise from poor pricing policies) will be avoided. Since other chapters deal with water, wastewater, wastes, and pressures on natural resources, only the main points are highlighted here.

Water use in agriculture:[36] Irrigated areas approximately doubled to 71 million hectares in the period 1970–95 (roughly one-third of the area under crops and pasture is irrigated). The number of tubewells rose from 15 to 90 thousand and dug wells from 6 to 10 million. While this has contributed greatly to increases in foodgrain production in the period, it is has imposed stresses on water resources:

While India is considered to be rich in terms of annual rainfall and total water resources, water is spatially and temporally very unevenly distributed: some river basins (including the Ganga Basin, and amounting to half the area of the country) fall into the category of water-scarce and water-stressed regions, and several others suffer from absolute scarcity .... In Haryana, while groundwater transformed the traditional cultivation into commercial cultivation, the average depth of the water table is estimated to have fallen by 1 to 33 cm annually in different parts of the state during the 1980s. In Gujarat, during the same period, water tables in over 90 per cent of all the observation wells monitored ... dropped by 0.5 metres to as much as 9.5 metres. ... Over-exploitation has also been significant in major cities.[37]

Yet the situation is not hopeless. Proposals on the following have been put forward in the literature cited:

Property rights: 'Groundwater is viewed essentially as a chattel attached to land. There exists, at the same time, no limit to how much water a land-owner may draw ... (Further) the landless have no legal access to groundwater. ... The legal framework for the management of groundwater, therefore, is conducive neither to equity nor to sustainibililty.'[38] Saleth (1996) makes the

[36]Goldar (2000), TERI (1997).
[37]TERI (1997).
[38]TERI (1997).

case for a water rights structure that specifies individual and collective limits to water withdrawals under which water resources are held by the state under the public trust doctrine.

• Electricity prices for agriculture: Electricity prices in rural areas have long been subsidized in the extreme. In Andhra Pradesh, for example, electricity tariffs to agriculture in the mid–1990s were one-fiftieth of the prices to industry and commerce. Such subsidies lead to excessive and unnecessary pumping and waste, and provide no incentive for the development of alternative methods of irrigation, such as drip irrigation.

• Water prices: Thirty years ago 'the Second Irrigation Commission recommended that charges for (for irrigation from surface waters) should be at least 5 per cent of the gross income from food crops and 12 per cent of that from cash crops. However ... receipts amount to only 1–3 per cent of the gross income.'(TERI 1997).

• Water losses: It is estimated that about 45 per cent of water is lost by seepage through unlined field channels and another 15 per cent in the field due to over-application (Saleth 1996).

• Research and Development (R&D) and incentives for the development of crops and practices suited to drip irrigation.

• Watershed protection through afforestation programmes, and further extension of agro-forestry on farmlands: Aside from protecting soils, such investments also improve microclimates, and provide a source of fodder, fuelwood, and mulch.

Chopra and Goldar (2000) also makes the point that there is still considerable potential for increases in agricultural production in rainfed areas (about two-thirds of agricultural lands in India). According to TERI (1997), notwithstanding current stresses 'India uses only 18 per cent of the available water resources whereas in Israel the figure is 86 per cent.'

Industry, homes, and municipal wastewater. The main concerns are the inter-related issues of (i) the expansion of safe water supplies and sanitation to unserved and poorly served populations; and (ii) the pollution of ground- and surface-water from industrial and municipal wastes. The expansion of water supplies and sanitation has been a consistent priority in development plans. It has been estimated that 60 per cent of all deaths in urban areas arise from water-borne diseases such as cholera, dysentery, and gastroenteritis.[39]

The pollution of industrial and municipal wastewaters, including pollution from sewage, presents a more daunting—yet, once again, tractable—problem. Both industrial and municipal wastewaters can be treated to a high level of

[39]World Bank (1996), cited by TERI (1997)

quality and recycled. Nor are the costs prohibitive. Chopra and Goldar (2000) have estimated the costs of addressing the water pollution problem to be US $0.62 per cubic metre for large-scale treatment plants and US $0.72 per cubic metre for small-scale plants; these are lower than those found in Europe and the US.[40] They conclude that the investment requirements for 'adequate treatment of wastewater from industries and urban households (are) about 0.5 per cent of the GDP (or) about 2.2 per cent of the expenditure of the urban household. It seems therefore that it should not be too difficult for the urban people to bear the cost of wastewater treatment in the cities, especially if a part of the cost of treatment is borne by government.' The issue is thus less one of cost, than of the capacity of the municipal authorities to charge for the services and recover costs, a policy which would greatly facilitate the financing of the further development of the services.

Solid wastes: The main problems arise from the volume of solid wastes, their complexity, and the institutional and managerial difficulties of their management and disposal:

*   The solid waste generated in Indian cities increased from 6 million tonnes in 1947 to 48 million tonnes in 1997, and on current trends would exceed five times this level in 50 years time.
*   More than one-fourth of the municipal solid waste (MSW) is not collected at all, and 90 per cent of the wastes that are collected are dumped in landfills. The cumulative area given to landfills is rising exponentially.
*   The landfills in turn 'are neither well equipped nor managed efficiently', and the accompanying seepage and pollution of soils and groundwater is extensive.[41]

The landfills include hazardous wastes from industry and hospitals, as well as the normal mix of pathogenic wastes from homes (diapers, contaminated food, and other debris). Aside from damaging people's health, there is damage to soils and groundwater resources from seepages, and to air from odorous gases.

While human and industrial waste cannot be eliminated, practices have long been evolving toward the minimization of the impact of waste on the environment and human health. Standard texts such as that by Kiely (1997) emphasize the importance of integrated waste management, with the following elements:

[40] The investment costs for primary, primary + secondary, and primary + secondary + tertiary treatment, are typically US $0.9, US $1.6 and US $2 per cubic metre in Europe and the US. Unit running costs are around 5–10 per cent of these figures. Source: David Butler (Imperial College Civil and Environmental Engineering Department), personal communication. Compare these figures with the costs of supplying potable water, typically US $0.5 per cubic metre, and the surveys by Whittington et al. (1994) and others of people's willingness to pay for potable water in developing countries, which is widely found to be several times these levels.

[41] TERI (1997)

- Reduction of waste generation at source, including, in the case of industry especially, through in-plant recycling and changes in process.
- Recycling of what is possible of paper, cardboard, glass, non-ferrous metals, and textiles. Design of a collection system that would support this process.
- Reuse of plastics, ferrous metals, and glass.
- Biogasification or composting the food fraction of MSW.
- Incinerating the remaining plastics or food waste.
- Landfilling the remainder, which according to Keily should amount to around no more than 20 per cent of overall waste in good practice situations, less than one-quarter of what India puts to landfill today.

The teaching of such practices and the municipal policies required to finance their application is standard in civil and municipal engineering at universities and colleges.

THE ECONOMIC BENEFITS OF ENVIRONMENTAL IMPROVEMENT

What would be the aggregate effects on economic growth of investments in environmentally improved technologies and practices? The data in Table 12.1 and the estimates in the case studies discussed above for energy, water, waste disposal, and transport suggest that the aggregate costs might amount to 2–3 per cent of GDP, similar to the estimates found in other countries in earlier studies (World Bank 1992). The economic benefits can be measured in terms of:

- The reduction of water-borne diseases from improved water supplies and sanitation;
- Improved water supplies for urban areas arising from reductions in polluted ground and surface waters;
- The health benefits of reduced outdoor air pollution from transport, electricity generation, and industry;
- The health and social benefits of improved systems for managing municipal and industrial solid waste;
- The health benefits of eliminating indoor air pollution from cooking fuels such as firewood and dung, and associated losses of soil nutrients;
- The elimination of soil degradation, which Ahluwalia and others estimated to be between 11–26 per cent of agricultural output in the 1990s, or 3–5 per cent of GDP.[42] These estimates are based on data on the salination and chemical contamination of soils and the depletion of topsoils, nutrients, and groundwater resources. Their lower estimate neglects the benefits of improved husbandry and resource conservation;

[42]'The Hidden Costs of Degradation', Chapter 11 in TERI (1997).

• Afforestation investments in the protection of watersheds and agricultural areas, which by improving micro-climates and providing a supply of recyclable nutrients have long been known to go beyond the purpose of stemming land degradation, to improve the yields of agriculture.

A World Bank study estimated the economic benefits of environmental improvement to be 4.5 per cent of GDP (Brandon et al. 1995). There are appreciable uncertainties in this estimate, particularly those arising from the estimates of health benefits (see Chapter 10). Even allowing for the uncertainties, however, the aggregate economic benefits of environmental improvement probably exceed the costs of achieving it by a large margin. TERI (1997) consider 4.5 per cent of GDP to be a lower bound estimate, since it neglects the costs to health of indoor air pollution, which afflict half the population.

WIN–WIN OPTIONS

There are the opportunities furthermore for improving economic efficiency and economic growth in ways that have environmentally desirable side effects:

(i) The elimination of subsidies for coal and nuclear power, which would encourage a more efficient use of coal and electricity (more technically, it would reduce 'dead-weight' losses).

(ii) The encouragement of load management programmes in the electricity industry.

(iii) The elimination of subsidies for rural electrification, which have long been a bone of contention between Indian economists and policy-makers. Along with (i) this would improve the financial performance of the electricity utilities; enable the utilities to improve and maintain supply; reduce waste in electricity consumption; reduce excessive irrigation pumping and pressures on groundwater resources; and lead to a more rational and sustainable use of groundwater resources. It would also encourage new technologies, such as solar pumping and drip irrigation.

(iv) The reduction of urban congestion through public transport systems, congestion pricing, and the creation of traffic-free zones.

(v) Cost-reflecting pricing policies for municipal services—water supplies, wastewater treatment, and the management of MSW in particular.

The long-run rate of economic growth of the Indian economy is thought to be around 4–5 per cent per year, that is two or more percentage points lower than what could be achieved in the long term. It is significant that a sizeable fraction of this difference is attributed to shortcomings in infrastructure management and pricing policies (Acharya 2002).

INCOME DISTRIBUTION AND ENVIRONMENTAL IMPROVEMENT

While limitations in the data preclude a satisfactory quantitative analysis of the effects of income distribution on the environment—and conversely, of the effects of environmental damage on income distribution—two points can be made. The first is that, as noted earlier, the worst effects of environmental damage bear overwhelmingly on the poorest members of society, who would stand to gain the most from the policies and practices discussed above. The second is that the economic costs are likely be small in relation to the benefits and also in relation to India's capacity to finance the required investments. The first point is evident if we consider the following:

- Indoor air pollution, caused by the burning of wood and dung as a cooking fuel, is often called the 'bottom rung' of the energy ladder. Its effects on the health of children who are exposed to it from birth are often compared to those of chain smoking.[43] It is the lowest income groups that have the least access to modern and cleaner fuels.
- Losses in the fertility of soils in regions where people are heavily dependent on fuelwood and dung for cooking fuels.
- Unsafe water supplies and sanitation. Once again, it is the lowest income people who have the worst access to safe water supplies and sanitation.
- The incidence of diseases and infections from unsafe practices of disposing of municipal and industrial wastes. Among the most affected are refuse workers and the women and children who earn a living as ragpickers: 'about 35,000 children work as ragpickers in Bangalore and about 80,000 in Delhi ... (The) majority of child ragpickers are between 8 and 15 years old and ... a large proportion of them start work when they are between 5 and 8 years old.'[44]
- The effect of depletion of groundwater on small farmers and the landless in over-irrigated areas. Again, the consensus of those who have looked at the problem is that it is these groups who have the greatest difficulty of obtaining access to irrigation water in regions where the groundwater table is being depleted. This process is encouraged by huge subsidies for rural electrification (which, of course, benefit the large farmers the most).

Lal (2000) also argues that it is the lowest income groups that will be the most vulnerable to climate change: to the increasing intensity of the monsoons on the one hand, and to droughts in the dry seasons on the other.

Policies to improve income distribution need to address the most pressing environmental problems directly—the provision of safe water and sanitation in low income areas, the reduction of indoor air pollution, the proper disposal

[43]World Bank (1992).
[44]TERI (1997).

of municipal effluents and wastes, the prevention of land degradation, land restoration, and the sustainable use of water in agriculture. The greatest social benefits of environmental improvement are thus those that would arise from addressing the environmental problems that mainly effect the lowest income groups. Few would surely dispute the conclusion that such policies would be a desirable component of the policies required to improve income distribution in the course of economic growth.[45]

As regards the affordability of addressing pollution problems faced by low income groups, this question is implicitly answered in the scenarios and studies discussed earlier. An improvement in income distribution over time might lead to the demands for energy, and the services of the water, waste-water, waste disposal, and transport services rising somewhat more rapidly than the various studies assumed; but, as shown, the effects on pollution would be virtually eliminated in the long term if environmental policies were put in place. (See, for example, the estimates for the case of higher growth rates, shown in Figure 12.5, which once again show that the overall determinant of environmental damage is not economic output but the kinds of technologies and practices used.) All the studies undertaken or cited here have shown that the costs would not be prohibitive. And there is an underlying consistency in the recommendations for generating the required finance— primarily the avoidance of unnecessary subsidies for polluting activities, and for policies to allow prices to reflect the costs of using the required technologies and practices. The main issue that remains concerns the design, monitoring, and enforcement of policies. There is no reason why India cannot aspire to prosperity on a broad basis and a substantial improvement in the environment and the health of her people.

CONCLUSIONS

The preceding analysis considered several of the most pressing environmental problems facing India today:
- Acid deposition and PM emissions from thermal power stations;
- The disposal of ash and water wastes from the rapidly expanding use of coal in electricity generation;
- Emissions of lead compounds, PM, carbon monoxide, nitrous oxides, and unburned hydrocarbons from vehicles in congested urban areas;
- Smoke and the damage to soils and watersheds from the use of dung, crop residues, and wood for domestic fuels;
- The emerging problem of climate change;
- The pressures on the use of groundwater and surface water resources for irrigation;

[45]Beckerman (1992) makes this point in relation to air and water pollution.

- The problem of increasing the supply of 'safe' water and sanitation services to households.
- The management of municipal and industrial solid waste.

This leaves several problems undiscussed, such as agro-chemicals, industrial chemicals, and the protection of forests and biodiversity. Nevertheless, a fair range of problems has been considered. The striking feature of the literature is the range and effectiveness of the technologies and practices developed by the engineers and scientists whose profession it is to solve environmental problems. From a scientific and technological viewpoint, there is no reason why India cannot aspire to addressing the problems discussed within the next two generations or so.

Economic analysis leads to the same conclusion. Earlier estimates were that a developing country would need to allocate 2–3 per cent of its GDP to environmental ends and achieve continual environmental improvement while sustaining economic growth. The estimates of Indian scholars cited here for particular problems, and the evidence in Table 12.1, are consistent with this. Put another way, this would shave 0.15 to 0.2 percentage points off India's current rate of economic growth, if there were no economic benefits to the policy. However, the benefits would be:

- Improvements in people's health in urban and rural areas from reductions in water-borne diseases and air pollution.
- Sustainable supplies and use of water resources for agriculture and industry.
- Reductions in river and groundwater pollution.
- Improvements in the fertility of soils over large areas of farm- and pasture-land
- The possibility of new energy technologies emerging to meet India's energy needs from its most abundant and least used energy resource (solar energy).

In addition there are substantial efficiency and environmental benefits to be gained from more rational pricing policies and institutional reforms. The evidence is that India's growth rate would be higher not lower with environmental policies in place. Furthermore, the poorest income groups would benefit the most from a concentration on priority areas—from the reduction of PM emissions from outdoor and indoor air pollution, the reduction of pollution from traffic, the provision of safe water supplies, the proper treatment of industrial and municipal waste water effluents and solid wastes, the development of more sustainable systems of water use in agriculture, and the protection of soils and natural resources. The conclusion must be that India's prospects for achieving economic prosperity on a broad basis will be improved by enlightened environmental policies, notwithstanding the growth of her population.

Appendix 12.1

KEY FEATURES OF THE SIMULATION MODEL

The equations in the model need to represent the following:

(i) The demand for the product or service in question, as a function of per capita incomes, prices, population, and other variables.[1]

(ii) The outputs of the different technologies and practices making up the total supply.

(iii) Costs.

(iv) Prices, based on costs plus or minus taxes or subsidies, and plus or minus the imputed taxes or subsidies arising from regulation or public policy, to feed into the demand and technical choice equations (i) and (ii).

(v) Emissions, which can be derived from the outputs from the technologies and practices making up total supply times their emissions co-efficients.

(vi) The accumulation of pollutants in the ecosystems, estimated from emissions, the natural rates of recovery of the ecosystems, and the effects of remediation policies.

(vii) The costs of environmental damage, as a function of (vi).

(viii) The net effects of (vii) minus (iii) on growth.

This is the approach followed here, with the following differences. Instead of making the technical choice variables in (ii) an endogenous function of prices, the possible patterns of technology choice over time are specified exogenously as 'scenarios'. The marginal costs are estimated from the technical choice equations, from which we can estimate the prices required to bring any given scenario about, and the total costs of moving from one scenario to another. Also, although it is possible to stipulate suitable forms for the relationships under (vi) and (vii), the data are not available to estimate them reliably, so their implications are dealt with descriptively. Let us consider the equations in more detail, and then turn to their application.[2]

---

[1] Ideally, demand would be studied by income group, but unfortunately neither the data nor the econometric relationships available permit the following model to look at distribution quantitatively. A discussion of distributional issues is provided in the section 'Income distribution and environmental improvement' of this chapter.

[2] The following is based on Anderson and Cavendish (2001).

Demand equations: The starting point is a demand-for-product relationship:

$$D_t = f(y_t, P_t, N_t) \qquad (E12.1)$$

where D_t denotes demand, y_t per capita incomes, P_t energy prices, and N_t population. Functional forms differ between studies depending on 'goodness-of-fit' among the alternatives, but for practical purposes the following often works well:

$$D_t/D_0 = (y_t/y_0)^\alpha (P_t/P_0)^\beta (N_t/N_0) \qquad (E12.2)$$

where α is the per capita income elasticity and β the price elasticity of demand. For convenience, demand has been expressed relative to demand in year 0. For commercial energy income elasticities are zero below a certain threshold or 'poverty line'(see the case study on household fuels), increase rapidly to around 1.5 as countries become more industrialized and motorized and household demand for energy-using appliances increases, and then decline to one-fifth or less of this at high per capita incomes as markets mature.[3] In the case studies of commercial energy use discussed here, the following relationship, derived from the studies of Judson et al. (1999), summarizes the change of elasticity with incomes quite well: $\alpha = \alpha_0 (1+r)^{-(y_t/y_0 - 1)}$, where $\alpha_0 = 1.5$ is the initial elasticity and $r \approx 0.1$ is the rate of decline of the elasticity with the growth of per capita income.

In this model, per capita incomes and population are treated as exogenous variables, and the consequences of alternative rates of growth of these quantities are explored through simulation. The price variables are partly endogenous, being derived from the cost equations, discussed next, and partly exogenous, being dependent on (the model's input) assumptions about taxes, regulation and the institutional impediments to price efficiency being achieved.

Supply and technology choice in pollution prevention and control: We now need equations to reflect the choice of technologies for providing the product or service in question. In all sectors of economic activity the demand D_t can be met in many ways, some much less damaging environmentally than others. Consider the emissions from a particular sector—electricity or road transport. Given the huge disparities in the emissions co-efficients between the polluting and low-polluting technologies listed in Table 12.1, and the variety of methods of pollution control, we need in principle separate equations for each technology. The study by Bose (1998) of automotive energy use and emissions in Bangalore, Kolkata, Delhi, and Mumbai (discussed in the text) is a good example. But for the purposes of the present paper, the main effects can be approximated by two groups of equations, one representing existing (polluting) technologies, the other new (low-polluting) technologies.

[3]Bates and Moore (1992), Dargay and Gately (1995), and Judson et al. (1999).

Let Q_t denote the total supply in period t, s_t the share of incremental investment in low polluting practices, δ the retirement rate of the capital stock, and subscripts c and d the low-polluting (clean) and polluting (dirty) options respectively. Assuming equilibrium between demand and supply, the incremental output required from new investments will be equal to incremental demands, Δd_t, plus the amount of capital stock retired, δq_t, where $q_t = q_{c,t} + q_{d,t}$. Thus both demand growth and the retirement of old practices provide an opportunity to introduce clean technologies and practices. A further possibility is to retrofit or retire early the older technologies. Let the rate of retrofitting and/or early retirement of the polluting technologies be denoted by the choice variable, r_t.[4] The output from the low-polluting technologies in period t thus equals the output from the capital stock newly installed in the period, plus the output from the capital stock left over from the preceding period, plus any retrofits or early retirements replaced by new investment:

$$q_{c,t} = s_t\,(\Delta d_t + \delta q_{t-1}) + (1 - \delta)\,q_{c,t-1} + r_t q_{d,t-1} \qquad \text{(E12.3)}$$

Similarly, for the polluting technologies:

$$q_{d,t} = (1 - s_t)\,(\Delta d_t + \delta q_{t-1}) + (1 - \delta)\,q_{d,t-1} - r_t q_{d,t-1} \qquad \text{(E12.4)}$$

Note that (E12.3) and (E12.4) summed satisfy the equilibrium condition $\Delta q_t = \Delta d_t$.

As noted earlier, there are two ways of treating the share of new investment in low polluting technologies, s_t. The first is to make it an endogenous function of pollution taxes or policies. The second is to make it an exogenous decision variable and to explore the implications of different paths for s_t. This enables us to consider alternative scenarios, estimate the costs of pollution abatement and, from this, the pollution taxes (or the imputed taxes if a regulatory route is chosen) ideally required for any given time path of abatement.

Equations (E12.3) and (E12.4) are the core of the model. They reflect a situation in which increases in demand plus the investments required to replace assets that are being retired can be met in one of two ways. The first is through continued investments in current technologies and practices. The other is through a change in technique or practice to provide the same product or service—kWh, motive power, heat and light and so forth—but with lower pollution levels. Both may be capable of marginal improvements and have rising marginal costs of abatement curves in the sense often depicted in economic texts. However, by far the largest effect on emissions arises from the substitution of one group of technologies for the other, as can be inferred from the data in Table A12.1. (This point applies with yet greater validity when more than two options for reducing pollution are considered.)

---

[4] For simplicity, the following relationships assume an exponential-decay type retirement function. It is not difficult to consider alternative forms such as a normal distribution round an expected plant lifetime. Cavendish and Anderson (1994).

Supply costs, policies, and prices: Supply costs are the sum of capital operating and maintenance costs. Let $k_{c,t}$ and $k_{d,t}$ denote the present worth of the lifetime capital and operating costs per unit of output from the capital stock installed in year t. The total costs c_t of the investments installed to meet any demand increment in period t are then:

$$c_t = k_{d,t} \Delta q_{d,t} + k_{c,t} \Delta q_{c,t} \tag{E12.5}$$

and the present worth of total costs, C_t, is:

$$C_t = \sum_{w=0}^{\infty} \beta_w c_{t+w} \tag{E12.6}$$

where β_w is the discount factor.[5]

Turning to prices, if the private costs of the low-polluting technologies are greater than those of the polluting options, the marginal costs of supply, c'_t, will be given by the marginal costs of the former. Assuming that costs are independent between periods, then $c'_t = k_{c,t}$, and the price is:

$$P_t = c'_t + e_t \tag{E12.7}$$

where e_t is the excise tax on the product. The estimate of P_t closes the demand-supply relationships in the model and enables us to estimate D_t. Finally, an estimate of the pollution tax (τ_t) required to encourage substitution can be obtained from:

$$\tau_t = c'_t - k_{d,t} \tag{E12.8}$$

This will usually be a minimum estimate of the pollution tax required, however, as more often than not there will be a history of procrastination on environmental policy, until the evidence becomes clear and overwhelming or until public pressures force the policy-makers' hands. In such situations the marginal benefits of pollution abatement may well exceed the marginal costs for a considerable period, justifying an initial pollution tax greater than that corresponding to the long-run equilibrium.

This is to oversimplify the situation, however, since the basis for estimating prices given here ignores the reality that regulatory policies frequently lead to large distortions between costs and prices—quite apart from distortions that may arise in current systems of taxes and tariffs. For example, coal is heavily subsidized in India and electricity heavily regulated and the disparities between prices and costs are appreciable.[6] There are three effects to consider. The first

---

[5] Another useful quantity to calculate is the average incremental financial costs of implementing a policy, namely $(k_{d,t} \Delta q_{d,t} + k_{c,t} \Delta q_{c,t})/\Delta q_t$, relative to the incremental financial costs of not implementing it, $k_{d,t}$. Affordability is a frequently raised issue, and different rates of substitution have very different financial requirements (see the case studies referred to in Chapter 12).

[6] The disparity between prices and social costs in urban transport can similarly be large because of the neglect of the external costs of congestion.

is the departure between prices and costs itself and the effects on demand. Eliminating subsidies, for example, acts to raise prices and reduce demand. Second, there is an effect on 'X-inefficiencies' and costs. For instance, the primary reason for the reforms currently taking place in the electricity sector in India is that state controls and regulations on the industry have led to poor plant availability and utilization, high losses in transmission and distribution (30 to 40 per cent, including theft, compared to 10 per cent in good practice situations), and reduced thermal efficiencies of power plants. It is anticipated that regulatory reform and openness to private investment will, by improving financial incentives, lead to reductions in such inefficiencies. As is widely observed there are significant 'win–win' opportunities for reducing costs and, by bringing prices and costs more into line, for environmental improvement. The third effect is to encourage substitution between one technology and another; in Europe and the US, for instance, this encouraged a shift from coal to gas, and also acted to make nuclear power yet more financially unattractive than it already was.

To represent the first two effects, the marginal cost variable in (E12.7) is multiplied by a quantity M_t, representing the ratio of actual marginal costs to those that obtain in 'good practice' situations found when prices reflect cost, and another quantity $(1 - S_t)$, where S_t denotes the effective subsidy arising from regulatory or public finance policies relative to total costs. (The basis on which these are estimated is explained in the case studies discussed earlier.) The price equation is then:

$$P_t = c_t' . M_t (1 - S_t) + e_t \qquad \text{(E.12.9)}$$

Several scenarios discussed next will consider the effects on costs and the environment of a gradual reduction of removing the distortions in question. The third effect (on substitution) will necessarily have to be analysed through the scenario variables given the construction of the model.

Changes in costs over time: It is often necessary to allow for the point that costs are not static quantities, but change over time with technical progress and scale economies. This is as true for environmental innovations as it has been historically for most other sectors of economic activity. Table A12.1 provides examples for several technologies in the energy sector.

TABLE A12.1: *Learning rates for selected energy technologies*

Technology	Period	Learning Rate, per cent
Wind:		
OECD	1981–95	17
US	1985–94	32
California	1980–94	18
Denmark	1990–4	8

(contd...)

(Table A12.1 continued)

Technology	Period	Learning Rate, per cent
Solar PV:		
EU	1985–95	32
World	1976–92	18
Ethanol (Brazil)	1979–95	20
Electrolytic Hydrogen from renewables	—	18
Compact Florescent Lamps (US)	1992–8	16
Gas Turbine Combined Cycle Power Plants:		
OECD	1984–94	34
EU	n.g.	4
Gas Pipelines:		
Onshore	1984–97	4
Offshore	1984–97	24
Oil Extraction from the North Sea	n.g.	25
Coal for Electric Utilities	1948–69	25
Nuclear Power (OECD)	1975–93	6
Electric Power Production	1926–70	35

Note: n.g. = not given.

Source: Except for electrolytic hydrogen, which is based on the review by Ogden (1999), the estimates are quoted from McDonald and Shreattenholzer (2001), who quote estimates for several other technologies. Note that for electrolytic hydrogen, the estimates are based on engineering studies, while for the other technologies they are estimated from historical data.

These estimates show that:

- There is much historical evidence in the energy industry that costs decline appreciably with innovation, investment, and operating experience.
- The effects are notably strong for—but are not confined to—renewable energy.
- Even for particular technologies, on which substantial experience has already been gained, the estimates show a wide range.

The learning-by-doing effects are most important in the early phases of a technology's development. When it occupies around 0.001 per cent to 0.01 per cent of the energy market, even a 100-fold expansion still leaves it occupying only 0.1 per cent to 1 per cent of the market; but experience accumulates rapidly in this period, and costs may decline several-fold. In contrast, when it occupies a larger share, the cost reductions are still significant (as, for example, with gas-turbine power plant) but are small in comparison. In other words, there can be a phase of rapid catch-up.

Costs decline with learning-by-doing, represented by the cumulative volume of investment. A commonly used cost function to represent learning by doing is:

$$c_{ct} = \left(\sum_0^t q_{cv} \right)^{-b}$$ (E12.10)

where b is the rate of learning. The learning effects are especially important for new and emerging technologies, such as renewable energy, when the cumulative volume of investment and output may increase several-fold from a small base.

Emissions: Letting $\theta_{c,jt}$ and $\theta_{d,jt}$ denote the emissions of pollutant j per unit output of the low-polluting and polluting practices respectively,[7] then the total emissions of the pollutant, denoted by $E_{j,t}$, are given by:

$$E_{j,t} = \theta_{c,j,t} \, q_{c,t} + \theta_{d,j,t} \, q_{d,t}$$ (E12.11)

Once substitution to the low-polluting practices is complete, so that $q_t = q_{c,t}$, the long-term level of emissions relative to their initial levels is given by:

$$E_{j,t}/E_{j.0} = (\theta_{c,j,t}/\theta_{d,j.0}) \cdot (q_t/q_0)$$ (E12.12)

The ratio of $\theta_{c,j0}$ to $\theta_{d,jt}$ can range from 10^{-1} to 10^{-3} and even less in the energy sector, so that once the new technologies are developed and substituted for the old ones, very large reductions in polluting emissions can be accomplished even in the presence of large output increases. In many cases, a new technology changes the levels of several pollutants simultaneously, as when gas is substituted for coal, tailpipe controls are installed on vehicles, or when modern methods are introduced for industrial and municipal wastewater treatment. So a clean technology can often bring about multiple environmental benefits.

Accumulations, irreversibilities, and environmental damage: In most situations, environmental damage is a function less of emissions than of the concentrations (or accumulations) of the pollutants in the ecosystem, and the length of time the ecosystem is exposed to the pollutants. A simple way of estimating accumulations and exposure times is through relationships like:

$$A_t = (1-d)A_{t-1} + E_t - R_t \, A_t$$ (E12.13)

where A_t is the concentration or net accumulations of the offending pollutant in a particular environment, d the natural rate of recovery, and R_t, a policy variable, is the rate of remediation through physical investment and clean-up. Since d, and also R_t, differ between pollutants, a separate equation is needed for each pollutant.

---

[7]For simplicity we have assumed fixed pollution coefficients. In reality, these coefficients—like those for unit costs—can be reduced through R&D and learning-by-doing: this could be modelled through an equation linking current levels to past expenditures. Doing this would reinforce the results derived here concerning the potential size of external benefits accruing to investments in innovative clean technologies.

Environmental impact, economic damage, and feedback on growth and development:
The last step in the analysis is to estimate the impact of pollution on the
people's health and the environment. There are usually several effects to
consider, for example, relating to:

- Health: morbidity and mortality (virtually all airborne pollutants have
  deleterious effects above certain thresholds);
- Crops (yields may be reduced through acid deposition);
- Forests and lakes (acid deposition);
- Buildings, vehicles, and equipment (PM and acid deposition).

In addition, all such effects have economic consequences:

- Ill-health leads to losses in working hours and labour productivity, and
  entails significant expenditures on health care that would otherwise be
  avoided—and would become available for other purposes—if pollution
  were reduced to socially satisfactory levels.
- Reductions in the yields of crops lead to economic losses in agriculture.
- The damage to buildings, vehicles, and equipment require appreciable
  expenditures on restoration and replacement.

Attempts have been made to put economic values on these effects in some
countries so that the economic damage caused by pollution can be estimated,
though the quantitative results are uncertain and controversial.[8] What is not
uncertain, however, is that environmental damage has negative effects on
economic growth, even if the effects have so far proven difficult to quantify.
It reduces the health and productivity of the labour force, the yield of natural
resources, and it uses resources for the maintenance of environmental assets
and the remediation of environmental damage that would otherwise go into
investment or the enjoyment of consumption.

[8]Jones-Lee (1994). Another book which makes some estimates for the case of traffic is
Maddison et.al. (1996). A recent example of cost-benefit analysis is the book by ApSimon et al.
(1997). There has also been a major European Union (EU) study of external costs for several
pollutants from energy production and use. It is known as the 'externE' project; results are available
on the web.

13

India's Urban Environment:
Current Knowledge and Future Possibilities

BHASKAR VIRA AND SHIRAZ VIRA

India's towns and cities are significant centres of production, employment, and income generation and are estimated to contribute about 60 per cent of the country's GDP (UNCHS and HUDCO 2001). Despite the important economic role of cities rapid population growth is degrading the urban environment and placing strains on natural resources, thus undermining sustainable and equitable development. The most critical environmental concerns in India's cities include problems relating to water supply, sanitation, drainage, solid waste management (SWM), transport, and pollution from urban wastes and emissions. This chapter focuses on three specific issues in its discussion of 'the urban environment'—solid waste, water (availability and quality), and air. We recognize, however, that the term 'environment' could potentially include a number of additional dimensions, such as the quality of social infrastructure, the availability of shelter and recreational space, or the type of architecture.

Urban settlements, especially large cities, draw heavily on natural resources such as water, forests, and soil. If not properly managed, cities generate waste in a manner that pollutes air and water sources, and degrades renewable resources. Many of these problems of waste, air pollution, and water pollution have increased beyond both the absorptive capacity of nature and the handling capacity of institutions. It is this combination of lack of institutional capability and demographic pressures that explains the current state of the environment in India's cities. Future trends, by implication, will depend on the way in which demographic factors change, but also very largely on ways in which urban governance is transformed over the coming decades.

MUNICIPAL SOLID WASTE

With increasing urbanization and changing lifestyles, management of MSW has emerged as a major environmental issue in India. Municipal solid waste is a heterogeneous mixture of paper, plastic, cloth, metal, glass, and organic matter generated from households, commercial establishments, and markets. On account of unregulated land use across many urban areas (such as commercial and small-scale manufacturing activity) and the presence of unauthorized industrial and health care activities (such as clinics or nursing homes) within residential areas, there is a possibility that hazardous wastes are also present in the municipal waste system (Bhide and Shekdar 1999; Joardar 2000; TERI 1998).

Generation of solid waste

Data issues: There are serious problems associated with the ways in which municipalities actually calculate the amount of solid waste that is generated, and this has implications for the accuracy of the solid waste data. The Central Pollution Control Board (CPCB) points out that there are no authentic reports available on the generation of solid waste in most Indian cities (CPCB 1995). A per capita generation figure is usually arrived at by estimating the total generation of solid waste and dividing this by the population of the city. In the absence of house-to-house collection data, the quantity of waste generation is assessed in indirect ways like typical area study, weighing trucks, or using the density and correction factor method. Bhide and Shekdar (1999) suggest that very few disposal sites have a weighbridge. The estimate of waste is, therefore, made by multiplying the number of trips made by the tonnage of the vehicles. This is problematic as the designed capacity of the trucks is different from the load they carry, which varies depending on the substance being carried, and the extent of compaction. Bearing in mind these inaccuracies in data collection and reporting, any analysis based on published official data must be taken as only roughly indicative of the actual state of solid waste generation in India's cities.

Current trends: According to the CPCB, the total MSW generated by the 23 million plus cities (as per the 1991 Census) was 30,058 tonnes per day (CPCB 2000a). The total solid waste generated by all 299 Class I cities was estimated at 48,134 tonnes per day (CPCB 2000b), while that produced by 345 Class II towns was estimated at 3401 metric tonnes per day (CPCB 2000c). The average per capita generation of solid waste was 0.449 kg per day for the million plus cities, 0.376 kg per person per day for all Class I cities (100,000 population and above), and 0.152 kg per person per day for Class II towns (50,000–99,999). Out of the 113 Class II towns that responded, 56 towns fell under the category of less than 0.15 kg per capita per day generation of solid waste.[1]

Among the larger cities, Chennai generates the highest amount of waste per capita at 0.657 kg per day, while Kolkata generates 0.347 kg per day, well below the average for all metrocities. Kochi, which has the lowest population among the million plus cities (approximately 1 million) produces well above the average level of waste at 0.514 kg per capita per day, more than that generated in each of the three mega-cities, Mumbai, Kolkata, and Delhi. Similarly, the per capita generation of solid waste in Class I cities ranged between 0.1 kg per day for Junagadh to 0.929 kg per day for Jalgaon. The per capita generation of solid waste in Class II towns ranged from 0.019 kg per day for Puliyangudi in Tamil Nadu to 0.747 kg per day for Virar in Maharashtra.

The data suggest that within each size class, there is considerable variation, and that it would be simplistic to conclude that per capita solid waste generation increases monotonically with city size.[2] Other studies on per capita solid waste generation (for example, by the Operations Research Group in 1989, CPCB in 1997, and the National Institute for Urban Affairs (NIUA) in 1997) indicate similar sorts of differences between different cities. The broader literature (for instance, Bhide and Shekdar 1999; Joardar 2000; Rohilla and Bansal 1998; van Beukering 1994) provides some interesting case studies, but does not allow us to compare differences in solid waste generation across cities and towns in a more general sense. Overall, these trends suggest that it is difficult to conclude that urban growth is necessarily associated with higher levels of per capita waste generation.

Projections: In a report commissioned by the Supreme Court on Solid Waste for Class I Cities (Supreme Court 1999), total waste generated in 1991 by 217 million people living in urban areas was estimated at 23.86 million tonnes per year. The prediction was that this would cross 39 million tonnes by 2001. An alternative estimate by TERI (2001) suggested that solid waste generated in Indian cities increased from 6 million tonnes in 1947 to 47.8 million tonnes in 1997.[3] TERI uses the same method for making projections up to the year

---

[1]Out of 299 Class I cities, 210 cities responded to questionnaires sent out by CPCB and the Environment, Protection, Training, and Research Institute (EPTRI), while only 113 Class II towns out of a total of 345 responded to these. For the non-respondents, total solid waste generation was estimated on the basis of average solid waste generation in each size class.

[2]A recent survey by the National Institute for Urban Affairs (NIUA) (Raghupathi 2002) confirms that there is considerable variation in levels of per capita solid waste generation in urban India.

[3]TERI's method is based on surveys that estimate the average solid waste generated per head per day by the urban population. In 1971, the solid waste generated was estimated at 374 grams per capita per day (Bhide and Sunderesan 1984); in 1981, 432 grams (Nath 1984); and, in 1995, 456 grams (EPTRI 1995). These estimates are used to assume an annual growth rate of per capita solid waste generation of 1 per cent before 1980 and 1.33 per cent after 1990. Combining these per capita figures with population data allows TERI to make a backward and forward projection of quantities of MSW generated over the period 1947–1997.

2047. Assuming that daily per capita waste generation in 1995 was 0.456 kg (based on the Environment, Training, and Research Institute (EPTRI) estimate), per capita waste generation increases by 1.33 per cent per annum, and given an urban population of 796 million by 2047, TERI projects that solid waste generated by urban India in 2047 would increase to approximately 263 million tonnes, more than a five-fold increase over the 50-year period after 1997 (TERI 2001).

Recognizing that the use of overall national averages for solid waste generation is likely to lead to no more than an approximate estimate, a similar methodology can be combined with the present population projections (see Chapters 5 and 6). These projections suggest an urban population of 505.8 million by 2026. Although these projections do not provide separate figures for Class I cities, current trends suggest that such cities will constitute between 75 per cent and 80 per cent of the total urban population in 2026.[4] An assumption of 75 per cent yields a population of 379.35 million in Class I cities, while assuming 80 per cent suggests that this number will be 404.64 million.

Three different estimates of daily per capita waste generation are available— from the Supreme Court report (0.301 kg in 1991), the CPCB (for Class I cities, 0.376 kg in 1999; for Class II towns, 0.152 kg in 1999), and from EPTRI (0.456 kg in 1995). We assume a growth rate of per capita waste generation of 1.33 per cent per annum, following TERI. The estimated population figures for Class I cities and other cities and towns are combined with per capita averages for per capita solid waste generation in Class I and Class II cities from the CPCB data, adjusted for a growth rate of 1.33 per cent. The averages suggested by the Supreme Court and EPTRI are not broken down by the size of the city, so the aggregate population figures for 2026 can be used for these projections. This procedure produces a range of estimates for solid waste generation in 2026 varying between 84.40 million tonnes (using disaggregated CPCB averages and assuming that 75 per cent of the urban population lives in Class I cities) and 126.80 million tonnes (using TERI/EPTRI averages, and assuming that the entire urban population generates similar levels of waste per capita).[5] Details are given in Table 13.1, where '(75)' and '(80)' refer to assumptions that 75 per cent and 80 per cent respectively of the population live in Class I cities.

[4]The proportion of population in Class I cities was 44.87 per cent in 1951, 51.72 per cent in 1961, 57.15 per cent in 1971, 61.34 per cent in 1981, and 64.91 per cent in 1991 (Dyson and Visaria 2002).

[5]TERI's population projections for 2019 are for an overall urban population of 489 million, of which 362 million will live in Class I cities (TERI 2001). Chopra and Goldar (2000) estimate that the overall urban population in 2020 will be 512.7 million, of which 410.16 million will live in Class I cities. Using these projections, and the CPCB data for waste generation in Class I and Class II cities, yields overall annual solid waste generation figures of 73.88 million tonnes in 2019 (using TERI population figures) and 81.80 million tonnes in 2020 (using Chopra and Goldar's population figures). This would suggest that TERI's own projections of 111.76 million

TABLE 13.1: *Projected urban MSW generation in 2026*

	Kg per capita per day	*Annual (million tonnes)*
CPCB (75) Class I	0.537	74.38
CPCB (75) others	0.217	10.02
CPCB (75) total	–	84.40
CPCB (80) Class I	0.537	79.34
CPCB (80) others	0.217	8.02
CPCB (80) total	–	87.36
Supreme Court	0.478	88.24
TERI/EPTRI	0.687	126.80

Note: See text for explanation.

Disposal and management of solid waste: The Mid-term Appraisal of India's Ninth Five-Year Plan (Planning Commission 2000) acknowledges that the management of urban solid waste is one of the most neglected areas of urban development in India. Local authorities are responsible for SWM in towns and cities. A major portion of the waste collected is disposed of at dumpsites, most of which are not sanitary landfills, but unmanaged dumping grounds. The CPCB disposal figures for solid waste claim a disposal rate between 75 per cent and 100 per cent. These figures, however, do not necessarily reflect the situation on the ground. For example, Bhooshan (1998) suggests that Kochi faces a severe shortage of municipal services. Given its high per capita generation of solid waste (0.514 kg), for the local authority to claim 100 per cent disposal of waste seems unrealistic. Similarly, according to municipal records, Surat, which achieved notoriety due to an outbreak of plague in the city in 1994, produces 1040 tonnes of refuse, of which 920 tonnes are disposed of every day. But, unofficial estimates suggest that at least 250 tonnes of garbage out of 1250 tonnes generated every day are left uncollected (Ghosh and Ahmad 1996).

The life of existing disposal sites in the million-plus cities varies from one to ten years. In almost all cities and towns, finding a suitable disposal site is a major problem faced by the municipalities and corporations owing to stiff resistance from the public towards location of dumping sites in their neighbourhood. Furthermore, land is becoming an increasingly scarce resource in urban India. TERI (2001) estimates that the cumulative requirement of land for disposal of solid waste in 1997 was nearly 10 sq km, and that this can be expected to increase to about 1385 sq km by 2047, assuming an average collection efficiency of waste of 72.5 per cent. A recent report (UNCHS and HUDCO 2001) suggests that the land required for waste disposal in 1997

---

tonnes by 2019, derived using the higher per capita generation figure (0.456 kg in 1995) as an all-India average, are probably on the high side.

was 20.2 sq km, and projects that this will increase to 169.6 sq km by 2047.

If land for the disposal of solid waste is likely to become increasingly scarce, it is important to consider alternative methods for dealing with waste, including incineration, waste minimization, recycling, and reuse. Incineration of waste has not been successful in India, primarily due to the poor quality of wastes in terms of their low calorific value, high moisture content (average 30 per cent–50 per cent) and high silt content (average 50 per cent) (Joardar 2000). Furthermore, trends worldwide suggest a shift away from incineration for most types of waste, except biomedical waste.

In the area of waste minimization, while individual cities like Chennai, Pune, and Bangalore have made considerable progress, these are isolated cases and can be attributed more to NGO efforts than systematic government initiatives. On the other hand, the existing recovery of materials from waste for re-use or recycling, and the intensity with which limited resources are used in India is already quite remarkable. Furthermore, there are considerable differences in the scale and type of waste generated by households. Households in poorer city districts often generate half the city average and perhaps a third or quarter of the average waste produced in wealthy districts (Hardoy et al. 1992). Poorer households often separate glass, metals, and paper from their wastes since these can be sold. Their vegetable wastes may go to feeding livestock; they may also go to making compost if they have access to land on which food can be grown.

Overall, SWM is more an administrative and institutional problem than a technological one. Most municipal corporations realize that they need to generate more revenue from recycling waste to cover the high costs of other solid waste operations (CPCB 2000a; Vagale 1998; Venkateswarlu 1998). If these local bodies were to restructure their waste management system to separate organic matter and compost it, extract recyclables and recycle them, and only dump the remaining grit, rubble, etc., requirements of land for waste disposal could reduce dramatically, and substantial wealth could be generated from waste.

WATER AND SEWAGE

Ensuring adequate supplies of potable drinking water and sanitation facilities to urban areas has been a priority for Indian planners since the First Five-Year Plan. Despite this emphasis, the Mid-term Review of the Ninth Five Year Plan admits that accurate data on coverage for these facilities are not available (Planning Commission 2000). The document reports that coverage at the beginning of the Ninth Plan (1997) was estimated at 90 per cent of the urban population for potable drinking water, and 49 per cent of the urban population for sanitation (Planning Commission 2000: 432). These are average figures, which fail to capture the extent of variation in terms of access to these facilities within regions and within urban settlements. In particular, such statistics do not reflect the situation in slum and squatter settlements and peri-urban areas, where service provision is usually much worse (Cairncross 1990; Hardoy et al. 1992; Kundu 1992; TERI 1998). In addition, surface water resources, which are the principal source of water in urban areas, are becoming increasingly polluted. This is threatening the water supply system, particularly in metropolitan cities.

Water supply and availability: Data from the CPCB suggest that about 88 per cent of the population in Class I and Class II cities are covered by an organized source of water supply. Slightly over a quarter of the Class I cities and 14 per cent of Class II towns and cities report 100 per cent water supply coverage, while about one-sixth of such towns and cities report less than 75 per cent coverage. Details are in Table 13.2.

TABLE 13.2: *Coverage of water supply in urban areas*

Type	No.	Population	Per cent of pop. covered	Extent of coverage			
				100 per cent	*75–100 per cent*	*50–75 per cent*	*<50 per cent*
Million +	23	70.996 m.	90	6 (26%)	14 (61%)	3 (13%)	0 (0%)
Class I	299	139.966 m.	88	77 (26%)	158 (53%)	43 (14%)	10 (3%)
Class II	345	23.646 m.	88	50 (14%)	222 (64%)	44 (13%)	10 (3%)

Notes: (1) Here and in Tables 13.4 and 13.5 the million plus cities and those in size classes I and II shown are those that were identified by the 1991 Census. The million plus cities are Class I cities, but data on these cities are reported separately as well. The 299 Class I cities thus include the 23 million plus cities.
(2) For Class I and Class II cities, data on coverage do not add up to 100 per cent on account of incomplete reporting in the original documents.
Sources: CPCB (1997, 2000d, 2000e).

In terms of levels of water supply, the average availability of water in metrocities is 214 litres per capita daily (lpcd), while that in all Class I cities is 183 lpcd, and in Class II cities 103 lpcd (Table 13.3). The CPCB classifies towns and cities into four different categories, depending on average levels of water availability—low for areas with less than 100 lpcd, normal for areas with supply between 100 and 200 lpcd, high for areas with supply between 200 and 300 lpcd, and very high for areas reporting more than 300 lpcd. On this basis, Table 13.3 shows that while only 9 per cent of metrocities have a below-normal level of water supply, the situation for all Class I and Class II cities and towns is considerably worse.

What is striking about water supply data within these size classes is the extent of variation between cities and towns. Among the metrocities, Delhi has a high water supply of 341 lpcd, while Madurai reports a very low supply of 74 lpcd. Similarly, supply levels in Class I and Class II cities vary from

TABLE 13.3: *Water supply levels in urban areas*

Type	Av. lpcd	Supply level (no. and per cent of cities/towns)				Variation	
		Low <100	Normal 100–200	High 200–300	Very high >300	Highest	Lowest
Million +	214	2 (9%)	12 * (52%)	8* (35%)	1 (4%)	341 lpcd (Delhi)	74 lpcd (Madurai)
Class I	183	109 (36%)	138 (46%)	36 (12%)	16 (5%)	584 lpcd (Tiruvannamalai)	9 lpcd (Tuticorin)
Class II	103	203 (59%)	120 (35%)	18 (5%)	4 (1%)	776 lpcd (Dhrangadhara)	7 lpcd (Payyannur)

Notes: (1) The million plus cities are Class I cities, but data on these cities is reported separately as well. The 299 Class I cities, thus, include the 23 million plus cities.
(2) The threshold between normal and high supply level in metrocities is 214 lpcd, which is the average supply level for these cities.
*see note (2).
Sources: CPCB (1997, 2000d, 2000e).

single figures to between three and four times the 'normal' figure, as defined by CPCB. A further problem with the aggregate CPCB data is that, since it provides only an overall supply figure, disparities in water distribution within each city are not clear. CPCB (2000d) cites an independent study on disparities done by the Operations Research Group in 1995, which indicates that per capita availability of water varies between 36 lpcd and 310 lpcd within the metrocities.[6] Despite the fact that water supply systems are designed for 24-hour service at 150–200 lpcd, water is generally available for one to six hours, with average per capita consumption between 80 and 100 lpcd (Venkateswarlu 1998). Within slum areas, water availability tends to average between 25 and 27 lpcd and is considerably below the desirable minimum level of 40 lpcd as fixed by the National Drinking Water Mission (EGCIP 1996).

Wastewater generation: In the urban context, wastewater includes industrial and domestic wastewater. Though CPCB reports figures for domestic wastewater, it does not provide a breakdown for industrial wastewater for all cities. There is very little analysis of the generation and collection of wastewater in towns and cities (Heggade 1998; Misra1998; Singh and Steinberg 1996; Venkasteswarlu 1998). This is partly to do with data availability and the CPCB, in its own reports, regularly comments on the inadequacy of information on wastewater generation and collection.[7] Table 13.4 summarizes the data on wastewater generation, collection, and treatment, reported in CPCB documents.

[6]In the case of Delhi, which has a very high average of 341 lpcd, some areas get over 450 lpcd (New Delhi Municipal Corporation area and Delhi Cantonment), while others get less than 35 lpcd (Mehrauli, Narela) (Buch 1993; Misra and Misra 1998).
[7]Forty-four per cent of Class I cities and 68.4 per cent of Class II towns failed to furnish information on wastewater generation in response to CPCB questionnaires. In these cases, CPCB

TABLE 13.4: *Wastewater in urban areas*

Type	No.	Response Rate	Generation	Collection	Treatment capacity	Untreated
Million +	23	100%	9275.0 mld	7471.1 mld (80.55%)	2923.0 mld (31.51%)	6352.0 mld (68.49%)
Class I	299	56%	16662.5 mld	11938.2 mld (71.65%)	4037.2 mld (24.23%)	12625.3 mld (75.77%)
Class II	345	32%	1649.6 mld	1090.3 mld (66.09%)	61.5 mld (3.73%)	1588.1 mld (96.27%)

Note: The million plus cities are Class I cities, but data on these cities is reported separately as well. The 299 Class I cities, thus, include the 23 million plus cities.
Sources: CPCB (1997, 2000d, 2000e).

Of the total wastewater generated by Class I cities, about 59 per cent comes from the million-plus cities. Within the metrocities, the four largest—Mumbai, Kolkata, Delhi, and Chennai—generate 58.5 per cent of the overall wastewater. The figures for installed treatment capacity suggest that a very large proportion of urban wastewater re-enters the hydrological system untreated and contributes to pollution. Out of an estimated total wastewater generation of 18312 million litres per day (mld) from Class I and Class II cities combined, as much as 14213 mld (77.62 per cent) is untreated. Where wastewater treatment facilities exist, they do not function properly, and remain closed most of the time due to improper design and poor maintenance, together with a non-technical and unskilled approach. The Centre for Science and Environment's Second Citizen's Report claims that out of India's 3119 towns and cities only 209 have partial sewage and sewage treatment facilities and eight have full facilities (CSE 1985). Table 13.5 provides more details on sewage coverage in metropolitan, Class I, and Class II cities, according to CPCB data.

The CPCB data suggest that slightly over 25 per cent of Class I cities, and less than 5 per cent of Class II towns, have either primary or secondary treatment facilities. Among the metrocities, Delhi stands out as having the highest treatment capacity, and has five treatment plants with a further four under construction.[8] Chennai also has five treatment plants, and the percentage of population served by sewage treatment is 93 per cent, which is

---

estimated waste water generation as 80 per cent of the total volume of water supply, following recommendations of the Manual on Sewerage and Sewage Treatment published by the Central Public and Health and Environmental Engineering Organization (CPHEEO).

[8]While the installation of new facilities in Delhi has increased treatment capacity from 450 million litres per day (mld) in 1977 to 1270 mld in 1997 it has not ben able to meet the demands created by the increased flow of wastewater, which rose from 960 mld in 1977 to 1900 mld in 1997.

TABLE 13.5: *Sewage in urban areas*

Type	No.	Population	Per cent of pop. covered	No. and per cent with treatment	Sewarage coverage level (no. and per cent)		
					>75 per cent	50–75 per cent	<50 per cent
Million +	23	70.996 m.	78%	19 (82.61%)	19 (80.55%)	4 (31.51%)	0 (68.49%)
Class I	299	139.966 m.	70%	76 (25.42%)	160 (71.65%)	92 (24.23%)	47 (75.77%)
Class II	345	23.646 m.	66%	17 (4.93%)	160 (66.09%)	151 (3.73%)	34 (96.27%)

Note: The million-plus cities are Class I cities, but data on these cities is reported separately as well. The 299 Class I cities, thus, include the 23 million plus cities.
Sources: CPCB (1997, 2000a, 2000b).

very high compared to Mumbai where it is only 65 per cent (CPCB 1997). Among the other million-plus cities, Pune has the highest treatment capacity (981 mld) and 85 per cent of the population is served by sewage treatment, while Jaipur has the lowest treatment capacity at 27 mld.

Much of this waste water gets into neighbouring rivers. Most of India's rivers are literally open sewers. On the river Ganga alone, 114 cities each with 50,000 or more inhabitants dump untreated sewage into the river every day (Agarwal 1999).[9] The untreated water is often highly polluted. Pollution from pesticide leaching and toxic metal leaching from industrial effluents has had serious health effects on people all over the country. For instance, a World Bank study estimates that some 30.5 million DALYS (disability adjusted life-years) are lost each year in India due to poor water quality, sanitation, and hygiene (*Down to Earth* 1996).

Urban water—The future: TERI (2001) and Chopra and Goldar (2000) provide some estimates of water demand from urban areas in the medium term. TERI assumes that per capita supply will be 135 litres per person per day, and projects an annual demand of 24.10 billion cubic metres (BCM) in 2019. Chopra and Goldar assume that Class I cities will receive 220 lpcd, while Class II towns and smaller towns will receive 165 lpcd. With their population projections, this yields an estimate of 39.11 BCM in 2020. Projections made by the National Commission on Integrated Water Resource Development use two scenarios: in the high water requirement scenario, the norm for urban areas is 220 lpcd, whereas in the low water requirement scenario, the norm is 165 lpcd for Class I cities and 110 lpcd for Class II cities. These four alternative urban water

[9]For detailed dicussion on river pollution due to untreated sewage see the *Citizen's Fifth Report*, CSE (1999a).

supply norms allow us to make some estimates for urban water demand in 2026 (Table 13.6).[10] Water demand for 2026 is projected to vary between 24.92 BCM (using TERI's 135 lpcd norm) and 40.62 BCM (using the National Commission's high water requirement norm of 220 lpcd).

TABLE 13.6: *Projected annual urban water demand (BCM) under alternative population projections*

	TERI (2019)	Chopra (2020)	Present Study (2026)[1]	Present Study (2026)[2]
TERI/MoUD	24.10	25.26	24.92	24.92
NC low	26.90	28.82	27.92	28.43
Chopra	36.72	39.11	38.08	38.58
NC high	39.27	41.17	40.62	40.62

Notes: MoUD = Ministry of Urban Development; NC = National Commission on Integrated Water Resources Development.
[1]Assumes Class I cities are 75 per cent of the total urban population in 2026.
[2]Assumes Class I cities are 80 per cent of the total urban population in 2026.
Source: TERI (2001); Chopra and Goldar (2000).

As far as wastewater and sewage is concerned, the poor quality of current information makes forecasting even more hazardous than usual. The studies by TERI (2001) and Chopra and Goldar (2000) do make medium-term projections about the pollution load (Biological Oxygen Demand—BOD) due to urban wastewater discharge. TERI (2001) suggests that BOD due to urban water pollution will be 5.83 million tonnes in 2019, compared with their estimate of 3.75 million tonnes in 1997. Chopra and Goldar (2000) project urban BOD in 2020 to be 4.99 million tonnes, rising from an estimated 2.24 million tonnes in 1995. Given the low level of treatment that is currently available in most Class I and Class II towns and cities, such projections are extremely sensitive to assumptions about the management of wastewater in urban India. If there were to be substantial investment in upgrading sewage treatment facilities in urban areas, one could expect pollution loads to rise less dramatically. If local authorities are unable or unwilling to make such investments, the implications for urban water pollution are very serious indeed.

AIR POLLUTION

Indian cities are among the most polluted in the world, with concentrations of a number of air pollutants being well above recommended World Health Organization (WHO) levels. The major pollutants are SO_2, NO_x, CO, hydrocarbons, photochemical oxidants, metals, and other gases and vapours. According to analysts, the major sources of air pollution are industries, thermal

[10]The table reports on projections based on 75 per cent and 80 per cent of the projected urban population residing in Class I cities in 2026.

power plants, and motor vehicles (TERI 1998). Trends indicate that transport in cities is a key factor, often responsible for 60 to 70 per cent of the local air pollution (CSE 1996; HUDCO and UNCHS 2001; Parikh 1999). The other major sources of air pollution are industries (toxic gases) and thermal power plants (fly ash and SO_2). Air pollution in Indian towns and cities is responsible for serious health ailments. For instance, a widely-cited World Bank study (Brandon and Homann 1995) estimated that 40,351 premature deaths per year across 36 Indian cities could be attributed to air pollution alone.[11]

Data issues: Air pollution is monitored by the National Ambient Air Quality Monitoring System (NAAQM). The NAAQM network is operated through the respective State Pollution Control Boards, the National Environmental Engineering Research Institute (NEERI), Nagpur, and also through the CPCB. The pollutants monitored (which concern this study) are SO_2, nitrogen dioxide (NO_2), and SPM besides meteorological parameters, like wind speed and direction, temperature, and humidity.

The NAAQM does not measure other harmful pollutants such as CO, hydrocarbons, and ozone which contribute significantly to pollution levels. Small particles (particles with a size of less than 10 microns or PM 10) are not monitored separately on a routine basis in any of the metrocities. However, short-term monitoring of PM 10 levels in Delhi by CPCB shows that on average nearly 40 per cent of total SPM is PM 10. Analysts point out that it is these particles that are the most dangerous (Agarwal 1999; Kandlikar and Ramachandran 2000). Since CPCB does not monitor these important pollutants, it is difficult to get an accurate overall picture of air pollution in the metrocities.

It is necessary to bear in mind these limitations while examining air quality data for India. The CPCB itself admits that the large number of items of equipment and personnel involved in sampling and chemical analysis increases the variation caused by differences in recording equipment and human error (CPCB 2000f). Problems are also caused by frequent changes in the location of monitoring stations. This results in gaps in the data which in turn affect the average values and observed trends. Therefore, CPCB concludes, the data are merely indicative and not definitive.

Current trends: CPCB's (2000f) analysis of air quality trends over the nine-year period between 1990 and 1998 suggests that SPM levels remained consistently high in various cities over this period, while SO_2 and NO_2 levels were within permissible limits for most cities. However, there is also great variation, with average recorded levels of each of the three pollutants fluctuating considerably over this period in most cities. Trends are constant in some cities, worsening

[11]Other recent studies referring to links between health and air pollution include a report by Cropper et al. (1997), Kandlikar and Ramachandran (2000), and Parikh (1999).

in some, while they are improving in others, and the data show no overall pattern. SPM provides most cause for concern, and CPCB concludes that the data suggest that annual averages for both residential and industrial areas have probably 'been frequently violated at most cities' (CPCB 2000f: 95). Table 13.7 summarizes the CPCB data, showing the permissible limit, as well as the lowest and highest recorded mean of average values, for each pollutant in residential and industrial areas over this period.

TABLE 13.7: *Range of air quality data recorded by CPCB between 1990 and 1998*

Pollutant	Safe limits	No. of cities for which data are available	No. of cities exceeding safe limits	Recorded low	Recorded high
SPM					
Residential	140	16	16	99 (Chennai)	390 (Kanpur)
Industrial	360	16	5	123 (Chennai)	457 (Kanpur)
SO$_2$					
Residential	60	16	1	5.27 (Chandigarh)	74.02 (Howrah)
Industrial	80	16	0	8.91 (Nagpur)	46.27 (Pondicherry)
NO$_2$					
Residential	60	16	2	15.42 (Kanpur)	127.09 (Howrah)
Industrial	80	16	1	23.2 (Bangalore)	185.6 (Howrah)

Source: CPCB (2000f).

A survey of smaller towns and cities by the Centre for Science and Environment found high air pollution levels in many (*CSE* 1999b). Available case study evidence confirms this. For instance, a report released in January 1999 by the World Resources Institute in Washington, pointed out that Rajkot in Gujarat is the fifth most polluted city in the world with regard to air pollution (cited in *CSE* 1999b). A relatively small city, Dehra Dun (now the capital of Uttaranchal) registered the highest SPM level in the country in 1992, an extremely high 4809 ug/cum. Agra is also highly polluted with annual average SPM levels exceeding the limits permissible even in industrial areas (TERI 1998). Similarly, Pondicherry, Kota, Gajraula, Shimla, and Rohtak are a few other examples of smaller cities or towns which have regularly exceeded the SPM, SO$_2$, and NO$_x$ permissible limits.

Data on each of these air quality indicators separately do not necessarily provide a good indication of overall air quality in a city. Using CPCB data for 1993 and 1994, TERI (1998) constructed a single index, which provides an indication of the cumulative effect of the three pollutants on air quality in urban India. According to TERI's air quality index, out of 62 cities for which data were available, 20 had 'dangerous' levels of pollution, while the situation was judged to be 'bad' in 14, 'poor' in nine, 'fair' in 12, and 'good' in seven.

Causes of air pollution: The process of development and industrialization is typically associated with an increase in the scale of economic activity. This is likely to lead to higher levels of pollution, unless it is mediated by the adoption of improved technology and/or a shift in the structure of production and consumption away from polluting sources. Such shifts may occur because of changes in preferences, or may be forced upon producers and consumers due to government policy. Analysts suggest that the major factors behind an increase in air pollution in India are the transport sector (especially the growth of motor vehicles), industrial production, and the generation of thermal power (TERI 1998).

Vehicular air pollution: The number of vehicles increased by about 17 million (almost three-fold) in the seven years between 1986 and 1993 (CSE 1996), well above the rate of population growth over this period.[12] In 1994, the 23 metropolitan cities had 9 million vehicles, accounting for nearly 33 per cent of the total vehicle population in the country (Venkateswarlu 1998). Almost 48 per cent of these were registered in just three metros, Delhi (29 per cent), Mumbai (11.5 per cent), and Kolkata (8.3 per cent). During the year 1995–6, registered vehicle numbers increased by about 15 per cent in the 23 million-plus cities. The most rapid increases were in Hyderabad (37 per cent), Nagpur (53 per cent), Kochi (280 per cent), Bhopal (80 per cent), Varanasi (53 per cent), Madurai (44 per cent), and Ludhiana (75 per cent), while Surat and Indore saw significant declines in registered vehicle numbers (29 per cent and 30 per cent respectively).

Delhi has a disproportionately large share of the country's vehicular population. The city has witnessed a phenomenal rise in the number of vehicles over the years. In 1975, there were 235,000 vehicles, increasing to 841,000 in 1985, and 2,629,000 in 1996. Projections suggest that there will be 4.6 million vehicles in 2004, and about 6 million vehicles in 2011 (NCRPB 1999). The growth in number of motor vehicles has been more rapid than the growth of both road length and of human population (Pandey 1998). Estimates suggests that vehicular emissions in Delhi account for as much as 64 per cent of the total pollution load in Delhi, while thermal power plants contribute about 13 per cent, industrial activity 12 per cent, and the remaining 8 per cent are contributed by domestic sources (CSE 1996; TERI 2001).[13]

With a growing concentration of vehicles in the metrocities (and with similar trends in the Class I cities) it is clear why motor vehicles have been

---

[12]Vehicles include two-wheelers, three-wheelers, cars, jeeps, taxis, buses, trucks, tractors, and trailers.

[13]Revised estimates suggest that the share of vehicular pollution in Delhi is even higher (67 per cent in the 1997 White Paper on Pollution in Delhi and 70 per cent in the June 1999 issues of *Parivesh,* the newsletter of the CPCB) (TERI 2000).

singled out as the dominant source of air pollution. TERI (1998) reports that vehicles in major metropolitan cities account for 70 per cent of CO, 50 per cent of all hydrocarbons, 30–40 per cent of NO_x, 30 per cent of SPM and 10 per cent of SO_2 pollution (Table 13.8; and also Chapter 12). Until stringent emission norms are observed and suitable fuels are identified and used, air pollution will continue to be a problem in the cities. It is important for alternative fuels like compressed natural gas (CNG), LPG, and propane to be used more widely. It is also important to phase out poorly maintained vehicles running on Indian roads. Vehicular pollution can only be dealt with as part of an integrated and comprehensive strategy for containing air pollution and dealing with the transport needs of India's urban population.

Industrial pollution: In metropolitan cities and smaller towns and cities of India, the policy for industrial location has prevented large industries from being set up within urban boundaries, but the fringes and adjoining areas have become industrialized. In some cases, tax and financial incentives were preferentially available in the fringe areas of metropolitan cities. The Thane–Belapur area adjoining Mumbai; Noida, Gurgaon, and Faridabad near Delhi; and Hosur near Bangalore are some examples of industrial expansion near metropolitan cities.

Small-scale industries are major polluters. India has over 3 million small-scale units accounting for over 40 per cent of the industrial output in the country. Delhi and Mumbai both have a large number of small-scale units (Shah and Nagpal 1997). In general, while the larger industries are better organized to adopt pollution control measures, the small-scale sector is far less equipped (both financially and technically) to handle the problem. Therefore, the aggregate potential to pollute is high (TERI 1998).

TERI (1998) quotes World Bank estimates that suggest that pollution is concentrated amongst a few industrial sub-sectors. Further, there is often little relation between a sector's contribution to industrial output and its contribution to pollution. The most polluting sectors in India are petroleum refineries, textiles, pulp and paper, and industrial chemicals (which contribute about 87 per cent of sulphur emissions and 70 per cent of nitrogen emissions), and iron and steel and non-metallic products (which account for 55 per cent of particulate emissions). TERI (1998) also estimates that the aggregate pollution load from thermal power stations increased from 0.3 million tonnes in 1947 to 15 million tonnes in 1997, with SPM comprising 86 per cent of the total in 1997 (Table 13.8).

Projections and policy responses: It is particularly difficult to make projections about the future of air pollution in Indian cities, given the lack of detailed current data, as well as the sensitivity of such pollution to changes in policy, especially with respect to vehicular and industrial emissions. Vehicular emissions can be controlled by greater efficiency in combustion, use of alternative fuels, as well as the provision of suitable and reliable mass transport systems. Industrial pollution is sensitive to the adoption of energy efficient and environmentally-sensitive technology, which could occur due to a number of factors including policy, global market pressures, as well as expectations of investors and consumers.[14]

TERI (2001) makes specific assumptions about potential future trajectories in the transport, domestic, manufacturing, and power sectors, and projects emission trends for the medium term (2019) and long term (2047). Table 13.8 summarizes these projections, which include a base case forecast (B), and an alternative (lower emissions) scenario that includes the impacts of adoption of new policy measures and new technology. In the base case, emissions due to vehicles and manufacturing are projected to increase, while the installation of electrostatic precipitators in the power sector is expected to contribute to a reduced emission load, especially of SPMs. In the domestic sector, the use of cleaner fuels associated with greater urbanization is expected to reduce emission levels.

In the alternative (A) scenario, improved ventilation, improved stoves, and cleaner fuels may lead to lower emissions in the domestic sector than in the base case. In the transport sector, the adoption of higher emission norms, change of fuels and control of vehicle numbers may contribute to lower future emissions. In manufacturing, measures could include improvement of efficiency, implementation of existing environmental standards, greater material re-use, and appropriate industrial location. In the power sector, the use of better quality fuels and pollution control technologies, coupled with appropriate economic incentives, are seen as possible contributors to a lower future emissions load. The projections are most sensitive to the adoption of measures in the power sector, as can be seen from the difference between the base and alternative case scenario in terms of SPM emissions.

Some of these measures have already been introduced, although it is too early to assess their impacts on urban air pollution. For instance, in Delhi, the Supreme Court (July 1998) has directed that all public transport should use only CNG. However, there is still debate over which fuel to use, with some groups recommending the use of ultra low-sulphur diesel as an alternative due to its efficiency and availability (CSE 2001; Bose et al. 2001). Many observers have noted a considerable drop in air pollution levels in Delhi. The introduction of unleaded petrol from 1995 (for new passenger cars) and from 1998 for all vehicles also appears to have had an impact, and the recorded lead content in the atmosphere near traffic intersections in Delhi has reduced by more than 60 per cent (CPCB 1999). It is important to note, however, that many of the debates and Supreme Court orders on reduction of air

---

[14]Chapter 12 models the impact of technology and policy adoption on emissions, and discusses some of these issues in greater detail.

TABLE 13.8: *TERI projections for urban emissions (all sectors, in million tonnes)*

Year	Vehicles						Domestic		Manufacturing*		Power		
	CO	HC	NOx	SO$_2$	SPM	Total	CO	SPM	SPM	SPM	NOx	SO$_2$	Total
1997	4.25	0.02	0.18	0.04	0.03	4.52	7.08	1.00	0.98	11.92	1.73	1.34	14.99
2019 (B)	16.12	0.07	0.54	0.12	0.09	16.94	5.26	0.71	1.87	6.28	3.18	3.30	12.76
2019 (A)	9.27	0.04	0.36	0.07	0.05	9.79	3.78	0.52	1.67	0.50	1.99	2.28	4.77
2047 (B)	71.57	0.23	1.82	0.49	0.34	74.45	3.05	0.38	3.53	10.76	6.48	0.91	18.15
2047 (A)	25.11	0.07	0.67	0.13	0.09	26.07	2.27	0.26	1.66	0.76	3.86	0.49	5.11

Notes: *Data for the manufacturing sector relate to seven major industries: copper, aluminium, steel, cement, fertilizers, textiles, and PVC (polyvinyl chloride). See text for explanation of '(B)' and '(A)'.

Source: TERI (2001).

pollution, fuel use, etc. have pertained mainly to Delhi. If they are to have a wider impact, similar policies must be applied across other cities and towns in urban India where the problems of air pollution are as precarious. Some effort is being made towards this; for example, the use of unleaded petrol and CNG for commercial vehicles is being proposed in all cities and towns (UNCHS and HUDCO 2001). A Supreme Court judgment in April 2002 has directed the Government of India to extend supply of CNG to other cities.

POSSIBLE FUTURES FOR THE URBAN ENVIRONMENT

This chapter has highlighted the lack of reliable data on the state of India's urban environment, focusing on solid waste, water and sewage, and air pollution. Individual researchers and organizations do not have the capacity to generate the required primary data on a wide enough scale, so the onus remains upon official data collection sources to improve and upgrade their operations. There needs to be a serious investment in improving the extent and the quality of information that is available, so that the policy community can make decisions about urban environmental futures on the basis of good empirical knowledge.

The information that is available suggests that urban environmental problems are already quite considerable, and likely to worsen in the coming years. There are problems in the largest cities (the million-plus), but similar trends are reported from the smaller towns and cities as well, so it is clear that the deterioration in environmental quality is affecting all of urban India. Further, problems are beginning to extend beyond the urban as traditionally defined, and are affecting the rural–urban fringe, and peri-urban areas as well.

Many authors (as well as environmental institutions such as CSE and TERI) who have written about urban environmental problems in India (Gnaneshwar 1995; Hardoy 1992; Jain et al. 1995; Nath 1989) claim that it is probably misleading to refer to many of the most pressing environmental problems as 'environmental' since 'they arise not from some particular shortage of environmental resources (such as land or fresh water) but from economic or political factors which prevent poorer groups from obtaining them and organising to demand them'. They point out, for example, that the severe shortage of water supplies for much of the developing world's urban population is a serious environmental problem but rarely is its cause environmental; in most cities it is not a shortage of freshwater resources but government's refusal to give a higher priority to water supply (and the competent organizational structure that its supply, maintenance, and expansion requires). It is the same with land; most cities or metropolitan areas in the developing world have sufficient unused or under-utilized land sites within the current built-up area to accommodate most, if not all, the low-income households currently living in very overcrowded conditions.

Some issues appear to be strongly driven by the size of the population, since they relate to the volumes generated or demanded by urban dwellers. These include the total amount of MSW generated, the demand for water, as well as the quantity of wastewater generated. It has been possible to examine some future scenarios for these indicators, using a range of plausible assumptions about per capita generation rates and/or demands. For some other issues, notably air pollution, the poor current state of knowledge, and the complexity of causal mechanisms, makes forecasting difficult. However, the chapter has reported on predictions that have recently been made in this context by other independent researchers.

Any such prediction exercise is fraught with danger, especially given the manner in which urban environmental quality is linked with personal consumption choices, production technologies and methods, as well as the role of policy in directing incentives for such activities. Changes in the urban environment depend on strategies adopted by the government, changes in environmental legislation and the stricter enforcement of existing legislation, the demand for better living conditions by urban residents, as well as the ability of local authorities to perform their functions on their own or in partnership with others.

If there is a desire for an improvement in environmental standards, and this is supported by the availability of real alternatives for consumers and producers, the evidence suggests that significant changes are possible. Examples that are widely cited include the transformation in Surat following the 1994 plague, and the dramatic improvement in air quality in Delhi after the implementation of higher emission standards and the phasing out of leaded fuel, among others. However, these experiences are relatively recent, and it is difficult to draw any firm conclusions from them about the future of urban environmental quality and governance. There are at least as many cases where attempts to improve environmental standards or to ensure greater compliance with existing laws have met with considerable resistance. In Delhi, the controversy about relocation of non-conforming industrial units from residential areas, as well as the ongoing debate about the appropriate choice of fuel for public transport, are two examples. Here, a complex web of interests (consumers, businesses, workers, the judiciary, and various branches of the executive from the national government to municipalities) is involved, and this has made the process of political implementation of desirable changes very difficult.

India currently has weak institutions and infrastructure on which to base effective action to address urban environmental problems. The master planning approach was not able to curtail congestion, traffic jams, pollution, marginalization of the poor, and other serious environmental situations. Related strategies to 'balance' urban growth and to promote small and medium cities as 'counter magnets' and growth centres have not produced the desired impact. Added to this is the lack of coordination between different agencies responsible for various urban tasks within a city. Sewerage, drainage and solid waste services (including street cleaning) are often the responsibility of different agencies, yet their design, implementation, and management need to be carefully coordinated. Drainage systems, for example, cannot work in most developing world cities without SWM which keeps drains clean. Drainage networks need coordinated action at household, neighbourhood, and city level—and beyond the city for those living 'downstream' of the city—yet rarely do their design and operation take account of this fact. Our assessment of the urban situation suggests that many urban problems may arise due to a lack of perspective and appropriate structures of governance for planned urban development in India, and it is these links which need further investigation.

The main reason for the failure of urban planning can be seen in the weak revenue situation of urban local bodies which have lived through the painful experience of the 'resource crunch' of the 1990s. And this weak tax income has been accentuated by political populism which has prevented urban local bodies from exploiting whatever revenue potential exists. At the local level, the authorities have inadequate budgets, large backlogs in providing basic infrastructure, and a resource base that is not capable of generating the capital required to address the backlog. The 74th Amendment to the Constitution has transferred powers to local bodies to raise tax and non-tax revenues to enable them to exercise their responsibility of planning and development. However, analysts remain sceptical about the extent to which the constitutional amendment will be translated into any real improvement in the financial position of urban local bodies (Kundu 2000).

It is difficult to say, on the basis of the evidence, whether current trends in urban environmental quality will continue, worsen or improve over the next couple of decades. Given the rapid changes that have taken place in the Indian economy in the last few years, and the greater exposure of producers and consumers to the forces of globalization, the pressures on the environment are likely to increase. At the same time, new opportunities to tackle potential environmental problems are also emerging. These include a significant commitment to empowering urban local government under the 74th Amendment to the Constitution, a greater sensitization (especially of the urban middle classes) to issues of environmental quality, new technological possibilities in the production sector, as well as new models of service provision and delivery, which recognize the role of other participants (including the private sector, NGOs, and community-based organizations, and citizens' groups). While we cannot make firm forecasts about future trends, what is certain is that urban environmental quality issues will become increasingly important over the short and medium term, and are likely to be the subject of considerable research activity and policy debate during this period.

14

Water

BHASKAR VIRA, RAMASWAMY IYER, AND ROBERT CASSEN

A particularly powerful impact of population growth is likely to be on future demand for water, because of the strong link between food demand and population numbers, and the fact that agriculture takes a very large share of India's water supplies. However, a number of factors mediate the influence of population growth on resource availability and environmental quality. An important question is to try and assess how rising demand is going to be met. To answer the question, we have to look first at the overall supply of water and the factors affecting its availability and quality, the existing pattern of demand, and the factors that are likely to influence future water demand over the medium term. This chapter attempts to do just that.

WATER AVAILABILITY

The total amount of water that is available to a country is largely determined by natural phenomena.[1] In India's case, the main sources are rainfall and the melting snows and glaciers of the Himalayas—these are what ultimately feed the rivers, canals, and groundwater tables. The amount of water that is useable for human purposes is potentially influenced by the likelihood of climate change, and by the amount of pollution, which reduces effective availability.

---

[1]Within regions, there may be a limited amount of water flowing across international boundaries. But water is not really an internationally tradeable commodity. Importing water-intensive foods, though, may for some countries be a useful way of responding to rising water demand.

The annual water resources of the country, measured in terms of the flows at the terminal points in the river systems, have been estimated by the National Commission on Integrated Water Resources Development (NCIWRD) as 1953 billion cubic metres (BCM). Groundwater availability has been put at 432 BCM.[2] As against these 'availability' figures, the NCIWRD estimates that the annual 'useable' water resources of the country are 690 BCM of surface water and 396 BCM of groundwater, making a total of 1086 BCM. The present quantum of use is put at around 600 BCM. The average annual precipitation by way of rain and snow over India's landmass is 4000 BCM, but this masks considerable temporal and spatial variability. Approximately 80 per cent of the total annual rainfall arrives during the two-and-a-half months of the south-west monsoon between June and September. There are wide variations in rainfall between regions, ranging from 100 mm in parts of Rajasthan to 11,000 mm in the eastern part of Meghalaya (NCIWRD 1999). This variation is reflected in water availability in the major river systems, with nearly 60 per cent of the country's freshwater resources concentrated in the Ganga–Brahmaputra–Meghna basin, which makes up just 33 per cent of the country's land area. In contrast, 64 per cent of the land area is served by only 29 per cent of available freshwater.

The effects of climate change: The mean temperature increase over India, measured since 1881, has been estimated at 0.57 degrees Celsius (°C) per century.[3] There has been no trend in rainfall for the country as a whole, just seemingly random fluctuations for a century; but the 1990s saw an increasing trend on the west coast, northern Andhra Pradesh and north-west India, and a decreasing trend over eastern Madhya Pradesh and north-east India. There has also been an increase of atmospheric CO_2 with no detectable effects.

Climate change models predict an average increase of temperature of 2.7°C relative to 1961–90 for the 2050s decade, and 3.8°C for the 2080s, due to greenhouse gases. However, when the effects of sulphate aerosol are included, this reduces to 1.9°C for the 2050s and 3.0°C for the 2080s. Warming will be higher in winter months than in summer. The frequency of extreme warm days will probably rise.

Different models give different results for rainfall: most predict a rise of annual rainfall, steadily reaching something of the order of 7.5–10 per cent higher precipitation by the 2080s, but this divides into reductions in winter rainfall, especially in the central plains, and increases in monsoon rainfall. These are not wholly positive prospects. 'The decline in winter-time rainfall over India is likely to be significant and may lead to droughts during the dry summer months in many states of India.' While they are hard to model, it

[2]Treating these figures as distinct could lead to some double counting, in view of the complex interactions between surface and groundwater.

[3]The data and quote in this section are from Lal (2000).

seems likely that existing interannual fluctuations in monsoon rainfall will intensify, with more frequent flashflooding.

Another risk of climate change is that it may reduce or alter the timing of snow- and glacier-melt in the Himalayas.[4] Increasing volatility of temperature is also a probability, so that melt-water flows may become more variable, both in volume and time. The Indus, Ganga, and Brahmaputra systems all depend on the Himalayan glaciers and snow-melt. Since the three rivers account for more than 50 per cent of India's total water supplies, these effects of climate change, though uncertain, could have a very major influence on available water if they turn out to be negative.

All these predictions derive from models with scenarios based on numerous assumptions; to these must be added the natural fluctuations in weather, so all the results are far from certain. Available studies, at least those concerning agriculture, appear to suggest that the positive effects of precipitation increases are likely to be outweighed by the negative effects of temperature increase. These averages almost certainly hide the fact that some parts of India are likely to lose while others gain. In general, the estimated impacts are thought to be modest in the next two or three decades (other than locally); they also arrive gradually and over a period of decades. The impacts on water issues outside agriculture seem to have been little studied.

The effects of pollution: Water quality has already deteriorated considerably, with the major pollution sources being municipal (urban) wastewater and industrial effluents. Chopra and Goldar (2000) estimate the BOD pollution load due to municipal and industrial sources to be 2.74 million tonnes in 1995 (which is equivalent to a pollution load ratio of 6.09 thousand tonnes per BCM of surface water). The other main area affected by pollution is groundwater: over-pumping in some coastal districts has let in sea-water; in others, contaminants such as fluorides and arsenic have been released from rock-strata; in yet others, agricultural chemicals and industrial wastes have seeped into aquifers.

In general, while the extent of contamination is documented in many places in terms of water quality for rivers, irrigation canals, and groundwater, the effect on available water quantities for various purposes is little known. There are very few estimates of the extent to which pollution reduces the volume of available water. Chopra and Goldar (2000) cite a study which suggests that there is a 6 to 7 per cent decrease in available groundwater due to sewage, wastewater, and garbage. Since current levels of wastewater treatment are extremely low (see Chapter 13 for more details), Chopra and Goldar conclude

---

[4]There is already evidence of glacier retreat, amounting (for some glaciers) to several metres a year. But it is not yet clear what the implications are for overall flow from that source. So far, there is no evidence of significant changes in flows from glaciers to nearby dams or rivers, but this cannot continue indefinitely. Lal (2000, 2001).

that effective control of water pollution could augment water supply by as much as 200 BCM.

DEMAND FOR WATER

The parameters for future water demand are likely to be determined largely by the manner in which India resolves the problem of meeting increasing demand for food. Agriculture uses most of India's fresh water, taking about 80 per cent, while industry and domestic use account for the rest. Growing domestic and industrial needs must be met in part from water currently consumed by agriculture, while agriculture itself has to expand considerably. This implies that considerable improvements will be needed in the efficiency of water-use.

If population figures grew more slowly, it is probable that incomes would rise more quickly, with a possible consequent demand for more meat and vegetables and a declining demand for staples such as wheat and rice. Grain-fed cattle are very water intensive.[5] Demand for agricultural products, however, would not grow by the additional 40 per cent which a 400 million increase in population is likely to require. Income increases will also raise the share of manufacturing and services in the economy relative to agriculture, so the GDP per unit of production should become less water-intensive over time, as the non-agricultural sectors are less dependent on water.

Another effect of population growth is to raise the need for domestic water supplies—for drinking, cooking, bathing, sanitation, and hygiene—as well as water required in production. Need can be quantified quite easily; then estimates can be made tying individual needs to growth in numbers. Projecting need is one thing; what will actually happen is something else. Little can be understood about how India's future water requirements will be met without a discussion of how things work currently. The impact of population growth is particularly significant as a driver of water demand in the agricultural and urban sectors, and these are examined in some detail.

Agriculture: A complete account of Indian agriculture and irrigation would look at three systems: rainfed, canal- and tank-irrigated, and groundwater irrigated. There is no simple relationship in this case between population and water demand, only a relationship mediated by property rights, policies, and institutions. Indian agriculture is heavily dependent on irrigation, which has been the source of most of the recent increases in output and yields. For the last three decades India has managed both to keep food growing faster than population, and to move from periodic food scarcity and import dependence to national self-sufficiency (Chapter 11 has more details). Estimates suggest that this can continue with current technology at least till 2010.

[5]Cohen (1995) has modelled income changes and income distribution to exhibit such effects.

However, the implications for water use and availability are serious, primarily due to the inefficiency of current use patterns in agriculture. Even small reductions in water use in agriculture would potentially release substantial amounts for other uses.

The main sources of food production gains in the recent period have been the new wheat varieties, grown chiefly in the post-monsoon winter (*rabi*) season, depending especially on groundwater irrigation; and improved varieties of rice, grown principally in the monsoon season (half of it unirrigated). Output and yields have risen much more slowly, and mainly in irrigated areas. Tubewells and groundwater have contributed about 80 per cent of the increase in irrigation in recent decades, mostly through private development. However, average yields of irrigated agriculture in India are relatively low in comparison with other countries; if these were to increase, there could be substantial savings in water use (Iyer 2001).

To illustrate some of these issues more clearly, let us examine an area of water scarcity: Gujarat in western India. There were frequent and increasing reports of localized droughts in the area in the 1970s and 1980s, to the extent that it was claimed that rainfall was diminishing. In fact, over 30 years there had been no discernible trend in rainfall, though there were frequent annual peaks and troughs, including three consecutive below-average years in the mid-1980s (Mehta 2001). Water tables in the state as a whole declined in the 1980s by amounts varying locally from 1 to nearly 10 metres (Bhatia 1992).

Population growth appears to have had a relatively small direct impact on these patterns. While the population has grown at around 2 per cent, the number of private tubewells dug grew by 80 per cent just in the first half of the 1980s. In the 25 years up to 1985, the area under canal irrigation rose from 652 sq km to 4892 sq km; the area under well irrigation rose from 5677 to 17,370 sq km. In 1960, most of the wells would have been dug wells, and the great majority of the additions were tubewells. The area under well irrigation trebled while the population barely doubled. And water use has intensified as there has been a big increase in high-value and water-intensive crops.

The increase in drought experiences relates strongly to the excessive pumping of groundwater. The growth of tubewells was initially quite unregulated. Property rights under the law entitle anyone to pump any amount of water from a well dug on his own land, even if this reduces the water table below the reach of neighbouring wells. Once farmers have access to a groundwater source, the rate of pumping is determined by the quantity needed for their own use or the quantity that can be sold to their neighbours, and (most importantly) by the price of electricity or diesel fuel to run the pumps. Electricity has commonly been free or subsidized, so there has been no incentive to conserve water. Once a borewell exists, extraction is mainly a function of the price of power, and as long as this is kept artificially low, over-exploitation of groundwater is likely to continue.

Reduced plant cover and increased run-off, and reduced percolation due to soil changes, have meant that groundwater recharge rates have been inadequate. Coupled with over-pumping, this has resulted in a dramatic fall in the water table. The whole area has seen something of a groundwater disaster, as over-pumping has also let in saline water in coastal regions, up to 7 km inland from the coast. Fluoride content and other pollutants have also increased in various areas, frequently exceeding safety limits. This has resulted from over-pumping, and from agricultural chemicals and industrial pollution seeping into the water table.

Apart from the ecological implications of such use patterns, there have also been serious distributional consequences. The richer farmers dug deeper wells and often deprived their poorer neighbours of well water, if they had any. First attempts to regulate were by controlling the depth to which digging could be done with the support of public loans, but the rich farmers simply financed their own wells. Regulation was later introduced to forbid wells below a specified depth within a given range of existing wells, but this mainly stabilized the status quo, and conferred monopoly rights on those who already had deep wells. 'Waterlords' emerged as well as landlords—often selling water back to the very neighbours whose wells they had emptied. There is now an extensive water market, both for irrigation and for drinking purposes. Thousands of villages have become waterless, and are dependent on water delivered by tanker.

At the same time the absence of incentives for water conservation leads to wholly inappropriate crop mixes. Sugar is quite extensively grown—but it is a highly water-intensive crop which would probably not be grown at all in a state like Gujarat if water were sensibly priced or otherwise regulated. The water troubles of Gujarat have thus stemmed from a combination of inappropriate property rights, laws, and institutions, and the attempts of farmers to enrich themselves in a setting of price and other incentives which are ill-designed for making sense of the water economy.

A large share of future growth in population will be in the Ganga–Brahmaputra basin, where water is not yet scarce in overall volume. In 1991, the basin held 42 per cent of India's population, but the population in the basin is growing faster than in the rest of India, and will probably be over 50 per cent by mid-century. The area is home to some of the world's largest canal irrigation systems (the Sarda Sahayak system alone has some 9960 km of canals). The development and current status of these canal irrigation systems is a further major facet of the agriculture–irrigation story.

While canal irrigation has brought water to hundreds of thousands of farmers, it has also had its problems. Farmers near the head of the canal get abundant, often too much, water while those at the tail-end get too little and unreliably. Water-intensive cropping at the head pre-empts the available flow of water, leaving little for those at the tail-end (Iyer 2001). Rich farmers who can bribe the water engineers are the only ones who get the water more or less in the amounts and at the times they want it (Wade 1982). This money power is also an important source of political power, which is able to influence the planning, design, location, and operation of irrigation projects, thereby enhancing inequalities. In some canal-irrigated regions, continued preference by farmers for tubewell water reflects perceptions that the latter allows them greater direct control over the timing and amount of water use. As a result, many farmers see the chief virtue of the canal system as its capacity to recharge the water table through seepage, which is often as high as 60 per cent of the canal surface flow.

As with groundwater, there is a serious pricing and management problem. Charges do not cover costs, so the surface irrigation system does not generate the revenues needed for its own maintenance, which suffers accordingly. Furthermore, prices do not encourage conservation. There are also major ecological problems; waterlogging and salinization are endemic, especially near the headwaters, and this results in the loss of valuable agricultural land. Although estimates of the extent of these problems vary widely, a 1991 report of the Ministry of Water Resources suggested that the extent of waterlogged land in the country was 2.46 million hectares, and that of salt-affected land was 3.30 million ha. (Iyer 2001). Paradoxically, excessive groundwater pumping in such areas actually helps prevent waterlogging by lowering the water table.

Unlike Gujarat, or the agriculturally very successful Punjab, where groundwater use is near the limits of availability, in the Gangetic plain it is estimated that less than 20 per cent of potentially useable groundwater is currently drafted. While there are periodic problems due to the low-season flow of the Ganga, the area clearly has the potential to meet greatly increasing food needs, though many problems will have to be solved to achieve this sustainably. One is a shortage of power, an important obstacle to the exploitation of groundwater in the plain. While parts of the water table are quite shallow, there is also underground water at depths of 1000 metres or more. Furthermore, the same equity and ecological issues which afflict groundwater use in Gujarat are found in the Gangetic plain. A particular problem is that in areas where farmers are predominantly poor and owners of very small and often scattered plots of land, only collective solutions are really feasible. The difference is that there are resources potentially adequate to respond to very much higher levels of demand (Chapman and Thompson 1995; Kahnert and Levine 1993).

Urbanization: Urban water demand clearly has a strong population component; every single individual needs a water supply, and every individual contributes to waste disposal problems, which affect demand for water and water quality (see Chapter 13 for more details of current and projected trends). Minimum individual need for drinking, food, and sanitation purposes is commonly put at 100 litres per day (lpd). But simply multiplying such a number by the number of additional individuals, while it produces a figure for need, does not say anything about demand. Urban slum dwellers in India make do with

40–50 lpd or less, while the wealthy use 250 lpd or very considerably more. There is the same distortion of use-patterns by chaotic pricing structures, or lack of pricing. There is little cost recovery by many municipal authorities for water supply even when expensively pumped over long ⟍⟍⟍ance ⟍⟍⟍ in Bangalore. The rich often get their water free, while the poor have ⟍⟍⟍ for water delivered by tanker. Large establishments such as hotels and industrial units, which require very regular supplies, often pay private suppliers too.

There is much evidence that even quite poor consumers are willing to pay within reason for reliable supplies, and could often be supplied collectively for less than they have to pay privately, but such evidence is commonly, though not always, ignored. There are other huge inefficiencies in urban water systems such as waste, leakage, and installation of domestic pumps and wells (which deplete supplies at the expense of others). In Hyderabad, waste is equal to more than 40 per cent of the current gap between supply and demand. In many cases, it would be cheaper for authorities to introduce pricing, control pollution, and take other remedial measures, but it is often politically easier to arrange for increased supply by large public works. As a long-term option, however, the latter is simply economically infeasible in most cases, and will also contribute unnecessarily to inter-sectoral competition for water (Saleth and Dinar 1997).

There are already acute water shortages in many urban areas especially at dry times of the year, and conflicts between users: between the demand of agriculture and the demand of urban consumers in areas around Hyderabad or Delhi. In 1994, the Haryana authorities reduced supplies to Delhi by 274 million litres per day (mld), arguing that this water was needed for irrigation needs in their state. Water riots have been reported in urban Rajasthan. There have been newspaper reports of water tankers moving under armed guard in Bhopal in the summer, and of industrial units in Tamil Nadu raiding rural water sources. It is unclear how widespread these problems are, but urban water shortage is as much a current problem as a future one—a problem which will only get worse if appropriate measures are not taken.

Demand scenarios: In recent years, there have been several projections of India's future water requirements. Table 14.1 presents the results of three important studies: (i) the estimates made by the Working Group (WG) of the National Commission on Integrated Water Resources Development Plan (WG 1999) and adopted by the Commission in its report to the Government of India (NCIWRD 1999); (ii) *India Water Vision 2025* (IWV) prepared by the India Water Partnership, an informal body loosely affiliated to the Global Water Partnership, as part of the preparations for the World Water Forum held at The Hague in March 2000 (IWP/IHD 2000); and (iii) the final report (October 2000) of a study of sustainable water resources development by Chopra and Goldar (2000).

Although the studies differ in some ways, they are not widely divergent.

TABLE 14.1: *Estimates of water requirements, by sector*

		Irrigation	Domestic use	Cattle	Industry	Power	Navigation	Env & ecology	Losses	Total
WG	2010 L	543.00	42	4.8	37	18	7	5	36	694.00
	2010 H	557.00	43	4.8	37	19	7	5	36	710.00
	2025 L	560.00	55	5.2	67	31	10	10	42	784.00
	2025 H	611.00	62	5.2	67	33	10	10	42	850.00
	2050 L	628.00	90	5.9	81	63	20	20	65	973.00
	2050 H	807.00	111	5.9	81	70	15	20	65	1180.00
IWV	2025 L	730.60	70	–	12	30	–	77	–	1027.00
	2025 M	805.60	–	–	–	–	–	–	–	–
	2025 H	866.60	–	–	–	–	–	–	–	–
KC/BG	2020 BAU	677.30	67.52	–	27.91	8.19	–	78	42	920.92
	2020 HG	804.20	67.52	–	41.58	11.47	–	78	42	1004.77
	2020 SS	768.37	45.01	–	27.72	5.00	–	78	42	964.09

Notes: All figures are in billion cubic metres (BCM)

Demand projections: L: low; M: medium; H: high

BAU: business as usual; HG: high growth; SS: sustainable scenario

Totals are estimated by the original studies. The components do not always add up to these totals, but the discrepancies are not explained in the studies.

Sources: Chopra and Goldar (2000); IWV/IHD (2000); WG (1999).

Broadly speaking, all three agree on the quantum of water availability; their population projections are mainly based on the revised UN estimates (1994), and they adopt roughly similar percentages for the urban component; they envisage an addition (of different degrees) to the irrigated area; the norms that the WG adopts for rural and urban water supply are used by IWV and Chopra and Goldar with some modifications; there are some minor differences in other respects (such as the provision for environment/ecology). The total water requirements projected by the WG (973 to 1180 BCM in 2050) are relatively lower than IWV's projections (1027 BCM in 2025) or Chopra and Goldar's (920.92 bau, 1004.72 high growth, and 964.9 sustainable scenario in 2020).

All three studies envisage an effort at sustainability. While IWV and Chopra and Goldar project a separate sustainable scenario (on the basis of certain measures and investments), WG's projections assume that certain steps to ensure economy, efficiency, and conservation will be taken, and predict a fragile balance between supply and demand on that basis. IWV and Chopra and Goldar also seem to adopt a similar position of a cautious but not an alarmist view of the future. The consensus of these studies seems to be that the situation will be difficult, and localized water problems may intensify; but there need not be a crisis for India as a whole if the right supply and demand-side measures are adopted in time (Iyer 2001).

RESPONSE OPTIONS

There are at least four different central departments responsible for water-related issues: the ministries of water resources, rural development, agriculture, and urban development. Due to this multiplicity of agencies involved in the management of water, there has been very little coordination or a unified response. A more significant problem for a coordinated approach is that the management of water resources is a state subject, and one over which the central government actually has very limited jurisdiction. State governments have typically been reluctant to take steps that are perceived to be electorally damaging, and this has resulted in a number of populist measures that have encouraged the wasteful use of water within states, and also led to serious interstate conflicts over the sharing of water resources.

The standard response to the perceived current and potential scarcity of water in India has been an engineering one, designed to enhance storage and transport of available water, and to attempt to increase the efficiency of existing and new delivery systems. While supply-side measures have been dominant, very little attention has been paid to managing demand or attempting to promote water conservation measures.

Augmenting water supply: An obvious implication of the nature of precipitation in India is the need for water storage to deal with temporal fluctuations, and for the transport of water to correct for the spatial concentration of rainfall. The engineering solution to these challenges has been a programme of large storage construction (dams), augmented by an extensive canal network to service the requirements of deficit areas. This approach has come under considerable criticism (McCully 1996). The debate has become increasingly heated, and has been caught up in a broader conflict between top-down, technocratic, and interventionist approaches to development that are being challenged by what are proposed as more bottom-up, participatory, and locally appropriate alternatives. The debate has been exemplified in India by a number of protest movements against big dams, the most well known of which is the controversy over the Sardar Sarovar project in the Narmada Valley (Baviskar 1995).

The Government of India's reaction to the report of the World Commission on Dams (WCD) illustrates the intensity of this debate. The WCD report concluded that although dams have made a considerable contribution to human development, this has been accompanied in many cases by unacceptable social and environmental costs, and argued for a more careful consideration of alternatives. The Government of India reacted by rejecting the conclusions of the WCD India country report, arguing that the development guidelines proposed by the WCD were wholly incompatible with Indian development imperatives. The official response to the WCD confirmed the Government of India's resolve to 'continue with its programme of dam construction to create another 100 BCM of storage in the next 25 years or so to ensure continued self-sufficiency in food grain production and to meet the energy and drinking water needs of a growing population' (MWR 2001).

Despite this official commitment to an on-going programme of large storage construction, there has been considerable internal debate in India over alternative modes of storage, especially tanks, small and medium-sized dams, and in situ capture through soil and water conservation (integrated watershed development) and rainwater harvesting. These alternatives attempt either to augment or enhance the availability of water through a variety of sources, or to improve the efficiency of existing sources. There are numerous case studies of successful revitalization of traditional collective water-management systems, as well as new approaches that seek to create local management institutions through grassroots and community mobilization (for instance, the cases documented by the CSE (CSE 1999)). The poor performance of bureaucratic structures for canal management have also led to institutional restructuring of these systems, with participatory water users' associations being formally established in states such as Andhra Pradesh and Maharashtra, in an attempt to deliver water more efficiently and equitably to their members. However, there can be no complacency about these measures as a panacea; a study in Gujarat, for example, found water-harvesting schemes more successful in storing water than in delivering it to recipients, especially the poorer ones (Shah 2001).

It is difficult to quantify precisely the impact of these alternative measures on the aggregate availability of water in the country, or to estimate their local hydrological consequences if they are adopted on an extended scale. Take the case of in situ rainwater harvesting. Chopra and Goldar (2000) project an additional runoff capture of 142 BCM through these means, but the basis for this estimation has not been given. Assuming that 142 BCM of runoff are captured through local water harvesting and watershed development, what will the impact be on availability lower down? It is possible that water levels in wells and aquifers will rise, as has been observed in various places. However, flows in the streams and rivers further downstream may well be reduced, given that the runoff is being intercepted at earlier stages. Some of the captured water will no doubt become 'return flows' but that will necessarily be only a part of the water intercepted. Some of it will also get polluted or contaminated in the processes of use. What is relevant here is the net impact, in terms of a substantial addition to available and useable water (in the NCIWRD's sense). As the useable surface water (690 BCM) is currently only a fraction of the available water (1953 BCM), and as that in turn is only a fraction of overall precipitation (4000 BCM), it seems reasonable to assume that the capture of more rainwater will add to the availability of water for use. However, there does not appear to be any clear indication about the quantum of likely addition to existing water supplies, other than the figure of 142 BCM mentioned by Chopra and Goldar (2000).

The other possibility that has not been explored to any extent is that of large-scale migration as a response to perceived water scarcity. In effect, this would be a process that brings the people to water instead of the technocratic engineering solution that has been attempting to deliver water to the people. If circumstances do drive such movements of people away from water-scarce areas towards regions of abundance, this is likely to result in a significant concentration of human populations in the rain-abundant districts of the northern and eastern states, and away from the dry and semi-arid hinterland towards the coasts. The resultant potential for conflict between existing residents and incoming migrants is very high indeed, and would lead to increased political and social tensions. However, at present, such widespread population movements seem a relatively remote possibility, despite recent studies that report 'distress' migration as a local response to environmental degradation (Chopra and Gulati 2001).

Demand management: Inefficiency in water use in India has been seen as a serious problem by many analysts (Iyer 2001; Singh 2001). Low charges fail to cover the basic O&M costs of most irrigation systems, and under-pricing of irrigation water (as well as power) results in over use of both surface and groundwater sources. Similarly, most urban water supply systems fail to recover their costs, and provide a variable and unreliable service at best (see also Chapter 13). There are a number of economic measures that have been proposed to deal with these inefficiencies, including volumetric pricing of irrigation water, cost-recovery norms for the supply of rural and urban water, and pricing of electricity for groundwater pumping (Singh 2001). Technological interventions, such as greater use of drip irrigation and changes in cropping patterns, have also been suggested as ways to manage water demand.

Despite the clear awareness of the scope of such measures, and the need for their adoption, there is little political will to implement the reforms that would facilitate such an approach to demand management. Part of the difficulty lies in the existing division of responsibilities between the centre and the states with respect to water resources and their management. Thus, while demand management is widely seen as being important, there are few policy champions who are willing to take this issue forward in any meaningful way because of the risk of alienating vital political supporters, such as farmers and consumers.

In 2000, the MWR launched a series of six reports on water resources management in collaboration with the Ministry of Urban Affairs, the Ministry of Rural Affairs, and the World Bank. The reports recommended a comprehensive approach that would simultaneously combine changes in policy, institutions, legal and regulatory framework, economic and financial incentives, and the strengthening of data, technological, and information systems. However, the National Water Policy (MWR 2002) released in April 2002 failed to articulate a clear strategy to take these recommendations forward. While emphasizing the need to improve the efficiency of utilization in all the diverse uses of water, and to foster an awareness of water as a scarce resource, the new policy contains no guidelines for implementing such reforms. The policy instead speaks generally about the need to promote conservation consciousness through education, regulation, incentives and disincentives, without any elaboration of how these measures would actually be made to work, or clearly outlining the respective roles of central and state governments, as well as community-based organizations in these processes.

BEYOND THE DEMAND–SUPPLY CALCULUS

The use of estimates of water supply and projections of future demand to explore water scarcity reflects the sort of thinking that characterized perceptions of an imminent crisis in fuelwood availability that alarmed environmentalists in the 1970s. A number of studies subsequently demonstrated that people's responses to scarcity were an important endogenous factor that influenced demand patterns, so simplistic projections based on current consumption trends were unhelpful as a prediction of future resource scarcity (Dewees 1989). It is likely that predictions about water scarcity that simply use a mechanistic demand–supply calculus will also be inaccurate. For instance, Mehta (1998) reports from parts of western India where rural people devise ways of coping with localized water scarcity, and argues that the temporal and cyclical dimensions of scarcity are an important part of such indigenous responses. What this suggests is that trends in future demand for water are not independent of human perceptions of need, and that perceptions of scarcity are as often manufactured as they are real (Mehta 2001).

Studies that project future water-use scenarios for India all operate within the restrictive framework of a demand–supply calculus. They share similar ideas of growth and development; and they have similar understandings of sustainability (some measures of efficiency and economy on the demand side and a degree of augmentation on the supply side). None of them envisages radical departures from the past. The sustainable scenario that they talk about is largely the BAU scenario with some efficiency/conservation measures added. Essentially, the approach is to proceed from projections of demand to supply-side answers. Environmental and ecological concerns are seen not as limits on our draft on nature but as yet another category of demand for which an allocation has to be made, taking the total water requirements higher.

If we go simply by the demand–supply calculus and by prevailing notions of development, difficulties may well be inevitable given the pressures of a growing population and its associated water needs. They can perhaps be averted, but not merely by supply-side solutions, whether large scale and centralized or small scale and local. There may also be a need for fairly radical changes in people's ways of living. This is not seriously discussed in the WG/NCIWRDP/ IWV Reports (though some pro forma references are made to lifestyle changes).

A radical departure from current thinking will undoubtedly be fraught with serious difficulty and will pose formidable challenges. If no more than moderate improvements in efficiency and economy in water-use are likely, and there is no change in ideas of development, the numbers can quickly add up to suggest serious water scarcity, and to justify continued reliance on massive supply-side projects. However, if we recognize the diversity of potential responses, both on the supply and demand sides, and acknowledge the importance of ensuring more equitable and even distribution of existing water resources, large-scale engineering interventions will be seen as just one part of a more integrated approach to meeting India's future water needs.

CONCLUSION: POLICY ISSUES AND PROSPECTS

Many mistakes have been made in water policy in the Third World. Some have come from inappropriate modelling of supply and demand scenarios, and others from ignoring the actual factors that determine water availability and use. As can be seen from the brief description given here, these factors include social inequalities, inappropriately defined property rights, absence of pricing and regulatory systems—often not just for water but for the whole of agriculture, whose pricing and trade protection often lead to seriously sub-optimal crop mixes.

Water scarcity and conflicts have already occurred in many contexts in India, from local rural droughts to interstate water disputes. It is obvious that population growth will operate as a major background factor increasing demand for water. However, water use is more properly seen to depend on a complex interplay between incentives, property rights, the distribution of wealth and assets, technology, and the behaviour of the economy. The extent of the challenge can be gauged from the fact that growing agricultural needs must be met by greater efficiency in water use, at the same time as growing non-agricultural needs are met from the same source. The implications of climate change assessments reinforce the importance and urgency for India to move towards improved water storage.

Whether India will solve its water problems is a matter of policies and politics. State governments in the 1990s have legislated free water and electricity for all farmers, the antithesis of an intelligent water strategy. As long as Indian politics remain in the grip of populist leaders and the large-farmer 'vote-bank', such trends are likely to continue. Most senior Indian politicians and bureaucrats do not treat environmental and resource scarcity issues as high priorities. It is likely that the continuation of current trends will force these issues more explicitly on to the public agenda, but it is far from certain that this will take place in the short term.

There are encouraging signs that things are changing, at least in some areas. There are many successful schemes and grassroots movements that are increasing awareness and public concern. There is evidence that where there is greater understanding of the local context for water management, a lot can be done. If existing knowledge about how to cope with increasing water demand is applied appropriately, India's water problems can be addressed, at least in the relatively water-abundant areas. However, if current practices remain in force, given the extent of pollution, waste and misuse of water, and the lack of incentives for efficient use and conservation, problems could become extremely serious even in these areas.

In dry areas, there are promising initiatives, such as farmer-centred irrigation management schemes, that have already been tried and introduced in some states. Although such schemes have significantly raised water prices, farmers have asserted control and have generally welcomed them. Best practice in watershed management and soil-water conservation has led to the creation of new guidelines which are being implemented in a number of catchments. Above all, two chief ministers at the head of state governments, in Andhra Pradesh and Madhya Pradesh, have carefully cultivated their political constituencies by delivering real developmental benefits for ordinary people. They have both been active in promoting new methods of resolving water problems, and have championed innovative reform programmes. Opinions differ as to the extent of success even in these promising cases. In the rest of the country, there is even further to go. Vested interests have to be challenged, poor practice and malpractice have to be set right, and inaction has to be turned to action.

What is important is to recognize that responses to population numbers cannot be based solely on estimates of need, and plans to meet need. It is important to start with an understanding of how water use operates in its several and diverse local contexts, and to appreciate that the solutions are likely to emerge from a mix of policies from central and state governments, and from action by NGOs and institutions, and community and participatory groups. Needs are unlikely to be met by increasing supply unless the factors that govern use are themselves modified. This is unlikely to happen on any adequate scale until Indian politics and civil society make it happen.

It has to be said that current policies are failing to address these complex problems. Pollution is getting worse, not better; in Delhi, for example, the volume of polluting waste-water is growing faster than treatment capacity.[6] Hardly anything is being done on the water and electricity pricing and regulation front, or more generally on the containment of demand. There are some modest signs of acceleration in the development of better storage schemes, but on a very piecemeal basis. There is debate over the technical solutions, although it is generally believed that these are potentially adequate to the challenges ahead. Arguments are especially heated over the issue of large dams, and the view of them taken here is that these should be instruments of last resort. Overall, the trends are ominous; both population growth and climate change, although working slowly, point in the same direction. More difficult decisions have to be made, and a greater sense of urgency is needed in implementing them. This is hardly a matter of future problems—most of them are already in evidence.

[6]Chapter 13 discusses this issue in further detail.

15

Common Pool Resources:
Current Status and Future Prospects

BHASKAR VIRA

I n poor countries, CPRs[1] make a valuable contribution to the sustainable livelihoods of rural populations. This includes the collection of fuelwood, fodder, crop wastes, cow dung, organic manure, small timber, and other products that are derived from the bark, seeds, flowers, and fruit of trees, as well as water for drinking, cooking, and irrigation, and local fisheries. The existence of imperfect factor markets results in an intimate link between the rural economy and its natural resource base. Inadequate rural employment opportunities, especially in the slack season, imply that the local commons can make substantial contributions to household incomes. Another important function of local CPRs is as insurance against uncertainty, in the absence of complete contingent markets. Access to such resources serves to pool risks associated with natural disasters and crop failure. Furthermore, for landless populations, access to local CPRs may be the only available non-human asset.

What makes the issue particularly interesting is that CPRs have other, conflicting, claims upon them. Forests, for instance, have been an important source of raw material in the production process, and support a number of major and minor industries such as saw mills, paper, plywood, match-making,

---

[1] A definitional clarification is required at the outset. Common pool resources may be managed under a variety of regimes. They can be open access resources with no rules in operation. They could be found on private or state land and used by others either informally, or illegally. They could also be managed under common property regimes. The literature frequently fails to distinguish between the resource itself (common pool) and the regime under which it is managed (common property as one possibility). To avoid this confusion, this chapter will not refer to common property resources, but will use the term common pool resources.

polyfibres, pharmaceuticals and chemicals, and oils. In the commercial sector, timber dominates the forest economy, while there is a growing market for non-timber forest produce. Forests also perform vital ecological functions, such as providing stability to soil, water, and climatic regimes, and serve as storehouses of biological diversity. In addition, forests are valued as places for recreation and as areas of outstanding natural beauty.

This chapter suggests that dynamic internal and external processes are impacting on the context within which local CPRs are used (and conceptualized) in India. While the large rural sector continues to depend on such resources as a safety net, there are also new opportunities emerging due to the development of products and services derived from sustainable commons management. Existing uses of CPRs may be affected by changing social, economic, and ecological dynamics.

CONCEPTUALIZING CPRs

The literature on CPRs in India has devoted considerable attention to documenting their role in the rural household economy. Most research on CPRs has focused primarily on their role in mitigating failures of other resource provisioning systems, especially their role as a safety net for those who may not have access to products and services through alternative mechanisms. As they provide for the subsistence needs of asset-poor individuals and groups, CPRs are seen to be important for poverty alleviation.

This is a negative, or defensive, view of the contribution that CPRs make to the developmental process. In such a perspective, CPRs are useful because they prevent people from falling further into deprivation. If this is true, such resources may be expected to become less important with higher levels of development. However, a more positive approach to development requires a shift in focus towards providing people the means with which to lead better lives. Senior planners in India have recently argued for a shift in developmental priorities from funding safety net programmes to asset creation (Saxena 2000). If the mindset of policy-makers is beginning to move from the prevention of acute destitution (poverty alleviation) to the promotion of economic and social opportunity (sustainable livelihoods), one needs to consider whether the role of CPRs also needs to be reconceptualized. CPRs need to be seen not only as a safety net, but also in terms of their contribution to positive opportunities for social and economic development.

Outputs from CPRs: A shift towards a more positive view of the development process does not necessarily dilute the emphasis on CPRs as providers of specific products that overlap with household production and consumption strategies. What may need to change, however, is the manner in which such consumptive use is conceptualized. Harvesting of resources for self-consumption is sometimes seen as a more legitimate demand than their production for sale in markets. For instance, India's 1988 Forest Policy Resolution suggests that 'rights and concessions from forests should primarily be for the bonafide use of the communities living within and around forest areas, specially the tribals' (Ministry of Environment and Forests (MOEF) 1988). The language implies a distinction between such uses and other resource uses that cater to the needs of more distant consumers. The domestic requirements of tribals and the poor are highlighted by the resolution as the first charge on forest produce, but it is not clear whether these domestic requirements extend to the use of forest produce as a source of sustainable rural incomes.

However, resource gatherers and users who optimize their allocation of labour and other inputs in the production process may wish to generate marketable surpluses from CPR-based activity. As long as such activity does not exceed the ecological limits of the resource base, it may be unnecessary to make a distinction between subsistence uses and the production of goods for the market.[2] If CPRs are understood as part of rural household production systems, their contribution to domestic consumption (subsistence) and towards income generation should not be seen as fundamentally very different.

Looking ahead, as the rural economy becomes further integrated into the market, CPRs may become increasingly valued as a source of income for rural households. As resource users shift away from subsistence-dominated activities and self-consumption, the generation of surpluses for sale in the market is likely to become more important. Associated with such a shift are likely to be significant changes in control over such resources and decisions over their use. For instance, much anecdotal evidence suggests that once a resource acquires market value, it becomes subject to capture by more powerful agents.

There may be limits to the extent to which one can expect CPRs to provide a long-term source of sustainable rural incomes. Outputs from CPRs are valuable as long as there remains a buoyant market for them. Extrapolation of cases of successful market-based exploitation of CPRs may not always be appropriate, since the wider adoption of such strategies may create a glut in the market and depress prices (as with eucalyptus farming in north-west India in the 1980s (Saxena 1994)). Furthermore, the demand for such products may also suffer because of the increased availability of substitutes, or because CPR-use itself is considered an inferior form of consumption. Other products may then eventually replace products from CPRs. For instance, fuelwood and

---

[2]It could be argued that allowing production for the market itself creates incentives to overexploit resources, thus exceeding ecological limits. However, there is no evidence that conclusively demonstrates that the introduction of markets for specific resources is necessarily associated with their subsequent overexploitation. Under appropriate regulatory systems, resource exploitation to generate marketable surpluses can be ecologically sustainable. Equally, subsistence-oriented systems have been known to result in overuse and resource degradation.

animal dung as sources of domestic energy are often seen as more primitive than modern stoves that use kerosene and gas. In this sense, one must recognize that the flows of goods from CPRs may be currently valuable, but are potentially substitutable by other goods. Thus, it is important to look at market conditions and opportunities quite closely when projecting forward from current resource use trends.

Services from CPRs: CPRs also provide important services, playing a role in regulating the hydrological cycle, contributing to soil fertility through nutrient cycling, helping conserve biodiversity, as well as serving as sinks for greenhouse gases. There is a spatial dimension to these service functions: some benefits may be local, as in the supply of irrigation and nutrients to local agriculture (Kumar 2001); others may benefit resource users downstream, such as the impact of land use on water availability in a catchment (Nathan and Kelkar 2001); while some functions may be global, such as biodiversity benefits or carbon sinks.

Resource management issues become considerably more complex, since internalization of such externalities would require the creation of a system of financial transfers between downstream beneficiaries and those whose local resource-use practices ensure the continued flow of these services. Schemes such as the farm management programme in upstate New York, which was initiated due to concern over water quality in New York City (Gandy 1997), suggest that partnerships between regulators, upstream resource users, and downstream beneficiaries may well provide a way of managing resources in order to capture some of these ecological service functions.

What is distinctive about the service functions from CPRs is that, in many cases, there are no alternatives, or the alternatives are not cheap. For instance, in the New York example, filtration of water for urban supplies was seen to be considerably more expensive than adaptation of upstream resource-use practices. If there are no easy substitutes, these ecosystem functions are vital and irreplaceable, as captured by the notion of critical natural capital. Looking ahead, if other goods increasingly substitute for outputs from CPRs, the primary reason to maintain such resources may be to protect and manage their ecosystem and ecological functions. Such arrangements are likely to demand increasingly complex negotiation between those who represent the resource interests of local users and those who are affected by the externalities (positive and negative) of specific resource use practices.

CURRENT STATUS OF CPRs IN INDIA

Interest in CPRs in India, both from a policy and a research perspective, dates back at least till the early 1980s. In terms of assessing the status of such resources, Jodha's seminal work from the mid-1980s remains the most extensive village-level study, although a number of micro-level assessments have been conducted subsequently. Since 1999, researchers have had access to a large-scale data set that reports on the current status of CPRs in the country, based on a survey of 78,990 rural households in 5114 villages conducted by the NSSO (NSSO 54th round).

The NSSO data set is unique, in that it is the only such comprehensive countrywide study of CPRs anywhere in the world. However, there are reasons to believe that the enumeration process of such a survey is likely to be less accurate than in-depth long-term ethnographic field research. For instance, if illegality is involved in the use of some types of common resources, respondents may be unwilling to reveal such use patterns to enumerators with whom they are unfamiliar. Despite these obvious limitations, the NSSO data allow us to make a systematic assessment of the current status of CPRs in India in a manner that has not been possible until now. It also provides a very useful baseline against which one would hope to be able to measure future trends, given that the sampling strategy that is used by the NSSO is comparable across different enumeration rounds.

Extent of CPRs: The NSSO data on CPRs were collected using two different criteria—the de jure and the de facto methods. The extent of CPRs was estimated on the basis of the legal status of the land (de jure), including only those resources that were 'within the boundary of the village and were formally (that is, by legal sanction or official assignment) held by the village panchayat or a community of the village' (NSSO 1999). Information on the extent to which rural households used such resources was collected on the basis of actual use patterns (de facto), regardless of the legal status of the land. This included uses that occur on state (revenue and forest) lands, as well as conventional (often seasonal) uses of private lands.

The data on the extent of resources are reported in Table 15.1, and suggest that even by the restrictive de jure definition, a substantial proportion (15 per cent) of the total land area is classified as local CPRs.

The data also suggest that 23 per cent of reported CPR land is community pasture and grazing lands, while 16 per cent is village forests and woodlots, and 61 per cent is attributed to the 'other' category. 'Other' includes the village

TABLE 15.1: *NSSO estimates of CPRs in India*

Indicator (all-India figures)	NSSO estimates
Share of CPRs in total geographical area	15 per cent
Common pool land resources per household (in ha.)	0.31
Common pool land resources per person (in ha.)	0.06
Reduction in CPR land in last 5 years (per 1000 ha.)	19 ha. (0.38 per cent per annum)

Source: NSSO (1999).

site, threshing floors, and other barren and waste land. The NSSO report considers this figure (which is equivalent to 9.15 per cent of the total geographical area) to be inordinately high (NSSO 1999). The report suggests that it is possible that some 'free access' revenue land was 'misidentified' as de jure common pool land (defined for the survey as land which is under the legal control of the village or community).

Given these qualifications, it is instructive to compare the NSSO results with those that have been obtained by other methods. Chopra and Gulati (2001) reclassify India's agricultural land use statistics data for 1991 to estimate the extent of CPRs in 16 major states. Chopra and Gulati (2001) calculate common pool land resources as the sum of private land to which common access may exist, cultivable wastes and fallows other than current, common pastures and grazing land, and protected and unclassified forests. Two series are reported in Table 15.2, including and excluding forest areas (for purposes of comparison, the series that excludes forests is more useful, since the use of the de jure approach for the NSSO study excluded forest areas).

TABLE 15.2: *Alternative estimates of common pool land resources*
(total CPR land/total geographical area)

State	NSSO (1998)	Chopra & Gulati (1991)	Chopra & Gulati (1991, non-forest)	Jodha (mid-1980s)
Andhra Pradesh	0.09	0.220	0.160	0.110
Assam	0.07	–	–	–
Bihar	0.08	0.300	0.160	–
Gujarat	0.27	0.170	0.140	0.110
Haryana	0.03	0.040	0.009	–
Himachal Pradesh	0.12	0.930	0.290	–
Jammu & Kashmir	–	0.012	0.000	–
Karnataka	0.10	0.170	0.110	0.160
Kerala	–	0.080	0.050	–
Madhya Pradesh	0.22	0.320	0.150	0.240
Maharashtra	0.11	0.260	0.190	0.150
Nagaland	0.08	–	–	–
Orissa	0.11	0.310	0.090	–
Punjab	0.01	0.070	0.014	–
Rajasthan	0.32	0.350	0.340	0.140
Sikkim	0.14	–	–	–
Tamil Nadu	0.12	0.210	0.180	0.100
Tripura	0.01	–	–	–
Uttar Pradesh	0.12	0.130	0.030	–
West Bengal	0.02	0.070	0.010	–

Sources: Chopra and Gulati (2001); Jodha (1986); NSSO (1999).

The results of the NSSO and those obtained by Chopra and Gulati are similar for six states (Haryana, Karnataka, Orissa, Punjab, Rajasthan, and West Bengal), but are substantially different for eight others (Andhra Pradesh, Bihar, Gujarat, Himachal Pradesh, Madhya Pradesh, Maharashtra, Tamil Nadu, and Uttar Pradesh). The broad patterns of both studies, however, suggest that CPRs are most important for states in the arid and semi-arid zones, and in the Himalayan regions, while the agriculturally dominated states of the Indo-Gangetic plains have a relatively low proportion of CPR land. Bihar and Uttar Pradesh seem to be exceptions, but this is probably because the data include the new states of Jharkhand and Uttaranchal respectively, areas that have a higher proportion of CPR land. Table 15.2 also reports Jodha's (1986) estimates based on extensive micro-level fieldwork. Interestingly, these are fairly similar to the NSSO data, except for Gujarat and Rajasthan.

The Chopra and Gulati methodology can be applied to data at an all-India level for 1990–1, and this allows for a rough estimation of common pool land resources across the country, based on a reclassification of land use data. This procedure suggests that non-forest CPRs in India in 1990–1 were 48.69 million hectares (Table 15.3), which is 14.81 per cent of the total land area, a figure which is remarkably close to the 15 per cent reported by the NSSO survey.

The NSSO data report a quinquennial rate of decline in the area of CPRs of 1.9 per cent. The largest decline is reported from the Gangetic belt, probably reflecting pressures to bring land under cultivation in these areas. However, evidence from some earlier micro studies has suggested a much

TABLE 15.3: *Estimation of common pool land resources using land-use data*

Land use type	1990–1
1. Total Geographical Area (ASI)	328.73
2. Owned land (AC)	165.51
3. Net sown area (ASI)	143.00
4. Current fallows (ASI)	13.70
5. Private land with common access (2–3–4)	8.81
6. Cultivable wastes (ASI)	15.00
7. Other fallows (ASI)	9.66
8. Common pastures & grazing land (ASI)	11.40
9. Land under misc. tree crops (ASI)	3.82
10. Non-forest CPR (5+6+7+8+9)	48.69
11. As per cent of total area	14.81
12. Protected forest (SFR)	23.30
13. Other forest (SFR)	12.21
14. CPR including forests (10+12+13)	84.20
15. As per cent of total area	25.61

Sources: Agricultural Statistics of India (ASI, 2002); Agricultural Census (AC, 2002); State of Forest Report (SFR, 1991).

more rapid decrease in CPR land. For instance, in his study of 14 Karnataka villages, Pasha (1992) reported a decline of 33 per cent over a 20-year period. Jodha's (1986) study of 82 villages from seven states in the arid and semi-arid zone during the 1980s reported a decline of between 31 per cent and 55 per cent over a 30-year period.

These differences in the data reflect the different methodologies that have been adopted for estimation, and are not surprising. For instance, some authors have pointed out that land use data may not be a good indicator, since they do not register decline in actual access to common lands (Iyengar and Shah 2001). Despite these differing estimates, the overall pattern from all sources suggests that CPRs continue to play an important role in many parts of rural India. Furthermore, most studies are in general agreement about the broad orders of magnitude that are involved, from an insignificant amount in some states up to about 35 per cent of the geographical area in others. There is also general agreement that these resources are facing pressures from competing land uses, in some cases affecting their legal extent, but usually impacting more on access and use than on their de jure status.

Use of CPRs: Table 15. 4 reports data from the NSSO survey on the use of CPRs. These data were collected on a de facto basis, without consideration of the legal status of the land on which CPRs were located. About half of the surveyed households reported collection from CPRs, with the major uses being fodder for grazing and fuelwood.

TABLE 15.4: *Use of CPRs*

Indicator of use		NSSO
Households reporting collection of any materials from CPRs		48 per cent
Collections per household	Average value	Rs 693
	As per cent of consumption expenditure	3.02 per cent
Fodder	Households reporting grazing on CPRs	20 per cent
	Households possessing livestock	56 per cent
	Households collecting fodder from CPRs	13 per cent
	Households cultivating fodder on CPRs	2 per cent
	Average quantity of fodder collected (365 days)	275 kg
Fuelwood	Households reporting collection of fuelwood from CPRs	45 per cent
	Per cent of households reporting use of fuelwood	62 per cent
	Per cent of households reporting sale of fuelwood	1 per cent
	Average quantity of fuelwood collected (365 days)	500 kg
	Average quantity of fuelwood sold (365 days)	24 kg
	Share of fuelwood in value of collection from CPRs	58 per cent
Common water resources	Per cent of households utilizing for irrigation	20 per cent
	Per cent of households utilizing for livestock rearing	23 per cent
	Per cent of households utilizing for household enterprise	30 per cent

Source: NSSO (1999).

By comparing the data on fuelwood collection with earlier estimates from the consumption expenditure survey of the NSSO 50th round, the NSSO report (NSSO 1999) concludes that roughly half of all fuelwood consumed is collected from CPRs. This indicates the level of dependence of the rural population on such resources for access to fuelwood. However, the reported figures on fuelwood collection may not be very accurate, since respondents may have been reluctant to reveal their illegal use of government lands. For instance, the data suggest that respondents reported that a little over 40 per cent of fuelwood was collected from sources other than village forest or common land and government forest. These 'other' sources are private farmlands, on which free collection is likely to be limited, and wastes and fallows, which are unlikely to produce this amount of fuelwood. Most field research, on the other hand, suggests that there is considerable illegal fuelwood collection from government forests, so the reported figure of 27 per cent from such sources is likely to be an underestimate. Methodologically, this reveals the differences between a short survey technique such as that employed by the NSSO and in-depth case study research. This may be especially important when dealing with the complexities of rural CPR use, given that some types of use are likely to involve illegality.

The NSSO figures suggest that CPR collections contribute about 3 per cent of total consumption expenditure in the surveyed households, with some variation at the state level (the highest reported figure is from Orissa, 5.59 per cent). Although the survey does not report contributions to household income or employment, some evidence is available from micro-level studies. For instance, in his study of India's drylands, Jodha (1986) estimated that local commons provided between 18 and 31 days of exclusive employment per adult worker in poor households during the reference year, and that this was marginally higher than employment on their own farms. Despite arguing that these were probably substantial underestimates, Jodha also found that incomes from local commons contributed more than a fifth of income from all other sources for the poor (varying between 15 per cent and 23 per cent). Pasha (1992) studied 14 villages in Karnataka and reported that the contribution of CPRs to rural incomes varied between 6.2 per cent (non-poor households) and 10 per cent (poor households). In their study from West Bengal, Beck and Ghosh (2000) reported a contribution of 12 per cent to household income.

As with the data on the extent of CPR land, the figures for CPR use demonstrate the continuing importance of such resources for rural India. There are differing estimates, especially between the figures in the NSSO survey and those reported in some micro studies. However, there is no disagreement about the overall contribution that CPRs make, and their continuing relevance to rural livelihoods. Furthermore, it is important to appreciate the importance of the NSSO data set as the first systematic attempt to quantify the contribution of CPRs on a countrywide scale, and to recognize that this provides a good baseline against which to measure future trends.

Patterns of CPR use may be impacted by factors that are operating at a much broader level, such as overall economic growth rates (leading to changes in demand for CPRs); shifts in the structure of production (from the primary to the tertiary sector); as well as research that results in the identification of new products and services (such as the use of forests as carbon sinks). Demographic factors may be particularly important: overall population growth is likely to affect demand for CPRs, but the structure of this growth may also be relevant. Increases in rural–urban migration are likely to alter the nature of consumption demand for CPR-products, but would also change the availability of rural labour, which may have an impact on household production strategies. The incidence of poverty is also likely to be an important factor, since most estimates suggest that the rural poor, especially the landless, disproportionately use CPRs. The next section considers the impact of these wider social and economic drivers on the use of CPRs in India.

FUTURE PRESSURES ON CPRs

Population pressures are frequently seen to be an important factor behind the reduced availability and use of CPRs, especially for the rural poor (Beck and Ghosh 2000). The NSSO data provide some insight into the extent to which population has an impact on CPR use. The data also allow for some interstate comparisons of the potential pressures on such resources.

Tables 15.5 and 15.6 report data on the use of fuelwood and fodder resources, broken down by village size. The smallest villages report the greatest dependence on CPRs, and there is a clear negative relationship between village size and extent of fuelwood use and collection, as well as grazing and fodder collection. While dependence on fuelwood is significant even in larger villages, grazing on CPRs appears to hit some sort of lower threshold in villages in size classes above 200. One explanation may be that this threshold reflects the carrying capacity of village common lands for supporting grazing, and that this forces livestock owners to depend on a greater use of private fodder resources in larger villages. There are few such alternatives available for rural energy supplies, so fuelwood use is high, even though reported collections from CPRs do drop slightly in larger villages.

The data allow us to speculate on two types of pressures that may be affecting CPRs, operating on the demand and supply sides. On the demand side, if there are substitutes available, one may expect CPR use to decline as alternative consumption possibilities emerge. Assuming that the larger villages indicate a higher level of development, they are likely to have more alternative sources

TABLE 15.5: *Fuelwood use by size of village*

Size of village, persons (1991)	Per cent of households	Common land/ household	Per cent of households reporting		
			Fuelwood collection	Fuelwood use	Fuelwood sale
< 100	1.4	6.28	87.7	93.7	8.0
101–200	1.1	0.56	71.3	78.9	0.6
201–600	11.2	0.55	52.8	66.5	2.3
601–1200	19.7	0.31	48.4	64.9	1.3
1201–2000	19.6	0.19	44.8	61.7	0.9
2001–5000	32.3	0.15	40.8	60.9	0.6
5000 +	14.7	0.09	37.0	55.3	0.3
All	100.0	0.31	44.8	62.3	1.1

Source: NSSO (1999).

TABLE 15.6: *Access to grazing/fodder by size of village*

Size of village, persons (1991)	Per cent of households	Common land/ household	Per cent of households reporting grazing on CPRs	Per cent of households possessing livestock reporting use of CPR for fodder	
				Collection	Cultivation
< 100	1.4	6.28	72.7	68.6	0.8
101–200	1.1	0.56	41.5	29.1	1.2
201–600	11.2	0.55	28.6	20.9	3.2
601–1200	19.7	0.31	26.2	21.0	3.2
1201–2000	19.6	0.19	19.7	20.1	4.7
2001–5000	32.3	0.15	14.2	22.8	3.0
5000 +	14.7	0.09	9.9	23.5	3.2
All	100.0	0.31	19.7	22.7	3.4

Source: NSSO (1999).

of fuel and fodder, reducing use because of greater substitution possibilities. On the supply side, a higher population may exert greater pressure on the resource. According to this hypothesis, the data from the larger villages reflects the fact that they probably have too large a human and livestock population to sustain widespread access to and use of common resources, reflected also in the much lower availability of common land per household in such villages.

Looking to the future, it is difficult to make any sensible projections about the impact of increasing human populations (and associated livestock) without taking into account shifts in demand (due to preferences or substitution possibilities) and supply (because of resource depletion or regeneration). Furthermore, there is considerable variation in availability and use of CPRs at the state level, so an aggregate projection at the national level is somewhat meaningless.

In order to investigate differences that operate at the state level, an index of CPR access and use was constructed from the NSSO data. The index was constructed using data on five indicators: CPR availability per household; reported value of collection as a proportion of consumption expenditure; percentage of households reporting fuelwood collection; percentage of households possessing livestock and reporting grazing; and percentage of households collecting fodder. Each indicator was normalized using national averages, and these were then aggregated. The procedure yields an index of CPR access and use relative to the national average, where the national average is 1.[3] A similar procedure was used to create state-level indices for estimated population growth over 2001–26 (see Chapter 5 for details of these projections), and the incidence of poverty (as discussed in Chapter 9). The analysis reported in Table 15. 7 attempts to investigate the pressures of these factors on the safety net functions of CPRs.

TABLE 15.7: *State-level safety net pressures on CPRs*

	High population and poverty pressure	Moderate population and poverty pressure	Low population and poverty pressure
High CPR access and use	Rajasthan Madhya Pradesh	Gujarat Orissa Maharashtra Karnataka	Andhra Pradesh
Moderate CPR access and use	Bihar Uttar Pradesh	Haryana Tamil Nadu	
Low CPR access and use		West Bengal	Punjab Kerala

Table 15. 7 suggests that there are seven states where CPR access and use is currently high. Of these, Rajasthan and Madhya Pradesh are likely to experience significant demands on safety net functions due to population growth and a high incidence of poverty in the period to 2026. Such pressures are likely to be moderate in Gujarat, Orissa, Maharashtra, and Karnataka, while they are low in Andhra Pradesh. Of the four states where CPR access and use is moderate, Bihar and Uttar Pradesh face high demographic and poverty related pressures on CPR in the future, while these will be moderate in Haryana and Tamil Nadu. Finally, of the three states with low current levels of CPR access and use, West Bengal faces moderate pressure due to

[3]Data refer to 14 major states, and were unavailable for Himachal Pradesh and Jammu and Kashmir. Data for Uttar Pradesh, Madhya Pradesh, and Bihar refer to undivided states (that is, including Uttaranchal, Chhatisgarh, and Jharkhand, respectively).

population growth and poverty, while these pressures are low in Punjab and Kerala.

According to this analysis, demands on CPRs to act as a safety net are likely to be concentrated in the northern states, but these are characterized by different current levels of CPR access and use. The ability of the resource base to cope with these pressures may be quite limited, especially if there are other competing demands on CPRs. This situation is in stark contrast to that which is likely to prevail in Andhra Pradesh. Here, although current access and use of CPRs is high, demographic and poverty pressures are projected to be low. In such circumstances, there may be considerable scope for CPRs to serve a role as drivers of development or to provide broader ecological services.

Medium-term projections for the Indian economy vary in their optimism regarding growth rates,[4] but any predictions relating to the future of CPRs must be placed in this overall context. At the state level, the growth experience of the 1990s has been quite varied (Sachs et al. 2002; see also Chapter 10). The impact of growth on CPRs is ambiguous. As alternative consumption possibilities become available, the pressure due to safety net functions can be expected to decline. However, other demands (from the market, and for ecological services) are likely to emerge, which may create new conflicts. According to Sachs et al. (2002), the fastest growing states in the 1990s were Gujarat, Maharashtra, Tamil Nadu, West Bengal, Kerala, and Rajasthan. If there is a growth dividend that reduces safety-net pressures on CPRs, this is likely to be most significant in Rajasthan, Gujarat, and Maharashtra. Tamil Nadu, West Bengal, and Kerala face less pressure, so are likely to be able to explore alternative uses of CPRs. In the remaining states, current economic growth trends do not offer any real relief from the pressures that are documented in Table 15. 7.

POLITICAL AND POLICY FUTURES

What this discussion of alternative CPR futures does not adequately capture are the political dimensions of access to resources. The conflict between local values and the production of goods and downstream benefits, such as urban water supplies and other ecological services, has a spatial dimension, since resource users and other potential beneficiaries may be quite far apart. Recent policy initiatives for CPRs in India, such as Joint Forest Management and Guidelines for Integrated Watershed Development, have emphasized

[4]For instance, recent official pronouncements have revised estimates from an optimistic 8 per cent per annum to 6 per cent. The Planning Commission has adopted a target growth rate of 8 per cent over the Tenth Five-Year Plan period (2002–7), but recognizes the need for considerable economic and political reform in order to achieve this rate (Planning Commission 2001a). Chapter 10 estimates growth over the next five years to vary between 4 per cent and 6 per cent per annum, probably averaging 5 per cent over the period.

decentralization and management of CPRs by local communities. However, an increase in the relative importance of downstream service functions may re-introduce the resource interests of distant, non-local, stakeholders into management systems. For instance, the benefits of using land resources as carbon sinks may impact on a diffused global community (and perhaps even unborn future generations), stakeholders that are quite far from the local resource users who may have to adapt their land management practices.

Policies towards CPRs are likely to reflect ideological and organizational principles that govern wider economic processes. Current policies towards the Indian economy are dominated by objectives that emphasize sound micro- and macroeconomic management, and include, among others, the liberalization of markets, export promotion, the reduction of wasteful public expenditure, and managing the monetary sector (interest and exchange rates). There is growing consensus on the desirability of these policies, driven in part by external pressures, but also increasingly due to their adoption by national policy-makers as aspects of basic economic governance. The reform process is associated with a shrinking role for the state and a greater emphasis on private enterprise.

At a fundamental level, these two agendas are mutually incompatible. Supporters of decentralized natural resource management advocate such strategies as a means of ensuring access to the poorest, and as a strategy to empower groups that have historically been excluded from access to decision-making; there is an agenda of radical rural reform behind such proposals. The proponents of economic liberalization see no such need for radical restructuring. Indeed, they are likely to reject such decentralization strategies if they are seen to be incompatible with the push towards higher economic growth rates, or to pose a significant threat to the power of established interests.

Although there appears to be a basic disjuncture between the collective ethos implied by moves towards decentralized governance of CPRs, and the individualistic emphasis that is dominant in many other sectors of the Indian economy, these processes also share some similarities. The motivation for reform in both cases is a perception that the state and its functionaries are incapable of managing resources (in the case of the rural commons) and economic activity (in the case of liberalization), and that these functions need to be minimized. The minimal state, reduced to its basic regulatory functions, is compatible both with community-based natural resource management and with privatization.

The experience of Joint Forest Management through the 1990s, however, suggests that the bureaucracy does not necessarily view the programme as one which undermines its own role in natural resource management (Sundar et al. 2001). Instead, the participation of local resource users in the protection and regeneration of degraded forest lands is seen as promoting the objectives of the forest department, and is not really perceived as a threat to the current dominance of the state in this sector. The process is one in which the state retains its controlling interests, but forges partnerships with a wide range of stakeholders to implement its strategies.

The principle of state–society partnerships for the management of local CPRs is one that could be extended further. In the case of forests, for instance, proposals for the greater involvement of the private sector in regenerating degraded lands have been put forward, but have also been successfully resisted at the highest levels of policy-making (Planning Commission 1999). At the same time, specific industries (especially mining) have been pushing for the easing of regulations regarding their ability to operate in scheduled (tribal) areas, as well as the lifting of restrictions on the transfer of land to non-tribals. There appear to be contradictory processes at work, simultaneously pushing for a celebration of the collective and communities (in the case of decentralized natural resource management), as well as the market and individuals (in the case of greater private sector involvement).

It is important to recognize, however, that these different stakeholders occupy very different positions in local and national political structures. Shifts in the relative importance of different CPR functions are likely to be intimately linked to shifts in the locus of control over resources. Any change, whether conceptual or material, is likely to have significant political implications, as existing resource users seek to defend their claims against those of other, perhaps newer, claimants. Policy perspectives on such changes will have to recognize the incompatibility of some of these competing uses. Consequently, complex political negotiation and accommodation strategies may be needed in order to reconcile future claims over the management of CPRs.

CONCLUSIONS

This chapter has provided some evidence that CPRs continue to play an important and increasingly complex role in the Indian economy. Current uses of CPRs continue to be important in most Indian states, and it is likely that population growth and a high incidence of poverty will add to the pressure on such resources. Given the multiple constituencies that derive benefits from such resources, and the plurality of policy objectives that are pursued through these resources, decision-makers are likely to be forced to make difficult choices about the types of uses that can be accommodated and those which have to be denied access. Specific outcomes are likely to be associated with negative impacts on some constituencies, and the politics of resource access and use may be critical in determining actual 'futures'. Products and services that are derived from such resources will ultimately depend on policy choices and the nature of political negotiation that takes place between key stakeholders in this sector.

The chapter has highlighted the need to examine the CPR sector in the context of wider economic policy reform processes in the Indian economy.

What these policy processes share is a critical re-examination of the role and functions of the state in the context of resource allocation and use, and the need to include a wider set of participants in the process of decision-making. There are crucial differences, however, with one vision of the future pointing towards a rapidly expanding and individualized market-based economy, while the other envisages a decentralized system of local governance with a strong emphasis on collective institutions and values. Ideologically, these alternative futures represent opposite ends of the political spectrum, and it remains to be seen whether the basic differences between these reform agendas can be reconciled.

At a more fundamental level, the chapter has argued that the very nature of CPRs and their linkages with development may need to be reconceptualized in the light of emerging national and global pressures. A singular focus on the safety-net functions of CPRs may be myopic given the potential for CPRs to contribute to more positive developmental futures. The exploitation of market-based opportunities for the use of CPRs has not been incorporated into current Indian policies in this sector. Nor has there been much attention to their role in the provision of ecological services. It is likely that these alternatives will be the subject of considerable debate in the future.

16
Lessons and Policies

T he projections made for this book imply a population of 1.4 billion in India by 2026, and somewhere between 1.5 and 1.7 billion by 2050. We have explored many of the implications of this prospect for India's development especially in relation to urbanization, the economy and the social sectors, food and agriculture, and the environment. One major conclusion from our research is the importance of conducting these analyses at the state level rather than the national level. For example, the population projections and the analysis of future trends in poverty would both look very different if they were made on an all-India basis. This reflects the very considerable geographical and cultural diversity of the country as well as the very different socio-economic conditions and trends that prevail in different states. There is as much diversity within states, but we have not been able to discuss India's smaller administrative units here.

In fact, this chapter on policies shares one thing with the rest of the volume: it is far from complete in its coverage. We reflect relatively little on international aspects of policy, just as we have spent little time on the implications of globalization for India, or on what India's future development implies for the international community. There are limits to what can be done. Most of our recommendations are for governmental policies at the centre and state levels, though clearly many of the issues we treat require action at every level, from the central government to local community groups. Indeed, NGOs and other institutions in the Third Sector are likely to play a more prominent role in the future than in the past: there may be something of a withdrawal of the state from various sectors, much as has happened elsewhere in the world.

The prospective addition of around 600 million to India's population will have major administrative and political implications, which we have not discussed hitherto. It could work against the maintenance of the country's political cohesion. Since 1977 representation in Parliament has been frozen on the basis of the results of the 1971 Census. The rationale of the constitutional amendment which established this 'freeze' was that those states, predominantly in the south, which were successful in reducing their rates of population growth should not be penalized by a loss of political representation in Parliament. Consequently the relative 'value' of votes cast by people in northern states like Bihar, Madhya Pradesh, Rajasthan, and Uttar Pradesh has fallen, because their populations have increased greatly while their political representation has not. The freeze was due to be lifted around the time of the 2001 Census when a reallocation of parliamentary seats was to occur on the basis of its results. But the National Population Policy recommended that the freeze be extended to 2026 (Department of Family Welfare 2000: 11).

The 2001 Census revealed a widening divergence of population growth rates between the main northern and southern states. And our population projections indicate that demographic growth rates in the northern states will continue to be significantly higher than those in the south for decades to come. The freeze cannot continue indefinitely. But its eventual lifting and amendment could be a serious source of tension between the country's north and south. Such tension will only be heightened by the widespread southern perception that the populous northern states are economically backward and contribute less than their fair share to central government resources.

The most populous states already experience difficulties because of their sheer demographic scale. And the larger they become the more likely they will be to contain linguistic minorities which are sufficiently numerous to agitate for the formation of entirely new states. The creation in the year 2000 of Jharkhand, Chhatisgarh, and Uttaranchal—all states with strong tribal representations—from Bihar, Madhya Pradesh, and Uttar Pradesh respectively, illustrated these processes well. And the creation of 127 new districts between 1991 and 2001 was also partly to help cope with administrative problems arising from increasing population size. Many districts have populations of 2–4 million, and two (in West Bengal) have populations of 10 million, comparable in size to those of Tunisia or Sweden. So by 2026 there will quite possibly be several new states and many more districts.

It is hard to foresee the political and administrative implications of projected demographic growth. Given the differential rates of growth, Uttar Pradesh will become still more of a population giant, and other fast growing states will increase their weight in the total. Some would argue that the centre is already losing power relative to the states, and these trends will only increase that tendency. With increasing decentralization of power and possible further splitting of some states, especially the bigger ones, it is possible that the problem will dissolve of itself. It is beyond the scope of this book to speculate further about such matters. We can only highlight the prospect of future uneven demographic growth. Combined as it may be with increasing economic divergence, or at least a lack of convergence, there could indeed be increasing tensions. There is a problem in any case about how 1.5 billion people can be adequately represented in a national parliament, particularly a people so diverse. Decentralization of power may be inevitable. At the same time there are many reasons to value a strong central government for national policy-making. These are problems with which India will have to grapple.

POPULATION SIZE

It follows from the analysis made in this book, and as successive Indian governments have concluded, that the country would be better off with slower demographic growth. The main way to achieve this is for the government to increase its commitment to the provision of safe, effective, accessible, and affordable contraception for all those who need it. The importance of this is underscored by the fact that in the late 1990s around a quarter of all births were unwanted (IIPS and ORC Macro 2000: 126). The country can attain an ultimate population lower than our standard projection, but only if measures are taken to facilitate the pace of fertility decline, particularly in the large northern states. In addition, it will be desirable to continue to maintain family planning programmes in all the country's states even after they have attained levels of fertility around or below the replacement level (that is, approximately two births per woman).

Declines in birth rates translate into big reductions in population size only over the longer run. Consequently, the full implications of policies and programmes in this realm of public action are delayed. Unfortunately, politicians tend to have short rather than longer term time horizons. But this is too crucial a matter to be neglected. A greater sense of reality somehow needs to be introduced into the ways in which population issues are understood and treated within India's policy and planning establishment. There is no better illustration of this requirement than the element of fantasy which has repeatedly characterized the country's stated objectives for lowering the birth rate. In 1968, for example, the Ministry of Health set as its goal the reduction of the birth rate from 41 to 23 births per 1000 population by 1978–9—a level not attained by 2001, when the birth rate was still about 25. The National Population Policy document issued in the year 2000 set the medium-term objective of achieving replacement fertility by 2010 (Department of Family Welfare 2000: 2). But our population projections indicate that total fertility will probably not fall to this level until around 2016–21. It is unclear what is achieved by setting such unrealistic goals.

FERTILITY

Fertility will certainly continue to decline—for example, as the steady reduction in the average size of landholdings makes people realize that family limitation can help them fulfil their rising aspirations both for themselves and their children. Increasing educational levels too may contribute to a slightly faster rate of fertility decline. Indeed, fertility decline is far from dependent on family planning alone. Much will depend upon the performance of various broader socio-economic programmes. The National Population Policy recognizes this in giving prominence to such goals. Greatly increased attention needs to be given to achieving the following objectives of the Policy stated for the year 2010: (i) the attainment of compulsory and free school education up to the age of 14 years, and the reduction of drop-out rates to under 20 per cent at primary and secondary school levels for both boys and girls, (ii) the reduction of the IMR to 30 infant deaths per 1000 live births, and the MMR to less than 100 per 100,000 births, (iii) the achievement of universal childhood immunization against all vaccine preventable diseases, (iv) raising institutional deliveries to 80 per cent, and those by trained persons to 100 per cent, and (v) the promotion of delayed marriage for women to 18 years, and preferably to over 20 (Department of Family Welfare 2000: 2). These may be yet more unrealistic targets, but moving in their direction is clearly desirable. Their attainment by 2010 will require both increased financial resources and big improvements in the functioning of several social sector programmes (perhaps especially education). This point needs to be stressed. It is one thing to say that the unmet needs relating to basic reproductive and child health services, supplies, and infrastructure will be addressed, and another actually to bring major changes about.

Approving of provision of family planning and reproductive health services does not imply support for a return to the 'tyranny of the targets' in family planning. Among other things, the setting of targets for numbers of contraceptive 'acceptors' in the past took little account of local conditions, put undue pressure on health workers and often their clients at all levels, and led to significant biases in the statistics on family planning acceptance. Accordingly, it is heartening that the National Population Policy 2000 affirms the government's commitment to 'voluntary and informed choice and consent of citizens while availing of reproductive health care services, and [the] continuation of the target free approach in administering family planning services.' (Department of Family Welfare 2000: 2).

It is hard to believe either that incentive schemes are valuable or that they would make much difference to the pace of future fertility decline. Evidence suggests that in the 1990s the incentives paid to sterilization and intra-uterine device (IUD) acceptors were responsible for only a small proportion of total acceptances (Visaria et al. 1995). Moreover, the payment of incentives promoted petty fraud and tended to distract providers from their obligation to supply services of good quality. The National Population Policy does mention five different schemes which entail incentive payments. But it would probably be better if the money were used instead to improve basic family planning service provision. The population policies of several states also include mention of disincentives aimed at reducing fertility. Thus it is proposed that people who have married below the minimum marriage age, or those with more than two children, should be barred from contesting elections, entering educational institutions, and applying for state government jobs. The proposals of Madhya Pradesh and Rajasthan probably go furthest in such respects. However, these policies are highly suspect. They carry the obvious risk that they will be used to harass the poor and disadvantaged. Questions also arise as to how age will be verified where birth registration coverage is highly deficient. Moreover, the linking of family size to the right to contest political elections is plainly undemocratic.

The removal of family planning targets may actually help matters, inasmuch as health workers should be able to pay greater attention to the needs of their clientele. Moreover, if all pregnancies were to be registered, perhaps linked to the desirable, but probably still distant, goal of raising birth and death registration coverage to 100 per cent, then the provision of prenatal, natal (that is, at delivery), and postnatal care to all pregnant women would become more achievable. In any event, particular attention must be given to the perfectly feasible and very important objective of realizing universal childhood immunization for all the country's states.

India's family planning programme is often maligned. For example, it is sometimes described as a 'failure'. But such a description is both sweeping and unjust. While the quality of the programme's services can and must be greatly improved, there is no doubt that for many couples the programme has made contraception much more accessible. In short, the programme has facilitated the country's fertility decline. Those in India who denigrate the contribution of the programme are closing their eyes to an important agent of past —and future—change. However, the programme needs to give greater emphasis to providing reversible forms of contraception, especially the pill and the IUD, although sterilization will doubtless remain the main contraceptive method for the foreseeable future. It is unlikely that injectable contraceptives will be included in the national programme any time soon. But such methods should be made available to those women who want them and are prepared to pay for them.

Despite our reservations about the incorporation of disincentives into some state-level population policies, the increasing formulation of population policies at the state level is a welcome development, especially as it may signify greater willingness of politicians to address population matters, and help the setting up of appropriate institutional structures and programmes at the state, district, and sub-district levels. Although it did not actually publish a formal policy document, Tamil Nadu really led the way in developing its own population policy. And, at the start of the twenty-first century, Andhra Pradesh, Madhya Pradesh, Rajasthan, and Uttar Pradesh all had population policies of their own. However, as with the National Population Policy, there is a tendency for state governments to be unrealistically ambitious in specifying their aims for future fertility and mortality decline. It remains to be seen to what extent states will use their own resources to supplement central government funds. Also, the proposals for administrative re-organization of population programme activities at the state-level may sometimes be difficult to achieve, although moves in this direction must be welcomed. Finally, state-level policy documents usually mention the potential for NGOs to increase family planning acceptance and improve health conditions. But such organizations are often few on the ground, and they tend to be concentrated in more developed districts. Nevertheless, it is to be hoped that NGOs will help to ensure that state and national population policies do not remain mere pronouncements of desirable goals.

Mention must be made of HIV/AIDS here, as controlling it is part of fertility as well as health policy. The policy and programme areas which require greater attention lie in both prevention and treatment, and are well known. They include, for example, information, education, and communication efforts (IEC), condom promotion, improving HIV surveillance, and providing care and support for those affected by HIV/AIDS. The experience of countries like Botswana and South Africa shows how, within the space of just a few years, levels of HIV infection can rise from virtually zero to over 20 per cent of the entire adult population. India's considerable social, cultural, and economic heterogeneity probably provides some degree of insurance against such a thing happening at the national level in the near future. But that same heterogeneity raises the distinct possibility that it could happen in some of the states. Much more needs to be done perhaps, especially, in the area of IEC. We return to the subject of HIV/AIDS in the section that follows.[1]

MORTALITY AND HEALTH

A major part of India's health agenda continues to revolve around maternal and child care. Mortality levels have fallen throughout India, partly aided by the decline in fertility, which helps to improve the survival chances of infants and young children, and also of mothers, by lowering exposure to the risks of pregnancy. Yet in the absence of universal immunization, lack of control of basic diarrhoeal diseases, and poor obstetric facilities, mortality among

[1] Much of this and the previous section has relied on Visaria (2000c).

women and children continues to remain unacceptably high and has considerable scope for further reductions. These will only be possible with effective implementation of measures to combat vaccine-preventable illnesses, and easy availability of emergency obstetric care. The technology and impact on mortality reduction are well established and known. What are lacking are infrastructural development and the political and administrative will to implement the programmes. The main instrument for tackling child health issues, the Integrated Child Development Scheme (ICDS), has now over 5500 projects spread throughout the country. It has a number of well-known deficiencies, not least a lack of integration with other health services, to which successive government reports have drawn attention. But, as with so many programmes, the policies and excellent intentions are in place; performance lags behind (Kapil and Pradhan 2000).

Given the strong preference for sons in India and the mounting evidence of its increasing manifestation in female-specific abortions in some parts of the country, the relative death rates of females at childhood ages have not improved; indeed, if anything, the situation has worsened. While it is difficult to address son preference and such cultural practices directly by programme measures, there remains a need to develop and propagate culturally sensitive IEC messages about equality between the sexes and the value of girl children and women.

The adult mortality of females has improved appreciably faster than that of adult males. The age group at which the male death rate exceeds that for females dropped from 40–4 in 1971 to 30–4 by 1996. But adult mortality among both males and females will be a subject of greater concern in the years ahead because of the likely spread of HIV/AIDS, which could well become the country's leading cause of death at some point in the first or second decade of this century. The spread of HIV/AIDS will slow down the overall rate of decline of mortality in India, and its increasing presence in the general population will stimulate and interact with other infections such as hepatitis, diarrhoea, malaria, and, especially, TB. A strategy and concerted efforts for their effective treatment and control are required urgently. Here, perhaps above all, there needs to be much greater political commitment and foresight, and greater financial resources allocated, at both the national and the state levels. Denial has been a common human reaction in the face of HIV/ AIDS, especially since the chief mode of transmission of the disease is through sexual relations. [2] Moreover, politicians everywhere have very short-term time horizons. At present, policy-makers seem not to have grasped the magnitude

[2]According to the 1998–9 NFHS surveys, only 11.7 and 20.2 per cent of ever-married women in Bihar and Uttar Pradesh respectively had heard about HIV/AIDS, and even among those women who had heard of the disease levels of ignorance regarding its transmission and ways to avoid becoming infected were great (IIPS and ORC Macro 2000: 230–35).

of the danger. There is inadequate data collection for surveillance, inadequate IEC work, and inadequate availability even of the low-cost and effective treatments that can help, such as Nevirapine to prevent transmission from mother to child. The potential for calamity is clear. It can be avoided, but one can have no certainty at present that it will be.

Other communicable diseases continue to pose heavy threats, not least malaria. National Malaria Control Strategies have been adopted in recent years to identify high-risk areas and introduce remedial schemes, but the resurgence of malaria, even in parts of the country where it was not previously endemic, points to flaws in the control measures. Development projects and urban expansion have often led to the creation of new vector breeding grounds, and malaria control has become highly complex. The management and control or restriction of the transmission of malaria will require, in addition to public measures, locally-based community participation approaches. Control depends on curing malaria sufferers as well as eliminating the vector. There is a long way to go.

India has a continuing high level of communicable diseases, together with nutritional deficiencies and reproductive health problems—the ailments common to many developing countries. At the same time non-communicable diseases that are linked to new patterns of behaviour and growing environmental pollution are responsible for the country currently experiencing a double burden of disease. Many infections can be effectively controlled by provision of safe water and better sanitation. These require effective public health interventions and should receive greater priority than they do. Non-communicable diseases require long-term interventions, many of which are more costly than most Indians can afford. At the same time these diseases are exerting new pressures on already overburdened health systems. This is an area in which much more preventive work is essential.

Given limited resources, priorities and strategies will have to be clearly set to address the twin burdens. The major scourge of respiratory diseases can be conquered, but it requires greater individual and social awareness and stronger public programmes to reduce the incidence of tobacco consumption, lower atmospheric pollutants released by industrial units and vehicles, and increase the use of cleaner fuels in transport and in the home. While the cost of alternative sources of energy may be beyond the reach of poor households, the aggregate cost of treating respiratory ailments arising from breathing heavily polluted air will far exceed the cost of making cleaner fuels available at affordable rates.

MIGRATION AND URBANIZATION

It is inevitable that India will become increasingly urbanized in the future. And this aspect of growth requires much greater acceptance and attention from policy-makers. The process of urbanization, that is, the rise in the proportion of the total population living in urban areas, is probably a good thing on balance. Indeed, it is a sign of development. Incomes tend to be greater in urban areas; and in the late 1990s life expectation was about seven years higher in urban than in rural India (Registrar General, India 1999a). Furthermore, in many respects urban living is a relatively efficient way of delivering basic services such as health and education.

However, while urbanization is to be welcomed, rapid urban growth is not. The country will definitely experience very considerable urban growth during the next few decades. And this will worsen greatly the already acute pressures on urban infrastructures—water, sewage, housing, transport, and so forth. If urban living conditions are going to be improved from their current, frequently abysmal state, the urban sector will need to get a significantly larger share of government resources in the future. The past record of inexcusable inaction in confronting urban problems must also be reversed. Issues of urban governance and management will be critical to this. More accountable and democratic institutions of urban self-government will need to revise key regulations (for example, the legal framework relating to the use of land for housing), strengthen the enforcement of key policies and rules (such as those for traffic and pollution), and facilitate the greater use of new technologies (for example, through the promotion of water recycling and bio-gas plants) (Visaria 1997). Most problems should be easier to manage if urban population growth is slowed; and here the promotion of family planning in both rural and urban areas can play a key role.

The future of urban areas cannot be considered in isolation from the future of rural areas. Urban areas exist within their rural hinterlands and they share common concerns, such as water, waste disposal, and transport. Also, although rural to urban migration accounts for only a minority of urban population growth, both the urban and the rural sectors are intimately connected through migration. So developing regional perspectives and institutions for planning will be essential (Centre for Policy Research 2001). And such developments must protect the interests of rural people and promise them a better life, for example, with respect to electricity, transport, and the provision of educational and health facilities.

EDUCATION

At the turn of the century, 25 per cent of girls aged 6–10 years and 38 per cent of girls aged 11–14 in rural India were not currently attending school. Our projections suggest that even under the most optimistic scenario, 16 per cent of girls in Bihar will not complete elementary education even by 2026. These figures alone give an indication of the magnitude of the task of making elementary education available for all in India, and suggest that recent educational progress is not a cause for complacency.

Public policy should focus on strengthening the quantity and quality of the supply of education since improving supply of schooling is more amenable to policy than stimulating demand for it. There is, in any case, ample evidence that demand for education of decent quality is greater than supply.

A number of government interventions contributed to the educational improvements of the 1990s including mid-day meals, decentralization of educational powers to panchayats, education guarantee schemes, and centrally and externally funded education programmes such as the total literacy campaigns, and district-level planning, teacher training, and curriculum development. It would be desirable, therefore, to continue with and enhance these schemes. This is indeed intended by the Government of India under its Sarv Shiksha Abhiyan campaign.

But the universalization of elementary education in India requires a much greater financial outlay from the government than hitherto provided. There is an enormous need for improved educational facilities, and for more teachers to reduce excessively high pupil–teacher ratios where these exist. However, there is much scope for improvement via better use of existing resources, such as the teachers already in place. Increased accountability of teachers to their local communities would reduce teacher absenteeism and negligence; but state governments have lacked the political courage to implement measures to achieve this because of the resistance by teachers' unions. Greater political will is needed to push through mechanisms to raise teacher accountability.

The spread of private schooling is the greatest at the primary level of education, less at the junior level, and even less at the secondary level. This is perverse from the point of view of equity and needs correction. Providing good quality government primary schools will prevent the further development of a dualistic structure in education whereby well-off children go to the private schools and poor children to the impoverished and often dysfunctional government schools.

EMPLOYMENT

The experience of the 1990s, at both the all-India and the state levels, has demonstrated that the policy solution for adequate employment generation does not lie solely in economic growth. Our projections too show that rapid economic growth may not be a sufficient condition for adequate employment generation in future. But the higher projected unemployment rates associated with slower growth show that it is a necessary one. Achieving rapid economic growth is, therefore, one of the keys to employment generation.

A distinct policy goal, though one which is clearly related to encouraging an overall high rate of economic growth, is to stimulate the growth of strategic sectors, sub-sectors, and activities. These may already exist or could be just emerging, and are, or have, the potential to be particularly labour intensive. The state-level story demonstrates that recent successes in bringing down unemployment have depended on a combination of high economic growth and high employment intensity of output.

Agriculture is a strategic sector in the sense that it still absorbs the majority of the rural workforce, but its recent poor performance in generating employment will have to be reversed in the future if it is to assist the employment situation. Many doubt its capacity to become more labour absorbing. But others argue that its potential is substantial, particularly in lagging regions such as Bihar and Uttar Pradesh. The diversification of agriculture into allied activities such as dairy, floriculture, and food processing also has considerable labour-using potential. For these potentials to be realized, Chadha and Sahu (2002) maintain that the crucial role of public sector investment in rural infrastructure and other supporting institutions must be restored. As such investment must come from the state governments, their fiscal predicaments are a major constraint (Ahluwalia 2000).

In the rural and urban non-agricultural sector, recent positive growth and employment trends in several service activities suggest that they will be major sources of employment in the future. Such sectors include retailing and financial services. IT-related services also continue to have promise, both internationally and in the domestic market. Although the recent performance of community, social, and personal services has been poor, many scholars argue that the need to meet the shortage of teachers, nurses, and doctors will provide many jobs (Planning Commission 2001b, 2002b). Some labour-intensive export oriented manufactures, such as garments, have also recently done well, and continue to have good prospects. Perhaps the success of China in this area is an example to emulate. Other emerging labour-intensive activities include tourism and construction. Efforts to remove infrastructural, legislative, and resource constraints on the development of these activities need to be increased. In rural areas, policy interventions to reduce barriers to entry for the poor into productive non-farm employment, such as lack of education and credit, are also needed (Lanjouw and Shariff 2002).

The 1990s witnessed only sluggish growth in organized sector employment. It is unlikely that the absolute public sector job losses which have been behind this trend will soon be reversed, as further retrenchment seems likely. The organized private sector shows a more encouraging trend, but has only a small employment share. In these circumstances, policy-makers must recognize that the informalization of employment, with the unorganized sector providing the overwhelming bulk of work, will continue to be the context in which most jobs will be generated in the future, and address the implications for employment quality. Raising employment quality in the unorganized sector requires policies that will accelerate income and productivity growth, necessary for ensuring the viability of unorganized enterprises in an environment of increasing global and domestic competition. Trends in these variables during the 1990s have been promising. To enhance them, policy attention should be given to finding ways of extending credit to the unorganized sector, through both bank and non-bank sources like self-help groups, and improving the specific infrastructural needs of unorganized sector workers, not least women workers. Policy should encourage inter-firm linkages and sub-contracting between large and small firms in which there is scope for technology and skill transfer to unorganized workers. Such linkages would be facilitated by the formation of a single agency which maintains a list of firms engaged in or with capability to engage in sub-contracting, together with information about their products, capacity, and technology.

Future increases in the participation of women in the unorganized sector also suggest the need to expand facilities to assist them with child and elder care, areas which have been vulnerable to government expenditure cuts during the reforms period. Ensuring basic social security, such as minimum wages, is also important. The Planning Commission's Task Force also suggests phasing out the SSI reservation policy, as has recently been done for garments and soon will be for leather goods and toys; this will help to promote greater economic efficiency at every scale of production. Under India's freer trade policy, the restrictions now stifle both export and domestic competitiveness (Planning Commission 2002b).

Although it has only a small employment share, the organized private sector has contributed to providing high quality jobs during the 1990s. Its expansion should, therefore, be encouraged. It is often argued that labour market rigidities resulting from India's various labour laws inhibit employment growth in this sector, so that there is a case for modifying these laws. Employers of over 100 workers cannot undertake retrenchment and closure without the permission of the appropriate state government. The alleged result is that they avoid hiring workers, so that the growth of labour-intensive sectors is curbed and flexibility and competitiveness are impaired. The debate about the 'jobless growth' in organized manufacturing in the 1980s centres around the accuracy of such arguments (Besley and Burgess 2002; Bhalotra 2002; Dev 2000). Experts who state that the adverse impact of labour laws tends to be overplayed point out that this sector performed better in the 1990s without their modification (Bhalotra 2002). Nevertheless, they are not ideal in a liberalized environment where flexibility to restructure and adapt to changing technology and market conditions is paramount. Amending the law so that India's situation becomes similar to those elsewhere, therefore, seems sensible (Planning Commission 2002b). Because the immediate impact of such reform may be more firings than hirings as employers discharge excess labour, setting up compensatory social security measures will also be necessary (Ghose 1999). The Planning Commission's Task Force recommends that such measures be based on compulsory contributions by both workers and employers, involving no government liability (Planning Commission 2001b).

If India's employment strategy is to involve encouraging the growth of labour-intensive sectors and improving the quality of unorganized sector employment, supportive policies on the supply-side of labour are essential. Principal among these are policies that aim to develop education and skills training in appropriate directions. In the past, training has been largely geared towards meeting the needs of the organized sector. A shift in focus towards the needs of the informal sector and specific strategic activities is necessary for the future. Without such a shift, the mismatch between the aspirations of educated job-seekers and available jobs, as well as skill shortages in other areas, will deepen as the future educational attainment of the labour force rises. Wood and Calandrino (2000) argue that the need for appropriate training policies is increased in an open economy, where the acquisition of modern technological and commercial knowledge and production methods raises the demand for skilled labour.

In terms of formal training, policies must address the low demand for vocational education, perhaps via its better integration into general education at the school level. Problems on the supply-side of formal vocational training also require remedy. There is a need to improve the market relevance of training courses, perhaps through greater industry and employer involvement. Funding constraints could be eased by facilitating private sector participation, so far discouraged because public sector training courses are highly subsidized (Planning Commission 2001b). Skill shortages in growth areas, such as for software engineers, must also be addressed to prevent such sectors pulling skilled workers out of other activities (Arora and Athreye 2001). An expansion in the number of institutes providing specialized technical education is required. Increasing the flexibility of the system so that training can be undertaken during employment at times and locations convenient for informal sector workers would also be beneficial. Increasing the efficiency of enterprise-based training is important here (Dev 2000). Training in multi-skills, including production skills, marketing, accounting, and management would also be useful for informal sector workers, including the self-employed (Planning Commission 2001b). The need to enhance female access to education and training will also increase as women's participation in the labour force rises.

POVERTY

According to current trends, plausibly projected, there could still be 190 million poor people in India by 2026, three-quarters of them in the five poor states of Bihar, Madhya Pradesh, Orissa, Rajasthan, and Uttar Pradesh. These are the states with the most poverty, and mostly slow economic growth and high population growth.

Almost everything this book discusses has implications for the poor, whether it is education, health, family planning, employment, or the environment: they are all fields where current performance hurts the poor in particular.

Policies that enhance economic growth, and agricultural growth, will favour the reduction of poverty. The lives of poor people are most threatened by potential shortages of water and low water quality, and by air pollution; pressures on CPRs also bear most heavily on the poor, and on women in particular.

Tendulkar (1992) sets out a useful framework for policy discussion. He divides the poor into those outside and inside the mainstream of economic activity. The former are to be taken care of by social security measures; the latter he divides further into the chronically poor and those whose poverty is transient. Transient poverty can be taken care of by growth, and by relief schemes or insurance that provide temporary income and reduce vulnerability to shocks. Those who are persistently poor require various forms of help. Those who are self-employed in commodity producing sectors, both rural and urban, need assets, technology, credit, and marketing facilities; in the urban informal sector, they need mainly credit and marketing. The wage-dependent need more and better-rewarded employment. Nagaraj (1999) provides a further helpful distinction for employment—between those denied the utilization of skills and those denied the acquisition of skills. The former are part of the problem of labour demand, particularly in the more advanced states where there is already a fair spread of education and modernization; the latter are found among those living within traditional support systems or engaged in household enterprises, most particularly in the poorer states.

Since half of India's poor are in the persistent category, the country's anti-poverty programmes can, at best, have only a limited impact. They are excessively scattered and unrelated to basic processes in the economy. They focus on regions with particular problems, such as drought prone areas; subsidy programmes such as the Targeted Public Distribution System (TPDS) for food; a number of employment related schemes, and social security measures for the very poor. Most of them have been shown to be inefficient in terms of the proportion of expenditure actually reaching the poor, and in terms of their lasting effects. A process of rationalization of the schemes has been in train. Certainly many parts of the food and employment schemes and social security deserve to be maintained, to the extent that they provide relief to people in great need; but greater efforts are needed to prevent leakage, and to ensure that all those in need are reached.

But greater impacts on poverty could be made by improved performance in the social sectors and the environment generally, concentrating on the states with the greatest backlogs. Better health and nutrition and better education for all, and clean air and water are the best anti-poverty programmes. To these must be added reproductive health services and family planning, again most needed in the poorest states: they too are pro-poor measures in themselves for high fertility households.

It cannot be said that the funds do not exist to achieve these aims. Anti-poverty programmes themselves absorb very large resources, a considerable share of which could be beneficially re-directed. State-level social expenditures are held back because of the fiscal deficits of the states, which are themselves the result of misguided subsidies, particularly for water and electricity. They are subsidies that do not benefit the poor; they are also damaging to the environment. In the end a large share of the persistence of poverty goes back to governance. India's political processes do not serve the poor well in terms of the sectoral programmes which should be lifting them out of poverty. They also result in deficiencies of economic management in many states and, as far as economic reforms are concerned, at the centre as well.

The majority of the poor remain in rural areas, and measures to redress poverty must concentrate on enhancing both agricultural growth and non-farm employment. Yet India, for all its anti-poverty commitment, has not seen the increases in the key investments—irrigation, rural roads, and agricultural research—that would help to achieve this. These investments commonly have high rates of return and large impacts on poverty reduction in backward areas in particular (Lipton 2002). A particular emphasis will be needed on water measures for the poor. As water becomes increasingly scarce and some forms of regulation or market-based pricing for water are introduced, as eventually they will be, it will be essential to ensure the redistribution of water to the poor, and water-yielding assets, as well as action to improve water quality. As Chapter 14 notes, better practices for water storage are slowly being introduced in India, but the provision for ensuring the equitable distribution of the stored water lags behind.

Anti-poverty strategies the world over rightly give an important place to the empowerment of the poor, and their involvement in the design and management of schemes intended for their benefit. India has made considerable strides in these directions: in education, giving local communities a role in monitoring schools and teachers; in water, moving to farmer-managed watershed development; in a range of activities devolving budgets and management to panchayats and pushing decentralization. Much of this experience has been positive; but much has not—instead of empowering the poor, it has empowered local vested interests. Like markets, devolution and decentralization cannot be guaranteed to help the poor. There is an indispensable role for the state. But frequently public action by state institutions has not delivered either.

'Good governance' is not just a slogan. Corruption, malfeasance, and nonfeasance have all to be tackled if the state is to serve the poor as it should. Policies to redress poverty require the positive engagement of central and state governments as well as NGOs, local communities, and groups of beneficiaries. With greater accountability and transparency India's own resources will be adequate to overcome poverty. Accountability is needed most particularly in public services that affect the poor: health, education, the police perhaps more than any other, as well as the general workings of the bureaucracy. If resources are not invested or distributed where they are needed, and policies are not framed to benefit the poor or to ensure that the poor receive the benefits meant for them, this study's projections of slow poverty decline could become a reality. It is ultimately down to politics. If more of India's politicians see electoral promise in genuinely addressing the needs of the poor, poverty can and will decline much faster.

Finally, it bears repetition in a population-centred book that bringing family planning and reproductive health services to those who want them is a measure that favours the reduction of poverty, both at the household level, in improving the lives of women and children, and on a wider basis, since fertility decline from high levels hastens the arrival of the 'demographic bonus' and permits faster economic growth, while reducing pressures on labour markets, public services, and fragile environmental resources.

ECONOMIC GROWTH

The requirements for growth in India are fairly well known; putting them in place has proved politically difficult in recent years. Reaching faster economic growth requires policies at macro and micro levels. Savings have to rise. In the 1990s household savings did so and they can be expected to continue to rise, perhaps with the help of the demographic bonus. But government savings fell. These trends continued in 2000–1 (Ministry of Finance 2002). The main improvement in savings should come from the government sector. A major improvement is needed in the fiscal deficit, which in turn calls for measures which have proved difficult to implement: reduction of subsidies that do not reach the poor, increases in taxes, cuts in government employment, closing or privatization of loss-making public sector enterprises. They are all feasible, but require political will.

Greater FDI could make a contribution as well but that requires improvements in the investment climate. Such improvements are needed for raising the efficiency of investment. But this means tackling the remaining constraints to domestic and international competition—the stalled programme of reform discussed in Chapter 10.

A similar story can be told about growth at the state level, where the policy agenda is similar. One positive recent development has been the Medium Term Fiscal Reform Programme by which the states reach agreement with the centre on fiscal reform, with some incentives from the centre for them to do so. But by mid-2002 only Orissa, of the five large, poor states, had signed such agreements. It is in the poor and slowly-growing states of Bihar and Uttar Pradesh, in particular, that these measures are most needed.

Higher investment will not achieve its maximum effect without improvements in efficiency. Chapter 10 detailed a number of areas where central and state regulation still limit competition, and despite the changes under the reform process there is considerable scope for further de-regulation, in agriculture, transport, mining, pharmaceuticals, and in the policy of reservation for the small-scale sector. Fear of unemployment is a factor in preventing further reform, but most analysts agree that there would be major gains in employment overall, and what is needed are adequate safety nets to protect those who would lose out, as some inevitably will. The same analysis applies to international competition, where again the country has more to gain than to lose from further liberalization. India remains one of the world's most protected economies. In fact, the finance minister, introducing the Budget for 2001–2, announced reductions in tariffs to 'East Asian levels' over three years—these are half Indian levels or less (Planning Commission 2001a).

It is widely agreed that India's growth is seriously constrained by inadequate infrastructure. Energy and transport deficiencies affect industry and rural production alike, and irrigation and water management lag well behind what is required. The needs of rural areas for better roads, electricity, and telecommunications are well known. Sanitation—urban and rural—should also be added to the list. It is not just a health matter, but something that affects foreign investment and tourism, and, therefore, growth and employment. While private funding for infrastructure can play a part, and new mechanisms exist to encourage it, such as the Infrastructure Development Finance Company (IDFC), the main burden rests with the public sector. This makes all the more necessary the kinds of fiscal correction at state and central levels already referred to.

Further reforms are also called for in finance and banking. The banking system as a whole suffers from high costs of credit and poor quality of service. The costs are not only due to high interest rates, but also due to inefficiencies in intermediation. Many studies and reports have pointed to the combination of increased competition and regulation that would create a healthier financial sector with lower costs, less delay in the granting of credits, fewer non-performing loans, and more efficient service. Two sectors need particular attention, the service sector, responsible for so large a share of employment, but one whose financial needs are not well addressed by banks currently; and the informal sector. Banks can play a role in lending to informal enterprises; non-bank intermediaries also have a major part to play. A scheme to link banks with self help groups (SHGs) had provided credits to almost 2 million poor families by September 2000; 85 per cent of the SHGs assisted were women's groups. Further activities are in train to link official agencies, banks, NGOs, and SHGs. But more fundamentally the greatest need is for reduction of public sector dominance in the financial system, including privatization of many public financial institutions.

Raising the rate of economic growth is important if the country's goals for improving human welfare are to be achieved. Growth by itself is not enough to redress poverty and generate higher levels and better quality of employment. An important conclusion of the present study is that faster growth need not come at the expense of environmental damage; on the contrary, many of the measures needed for environmental enhancement and conservation have high rates of return and will add to growth and welfare. The economist would have to point to one measure in particular that stands out as contributing to a large number of policy objectives: the reduction of misplaced subsidies, particularly those for water and electricity. These do nothing for the poor, but harm the environment, and create a financial situation that raises the cost of credit in general, thereby reducing economic growth, and severely restricting all the expenditures which would help the poor—not least, those for education and health.

FOOD AND AGRICULTURE

Patterns of food consumption are becoming more diverse and will continue to do so for the foreseeable future. While levels of per capita cereal consumption have tended to fall, there have been significant rises for non-cereal foods especially vegetables, fruits, and milk. Virtually all this past growth in the consumption of non-cereal foods has come from increased domestic output, most of which has had only modest assistance from the government. However, perhaps particularly in relation to vegetables and fruits, keeping up with projected demand growth in the future may well require increased governmental attention. In recent decades the prices of non-cereal foodstuffs have risen appreciably faster than the prices of cereals (Hanchate 2001). Both greater efforts by government to promote vegetable and fruit production, and greater openness to the import of some non-cereal foodstuffs, could help to mitigate such a trend in the future.

The main aims of the government's extensive involvement in the agricultural sector since 1947 have been national self-sufficiency in cereal production and the maintenance of adequate cereal stocks. To these ends, farmers have benefited from various kinds of financial support (for example, subsidized irrigation and power supplies, and the provision of cheap credit), which have comprised the bulk of government spending on agriculture. In the 1990s expenditure on the procurement, storage, and distribution of rice and wheat rose sharply. And the high government-determined procurement prices that prevailed were at odds both with market signals and the growth of vast stockpiles of grain (which by the end of 2001 exceeded 65 million tonnes). The continuation of these policies in support of cereal production is extremely expensive; it distorts the allocation of agricultural resources; and it increases problems of agricultural sustainability (Ramaswami 2002). In addition, such a policy stance hampers the ability of Indian agriculture to cope with a likely scenario in which demand growth will shift increasingly towards higher levels of non-cereal food consumption. Therefore, at the start of the twenty-first century, the government's policy towards agriculture is at a critical stage. There must be a major reduction in its stress on cereal production, and increased emphasis on promoting the cultivation of non-cereal foods.

Of course, a reduction in the artificially high support prices paid for rice and wheat will complement market forces in giving greater impetus to the production of non-cereal foodstuffs. The pace with which the production side responds to increasing demand will also be influenced by considerations that lie well beyond the control of most farmers. Thus, as for cereals, higher levels of fruit and vegetable production will require more investment in irrigation, the development of new technologies both to raise yields and improve product quality, and the promotion of non-cereal crop cultivation through increased agricultural extension activities. Also, vegetables and fruits tend to be extremely perishable. It has been estimated that about half the country's total horticultural output is lost through wastage (Singhal 1999: 134). Therefore the growth of markets for fruit and vegetables will also hinge critically on the expansion of cold storage facilities and improved transport networks.

An equally critical infrastructural requirement will be the development of efficient and reliable marketing and distribution systems. This is because, as one analyst has put it: 'farmers in India receive much lower prices for their produce and the consumers pay much higher prices for agricultural commodities ... because of the existence of too many intermediaries between the farmer and the consumer' (Singhal 1999). The private sector will be central to many of the developments that will be required to bring about major rises in the production of non-cereal foods. But there will be an important role for the government too, for example, in relation to transport facilities and the provision of an effective regulatory framework to promote healthy competition.

The establishment of the WTO in 1995 has accelerated the expansion of international trade in agriculture. And the gradual implementation of various WTO agreements should have a major effect on the market conditions facing all countries which either export or import agricultural products. In general, it seems probable that the first decades of the new century will see a considerable liberalization of world agriculture. Trade barriers will be reduced, market access will be increased, subsidies and levels of domestic support will tend to fall.

A detailed assessment of India's future trade competitiveness in the face of these developments is difficult. This reflects the generally high level of international protectionism which has prevailed in the past, and the considerable uncertainties which are attached to the speed and nature of the future reforms to be brought about under the WTO. According to Rao and Gulati (1994) in the past India's trade policy generally 'favoured industry and discriminated against agriculture'. However, they consider that the economic reform process initiated in the country from the early 1990s, as well as the likely sway of future reforms which will be agreed to under the WTO, should both help to bring about a corrective adjustment in the terms of trade between the country's industrial and agricultural sectors. Certainly, a reduction in the high subsidies underpinning cereals, and other targeted food crops like sugarcane, should help to rationalize the country's agricultural production structure. There should be a more efficient allocation of basic resources and inputs (for example, land, labour, irrigation, power). Accordingly, a diversification towards much greater cultivation of non-cereal crops, which are also often fairly labour intensive, seems to be an appropriate strategy for India in the international context too. The government needs to do much more to help modernize the country's agriculture and enhance its trade competitiveness. Key areas for attention are: increased promotion of agro-processing industries; the establishment of systems of product quality certification; the setting up of commodity and futures exchanges; and the development of sustainable and affordable crop insurance programmes for farmers (Gulati 2002).

Various authorities have noted a general falling-off in governmental attention to agriculture and rural investment. This is despite findings that such investments often have very high payoffs in general and also contribute more than most expenditures to the reduction of poverty. This is equally true for India's agricultural research, which has in the past made major contributions to productivity. Stronger research efforts will be required all the more in an era where questions arise about the need for GM crops, and about increasing yields in ways that are pro-poor and environmentally sustainable.

The large increase in chemical fertilizer use which will happen during the next few decades has significant implications for policy. India's use of organic matter to enhance the structure of its farmland soils, increase water retention, and raise nutrient levels, is quite insufficient. Indeed, many farmers are unaware of the full benefits of organic inputs (for example, compost), and much waste matter which could profitably be employed for these purposes (for example, farmyard manure) is wasted. The yield response to chemical fertilizers will be boosted by the greater incorporation of organic matter into the soils. There is certainly going to be a major rise in chemical fertilizer applications, but for reasons of efficiency much more attention must also be paid to improving the mix of nitrogen, phosphate, and potash within the overall application load. Moreover, as levels of chemical fertilizer use rise, so greater attention must be paid to the management of the applications, both for reasons of efficiency and to avoid various environmental problems.

Finally, a word is required about food consumption and poverty alleviation. Irrespective of problems of data interpretation and estimation, there is no doubt that the poorest sections of India's population experience a monotonous, inadequate diet. Average levels of nutritional intake are far below any recommended international standards (Hopper 1999). Therefore the need for the continuation of a food assistance programme targeted at the poorest quintiles is compelling. But the TPDS needs further reform, or even replacement by a new form of food assistance, for instance, one based on food stamps, which have been shown to work well in many other countries, or grain pass-books (Srivastava 2001).

INDUSTRY, ENERGY, AND TRANSPORT

A key message of our analysis is that India can cope with increasing industrialization and energy use while conserving the environment. And it can achieve this without reducing economic growth, indeed, while actually enhancing growth. Whether it will succeed in these objectives is another matter.

We would support as a first measure the long-standing arguments for more rational, cost-reflecting, pricing and regulatory policies for energy and transport (including urban transport and congestion management). This would include, in particular, the reduction of misdirected subsidies in these fields. Electricity subsidies figure as an object of policy reform in several of our chapters, but there are also misdirected subsidies in transport, some of which could be better used to encourage environmental improvements and innovative technologies. Technology is the principal key to environmental improvement when it comes to industrial and vehicle pollution and the use of energy; but there are also important roles for the public sector, especially in further developing public transport and its infrastructure to make transport more efficient and less polluting. Incentives for innovative environmental technologies (as, for example, in renewable energy) and the removal of disincentives (as is arguably desirable for the tax regime affecting wind energy) have a major part to play. They should always bear in mind the positive externalities of innovation, where these exist.

Improved pricing and incentives have to be combined with appropriate market regulation, as, for example, with pollution from coal-fired power stations, which requires either direct regulation or a derivative of it such as pollution permits. There is a variety of well-tested approaches to environmental policy-making, and India, like other countries, has no shortage of options. Policies work, in the sense that people and industry do change practices and technologies in response to them, in ways that reduce environmental damage by orders of magnitude while permitting economic activity and incomes to grow.

The climate for environmental policy reform is still unsatisfactory. Politicians and civil servants are frequently not gripped with the importance of environmental objectives and the damage caused by environmental pollution. As our analysis makes clear, many improved practices will be adopted by private parties if the right incentives and disincentives are in place. Many more need public support, which can be eminently justified by improved health and the conservation of ecological services.

On a long term basis more could be done to foster a better climate for policy by enhancing education in secondary schools and at the undergraduate and graduate level in universities. There should be a special focus on what improved technologies and practices can accomplish, and to show why India, like other countries, may aspire to achieving both material prosperity and a better environment. Specialist courses are also desirable in subjects such as renewable energy, energy policies, transport management and policies, in addition to the long-standing courses in water supply, sanitation, waste management, and municipal engineering more generally. NGOs can make an important contribution. India's Centre for Environment Education, for example, has won international awards; there is scope for far greater expansion of the kinds of activities it and other environmental NGOs undertake. Much of the progress India has made in environmental policy has been due to the work of one man, Anil Agarwal, and the organization he created, the CSE. NGOs and the law courts have been taking the initiative in environmental action. Where they have led, the government should follow far more energetically than it does.

India could become a polluting giant, to the detriment of its own citizens and the world beyond. But it has every incentive to try to reverse current trends and move towards sustainability in every field of activity. This would bring benefits to all its people, rich and poor, and make a contribution internationally to reducing pollution that spreads beyond its borders, as well as to slowing global warming and climate change.

THE URBAN ENVIRONMENT

The most critical environmental concerns in India's cities are water supply, sanitation, drainage, SWM, transport, and pollution from urban wastes and emissions. Waste, air, and water pollution have increased beyond both the absorptive capacity of nature and the handling capacity of institutions. It is this combination of lack of institutional capability and demographic pressures that explain the current state of the environment in India's cities.

Some issues appear to be strongly driven by the size of population, since they relate to the volumes generated or demanded by urban dwellers. These include the total amount of solid waste generated, the demand for water, as well as the quantity of wastewater generated. But there are difficulties in forecasting India's urban environmental future owing to inadequate knowledge about environmental issues, largely due to lack of reliable data. Where data are available they are of relatively poor quality. In addition, India has weak institutions and infrastructure on which to base effective actions to address its urban problems. When it comes to environmental issues, a complex web of interests is involved (consumers, businesses, workers, the judiciary, and various branches of the executive from the national government to municipalities), and this has made the process of political implementation of desirable changes very difficult.

Urban environmental problems are often the result of economic or political factors. Changes in the urban environment depend on strategies adopted by the government, changes in environmental legislation and the stricter enforcement of existing legislation, the demand for better living conditions by urban residents, as well as the ability of local authorities to perform their functions, including partnerships with other interested parties. The main reason for the failure of urban planning can be seen in the weak revenue situation of urban local bodies. Local authorities have inadequate budgets, large backlogs in providing basic infrastructure, and a resource base that is not capable of generating the capital required to address the backlog. The 74th Constitutional Amendment, however, has gone some way towards empowering urban local government.

Many successful schemes have shown the way to manage solid wastes in a number of towns and cities. But they are mostly carried out by NGOs rather than municipal authorities. Poorer households already engage in active recycling of waste, and there are considerable opportunities for this to be done on a larger scale, which could even earn revenue. Doing better is more an organizational than a technical problem, and there is much scope for best practices to be widely copied.

Liquid waste is another matter. Mains sewage is completely absent for the vast majority of India's towns and cities, and wastewater treatment facilities are unable to keep up with the volume of liquid waste generated. This is due to lack of adequate funding. Also, even where treatment plants exist they are often not functioning due to inadequate maintenance. The extent of river pollution from these sources is reaching critical levels in many places, and requires urgent action and investment if the country is not to become prey to even worse health problems and water shortages than there already are at present. This is in part a local matter. But the central government has largely neglected problems of urban finance, and it is high time it gave them proper attention.

There is a need for alternative fuels such as CNG, LPG, and propane to be used much more widely. CNG has been successfully introduced for public transport in Delhi. Together with retiring older vehicles and introducing higher environmental standards for new ones, Delhi has made valuable strides in reducing pollution. The recent improvement in its air quality is a good illustration of this book's thesis, that many pollution problems are susceptible to affordable technological solutions, far outweighing any effect of population growth. Steps are in fact being taken to extend supply of CNG to other cities, with a recent Supreme Court judgment directing the government to make this happen.

Other key measures to control vehicle pollution are to introduce congestion pricing and management and further develop public transport.

These would encourage a more rational and efficient urban transport system, improving economic productivity as well as the urban environment.

WATER

The discussion in Chapter 14 ended with the observation that India's water problems are not just things of the future, but are already pressing. The greatest impact of further population growth could well be felt here. The combination of growing pollution and climate change could reduce the amount of available water, while growing human numbers will inevitably increase demand. This comes about particularly as a result of the demand for food and agricultural products, since agriculture takes about four-fifths of the fresh water supplies. Water use does not depend on these basic factors alone, but is influenced by laws, property rights, social inequalities, markets and the lack of markets, institutions, and technologies. The list could be continued. Consequently, policies to address the country's impending water problems will need to be more detailed.

Various studies have shown that in basic supply and demand terms, India can meet its future water needs on a national basis, though with inevitable difficulties in some regions. The principal goal must be to realize greater efficiency in the use of water, which can be achieved by controlling pollution, greater use of water pricing and regulation, and by greatly enhanced water storage facilities. A National Water Policy has been published with thorough attention to most of the main issues. But the policy was lacking in one key ingredient: a set of detailed steps for its implementation.

Water issues are beset with political difficulties and conflicts of interest at every level. Pollution is often due to lack of resources on the part of urban authorities to install adequate protective facilities, but raising the revenue required can be politically difficult. There are less defensible problems where corporations defeat environmental controls, though this too can be due to the politics of opposing corporate interests, not to speak of corruption. More understandable conflicts arise where polluting industries employing large numbers of people would be less viable under stronger environmental regulation. As we show, in the large-scale sector of manufacturing, there is usually a technological solution that will pay the investor, or will have high social returns if induced by government policy. But in the small-scale sector this may not be true. Here, cleaner technology may not be available, or, at least, not at a low cost. As Chapter 14 observes, the pollution trends are in the wrong direction, and clearly the political issues are far from being tackled.

Only limited progress is being made in water pricing and regulation. Canal irrigation needs to be put on a self-financing basis if proper maintenance is to be ensured and further investment made on a sustainable basis; instead, the canal system is heavily subsidized. Coupled with the lack of regulation of groundwater use, and the subsidies to electricity which encourage over-pumping, there is little incentive for careful water management anywhere in agriculture. Successful farmer-managed irrigation schemes and water-harvesting have been put in place in some parts of the country and are showing promising results. They need to be far more widespread with enabling policies. As it is, the difficulties of proceeding with small-scale measures may give too free a rein to large-scale water projects, which this book sees as instruments of last resort.

A somewhat similar analysis applies to urban water. There are few incentives to conserve water, and great inequalities in use, with the better-off households receiving ample water at no cost, while the poor have limited supplies, for which they often have to pay. Municipal authorities are reluctant to deal with the real issues, which require pricing and regulation. They frequently concentrate instead on increasing supplies, possibly requiring large works which again will not be funded by consumers, adding to deficit problems.

The costs of needed public investment in water have been estimated at modest percentages of GDP. Of course, if one adds all these 'needed investment' figures together over the whole range of policies discussed here they come to substantial amounts. But as with the investments discussed earlier in this chapter, they have high returns, and the costs of not undertaking them will be very considerable in human and political terms, as well as in productivity. As has been repeatedly pointed out, large savings may be made by removing misguided subsidies and programmes which do not reach their intended beneficiaries. India will have to afford the water investments that the present and the future require.

The country will be forced to address its problems as shortages mount and conflicts grow between competing users. Resolving these issues while protecting the poor is perhaps the greatest challenge India faces from its growing population. It may become impossible to match supply with unfettered demand, and changes in lifestyles and demand management will have to be faced as solutions to what is already a difficult situation, one that will only become more difficult.

COMMON POOL RESOURCES

CPRs constitute roughly 15 per cent of the total land area, but there are varia-tions at the state level. These resources are subject to the multiple, competing demands of diverse stakeholders. They have traditionally been seen as pro-viding safety nets for the rural poor. They also have important functions as sustainable sources of rural livelihoods and as providers of ecological services, which are going to become increasingly important in India. There are differ-ential pressures on these resources due to growing populations and a high incidence of poverty. Our analysis suggests that Rajasthan, Madhya Pradesh, Bihar, and Uttar Pradesh are likely to experience severe pressures, while the demands from these sources are likely to be low in Andhra Pradesh, Kerala, and Punjab. This implies that strategies to deal with CPRs need to be sensitive to state-level variations: the adoption of a single strategy for the entire country is inappropriate.

Stakeholders with interests in CPRs range from poor rural households to large corporate enterprises. Policy in this sector must attempt to reconcile the diverse objectives of these stakeholders, while recognizing that they are endowed with differential power and political influence. Private sector companies press for land use rights for mining or for a role in regenerating degraded land. Public sector agencies may not wish to see their role in natural resource management diluted. There can also be differences of interest between local users of CPRs and people further off who depend on ecological services, in water for example, that the local users may affect. Whatever the roles of markets and NGOs and user groups, there remains an indispensable role for government to reconcile these competing claims.

Under strategies towards CPRs over the last decade there have been attempts to decentralize control to local users. Some have enjoyed notable success, in schemes such as Joint Forest Management and Integrated Watershed Development. Rural governance has been restructured with the Panchayati Raj Act, and its extension to scheduled areas, both of which give much greater control to village communities over their natural resources. While these policy initiatives would be steps in the right direction, they are long overdue, and their wider effectiveness depends on a more substantive political decentralization of the polity, which is much more difficult. Rural society in many parts of India is still hierarchical and non-participatory, and initiatives in the CPR sector have to be considered in this wider social and political context.

What appears to present additional challenges to the current agenda of reform in this sector is the emergence of a number of new demands on CPRs. While conflict has historically revolved around the competing claims of the state, rural users and industry, ecological concerns and growing influences from the global economy and civil society mean that the context for CPR policy has become far more complex. Issues of governance and collaboration— between the centre, states, and local communities, as well as international agencies—are going to continue to dominate the political debate.

References

Acharya, P. (2002), 'Education: Panchayat and Decentralization. Myth and Reality', *Economic and Political Weekly*, Vol. 37 No. 8, pp. 788–96.

Acharya, S. (2002a), 'India's Medium-Term Growth Prospects', *Economic and Political Weekly*, Vol. 37 No. 28, pp. 2897–906.

_____ (2002b), 'Macroeconomic Management in the Nineties', *Economic and Political Weekly*, Vol. 37 No. 16, pp. 1515–38.

Agarwal, A. (1999), *Engines of the Devil—Why Dieselisation of the Private Automobile Fleet Should be Banned—The Case of Delhi*, New Delhi: CSE.

_____ (1998), 'False Predictions', *Down to Earth*, Vol. 7 No. 1.

_____ (1996a), 'Pay-Offs to Progress', *Down To Earth*, Vol. 5 No. 10, pp. 31–9.

_____ (1996b), *Slow Murder: The Deadly Story of Vehicular Pollution in India*, New Delhi: CSE.

Agrawal, A. N., H. O. Varma, and R. C. Gupta (1993), *India: Economic Information Yearbook, 1992–3*, New Delhi: National Publishing House.

Agrawal, P. K. (2002), 'Emerging Obesity in Northern Indian States: A Serious Threat for Health', Paper presented at the International Union for the Scientific Study of Population (IUSSP) Regional Population Conference on Southeast Asia's Population in a Changing Asian Context, Bangkok, 10–13 June.

Agricultural Census (2002), 'Distribution of Operational Holdings: All India', Agricultural Census Division, Ministry of Agriculture. New Delhi: Available at http://agricoop.nic.in/statistics/hold1.htm.

Agricultural Statistics of India (2002), 'Distribution of Agricultural Land by Different Usages in India from 1950–51 to 1997–98', Agricultural Statistics at a Glance, Ministry of Agriculture. Available at http://agricoop.nic.in/statistics/land1.htm.

Ahluwalia, M.S. (2002), 'State-Level Performance Under Economic Reforms in India', in A. O. Krueger, (ed.), *Economic Policy Reforms and the Indian Economy*, Chicago: University of Chicago Press, pp. 91–122.

_____ (2000), 'Economic Performance of States in Post-Reforms Period', *Economic and Political Weekly*, Vol. 35 No. 19, pp. 1637–48.

_____ (1978), 'Rural Poverty and Agricultural Performance in India', *Journal of Development Studies*, Vol. 14 No. 3, pp. 298–323.

Ahmed, K. (1994), 'Renewable Energy: A Review of the Status and Costs of Selected Technologies', *World Bank Technical Paper*, No. 240, *Energy Series*, Washington, D.C.: World Bank.

Akhtar, R. and A. T. A. Learmonth (1985), 'The Resurgence of Malaria in India, 1965–76', in R. Akhtar, and A. T. A. Learmonth, (eds), *Geographical Aspects of Health and Disease in India*, New Delhi: Concept Publishing Company, pp. 107–23.

Ambirajan, S. (1976), 'Malthusian Population Theory and Indian Famine Policy in the Nineteenth Century', *Population Studies*, Vol. 30 No. 1, pp. 5–14.

Anand, S. and J. Morduch (1998), 'Poverty and the "Population Problem"' in M. Livi-Bacci, and G. De Santis, (eds), *Population and Poverty in the Developing World*, Oxford: Clarendon Press, pp. 9–24.

Anand, S. and A. V. Shekdar (1999), *Solid Waste Management in Delhi, India* (mimeo), Nagpur: National Environmental Engineering Research Institute.

Anderson, D. (2002), 'Modelling the Environment', India Project Working Paper, Department of Social Policy, London School of Economics.

_____ (2001), 'Technical Progress and Pollution Abatement—An Economic View of Selected Technologies and Practices', *Environment and Development Economics*, Vol. 6 No. 3, pp. 283–311.

Anderson, D. and W. Cavendish (1994), 'Efficiency and Substitution in Pollution Abatement: Three Case Studies', *World Bank Discussion Paper*, No. 186, Washington, D.C.: World Bank.

_____ (2001), 'Dynamic Simulation and Environmental Policy Analysis: Beyond Comparative Statics and the Environmental Kuznets Curve', *Oxford Economic Papers*, 53: 721–46.

Andreadakis, A. (1996), 'Pretreatment of Industrial Wastewaters II: Proceedings of an International Conference on Wastewater Treatment (Athens)', *Water Science and Technology*, Vol. 36, pp. 2–3.

Angrist, Joshua D. and V. Lavy (1999), 'Using Maimonides' Rule to Estimate the Effect of Class Size on Scholastic Achievement', *Quarterly Journal of Economics*, Vol. 114 No. 2, pp. 533–75.

Appleton, S., J. Hoddinott, and J. Knight (1996), 'Primary Education as an Input into Post-Primary Education: A Neglected Benefit', *Oxford Bulletin of Economics and Statistics*, Vol. 58 No. 1, pp. 211–9.

ApSimon, H. M., D. Pearce, and E. Ozdemiroglu (1997), *Acid Rain in Europe: Counting the Cost*, London: Earthscan.

Archer, M. and R. Hill (2001), *Clean Energy from Photovoltaics*, London: Imperial College Press.

Arnold, F. and T. K. Roy (2002), 'Sex Ratios and Sex-selective Abortions in India: Findings from the 1998–9 National Family Health Survey', Paper presented at the Workshop on Sex Ratio of India's Population, held at the International Institute for Population Sciences, Mumbai, 10–11 January.

Arora, A. and S. Athreye (2001), 'The Software Industry and India's Economic Development', *World Institute for Development Economics Research (WIDER)*

Discussion Paper, No. 2001/20. Helsinki: United Nations University/World Institute for Development Economics Research (UNU/WIDER).

Asthana, M.D. (2002), 'Projection of Employment Generation in Agriculture and Allied Sector of India in 10th Five Year Plan Period', Paper presented at the Workshop on India's Future: Population, Environment, and Human Development, New Delhi, January.

——— (2001), 'Introduction', in M. D. Asthana, and P. Medrano, (eds), *Towards Hunger Free India*, New Delhi: Manohar Publications.

Baddeley, M., K. McNay, and R. H. Cassen (2003), 'Divergence in India: Economic Growth at the State Level, 1990–7', *Wellcome Project Working Paper*, London: London School of Economics.

Bajpai, N. (2001), 'Sustaining High Rates of Economic Growth in India', *Center for International Development (CID) Working Paper*, No. 65. Cambridge, Mass.: CID, Harvard University.

Bajpai, N. and J. D. Sachs (1999), 'The Progress of Policy Reform and Variations in Performance at the Sub-National Level in India', *Harvard Institute of International Development (HIID) Development Discussion Paper*, No. 730. Cambridge, Mass.: HIID, Harvard University.

Bandyopadhyay, J. (2002), 'A Critical Look at the WCD Report in the Context of the Debate on Large Dams on the Himalayan Rivers', *International Journal of Water Resource Development*, Vol. 18 No. 1, pp. 127–45.

Banerji, A. (2002), 'Top Indian Incomes', Paper presented to the World Bank Workshop on Poverty Estimates, New Delhi, January.

Bansil, P. C. (1999), *Demand for Foodgrains by 2020 AD*, New Delhi: Observer Research Foundation.

Banthia, J. and T. Dyson (2000), 'Smallpox and the Impact of Vaccination Among the Parsees of Bombay', *The Indian Economic and Social History Review*, Vol. 37 No. 1, pp. 27–51.

——— (1999), 'Smallpox in Nineteenth Century India', *Population and Development Review*, Vol. 25 No. 4, pp. 649–80.

Basu, A. M. (1992), *Culture, the Status of Women and Demographic Behaviour*, Oxford: Clarendon Press.

——— (1986), 'Birth Control by Assetless Workers in Kerala: The Possibility of a Poverty Induced Population Transition', *Development and Change*, Vol. 17 No. 2, pp. 265–82.

Bates, R. M. and E. A. Moore (1992), 'Commercial Energy and the Environment', Policy Research Working Paper, World Bank, Energy Policy Research Division, Washington, D.C.

Baviskar, A. (1995), *In the Belly of the River: Tribal Conflicts over Development in the Narmada Valley*, New Delhi: Oxford University Press.

Beck, T. and M. G. Ghosh (2000), 'Common Property Resources and the Poor: Findings from West Bengal', *Economic and Political Weekly*, Vol. 35 No. 3, pp. 147–53.

Becker, C. M., J. G. Williamson, and E. S. Mills (1992), *Indian Urbanization and Economic Growth Since 1960*, Baltimore and London: Johns Hopkins Press.

Beckerman, W. 1992, 'Economic Growth and the Environment: Whose Growth? Whose Environment?', *World Development*, Vol. 20 No. 4, pp. 481–97.

Benabou, R. (1994), 'Human Capital, Inequality, and Growth: A Local Perspective', *European Economic Review*, Vol. 38 No. 4, pp. 817–26.

Besley, T. and R. Burgess (2002), 'Can Labour Regulation Hinder Economic Performance? Evidence from India', *Suntory and Toyota International Centres for Economics and Related Disciplines (STICERD), Development Economics Research Programme (DEDSP) Paper*, No. 33, London: London School of Economics.

Bhalla, G. S. (2001), 'Political Economy of Indian Development in the 20th Century: India's Road to Freedom and Growth', *Indian Economic Journal*, Vol. 48 No. 3, pp. 1–23.

Bhalla, G. S. and P. Hazell (1997), 'Foodgrains demand in India to 2020', *Economic and Political Weekly*, Vol. 32 No. 52, pp. A150–A154.

Bhalla, G. S., P. Hazell, and J. Kerr (1999), Prospects for India's Cereal Supply and Demand to 2020, *Food, Agriculture and the Environment, Discussion Paper 29*, Washington. D.C.: International Food Policy Research Institute.

Bhalla, S. (2001), 'Assessing the Quality of Employment Growth Using National Sample Survey Data', Paper presented at the NSSO Golden Jubilee Seminar on Understanding Human Development through National Surveys, Gokhale Institute of Economics, Pune, 6–7 April 2001.

Bhalotra, S. (2002), 'The Impact of Economic Liberalisation on Employmentand Wages in India', Geneva: International Policy Group, International Labour Office.

_____ (1998), 'The Puzzle of Jobless Growth in Indian Manufacturing', *Oxford Bulletin of Economics and Statistics*, Vol. 40 No. 1, pp. 5–32.

Bhat, Mari P. N. (2002a), 'India's Changing Dates with Replacement Fertility: A Review of Recent Fertility Trends and Future Prospects', in United Nations, *Completing the Fertility Transition*, Report No. ESA/P/WP.172/REV./. New York: United Nations Population Division, 376–91.

_____ (2002b). 'Returning a Favour: Reciprocity Between Female Education and Fertility in India', *World Development*, Vol. 30, No. 10, pp. 1791–1803.

_____ (2001a), 'Indian Demographic Scenario, 2025'. Discussion Paper Series N. 27, Delhi: Institute of Economic Growth.

_____ (2001b), 'Generalised Growth-Balance Method as an Integrated Procedure for Evaluation of Completeness of Censuses and Registration Systems, A Case Study of India, 1971–1991', typescript, Delhi: Institute of Economic Growth.

_____ (2001c), 'A Demographic Bonus for India? On the First Consequence of Population Ageing', Address to the Population Research Centre, University of Groningen, Netherlands, 22 November 2001.

_____ (1998), 'Demographic Estimates for Post-Independence India: A New Integration', *Demography India*, Vol. 27 No. 1, pp. 23–57.

_____ (1996), 'Contours of Fertility Decline in India: A District Level Study Based on the 1991 Census', in K. Srinivasan, (ed.), *Population Policy and Reproductive Health*, New Delhi: Hindustan Publishers, pp. 96–177.

_____ (1989), 'Mortality and Fertility in India, 1881–1980' in T. Dyson, (ed.), *India's Historical Demography*, London: Curzon Press, pp. 73–118.

Bhat, Mari P. N. and S. I. Rajan (1990), 'Demographic Transition in Kerala Revisited', *Economic and Political Weekly*, Vol. 25 Nos. 35–6, pp. 1957–80.

Bhat, Mari P. N. and F. Zavier (1999), 'Findings of National Family Health Survey, Regional Analysis', *Economic and Political Weekly*, Vol. 34 Nos. 42–3, pp. 3008–33.

Bhat, Mari P. N., K., Navaneetham, and S. I. Rajan (1995), 'Maternal Mortality in India: Estimates from a Regression Model', *Studies in Family Planning*, Vol. 26 No. 4, pp. 217–32.

Bhat, Mari P. N., S. H. Preston, and T. Dyson (1984), *Vital Rates in India, 1961–1981*, Committee on Population and Demography, Report No. 24, Washington, D.C.: National Academy Press.

Bhatia, B. (1992), 'Lush Fields and Parched Throats: The Political Economy of Groundwater in Gujarat', Working Paper No. 100, Helsinki: World Institute for Development Economics Research.

Bhattacharya, D. (1989), 'Trends of Population in the Indian Sub-continent: C2001 BC–2001 AD', in S. N. Singh, M. K. Premi, P. S. Bhatia, and A. Bose, (eds), *Population Transition in India, 2.* Delhi: B. R. Publishing Corporation, pp. 347–55.

Bhattacharya, S. and U. R. Patel (2002), 'Financial Intermediation in India: A Case of Aggravated Moral Hazard?', Paper presented at the Third Annual Conference on Economic Policy Reform in India, Center for Research on Economic Development and Policy Reform, Stanford University, CA, 3–4 June.

Bhide, A. D. and B. B. Sunderesan (1984), 'Street Cleansing and Waste Storage and Collection in India', in J. R. Holmes, (ed.), *Managing Solid Wastes in Developing Countries*, Chichester: John Wiley, pp. 139–50.

————— and A. V. Shekdar (1999), 'Solid Waste Management in Delhi, India', unpublished paper, Nagpur National Environmental Research Institute.

Bhooshan, B. S. (1998), 'Kochi: The Queen of the Arabian Sea', in R. P. Misra, and K. Misra, (eds), *Million Cities of India*, New Delhi: Sustainable Development Foundation, pp. 560–82.

Birdsall, N., A. C. Kelley, and S. W. Sinding, (eds) (2001), *Population Matters: Demographic Change, Economic Growth and Poverty in the Developing World*, Oxford: Oxford University Press.

Blanchet, D. E. (1991), 'On Interpreting Observed Relationships Between Population Growth and Economic Growth: A Graphical Exposition', *Population and Development Review*, Vol. 17 No. 1, pp. 105–14.

Bloom, D. E, and D. Canning (2001), 'Cumulative Causality, Economic Growth, and the Demographic Transition', in N. Birdsall, A. C. Kelley, and S. W. Sinding, (eds), *Population Matters: Demographic Change, Economic Growth, and Poverty in the Developing World*, Oxford: Oxford University Press.

—————, D. Canning, and P. N. Malaney (2000), 'Demographic Change and Economic Growth in Asia', *Population and Development Review*, Vol. 26 Supplement, pp. 257–90.

————— and P. Godwin, (eds), (1997). *The Economics of HIV and AIDS: The Case of South and South East Asia*, New Delhi: Oxford University Press.

————— and J. G. Williamson (1997). 'Demographic Change and Human Resource Development', in Asian Development Bank, (ed.), *Emerging Asia*, Manila: Asian Development Bank, pp. 141–97.

Bongaarts, J. (1978), 'A Framework for Analyzing the Proximate Determinants of Fertility', *Population and Development Review*, Vol. 4 No. 1, pp. 105–32.

Booth, B. E., M. M. Verma, and R. S. Beri (1994), 'Fetal Sex Determination in Infants in Punjab, India: Correlations and Implications', *British Medical Journal*, 309, pp. 1259–61.

Bose, A. (1980), *India's Urbanization 1901–2001*, New Delhi: Tata McGraw Hill.

Bose, R. K. (1998), 'Automotive Energy Use and Emissions Control: A Simulation

Model to Analyse Transport Strategies for Indian Metropolises', *Energy Policy,* Vol. 26 No. 13, pp. 1001–16.

Bose, R. K., S. Sundar, and K. S. Nesamani (2001), *Clearing the Air—Better Vehicles, Better Fuels,* New Delhi: Tata Energy Research Institute.

Boserup, E. (1981), *Population and Technological Change: A Study of Long-Term Trends.* Chicago, Ill.: University of Chicago Press.

―――― (1965), *The Conditions of Agricultural Growth: The Economics of Agrarian Change Under Population Pressure,* Chicago, Ill.: Aldine Press.

Brandon, C., K. Hommann, N. M. Kishor (1995), 'The Cost of Inaction: Valuing the Economy-Wide Cost of Environmental Degradation in India,' Paper presented at the UNU Conference on the Sustainable Future of the Global System, United Nations University/Institute of Advanced Studies, National Institute of Environmental Studies, Tokyo, Japan.

Buch, M. N. (1993), *Environmental Consciousness and Urban Planning,* New Delhi: Orient Longman.

Cairncross, S. (1990), 'Water Supply and the Urban Poor' in S. Cairncross, J. Hardoy, and D. Satterthwaite, (eds), *The Poor Die Young,* London: Earthscan Publications, pp. 109–26.

Caldwell, J. C. (1998), 'Malthus and the Less Developed World: The Pivotal Role of India', *Population and Development Review,* Vol. 24 No. 4, pp. 675–96.

Caldwell, J. C., P. H. Reddy, and P. Caldwell (1985), 'Educational Transition in Rural South India', *Population and Development Review,* Vol. 11 No. 1, pp. 29–51.

―――― (1983), 'The Social Component of Mortality Decline: An Investigation in South India Employing Alternative Methodologies', *Population Studies,* Vol. 37 No. 2, pp. 185–205.

―――― (1982), 'The Causes of Demographic Change in South India: A Micro Approach', *Population and Development Review,* Vol. 8 No. 4, pp. 689–724.

Case, A. and A. Deaton (1999), 'School Inputs and Educational Outcomes', *Quarterly Journal of Economics,* Vol. 114 No. 3, pp. 1047–894.

Cassen, R. H. (2002), 'Well-being in the 1990s: Towards a Balance Sheet', *Economic and Political Weekly,* Vol. 37 No. 27, pp. 2789–94.

―――― (1978), *India, Population, Economy, Society,* London and Basingstoke: Macmillan.

―――― (1976), 'Population and Development: A Survey', *World Development* Vol. 4 No. 10 and 11, pp. 785–830.

Cassen, R. H. and V. Joshi, (eds), (1995), *India: The Future of Economic Reform,* Oxford and Delhi: Oxford University Press.

Cayton, H., N. Graham, and J. Warner (2002), *Dementia* (2nd edition), London: Class Publishing.

Central Pollution Control Board (CPCB) (2000a), *Status of Solid Waste in Metrocities,* New Delhi: CPCB, Ministry of Environment and Forests.

―――― (2000b), *Status of Solid Waste Generation, Collection, Treatment, and Disposal in Class I Cities,* New Delhi: CPCB, Ministry of Environment and Forests.

―――― (2000c), *Status of Solid Waste Generation, Collection, Treatment, and Disposal in Class II Towns,* New Delhi: CPCB, Ministry of Environment and Forests.

―――― (2000d), *Status of Water Supply and Wastewater Generation, Collection, Treatment, and Disposal in Class I Cities,* New Delhi: CPCB, Ministry of Environment and Forests.

_____ (2000e), *Status of Water and Wastewater Generation, Collection, Treatment, and Disposal in Class II Towns,* New Delhi: CPCB, Ministry of Environment and Forests.

_____ (2000f), *Air Quality Status and Trends in India,* New Delhi: CPCB, Ministry of Environment and Forests.

_____ (1999), 'Auto Emissions' in *Parivesh* Vol. 6 No. 1, New Delhi: CPCB, Ministry of Environment and Forests, p. 4.

_____ (1997), *Status of Water Supply and Wastewater Generation, Collection, Treatment and Disposal in Metrocities* (1994–5), New Delhi, CPCB, Ministry of Environment and Forests.

_____ (1995), *Management of Municipal Solid Waste,* New Delhi, CPCB, Ministry of Environment and Forests.

_____ (1993), *Pollution Statistics Delhi,* New Delhi, CPCB, Ministry of Environment and Forests.

Centre for Policy Research (2001), *The Future of Urbanisation,* New Delhi: Centre for Policy Research.

Centre for Science and Environment (CSE) (2002), 'Back-pedalling on Norms', *Down to Earth,* CSE, 31 January, Vol. 10 No. 17, p. 6.

_____ (2001), *The Smokescreen of Lies—Myths and Facts about CNG,* New Delhi: CSE.

_____ (1999a) *Citizen's Fifth Report—Part I, National Overview,* New Delhi: CSE.

_____ (1999b), 'Polluted and Ignored, *Down to Earth,* Vol. 8 No. 11, pp. 38–42.

_____ (1999c), *State of India's Environment: The Citizens' Fifth Report, Part II, Statistical Tables,* New Delhi: CSE.

_____ (1999d), *Engines of the Devil—Why Dieselisation of the Private Automobile Fleet Should be Banned—The Case of Delhi,* New Delhi: CSE.

_____ (1996), *Slow Murder: The Deadly Story of Vehicular Pollution in India,* New Delhi: CSE.

_____ (1985), *The Citizens' Second Report—State of India's Environment,* New Delhi: CSE.

Chadha, G. K. and P. P. Sahu (2002), 'Post-Reform Setbacks in Rural Employment: Issues that Need Further Scrutiny', *Economic and Political Weekly,* Vol. 37 No. 21, pp. 1998–2026.

Chapman, G. P. and M. Thompson (eds) (1995), *Water and the Quest for Sustainable Development in the Ganges Valley,* London: Mansell Publishing.

Chapman, G. P. and P. Pathak (2000), 'Indian Urbanisation and the Characteristics of Large Indian Cities Revealed in the 1991 Census', in C. Z. Guilmoto and A. Vaguet, (eds), *Essays on Population and Space in India,* Pondicherry: French Institute of Pondicherry, pp. 97–116.

Chatterjee, M. (1990), 'A Report on Indian Women from Birth to Twenty', New Delhi: National Institute of Public Cooperation and Child Development.

Chaudhuri, S. (2002), 'Economic Reforms and Industrial Structure in India', *Economic and Political Weekly,* Vol. 37 No. 2, pp. 155–62.

Chelliah, R. J. and R. Sudarshan (eds) (1999), *Income Poverty and Beyond: Human Development in India,* New Delhi: Social Science Press.

Chen, B. H., C. J. Hong, M. R. Pandey, and K. R. Smith (1990), 'Indoor Air Pollution in Developing Countries', *World Health Statistics Quarterly,* Vol. 43 No. 3, pp. 127–37.

Chopra, K. and B. Goldar (2000), *Sustainable Development Framework for India: The*

Case of Water Resources (mimeo), Final report for the United Nations University, 'Tokyo Project on Sustainable Development Framework for India', Delhi: Institute of Economic Growth.

Chopra, K., B. Goldar and S. C. Gulati (2001), *Migration, Common Property Resources and Environmental Degradation: Interlinkages in India's Arid and Semi-Arid Regions*, New Delhi: Sage.

Chopra, K., and S. C. Gulati (2001), *Migration, Common Property Resources and Environmental Degradation: Inter-linkages in India's Arid and Semi-Arid Regions*, New Delhi: Sage Publications.

Chua, S. (1999), 'Economic Growth, Liberalization and the Environment: A Review of Economic Evidence', *Annual Review of Energy and the Environment,* Vol. 24 No. 1, pp. 391–430.

Claeson, M., E. Bos, and I. Pathmanathan (1999), 'Reducing Child Mortality in India, Keep up the Pace', Health Nutrition and Population (HNP) discussion paper, Washington, D.C.: World Bank.

Coale, A. J. and E. M. Hoover (1958), *Population Growth and Economic Development in Low-Income Countries*, Princeton, NJ: Princeton University Press.

Cohen, J. (1995), *How Many People can the Earth Support?* London and New York: W. W. Norton.

Commander, S. (1989), 'The Mechanics of Demographic and Economic Growth in Uttar Pradesh; 1800–1900', in T. Dyson (ed.), *India's Historical Demography*, London: Curzon Press, pp. 49–72.

Cropper, M. L., N.B. Simon, A. Alberini, and P. K. Sharma (1997), 'The Health Benefits of Air Pollution Control in Delhi', in *American Journal of Agricultural Economics,* Vol. 79 No. 5, pp. 1625–9.

Crow, B. (1995), *Sharing the Ganges: The Politics and Technology of River Development*, New Delhi: Sage.

Dargay, J. and D. Gately (1995), 'The Response of World Energy and Oil Demand to Income Growth and Changes in Oil Prices', *Annual Review of Energy and the Environment,* Vol. 20 No. 1, pp. 145–78.

Das, N. P. and D. Dey (2000), 'Demographic Transition in Gujarat', Dr D. T. Lakdawala Memorial Trust Occasional Paper Series No. 2, Ahmedabad: Lakdawala Memorial Trust.

Das Gupta, M. (1995), 'Fertility Decline in Punjab, India: Parallels with Historical Europe', *Population Studies,* Vol. 49 No. 3, pp. 481–500.

Das Gupta, M. and P. N. Mari Bhat (1998), 'Intensified Gender Bias in India: A Consequence of Fertility Decline', in M. Krishnaraj, R. M. Sudarshan, and A. Shariff, (eds), *Gender, Population and Development.* New Delhi: Oxford University Press, pp. 73–93.

———— (1997), 'Fertility Decline and Increased Manifestation of Sex Bias in India', *Population Studies,* Vol. 51 No. 3, pp. 307–15.

Dasgupta, S., B. Laplante, H. Wang, and D. Wheeler (2002), 'Confronting the Environmental Kuznets Curve', *Journal of Economic Perspectives,* Vol. 16 No. 1, Winter: pp. 147–68.

Datt, G. and M. Ravallion (2002), 'Is India's Economic Growth Leaving the Poor Behind?', Paper presented to the World Bank Workshop on Poverty Estimates, New Delhi, January.

———— (1998), 'Why Have Some Indian States Done Better Than Others in Reducing Poverty?', *Economica*, Vol. 65 No. 257, pp. 17–38.

Davis, K. (1951), *The Population of India and Pakistan*, Princeton: Princeton University Press.

Deaton, A. (2001), 'Adjusted Indian Poverty Estimates for 1999–2000', *Research Program in Development Studies (RPDS) Working Paper*, No. 209, Princeton NJ: RPDS, Woodrow Wilson School, Princeton University.

Deaton, A. and J. P. Drèze, (2002). 'Poverty and Inequality in India: A Reexamination'. *RPDS Working Paper*, No. 215, Princeton NJ: RPDS, Woodrow Wilson School, Princeton University.

Department of Family Welfare (2000), *National Population Policy 2000*, New Delhi: Department of Family Welfare, Government of India.

Desai, M. (1995), 'Poverty and Capability: Towards an Empirically Implementable Measure', in M. Desai, (ed.), *Poverty, Famine and Economic Development: The Selected Essays of Meghnad Desai*, Vol. 2, Cheltenham: Edward Elgar.

Dev, M. (2000), 'Economic Liberalisation and Employment in South Asia', *Center for Development Research (ZEF) Discussion Paper on Development Policy*, No. 29, Bonn: Center for Development Research (ZEF), University of Bonn.

Devi, R. S. and S. Das (1999), 'Environmental Factors of Malaria Persistence: A Study of Valiyathura, Thiruvananthapuram City', Kerala Research Programme on Local Level Development, Discussion Paper Series, Trivandrum: Centre for Development Studies.

Dewees, P. (1989), 'The Woodfuel Crisis Reconsidered: Observations on the Dynamics of Abundance and Scarcity', *World Development*, Vol. 17 No. 8, pp. 1159–72.

Dholakia, R. (1997), *The Potential Economic Benefits of the DOTS Strategy Against TB in India*, TB Research Series, Geneva: World Health Organization.

Dopico, F. (1987), 'Regional Mortality Tables for Spain in the 1860s', *Historical Methods*, Vol. 20 No. 4, pp. 173–80.

Drèze, J. (1990), 'Famine Prevention in India', in J. Drèze and A. Sen, (eds), *The Political Economy of Hunger, Volume 2, Famine Prevention*, Oxford: Clarendon Press, pp. 13–122.

———— (1988), *Famine Prevention in India*, Discussion Paper No. 3, Development Economics Research Programme, London: London School of Economics.

Drèze, J. and M. Murthi (2001), 'Fertility, Education, and Development: Evidence from India', *Population and Development Review*, Vol. 27 No. 1, pp. 33–63.

Drèze, J. and H. Gazdar, (1997), 'Uttar Pradesh: The Burden of Inertia', in J. Drèze, and A. Sen, (eds), *Indian Development: Selected Regional Perspectives*, Oxford and Delhi: Oxford University Press, pp. 22–128.

Drèze, J. and G. Kingdon (2001), 'School Participation in Rural India', *Review of Development Economics*, Vol. 5 No. 1, pp. 1–24.

Drèze, J. and A. Sen (2002), *India: Development and Participation*, Oxford and Delhi: Oxford University Press.

Drèze, J. and P. V. Srinivasan, (1995), 'Widowhood and Poverty in Rural India: Some Inferences from Household Survey Data', *London School of Economics/Suntory Toyota Development Economics Research Programme Working Paper*, No. 62, London: London School of Economics.

Duraisamy, P. (2000), 'Changes in Returns to Education in India, 1983–94: by Gender, Age-Cohort, and Location', *Center Discussion Paper*, No. 815, New Haven, Conn.: Economic Growth Center, Yale University.

Durand, J. D. (1977), 'On the Populousness of Ancient Nations', *Population and Development Review*, Vol. 3 No. 3, pp. 253–96.

Dyson, T (2002a), 'On the Future of Human Fertility in India', in *United Nations Expert Group Meeting on Completing the Fertility Transition* (ESA/P/WP.172). New York: United Nations Population Division, CP.6–3—CP. 6–21.

—————— (2002b). 'New Population Projections for India', India Project Working Paper, Department of Social Policy, London School of Economics.

—————— (2001), 'The Preliminary Demography of the 2001 Census of India', *Population and Development Review*, Vol. 27 No. 2, pp. 341–56.

—————— (1997), 'Infant and Child Mortality in the Indian Subcontinent, 1881–1947', in A. Bideau, B. Desjardins, and H. P. Brignoli, (eds), *Infant and Child Mortality in the Past*, Oxford: Clarendon Press, pp. 109–34.

—————— (1989a). 'Indian Historical Demography: Developments and Prospects', in T. Dyson, (ed.), *India's Historical Demography*, London: Curzon Press, pp. 1–15.

—————— (1989b), 'The Historical Demography of Berar, 1881–1980', in T. Dyson (ed.), *India's Historical Demography*, London: Curzon Press, pp. 150–96.

—————— (1989c). 'The Population History of Berar Since 1881 and its Potential Wider Significance', *The Indian Economic and Social History Review*, Vol. 26 No. 2, pp. 167–201.

Dyson, T. and A. Hanchate (2002), 'Prospects for Food and Agriculture', Paper presented at the Workshop on India's Future, India International Centre, Delhi, January, 14–15.

—————— (2000), 'India's Demographic and Food Prospects, State-level Analysis', *Economic and Political Weekly*, Vol. 35 No. 46, pp. 4021 36.

Dyson, T. and A. Maharatna (1991), 'Excess Mortality During the Great Bengal Famine: A Re-evaluation', *The Indian Economic and Social History Review*, Vol. 28 No. 3, pp. 281–97.

Dyson T., and M. Moore, (1983), 'On Kinship Structure, Female Autonomy and Demographic Behaviour in India', *Population and Development Review*, Vol. 9 No. 1, pp. 35–75.

Dyson T., and P. Visaria (2002), 'Migration and Urbanisation: Retrospect and Prospects', Paper presented at the Workshop on India's Future, India International Centre, Delhi: January 14–15.

Easterly, W. (2001), *The Elusive Quest for Growth: Economists' Adventures and Misadventures in the Tropics*, Cambridge, Mass.: Massachusetts Institute of Technology Press.

Eastwood, R., and M. Lipton (2001), 'Demographic Transition and Poverty: Effects Via Economic Growth, Distribution and Conversion', in N. Birdsall, A. C. Kelley, and S. W. Sinding, (eds), *Population Matters: Demographic Change, Economic Growth and Poverty in the Developing World*, Oxford: Oxford University Press, pp. 213–59.

Eberstadt, N. (1981), 'Recent Fertility Declines in Less Developed Countries and What Population Planners May Learn From Them', in N. Eberstadt (ed.), *Fertility Decline in Less Developed Countries*, New York: Praeger, pp. 37–60.

Ekins, P. (1997), 'The Kuznets Curve for the Environment and Economic Growth: Examining the Evidence', *Environment and Planning Annals*, 29, pp. 805–30.

Environment Protection, Training, and Research Institute (1995), *Status of Solid Waste Disposal in Metropolis Hyderabad*, Hyderabad: EPTRI.

Eswaran, M., and A. Kotwal (1994), *Why Poverty Persists in India: An Analytical Framework for Understanding the Indian Economy*, Delhi: Oxford University Press.

Evans, L. T. (1998), 'Greater Crop Production, Whence and Whither?', in J. C. Waterlow, D. G. Armstrong, L. Fowden, and R. Riley, (eds), *Feeding a World Population of More than Eight Billion People*, New York: Oxford University Press, p. 89–97.

Evenson, R. E. (1993), 'India: Population Pressure, Technology, Infrastructure, Capital Formation and Rural Incomes', in C. L. Jolly, and B. B. Torrey, (eds), *Population and Land Use in Developing Countries: Report of a Workshop*, Washington D.C.: National Academy Press, pp. 70–97.

Evenson, R. E., C. E. Pray, and M. W. Rosegrant, (1999), 'Agricultural Research and Productivity Growth in India', Research Report 109, Washington, D.C.: International Food Policy Research Institute.

Expert Group on Indian Railways (2001), *The Indian Railways Report 2001: Policy Imperatives for Reinvention and Growth*, New Delhi: National Council of Applied Economic Research (NCAER).

Expert Group on the Commercialisation of Infrastructure Projects (EGCIP) (1996), The India Infrastructure Report, Vol. 1, New Delhi: EGCIP, Ministry of Finance, Government of India.

Fan, S., P. Hazell, and S. Thorat (1999), 'Linkages Between Government Spending, Growth, and Poverty in Rural India', *Research Report*, No. 110, Washington, D.C.: IFPRI.

Fertilizer Association of India (1998), *Fertilizer Statistics*, New Delhi: The Fertilizer Association of India.

Filmer, D., E. M. King, and L. Pritchett (1998), 'Gender Disparity in South Asia: Comparison Between and Within Countries', Policy Research Working Paper 1867, Washington, D.C.: World Bank.

Food and Agriculture Organization (FAO) (2000a), *FAOSTAT*, Rome: FAO.

_____ (2000b). *Food Balance Sheets*. Rome: FAO.

_____ (2000c). *Nutrition Country Profiles, India*. Rome<http://www.fao.org/WAICENT/FAOINFO/ECONOMICS/ESN/ncp/ind-e.htm>

_____ (1987), *World Crop and Livestock Statistics*, pp. 1948–85, Rome: FAO, <http://www.fao.org>

Fuller, B. (1986), 'Raising School Quality in Developing Countries: What Investments Boost Learning?', *World Bank Discussion Paper*, No. 2, Washington, D.C.: World Bank.

Gaiha, R. (1988), 'On Measuring the Risk of Rural Poverty in India', in T. N. Srinivasan, and P. K. Bardhan, (eds), *Rural Poverty in South Asia*, Oxford: Oxford University Press, pp. 219–61.

Galloway, P. (1986), 'Long-Term Fluctuations in Climate and Population in the Preindustrial Era', *Population and Development Review*, Vol. 12 No. 1, pp. 1–24.

Ganatra, B., S. Hirve, and V. N. Rao (2001), 'Sex-selective Abortion: Evidence from a Community-based study in Western India', *Asia-Pacific Population Journal*, Vol. 16 No. 2, pp. 109–24.

Gandy, M. (1997). 'The Making of a Regulatory Crisis: Restructuring New York City's Water Supply,' *Transactions of the Institute of British Geographers*, Vol. 22 No. 3, pp. 338–58.

Geddes, A. (1947), 'The Social and Psychological Significance of Variability in Population Change', *Human Relations*, 1, Vol. 1 No. 1, pp. 181–205.

George, S. and R. S. Dahiya (1998), 'Female Foeticide in Rural Haryana', *Economic and Political Weekly*, Vol. 33 No. 12, pp. 2191–8.

Ghose, A. K. (1999), 'Current Issues of Employment Policy in India', *Economic and Political Weekly*, Vol. 34 No. 36, pp. 2592–608.

Ghosh, A. and S. S. Ahmad (1996), *Plague in Surat—Crisis in Urban Governance*, New Delhi: Concept Publishing.

Glaister, S. and R. Layard, (eds) (1994), *Cost-Benefit Analysis*, 2nd edn., Cambridge: Cambridge University Press.

Gnaneshwar, V. (1995). 'Urban Policies in India—Paradoxes and Predicaments', *Habitat International*, Vol. 19 No. 3, pp. 293–316.

Goldar, B. N. (2000), 'Employment Growth in Organized Manufacturing Sector', *Economic and Political Weekly*, Vol. 35 No. 14, pp. 1191–5.

Goldemberg, J. (1998), 'Leapfrog Energy Technologies', *Energy Policy*, Vol. 26 No. 10, pp. 729–41.

Goswami, O., D. Dollar, A. K. Arun, S. Gantakolla, V. More, A. Mookherjee, T. Mengistae, M. Hallward-Driernier, and G. Iarossi (2002), 'Competitiveness of Indian Manufacturing: Results from a Firm-Level Survey', Paper presented at a conference organized by the Confederation of Indian Industry and the World Bank, New Delhi, January. Available at http://lnweb18.worldbank.org/sar/sa.nsf/Attachments/wbcii/$File/FACSReport.pdf

Goujon, A. (2002), 'Education Prospects in India', Vienna: Institute for Demography of the Austrian Academy of Science (unpublished paper).

Goujon, A., and K. McNay (2003), 'Projecting the Educational Composition of the Population of India: Selected State-level Perspectives', *Applied Population and Policy*, Vol. 1 No. 1, forthcoming.

Govinda, R. (ed.) (2002), *India Education Report: A Profile of Basic Education*, New Delhi: Oxford University Press.

Gray, G. (1998), 'Anti-Retrovirals and their Role in Preventing Mother to Child Transmission of HIV-1', in *The Implications of Anti-retroviral Treatments*, Geneva: World Health Organization.

Griffiths, P., Z. Matthews, and A. Hinde (2000), 'Understanding the Sex Ratio in India: A Simulation Approach', *Demography*, Vol. 37 No. 4, pp. 477–88.

Grobler, A. (1998), *Technology and Global Change*, Cambridge: Cambridge University Press.

Grubb, M. (1997), 'Technologies, Energy Systems and the Timing of CO_2 Emissions Abatement', *Energy Policy*, Vol. 25 No. 2, pp. 159–72.

Guhan, S. (1995), 'Centre and States in the Reform Process', in R. Cassen, and V. Joshi, (eds), *India: The Future of Economic Reform*, Oxford and Delhi: Oxford University Press, pp. 71–111.

——— (1986), 'Rural Poverty Alleviation in India: Policy, Performance and Possibilities', in S. Subramanian, (ed.) (2001), *India's Development Experience: Selected Writings of S. Guhan*, New Delhi: Oxford University Press, pp. 15–46.

Guilmoto, C. Z. (2000), 'The Geography of Fertility in India (1981–1991)', in C. Z. Guilmoto and A. Vaguet, (eds), *Essays on Population and Space in India*, Pondicherry: French Institute of Pondicherry, pp. 37–53.

Guilmoto, C. Z. and S. I. Rajan (2001), 'Spatial Patterns of Fertility Transition in Indian Districts', *Population and Development Review*, Vol. 27 No. 4, pp. 713–38.

Gulati, A. (2002), 'Challenges to Punjab Agriculture in a Globalizing World', Policy Paper, Washington, D.C.: International Food Policy Research Institute.

Gulati, A. and S. Bathla, (2001), 'Capital Formation in Indian Agriculture: Re-visiting the Debate', *Economic and Political Weekly*, Vol. 26 No. 20, pp. 1697–708.

Gupta, I. (1998), 'Planning for the Socio-economic Impact of the Epidemic: the Cost of Being Ill', in P. Godwin, (ed.), *The Looming Epidemic: The Impact of HIV and AIDS in India*, New Delhi: Mosaic Books, pp. 94–125.

Gupta, R. and V.P. Gupta (1996), 'Meta-analysis of Coronary Heart Disease Prevalence in India', *Indian Heart Journal*, Vol. 48, pp. 241–5.

Gwatkin, D. R. (1993), 'Distributional Implications of Alternative Strategic Responses to the Demographic-Epidemiological Transition: An Initial Inquiry', in J. N. Gribble and S. H. Preston, (eds), *The Epidemiological Transition: Policy and Planning Implications for Developing Countries*, Washington D.C.: National Academy Press, pp. 197–228.

Habib, I. (1982), 'Population', in T. Raychaudhuri and I. Habib, (eds), *Cambridge Economic History of India, Volume I, c. 1200–c. 1750*, Hyderabad: Orient Longman, pp. 163–71.

Haddad, L. (2002), 'Nutrition', in International Food Policy Research Institute (IFPRI), *Sustainable Food Security for All by 2020: Proceedings of an International Conference*, Bonn, Germany, September 4–6, 2001, Washington, D.C.: IFPRI, pp. 55–9.

Hanchate, A. (2001), 'Trends in the Composition of Food Consumption and their Impact on Nutrition and Poverty in Rural India', unpublished typescript, Department of Social Policy, London School of Economics.

Hanushek, E. (1995), 'Interpreting Recent Research on Schooling in Developing Countries', *World Bank Research Observer*, Vol. 10 No. 2, pp. 227–46.

—— (1992), 'The Trade-Off Between Child Quantity and Quality', *Journal of Political Economy*, Vol. 100 No. 1, pp. 84–117.

—— (1986), 'The Economics of Schooling: Production and Efficiency in Public Schools', *Journal of Economic Literature*, Vol. 24 No. 3, pp. 1141–77.

Hardoy, J. E., D. Mitlin, and D. Satterthwaite (1992), *Environmental Problems in Third World Cities*, London: Earthscan.

Harriss, B., S. Guhan, and R. H. Cassen (eds) (1992), *Poverty in India: Research and Policy*, Bombay: Oxford University Press.

Heggade, O. D. (1998), *Urban Development in India—Problems, Policies and Programmes*, New Delhi: Mohit Publications.

Hirway, I. (2002), 'Employment and Unemployment Situation in 1990s. How Good are NSS Data?', *Economic and Political Weekly*, Vol. 37 No. 21, pp. 2027–36.

Holdren, J. P. and K. R. Smith (2000), 'Energy, the Environment and Health', in *World Energy Assessment: Energy and the Challenge of Sustainability*, New York: United Nations Development Programme and World Energy Council, pp. 61–110.

Holtz-Eakin, D. and T. Selden, (1995), 'Stoking the Fires? CO_2 Emissions and Economic Growth', *Journal of Public Economics*, Vol. 57 No. 1, pp. 85–101.

Hopper, G. R. (1999), 'Changing Food Production and Quality of Diet in India', *Population and Development Review*, Vol. 25 No. 3 pp. 443–77.

ICMR (1989), *Evaluation of the National Nutritional Anaemia Prophylaxis Programme*, New Delhi: Indian Council of Medical Research.

IIPS and ORC Macro (2000), *National Family Health Survey, India, 1998–9 (NFHS-2)*, Mumbai: International Institute for Population Sciences.

———— (1995), *National Family Health Survey (NFHS-1), 1992–3: India*, Mumbai: International Institute for Population Sciences.

India Water Partnership/Institute for Human Development (IWP/IHD) (2000), 'India Water Vision 2025: Report of the Vision Development Consultation', New Delhi: IWP/IHD.

Intergovernmental Panel on Climate Change (IPCC) (2001), *Synthesis Report*, Cambridge: Cambridge University Press.

Irudaya Rajan, S. and U.S. Mishra, (1996), 'Fertility Transition in Kerala: Implications for Educational Planning', *Productivity*, Vol. 37 No. 3, October-December, pp. 386–96.

Iyengar, S. and A. Shah (2001), 'CPR in a Rapidly Developing Economy: Perspectives from Gujarat', Paper presented at a workshop on 'Policy Implications of CPR Knowledge with Respect to Common Pool Resources in India', Delhi: Institute of Economic Growth.

Iyer, R. (2001), 'Water: Charting a Course for the Future: I', *Economic and Political Weekly*, Vol. 36 No. 13, pp. 1115–22.

Jain, A. K. (1985), 'Determinants of Variations in Infant Mortality in Rural India', *Population Studies* Vol. 39 No. 3, pp. 407–24.

Jain, A. K. and A. L. Adlakha (1982), 'Preliminary Estimates of Fertility Decline in India During the 1970s', *Population and Development Review*, Vol. 8 No. 3, pp. 589–606.

Jain, A. K., A. L. Adlakha, P. S. Satsangi, and D. P. Kothari (1995), 'Urbanization and Energy Related Problems in Indian Cities', *Energy Sources*, Vol. 16 No. 1, pp. 177–82.

Jain, L. R. and B. S. Minhas (1991), 'Rural and Urban Consumer Price Indices by Commodity Groups', *Sarvekshana*, July–September, 1–2.

Jain, M. K., M. Ghosh, and W. B. Kim (1993), *Emerging Trends of Urbanization in India: An Analysis of 1991 Census Results*, Occasional Paper, No. 1 of 1993, New Delhi: Office of the Registrar General.

Jain, N. K. (2000), *Nabhi's Compilation of Ninth Five Year Plan 1997–2002*, New Delhi: Nabhi Publications.

James, K. S. (1999), 'Fertility Decline in Andhra Pradesh: A Search for Alternative Hypotheses', *Economic and Political Weekly*, Vol. 34 No. 8, pp. 491–9.

Jeffery, P. and R. Jeffery, (1996), 'What's the Benefit of Being Educated? Women's Autonomy and Fertility Outcomes in Bijnor', in R. Jeffery and A. M. Basu, (eds), *Girls' Schooling, Women's Autonomy and Fertility Change in South Asia*, New Delhi: Sage, pp. 150–83.

Joardar, S. D. (2000), 'Urban Residential Solid Waste Management in India—Issues Related to Institutional Arrangements', *Public Works Management and Policy*, Vol. 4 No. 4, pp. 319–31.

Jodha, N. S. (1986), 'Common Property Resources and Rural Poor in Dry Regions of India', *Economic and Political Weekly*, Vol. 31 No. 27, pp. 1169–81.

Johansson, T. B., H. Kelly, A. K. N. Reddy, and R. H. Williams (1993), *Renewable Energy: Sources for Fuels and Electricity*, Washington D.C.: Island Press.

Jolly, C. L. and B. B. Torrey (1993), *Population and Land Use in Developing Countries: Report of a Workshop*, Washington D.C.: National Academy Press.

Jones-Lee, M.W. (1994), 'Safety and the Saving of Life: the Economics of Safety and Physical Risk', in S. Glaister, and R. Layard, (eds), *Cost Benefit Analysis*, Cambridge: Cambridge University Press.

Joshi, P. D. (1998), *Changing Patterns of Consumption Expenditure in India and Some Selected States*, Sarvekshana Analytical Report, No. 2. New Delhi: Ministry of Planning and Programme Implementation.

Judson, R. A., R. Schmalensee, and T. M. Stoker (1999), 'Economic Development and the Structure of the Demand for Commercial Energy', *The Energy Journal*, Vol. 20 No. 2, pp. 29–57.

Kahnert, F. and G. Levine (eds) (1993), *Groundwater Irrigation and the Rural Poor: Options for Development in the Gangetic Basin*, Washington, D.C.: World Bank.

Kandlikar, M. and G. Ramachandran (2000), 'The Causes and Consequences of Particulate Air Pollution in Urban India: A Synthesis of the Science', *Annual Review of Energy and Environment*, Vol. 25 No. 1, pp. 629–84.

Kapil, U. and R. Pradhan (2000), 'Integrated Child Development Services Scheme (ICDS) in India: Its Activities, Present Status and Future Strategy to Reduce Malnutrition', *Journal of the Indian Medical Association*, Vol. 98 No. 9, pp. 559–66.

Kelley, A. C. (1988), 'Economic Consequences of Population Change in the Third World', *Journal of Economic Literature*, Vol. 26 No. 4, pp. 1685–728.

Kelley, A. C. and R. M. Schmidt 1994, *Population and Income Change: Recent Evidence*, World Bank Discussion Paper, No. 249, Washington, D.C.: World Bank.

Kiely, G. (1997), *Environmental Engineering*, London: McGraw-Hill.

Kingdon, G. G. (2002a), *Gender-Discrimination in the Intra-Household Allocation of Educational Expenditure in Rural India* (mimeo), Department of Economics, University of Oxford.

―――― (2002b), *The Spread of Private Schooling in India* (mimeo), Department of Economics, University of Oxford.

―――― (1998), 'Does the Labour Market Explain Lower Female Schooling in India?', *Journal of Development Studies*, Vol. 35, No. 1, pp. 39–65.

―――― (1996b). 'Student Achievement and Teacher Pay: A Case-Study of India', *Discussion Paper*, No. 74, London: Development Economics Research Programme, Suntory and Toyota International Centres for Economics and Related Disciplines (STICERD), London School of Economics.

―――― (1996a), 'Private Schooling in India: Size, Nature and Equity Effects', *Economic and Political Weekly*, Vol. 31 No. 51, pp. 3306–14.

Kingdon, G. G. and J. Drèze (1998), 'Biases in Education Statistics', *The Hindu*, 6 March.

Kingdon, G. G. and M. Muzammil (eds) (2002), *Teachers, Politics and Education in India: A Political Economy Case Study of Uttar Pradesh*, Oxford: Oxford University Press.

Kingdon, G. G. and Unni, J. (2001), 'Education and Women's Labour Market Outcomes in India', *Education Economics*, Vol. 9 No. 2, pp. 173–95.

Kishor, S. (1994), 'Fertility Decline in Tamil Nadu, India', in B. Egero, and M.

Hammarskjold, (eds), *Understanding Reproductive Change: Kenya, Tamil Nadu, Punjab, Costa Rica*. Lund: Lund University Press, pp. 66–100.

Klein, I. (1972), 'Malaria and Mortality in Bengal, 1840–1921', *The Indian Economic and Social History Review*, Vol. 9 No. 2, 132–60.

Knodel, J., N. Havanon, and W. Sittitrai (1990), 'Family Size and Education of Children in the Context of Rapid Fertility Decline', *Population and Development Review*, Vol. 16 No. 1, pp. 31–62.

Kothari, A. (2002), 'Environment, Food Security and Natural Resources', *Economic and Political Weekly*, Vol. 37 No. 4, pp. 289–92.

Krishnan, P. (2001), 'Culture and the Fertility Transition in India', WIDER Discussion Paper No. 2001/7, Helsinki: United Nations University.

Krishnan, T. N. (1998), 'Social Development and Fertility Reduction in Kerala', in M. Das Gupta, G. Martine, and L. C. Chen, (eds), *Reproductive Change in India and Brazil*, Delhi: Oxford University Press, pp. 37–64.

Krishnaswamy, U. (2000), 'Can the War Against Tuberculosis be Won?', *The Hindu Magazine*, 23 April, Delhi.

Krueger, A. (1999), 'Experimental Estimates of Education Production Functions', *Quarterly Journal of Economics*, Vol. 114 No. 2, pp. 497–532.

Krueger, A. O. (ed.) (2002), *Economic Policy Reforms and the Indian Economy*, Chicago: University of Chicago Press.

Kulkarni, P. M. (2000), 'Interstate Variations in Human Development Differentials among Social Groups in India', *Working Paper*, No. 80, New Delhi: National Council of Applied Economic Research (NCAER).

Kulshreshtha, A. C. and A. Kar (2002), 'Estimates of Food Consumption Expenditure from Household Surveys and National Accounts', Paper presented at the World Bank Workshop on Poverty Estimates, Delhi, January.

Kumar, K., M. Priyam, and S. Saxena (2001a), 'Beyond the Smokescreen: DPEP and Primary Education in India', *Economic and Political Weekly*, Vol. 36 No. 7, pp. 560–8.

———— (2001b), 'The Trouble with "Para-Teachers"', *Frontline*, Vol. 18 No. 22.

Kumar, P. (1998), *Food Demand and Supply Projections for India*, Agricultural Economics Policy Paper, New Delhi: Indian Agricultural Research Institute.

Kumar, S. (2001), 'Indigenous Communities' Knowledge of Local Ecological Services', *Economic and Political Weekly*, Vol. 36 No. 30, pp. 2859–69.

Kumar, S. and N. K. Sharma (2002a), 'Workers in Census 2001. Some Pertinent Issues', *Economic and Political Weekly*, Vol. 37 No. 18, pp. 1712–3.

———— (2002b), 'Rural Non-Farm Employment: An Analysis of Rural Urban Interdependencies', (unpublished paper).

———— (2000), *Urban Development, Infrastructure, Financing and Emerging System of Governance in India: A Perspective*, MOST Discussion Paper No. 48, Paris: UNESCO.

Kundu, A. (2002), 'Rural Non-farm Employment: An Analysis of Rural–Urban Interdependencies', Unpublished paper, New Delhi, Jawaharlal Nehru University.

———— (1992), *Urban Development and Urban Research in India*, New Delhi: Khama Publishers.

———— and S. Gupta (2000), 'Declining Population Mobility, Liberalisation and Growing Regional Imbalances, the Indian Case', in A. Kundu, (ed.), *Inequality,*

Mobility and Urbanisation, New Delhi: Indian Council of Social Science Research and Manak Publications, pp. 257–74.

Kuznets, S. (1974), *Population, Capital and Growth: Selected Essays.* London: Heinemann Educational Books.

Lahiri, S. and P. Dutta (2002), 'Sex Preference and Child Mortality in Some Selected Indian States: An Analysis Based on NFHS Data During 1992–93 and 1998–99', Paper presented at the workshop on Sex Ratio of India's Population, held at the International Institute for Population Sciences, Mumbai, 10–11 January.

Lal, D., R. Mohan, and I. Natarajan (2001), 'Economic Reforms and Poverty Alleviation: A Tale of Two Surveys', *Economic and Political Weekly,* Vol. 36 No. 12, pp. 1017–28.

Lal, M. (2001), 'Climatic Change—Implications for India's Water Resources', *Journal of Social and Economic Development,* Vol. 3 No. 1, pp. 57–87.

——— (2000), 'Climate Change and its Impacts on India', *Asia-Pacific Journal of Environment and Development,* Vol. 7 No. 1, pp. 1–41.

Lanjouw, P. and A. Shariff (2002), 'Rural Non-Farm Employment in India: Access, Income and Poverty Impact', National Council of Applied Economic Research (NCAER) Working Paper, No. 81, New Delhi: NCAER.

Leach, G. (1992), 'The Energy Transition', *Energy Policy,* February, pp. 116–23.

Learmonth, A. (1988), *Disease Ecology: An Introduction,* Oxford: Basil Blackwell.

Leclercq, François (2002), *The Impact of Education Policy Reforms on the Education System: A Field Study of EGS and Other Primary Schools in Madhya Pradesh* (mimeo), Centre de Sciences Humaines, Delhi.

Lee, R. D., A. Mason, and T. Miller (2001), 'Saving, Wealth, and Population', in N. Birdsall, A. C. Kelley, and S. W. Sinding, (eds), *Population Matters. Demographic Change, Economic Growth, and Poverty in the Developing World,* Oxford: Oxford University Press.

Lewis, W. A. (1954), 'Economic Development with Unlimited Supplies of Labour', *Manchester School of Economic and Social Studies,* Vol. 22 No. 2, pp. 139–41.

Lipton, M. (2002), 'What Productive Resources do the Poor Really Need to Escape Poverty?', in *Sustainable Food Security for All by 2020,* proceedings of an International Conference of the International Food Policy Research Institute (IFPRI) in Bonn, Germany in 2001, Washington, D.C.: IFPRI, pp. 66–72.

Lloyd, C. B. (ed.) (1993), *Fertility, Family Size, and Structure: Consequences for Families and Children,* New York, NY: Population Council.

Lutz, W. and A. Goujon (2001), 'The World's Changing Human Capital Stock: Multi-State Population Projections by Educational Attainment', *Population and Development Review,* Vol. 27 No. 2, pp. 323–39.

Lutz, W. and W. Sanderson (2002), 'Population and the Environment: Methods of Analysis', *Population and Development Review,* Supplement to Vol. 28.

Maddison, D., D. Pearce, O. Johansson, E. Calthrop, T. Litman, and E. Verhoef (1996), *The True Costs of Road Transport,* Blueprint Series, No. 5, London: Earthscan Publications.

Maharatna, A. (1996), *The Demography of Famines, An Indian Historical Perspective,* Delhi: Oxford University Press.

Mathew, D. A. (2002), 'Panchayats Alone are Not to Blame', *Economic and Political Weekly,* Vol. 37 No. 18, pp. 1767–8.

McAlpin, M. B. (1983), *Subject to Famine: Food Crises and Economic Change in Western India, 1860–1920*, Princeton NJ: Princeton University Press.

McCully, P. (1996), *Silenced Rivers: The Ecology and Politics of Large Dams*. London: Zed Books.

McDonald, A. and L. Shcreattenholzer (2001), 'Learning Rates for Energy Technologies', *Energy Policy*, Vol. 29 No. 4, pp. 255–61.

McEvedy, C. and R. Jones (1978), *Atlas of World Population History*, Harmondsworth: Penguin Books, pp. 182–5.

McMichael, T. (2001), *Human Frontiers, Environments and Disease*, Cambridge: Cambridge University Press.

McNay, K., P. Arokiasamy, and R. H. Cassen (2003), 'Why are Uneducated Women in India Using Contraception? A Multilevel Analysis', *Population Studies*, Vol. 57 No. 1, pp. 21–40.

McNeill, W. H. (1977), *Plagues and Peoples*, Harmondsworth: Penguin Books.

Measham, A. R., and M. Chatterjee (1999), *Wasting Away: The Crisis of Malnutrition in India*, Washington, D.C.: World Bank.

Measham, A. R., M. Chatterjee, K. D. Rao, T. D. Jamison, and J. Wang (1999). 'Reducing Infant Mortality and Fertility, 1975–1990: Performance at all-India and State Levels', *Economic and Political Weekly* Vol. 34 No. 2, pp. 1359–67.

Mehta, L. (2001), 'The Manufacture of Popular Perceptions of Scarcity: Dams and Water-Related Narratives in Gujarat, India', *World Development*, Vol. 19 No. 12, pp. 2025–41.

—— (1998), *Context of Scarcity: The Political Ecology of Water in Kutch, India*, unpublished Ph.D. dissertation, Institute of Development Studies, University of Sussex, UK.

Mencher, J. P. (1980), 'The Lessons and Non-lessons of Kerala: Agricultural Labourers and Poverty', *Economic and Political Weekly*, Vol. 15 Nos. 41–3, pp.: 1781–802.

Metcalf and Eddy, Inc. (1991), *Wastewater Engineering: Treatment, Disposal and Reuse*, New York: McGraw-Hill.

Mills, I. (1986), 'Influenza in India during 1918–19', *The Indian Economic and Social History Review*, Vol. 23 No. 1, pp. 1–40.

Ministry of Agriculture (2002), *Agricultural Statistics at a Glance*, New Delhi: Directorate of Economics and Statistics. Available at <http://agricoop.nic.in/stats.htm>.

—— (1999), *Basic Animal Husbandry Statistics*, New Delhi: Directorate of Economics and Statistics.

—— (1997), *Indian Agricultural Statistics, Volumes I and II, All-India, State-wise, and District-wise*. New Delhi: Directorate of Economics and Statistics.

Ministry of Environment and Forests (MOEF) (1988), *National Forest Policy Resolution*, New Delhi: Government of India.

Ministry of Finance (2001), *Economic Survey 2000/01*, New Delhi: Government of India.

Ministry of Health and Family Welfare (2000a), *Annual Report, 1999–2000*, New Delhi: Government of India.

—— (2000b), *National Population Policy 2000*, New Delhi: Government of India.

Ministry of Water Resources (MWR) (2002), *National Water Policy*, New Delhi: Ministry of Water Resources, Government of India.

—— (2001), 'Letter Rejecting the Report of the World Commission on Dams', Letter

No.2/WCD/2001/DT (PR) Vol. III, 2 February 2001, New Delhi: Ministry of
Water Resources, Government of India. Available at http://genepi.louis-jean.com/
cigb/Inde.htm accessed 01 July 2002.

Mishra, V. and R. D. Retherford (1997), 'Cooking Smoke Increases the Risk of Acute
Respiratory Infection in Children', *NFHS Bulletin*, No. 8, Mumbai: International
Institute for Population Sciences.

Misra, R. P. and K. Misra (eds) (1998), *Million Cities of India—Growth Dynamics,
Internal Structure, Quality of Life and Planning Perspectives*, Vols. 1 and 2, New
Delhi: Sustainable Development Foundation.

Mitchell, D. O., M. D. Ingco, and R. C. Duncan (1997), *The World Food Outlook*,
Cambridge: Cambridge University Press.

Mohan, R. (2002), 'Small-Scale Industry Policy in India: A Critical Evaluation', in
A. O. Krueger (ed.), *Economic Policy Reforms and the Indian Economy*, Chicago:
University of Chicago Press, pp. 213–302.

Montgomery, M., A. Kouame, and R. Oliver (1995), 'The Trade-Off between Number
of Children and Child Schooling: Evidence from Cote d'Ivoire and Ghana', *Living
Standards Measurement Study (LSMS) Working Paper*, No. 112, Washington D.C.:
World Bank.

Moomaw, W. R. and G. C. Unruh (1997), 'Are Environmental Kuznets Curves
Misleading Us? The Case of CO_2 Emissions', *Environment and Development
Economics*, Vol. 2 No. 4, pp. 451–63.

Mukherjee, S. B. (1976), *The Age Distribution of the Indian Population*, Honolulu: East–
West Center.

Murray, C. J. L. and A. D. Lopez (eds) (1996), *The Global Burden of Disease: A
Comprehensive Assessment of Mortality and Disability from Diseases, Injuries and Risk
Factors in 1990 and Projected to 2020*, Cambridge, Mass.: School of Public Health,
Harvard University.

Murthi, M., A. C. Guio, and J. Dréze (1995), 'Mortality, Fertility and Gender-bias in
India: A District Level Analysis', *Population and Development Review*, Vol. 21 No. 3,
pp. 745–82.

Nagaraj, K. (1999), 'Labour Market Characteristics and Employment Generation
Programmes in India', in B. Harriss-White and S. Subramanian, (eds), *Illfare in
India: Essays on India's Social Sector in Honour of S. Guhan*, New Delhi: Sage,
pp. 73–109.

Nagaraj, R. (2000), 'Indian Economy since the 1980s. Virtuous Growth or Polarisation?',
Economic and Political Weekly, Vol. 35 No. 32, pp. 2831–8.

——— (1994), 'Employment and Wages in Manufacturing Industries: Trends,
Hypotheses and Evidence', *Economic and Political Weekly*, Vol. 29 No. 4, pp. 177–86.

Narasimhan, R. L., R. D. Retherford, V. Mishra, F. Arnold, and T. K. Roy (2001),
'Comparison of Fertility Estimates for India's Sample Registration System and the
1992–3 National Family Health Survey', in J. F. Phillips and Z. A. Sathar, (eds),
Fertility Transition in South Asia, Oxford: Oxford University Press, pp. 78–98.

Natarajan, I. (1998), 'Demand Forecast for Biofuels in Rural Households', *International
Energy Agency Conference Proceedings, Biomass Energy: Data Analysis and Trends*. Paris:
International Energy Agency, pp. 181–91.

Natarajan, K. S. and V. Jayachandran (2001), 'Population Growth in 21st Century

India', in K. Srinivasan and M. Vlassoff, (eds), *Population-Development Nexus in India*. New Delhi: Tata McGraw-Hill, pp. 35–57.

Nath, K. J. (1984), 'Metropolitan Solid Waste in India', in J. R. Holmes, (ed.), *Managing Solid Wastes in Developing Countries*, Chichester: John Wiley, pp. 47–70.

Nath, V. (1989), 'Urbanization and Urban Development in India—Some Policy Issues', *International Journal of Urban and Regional Research*, Vol. 13 No. 2, pp. 256–81.

Nathan, D. and G. Kelkar (2001), 'Case for Local Forest Management: Environmental Services, Internalisation of Costs and Markets', *Economic and Political Weekly*, Vol. 36 No. 30 pp. 2835–45.

National AIDS Control Organization (2000a), *Combating HIV/AIDS in India 1999–2000*, New Delhi: Ministry of Heath and Family Welfare.

_____ (2000b), 'Surveillance for HIV Infection/AIDS cases in India', Available at www.naco.nic.in/vsnaco/indianscene/update.htm#8, Accessed February 2000.

National Capital Region Planning Board (NCRPB) (1999), *Delhi 1999: A Fact Sheet*, New Delhi: NCRPB.

National Council of Applied Economic Research (NCAER) (1996), *Human Development Profile of India: Inter-State and Inter-Group Differentials*, New Delhi: NCAER.

National Council of Educational Research and Training (NCERT) (1998), *Sixth All India Education Survey*, New Delhi: NCERT.

_____ (1992), *Fifth All-India Education Survey*, New Delhi: NCERT.

_____ (1982). *Fourth All-India Education Survey*, New Delhi: NCERT.

National Horticulture Board (2000), *Indian Horticulture Database 2000*, Gurgaon: Ministry of Agriculture.

National Institute of Occupational Health (1979), 'Comparative Epidemiological Studies of the Effects of Air Pollutants', in *Annual Report, 1979*, Ahmedabad: National Institute of Occupational Health.

National Sample Survey Organisation (NSSO) (2001), *Level and Pattern of Consumer Expenditure in India 1999–2000*, Report No. 457, New Delhi: Ministry of Statistics and Programme Evaluation.

_____ (1999), *Common Property Resources in India*, Results of the NSSO 54th Round, January–June 1998, Report No. 452(54/31/4), New Delhi: NSSO, 8, 19, pp. 32–3.

_____ (1998), *Attending an Educational Institution in India: Its Level, Nature and Cost*, Report No. 439 (52/25.2/1), New Delhi: NSSO.

_____ (1997), 'A Note on Economic Activities and School Attendance by Children of India', NSS 50th Round (July 1992–June 1994), *Sarvekshana*, Vol. 21 No. 2, issue 73 (October–December), New Delhi: NSSO.

NCIWRD (1999), 'Integrated Water Resources Development: A Plan for Action', Report of the National Commission on Integrated Water Resources Development, New Delhi: Ministry of Water Resources, Government of India.

Nilsen, H. (1998), 'Water Management at a Paper Mill', *Industry, Fresh Water and Sustainable Development*, Geneva and Nairobi: World Business Council for Sustainable Development/United Nations Environment Programme.

Nuclear Energy Agency (2000), *Nuclear Energy in a Sustainable Development Perspective*, Paris: Organization for Economic Cooperation and Development.

Ogden, J. M. (1999), 'Prospects for Building a Hydrogen Energy Infrastructure', *Annual Review of Energy and the Environment*, 24, pp. 227–79.

Operations Research Group (1990), *Family Planning Practices in India—Third All India Survey*, Baroda: Operations Research Group.

_____ (1989), *Delivery and Financing of Urban Services* (mimeo), Baroda: Operations Research Group.

_____ (1983), *Family Planning Practices in India—Second All India Survey*, Baroda: Operations Research Group.

OECD (Organization for Economic Cooperation and Development) (2001), *Education at a Glance*, Paris: Organization for Economic Cooperation and Development.

_____ (1992), *Projected Costs of Generating Electricity: Update, 1992*, Paris: OECD.

Overseas Development Administration (1993a), *People (Version 3.0)*, Computer programme developed by the Economic Planning Unit, Kuala Lumpur and the United Kingdom, London: ODA.

_____ (1993b), *People (Version 3.0)*, *User's Manual*, Economic Planning Unit, Kuala Lumpur and the United Kingdom, London: ODA.

Overseas Development Institute (2001), 'How have the Poor Done? Mid-Term Review of India's Ninth Five-Year Plan', *ODI Natural Resource Perspectives No. 66*, London: Overseas Development Institute.

Özler, B., G. Datt, and M. Ravallion (1996), *A Database on Poverty and Growth in India*, Poverty and Human Resources Division, Policy Research Department, World Bank.

Pai, S. (2002), 'Electoral Identity Politics in Uttar Pradesh', *Economic and Political Weekly*, Vol. 37 No. 14, pp. 1334–41.

Panayotou, T. (1998), 'Demystifying the Environmental Kuznets Curve: Turning a Black Box into a Policy Tool', *Environment and Development Economics*, Vol. 2 No. 4, pp. 465–84.

Pandey, M. R., P. R. Neupane, A. Gautam, and I. B. Shrestha (1990), 'The Effectiveness of Smokeless Stoves in Reducing Indoor Air Pollution in a Rural Hill Region of Nepal', *Mountain Research and Development*, Vol. 10 No. 4, pp. 313–20.

Pandey, R. (1998), 'Fiscal Options for Vehicular Pollution Control in Delhi', *Economic and Political Weekly*, Vol. 33 No. 45, pp. 2873–80.

Papola, T. S. (1997), 'Extent and Implications of Rural–Urban Migration in India', in G. Jones and P. Visaria, (eds), *Urbanization in Large Developing Countries*, Oxford: Clarendon Press, pp. 315–20.

Parikh, J. K., K. R. Smith, and V. Laxmi (1999), 'Indoor Air Pollution: A Reflection on Gender Bias', *Economic and Political Weekly*, Vol. 34 No. 9, pp. 539–44.

Parikh, J. K., K. R. Smith, V. Laxmi, and K. S. Parikh (2002), 'Reforms in the Power Sector', in K. S. Parikh and R. Radhakrishna, (eds), *India Development Report 2002*, New Delhi: Oxford University Press, pp. 116–27.

Parikh, K. S. (ed.) (1999), *India Development Report 1999–2000*, Mumbai and New Delhi: Indira Gandhi Institute for Development Research and Oxford University Press.

Parikh, K. S. and R. Radhakrishna, (eds) (2002), *India Development Report 2002*, New Delhi: Oxford University Press.

Pasha, S. A. (1992), 'Common Pool Resources and the Rural Poor: A Micro Level Analysis', *Economic and Political Weekly*, Vol. 27 No. 46, pp. 2499–503.

Pathak, P. and D. Mehta (1995), 'Recent Trends in Urbanisation and Rural–Urban Migration in India: Some Explanations and Projections', *Urban India*, Vol. 15 No. 2, pp. 1–16.

Pathania, V., J. Almeida, and A. Kochi (1997), *TB Patients and Private for-Profit Health Care Providers in India*, World Health Organization.

Patterson, J. W. (1985), *Industrial Wastewater Treatment Technology*, Butterworth: London.

Pearson, P. J. G. (1994), 'Energy, Externalities and Environmental Quality: Will Development Cure the Ills It Creates?', *Energy Studies Review*, Vol. 6 No. 3, pp. 199–216.

Pearson, P. J. G. and J. Pena-Torres (2000), 'Carbon Abatement and New Investment in Liberalised Electricity Markets: A Nuclear Revival in the UK?', *Energy Policy*, Vol. 28 No. 12, pp. 115–35.

Pender, J. (2001), 'Rural Population Growth, Agricultural Change, and Natural Resource Management: A Review of Hypotheses and Some Evidence from Honduras', in N. Birdsall, A. C., Kelley, S. W. Sinding, (eds), *Population Matters: Demographic Change, Economic Growth, and Poverty in the Developing World*, Oxford: Oxford University Press, pp. 325–68.

Planning Commission (2002a), *India: National Human Development Report*, New Delhi: Government of India.

———— (2002b), *Special Group on Targeting Ten Million Employment Opportunities Per Year: Employment Generating Growth* (online), New Delhi: Planning Commission, Government of India. Available at http://planningcommission.nic.in/tsk_sg10m.pdf

———— (2001a), *Approach Paper to the Tenth Five–Year Plan, 2002–7*. New Delhi: Government of India.

———— (2001b), *Report of the Task Force on Employment Opportunities*, New Delhi: Government of India.

———— (2000a), *Mid-Term Review of the Ninth Five–Year Plan, 1997–2002*, New Delhi: Government of India, Planning Commission. Available at: http://planningcommission.nic.in/midbody.htm

———— (2000b), *Mid-Term Appraisal of Ninth Five–Year Plan, 1997–2002*, New Delhi: Planning Commission, Government of India.

———— (1999), *Leasing of Degraded Forest Lands*, Working Group's Report to the Planning Commission on the Prospects of Making Degraded Forests Available to Private Entrepreneurs, Report Reprint Series No.1/99–PC, New Delhi: Planning Commission, Government of India.

———— (1997), *Ninth Five-Year Plan, 1997–2002*, New Delhi: Government of India.

Population Foundation of India (2000), *Population Growth in 21st Century India*, New Delhi: PFI.

Population Reference Bureau (2001), *2001 World Population Data Sheet*, Washington, D.C.: Population Reference Bureau.

Prabhu, K. S. (1996), 'The Impact of Structural Adjustment on Social Sector Expenditure', in C. H. H. Rao and H. Lindemann, (eds), *Economic Reforms and Poverty Alleviation in India*, New Delhi: Sage (Indo–Dutch Studies on Development Alternatives, Vol. 17, pp. 228–54).

Pradhan, B., and A. Subramanian (2000), 'Education, Openness and the Poor: Analysis of an All-India Survey of Households', *National Council of Applied Economic Research (NCAER) Discussion Paper*, No. DP020015, New Delhi: NCAER.

Pratichi Trust (2002), *Education Report*, http//www.amartyasen.net/pratichi.htm

Preston, S. H. (1979), 'Urban Growth in Developing Countries: A Demographic Reappraisal', *Population and Development Review*, Vol. 5 No. 2, pp. 195–215.

Preston, S. H., N. Keyfitz, and R. Schoen (1972), *Causes of Death, Life Tables for National Populations*, London: Seminar Press.

Pritchett, L. (2001), 'Where Has All the Education Gone?', *The World Bank Economic Review*, Vol. 15 No. 3, pp. 367–91.

——— (1997), 'Divergence, Big Time', *Journal of Economic Perspectives*, Vol. 11 No. 3, pp. 3–17.

PROBE Team (1999), *Public Report on Basic Education in India*, New Delhi: Oxford University Press.

Radhakrishna, R. (2002), 'Agricultural Growth, Employment and Poverty: A Policy Perspective', *Economic and Political Weekly*, Vol. 37 No. 3, pp. 243–50.

Radhakrishna, R. and A. N. Sharma (eds) (1998), *Empowering Rural Labour in India: Market, State and Mobilisation*, Delhi: Institute for Human Development.

Raghavachari, S., K. S. Natarajan, A. K. Biswas, and S. S. Bawa (1974), *The Population of India*, New Delhi: Ministry of Home Affairs.

Raghupati, U. (2002), 'Status of Water Supply, Sanitation, and Solid Waste Management in Urban India', Draft Report, New Delhi: National Institute of Urban Affairs.

Ramachandran, R. (1989), *Urbanization and Urban Systems in India*, New Delhi: Oxford University Press.

Ramachandran, V. (2001), *Gender and Social Equity in DPEP*, (draft), New Delhi: Education Resource Unit.

Ramachandran, V. K. (1997), 'On Kerala's Development Achievements', in J. Drèze and A. Sen, (eds), *Indian Development: Selected Regional Perspectives*, Oxford and Delhi: Oxford University Press, pp. 268–322.

Ramachandran, V. K., V. Rawal, and M. Swaminathan (1997), 'Investment Gaps in Primary Education. A Statewise Study', *Economic and Political Weekly*, Vol. 32 Nos. 1 and 2, pp. 39–45.

Ramasundaram, S. (1995), 'Causes for the Rapid Fertility Decline in Tamil Nadu: A Policy Planner's Perspective', *Demography India*, Vol. 24 No. 1, pp. 13–21.

Ramsey, C. B. (2000), 'Modelling the Health Impact of Domestic Energy Transitions in India', MSc dissertation, Department of Environmental Science and Technology, Imperial College, London.

Ramaswami, B. (2002), 'Efficiency and Equity of Food Market Interventions', *Economic and Political Weekly*, Vol. 37 No. 12, pp. 1129–35.

Rao, B. N., P. M. Kulkarni, and P. H. Rayappa (1986), *Determinants of Fertility Decline: A Study of Rural Karnataka*, New Delhi: South Asian Publishers.

Rao, C. H. H. and A. Gulati (1994), 'Indian Agriculture: Emerging Perspectives and Policy Issues', *Economic and Political Weekly*, Vol. 29 No. 53, pp. A-158–169.

Rao, C. H. H., A. Gulati, and H. Lindemann (eds) (1996), *Economic Reforms and Poverty Alleviation in India*. New Delhi: Sage (Indo–Dutch Studies on Development Alternatives 17).

Rao, V. K. R. V. (1983), *India's National Income 1950–80: An Analysis of Economic Growth and Change*, New Delhi: Sage.

Rath, G. K. and K. Chaudhry (1999), *Estimation of Cost of Tobacco Related Cancers—Report of an ICMR Task Force Study (1990–1996)*, New Delhi, Indian Council of Medical Research.

Ravallion, M., and G. Datt (1999), 'When is Growth Pro-Poor? Evidence From the Diverse Experiences of India's States', *World Bank Policy Research Working Paper*, No. 2263, Washington, D.C.: World Bank.

_____ (1996), 'How Important to India's Poor is the Sectoral Composition of Growth?', *World Bank Economic Review*, Vol. 10 No. 1, pp. 1–25.

Ravindran, T.K.S. (1999), 'Female Autonomy in Tamil Nadu: Unravelling the Complexities', *Economic and Political Weekly*, Vol. 34, Nos. 16–17, WS34–WS44.

Registrar General, India (2002a), *Sample Registration System Statistical Report 2000*, New Delhi: Office of the Registrar General.

_____ (2002b), 'Work Participation Rates (2001 Census). Substantial increase in female work participation rate', 30 January, No. 6, New Delhi: Office of the Registrar General. Available at: http://www.censusindia.net/results/eci6_page3.html

_____ (2001a). *Census of India 2001, Provisional Population Totals*, New Delhi: Office of the Registrar General. Available at http://www.censusindia.net

_____ (2001b), *Provisional Population Totals, Paper 1 of 2001, Supplement, District Totals*, New Delhi: Office of the Registrar General.

_____ (2001c), *Urban Agglomerations/Cities Having Population of More than One Million in 2001*. New Delhi: Government of India, Office of the Registrar General. Available at: http://www.censusindia.net/results/million_plus.html

_____ (2001d), *Rural–Urban Distribution of Population—India and States/Union Territories:2001*. Available at http://www.censusindia.net/results/rudist.html

_____ (2001e), *Population in the Age Group 0–6 and Literates by Sex–Urban Agglomerations:2001*. Available at: http://www.censusindia.net/results/UA.html

_____ (2001f), *Class 1 Towns with 1,00,000 and Above Population (Census 2001Provisional)*. Available at: <<http://www.censusindia.net/results/class.html>>.

_____ (2000), *Sample Registration System Statistical Report 1998*, New Delhi: Office of the Registrar General.

_____ (1999a), *Compendium of India's Fertility and Mortality Indicators 1971–1997*, New Delhi: Office of the Registrar General.

_____ (1999b), *Sample Registration System Bulletin*, Vol. 33, Part 2, New Delhi: Office of the Registrar General.

_____ (1998a), *State Profile 1991, India*, New Delhi: Office of the Registrar General.

_____ (1998b), *Census of India 1991, Migration Tables, Volume 2, Part 1*, New Delhi: Office of the Registrar General.

_____ (1998c), *Census of India 1991, Migration Tables, Volume 2, Part 2*, New Delhi: Office of the Registrar General.

_____ (1996), *Population Projections for India and States 1996–2016*, New Delhi: Office of the Registrar General.

_____ (1988), *Census of India 1981, Migration Tables, Part V-A and B(i) (Table D-1 and D-2)*, New Delhi: Office of the Registrar General.

_____ (1979), *Census of India 1971, Migration Tables, Part II—D(i)*, New Delhi: Office of the Registrar General.

Repetto, R. (1994), *'Second India' Revisited: Population, Poverty, and Environmental Stress Over Two Decades*, Washington, D.C.: World Resources Institute.

Retherford, R. D. and V. K. Mishra (2001), 'An Evaluation of Recent Estimates of Fertility Trends in India', National Family Health Survey Subject Reports, No. 19, Mumbai: International Institute for Population Sciences, pp. 36–9.

Rohilla, S. K. and S. P. Bansal (1998), 'Delhi's Solid Waste Disposal and Management-II' in S. K. Rohilla, P. S. Datta, and S. P. Bansal, (eds), *Delhi's Water and Solid Waste Management—Emerging Scenario*, New Delhi: Vigyan Prasar, pp. 38–65.

Rosegrant, M. R., M. Agcaoili, and N. Perez (1995), *Global Food Projections for 2020*,

Food, Agriculture and the Environment Discussion Paper 5, Washington D.C.: International Food Policy Research Institute.

Rostow, W. W. (1960), *The Stages of Economic Growth: A Non-Communist Manifesto,* Cambridge: Cambridge University Press.

Ruzicka, L. T. (1984), 'Mortality in India: Past Trends and Future Prospects', in T. Dyson and N. Crook (eds), *India's Demography: Essays on the Contemporary Population,* New Delhi: South Asian Publishers, pp. 13–36.

Säävälä, M. (2001), 'Fertility and Familial Power Relations: Procreation in South India', Nordic Institute of Asian Studies, Monograph Series N. 87, London: Curzon Press.

Sachithanandan, A. N. (1998), 'Chennai: A Coastal City of Colonial Origin,' in R. P. Misra and K. Misra, (eds), *Million Cities of India,* New Delhi: Sustainable Development Foundation, pp. 276–95.

Sachs, J. D., and N. Bajpai (2001), 'The Decade of Development: Goal Setting and Policy Challenges in India', *CID Working Paper,* No. 62, Cambridge, Mass.: Center for International Development, Harvard University.

Sachs, J. D., N. Bajpai, and A. Ramiah (2002), 'Understanding Regional Economic Growth in India', *CID Working Paper,* No. 88, Cambridge, Mass.: Center for International Development, Harvard University.

Sainath, P. (1996), *Everybody Loves a Good Drought : Stories from India's Poorest Districts,* New Delhi and New York, NY: Penguin Books.

Saksena, S., R. Prasad, R. C. Pal, and V. Joshi (1992), 'Patterns of Daily Exposure to TSP and CO in the Garhwal Himalaya', *Atmospheric Environment,* Vol. 26A, No. 11, pp. 2125–34, New Delhi: TERI.

Saleth, R. M. (1996), *Water Institutions in India: Economics, Law and Policy,* New Delhi: Commonwealth Publishers.

Saleth, R. M. and A. Dinar (1997), 'Satisfying Urban Thirst: Water Supply Augmentation and Pricing Policy in Hyderabad City, India', *Technical Paper No. 395,* Washington, D.C.: World Bank.

Satia, S. K. and S. J. Jejeebhoy (1991), *The Demographic Challenge: A Study of Four Large Indian States,* Mumbai: Oxford University Press.

Saxena, N. C. (2000), 'How Have the Poor Done? Mid-term Review of the Ninth Plan,' *Economic and Political Weekly,* Vol. 35 No. 41, pp. 3627–30.

———— (1994), *India's Eucalyptus Craze: The God that Failed,* New Delhi: Sage.

Selden, T. M. and D. Song (1994), 'Environmental Quality and Development: Is there a Kuznets Curve for Air Pollution Emissions?', *Journal of Environmental Economics and Management,* Vol. 27 No. 2, pp. 147–62.

Sen, A. (2000), 'Estimates of Consumption Spending and its Distribution: Statistical Priorities after the NSS 55th Round', *Economic and Political Weekly,* Vol. 35 No. 51, pp. 4499–518.

———— (1998), 'Rural Labour Markets and Poverty', in R. Radhakrishna and A. N. Sharma, (eds), *Empowering Rural Labour in India: Market, State and Mobilisation,* Delhi: Institute for Human Development, pp. 36–89.

Sen, A. K. (1985), *Commodities and Capabilities,* Amsterdam: North Holland.

Sen, G., A. Iyer, and A. George (2002), 'Structural Reforms and Health Equity: A Comparison of NSS Surveys of 1986–87 and 1995–96', *Economic and Political Weekly,* Vol. 37 No. 14, pp. 1342–52.

SFR (1991), *The State of Forest Report 1991,* Dehra Dun, Forest Survey of India. Available at: http://envfor.nic.in/fsi/sfr99/sfr.html

Shah, A. (2001), 'Who Benefits from Watershed Development? Evidences from Gujarat', *IIED Gatekeeper Series No. 97*, London: International Institute for Environment and Development.

Shah, G. (1997), *Public Health and Urban Development: The Plague in Surat*, New Delhi: Sage.

Shah, J. and T. Nagpal (eds) (1997), *Urban Air Quality Management Strategy in Asia (URBAIR) Greater Mumbai Report*, World Bank Technical Paper, No. 381, Washington, D.C.: World Bank.

Shah, T. (2000), 'Wells and Welfare in the Ganga Basin', Paper produced for the Policy, Institutions and Management Programme, Colombo: International Water Management Institute.

Shariff, A. (1999), *India: Human Development Report: A Profile of Indian States in the 1990s*, New Delhi: Oxford University Press.

Shariff, A., P. Ghosh, and S. K. Mondal (2002), 'State-Adjusted Public Expenditure on Social Sector and Poverty Alleviation Programmes', *Economic and Political Weekly*, Vol. 37 No. 8, pp. 767–87.

Sharma, V. P. (1996), 'Re-emergence of Malaria in India', *Indian Journal of Medical Research*, Vol. 103 No. 1, pp. 26–45.

Shaukat, N., J. Lear, A. Lowy, S. Fletcher, D. P. de Bono, and K. L. Woods (1997), 'First Myocardial Infarction in Patients of Indian Subcontinent and European Origin: Comparison of Risk Factors, Management and Long Term Outcome', *British Medical Journal*, Vol. 315 No. 7081, pp. 639–42.

Singh, D. P. (1998), 'Internal Migration in India: 1961–1991', *Demography India*, Vol. 27 No. 1, pp. 245–61.

Singh, K. (2001), *Water Conservation and Demand Management* (mimeo), Paper presented at the Second Biennial Conference of the Indian Society for Ecological Economics, December 2001.

Singh, K. and F. Steinberg (eds) (1998), *Urban India in Crisis*, New Delhi: New Age International Ltd.

Singhal, V. (1999), *Indian Agriculture 1999*, New Delhi: Indian Economic Data Research Centre.

Sinha, A. (1998), *Primary Schooling in India*, Delhi: Vikas Publishing House.

Skeldon, R. (1986), 'On Migration Patterns in India During the 1970s', *Population and Development Review*, Vol. 12 No. 4, pp. 759–79.

—— (1983), *Migration in South Asia: An Overview*, Bangkok: Economic and Social Commission for Asia and the Pacific.

Smith, K. R. (2000), 'National Burden of Disease in India from Indoor Air Pollution', *Proceedings of the National Academy of Sciences*, Vol. 97 No. 24, pp. 13286–93.

—— (1996), 'Indoor Air Pollution in India', *National Medical Journal of India*, Vol. 9 No. 3, pp. 103–4.

—— (1993), 'Fuel Combustion, Air Pollution Exposure and Health: The Situation in Developing countries', *Annual Review of Energy and the Environment*, Vol. 18 No. 1, pp. 529–66.

Smith, K. R., J. Jhang, and R. Uma (1999), 'Greenhouse-gas Emissions from Small-scale Combustion Devices in Developing Countries: Stoves in India', United States Environmental Protection Agency, Research Triangle Park, North Carolina.

Socolow, R. E. (1997), 'Fuels Decarbonisation and Carbon Sequestration', Report

No. 302, Princeton NJ: Princeton University, Center for Energy and Environmental Studies.

Solow, R. (1957), 'Technical Change and the Aggregate Production Function', *Review of Economics and Statistics*, Vol. 39 No. 2, pp. 312–20.

Sopher, D. (1980), 'Indian Civilisation and the Tropical Savanna Environment', in O. R. Harris, (ed.), *Human Ecology in Savanna Environments*, London: Academic Press, pp. 185–207.

Srinivasan, K. (1995), 'Lessons from Goa, Kerala, and Tamil Nadu: The Three Successful Fertility Transition States in India', *Demography India*, Vol. 24 No. 2, pp. 163–94.

Srinivasan, S., R. Mosdale, P. Stevens, and C. Yang (1999), 'Fuel Cells: Reaching the Era of Clean and Efficient Power Generation in the Twenty-First Century', *Annual Review of Energy and the Environment*, Vol. 24 No. 1, pp. 281–328.

Srinivasan, T. N., and P. K. Bardhan (eds) (1988), *Rural Poverty in South Asia*, Oxford: Oxford University Press.

Srivastava, L. (1997), 'Energy and CO_2 Emissions in India: Increasing Trends and Alarming Portents', *Energy Policy*, Vol. 25 No. 11, pp. 941–9.

Srivastava, R. S. (2001), 'Public Distribution System in Rural Uttar Pradesh', in M. D. Asthana and P. Medrano, (eds), *Towards Hunger Free India*, New Delhi: Manohar Publishers, pp. 481–503.

Statistics Canada (2001), *Places of Birth for Total Immigrants*. Available at: http://www.statcan.ca/english/census96/nov4/table1.html

Stewart, F. (1995), *Adjustment and Poverty: Options and Choices*, London and New York: Routledge.

Stewart, F. and O. Morissey (eds) (1995), *Economic and Political Reform in Developing Countries*, London : Macmillan.

Subramanian, S. (1995), *Gender Discrimination in Intra-Household Allocation in India*, (mimeo), Ithaca, NY: Department of Economics, Cornell University.

———— and A. Deaton (1991), 'Gender Effects in Indian Consumption Patterns', *Sarvekshana*, Vol. 14 No. 4, pp. 1–12.

———— (ed.) (2001), *India's Development Experience: Selected Writings of S. Guhan*, New Delhi: Oxford University Press.

Sudarshan, R. and N. Mishra (1999), 'Gender and Tobacco Consumption in India', *Journal of Women's Studies*, Vol. 5 No. 1, pp. 84–114.

Summers, R. and A. Heston (1991), 'The Penn World Tables (Mark 5): An Expanded Data Set of International Comparisons, 1950–88', *Quarterly Journal of Economics*, Vol. 106 No. 2, pp. 327–69.

Sundar, N., R. Jeffery, and N. Thin (2001), *Branching Out: Joint Forest Management in India*, Delhi: Oxford University Press.

Sundaram, K. (2001a). 'Employment and Poverty in the 1990s: Further Results from NSS 55th Round Employment–Unemployment Survey, 1999–2000', *Economic and Political Weekly*, Vol. 36 No. 32, pp. 3039–49.

———— (2001b), 'Employment–Unemployment Situation in the Nineties. Some Results from NSS 55th Round Survey', *Economic and Political Weekly*, Vol. 36 No. 11, pp. 931–40.

———— (2001c), 'Employment and Poverty in the 1990s: A Postscript', *Economic and Political Weekly*, Vol. 36 No. 34, p. 3326.

Sundaram, K. and S. D. Tendulkar (1988), 'Towards an Explanation of Inter-Regional Variations in Poverty and Unemployment in India', T. N. Srinivasan and P. K. Bardhan, (eds), *Rural Poverty in South Asia*, Oxford: Oxford University Press, pp. 316–62.

Supreme Court of India (1999), *Solid Waste Management in Class I Cities in India*, Report of the committee constituted by the Hon. Supreme Court of India, New Delhi: Supreme Court of India.

Suryanarayana, M. H. (2002), 'Poverty in India: Misspecified Policies and Estimates', *World Institute for Development Economics Research (WIDER) Discussion Paper*, 2002/ 15, Helsinki: United Nations University (UNU)/WIDER Publications.

―――― (2001), 'Social Cost of Economic Reform in India: Some Hard Evidence?', Paper presented to the workshop on 'Poverty and Human Development Monitoring System', Planning Department, Government of Karnataka and Institute for Social and Economic Change, Bangalore, 2–3 February 2001.

Swaminathan, M., and V. Rawal (1999), 'Primary Education for All', in K. S. Parikh, (ed.), *India Development Report 1999–2000*, Mumbai and New Delhi: Indira Gandhi Institute for Development Research and Oxford University Press, pp. 68–84.

Tata Energy Research Institute (2001), *Directions, Innovations, and Strategies for Harnessing Action (DISHA) for Sustainable Development*, New Delhi: TERI.

―――― (1998), *Looking Back to Think Ahead: Green India 2047*, New Delhi: TERI.

―――― (1997), *Looking Back to Think Ahead: Green India 2047*, P. K. Pachauri and P. V. Sridharan, (eds), New Delhi: TERI, 52, pp. 180–3, 271, 319.

Tavoulareas, S. E. and J. P. Charpentier (1995), 'Clean Coal Technologies for Developing Countries', *Technical Paper: Energy Series*, Washington, DC: World Bank.

Teitelbaum, M. S. (1997), 'Portents and Unpredictabilities: Responses to Very Low Fertility', in *United Nations Expert Group Meeting on Below-Replacement Fertility*, (ESA/P/WP.140), New York: United Nations Population Division.

Tendulkar, S. (1992), 'Economic Growth and Poverty', in B. Harriss, S. Guhan, and R. H. Cassen, (eds), *Poverty in India: Research and Policy*, Mumbai: Oxford University Press, pp. 27–57.

Tendulkar, S. D. (2002), 'Employment Growth in Factory Manufacturing Sector During Pre- and Post-Reform Periods', Unpublished paper, New Delhi: Delhi School of Economics.

Thamarajakshi, R. (2001), 'Demand and Supply of Food Grains in 2020', in M. D. Asthana and P. Medrano, (eds), *Towards Hunger Free India*, New Delhi: Manohar Publications.

Thapar, S. (1963), 'Family Planning in India', *Population Studies*, Vol. 17 No. 1, pp. 4–19.

Turkenburg, W. C. (2000), 'Renewable Energy Technologies', in United Nations Development Programme and World Energy Council (2000), *World Energy Assessment: Energy and the Challenge of Sustainability*, New York: United Nations Development Programme, pp. 119–272.

UNICEF (2000), *The State of the World's Children 2000*, New York: United Nations Children's Fund.

United Nations (2001), *World Population Prospects: The 2000 Revision*, New York: United Nations.

United Nations (2000), *World Urbanisation Prospects: The 1999 Revision*, New York: Population Division, United Nations Secretariat.

―――― (1999a), *The Demographic Impact of HIV/AIDS*, Report on the Technical Meeting of November 1998, New York: United Nations Population Division.

―――― (1999b), *World Population Prospects: The 1998 Revision, Volume III, Analytical Report*, New York: United Nations.

―――― (1983), *Manual X, Indirect Techniques for Demographic Estimation*, New York: United Nations.

―――― (1982), *Model Life Tables for Developing Countries*, New York: United Nations.

United Nations Centre for Human Settlements and Housing and Urban Development Corporation (2001), *The State of Indian Cities 2001*, New Delhi: UNCHS/HUDCO.

United Nations Development Programme (1999), *Household Energy Strategies for Urban India: The Case of Hyderabad*, Washington, D.C.: UNDP/World Bank.

United Nations Development Programme/World Bank Energy Sector Management Assistance Programme (1998), *India: Environmental Issues in the Power Sector*, Report No. 205/98, June, Washington, D.C.: UNDP/World Bank.

United Nations Environment Programme/World Health Organization (1992), *Urban Air Pollution in Mega-Cities of the World*, Oxford: Blackwell.

United States National Research Council (1992), *Nuclear Power: Technical and Institutional Options for the Future*, Washington, D.C.: National Academy Press.

Unni, J. (2002), 'Economic Growth and Quality of Employment in India', Unpublished paper, Ahmedabad: Gujarat Institute of Development Research.

―――― (2001), 'Gender and Non-Farm Employment in India', Paper presented at the Workshop on Rural Transformation in India: The Role of the Non-Farm Sector, organized by the Planning Commission of India, the Institute of Human Development, the World Bank and the Department for International Development (DFID), New Delhi, 19–21 September 2001.

US Bureau of the Census (1999), *World Population Profile: 1998*, Report WP/98, Washington D.C.: US Government Printing Office.

Vagale, L. R. (1998), 'Bangalore: A Garden City in Distress', in R. P. Misra and K. Misra (eds), *Million Cities of India*, New Delhi: Sustainable Development Foundation, pp. 339–57.

Vaidyanathan, A. (2000), 'India's Agricultural Development Policy', *Economic and Political Weekly*, Vol. 35 No. 20, pp. 1735–41.

―――― (1999), *Water Resource Management: Institutions and Irrigation Development in India*, New Delhi: Oxford University Press.

Van Beukering, P. (1994), 'An Economic Analysis of Different Types of Formal and Informal Entrepreneurs: Recovering Urban Solid Waste in Bangalore', *Resources, Conservation and Recycling*, Vol. 12 No. 3/4, pp. 230–51.

Van de Walle, D. (1985), 'Population Growth and Poverty: Another Look at the Indian Times Series Data', *Journal of Development Studies*, Vol. 21 No. 3, pp. 429–39.

Venkateswarlu, U. (1998), *Urbanisation in India: Problems and Prospects*, New Delhi: New Age International.

Vira, B. and S. Vira (2001), *Testing the Limits: An Analysis of Environmental Indicators in Metropolitan India* (mimeo), Department of Geography, University of Cambridge.

Visaria, L. (2002), 'The Proximate Determinants of Fertility in India', India Project Working Paper, Department of Social Policy, London School of Economics.

—— (2000), 'From Contraceptive Targets to Informed Choice: The Indian Experience', in R. Ramasubban and S. J. Jejeebhoy, (eds), *Women's Reproductive Health in India*, Jaipur: Rawat Publications, pp. 331–82.

—— (1996), 'Regional Variations in Female Autonomy and Fertility and Contraception in India', in R. Jeffery and A. M. Basu, (eds), *Girls' Schooling, Women's Autonomy and Fertility Change in South Asia*, New Delhi: Sage Publications, pp. 235–60.

—— (1988), 'Sex Differentials in Nutritional Status and Survival During Infancy and Childhood: Review of Available Evidence', Paper presented at the International Union for the Scientific Study of Population (IUSSP) Regional Population Conference on Women's Position and Demographic Change in the Course of Development, Asker, Norway: 15–18 June.

Visaria, L. and P. Visaria (1982), 'Population (1757–1947)', in D. Kumar, (ed.), *The Cambridge Economic History of India, Volume II: c. 1757–c. 1970*, Hyderabad: Orient Longman, pp. 463–532.

Visaria, P. (2000a), 'Urbanisation in India', Unpublished typescript.

—— (2000b), 'Statistical Tables', Unpublished typescript.

—— (2000c), 'Population Policy in India: Evolution, Performance and Challenges', Typescript, Delhi: Institute of Economic Growth.

—— (1999a), 'Labour Force in India: Retrospect and Prospect', Unpublished paper, New Delhi: Institute of Economic Growth.

—— (1999b), 'A Population Projection for India by Rural–Urban Residence, 1991–2051', Unpublished typescript.

—— (1998a), 'Unemployment Among Youth in India: Level, Nature and Policy Implications', *Employment and Training Papers*, No. 36, Geneva: Employment and Training Department, International Labour Office.

—— (1998b), 'Urbanisation in India: Retrospect and Prospect', Unpublished typescript.

—— (1997), 'Urbanization in India: An Overview', in G. Jones and P. Visaria, (eds), *Urbanization in Large Developing Countries*, Oxford: Clarendon Press, pp. 266–88.

Visaria, P. and A. K. Jain (1976), *India, Country Profile*, New York: The Population Council.

Visaria, P. and D. Kothari (1985), 'Data Base for the Study of Migration and Urbanisation in India: A Critical Analysis', Working Paper No. 2, Ahmadabad: Gujarat Institute of Development Research.

Visaria, P. and L. Visaria (1994), 'Demographic Transition, Accelerating Fertility Decline in 1980s', *Economic and Political Weekly*, Vol. 29 Nos. 51–2, pp. 3281–92.

—— (forthcoming), 'Demographic Characteristics of India's Population and Its Social Groups', Companion Oxford Encyclopaedia of Sociology and Anthropology, New Delhi: Oxford University Press.

Visaria, P., L. Visaria, and A. K. Jain (1995), *Contraceptive Use and Fertility in India*, New Delhi: Sage.

Wade, R. (1982), 'The System of Administrative and Political Corruption: Canal Irrigation in South India', *Journal of Development Studies*, Vol. 18 No. 3, pp. 287–328.

Weiner, M. (1990), *The Child and the State in India: Child Labor and Education Policy in Comparative Perspective*, Princeton, NJ: Princeton University Press.

—— (1982), 'International Migration and Development: Indians in the Persian Gulf', *Population and Development Review*, Vol. 8 No. 1, pp. 1–36.

Whittington, D., D.T. Lauria, D. Okun, and X. Mu (1994), 'Water Vending Activities in Developing Countries', in S. Glaister and R. Layard (eds), *Cost Benefit Analysis*, Cambridge: Cambridge University Press: pp. 448–63.

Williamson, J. G. (2001), 'Demographic Change, Economic Growth, and Inequality', in N. Birdsall, A. C. Kelley, and S. W. Sinding, (eds), *Population Matters. Demographic Change, Economic Growth, and Poverty in the Developing World*, Oxford: Oxford University Press.

Wood, A., and M. E. Calandrino (2000), 'When the Other Giant Awakens: Trade and Human Resources in India', *Economic and Political Weekly*, Vol. 35 No. 52 and 53, pp. 4677–94.

Woods, R. (2000), *The Demography of Victorian England and Wales*, Cambridge: Cambridge University Press.

———(1988), 'The Causes of Rapid Infant Mortality Decline in England and Wales', *Population Studies*, Vol. 42 No. 3, pp. 343–66.

Working Group on Perspective of Water Requirement (WG) (1999), *Report of the Working Group on Perspective of Water Requirements* (National Commission on Integrated Water Resources Development Plan), New Delhi: Ministry of Water Resources, Government of India.

World Bank (n.d.), Country Reports on Health, Nutrition, Population, and Poverty (Online). Available at: http://www.worldbank.org/poverty/health/data/index.htm (5 Feb. 2002).

——— (2002), *Poverty in India: the Challenge of Uttar Pradesh*, Report No. 22323–IN, Washington, D.C.: World Bank.

——— (2000a), *India: Reducing Poverty, Accelerating Development*, New Delhi: Oxford University Press.

——— (2000b), *World Development Indicators*, CD-ROM, Washington, D.C.: World Bank.

——— (2000c), *India: Alleviating Poverty through Forest Development*, Washington, D.C.: World Bank, Operations Evaluation Department.

——— (1998a), 'India—Water Resources Management: Groundwater Regulation and Management Report', Report No. 18324IN, Washington, D.C.: World Bank.

——— (1998b), 'India—Water Resources Management: Report on the Irrigation Sector', Report No. 18416IN, Washington, D.C.: World Bank.

——— (1997a), *India: Achievements and Challenges in Reducing Poverty*, Washington, D.C.: World Bank.

——— (1997b), *World Development Indicators 1997*, Washington, D.C.: World Bank.

——— (1996), *Rural Energy and Development: Meeting the Needs of 2 Billion People*, A World Bank Special Briefing Paper, Washington, D.C.: World Bank.

——— (1994), *World Development Report 1994: Infrastructure for Development*, Washington, D.C.: World Bank.

——— (1993a). *World Development Report 1993: Investing in Health*, Washington, D.C.: World Bank.

——— (1993b). *The East Asian Miracle: Economic Growth and Public Policy*, Oxford: Oxford University Press.

——— (1992), *World Development Report 1992: Development and the Environment*, Washington, D.C.: World Bank.

World Energy Council (WEC) (1998), *Survey of Energy Resources*, London: WEC.

World Health Organization (1999), *The World Health Report 1999: Making a Difference*, Geneva: World Health Organization.

World Resources Institute (1998), *World Resources 1998–99*, New York: Oxford University Press.

Xaxa, V. (2001), 'Protective Discrimination: Why Scheduled Tribes Lag Behind Scheduled Castes', *Economic and Political Weekly*, Vol. 36 No. 29, pp. 2765–83.

Zachariah, K. C. (1994), *Demographic Transition in Kerala in the 1980s*, Trivandrum: Centre for Development Studies.

Zerah, M. H. (2000), *Water—Unreliable Supply in Delhi*, New Delhi: Manohar Press and Centre de Sciences Humaines.

Index